# BASEBALL'S HALL OF FAME

# COOPERSTOWN

## WHERE THE LEGENDS LIVE FOREVER

# BASEBALL'S HALL OF FAME
# COOPERSTOWN
## WHERE THE LEGENDS LIVE FOREVER

*Written by*
**LOWELL REIDENBAUGH**

*Editor*
**JOE HOPPEL**

*Design*
**BILL PERRY**

*Associate Editors*
**CRAIG CARTER**
**DAVE SLOAN**

**ARLINGTON HOUSE, INC.**
**New York**

**—Photography Credits—**
Color:
Fred Kaplan—
Page 129 (2), 134, 137, 140-41.
Focus on Sports—
Page 130, 131, 132, 133, 135, 136, 138, 139, 142, 143, 144.
All black-and-white photos are from *The Sporting News* archives.

This 1986 edition is published by Arlington House, Inc., distributed by
Crown Publishers, Inc., 225 Park Avenue South, New York, New York
10003, by arrangement with The Sporting News Publishing Company.

Printed and Bound in the United States of America

Library of Congress Cataloging-in-Publication Data
Reidenbaugh, Lowell.
Baseball's Hall of Fame.
Enl. and updated ed. of: Cooperstown 1st ed. © 1983.
1. Baseball players—United States—Biography.   2. National Baseball
Hall of Fame and Museum.   I. Title.   II. Title: Cooperstown.
GV865.A1R43     1986        796.357′092′2       [B]        85-28707
ISBN 0-517-60739-5
h  g  f  e  d  c  b

# CONTENTS

Yogi Berra

Roberto Clemente

Joe DiMaggio

Lou Gehrig

Rogers Hornsby

Walter Johnson

Stan Musial

Tris Speaker

Ted Williams

*Color photographs 129–144*

The National Baseball Hall of Fame and Museum (above) is located in Cooperstown, N.Y. Seven of the illustrious players enshrined there (below) posed prior to the 1937 All-Star Game in Washington. Pictured are (left to right) Lou Gehrig, Joe Cronin, Bill Dickey, Joe DiMaggio, Charley Gehringer, Jimmie Foxx and Hank Greenberg.

# Introduction

A small minority of mortals is blessed with the ability to smite a speeding spheroid for prodigious distance, or to propel it with extraordinary velocity and accuracy, or to perform with uncommon grace and agility in halting the spheroid when it approaches within arm's reach.

Except for those distinctive attributes, the inhabitants of baseball's Hall of Fame in Cooperstown, N.Y., might well have been the patrolmen on the beat, the custodians at the local high schools or the grocers down the street.

But they were gifted beyond comparison and those gifts can be appreciated by the millions of people who have attempted to hit a curve ball or catch a sizzling line drive, reaping only futility for their efforts.

Superbly endowed as they were with physical talents, they also had the fierce determination to succeed and were willing to devote long hours of practice to master the intricacies required of major league performers.

Behind the plaques at Cooperstown are hours of bumpy bus rides, countless blue-plate specials in sleazy all-night eateries, dingy motels in forgotten hamlets and numberless games on corduroy fields rimmed by unpainted grandstands.

Despite their early career substandard lifestyle, the future Hall of Famers persisted because it was a livelihood that offered the hope for princely salaries and universal adulation.

Some, like Frank Frisch, Bob Feller and Al Kaline, leaped directly to the major leagues from the sandlots. Others, like Carl Hubbell and Dazzy Vance, drifted in the minors for years before their courses were reversed. Hubbell was discarded by the Detroit Tigers, Joe Cronin by the Pittsburgh Pirates and Vance by Pittsburgh and the New York Yankees before, at age 31, he found his niche as a strikeout king for the Brooklyn Dodgers.

Not all of the immortals attained stardom at their original positions. Babe Ruth, George Sisler and Bill Terry were pitchers before their batting talents demanded that they play daily. Jimmie Foxx started as a catcher, Hank Aaron as an infielder and Frank Chance as a catcher.

Terry, the young head of a family, questioned baseball as a profession until the Giants made him an irresistible proposition. He played the game on his own financial terms. Edd Roush was of a similar cut. When his terms were not met, he took a one-year sabbatical from the game.

While they were idols on the baseball field, many demonstrated human frailties during their off hours. Paul Waner made no effort to conceal his affinity for the flowing grape and grain. But his unconventional lifestyle never interfered with his ability to bat .300, or to compile more than 3,000 major league hits. When he was asked to go on the wagon in order to set an example for young players, he

readily agreed. But when he failed to collect a hit in an entire week, he was ordered to revert to old habits, and base hits barked again.

Throughout his incomparable career, Babe Ruth defied all dietary directives. Chocolate ice cream and pickled eels between games of a doubleheader never dimmed his effectiveness. A pint of bourbon with steak, eggs and hash browns for breakfast only served to fuel an afternoon of prodigious clouts.

They tippled in public and they tippled in private, much in the manner of those who made the turnstiles whirl, thereby producing the players with the handsome salaries that provided the means for excessive tastes.

They were human—the players, the managers, executives and umpires. The blacks, many of them denied the opportunity to enjoy major league acclaim, were great, famous and gifted in their own universe.

This volume is directed toward the humanizing of the 193 immortals whose performances have illuminated all phases of baseball since its inception. They emerged on the national conscience as unknowns. For varying periods they flashed spectacularly. Some faded with dignity, others departed in tragedy.

Roberto Clemente perished on a mission of mercy just months after rapping his 3,000th hit. Lou Gehrig, the seemingly indestructible Iron Horse, was forced into retirement at age 36 by a disabling affliction that came to be known later as "Lou Gehrig's Disease." He died two years later.

Ed Delahanty plunged to his death through an open draw bridge and Addie Joss, in his prime, was cut down by tubercular meningitis. Ross Youngs, termed by his manager, John McGraw, as the finest outfielder of his experience, was cut down by Bright's disease when barely 30 years old.

Even in retirement, there were those who walked with misfortune. Baseball has known no more poignant a scene than Babe Ruth, racked by cancer, waving farewell to Yankee Stadium fans. Automobile accidents terminated too soon the lives of Mel Ott and Frisch. Foxx choked to death on a piece of meat at the dinner table.

Some died as princes, some as paupers. Ty Cobb enjoyed a millionaire's luxury because of investments in General Motors and Coca-Cola. Hack Wilson, the all-time single-season RBI king and still National League home run champion, went to a penniless grave, clad in a suit and laid in a coffin donated by a charitable mortician.

They spanned the spectrum of humanity, these members of baseball's shrine. But, diversified as they were in many respects, they were united in their mastery of and devotion to the game that made them celebrities to all ages for all time.

# Hank Aaron

The pressure was almost suffocating. Everywhere he went, cameras focused on him. Every step he took was followed by a coterie of newsmen that would have made an oil prince proud. Hank Aaron was living in a goldfish bowl, at center stage and under blinding spotlights.

Whether another public figure could have retained his composure under such circumstances is doubtful. Aaron was in methodical pursuit of Babe Ruth's lifetime major league home run record of 714, held sacred since the Babe's retirement in 1935, and the closer he drew to the mark the less privacy he enjoyed.

"The thing I'll always remember," said an Atlanta teammate, "is the way he handles himself. And something else, none of this has changed him."

The pressure on the Braves' outfielder started to build during the 1973 season when he clouted 40 home runs, climbing within two of breaking Ruth's all-time standard. Aaron was 39 and in his 20th major league season.

On the first swing of the next season, Aaron tied Ruth's mark by tagging a Jack Billingham pitch for a home run at Riverfront Stadium in Cincinnati. Aaron sat out the second game of the series, then failed to connect in the third game.

Braves officials, wanting Aaron to both equal and surpass Ruth's record at Atlanta Stadium, had at one point announced their intentions of holding Aaron out of the entire Cincinnati series. Overruled by Commissioner Bowie Kuhn, the Braves lost out on "hosting" No. 714 but retained a shot at No. 715 with a home-opening series coming up against Los Angeles.

And the man and the hour did meet in Atlanta Stadium —on April 8, 1974. In the fourth inning, with the outfield clock standing at 9:07 p.m., Aaron belted a pitch from Al Downing over the left-field fence and into the Braves' bullpen, where it was caught by reliever Tom House.

Pandemonium rounded the bases with Hammering Hank. After touching home plate, he trotted to a box seat where a female spectator clasped him in a bear hug. Later, among popping champagne corks in the clubhouse, Aaron conceded: "I didn't know Mom was that strong."

Aaron hit 18 more home runs in 1974, but was not yet ready to call it a career. He returned to Milwaukee, where he had launched his magnificent big-league career in 1954, and served the American League Brewers for two years as an outfielder and designated hitter. He socked 22 more home runs for an overall total of 755.

Aaron, a native of Mobile, Ala., was a skinny shortstop with Indianapolis in the Negro American League when he was discovered by Dewey Griggs, a scout for the Braves. For $10,000, the National League club acquired Aaron on June 14, 1952.

After two seasons as an infielder with Eau Claire of the

A young, hopeful Henry Aaron handled second base duties for the Jacksonville Braves in 1953.

Northern League and Jacksonville of the Sally League, Aaron won a regular outfield berth with the Braves in 1954 when Bobby Thomson fractured an ankle during a spring exhibition game. Three years later, Hank was the league's Most Valuable Player, leading the Braves to a pennant and World Series upset over the New York Yankees.

Next to his home runs that tied and broke Ruth's record, Aaron's most satisfying hit may have been an infield single at Cincinnati on May 17, 1970. Before the largest

Hank Aaron had plenty of company (above) as he rounded the bases for the record-breaking 715th time in his illustrious career on April 8, 1974, in Atlanta. Aaron finished his career in 1976 (left) with the Brewers in Milwaukee, site of many of his early-career exploits.

Crosley Field crowd in 23 years, Aaron beat out a bouncer against Wayne Simpson in his first at-bat in the second game of a doubleheader.

With that safety, Aaron became the first major leaguer to collect 3,000 hits and 500 home runs.

As Aaron crossed the bag, a figure leaped over the fence behind first base and trotted toward the infield. It was Stan Musial, Aaron's boyhood idol and the only living member of the 3,000-hit club.

"It was getting awfully lonely," said The Man. "Con-gratulations, Henry."

The slugging outfielder would have preferred to hit a home run for his 3,000th hit. Ironically, he connected on his next at-bat. It was No. 570.

All-Star Game honors gravitated early to Aaron. At the finish, he had appeared in 24 midsummer classics, 23 for the National League and one for the American. Curiously, the career home run king clouted only two All-Star homers, his first in Detroit in 1971 and his second in Atlanta in 1972.

# Grover Cleveland Alexander

In 79 years of World Series competition, there have been few dramatic moments to match what occurred on October 10, 1926, at Yankee Stadium.

With the bases loaded and two out in the seventh inning of Game 7 and the Yankees attempting to overcome a 3-2 St. Louis lead, a 39-year-old righthander shuffled out of the Cardinals' bullpen and struck out rookie slugger Tony Lazzeri.

The aged reliever, who had pitched the Cardinals to a Series-tying 10-2 victory the previous day, was Grover Cleveland Alexander—known familiarly as Old Pete or simply Alex.

For the remainder of the contest, the Yankees swung ineffectually at Old Pete's offerings. They failed to collect even one hit and when Babe Ruth was thrown out on an attempted steal to end the game, the righthander from St. Paul, Neb., was truly Alexander the Great in St. Louis.

Alexander joined the Phillies in 1911 after winning 29 games the previous year for Syracuse of the New York State League. Purchased by the National League club for $500, Alex was promised that he would earn $250 monthly with the Phils if he made the grade.

Alex hurled his first game for the Phils in a City Series exhibition contest with the defending world champion Athletics in bandbox Baker Bowl. "You'll pitch five innings," informed catcher Pat Moran. "They'll be murder, but you'll learn something."

The game proved more of a learning experience for the A's than for Alexander, however. In five innings, the 24-year-old rookie allowed no runs and no hits, nor did he walk a batter.

Alex was scheduled to make his regular-season debut in New York, but a fire that destroyed the grandstand at the Polo Grounds the night of April 13 caused the game to be postponed. He bowed in at Boston, losing 5-4 in 10 innings. Curiously, Old Pete pitched his final game in Boston 19 years later, hurling the last two innings of a 5-1 defeat that was charged to the Phils' Phil Collins.

After his initial setback in Boston, Alexander won 28 games in 1911 to establish a modern major league rookie record that still stands. He lost 13 games overall that season.

One of the most distinguished efforts of his freshman season was a 12-inning marathon against Cy Young, who at age 44 was pitching his final major league game. Young, trying for his 512th victory, struggled through 11 scoreless innings before the Phils touched the Boston veteran for the game's only run.

Alex enjoyed his finest overall season in 1915 when he compiled a 31-10 record and a 1.22 earned-run average. Despite the short dimensions of his home park, Alexander registered 12 shutouts.

Grover Cleveland Alexander (left) in 1911, his rookie season.

In the opening game of the 1915 World Series at Baker Bowl, Alex scattered eight hits and defeated the Boston Red Sox, 3-1.

Old Pete chalked up 33 victories (including 16 shutouts) in 1916 and 30 in 1917 for a three-year total of 94. Despite his valiant efforts, the Phils were runners-up in both the 1916 and 1917 pennant races.

In 1917, Alexander hurled a Labor Day doubleheader in Brooklyn, winning the opener, 5-0, and taking the nightcap, 9-3.

On May 22, 1926, Alexander (above, shaking hands) was honored by the Cubs. Just over a month later, he was waived to St. Louis after repeated run-ins with Manager Joe McCarthy. Alexander (below) was sent to France in 1918 as a member of the 89th Infantry Division.

Alexander's best season was 1915, when he finished 31-10 with a league-leading 1.22 ERA for the Phillies.

Shortly after the close of the season, Alex, at his Nebraska home, read in the daily papers that he and catcher Bill Killefer had been traded to the Chicago Cubs for two players and $60,000.

After pitching only three games at the start of the 1918 season, Alex joined the Army and was sent to France where he served as an artillery sergeant. When he returned home, Alex was a changed man; he suffered fits of epilepsy throughout the remainder of his life.

Alexander won 27 games one season with the Cubs and

22 in another. On June 22, 1926, Alexander was waived to the Cardinals. He had run afoul of Chicago Manager Joe McCarthy with excessive drinking habits stemming from his epilepsy.

Alex, who posted 21 victories for St. Louis in 1927, tried to recapture some of his old magic in Game 2 of the 1928 World Series. But he yielded six hits and four walks in 2⅓ innings against the Yanks, and was charged with a 9-3 defeat. Relieving in the fourth and final game, Alex gave up four hits in 2⅔ innings.

# Walter Alston

Speculation ran wild on the identity of the new Brooklyn manager. When media people crowded into the Dodger offices on Montague Street on November 24, 1953, the popular candidate was shortstop Pee Wee Reese, who had declined the post once before.

When the door to the inner sanctum swung open, President Walter O'Malley, seated at his desk, pointed to a balding stranger at his side and announced: "This is Walter Alston. I've hired him as my manager to beat the Yankees next season."

Alston succeeded Chuck Dressen, who had failed to defeat the Yankees in the 1952 and '53 World Series. Dressen also had demanded a multi-year contract to pilot the Dodgers. Such a practice was foreign to O'Malley's policies and Dressen was deposed.

Alston, sometimes known as Smokey because of the fastball he displayed as a youthful pitcher, was a virtual unknown. Even in his little hometown of Darrtown, O., he was not a familiar figure.

A graduate of Miami (O.) University and an off-season science teacher and basketball coach, Alston appeared in one major league game, for the Cardinals, on the final day of the 1936 season. In his only at-bat, he struck out against Lon Warneke of the Cubs. In two chances at first base, he committed one error.

Alston did not appear in a major league uniform again until opening day of 1954 when the Dodgers, despite two home runs by Roy Campanella, lost to the Giants, 4-3.

In the 18-year interim, Walter completed his playing career (at Pueblo in 1947) and launched his managerial career (at Portsmouth, O., in 1940).

In 1947, Neal Hobbs, general manager of Pueblo (Western), conferred with Branch Rickey, then the Mahatma of Montague Street, over a manager for the Class A club. After a dramatic contemplation, Rickey removed the cigar from his mouth and announced, "I'm going to give you Walter Alston as your manager."

"Who is Walter Alston?" asked Hobbs.

"Alston is the man we're grooming to manage the Dodgers someday," advised Rickey, who had moved on to the Pittsburgh Pirates before Walter arrived in Flatbush.

By 1950, Alston was manager of the Montreal Royals. He had engraved impressive records at every stop, and Montreal was no exception. He won pennants in 1951 and 1952 and, after finishing second the next year, his Royals defeated Buffalo and Rochester in the '53 International League playoffs before beating Kansas City, a Yankee farm club, in the Junior World Series.

A direct opposite to Dressen, his pepperpot predecessor, the strong and unemotional Alston spoke little. He conducted no pep rallies, engaged in no dramatic confrontations with umpires.

**Walter Alston's only major league plate appearance came at the end of the 1936 season when he batted against the Cubs at Sportsman's Park.**

Alston did not make a show of discipline, but enforced it in his own style. When Don Newcombe refused to pitch batting practice, Alston ordered him to remove his uniform and leave the park. Newk was back a day later, minus several hundred dollars in penalties and lost pay.

Alston did not win the pennant in 1954, but he finished first in 1955 and followed with a dramatic World Series conquest of the Yankees that gave Brooklyn its only world title. His Dodgers repeated as league champions in '56. When the Dodgers transferred to Los Angeles in 1958 and Walter's "Boys of Summer" were past their prime, Alston fell to seventh. He rebounded in '59, however, guiding the Dodgers to a World Series title over the White Sox.

The Quiet Man never gloated in victory, nor bled in defeat. Unemotionally, he conducted postgame interviews regardless of the fortunes of the day. When the Dodgers lost a heartbreaking third game in the 1962 playoffs to the Giants, Alston answered probing inquiries outside the clubhouse while protecting his players from the press.

Working always on one-year contracts, Alston won seven pennants and four World Series titles in 23 years.

On September 27, 1976, Walter announced his retirement. Only Connie Mack and John McGraw had managed one club for a longer time.

# Cap Anson

The first of baseball's superstars, Cap Anson compiled impressive batting statistics whether pitchers threw from 45 feet, or 50 feet, or 60 feet, 6 inches.

The first baseman for Chicago's National League club was the first player to collect 3,000 hits in his career, the first to hit three consecutive home runs in a game, the first to clout five home runs in two consecutive games and the first to rap four doubles in a single contest. As a first baseman, he also was the first to complete two unassisted double plays in one game.

The reflexes of the 6-foot-1, righthanded hitter were so quick, it was said, that he never was hit by a pitched ball—no matter what the pitching distance.

Legend attributes to Anson the honor of being the first white child born in Marshalltown, Ia. As a teen-ager, Anson played with his father and brother on a town team that was the scourge of the state.

In 1869, Anson attended Notre Dame and is generally credited with organizing the university's first baseball team. He was a third baseman and captain.

Anson played five years with the Athletics of the National Association before shifting to the Chicago club—the White Stockings—of the fledgling N.L. in 1876. He was a third baseman and batted .343 for the first N.L. championship team.

Anson played the outfield and second base and also caught before concentrating on first base in 1879, the year he commenced his 19-year reign as manager of the team.

Cap was "neither the greatest, nor the most agile first baseman," one historian wrote. "Anson played only a few feet from the base and fresh, young Chicago infielders would throw the ball low to first so as to further bark his bruised shins.

"They enjoyed seeing him squirm, but Cap seemingly swallowed liberal doses from the Fountain of Youth and at times it looked as though he would go on forever . . . Fans in Chicago loved him and rooted for him whenever he came to bat. He also brought out the customers on the road, so they could root against him."

Anson won four batting championships, twice with averages over .400 and once with a .399 mark, and he managed the Chicagoans to pennants in 1880, 1881, 1882, 1885 and 1886.

Cap, also known as "Pop" before he stepped down as Chicago manager after the 1897 season, is frequently credited with being the father of spring training. In 1886, Anson shepherded his players to Hot Springs, Ark., to "boil out" after a winter of loading and swilling beer as home-town heroes.

Anson also pioneered inside baseball, coordinating infield and outfield play and originating other scientific ma-

**Major league baseball's original superstar was Cap Anson, the first player to amass 3,000 career hits and to hit three consecutive home runs in one game.**

neuvers quickly adopted by other clubs. A powerful figure himself, he showed the way in slugging for a purpose, not merely to drive the ball out of the park. At the plate, he stood with heels together and swung probably the heaviest bat of all time.

After leaving the Chicago club, Anson accepted an invitation to manage the Giants during the 1898 season. After three weeks, however, he quit. Anson said he couldn't accede to Owner Andrew Freedman's directives on the use of his personnel, nor could he accept a ban on talking to newspapermen.

Anson died in 1922, shortly after being appointed manager of a new golf club.

# Luke Appling

In his heyday as a shortstop for the Chicago White Sox, Luke Appling possessed perhaps the sharpest eye among major league batters.

He could foul off pitches almost at will, as the club secretary discovered on the day that he refused Luke's request for two new baseballs to give to admirers. "They cost $2.75 apiece," chided the secretary.

Appling held his tongue in disappointment, but the first time he came to bat that afternoon he worked the count to 3-and-2 and then fouled 10 pitches into the stands.

Looking toward the secretary sitting in a box seat, Appling shouted, "That's $27.50, and I'm just getting started."

Before he finished, the story goes, Appling distributed 23 souvenirs throughout the stands.

If Appling wasn't slicing baseballs into the stands, he was complaining about aches and pains that never seemed to forsake him. For years, he answered to "Old Aches and Pains," but the chief sufferers of his many, fancied maladies were opposing pitchers who felt the sting of Luke's bat.

Appling was a sophomore—and a three-sport star—at Oglethorpe University in Atlanta, with no intention of turning professional, when he suddenly found himself the shortstop for the Atlanta Crackers of the Southern Association in 1930. Before the end of the summer, he was acquired by the White Sox, with whom he played through 1950 (except for nearly two years of service in World War II).

The .310 lifetime hitter once declared that he owed his prowess as a batter to Lefty Grove, the hard-throwing lefthander of the Philadelphia A's.

In his first at-bat against Grove, Appling recalled, a high inside pitch nearly struck him. "I decided then," Appling noted, "that anybody who can duck away from his fastball doesn't have to worry about being beaned."

Luke's hitting accomplishments, which included two American League batting championships, were once attributed to his "studied carelessness" and the following incident was cited:

One day, while lounging around the batting cage, Appling noticed Bill Dickey of the Yankees draw his hand across his shirt in a gesture to his batterymate of the day. Luke interpreted the maneuver as a sign to pitch Appling inside.

On his first at-bat, Appling fell back from an inside change-up and doubled down the left-field line. Luke was a notorious right-field hitter for a righthanded batter.

On his next trip, Appling watched a fastball go by, then belted the second pitch, also a change-up, into the left-field stands.

When the bewildered pitcher later asked Appling if he

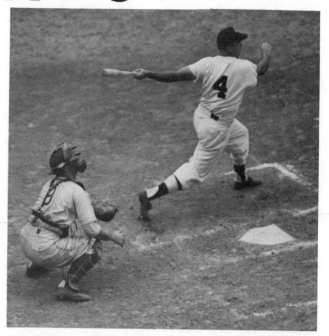

Luke Appling's batting stroke was still producing base hits in the late 1940s (above), but the 75-year-old former shortstop displayed a new dimension to his game in 1982 when he muscled up and hit a ball out of RFK Stadium during the Cracker Jack Old Timers Baseball Classic.

had stolen the Yankees' signs, the shortstop replied:

"Tell Dickey to keep his hands in his pocket or conduct his meetings in the clubhouse."

In his 17th year with the White Sox, Appling was tendered a day at Comiskey Park.

During his major league career, Appling hit only 45 home runs. However, in the Cracker Jack Old Timers Baseball Classic, played at Robert F. Kennedy Memorial Stadium in Washington in 1982, the 75-year-old Appling drove a Warren Spahn pitch over the fence to feature a 7-2 A.L. victory.

# Earl Averill

**Cleveland's Earl Averill crosses the plate after a Red Ruffing single during a six-run fifth inning for the American** **League during the 1934 All-Star Game at the Polo Grounds. Averill had reached base with a two-run double.**

No American League player had hit a home run in his first major league plate appearance until April 16, 1929. On that date, Cleveland's Earl Averill connected against Earl Whitehill, a crafty Detroit lefthander.

Averill had been acquired from the San Francisco Seals of the Pacific Coast League several months earlier. Billy Evans, general manager of the Indians, visited the West Coast to scout Roy Johnson, a teammate of Averill and more highly regarded as a major league prospect.

The longer Evans watched Johnson, the better he liked Averill. "There was something about the nonchalant Averill that won you over," Evans said. "I guess it was the easy, steady manner in which he did his work, without any great show."

The Indians took an option to purchase both outfielders. However, when Evans learned that the Tigers had offered $65,000 and two players for Johnson, he waived his option and bought Averill for $50,000.

Johnson proved a solid major leaguer, posting a lifetime batting average of .296. Averill, though, was an immediate star. And Earl compiled a .318 career average.

That initial home run remained Averill's foremost thrill throughout his 13-year major league career—no other Hall of Famer has homered in his first big-league plate appearance—but there were other remarkable achievements. Averill hit for the cycle at Philadelphia in 1933, and on September 17, 1930, he clouted four home runs in a doubleheader against Washington, three in one contest, and drove in 11 runs in the twin bill.

Earl was irked at day's end after the three-homer game. After all, he had just missed a record-tying fourth homer in the game when a long drive curved foul.

In 1931, Averill drove in seven runs in one contest, hit two home runs in a game three times and hit for a total of 10 bases twice and eight bases four times.

It is little wonder that on August 2, 1931, Boston pitchers decided that discretion was the better part of their repertoire and walked the lefthanded-hitting slugger all five times he appeared at the plate.

Averill played in five All-Star Games and numbered a double and a triple among his four hits. But the most-remembered All-Star play involving Averill did not include a hit.

In the 1937 classic at Washington's Griffith Stadium, Earl slammed a pitch from Dizzy Dean off the St. Louis hurler's foot. Attempting a comeback before the foot was healed completely, Dean put an unnatural strain on his arm, ending his career prematurely.

Averill, a product of Snohomish, Wash., a sawmill town in the big timber country, was named to Cleveland's all-time outfield in baseball's centennial year of 1969 along with Tris Speaker and Shoeless Joe Jackson.

# Home Run Baker

As a major leaguer, John Franklin Baker hit 96 career home runs, a reasonably good three-year total for a latter-day slugger, but hardly the kind of figure to inspire a nickname of "Home Run." But homers on successive days in the 1911 World Series did earn Baker such a sobriquet.

The Philadelphia A's third baseman rapped 11 home runs in the dead-ball season of 1911. The total was good enough to lead the American League, but incapable of stirring the public. What Baker accomplished on October 16-17, though, caught the fans' fancy.

The Giants won the Series opener and the teams were deadlocked in the sixth inning of Game 2 when Baker walloped a Rube Marquard fastball over the right-field wall in Philadelphia to account for a 3-1 victory.

The next day's New York newspapers featured a column by Christy Mathewson in which the Giants' ace criticized Marquard for the way he pitched to Baker. That afternoon, when Matty was within two outs of a 1-0 shutout, Baker homered into the right-field seats at the Polo Grounds and the A's went on to win, 3-2, in 11 innings. From that day forward, the Maryland farm boy was known as Home Run Baker.

Baker was a member of one of baseball's most illustrious units, the "$100,000 infield," which included Jack Barry, Eddie Collins and Stuffy McInnis.

In six World Series, Baker batted .363, compared with his regular-season lifetime mark of .307. He was devastating in the 1913 Series when he batted .450 and clouted another homer off Marquard.

After the A's four-game debacle at the hands of the Miracle Boston Braves in 1914, a Series in which Baker batted only .250, Owner-Manager Connie Mack didn't offer Baker a raise and the Philadelphia slugger sat out the 1915 A.L. season (playing semipro ball in Upland, Pa.). The following February, Baker was traded to the Yankees, for whom he appeared in the 1921 and 1922 Series (after voluntarily retiring in 1920 and again playing for Upland).

Home Run Baker, who, ironically, hit only 96 career homers, was a member of the Philadelphia A's in 1912.

Aside from his home runs in 1911, Baker is remembered as the Yankee whose sharply hit grounder between first and second base was converted into a 4-3-5 double play by the Giants that wrapped up the 1921 Series.

Although no gazelle, "Home Run" posted impressive stolen-base totals of 38 in 1911, 40 in 1912 and 34 in 1913.

Baker joined the A's late in the 1908 season at the conclusion of the Reading (Tri-State) campaign. He encountered Mack in the dining room of a Chicago hotel and announced: "Mr. Mack, I'm here."

"I see that you are," was the terse rebuttal.

To Baker's dismay, he discovered that Ed Walsh, the formidable spitballer, was scheduled to pitch that day's game. But Baker did not remain dismayed for long. "I fouled off a pitch, then Walsh threw me a ball, then I doubled over Fielder Jones' head in left field," Baker said.

Toughened by years of toil, Baker yielded to no intimidator. One year, when Ty Cobb slid into third base with spikes high, Baker went after the fiery Tiger and precipitated a near riot at Shibe Park. The A's and Tigers were deadly enemies thereafter.

Despite his differences with Mack in 1915, Baker remembered his old manager in 1924 when he spotted a burly, 17-year-old catcher in Maryland.

Mack was not instantly impressed. "We have enough catching," Connie told Baker.

"Play him anywhere," responded the old third baseman. "He has more power than anyone I've ever seen, including Babe Ruth."

Mack agreed to take a look, then several more. The prodigy was Jimmie Foxx, who hit 534 home runs in the majors.

Baker retired from the major leagues after the 1922 season. He managed briefly for Easton (Eastern Shore) and later served a one-year stint as president of the club.

He died in 1963 at age 77 after suffering a series of strokes.

# Dave Bancroft

No shortstop, it was said, was better than Dave Bancroft at fielding bad-hop ground balls or cutting off outfield throws and hanging up runners between bases.

On all-time, all-star teams of the first half of the 20th Century, Honus Wagner was the choice at shortstop. Bancroft ranked second—and only because the Flying Dutchman was a superior hitter.

As a rookie in 1915, Bancroft sparked the Phillies to their first National League pennant. He made the difference between the sixth-place club of 1914 and the pennant-winning performance of a year later, insisted Manager Pat Moran.

Bancroft, known as "Beauty" because of his superlative play, spent five years with the Phillies before Giants Manager John McGraw decided in June of 1920 that he needed Bancroft on his club.

The Polo Grounders, beaten out for the 1919 flag by the Cincinnati Reds, were deep in the second division after two months of the '20 race. Moreover, the Yankees were packing 'em in with their new hitting sensation, Babe Ruth, while the Giants were playing before expanses of empty seats.

At McGraw's suggestion, Giants President Charles Stoneham telephoned William F. Baker, president of the Phillies, and offered aging shortstop Art Fletcher, young pitcher Wilbur Hubbell and $100,000 for Bancroft. Baker was incredulous. No would-be trader had made such an extravagant offer in the immediate postwar period.

Baker hesitated to ask Stoneham to repeat the offer for fear it would be different the second time around. Stoneham demanded an answer, until Baker finally found his tongue and said: "I'll take the 9 o'clock train tomorrow and will be in your office at 11, when we can discuss the trade."

Good as his word, Baker, accompanied by the National League attorney as a witness, was in Stoneham's office on schedule and the deal was completed.

While the Giants failed to win the 1920 pennant with Bancroft in the ranks, they captured the next three flags with Dave at shortstop.

The new acquisition already had taken his position in the field for his first game as a Giant when catcher Pancho Snyder summoned Bancroft to a conference on the mound. "Maybe I should explain our signs to you," Snyder volunteered.

"Why, have they changed?" replied Bancroft. "If not, I know them already." Having mastered the system while with the Phils, Dave clearly was McGraw's type of brainy player.

One day in 1923 Bancroft reported to the Polo Grounds with a high fever, but insisted on playing. At game's end he collapsed in the clubhouse and the team physician was

**Dave Bancroft was a hopeful youngster in 1909 when he played shortstop for Duluth-Superior.**

summoned. "Call an ambulance," the doctor ordered, "this man has pneumonia."

"Imagine," marveled McGraw, "he played nine innings with pneumonia."

Despite his extreme admiration for Bancroft, McGraw agreed to trade him after the 1923 season so that Dave could manage the Boston Braves.

Through no fault of his own, but because the club was lacking in talent, Bancroft failed to inspire the Braves to great heights. After four seasons, he was dismissed by Judge Emil Fuchs, the club owner.

Bancroft caught on with the Brooklyn Dodgers for a couple years before returning to the Giants as a coach under McGraw. Whenever Little Napoleon was indisposed, Bancroft handled the managerial chores without loss of effectiveness. But his future as a Giant was sealed when McGraw retired in June of 1932. Dave finished the year under new Manager Bill Terry, then departed.

Bancroft briefly managed Minneapolis in the American Association and guided clubs in the low minors in his native Midwest before retiring to pursue his favorite pastimes, hunting and fishing.

# Ernie Banks

When the Chicago Cubs acquired Ernie Banks from the Kansas City Monarchs in 1953, they obtained more than a highly promising prospect. They acquired one of baseball's foremost good-will ambassadors.

In 19 years of major league competition, the shortstop-first baseman never lost his youthful enthusiasm, proclaiming regularly, "It's a great day for baseball, let's play two."

Banks could well appreciate the bounties derived from big-time baseball. He succeeded the hard way, through Negro league ball in which his salary was based on a percentage of the gate. "The most I ever got was $20 for a game in Hastings, Neb.," he recalled.

The Cubs bought Banks and a long-forgotten pitcher for about $25,000, but other clubs were well aware of the potential contained in the lithe and limber 22-year-old.

The White Sox made serious inquiries about Banks, but were unable to pin down Monarchs Owner Tom Baird on a price. Their ardor cooled when Banks, performing in a Negro all-star contest at Comiskey Park, failed to distinguish himself.

On the day that Banks donned a Cubs uniform for the first time, the club knew it had something special. Ernie walloped the first batting-practice pitch into the left-field bleachers at Wrigley Field, and never changed the tempo thereafter.

Before long, one American League executive said: "If I were permitted to pick one player out of the National League, it would be Banks."

Other experts hailed Banks for his good hands, his deadly aim and his ability to smother bad hops. "And how many shortstops can hit you a home run in the clutch?" asked Mel Ott, Hall of Fame outfielder.

In his second full season with the Cubs, Banks blasted 44 home runs. His most productive year in homers was 1958 when he socked 47 of his career total of 512.

Early in his career, Banks played 717 consecutive games, but removed himself from the lineup for fear that the pressures would jeopardize his career. He was shifted to first base in 1961 when an ailing knee reduced his mobility.

Mr. Cub, who did not play high school baseball because his Dallas alma mater did not field a team, was coveted frequently by rival clubs. One offer of $500,000 by the Cardinals received a flat "No" from Cubs Owner P.K. Wrigley.

One of Banks' more memorable days occurred on May 12, 1970, when he became the ninth member of the 500-homer club. The milestone was reached against Atlanta's Pat Jarvis in the second inning of a 4-3 Chicago victory.

During a standing ovation, Banks let his thoughts drift back to his first homer, a blast off Gerry Staley in St.

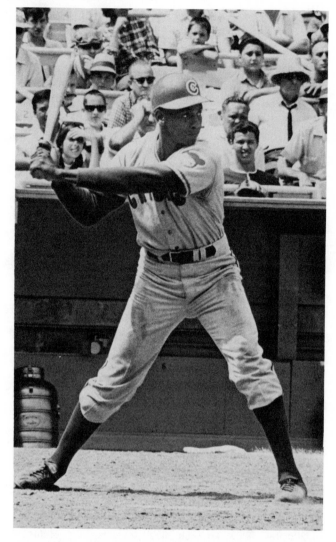

The booming bat of Ernie Banks produced 512 career homers, but never was enough to carry the Cubs to a pennant.

Louis on September 20, 1953.

Throughout his career, which ended in 1971, Ernie was highly respected for his even temperament. But there was a time, in 1959, when he accused an opponent of deliberately hitting him with a pitch. It was the third time during the season that Jack Sanford of San Francisco had nicked Banks and he was angry enough to announce on a post-game radio show that "his control is too good for him to have to do that."

While still at the height of his career, the Cubs' star tried his hand at politics, running as a Republican against the incumbent Eighth Ward alderman in Chicago. Ernie was soundly trounced, but not bitter. He consoled himself with the assurance that he had finished second which, at the time, was higher than the Cubs had finished during his career.

Banks approaches the plate and tips his hat to the Wrigley Field crowd (right) after hitting home run No. 500 in 1970. No. 14's defensive play (below) matched his hitting prowess and Banks was rewarded in 1982 by becoming the first Cub to have his uniform retired (above).

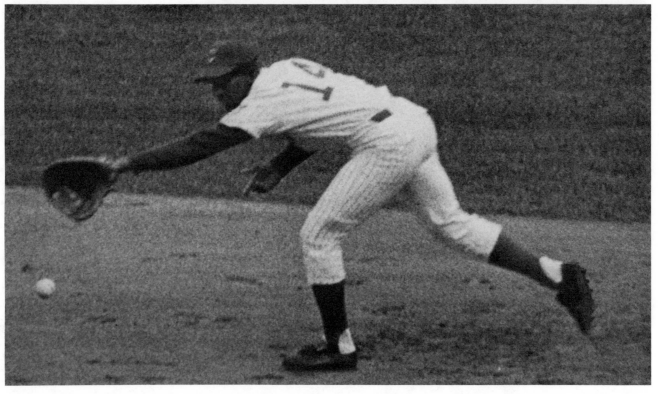

# Ed Barrow

If Edward Grant Barrow had accomplished nothing more, he would deserve a niche in the Hall of Fame for the influence he exerted on two of the first five players to be elected to the shrine.

In the mid-1890s, Barrow spotted a youngster with long, sweeping shoulders and bowed legs standing on the railroad tracks near Pittsburgh and heaving rocks into the Monongahela River. That chance discovery started Honus Wagner on the way to diamond immortality.

And, as manager of the Boston Red Sox, Barrow determined that one of his front-line pitchers possessed greater potential as a hitter than on the mound. There came the day in 1919 when he "called in Mr. Ruth and told him from now on you're an outfielder."

Barrow, a native of Springfield, Ill., and a boyhood resident of Nebraska, arrived in the major leagues in 1903 as manager of the Detroit Tigers. By 1918, he was manager of the Red Sox and produced a World Series championship at the expense of the Chicago Cubs.

In addition to converting Babe Ruth into an everyday slugger, Barrow wielded further influence on the Bambino in his Boston years.

On one occasion, the hot-tempered and poorly disciplined Ruth threatened to punch his boss in the eye. Barrow, although 50 years old, ordered Ruth into the clubhouse, bolted the door and started to remove his coat.

"Was there something you wanted to do?" began Barrow.

"No, Ed. I was just popping off," replied Ruth, half Barrow's age.

After the Babe socked 29 homers in 1919, he was sold to the Yankees for $125,000. Two years later, Barrow followed as business manager, having been recommended by Boston Owner Harry Frazee to Colonel Til Huston, co-owner of the New York club.

It was in the role as front-office chief that Barrow achieved his foremost success, organizing and developing the farm system that established the Yankees as the all-time kings of baseball.

To the New York media, Barrow was "Cousin Ed," but the title was not intended in the popular baseball sense as a soft touch. He was a hard-headed businessman as well as an astute judge of talent. Under his leadership, the Yankees hired the most discerning scouts who signed the most promising prospects.

Barrow's influence on the Yankees was instantaneous. The players, who had flouted Miller Huggins' authority for three years, were told in no uncertain terms by Barrow that the little skipper was their boss in the clubhouse, in the dugout and on and off the field.

The Yankees won pennants in the first three years of the Barrow administration. Before Barrow retired in 1945, they had captured 14 pennants and 10 world championships.

In constructing the Yankee empire, Barrow conceded that he took chances but the two greatest risks were the purchase of Tony Lazzeri and Joe DiMaggio. Tony had been the sensation of the Pacific Coast League, but was known to suffer from seizures. The Cubs and the Reds passed up the chance to buy the second baseman, but Barrow assigned a scout to follow Lazzeri for a period and, on the agent's recommendation, arranged for his purchase.

DiMaggio also was a PCL sensation, but suffered a knee injury that threatened his career. While other clubs were scared away by the injury, Barrow arranged for DiMaggio to undergo a physical examination. When the report showed no permanent damage, Barrow bought the San Francisco outfielder for $25,000.

At the depth of the Great Depression, Barrow created a national sensation by signing Ruth for $80,000, a salary peak that other players aspired to for two more decades. "And to think," Barrow mused years later, "I signed him for $7,500 in 1918."

Barrow was elected to the Hall of Fame by the Committee on Veterans on September 28, 1953, less than three months before his death in a Port Chester, N.Y., hospital.

**Edward Grant Barrow poses (below) with Mrs. Babe Ruth (left) and Mrs. Lou Gehrig.**

# Jake Beckley

Jake Beckley made up for his notorious scatter-arm with a bat that produced .300-plus averages 13 times.

By all measurements, Jake Beckley was one of the finest early-day players in the majors. In 20 years of major league competition, the lefthander batted more than .300 13 times. When he was on a hitting rampage, his cry of "Chickazoola" sounded a warning to pitchers that Beckley was after their scalps.

Great as Beckley was as a hitter, he also was the original scatter-arm. Any time Jake needed to throw the baseball, runners automatically headed for the extra base.

In the early 1900s, Beckley was tending first base for the Cardinals in a game against the Pirates, for whom Beckley had played some years earlier. When third baseman Tommy Leach of the Bucs laid down a bunt, Jake fielded the ball cleanly and tossed to pitcher Jack Taylor, covering the bag.

To nobody's surprise, the ball sailed a yard over Taylor's head and into foul territory.

Beckley lumbered after the ball as Leach raced around the bases. Instinctively, Jake knew that Leach would try to score, but he did not trust his erratic left arm with a throw to the catcher, so he did the only thing a smart first baseman would do. He retrieved the ball and ran toward the plate, sliding in head-first from one direction as Leach slid feet-first from another.

Leach not only was out, but he suffered two broken ribs in the collision. When Leach recovered from his injury, he became an outfielder—all because of Beckley's erratic throwing arm.

Despite his weakness as a thrower, Jake stayed around long enough to set a major league record for first basemen by playing in 2,368 games.

Beckley played only 34 games in his third minor league season, with St. Louis of the Western Association, before he was sold to Pittsburgh for $100 (regarded as a high price in 1888). In 71 games during the remainder of that National League season, Old Eagle Eye batted .343, one point less than Cap Anson, the league batting champion.

A dashing individual, Beckley was a crowd favorite with his bizarre style of play.

Once, when he disagreed with an umpire's decision that awarded a triple to Roger Bresnahan of the Giants, Jake grabbed the ball from the umpire and fired it toward the backstop screen. This time, his aim was unerring. Unfortunately for Jake, time had not been called. As the ball rebounded crazily, Bresnahan walked home with the run.

During his big-league career, Beckley developed a hidden-ball trick that was a bit different from other similar plays. He concealed the baseball under one corner of the bag, extracted it and then tagged out the runner.

It was a slick maneuver until the day Jake lifted up the wrong corner of the base—no ball. As Beckley scrambled to locate the ball, Honus Wagner took second base.

# Cool Papa Bell

Exaggeration may be the only way to illustrate the blinding speed that Cool Papa Bell possessed during his 27 years in the Negro leagues.

Satchel Paige delighted in telling how Bell, on a smash through the box, was struck by the ball as he slid into second base.

Hyperbole, sure, but there were instances when Bell completely flabbergasted the opposition with his speed afoot.

One year, while opposing a major league all-star team on the West Coast, Bell took off from first base with the pitch. As Paige bunted down the third-base line, Bell reached second and continued toward third. And as Roy Partee set to throw to first, Cool Papa brushed past him to score.

Partee was a major league catcher. The pitcher was Bob Lemon, a future Hall of Famer. At the time, Bell was 45 years old.

Bell once was credited with circling the bases in 13.1 seconds, four-tenths of a second faster than the accepted major league mark set by Evar Swanson.

"The field was wet," Cool Papa recalled almost apologetically. "I once did it in 12 seconds."

Because of his burning speed, Bell was able to play a shallow center field. While with the Homestead Grays, he teamed with catcher Josh Gibson to pick runners off second base.

When Maury Wills was on his way to a modern major league record for stolen bases in a season in 1962, Cool Papa pointed out to the Dodger speedster that if teammates stood deep in the batter's box the catcher would, by necessity, retreat a step, thereby giving Wills an edge in swiping bases.

"I never thought of that," Wills acknowledged.

"That's how we played in the Negro leagues," replied Bell, who is said to have stolen 175 bases in one 200-game season.

Incomplete statistics credit Bell with hitting over .400 several times, and competent observers insisted he would have been outstanding in the American League or National League if the color ban had been lifted earlier.

One gauge to Bell's abilities against major league pitching is his performance in barnstorming games against Bob Feller, Dizzy Dean, Bob Lemon, Earl Whitehill and Bucky Walters. Bell batted well over .350 against big-league pitching.

A native of Starkville, Miss., Bell turned professional in 1922 at age 19 when he joined the St. Louis Stars. Seeking to make the youngster's debut as easy as possible, Manager Frank Duncan cautioned him against nervousness.

Bell assured Duncan: "Back home I played before

**By 1940, Cool Papa Bell was in his late 30s, coaching and playing for the Kansas City Monarchs.**

crowds that sometimes were as large as one thousand."

A teammate standing nearby observed: "He's a cool one, isn't he?"

"Yeah," replied Duncan, "a cool papa." The name stuck.

According to John Holway, premier historian of Negro baseball, Cool Papa once yielded a Negro league batting championship to Monte Irvin under extenuating circumstances.

In 1946, Jackie Robinson's first year in Organized Baseball, Bell and Irvin went into the final day's doubleheader with Bell leading in the batting race, .402 to .398. Bell needed to play two games to qualify for the title.

After rapping two singles in as many official at-bats in the opener, Bell sat out the nightcap, forfeiting the championship to Irvin.

"The fans were mad," recalled Bell, "but they didn't know what we were doing. We wanted to give Irvin a chance to go to the majors. We would rather pass something on to a young guy to help the future of the black man. And I'm not the only older guy who kept his average down. We didn't have a future. We were too old."

# Chief Bender

Born on a reservation near Brainerd, Minn., educated at the Carlisle Indian School and a major league starting pitcher at age 19 . . . that was the story of Chief Bender, the crafty Chippewa who starred for the Philadelphia Athletics for more than a decade.

Before the start of the 1903 season, A's Manager Connie Mack was asked about the team's prospects. About his pitching, Mack said: "I think I will be able to put together a good staff. Albert Bender, who pitched for the Harrisburg A.C. last season under the name of Charles Albert, should help us."

Mack often referred to the Chief as Albert.

The 1903 season was only a couple hours old when Bender received a chance to display his wares. On opening day in Boston, Bender relieved Eddie Plank with the A's trailing, 6-0, and held the Red Sox at bay while the A's pulled out a 10-7 victory over Cy Young.

In his first starting assignment, against the New York Highlanders at Columbia Park in Philadelphia, Bender outpitched Clark Griffith, 6-0.

Chief appeared in five World Series and collected a winners' share three times. His two most notable performances were a four-hit, 3-0 victory over the Giants in 1905 when all five Series games produced shutouts, and a three-hit, 4-1 triumph against the Cubs in 1910.

Bender pitched his only big-league no-hitter in 1910, blanking Cleveland, 4-0. Cleveland's lone baserunner, aboard with a walk, was nailed by 20 feet while trying to steal.

The Chief never asked to be taken out of a game. He was durable and rarely missed a turn. In 1905, when he was 21, Bender shut out the Washington Senators in the first game of a late-season doubleheader. When the Nats forged an early 3-0 lead in the nightcap, Mack called on the Chief again, and he won that contest, too, as the A's rallied to win the game and the pennant.

Speaking of Bender, Mack once said, "If I had all the pitchers I ever handled, with one game coming up that I simply had to win, I would call on the Chief. He was my greatest money pitcher."

Prior to the start of the 1911 Series, Mack informed Bender: "I expect you to win the Series (against the Giants)." The manager then asked, "Albert, how much do you owe on your house?"

"None of your business," replied the Chief, smiling.

Eventually, he admitted there was $3,500 remaining on his mortgage.

Bender lost the Series opener to Christy Mathewson, but went on to win two games, including the 13-2 clincher. The next morning, Mack presented him with a check for $3,500.

**Chief Bender, the crafty Chippewa who starred for Connie Mack's Philadelphia A's, was a rookie in this 1903 photo.**

Bender's top salary with the A's was $5,000. After the 1914 season, in which Bender suffered one of the A's four Series defeats to the Miracle Braves, Federal League agents intensified their efforts to lure major leaguers to the new outlaw circuit.

A $5,000 signing bonus and an $8,500 annual salary made Bender a member of the Baltimore team in 1915.

"It was the biggest mistake of my life," he conceded. "If I had had somebody to advise me, I probably wouldn't have done it." Bender was 4-16 in 1915 for a Baltimore club that finished 47-107.

The Chief returned to Philadelphia in 1916—as a member of the Phillies—and appeared in his final major league game in 1925 when, at 41, he hurled one inning for the White Sox, yielding a walk and a home run.

Bender managed New Haven of the Eastern League for two seasons under George Weiss, later a Yankee executive.

In 1927, Bender was named manager of Johnstown (Middle Atlantic) for the second half of the season. He won seven games during the remainder of the campaign, including a one-hitter.

# Yogi Berra

Probably no major leaguer has had more anecdotes, real or fancied, told at his expense than the son of Italian immigrants who grew up in St. Louis hoping to become a Cardinal.

When folks joshed him by saying he'd never be mistaken for a matinee idol, Yogi Berra grunted: "I hit with a bat, not with my face."

As a young catcher with the Yankees, Yogi roomed with Bobby Brown, about to embark on a medical career. One night, Brown closed his medical tome at the same time Yogi closed his comic book, leading Berra to inquire: "How did yours turn out?"

Hitting and catching were Yogi's game, and he might have been a Cardinal except for $500, the bonus the Cardinals paid to his boyhood chum, Joe Garagiola, who preceded Berra to the majors.

When the Cards refused to match the bonus, Berra cast his lot with the Yankees. He went on to hit 358 career homers for the Yanks, then became the club's manager.

At a press conference announcing his appointment as manager for the 1964 season, Yogi was asked what he needed to find out about his new job.

"If I can manage," he replied straight-faced.

How had he prepared for the position, another wondered.

"You can observe a lot by watching," was the retort.

Yogi's replies created waves of laughter, but there were no guffaws when Berra stepped into the batter's box. He was a natural with a bat in hand. He helped propel the Yankees into 14 World Series, in which he batted .274, socked 12 homers, drove in 39 runs and earned about $100,000.

A compassionate sort, Berra cuffed Don Newcombe for three home runs in the 1956 Series. As he rounded the bases after one wallop, he glanced at the Brooklyn pitcher, a picture of despair, and shouted, "I hit a good pitch, Newk."

Yogi, who derived his nickname from a movie character, was not a selective hitter. He functioned on the theory that if he could reach a pitch with his bat, he should swing at it. A base on balls was something abhorred.

Berra was always a menace at the plate, but particularly when an opposing club walked a preceding batter to pitch to him.

In a game against Boston during Casey Stengel's regime, Yogi and Ol' Case had a difference of opinion on the bench. Stengel bet a beer that the opposition would walk Mickey Mantle intentionally to load the bases so that a lefthanded reliever could be brought in to pitch to the lefthanded-swinging Berra. Yogi took the wager.

With the bases jammed, righthander Skinny Brown was replaced by lefthander Bill Wight.

**Yogi Berra is welcomed home by Mickey Mantle after hitting a home run in the first game of the 1953 World Series against the Dodgers.**

"Okay," said Berra, "you win the bet, but I'm gonna change my stance."

"What stance you gonna use?" Stengel wondered.

"My home run stance with the bases loaded," Berra responded, and two pitches later he drove the ball over the right-field fence.

Berra also clouted a grand slam in the World Series (1956), was the first player to pinch-hit a Series homer (1947) and established dozens of other marks, most of which still stand.

The three-time Most Valuable Player managed the Yankees to the American League pennant in '64, but was deposed after losing the Series to the Cardinals. He won an N.L. flag as skipper of the Mets in 1973 and again was on the losing end of a seven-game Series, to the Oakland A's.

By 1972, Berra was giving umpires his two-cents worth as manager of the New York Mets.

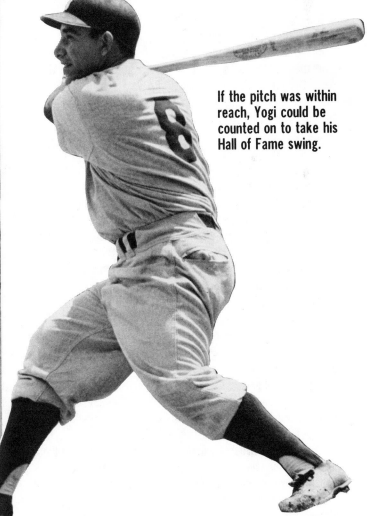

If the pitch was within reach, Yogi could be counted on to take his Hall of Fame swing.

Berra gathers in a foul pop during the third game of the 1949 World Series at Brooklyn's Ebbets Field.

# Jim Bottomley

One of the most popular players to wear a Cardinal uniform, Jim Bottomley starred on four pennant-winning clubs, two of which (the 1926 and 1931 teams) also captured World Series titles.

With a touch of swagger, a constant smile and a cap perched at a rakish angle, Bottomley came by his nickname of "Sunny Jim" honestly and, in his bachelor days, he was certain to attract thousands of extra customers to Ladies Days at Sportsman's Park.

Bottomley owed his professional baseball career to the fact that a St. Louis policeman was sitting in the stands on an afternoon in 1919 when Jim belted two home runs and three triples for a Nokomis, Ill., semipro team that paid the young first baseman $5 a game.

The policeman recommended Bottomley to Branch Rickey, manager of the Cardinals. Within a few years, Jim was a Redbird regular, one of the first products harvested in Rickey's budding farm system.

Bottomley's most memorable day as a major leaguer occurred on September 16, 1924, at Ebbets Field in Brooklyn.

Batting with the bases loaded in the first inning, Bottomley singled home two runs.

In the second, he doubled to left, driving in another run.

In the fourth inning, with Cardinals on second and third base, Brooklyn Manager Wilbert Robinson offered an intentional walk to Rogers Hornsby, probably figuring that the next batter, Bottomley, already had his quota of hits for the day.

Jim pulled a drive over the right-field wall and four runs scored.

In the sixth, one runner was aboard when Bottomley homered again, raising his runs-batted-in total for the day to nine.

When Bottomley singled in the seventh, two more runners crossed the plate. In the ninth, another single produced his 12th RBI, an all-time major league mark, and gave him a 6-for-6 day.

The old big-league record of 11 RBIs had been set, ironically, by Robinson in 1892.

Bottomley was voted the National League's Most Valuable Player in 1928 when he tied for the home run leadership (31), batted .325 and drove in 136 runs for the pennant-winning Cards. And in 1931 he enjoyed another 6-for-6 day (only two other players in big-league history have turned the trick twice).

A series of injuries forced Jim to the bench several times in '31. However, when his replacement, Rip Collins, also was shelved by injury in early August, Bottomley returned to the lineup in spectacular style. He collected 12 hits in four games and went on to wage a blistering battle with teammate Chick Hafey and Bill Terry of the Giants for

**Sunny Jim Bottomley's constant smile didn't relieve the agony he imposed on opposing pitchers.**

the batting title. Hafey finished at .3489, Terry at .3486 and Bottomley at .3482.

After the 1932 season, Bottomley was traded to Cincinnati, a chronic tail-ender. Though troubled with arthritis, he survived three seasons with the Reds, then was traded to the St. Louis Browns. When Hornsby was fired as the Browns' manager in July of 1937, Bottomley was named to succeed him, and he finished out the campaign.

After a minor league managerial stint at Syracuse, Bottomley retired from the game. However, in 1957, he signed with the Cubs as a scout and later was appointed manager of the Pulaski farm club in the Appalachian League.

Two games into his term as pilot, he suffered a heart attack and retired from baseball for good.

# Lou Boudreau

**Lou Boudreau was a performer whose brains matched his clutch bat. Boudreau was a rookie in 1938 (left) and**

**Cleveland's manager by 1942 (right), when he led off the All-Star Game at the Polo Grounds with a home run.**

Spectators rubbed their eyes in disbelief in 1946 when four Cleveland infielders suddenly took position on the right side of the diamond and the left fielder played deep shortstop.

The exaggerated deployment was designed by Cleveland Manager Lou Boudreau to blunt the slugging talents of Boston's Ted Williams, who had devastated Indians pitching in the first game of a doubleheader.

Boudreau was willing to concede a bunt single down the third-base line, if Williams' immense pride would permit, to deny a possible extra-base hit. The "Boudreau Shift" had its desired effect. Too proud to settle for a bunt single, Williams continued to swing away—into a subpar performance.

A graduate of the University of Illinois, the inventive Boudreau was a full-fledged major league shortstop at age 22. In his first full season, 1940, he led American League shortstops in fielding—a feat he also accomplished in seven of the next eight years.

Boudreau was a brainy performer, with a keen sense of anticipation. He also was capable of playing in pain. One time he played four weeks with what he thought was a pulled stomach muscle. It turned out to be appendicitis.

In 1948, Boudreau sat out several games to rest a badly injured ankle, but at a crucial spot in a critical game

with the Yankees he inserted himself as a pinch-hitter against Joe Page, the premier reliever of his time.

Boudreau singled through the box to drive in the deciding run, limping all the way to first base.

Boudreau was an assistant basketball coach at his alma mater in the winter of 1941-42 when he wrote to the president of the Cleveland club applying for the managerial post vacated by Roger Peckinpaugh.

Lou was interviewed by the board of directors and was awarded the job chiefly on the recommendation of an 82-year-old board chairman of a large paint company who insisted that the team needed new blood.

When he took over the Indians in 1942, Boudreau, at 24, became the youngest manager to head a team from the start of a major league season.

In 1948, the shortstop-manager drove Cleveland to a first-place tie with the Red Sox, then clouted two homers and two singles as he inspired the Tribe to an 8-3 victory in a one-game playoff for the American League pennant at Fenway Park.

Boudreau's .355 average and 106 runs batted in earned him the American League's Most Valuable Player award. In the Tribe's six-game World Series triumph over the Boston Braves, Boudreau contributed four doubles.

As a result of his achievements—and the fact that the

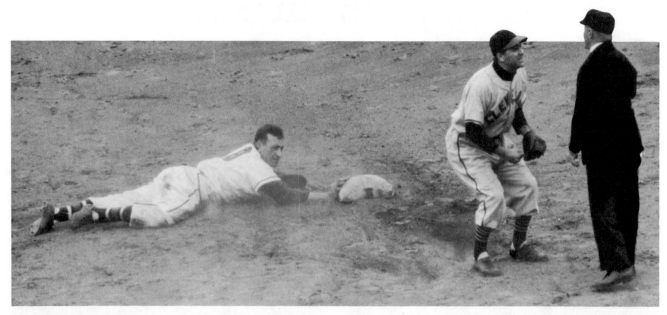

Boudreau argues (above) after umpire Bill Stewart had called Boston's Phil Masi safe on a pickoff attempt in

Game 1 of the 1948 Series. Boudreau was out (below) in Game 4 when he tried to stretch a double into a triple.

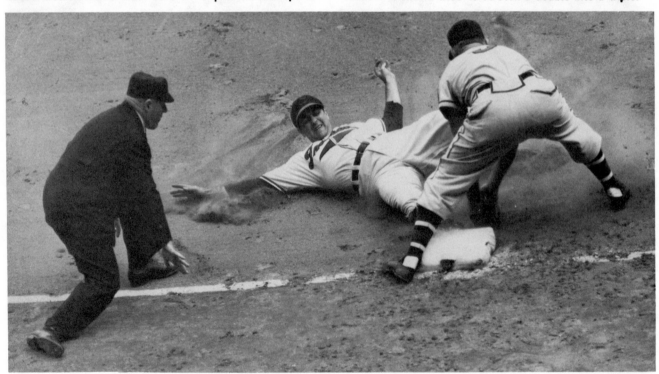

Indians set a major league mark with an attendance of 2.6 million—President Bill Veeck tore up Lou's $50,000 contract and gave him one for $75,000.

The love affair between Cleveland and Boudreau terminated two years later when a new general manager, Hank Greenberg, released Lou. Within a week, Boudreau signed with the Red Sox as utility infielder. One year later, he succeeded Steve O'Neill as manager.

Boudreau tried to revive the old Philadelphia Athletics in their first three seasons at Kansas City (1955-57), but

the players were not of a contending caliber and the A's finished as high as sixth only once.

In 1960, Boudreau took his baseball knowledge into the Cubs' radio booth. And when Owner Philip K. Wrigley made a managerial change, he called on the old shortstop. Lou replaced Charley Grimm, who took Boudreau's job in front of the microphone.

Lou completed the season on the field, but after a 54-83 record he retired permanently from an active role and returned to the broadcast booth.

30

# Roger Bresnahan

It was not true that Roger Phillip Bresnahan was born in Ireland, although for years he was known as the "Duke of Tralee," a monicker that he did very little to discourage.

But it is true that the Toledo-born catcher introduced shin guards to the big leagues. After taking foul tips on the shins and nursing cuts inflicted by baserunners' spikes, Bresnahan appeared on the field in 1907 with a protective device borrowed from cricket players.

The jeering was long and loud. Fred Clarke, manager of the Pirates, insisted that the guards represented a menace to runners sliding into the plate. Roger survived the ridicule, and that winter shin guards received formal approval from league officials.

Bresnahan was the batterymate of Christy Mathewson with the New York Giants when Matty enjoyed some of his greatest seasons. "I could've caught him sittin' in a rockin' chair," Bresnahan said of the fadeaway artist.

Although he gained his greatest fame as a catcher, and also played the infield and outfield, Bresnahan made his major league debut as a pitcher with the Washington club of the National League on August 27, 1897. Roger celebrated the occasion with a six-hit, 3-0 victory over St. Louis. He won three more games (losing none) that season.

Despite his impressive start, Bresnahan drifted back to the minors before surfacing to play in one game with the Cubs in 1900.

When John McGraw placed an American League club in Baltimore in 1901, Bresnahan jumped to the new organization. When McGraw tangled with A.L. President Ban Johnson in 1902 and accepted the manager's job with the New York Giants as a consequence, Bresnahan accompanied his boss to Gotham.

Bresnahan starred for the pennant-winning New York clubs of 1904 and 1905, catching superbly, batting leadoff and running the bases with excellent speed.

When the Cardinals were casting about for a new manager after the 1908 season, McGraw offered Bresnahan in a trade that stripped the St. Louis club of pitcher Bugs Raymond, outfielder John Murray and catcher George Schlei.

The Duke of Tralee lifted the Cardinals one notch in the standings in his first season and in 1911 St. Louis was in the thick of the race most of the year before winding up fifth.

Roger's work, nevertheless, pleased Owner Helene Robison Britton so much that she awarded her manager a five-year contract—and a civil contract calling for 10 percent of the club's profits.

When the Cardinals dropped to sixth place in 1912, Mrs. Britton wanted some questions answered. Bresnahan replied in syllables worthy of his crusty old mentor,

**Roger Bresnahan (shown in 1906), tired of bruised legs, introduced the shin guard to the major leagues in 1907.**

McGraw, and was fired.

Subsequently, Bresnahan received a $20,000 settlement for the unexpired portion of his contract and a $26,000 bonus to sign as a catcher with the Cubs.

In 1915, Roger was named the Cubs' manager, but he lasted only one season.

Bresnahan invested $40,000 of his baseball earnings in the Toledo club of the American Association, serving as a playing manager. He concluded his playing career in 1918 at age 39 and sold the franchise in 1922.

The Duke of Tralee pulled on the catching gear for the last time in 1943 when he was 64. Appearing in a war-bond game in New York, Bresnahan, for the first time, caught the pitches of Walter Johnson, former Big Train of the Senators, who was 56.

"He must have been quite a pitcher," Bresnahan said of the longtime standout, "because he's still fast."

# Dan Brouthers

Like Babe Ruth of a later generation, Dan Brouthers started his career as a pitcher. Unlike the Bambino, however, Brouthers shifted to first base rather than the outfield.

Also unlike Ruth, Dan never acquired even a small degree of fame on the mound. Pitching for Troy of the National League, Brouthers was victimized by 23 of his teammates' errors in one of his rare mound appearances.

Brouthers' tremendous power at bat became evident early, even to the most casual observer. Dan hit 14 home runs in 1884, a high figure for those times.

As the "Babe Ruth of his day," Brouthers set standards for long-distance hitting. In 1886, while playing for Detroit, Dan walloped a pitch out of Capitol Park in Washington that for years was recognized as the granddaddy of all prodigious pokes.

A Brouthers blow also sailed out of the Boston park in '86 and struck a structure known as Sullivan's Tower. That incident, in itself, was of little note, but when the impact unseated fans who were obtaining a cheap view of the game, it became a widespread news item.

A native of Sylvan Lake, N.Y., Dan made his major league debut in June of 1879 for Troy.

By 1881, Brouthers was with Buffalo of the National League and soon gained recognition as a member of that club's "Big Four" along with utilityman Hardie Richardson, third baseman Deacon White and shortstop Charlie Rowe.

Brouthers won batting championships in 1882 and 1883, becoming the first player to win consecutive crowns, but a sprained ankle in 1884 contributed to his batting decline to .325.

Brouthers enjoyed one of his most explosive days at the plate on September 10, 1886, when he clouted three homers, a double and single against old friend Jim McCormick in a game at the West Side grounds in Buffalo.

Several weeks later, after Dan completed the season with a .370 average, fans were stunned by the news that the financially strapped Buffalo club had sold the "Big Four" to Detroit. The price reportedly was $7,500, a sensationally high figure for that era.

When the Wolverines, as N.L. champions, won a post-season series from St. Louis, king of the American Association, in 1887, Brouthers was able to participate in only one of the 15 contests because of illness. Upon receiving his $200 winner's share, Dan requested that the money be divided among his teammates because he was of minimal importance to his club in the series. The offer was declined.

During the same season of '87, Dan joined John Montgomery Ward and Ned Hanlon in presenting several player requests to management. A meeting was held to discuss the reserve clause and to ask that a player's full salary be

**Dan Brouthers was known as the "Babe Ruth of his day," which spanned the 1880s and 1890s.**

spelled out in every contract.

Ownership rejected the contract plea, and in 1890 Brouthers jumped to the Players League.

An American Association campaign (1891) followed, then the old warrior spent five more years in the N.L. before going to the minors.

At the request of his old friend, John McGraw, Brouthers joined the Giants in 1904, but was unproductive in five at-bats.

Brouthers' association with Little Napoleon did not terminate when Dan took off his uniform for the last time, however. In 1907, Brouthers signed as a scout for the Giants and for more than 20 years served as a night watchman and press-box custodian at the Polo Grounds.

# Mordecai Brown

Because of two accidents, Mordecai Brown gained Hall of Fame stature as a major league pitcher.

The first mishap occurred when Brown was in his childhood. He stuck his right hand in a feed chopper on an uncle's Indiana farm and lost all but about an inch from his right index finger.

As a young man, Mordecai was playing third base when the pitcher on a semipro team fell and injured his shoulder. Pressed into duty as a pitcher, Brown attained immediate success.

Brown frequently asserted that his handicap was actually an advantage to him as a pitcher because it imparted a sharper break to his curveball.

Mordecai made his professional debut in 1901 with Terre Haute (Three-I) in his native Indiana after he was recommended to the club president by a brother of Cy Pfirman, later a National League umpire. Brown never signed a contract with Terre Haute, but received $40 a month.

After winning 23 games for Terre Haute and then 27 for Omaha in 1902, Brown went to the big leagues.

The righthander, called Three Finger by the fans but Brownie by his teammates, was a sub-.500 hurler with the eighth-place St. Louis Cardinals of 1903. However, he quickly became a mainstay of the Chicago Cubs' staff following his trade to Frank Selee's team after his rookie major league season.

The pitching duels between Brown and Christy Mathewson were historic engagements.

Brown's best-remembered triumph was pitched on October 8, 1908, in a game in which he was not the starter.

The contest was a replay of a game in which Fred Merkle earned undying notoriety for his failure to touch second base as the potential winning run crossed the plate. The earlier game—a 1-1 tie—had been called after nine innings when fans streamed onto the field.

Jack Pfiester was the Cubs' starter in the replay, but was lifted when the Giants scored one run in the first inning. Brown took over and held the Giants to four hits the remainder of the game and picked up a pennant-winning 4-2 decision over Mathewson.

Three years earlier the two righthanders had hooked up in a no-hit struggle for eight innings before the Giants nicked Brown for two ninth-inning safeties to pull out a 1-0 victory.

Matty gained the no-hitter. Brown never achieved the goal of all pitchers, although he posted seven one-hitters.

The two old titans of the mound bade farewell to major league pitching on September 4, 1916, battling head-on when Matty was manager of the Reds and Brown was wearing a Cubs uniform again after stints with three other

Mordecai Brown already was among baseball's premier pitchers in 1909 when he finished 27-9 for the Cubs.

teams. It was a sentimental matchup of Mathewson, 36, and Brownie, 39, with the younger one staggering to a 10-8 victory.

Brown scored his first World Series win against the Hitless Wonder White Sox of 1906, beating Nick Altrock, 1-0, in Game 4 after losing the opener to Altrock, 2-1.

But Brown's most satisfying achievement may have been his first appearance against Ty Cobb in the 1907 Series. The Detroit star had boasted he would hit .800 against Chicago pitching. Cobb went 1-for-4 against Brown and finished the Series with a .200 batting average.

The following year was Brown's most productive season in victories. Pitching 312 innings in 1908, Mordecai captured 29 decisions and walked only 49 batters.

# Morgan Bulkeley

When the National League was founded in 1876, Morgan G. Bulkeley, a man highly regarded in the worlds of finance and politics, was named president. Bulkeley was exactly what was needed to head a league of professional baseball clubs, a unit viewed with an air of suspicion in some quarters.

Officially, the election was conducted by the time-honored system of drawing names from a hat. Bulkeley's name was the first to be drawn. The second, Nicholas E. Young, was named secretary-treasurer.

Bulkeley accepted the office with the understanding that his term would be for one year only, after which he would be permitted to resign to devote his energies to other interests.

While Bulkeley was the nominal head of the new circuit, the force behind the chair was William A. Hulbert. A Chicagoan, Hulbert represented the brains behind the throne. Because he insisted that Bulkeley accept the presidency, Hulbert has never been enshrined at Cooperstown. Conversely, Bulkeley occupies a niche on the strength of his one-year presidency.

Bulkeley was a New England blueblood, descended from Mayflower settlers. An ancestor, the Rev. Peter Bulkeley, was said to have been the first settler of Concord, Mass.

Morgan's father had been an attorney and member of the state legislature before founding the Aetna Life Insurance Co. in 1850.

Morgan attended public schools in Hartford, Conn., where the family moved in the 1840s, but instead of pursuing his education and attending Yale, as his parents wished, he left school at age 14 and took a job as an errand boy at Aetna. Eventually, at 51, he received an honorary master of arts degree from Yale, and, in 1917, Trinity College conferred upon him an LL.D.

In 1852, Bulkeley left Hartford for Brooklyn, N.Y., where he obtained employment in his uncle's dry goods store. Seven years later, he was a partner in the business. At the outbreak of the Civil War, Morgan enlisted in the 13th New York Volunteers and saw action with General George B. McClellan in the Virginia Campaigns.

At the conclusion of the National League's first season, Bulkeley, as promised, yielded the president's chair to Hulbert. Bulkeley did not even attend the league meeting at which the Mutuals and Athletics were expelled for failure to complete their schedules.

Bulkeley founded and served for seven years as president of the United States Bank of Hartford. In 1879, he was elected president of Aetna and later head of Aetna's two subsidiary companies.

From 1880 to 1888, Morgan served as mayor of Hartford, donating his salary to the city's poor fund.

Bulkeley then served as governor of Connecticut from

**Morgan Bulkeley, a heavyweight in the worlds of finance and politics, became the first N.L. president in 1876.**

1888 to 1893. He was elected U.S. senator in 1905, serving until 1911.

He was a delegate to the Republican national convention from 1888 to 1896, being present for the nomination of William McKinley in '96. Bulkeley, himself, received 39 votes for the vice-presidential nomination.

Bulkeley was a member of the Grand Army of the Republic, being founder and department commander; a member of the Massachusetts Commandery of the Loyal Legion; Society of the Cincinnati Sons of the American Revolution; Society of Mayflower Descendants; Society of Colonial Wars, and Society of the War of 1812.

On Bulkeley's death, N.L. club owners, on the motion of Charles Ebbets of Brooklyn, adopted a resolution calling for the league to "inscribe on its records its appreciation of the invaluable aid rendered by him as a founder of the national game and . . . give expression of our honor to the man and of the deep regret at his death, we now convey these sentiments to the members of his family, and to those who were closely associated with him during his successful life."

# Jesse Burkett

There was a game in the New England League early in the century when Manager Jesse Burkett approached the plate as a pinch-hitter.

"Who ya batting for," asked the umpire politely.

"None of your business," growled Burkett, in his late 30s.

Turning to the spectators, the umpire called: "Burkett batting for exercise."

Through incidents such as that, Burkett came by his nickname of "The Crab" legitimately. Jesse did not display his dour disposition daily, though, and he generally was a congenial person, especially among young fans.

But the 5-foot-8, 155-pound Burkett was a scrapper. He once declared that he was forced to fight to succeed in a game of huskier athletes.

Once, while playing for the Cleveland Spiders in a National League doubleheader at Louisville, Burkett was ejected from both games. With teammates, he was escorted off the field by a police cordon. The next day he was fined $200 in police court for inciting a riot.

Burkett carried his short fuse to the American League after jumping from the St. Louis Cardinals to the Browns in 1902. An exchange of epithets with Manager Tommy Loftus of Washington led to Burkett punching his adversary in the nose. The next day he drew a $50 assessment.

Burkett, who was adept at bunting, shares with Ty Cobb and Rogers Hornsby the distinction of being the only players to hit .400 three times in the majors.

Jesse was past his 70th birthday when he attended a morning practice of Red Sox players in Boston. Noting that the players had difficulty laying down bunts, Burkett stepped into the batting cage and ordered the pitcher to throw as hard as he could.

The first pitch was bunted deftly down the third-base line, the second down the first-base line and the third was smacked on a line over second base.

As a star outfielder with Cleveland and St. Louis, Burkett amassed 200 or more hits in six of seven consecutive seasons (and had 199 in the other).

Jesse did not possess exceptional speed. Generally, he occupied the leadoff spot and reached base through his deftness with the bat. In a year in which he batted .400 (.402 in 1899), Burkett failed to win the batting title because Ed Delahanty of the Phillies batted .408. But Burkett did win championships with marks of .423 (1895), .410 (1896) and .382 (1901).

When his major league playing days were over, Burkett settled in Worcester, Mass., where he had played in 1889. In his adopted city, he led the team to four consecutive New England pennants and was an excellent hitter (leading the league in 1906 at .344). He also coached at Holy Cross from 1917 through 1920.

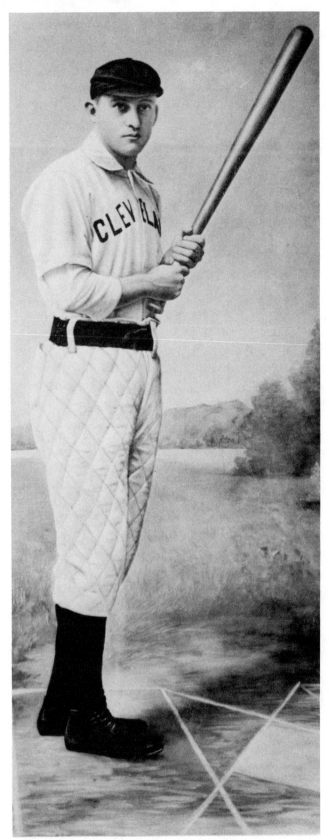

Jesse Burkett, a member of the Cleveland Spiders through most of the 1890s, was known as "The Crab."

# Roy Campanella

Baseball's all-time record crowd of 93,103 thronged the Los Angeles Memorial Coliseum in 1959—not for a World Series game, not for a decisive contest in a pennant race.

The fans flocked into the huge arena out of admiration and affection for a paralyzed ballplayer. The date was May 7 and the occasion was a benefit night for Roy Campanella.

From his wheelchair, the onetime catcher for the Brooklyn Dodgers intoned: "I thank God that I'm living to be here. I thank . . . every one of you from the bottom of my heart. It is something I'll never forget."

Nor will Campy's contributions ever be forgotten. A three-time Most Valuable Player, the rugged player was the heart of the Dodgers' lineup that dominated the National League in the 1950s. When the Yankees and Dodgers played the 1959 benefit in Los Angeles, they were performing for one of the most popular athletes ever.

When Campanella was injured in an automobile accident in January of 1958, he had turned 37 and Dodgers President Walter O'Malley had only recently announced that the club would shift from Brooklyn to Los Angeles for the '58 season. The catcher, driving toward his Long Island home in the early morning hours of a cold night, struck a slick spot in the road and his car slammed into a utility pole. Roy was pinned in the wreckage. Two vertebrae were fractured and Campanella was paralyzed below the waist. His career was over.

The son of an Italian father and a black mother, Campy joined a team known as the Bacharach Giants at age 15 for weekend games through Pennsylvania, New York, New Jersey and Connecticut. He performed for the Baltimore Elite Giants—spending winters in the Latin American leagues—before joining the Brooklyn organization in 1946, playing at Nashua (New England).

One of Campanella's favorite expressions was, "You gotta have a lot of little boy in you to be a good ballplayer," and he never lost his enthusiasm for the game. He bounced around behind the plate, chirping in his high-pitched voice. He caught every pitch with consummate ease and he swung the bat with an energy that bespoke a man in love with his work.

Campanella won Most Valuable Player awards in 1951, 1953 and 1955. He earned his first citation despite a series of injuries that would have crushed a less-determined spirit.

Before spring training, a hot-water heater exploded in his face. During spring training, he suffered a thumb fracture. Roy was beaned early in the '51 campaign, and he incurred lesser hurts during the season. With it all, the durable catcher played 143 games, batted .325, clouted 33 homers and batted in 108 runs.

When the Dodgers won the final game of the 1951

**Roy Campanella and umpire Bill Stewart are the picture of concentration as runner and ball converge on the plate during a 1951 game at Ebbets Field.**

regular season in Philadelphia, Campanella pulled a leg muscle running out a triple. His attempts to run thereafter were painful caricatures of the real Campy. He was sidelined after the first N.L. playoff contest against the Giants, a situation that might have had a more serious effect on the Dodgers' loss to the Giants than any other incident during the season.

When Campy received his third MVP plaque after the 1955 season, he announced: "When you win the first award, you're happy. When you win the second, you're very happy. But when you win the third, you're overwhelmed."

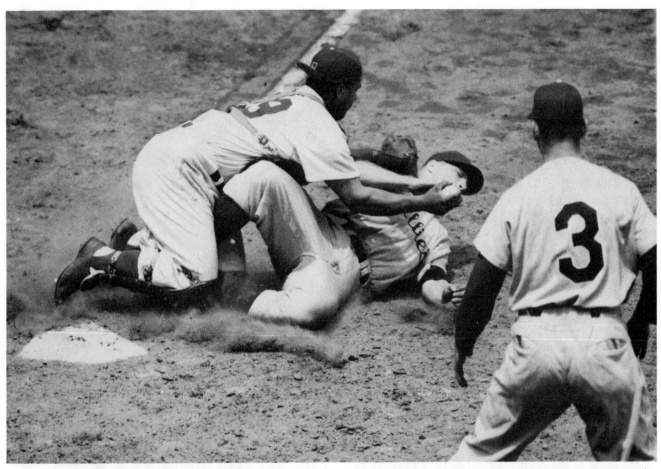

Campanella, a three-time MVP, was a tough competitor whether at bat or catching, as the Phillies' Richie Ashburn would have attested after his 1950 collision (above) with Campy at the plate. Campanella (below left with catch-er's mitt) is pictured with teammate Jackie Robinson and (below right) with former teammates Robinson, Don Newcombe (36) and Pee Wee Reese at an old timers game in 1964, six years after his crippling accident.

# Max Carey

Maximilian Carnarius had every intention of making his mark in life as a Lutheran minister. But as the years unfolded, he discovered he was destined for baseball immortality under the name of Max Carey.

Carey was a student at Concordia College in Fort Wayne, Ind., when, in the summer of 1909, he and a friend attended a Central League game in Carey's native Terre Haute. Max took one look at the South Bend shortstop and allowed that he could play the position more effectively.

The next day, Carey presented himself to the South Bend manager. He displayed a medal he had won as a sprinter and offered his services.

The offer was accepted, but the young theologian changed his name to protect his amateur status. He appeared in 48 games and although his statistics were unimpressive, he was invited back the following season.

By the next spring, however, Max had been replaced by a better fielding shortstop and he was shifted to the outfield, where he remained for the remainder of his career.

On August 20, 1910, Carey was purchased by the Pirates and saw action in two games in the closing days of the race. He made his major league debut in St. Louis on October 3, rapping two hits, including a triple, and scoring two runs.

Carey played 122 games in 1911, and proceeded to fall below the 100-game mark only once until his final year as an active player, 1929.

The break in his streak occurred in 1919 when he was limited to 66 games because of illness. Even so, Carey stole 18 bases and batted .307.

A switch-hitter, Carey enjoyed perhaps his most remarkable game on July 7, 1922. In an 18-inning game against the Giants, Max collected six hits and walked three times in nine trips to the plate. In addition, he stole three bases, including a theft of home. Despite his performance, the Pirates lost.

Carey's finest hour as a money player occurred in Game 7 of the 1925 World Series. The Pirates, who lost three of the first four games to the Senators, fell behind by four runs in the first inning of the deciding contest. But led by Carey's three doubles, a single and a stolen base, the Bucs rallied to defeat Walter Johnson.

There was a story behind the Pirates' manhandling of Johnson. As Carey explained years later: "Johnson beat us twice (in the first four games) and gave us just one run. He didn't figure to pitch again in the Series. After the fourth game, Jack Onslow (Pirates' coach) got into a cab with Bobby Veach (Washington) and asked how he had hit Johnson so well when he was with Detroit.

"Veach thought the Series was just about over, naturally, and never dreamed Johnson would pitch again. He told Onslow that when Johnson pulled his arm all the way back

The switch-hitting Max Carey enjoyed his best season in 1925, hitting .343 at age 35.

in his windup, it was a fastball; when he shortened his delivery, it was a curve."

Armed with that information, the Pirates solved Johnson for 15 hits in a 9-7 victory.

As a base stealer, Max was at his best in 1922 when he swiped 51 bases in 53 attempts for a .962 percentage. He was adroit at timing and getting a jump on the pitcher. He swiped bases cleanly, without the need to bowl over a fielder.

Good as he was as a hitter, Max maintained that he might have been even better if he had seen Ty Cobb play before 1924, when the Pirates and Tigers played an exhibition game.

Holding the bat almost vertically with his hands separated on the handle, and bent forward, Cobb was able to hit any type of pitch with a flick of the wrist.

Carey adjusted his style. And, the following year, when he was 35, Max enjoyed his finest season at the plate by batting .343.

# Alexander Cartwright

In 1938, while the Hall of Fame commission was finalizing preparations to celebrate baseball's centennial the following year at Cooperstown, N.Y., and establish Abner Doubleday as the father of the pastime, members were shocked by word from Hawaii that the game's legitimate parent was an almost-forgotten gentleman named Alexander Joy Cartwright Jr.

The incontrovertible evidence included a diary, clippings and other materials supplied by Cartwright's grandson Bruce. The information detailed Alexander's role in formalizing the first rules of the game.

Because the commission was too far along in its planning to turn back, the Doubleday myth was allowed to stand, but Cartwright's contributions were acknowledged and he was named to the shrine the same year.

A descendant of British sea captains, Cartwright spent his early years in New York City where he participated in the English game of rounders and other contests involving a ball and bases.

By 1842, when he was 22, Cartwright was one of a group of young executives who participated in a new game called "base ball" on 27th Street (where Madison Square Garden would be built later).

As the city expanded into the open spaces, the young gentlemen moved to a lot at Lexington Avenue and 34th Street. After three years of informal play, the group organized into the "Knickerbockers" club in 1845.

By 1846, Cartwright formulated a new set of rules for the game, dropping the rounders regulations that provided for a runner to be retired by being hit with a thrown ball. The new rules provided for foul lines, nine players to a team and nine innings to a game.

After several Sundays of practice, the Knickerbockers announced they were ready to meet any team that was willing to play under the new set of rules. The first challenger was the New York Nine. The site for the contest was an old cricket playground, Elysian Field, in Hoboken,

**Alexander Joy Cartwright, the legitimate "Father of Baseball," played a big role in formalizing the first rules of the game.**

N.J., a ferry ride across the Hudson River. The date was June 19, 1846.

Although he was the best Knickerbocker player, Cartwright umpired in the historic first game. Among his decisions was a six-cent fine against a player for swearing, payable on the spot.

Without Cartwright's talents, the Knickerbockers bowed, 23-1.

The discovery of gold in California aroused Cartwright's adventuresome spirit and, in the company of a dozen friends, Alexander set out for the West Coast.

At Pittsburgh, the group purchased a covered wagon and shipped it, along with supplies, to St. Louis, where the travelers arrived 42 days after leaving home.

The extended travel time was created by frequent stopovers devoted to demonstrations of the game called base ball.

The party arrived in San Francisco in July of 1849, but five weeks later, weary of the gold rush, Cartwright decided to book passage on a ship bound for New York by way of China.

Before reaching Hawaii, Cartwright fell sick and was put ashore at Honolulu. While convalescing, he became infatuated with the islands and decided to make his home there. In 1851, he was joined by his wife and three children.

A born organizer, Alexander soon formed the first fire department and became its chief engineer. He was president of the Chamber of Commerce and the stock board. For many years he was the administrator for the estates of Hawaii's king and queen and pioneered in baseball for the remainder of his life.

An imposing figure at 6-foot-2 and 210 pounds, the white-bearded Cartwright frequently visited the elementary schools and with chalk and blackboard explained to the children the game he had done so much to organize decades earlier in the United States.

Cartwright died on July 12, 1892. His death went virtually unnoticed in his native country.

# Henry Chadwick

In 1857, the baseball writer for the New York Clipper, a daily newspaper devoted to sports and the theater, grew so disgusted with the method for scoring a baseball game that he designed his own system.

By assigning numbers to the various positions, he was able to record the game play by play. At game's end, he could tally the statistics for each player and present to his readers an easily understood box score that provided a major boost to the meteoric rise of baseball as the national pastime.

The young inventor was Henry Chadwick, a British-born journalist whose first love was cricket but whose paramount interest was baseball.

Chadwick was born in Exeter, England, the son of the editor of the Western Times. Unquestionably, Henry's association with England had much to do with his position in filing a minority report in the early years of the century when a commission denoted Cooperstown, N.Y., as the birthplace of baseball.

Chadwick stoutly maintained that baseball was descended from the English game of rounders and never accepted what he referred to as the "Cooperstown myth."

Henry was 13 when, in 1837, he migrated with his family to the United States. For the next 71 years Chadwick called Brooklyn his home, an association that was linked to the borough's passionate love for baseball through the next century.

Chadwick joined the Clipper in 1857 and was sports editor until 1880 (except for the period when he served as a Civil War correspondent).

While with the Clipper, Henry also served as baseball writer for the Brooklyn Eagle. The job lasted 30 years, during which time he acquired the nickname of "Father Chadwick." The journalist terminated his affiliation with the Eagle in 1894.

Chadwick's writing style was trenchant and fearless and he was quoted nationwide. Like Judge Kenesaw Mountain Landis after him, Chadwick attacked gambling in baseball with all his energies. One chronicler asserted that baseball's freedom from scandal is a direct result of Chadwick's untiring efforts.

In Chadwick's heyday, virtually no baseball writers bylined their stories. Editors believed that anonymity assured more objective reporting.

Henry sought no such protection. Disdaining the use of a typewriter, he composed his essays in a handsome penmanship reflective of his English origins.

Chadwick served as editor of the Spalding Baseball Guide for 20 years. In 1904, he was presented a medal by the St. Louis Exposition, the only newspaperman to be honored by the World's Fair.

Later, President Theodore Roosevelt honored Chadwick

**Henry Chadwick, a former baseball writer, is credited with developing the modern method of baseball scoring.**

as the "Father of Baseball."

Chadwick authored a number of books—including "Beadle's Dime Base Ball Book" in 1880, "Haney's Base Ball Book of Reference" (from 1866 to 1870) and "DeWitt's Base Ball Guide" (from 1869 to 1880).

In Chadwick's declining years, National League club owners discussed a motion to award him a $500 annual pension. The move was vigorously opposed by Andrew Freedman, owner of the New York Giants. Freedman insisted that Chadwick was biting the hand that fed him.

In response, Chadwick boycotted Giants games during Freedman's ownership and A.G. Spalding, the publisher of the baseball guides, launched a move to oust Freedman from baseball, a move that proved successful.

Despite a fever, Chadwick attended opening day at the Polo Grounds in 1908. Pneumonia developed, and Chadwick died on April 20. In tribute to the man who had done so much for baseball, flags were flown at half staff at all major league parks.

Chadwick's close friend, Spalding, erected a handsome marker at the old writer's gravesite in Greenwood Cemetery in Brooklyn, and for years Dodgers President Charles Ebbets led an annual pilgrimage of old-timers to Chadwick's grave for wreath-laying ceremonies. The practice was followed faithfully until Ebbets' death in 1925. Fittingly, Ebbets also was buried in Greenwood, near the remains of his longtime friend.

# Frank Chance

Immortalized as the first baseman in Franklin P. Adams' lyrical lament of "Tinker to Evers to Chance," Frank Chance attained prominence as the "Peerless Leader" who managed the Chicago Cubs to four pennants and two world championships from 1906 through 1910.

Chance was a student at Washington College in Irvington, Calif., in 1898 and intent on becoming a dentist when Bill Lange, former major league outfielder, recommended him to the Cubs.

A catcher at the time, Chance made his major league debut on April 29 that year by playing the final inning of a 16-2 victory over Louisville.

Chance batted for the first time on May 11 and went hitless in two at-bats against Cy Young of Cleveland. The following day, the young catcher known as "Husk" collected his first major league hit, a single against Frank Wilson.

Chance continued to catch, with an occasional game in the outfield, until 1903. En route to Chicago from the club's training base in California, Bill Hanlon—projected as the Cubs' regular first baseman—quit the team. Chance was asked by Manager Frank Selee to fill in temporarily "until I can find a regular."

As a catcher, Chance had the unhealthy habit of sticking his fingers in the path of foul tips and was sidelined frequently. Such dangers did not exist at first base, and Chance adjusted quickly to the new position.

On August 1, 1905, ill health forced Selee to resign and Chance was named his successor by Jim Hart, who was in the process of selling the Cubs to Charles Webb Murphy. At the time of the change the Cubs were in fourth place, but Chicago played inspired baseball under Chance's dynamic direction and finished third.

Chance demonstrated his leadership qualities to the fullest in 1906 when he led the Cubs to a record 116 victories and a 20-game spread over second-place New York.

The Cubs were favorites entering the World Series, but were upset by their cross-town rivals, the White Sox, in six games.

As a manager, Chance was a scrapper and would drive umpires and opposition to distraction.

Chance, nicknamed the "Peerless Leader" by Chicago baseball writer Charley Dryden, also produced flags in 1907 and '08, scoring World Series conquests both years against the Detroit Tigers and their outfield phenom, Ty Cobb. The second year, Chance cuffed Detroit pitching for a .421 average and stole five bases.

The Cubs had a golden opportunity to capture a fourth consecutive pennant in 1909 but—despite winning 104 games—finished second to Pittsburgh. A large share of the blame for their "failure" was laid at the feet of catcher Johnny Kling, who chose to stay in Kansas City, to tend

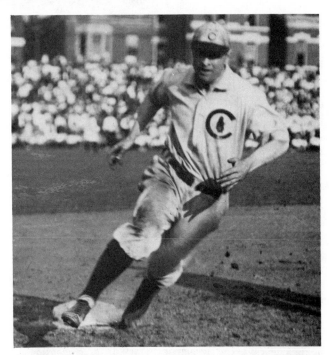

By 1910, Frank Chance, of "Tinker to Evers to Chance" fame, was known as the "Peerless Leader" of the Cubs.

to his billiard parlor and play semipro ball rather than accept a salary offer from management.

With Kling back in harness in 1910, the Cubs annexed their fourth flag under Chance but were beaten by the Philadelphia A's in the five-game World Series.

Chance played only 92 games in 1909 and never again reached the 100 mark, mainly because of headaches that were attributed to frequent beanings. He also became deaf in his left ear.

Frank remained the Cubs' manager until late September of 1912 when Owner Murphy announced succinctly: "Frank L. Chance is through as manager." Chance not only had made the Cubs the dread of the National League, he also had made Murphy a millionaire.

Chance, 35, was claimed on waivers by the Cincinnati Reds, but when an opportunity arose for Frank to manage the New York Yankees, the Reds stepped aside and the veteran first baseman was sold to the American League club for $1,700.

Serving the Yankees for two of the three years on his contract, Chance finished seventh and tied for sixth. Frequent friction with President Frank Farrell added to Chance's unpleasantness in New York.

After staying out of baseball for one season, Frank purchased the Los Angeles club of the Pacific Coast League and operated the franchise for two years before selling it at a profit.

Chance, who managed the Boston Red Sox in 1923, died of tuberculosis in 1924.

# Happy Chandler

When major league club owners started to vote for a successor to deceased Commissioner K.M. Landis on April 24, 1945, the name of a United States senator from Kentucky led from the first ballot.

The owners, meeting in Cleveland, reduced the list of candidates to three, then to two—the senator and Bob Hannegan, chairman of the Democratic National Committee. In the runoff, the Kentuckian was ahead, 12 votes to 4, when the executives—in a move for unity—decided to make the vote unanimous.

Albert B. (Happy) Chandler inspired ringing accolades from the owners.

"He'll give us a good administration," said American League President Will Harridge.

"He's the best choice we possibly could have made," added Senators Owner Clark Griffith.

Jack Zeller, representing the Tigers, chortled, "I think we've made a wise decision."

Yet within six years of the auspicious start, Chandler was on his way back to the Bluegrass State to resume his political career. On December 11, 1950, at a meeting in St. Petersburg, Fla., the owners voted down a new contract for Happy.

"It was the only election I ever lost where I got the majority of votes," Chandler said after receiving nine of the 12 votes required for reelection.

Between the starting gate and the finish line, Chandler ran a stormy race. Few, if any, decisions were universally endorsed.

Chandler made his first major decision less than a year after taking office. From his desk in Cincinnati, he announced that all players jumping to the Mexican League would be suspended automatically from Organized Baseball for five years. Three years later, all jumpers were granted amnesty.

When Branch Rickey, majordomo of the Brooklyn Dodgers, sought to introduce Jackie Robinson to the all-white major leagues in 1947 and owners voted 15-1 against the move, Chandler gave the blessings of his office. The commissioner's stand against discrimination opened a new and profitable era to the game.

While Happy won the admiration of the players by supporting their efforts for a pension plan, he angered executives with other actions. Del Webb, co-owner of the Yankees, and Fred Saigh, owner of the Cardinals, were openly hostile to the commissioner. Both were investigated for possible conduct detrimental to baseball.

Early in his reign, Chandler suspended Leo Durocher for an entire season for slugging a fan under the stands after a game in Brooklyn and for associating with known gamblers.

"I had to suspend him before he killed somebody,"

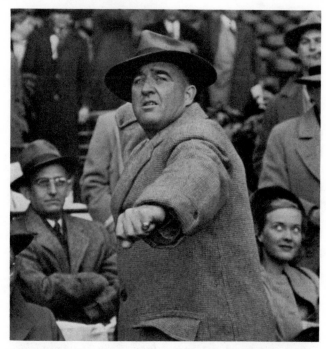

**A.B. (Happy) Chandler, newly elected baseball commissioner, officially opens the 1945 World Series in Detroit.**

Chandler explained years later. In the same decision, Chandler suspended Dodgers coach Charley Dressen for 30 days and fined the Yankees and Dodgers undisclosed amounts for airing a dispute publicly.

In 1949, after Durocher had become manager of the Giants, the New York club was fined $2,000 and the Lip and coach Fred Fitzsimmons were penalized $500 each as a result of a tampering case involving Fitzsimmons while he was employed by the Boston Braves. The same year, Leo was suspended briefly while Happy investigated allegations that he had struck another fan. Durocher was restored to good standing when the probe found Leo blameless.

The New York press, almost to a man, launched a full-scale attack on Chandler. "They even found fault when I said I love baseball," Happy quipped.

When Leslie O'Connor, general manager of the White Sox, signed a high school player, he was fined $500. His refusal to pay led to O'Connor's suspension and some heated words before the matter was settled.

After leaving office in 1951, Chandler returned to Kentucky where he was born (Corydon) and where he went to college (Centre). A life-long Democrat, he won two terms as governor and was instrumental in the construction of the University of Kentucky medical center that bears his name.

Chandler was elected to the Hall of Fame by the Veterans Committee in 1982, joining Earle Combs as the only Kentuckians in the shrine.

# Oscar Charleston

To be compared favorably with Ty Cobb is a supreme compliment for any baseball player. But to be likened to Ty Cobb AND Tris Speaker is an extravagance known but to a few.

Among that choice minority is Oscar Charleston. The one who gazed upon Oscar and saw the Georgia Peach and the Gray Eagle "rolled into one" was Judy Johnson, a veteran of Negro league competition and a longtime major league scout.

By virtually every yardstick, Charleston was a complete player. James (Cool Papa) Bell, himself a Hall of Famer, assayed Oscar in this manner:

"I could outrun Charleston a bit and maybe others might do this or that better than him. But putting it all together—the ability to hit, run, field, throw and hit with power—he was the best I ever saw."

Charleston's career was spent in the Negro leagues, where statistics were kept with a quaint indifference.

In 1925, for instance, playing for the Harrisburg (Pa.) Giants, "Charlie" was credited with a .430 average and 14 homers, both tops for the league. In 1929, with the Philadelphia Hilldale Daisies, he reportedly batted .392 with 98 hits in 250 at-bats and collected 37 extra-base hits. He also stole 22 bases in '29 and—like Cobb—slid with spikes gleaming.

"He was so fast," trumpeted an ancient publicity release, "that he makes Ty Cobb look like Ham Hyatt."

(Hyatt was a slow-moving first baseman-outfielder with several major league clubs in the pre-World War I era.)

The seventh of 11 children, Oscar was 15 when he followed an older brother's example and enlisted in the Army. As a member of the 24th Infantry in the Philippines, the teen-ager developed his sprinting talents. When he was discharged in 1915, he was ready to unleash his blinding speed for a baseball team and chose the Indianapolis ABCs in his native city.

Charleston was not only a speedster on the basepaths, he also moved briskly from one club to another. From the ABCs, his course led to the Lincoln Stars of New York, Chicago American Giants, St. Louis Giants, St. Louis Stars, Harrisburg, Philadelphia Hilldale, Homestead Grays and Pittsburgh Crawfords.

But, regardless of where he spent his summers, Oscar always headed south for the winter—to Cuba, where he was a national hero, or other Caribbean countries. He was a 12-month player.

As a rookie with the ABCs, Oscar earned $50 a month. The next season it was $350 monthly. As his paycheck swelled, so did Charleston's reputation on the diamond. He was particularly adept at the swinging bunt.

In the field, Charleston never ceased to dazzle and amuse spectators, frequently doing a backflip after making

**Oscar Charleston (left), shown with Hall of Famer Josh Gibson, displayed his vast talents in the Negro leagues.**

a circus catch.

But his power was the favorite subject among his legion of admirers.

In 1921, the St. Louis Giants, featuring Charleston, engaged in a five-game, postseason series with the Cardinals. The National Leaguers won three contests, but Oscar won the headlines, clouting four home runs in one game, two off Redbird ace Jesse Haines.

As the years started to take their toll on his once-svelte figure, Oscar shifted from the outfield to first base, where he finished his playing career. In 1932, Charleston was appointed playing manager of the Crawfords, an independent club that also numbered Bell, Johnson, Paige and Josh Gibson, all future Hall of Famers. Approaching his 36th birthday, Oscar still batted .363 with 13 homers.

Charleston managed the Philadelphia Stars from 1941 to 1944 and, at age 48, was a member of the Brooklyn Brown Dodgers in '45. The Brown Dodgers folded after one season, and for a number of years Charleston worked in the baggage department of the Pennsylvania Railroad in Philadelphia.

In 1954, Charleston returned to managing, joining the Indianapolis Clowns. The Clowns had barely completed their schedule when Oscar suffered a heart attack. He died at Philadelphia General Hospital on October 5, 1954, nine days before his 58th birthday.

# Jack Chesbro

Of all the wild pitches thrown in the major leagues, none bore so heavily on a pennant race nor created so much lasting notoriety as the errant delivery that sailed over the catcher's head in New York on October 10, 1904.

The unbridled pitch was uncorked by Jack Chesbro and enabled a Boston player to score the run that clinched the American League pennant for the Red Sox.

Chesbro was an instant goat. Almost forgotten were the righthander's 41 victories, a record for the 20th Century. Virtually ignored, too, were his six shutouts, a one-hitter, a two-hitter, a three-hitter, eight four-hitters, six five-hitters and a 14-game winning streak. To many, Chesbro had thrown away New York's first A.L. pennant, for which fans would have to wait 17 more years.

Chesbro's wild pitch occurred in the ninth inning of the first game of a doubleheader between the Highlanders, later the Yankees, and the Red Sox, who were seeking their second consecutive pennant.

The teams were deadlocked, 2-2, and New York—1½ games behind Boston at day's start—needed to sweep the twin bill to win the title.

Chesbro, making his 55th appearance of the season, battled Bill Dinneen evenly for eight innings, but in the ninth Boston catcher Lou Criger beat out an infield single. A sacrifice and infield out moved him to third base. Chesbro worked the count on Freddie Parent to 0-and-2, then fired the next pitch over catcher Jack Kleinow's head as Criger danced home.

The Highlanders won the second game, but it was scant solace for the 30,000 fans who jammed the park and ringed the outfield 12 deep.

Chesbro refused to blame anyone else for the crucial mistake. Some critics insisted Kleinow should have made a better effort to catch the ball, while others stoutly maintained it was uncatchable.

Chesbro, nicknamed Happy Jack because of his positive personality while working at a mental institution in Middletown, N.Y., in 1894, was in his second season with the Highlanders, having jumped from the Pittsburgh Pirates when the American League transferred the Baltimore franchise to Gotham.

He never again approached the brilliant performance of 1904. From a 41-13 record, he slumped to 19-13 in 1905 and was 24-16 in 1906.

An ankle injury contributed to his 10-10 log in 1907. Struggling gamely to reach the 200-victory mark, Happy Jack posted a 14-20 record in New York's cellar season of 1908. He then suffered four losses in as many decisions in 1909, the last one after being traded to the Red Sox, and finished with 198 career victories.

Chesbro coached the Amherst College team in 1911 while continuing to pitch in semipro games. He attempted

**One wild pitch diminished the glory of Jack Chesbro's 41-victory season in 1904.**

a comeback with the Highlanders in 1912, but was no more impressive than he had been in 1909 and did not appear in a regular-season game.

In 1924, Clark Griffith, Jack's former New York skipper who had become president of the Washington Senators, hired his old ace as pitching coach, but the club's financial straits led to Chesbro's early release.

Jack retreated to his Conway, Mass., home, where he stabled some trotting horses and spent idle hours hunting abundant wildlife.

Chesbro was preparing for his daily chores on November 6, 1931, when he died of a cerebral hemorrhage.

# Fred Clarke

The management of the Savannah baseball team had ample reason to be distressed during the 1894 season. The Southern League club was in Memphis, railroad and hotel creditors were screaming for payment and the club's coffers were dry. No ninth-inning, bases-loaded jam was ever so ominous.

When spirits were at their lowest, relief arrived from an unexpected source. In Louisville, Barney Dreyfuss, owner of the local National League club, offered to pick up the tab for one small consideration—the contract of outfielder Fred Clarke.

Circumstances did not invite bargaining. The offer was accepted, and the 21-year-old Clarke was on his way to Louisville.

Clarke joined the Colonels on June 30. While teammates suited up for the game against Philadelphia, the newcomer sat implacably in the clubhouse. He had been promised a $100 bonus, he revealed, and until Dreyfuss paid up, he had no intentions of playing.

Shortly, Clarke was $100 richer. Swinging an undersized bat he had brought with him, he ambled toward the field as others jeered: "Pitchers will saw that thing off in your hands."

For this one time, the fiery youngster held his tongue. And three hours later, teammates were wondering what manner of prodigy had been acquired in exchange for hotel and railroad debts.

For the only time in major league history, a rookie broke in with a 5-for-5 performance in a nine-inning game. Clarke belted four singles and a triple in a 13-6 loss.

As a youngster in Iowa, Clarke delivered a Des Moines newspaper, the circulation manager of which was Edward Barrow (later the architect of Yankee dynasties). "He never stopped hustling," Barrow once recalled.

At age 19, Clarke read an advertisement in The Sporting News seeking players for the Hastings team in the Nebraska State League. He made the club and two years later he was in the majors.

In mid-season of 1897, Dreyfuss appointed his 24-year-old star as manager of the Louisville club. Fred failed to produce an instant miracle, but he did excite Kentucky fans with his .406 batting average (the highest mark of his career).

The average, however, was good for only second place in the N.L. race. Willie Keeler of Baltimore batted .432.

Ball parks made little difference to Clarke in his super season. He batted .407 at home, .404 on the road. Fred was more than a hitter; he could patrol left field with the best. He made four assists in one game, and he registered 10 putouts in another.

When the N.L. went from 12 to eight clubs in 1900, Dreyfuss shifted his franchise to Pittsburgh, where Clarke

In 1903, Fred Clarke hit .351 and managed the Pittsburgh Pirates into the first modern World Series.

became an immediate favorite and the team, known as the Pirates, became an instant power in the league.

The Pirates captured pennants in 1901, 1902 and 1903, capping the last season with an appearance in the first modern World Series (which they lost to the Boston Red Sox).

The club's postseason fortunes were better in 1909 as the Bucs beat the Detroit Tigers in seven games.

Clarke, who was replaced as the Pirates' manager after the 1915 season, appeared at the plate for the last time on "Fred Clarke Day," September 23, 1915. Nearly 43, the old warrior played four innings and batted twice. He collected one single, his 2,703rd major league hit, (off Dick Rudolph of Boston), then called it a career.

Fred came out of retirement to serve as a Pirate coach in Pittsburgh's world-championship season of 1925, and the next year he was a club vice president and assistant manager.

Clarke retired to his Winfield, Kan., farm, "the Little Pirate Ranch," where he lived until his death at age 87 in 1960.

# John Clarkson

Great as he was, John Clarkson was not an easy player to handle. He was walking testimony to the maxim that a manager, to be successful, must be able to handle all types of temperaments.

At Clarkson's death in 1909, his old Chicago manager, Adrian (Cap) Anson, exclaimed: "Clarkson was one of the greatest pitchers of all time, certainly the best Chicago ever had. Many regard him as the greatest, but not many know of his peculiar temperament and the amount of encouragement needed to keep him going. Scold him, find fault with him and he could not pitch at all. Praise him, and he was unbeatable. In knowing exactly what kind of ball a batter could not hit and in his ability to serve up just that kind of a ball, I don't think I have ever seen the equal of Clarkson."

Fortunately for Clarkson and the Chicago White Stockings, Anson was enough of a psychologist to create a premier pitcher.

The son of a well-to-do manufacturing jeweler, John was one of three brothers to pitch in the major leagues.

A handsome youth, Clarkson, it was written, "seemed to have at all times a reserve of strength that never failed him. In the early days his speed was his big asset and when his famous fastball fell by the wayside, he developed a curveball with a peculiar drop and cultivated a change of pace. In his later years his wonderful control and precise knowledge of the batter who faced him still enabled him to continue to pitch winning ball long after his famous curve and fastball were but memories."

Anson discovered Clarkson pitching for Saginaw in 1884 and acquired him immediately. John won 10 games the remainder of that season and followed with marks of 53-16 and 35-17 as the club won consecutive pennants.

After winning 38 games in 1887, Clarkson was sold to Boston for $10,000, an astronomical price in that era. The previous winter, batterymate Michael (King) Kelly had been peddled to the same club for the same price.

In 1889, Clarkson worked 629 innings, earning $2,000 on a contract that spelled out a system of fines ($25 for the first offense, $50 for the second and $100 for the third) if John overindulged in spirituous liquors.

John was not above injecting a trace of merriment into a game. Once, when an umpire refused to call a game because of darkness as Clarkson thought he should, the pitcher threw a lemon to the batter. When the umpire ruled the pitch a strike, and the catcher held up the piece of citrus, the game was called.

In 1890, while many of his teammates were jumping to the Players League, Clarkson remained loyal to the National League. Some maintained that John's loyalty was purchased for $10,000. Clarkson maintained that his responsibilities as baseball coach at alma mater Harvard

John Clarkson, pictured in 1885, won 53 games that season for the Chicago White Stockings.

necessitated his remaining in the Boston area. Whatever the reason for his posture, Clarkson found his popularity plummeting among his peers.

John closed out his career in 1894 when he split 16 decisions with Cleveland, finishing with 327 lifetime victories.

The previous January, Clarkson and his close friend, catcher Charley Bennett, were riding a train westward on the first segment of a planned hunting trip.

When the train stopped at Wellsville, Kan., Bennett alighted to stretch his legs on the station platform. As the train pulled out, Bennett slipped on the icy boards and fell beneath the wheels of the cars. Clarkson remained with his buddy through the harrowing experience that cost Bennett part of both legs.

Clarkson was never the same mentally thereafter. For a while he operated a cigar store in Bay City, Mich., but the mental sharpness of his youth was gone.

While visiting relatives in Cambridge, Mass., in 1909, Clarkson died of pneumonia on February 4 at age 47.

In a tribute to the old master, Editor Francis Richter of Sporting Life wrote: "On all counts the deceased will always rank in history as one of the few great masters of the art of pitching."

# Roberto Clemente

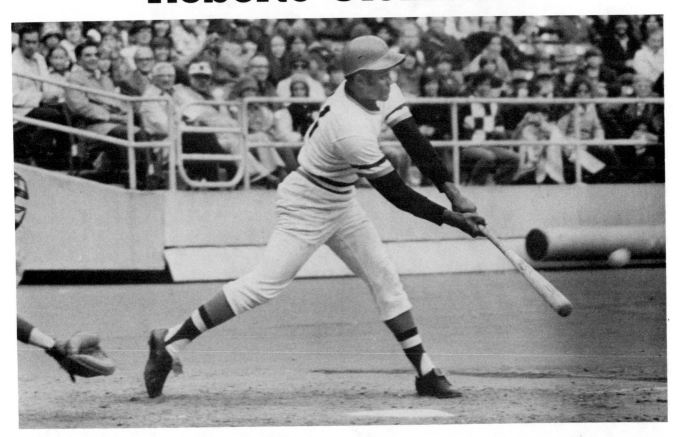

**When Roberto Clemente connected (above) for his 3,000th career hit, a double off the Mets' Jon Matlack at Pittsburgh's Three Rivers Stadium in 1972, nobody realized it would be his last.**

On September 30, 1972, Roberto Clemente collected his 3,000th major league hit, a double off Jon Matlack of New York at Three Rivers Stadium.

Three months later, the 11th member of the "3,000 Hit Club" forfeited his life in dedication to the welfare of mankind. The Puerto Rican star and four others were killed when their cargo plane carrying food, clothing and medical supplies to earthquake-stricken Nicaragua crashed only moments after takeoff from San Juan.

Clemente was one of baseball's all-time best bargains. Roberto had batted .257 in 87 games for Montreal (International) in 1954, his first professional campaign, and the parent Brooklyn Dodgers were so confident that the young outfielder would slip unnoticed through the player draft that he was left unprotected.

The Dodgers erred. Brooklyn's onetime front-office chief, Branch Rickey, selected Clemente for the Pirates, paying $4,000 for his contract. Roberto was a Pittsburgh regular for the next 18 years.

Renowned as a hitter (.317 lifetime average), Clemente was equally accomplished as a fielder. His arm ranked among the strongest of his era. On one occasion at Forbes Field, he caught a drive against the gate in right-center field and rifled the ball to the plate, 460 feet away.

It arrived on the fly.

Another time, Roberto threw out a runner on a bunt. It was a freak play, of course. With runners on first and second base and a sacrifice in order, the Pirates' strategy was for the third baseman to break for the plate and the shortstop to cover third for a forceout.

When the batter botched the bunt and popped a fly to the vacated shortstop position, the runners held up momentarily, only to discover that Clemente had raced in from right field, grabbed the ball and fired to third base ahead of the lead runner.

Throughout a large part of his career, Clemente complained of back pains. The aches were widely discounted by teammates, who cited his superior performances as being inconsistent with a player in pain.

However, a chiropractor confirmed that Roberto did suffer from an arthritic spine, the result of a whiplash from an auto accident some years earlier.

Another pain, although unrelated to the playing field, was Roberto's resentment toward media representatives who never ceased shouting the praises of Willie Mays while consigning the Pirate star to a considerably lesser role. Both players caught fly balls basket-style and both possessed strong, accurate arms. If the Giants' star had any

In 1964, Clemente (left) led the National League with a .339 average. Though Clemente missed connections (above) on a 1969 play at Chicago's Wrigley Field, he was known as one of the game's premier defensive outfielders throughout his career.

edge, it was in his flamboyant personality.

The son of a sugar plantation foreman, Clemente was still in high school when he started playing for Santurce of the Puerto Rican Winter League. Representatives of 10 major league clubs attended Clemente's high school commencement, one offering the young star $30,000 to sign with the Milwaukee Braves.

But Roberto kept an earlier commitment and accepted a $10,000 bonus from Brooklyn scout Al Campanis.

Clemente, a four-time batting champion in the majors, captured five assist titles, including one as early as 1958 when he threw out 22 runners. While most runners accorded him total respect, there were still some venturesome souls as late as 1967 when Roberto led outfielders in assists for the last time.

Clemente appeared in two World Series, both seven-game events. In 1960, he hit safely in every game as the Pirates scored their storybook upset of the Yankees, but

he was even more impressive in 1971.

Again, Roberto hit safely in each contest. He hit safely twice in each of the first two games, both defeats in Baltimore against the favored Orioles. He contributed five hits when the Bucs swept three games at Three Rivers Stadium and added three more back in Baltimore, including a second home run that accounted for the Series-deciding tally in a 2-1 triumph. Roberto's .414 average, with two homers and two doubles, earned the Series Most Valuable Player Award for the 37-year-old superstar.

In recognition of Clemente's baseball accomplishments and his humanitarian efforts, a special election was conducted among baseball writers in 1973. Roberto was named to the Hall of Fame without the customary five-year wait.

During the '73 season, Pittsburgh players wore patches on their sleeves displaying their former teammate's uniform No. "21" within a black circle.

# Ty Cobb

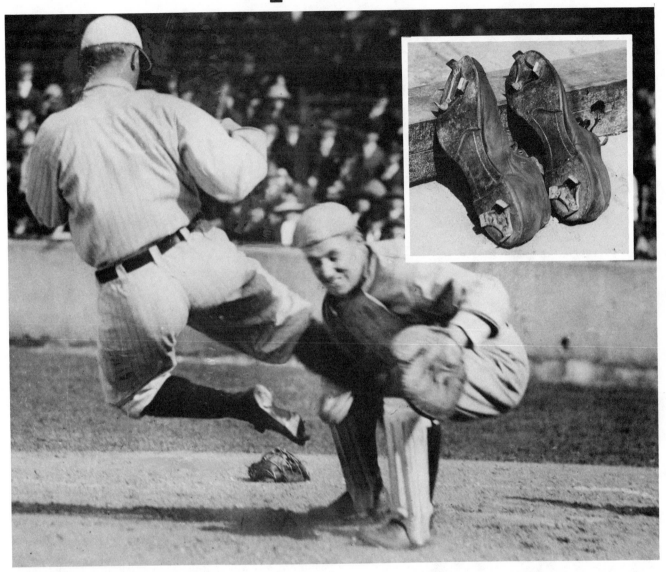

**The notorious baserunning techniques of Ty Cobb victimized many infielders and catchers, including St. Louis Browns' catcher Paul Krichell (above) in 1912. The sharpened spikes (inset) were a Cobb trademark.**

When the first Hall of Fame balloting was conducted in 1936, Ty Cobb polled 222 of 226 votes to lead all candidates from the 60-year-old major leagues. While many pondered the qualifications of those who left the Georgia Peach off their ballots, others interpreted the results as positive proof that Cobb was the greatest player of all time.

Throughout his illustrious career and into retirement, Cobb insisted that he was not superbly endowed as an athlete, only that he had greater desire. That flaming determination was expressed to a minor league roommate in 1905. When Nap Rucker, later a Brooklyn pitcher, returned to the hotel room first and bathed ahead of Cobb, Ty censured him.

"Oh," said Rucker, "did you want to be first today?"

"I've got to be first all the time—in everything," snapped Cobb.

Ty paid a steep price for success. He would practice sliding until his legs were raw. He would place blankets along the base line and practice bunting a ball dead on the blanket. During winter months he hunted through daylight hours in weighted boots so that his legs would be strong for the upcoming campaign. He overlooked no opportunity to gain an edge over opponents, most of whom disliked Ty personally but admired his drive to succeed.

Cobb appreciated the value of a dollar and engaged in annual haggles with Detroit executives before signing his contract. One season he did not sign until May 1. These protracted encounters did not stem from avarice, only Ty's appreciation of his value to the Tigers.

Cobb's brilliant bat produced 4,191 hits and made him one of the two dominant hitters of his era. The other, of course, was New York's Babe Ruth, who posed (above) with Cobb in 1928.

Cobb's earnings were invested wisely, chiefly in General Motors and Coca-Cola stocks, which made him a wealthy man and probably baseball's first millionaire.

But Cobb's intimidating playing style, his spikes-high slides and his brawls were what many remembered best. A photo of airborne Cobb sailing feet-first toward a catcher did nothing to dispel Ty's ferocity. Nor did an overzealous slide into third baseman Frank (Home Run) Baker of New York. There was no mistaking Cobb's intentions when he filed his spikes on the dugout steps before a game.

Perhaps his most violent fight was with Buck Herzog, longtime National Leaguer, after an exhibition game in Dallas. Herzog, who had been spiked by Cobb in a play at

second base that afternoon, went to Cobb's hotel room that evening and challenged the snarling Tiger to a fight. Cobb did not decline.

With furniture placed against the walls, and Detroit catcher Eddie Ainsmith serving as referee, Cobb (nearly 6-foot-1) and Herzog (5-11) slugged it out in primitive brutality.

"I got the hell kicked out of me," Buck mumbled, "but I knocked him down and with that swelled head of his, he'll never get over the fact that a little guy did that to him."

Ty also took on umpire Billy Evans, but his most notable brawl was with a grandstand heckler at Hilltop Park in New York in 1912. Cobb stormed into the stands and punched the spectator. When the Tigers arrived in Philadelphia, Cobb was notified by league offices that he had been fined and suspended.

Rallying behind their star outfielder, Detroit players voted to strike. The Tigers, facing a $5,000 fine if they failed to field a team the next day, recruited sandlotters to wear Detroit uniforms. The A's crushed the quasi-Detroiters, 24-2. The strike lasted for only one game.

If Cobb could inflict pain, he also could endure it. Grantland Rice wrote: "I recall when Cobb played a series with each leg a mass of raw flesh. He had a temperature of 103 and the doctors ordered him to bed for several days, but he got three hits, stole three bases and won the game. Afterward he collapsed at the bench. . . ."

It was little wonder that Tyrus Raymond Cobb, the son of a Georgia schoolmaster and state senator, departed the game in 1928 with countless records engraved in granite.

# Mickey Cochrane

The Philadelphia Athletics were in desperate need of a catcher after the 1924 season. Cy Perkins, the A's No. 1 catcher, was coming off a .242 season.

The best prospect in the minor leagues was a 21-year-old fireball with Portland of the Pacific Coast League.

"They wanted $100,000 for him," the A's Connie Mack recalled three decades later, "and we were ready to pay it. But we discovered the whole franchise could be had for $120,000, so we bought the club."

The bright prospect was Mickey Cochrane, once likened to an incendiary bomb. In the 1920s and early 1930s he was the king of catchers, driving the A's to three pennants and managing the Tigers to two more, all within seven years.

Cochrane possessed the ability to carry a team, a trait he demonstrated during his years at Boston University. Intercollegiate football at the time was in its infancy at BU, and Mickey served as coach, trainer, punter, passer, ballcarrier and spiritual leader.

When Cochrane arrived at his first training camp with the A's, veteran third baseman Jimmie Dykes took one look at him and snorted, "If that guy's worth $100,000, I'm worth $300,000."

Through endless hours of toil (Mickey chased pop fouls until he "caught 'em in my sleep"), Cochrane soon proved his 100-grand value.

Cochrane scaled his first peaks from 1929 through 1931 when the A's won pennants each season. From his No. 3 spot in the lineup, the lefthanded-hitting catcher batted .331, .357 and .349. He averaged 129 games a season and 87 runs batted in.

When Mack was forced to sell his high-salaried stars in the depths of the Great Depression, Cochrane was sold for $100,000 to Detroit, where he was named manager.

Cochrane produced a pennant winner in his first season, 1934, but the Tigers lost the seven-game World Series to the St. Louis Cardinals' Gas House Gang.

The next season Mickey caught 100 games for the last time and batted .319. As in '29, Cochrane faced the Cubs in the World Series.

The Tigers won three of the first five games and were deadlocked, 3-3, in the ninth inning of the sixth contest when Cochrane rapped a one-out single, moved up on an infield out and scored the winning run on Goose Goslin's single.

"It was my greatest day in baseball," the playing manager declared later.

A new Yankee steamroller dethroned the Tigers in 1936, a year before Cochrane's career ended with dramatic and tragic suddenness on May 25, 1937. Mickey came to bat with a runner on first base and ran the count to 3-and-1 against Yankee righthander Bump Hadley. Crowd-

**Mickey Cochrane was a tough scrapper who had the ability to literally carry his team.**

ing the plate for a better chance to pull the ball, Mickey lost sight of the next pitch when it was about six feet from the plate.

The ball struck Cochrane on the right temple, about an inch above the eyebrow. Mickey collapsed at the plate and was unconscious for 10 days with a fractured skull. He never batted again.

Forced to manage from the bench, Mickey was no longer the inspirational force he was while active. He was replaced as pilot in August of 1938.

Cochrane served as a Navy officer in World War II and coached and scouted in succeeding years. He served as general manager of the A's in Mack's last season as manager (1950) and for a while operated a dude ranch in Wyoming. He died in 1962 at age **59**.

# Eddie Collins

When a young shortstop named Sullivan broke in with the Philadelphia Athletics on September 17, 1906, handling six chances flawlessly and rapping a single off Ed Walsh of the White Sox, few suspected that he was playing under an assumed name or that he would blossom into one of the most brilliant second basemen of all time.

According to one account, Eddie Collins acquired his pseudonym the day he joined the A's. Connie Mack was chatting with Tim Murnane, a former major league pitcher who, in 1906, was a Boston sportswriter.

Fearing that Murnane would recognize Collins as the quarterback of the Columbia football team, thereby endangering Eddie's amateur status, the quick-thinking A's manager addressed him as "Sullivan."

The details may be apochryphal, but ironically Eddie discovered when he returned to Columbia for the fall semester that he had lost his eligibility—not for having been discovered as a member of the A's, but for having played semipro ball earlier to finance his education.

The six games that Eddie played in 1906 represented the start of the longest major league playing career, 25 years, in the 20th Century. Collins remained active through the 1930 campaign.

Whether Collins was history's finest second baseman will never be resolved satisfactorily. But Mack, who managed in the majors for more than half a century, termed him "the finest infielder of all time."

Ty Cobb, an opponent for many seasons and a teammate for two years (1927-1928), declared flatly that Collins was the premier keystoner. In addition to a lifetime batting average of .333, Collins was a greyhound on the bases. Twice he stole six bases in one game, and his lifetime total of 743 thefts ranks behind only Lou Brock and Cobb on the modern list.

Collins stole 67 bases in 1909, 81 in 1910 and 62 in 1912. He shares with Brock the career World Series stolen base record of 14.

Collins was a member of the "$100,000 Infield" that

Eddie Collins, shown in 1926, was Ty Cobb's pick as the best second baseman of his era.

sparked the A's to four pennants in five years (1910-14). He won the Chalmers Award as the league's Most Valuable Player in 1914.

At the end of the 1914 season, after the A's were upset by the Miracle Braves in the four-game World Series, Eddie was sold to the White Sox for $50,000. He remained with the Sox for 12 years, managing them in 1925-26 before returning to the A's.

Upon joining Chicago, Collins negotiated a contract for a reported $15,000, double the salary of any teammate. His relatively high pay accentuated Eddie's unpopularity with some teammates, notably shortstop Swede Risberg and first baseman Chick Gandil, who never talked to the man playing between them.

Eddie, nicknamed "Cocky" for his aggressive style of play, performed for the Sox in the World Series of 1917 and 1919. In Game 6 of the 1917 Series, he gained the spotlight as the baserunner who was chased across the plate by third baseman Heinie Zimmerman of the Giants. Collins noted the plate had been left unprotected.

In 1919, Collins was one of the Chicago players who made an honest effort to beat the Reds in the Series. Eight other players—so called "Black Sox"—were accused of trying to fix the classic.

Collins was a playing coach with the A's when the Yankees offered him the post as manager following the death of Miller Huggins in 1929. Eddie declined, having been assured that he was being groomed as the successor to Mack (then in his late 60s). Mack, though, ended up managing the A's through 1950.

When Tom Yawkey offered the general managership of the Red Sox to Eddie in 1933, Mack insisted that he take it. In that post, Collins built the Sox from chronic tailenders into pennant contenders. He personally scouted second baseman Bobby Doerr at San Diego and acquired an option to purchase Ted Williams from the same club.

Collins continued to occupy the general manager's chair until 1951 when he suffered a cerebral hemorrhage and died.

# Jimmy Collins

If Walter Preston had played third base in a more acceptable fashion, Jimmy Collins may never have had the opportunity to become a Hall of Famer.

Preston was playing for Louisville of the National League in 1895 when the Baltimore Orioles—featuring John McGraw, Willie Keeler and Hughey Jennings—laid down seven successive bunts, all of which Preston misplayed.

After the seventh tantalizer, Manager John J. McCloskey summoned Fred Clarke into a conference. "I'll give you $50 more a month if you'll play third base," McCloskey told his left fielder.

Clarke wanted no part of the position, but he had a suggestion. "Why don't you move that fellow Collins from center field?" asked Clarke. "I understand he played third base at Buffalo."

Collins was a third baseman thereafter. He had been purchased only recently from the N.L.'s Boston club for $1,500, with the understanding that he could be repurchased for the same amount at the close of the season.

Collins later recalled that day in Louisville: "McGraw bunted and I came in as fast as I dared, picked up the ball and threw it underhanded to first base. He was out. Keeler tried it and I nailed him by a step. I had to throw out four bunters in a row before the Orioles quit bunting."

In a game against Boston, Collins collected four hits and handled 16 chances. Boston newspapers raised such a clamor that the local club exercised its option to reacquire Collins.

Collins had made his professional debut with the Buffalo (Eastern) club on May 25, 1893, contributing two singles to his club's 11-inning, 8-7 victory over Erie.

Back with Buffalo the next year, Collins became an instant favorite with the fans. Possessing quick, sure hands, he revolutionized the playing style of third basemen. He was the first to play away from the bag, and the first to play shallow in bunting situations so he could race in, grab the ball barehanded and, in one fluid motion, fire to first base ahead of the runner.

An ankle injury limited Collins to 83 games for Boston in 1896, but he batted .300. He was a member of the foremost infield of the 19th Century, a unit also consisting of Fred Tenney at first base, Bobby Lowe at second and Herman Long at shortstop. The foursome pioneered numerous defensive strategies that soon were adopted by other teams.

In five seasons with the Beaneaters, Jimmy failed to register 300 assists only once and totaled 376 one year.

One of Jimmy's assists was a show-stopper in Philadelphia when Collins, it was said, dived toward the bag, grabbed an Ed Delahanty smash with his bare hand and threw out the hometown hero. The game was interrupted

Jimmy Collins, pictured with heavyweight fighter John L. Sullivan, revolutionized the art of playing third base.

until the crowd ceased cheering.

When the American League emerged as a new major circuit, Collins accepted an offer to serve as manager-third baseman for the Red Sox. Jimmy's first contract called for a $5,500 salary, but later he earned $18,000 a year, a princely salary based on a $10,000 salary and 10 percent of the club's profits over $25,000.

After directing Boston to second-place A.L. finishes in 1901 and 1902, Collins directed a pennant winner in 1903. In the first modern World Series that followed, the Sox won five of eight games from the Pittsburgh Pirates.

The Red Sox won the A.L. title again in 1904, but there was no World Series because John McGraw did not consider the newcomers worthy of facing the proud Giants, pennant winners in the N.L.

By 1905, the Sox were a fourth-place club and when they hit the bottom the next season, Collins was dismissed as manager. Jimmy remained with Boston as a player until June of 1907 when he was traded to Philadelphia, where he closed out his major league career in 1908.

After managerial ventures at Minneapolis (American Association) and Providence (Eastern), Jimmy returned to Buffalo, where he lived comfortably off real estate investments until the Depression of the 1930s wiped him out. Thereafter he worked for the city's Park Department.

Early in 1943, Collins fell on the sidewalk near his home. Pneumonia developed during his hospitalization, and Jimmy died 12 days later.

# Earle Combs

**Earle Combs, one of the more overlooked elements of the Yankees' devastating 1927 machine, takes a healthy cut** **at a pitch during the second game of the 1927 World Series against the Pittsburgh Pirates.**

It is doubtful that any Hall of Famer suffered through so horrendous a debut in professional baseball as Earle Combs.

Combs had been an elementary school teacher in the Cumberland Mountains and then had taken a $40-a-month job with a coal company. In turn, he played with a semipro team in Lexington, Ky., where he was discovered by Cap Neal, a scout for the Louisville team of the American Association.

Combs won the center-field position with the Colonels, but after the first game he wasn't sure that he wanted the job. He committed two errors on ground balls early in the contest and in the ninth inning, with the Colonels leading by one run, a batter grounded up the middle.

"I'll stop this if it kills me," Combs promised himself before the ball skipped through his legs and rolled to the wall as the batter and two other runners circled the bases.

In the clubhouse, sitting dejectedly in front of his locker, Combs was consoled by his manager, Joe McCarthy. "I know how you feel," McCarthy began. "But don't feel that way anymore. You're my center fielder. It won't be long before you know how to field ground balls."

With that pat on the back, Combs developed into a superlative ballhawk and, with batting averages of .344 and .380, was sold to the Yankees for $30,000 after the 1923 season.

Combs demonstrated his preparedness by batting .400 in his first 24 games as a Yankee. A fractured leg sidelined him for the rest of the season.

In Louisville, the swift Combs had been known as the "Mail Carrier," but in New York he was the "Waiter," waiting to be driven around the bases by the explosive bats of Murderers' Row. As a leadoff batter, he could wangle a base on balls, if necessary, but he also could bunt in all directions and he could drill the ball with the best. In his first complete season, Earle rapped 203 hits and batted .342.

In 1926, the Kentucky Colonel batted .299—and there's a story that partially explains that figure.

The Yankees clinched the pennant in St. Louis on a Saturday and the next day clowned through a meaningless doubleheader with the Browns, who, entering into the spirit of the occasion, let anyone pitch.

Not to be outdone in the shenanigans, Combs struck out deliberately. When the official averages were released, it was discovered that the strikeout had cost Earle a .300 mark. The following year, he batted .356.

The '27 season was climaxed by the Yankees' four-game World Series sweep over the Pirates. Combs scored the deciding run in the final game when Johnny Miljus uncorked a wild pitch in the last inning.

Combs and his first manager, McCarthy, were reunited in New York in 1931 when Joe took over the Yankees. And McCarthy was in the dugout on a steamy July afternoon in 1934 when Combs crashed into the concrete wall at Sportsman's Park in St. Louis.

The outfielder suffered a fractured skull and a broken collarbone and arm, but thanks to the surgical wizardry of Dr. Robert F. Hyland, Combs was repaired sufficiently well to play one final season for the Yankees, in 1935.

After coaching for the Yankees, Browns, Red Sox and Phillies, Combs returned to Kentucky where, among other interests, he served as a state banking commissioner and a regent at his alma mater, Eastern Kentucky.

# Charles Comiskey

In more than 50 years of baseball experience, Charles A. Comiskey scaled the loftiest peaks and plumbed the lowest valleys of emotion, all created by championships and scandal-racked ball clubs.

Comiskey was a pitcher when he arrived in St. Louis to play for Chris Von der Ahe's Browns in 1882. After two games, he developed a sore arm and was about to be dismissed when he convinced the owners he was a better first baseman than the incumbent.

Comiskey was not long in proving his point. He revolutionized the style of play at the position. Playing yards off the base, he taught pitchers how to cover the bag on ground balls hit to the right side.

By 1883, Comiskey was managing the Browns, whom he led to American Association pennants from 1885 through 1888. In those four seasons, Comiskey arranged championship series with the National League titlists. The first year, the Browns and Chicago Colts split the first six games and the seventh and last contest resulted in a tie.

The following year, the Browns defeated Cap Anson's Chicago team, four games to two. St. Louis then lost to Detroit in 1887, 10 victories to five, before bowing to New York, four games to two, in 1888.

After a second-place finish in 1889, Comiskey accepted the managerial reins of the Chicago entry in the Players League. However, he returned to St. Louis in 1891 when he replaced his old boss, Von der Ahe, as manager.

When the N.L. absorbed the A.A. in 1892, Comiskey was named manager of the Cincinnati Reds. Three seasons with the Reds proved uneventful, but they did afford an opportunity to meet Byron Bancroft Johnson, a local sportswriter. Together, the two men plotted the birth of a new major league, the American, which emerged from the old Western League in 1901. Comiskey was given the franchise in his native Chicago.

One of Comiskey's first acts was to induce Clark Griffith to jump from Chicago's N.L. club, and Griffith pitched the White Sox to the first A.L. pennant.

About this time, Chicago journalist Hugh E. Keough referred to Comiskey as the "Old Roman," a name that followed him the rest of his life.

In 1906, the White Sox, with a team batting average of .228, won the pennant and then stunned the baseball world by upsetting Frank Chance's lordly cross-town Cubs.

By 1915, Comiskey and John McGraw of the Giants were ready to spread the baseball gospel around the world. At the conclusion of a global tour that played to crowned heads and commoners, Comiskey hosted a banquet for 700 in Chicago.

Comiskey was a generous host, and loved to invite as many as 100 congenial spirits to his summer home in Eagle River, Wis. He paid tuition at Notre Dame for the

Charles A. Comiskey, alias the Old Roman, is pictured with his grandson at his summer home in Eagle River, Wis.

sons of pitcher Ed Walsh and catcher Billy Sullivan, and gave 10 percent of his revenue to the American Red Cross in World War I, but his players—even the superstars— were grossly underpaid. A $15,000 salary to Eddie Collins in 1915 was double the pay of any other Chicago player.

The White Sox won the 1917 World Series over the Giants and were league champions again in 1919. Before the first game of the 1919 Series in Cincinnati, rumors were rampant that gamblers had gotten to some Chicago players.

After the Chisox lost the first two games, performing in a most suspicious fashion, Comiskey was crushed. "I blame Ban Johnson for allowing the Series to continue," he blurted tearfully a short time later. "If ever a league president blundered in a crisis, Ban did."

The Series was permitted to continue, to a Cincinnati victory, and eight Chicago players were banished from Organized Baseball for their roles in a conspiracy to fix the outcome.

Comiskey never recovered from the blow; some observers said the Black Sox episode even affected his health.

At age 72, Comiskey died in 1931 at his summer home in Eagle River.

# Jocko Conlan

It was apparent from the way he walked, from the manner in which he thrust his chin and chest forward, that Jocko Conlan was an umpire—and one of the best.

Conlan's ability to umpire a flawless game was emphasized best perhaps in a letter he received early in his career from Bill Klem, the patron saint of umpires. "You are one man," wrote the Old Arbitrator, "who could have umpired in the old days."

In "the old days," only one umpire officiated a game.

Jocko was a legend long before he retired in 1964. Every player had a favorite tale to tell of the jaunty little fellow who wore his chest protector on the outside of his jacket and could keep up a running line of chatter with the most garrulous of persons.

The colorful career of John Bertrand Conlan was born the day that Red Ormsby was felled by a sunstroke and was unable to work a White Sox game in St. Louis in 1935. Jocko was a Chicago outfielder who had been sidelined by a thumb fracture suffered in a clubhouse wrestling match.

Managers Jimmie Dykes of Chicago and Rogers Hornsby of St. Louis settled on Conlan as a fit replacement. Conlan performed in such grand style—he even called out teammate Luke Appling on an attempted triple—that his course was clearly set for the future.

When Conlan arrived as an umpire in the National League in 1941 after a five-year apprenticeship, the old circuit brightened perceptibly. The little fellow took on all comers and nobody ever gained a decision over him. Jocko, for instance, engaged in a shin-kicking episode with Leo Durocher. The Lip was bruised twice in that encounter—once by the league president and once when his toes banged into Jocko's shin guards.

Durocher was perhaps one of Jocko's ongoing dislikes. Once he invited Leo to take a punch at him. "Why?" asked Durocher. "So I can knock your block off," shot back Conlan.

Conlan was not above editorializing on occasion. In the ninth inning of the final game of the 1951 N.L. pennant playoffs, he sauntered to the mound to determine Brooklyn Manager Chuck Dressen's decision on a pitching change. Starter Don Newcombe was faltering.

"Branca," said Dressen.

"Branca!" snorted the incredulous Jocko, "a fastball pitcher?"

Branca it was, rather than curveballers Clem Labine or Carl Erskine, and Bobby Thomson socked the pitcher's second pitch for a three-run homer that won the pennant for the Giants.

Jocko insisted on abiding by the rules, usually. When a Cincinnati organist insisted on performing during game action, Jocko delivered an ultimatum that said, in effect:

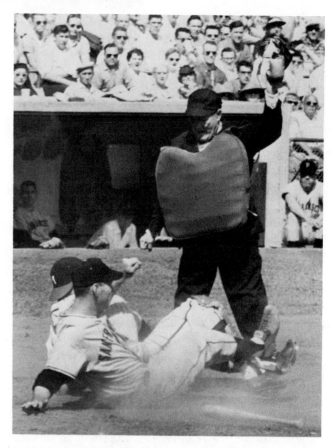

Jocko Conlan, shown making a call at the plate during a 1959 game, was a small man with a big heart.

"Play between innings, otherwise shut up."

Conlan was asked if there was a league rule on the matter.

"There sure is," he said. "I just made it."

If fan reaction ever alarmed Jocko, he never admitted it. He did confess, however, that his worst rhubarb was at the Polo Grounds in his rookie year of 1941. Missiles of all manner sailed out of the stands after Conlan ejected all-time favorite Mel Ott for protesting a strike.

Conlan had the utmost admiration for Walter O'Malley, president of the Dodgers. During a game at Ebbets Field, a foul tip struck Jocko on the throat. For 48 hours he was hospitalized while a throat specialist and nurses, all at O'Malley's expense, stood guard at the umpire's bedside.

When Jocko revealed in 1964 that he was about to retire, he was accorded farewell salutes in virtually every city he visited.

In Chicago, where Conlan grew up as a South Side rooter for the White Sox, N.L. President Warren Giles declared: "I know of no one who has been more dedicated to his profession, more loyal to the game in which he has been such a big part, and I hate to see him hang up his spikes."

# Tommy Connolly

Tommy Connolly, who never played a game of baseball, officiated at the first American League game in 1901, the first games at Comiskey Park, Shibe Park, Fenway Park and Yankee Stadium and, with Hank O'Day, called the first World Series in 1903.

A native of Manchester, England, Connolly was a cricket player when, as a teen-ager, he migrated with his parents to the United States and settled in Natick, Mass. There he appointed himself a batboy for a local baseball team. He graduated to the New England League where, on April 28, 1894, he called a game between Fall River and Portland.

Tim Hurst, famed 19th Century umpire, spotted Connolly and recommended him to Ban Johnson when the former Cincinnati sportswriter organized the American League.

Connolly's first assignment was the Cleveland-Chicago season opener at the White Sox's ball park. Because all other A.L. openers were rained out, Connolly earned the distinction of umpiring the first game in the new major league. The Sox won, 8-2, in 1 hour, 30 minutes.

Tommy was known as Mr. Connolly by generations of players. He wore high, hard collars and his tie was always held in place by a jeweled stickpin. He dressed neatly and conservatively, figuring he was a prominent part of an American subculture.

Everything Connolly did was to upgrade his profession. He was quiet and subdued. He did not cater to the crowd or engage in theatrical gestures. He believed that the most efficient umpire was the one who attracted the least attention. He enjoyed the respect of all the players, and in one 10-year period did not eject a single player.

Babe Ruth once felt the sting of Tommy's temper and ever after greeted the arbiter with: "Hi ya, Tommy, you old son of a gun. Remember the day you tossed me?"

Tris Speaker once made the mistake of accusing Connolly of prejudice in making a decision against his Indians.

"I'll never forget the way Tommy looked at me," remembered Speaker. "His face turned purple and I thought his neck was about to burst. But his voice was almost a whisper. 'Tris,' he said, 'of course, you're out of the game. And unless you change your way of thinking, you'll be out of baseball for life.' "

Ty Cobb said of the umpire: "You can go so far with Tommy, but when you see his neck get red, it's time to lay off him."

It was against Cobb that Connolly made one of his most unpopular decisions. In the heat of a pennant race, the first-place Tigers were trailing the second-place team late in a game. A runner was on second base and the pitcher was attempting to walk Cobb intentionally. On the third pitch, Cobb stepped across the plate and smacked an apparent triple.

Tommy Connolly held the distinction of umpiring the first American League game in 1901.

"What could I do but declare Cobb out and send the runner back to second base?" asked Connolly. "I thought the players and fans would attack me, but fortunately there were a lot of police there and the Detroit newspapers the next day backed me up."

Of Connolly it was written that "he probably knew more firemen than any man in America." In his off-hours, the umpire frequented fire stations where his Irish wit and eagerness to talk baseball made him a popular visitor.

Connolly also demonstrated a willingness to help a young player over rough spots.

Once, when bench jockeys were hassling a rookie over the way he was toeing the rubber, Connolly called time, strolled to the mound and advised the pitcher: "Son, there are right and wrong ways to pitch in this league. Let me show you the right way. I'll take care of that wrecking crew in the dugout and from what you've shown me today, you'll be up here a long time." Eddie Plank was forever grateful.

After 30 years of active service, Connolly was appointed umpire-in-chief by American League President Will Harridge in 1931. He held the post until his retirement in 1954, seven years before his death at age 90.

# Roger Connor

History does not record the direction of Jim Mutrie's gaze when the New York manager shouted to his players, "Come on, you Giants," but there is an excellent chance that he was looking at Roger Connor.

Connor, a 6-foot-2, 210-pound first baseman, was a giant in more ways than one. A bat was a genuine shillelagh for the Connecticut Irishman, who clouted 132 home runs from 1880 through 1897 in an era when the homer was a rarity and almost held in disrepute.

Until the advent of Babe Ruth and the lively ball, Connor reigned as the all-time home run king. One of his homers was especially memorable. It was socked at the old Polo Grounds at 110th Street and Fifth Avenue and sailed over the right-field fence onto 112th Street.

Several members of the New York Stock Exchange, occupying box seats, were so smitten by the Herculean clout that they took a collection for the slugger known as "Dear Old Roger."

When the contributions were totaled, the fans were able to present a $500 gold watch to their hero.

Home runs weren't Connor's only claim to fame. Roger's career total of 227 triples was exceeded only by Sam Crawford, Ty Cobb, Honus Wagner and Jake Beckley.

Roger was one of eight children born to Irish immigrants in Waterbury, Conn., his lifelong home. A younger brother Joe, a catcher, played for Cleveland, Milwaukee and New York in the American League and Boston in the National.

Connor entered professional baseball as a lefthanded third baseman, and became a first baseman only because of a dislocated shoulder that handicapped his throwing.

Connor enjoyed one of his biggest days at the plate on May 9, 1888, when he clouted three home runs against Indianapolis. On May 31, 1890, while playing for the New York team in the Players League, Connor was one of three players who homered in the same inning against Pittsburgh hurler John K. Tener, later governor of Pennsylvania.

Roger's most productive game occurred on June 1, 1895, when he was a member of the St. Louis Browns. Playing against his old teammates, the Giants, handsome, mustachioed Roger rapped two doubles, a triple and three singles in a 6-for-6 performance that highlighted a 23-8 rout against Jouett Meekin, who pitched the entire game.

Connor left the majors in 1897 and the following season purchased the Waterbury club of the Connecticut League. There Roger served as manager-first baseman, his wife worked in the box office and his adopted daughter sold tickets.

Roger batted .319 in 1898 and the next season, at 42, led the league with a .392 average.

In 1902, when Connor was managing and operating the

Roger Connor (pictured in 1887) was one of baseball's biggest power threats in the 1890s.

Springfield club in the Connecticut League, a young umpire officiated a game with Meriden. First, the arbiter's calls angered Meriden players, then the umpire incurred the wrath of the Springfield players with more unpopular calls.

At game's end, the young umpire feared the worst from the bespectacled, fierce-looking Springfield pilot. But Bill Klem was relieved when Roger extended his hand and declared: "Young man, let me congratulate you for umpiring a fine ball game."

After retiring from baseball, Connor served as a school inspector for the city of Waterbury.

Late in Connor's career, the slugger's wife gave Roger a handsome weather vane fashioned from two baseball bats. The vane was a Waterbury landmark for years, even after one of the bats was broken in a storm and the home was sold by the Connors.

# Stan Coveleski

In 1921, when the Cleveland Indians were in spring training at Dallas, Tex., Manager Tris Speaker arranged an outing for the players at his farm in nearby Hubbard.

As Speaker was preparing the barbecue, pitcher Stan Coveleski suggested to young shortstop Joe Sewell that they take a rowboat ride on a nearby lake. Sewell consented.

As they approached the middle of the lake, Coveleski asked Sewell if he could swim. "No," replied Joe.

"Now's as good a time as any," chirped Coveleski, shoving Sewell overboard a quarter mile from shore.

Sewell nearly drowned before a rescue party got to him. The near tragedy was nothing but good, clean fun to Coveleski.

Born Stanislaus Kowalewski in the coal-mining town of Shamokin, Pa., Stanley was preceded to the major leagues by older brother Harry (who acquired a reputation as a "Giant killer" in 1908 when the Phillies' hurler defeated New York three times in a five-game series).

Harry later starred for the Detroit Tigers, and for a period of 20 years the family name appeared regularly in major league box scores.

Curiously, the brothers faced each other on only one occasion.

"I was with Lancaster of the Tri-State League and Harry was already in the majors," Stanley remembered. "We faced each other in an exhibition game and when neither team scored in five innings our managers took us out.

"Harry refused to pitch against me in the majors. He told the Detroit manager never to use him when I was pitching. He explained to me, 'Win or lose, it would take something away from us. If I lose, they'll say I was laying down on purpose so you could win. If I win, they'll say you were laying down.'"

The younger Coveleski did little "laying down" during his major league career. The spitballer was especially brilliant in the 1920 World Series against Brooklyn.

In the first game he made 72 pitches, winning 3-1. In his second appearance, he made 78 pitches and won, 5-1. Coveleski's third outing in the nine-game Series was a 3-0 shutout in which he made 82 deliveries. In each contest, he yielded only five hits.

Control was Coveleski's foremost asset. In one regular-season game, he reportedly did not pitch a ball out of the strike zone until the seventh inning. In 1920, when he won 24 games, the righthander issued only 65 walks in 315 innings, an average of less than two every nine innings.

Coveleski was one of 17 spitball pitchers permitted to use the moist delivery after it was banned in 1920 and he capitalized on it fully.

Ordinarily, Stan did not try for strikeouts, but he altered his style in a game against Washington after Sam

Cleveland's Stan Coveleski was one of 17 pitchers permitted to throw the spitball after its ban in 1920.

Rice led off an inning with a triple.

"I threw spitballs to the next three batters and they struck out," he recalled. "Steve O'Neill was our catcher, the greatest I ever played with, and those balls were breaking so much he didn't catch a single one. But he did block them and we got out of the inning without them scoring."

Coveleski, who threw the spitter "about once in every five pitches," was traded to Washington after the 1924 season and responded with a 20-5 record for the pennant-winning Nats of 1925.

A rawboned righthander who once worked for $3.75 a week in the coal mines, Coveleski settled in South Bend, Ind., after retiring in 1928. He operated a service station for several years before settling into an easier lifestyle that afforded plenty of time for fishing.

# Sam Crawford

Charley Dryden, the noted baseball wit of the early 1900s, delighted in composing fictitious interviews such as the one that appeared in the Philadelphia North American.

"To what do you attribute your tremendous physique?" the writer allegedly asked Sam Crawford.

"Whacking wind-whipped whiskers in Wahoo," was the alliterative answer by the Detroit outfielder.

While readers chuckled over Dryden's fertile imagination, Crawford, the hardest-hitting barber to come out of Wahoo, Neb., was scarcely a laughing matter to pitchers.

"There never was a better hitter than Sam Crawford," declared Ed Barrow, the famed Yankee executive who was manager of the Tigers in 1903. "He was the Lou Gehrig of his day."

Sam was a product of Wahoo (pop. 2,100), where his father, operator of the general store, was reputed to be the strongest man in the town.

Nobody did more than Sam to popularize his hometown. For years a billboard on the outskirts of the community proclaimed, "The Home Town of Sam Crawford." The player's plaque at Cooperstown lists his nickname as Wahoo Sam.

The young Crawford wasted no time in reaching the major leagues. One summer he was accompanying about 12 other youths, riding a farm wagon across the Nebraska plains and playing games against other town teams wherever they could be found. One year later Crawford was in the majors, having played only 103 games in the minor leagues.

Sam joined the Cincinnati Reds in September of 1899, and immediately engaged in an unusual doubleheader. In the first game against Cleveland, Crawford drilled two singles; in the second game, against Louisville, the left fielder rapped two more singles and a triple. It was the first of Sam's record 312 triples, a mark that appears likely to withstand the ravages of time.

Tales of Sam's slugging prowess are endless. When League Park was built in Cleveland, a 45-foot-high screen was erected atop the right-field wall as a deterrent to Crawford's clouts. Sam paid it little heed. He simply lofted drives over the screen.

Although no speed merchant, Sam knew how to run bases. He stole 367 bases in his 19-year career, including 37 in 1911 and 41 in 1912.

During the war between the National and American leagues, Crawford signed contracts for 1903 with both Cincinnati and Detroit. When the leagues signed a peace agreement, Sam was awarded to Detroit, where he batted behind Ty Cobb.

For several periods during their years as teammates,

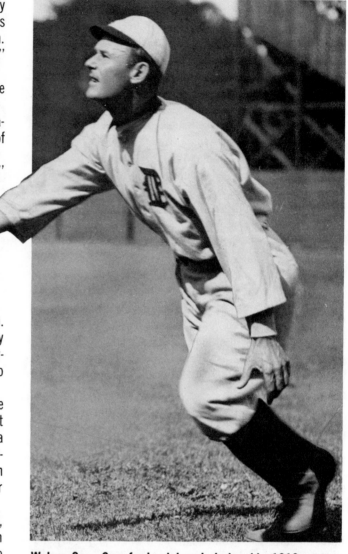

**Wahoo Sam Crawford, pictured during his 1910 season with Detroit, fell 36 hits short of the magic 3,000 level.**

Crawford and Cobb did not speak to each other. But when Hall of Fame electors failed to enshrine Crawford as quickly as Cobb thought they should, the old Georgia Peach campaigned vigorously for Sam.

After batting .173 in 61 games in 1917, Crawford departed the majors. He played four years for Los Angeles of the Pacific Coast League and, at age 41, was still capable of banging 199 hits for a .318 average in 1921.

When he was named to the Hall of Fame in 1957, Sam was living in a beach cabin in Pearblossom, Calif. He subscribed to a simple lifestyle, unrecognized by his neighbors as a former celebrity. He had no telephone "because people are always calling and wanting to talk." His spartan dwelling had an outside shower, constructed by Sam's own hands, and a television set, the gift of friends. The TV was not connected.

# Joe Cronin

Horatio Alger would have loved him. Hollywood could have done wonders with his story. He was the embodiment of the pluck-and-luck theme that transformed shoeshine boys into wealthy and influential magnates.

He even married the boss' daughter, but that wasn't important to the phenomenal success saga of Joe Cronin.

The son of Irish immigrants, Cronin grew up in the Mission District of San Francisco and attended the same high school that had launched Gentlemen Jim Corbett and Harry Heilmann toward athletic fame.

Joe attained his initial athletic prominence when, at age 15, he won the junior tennis championship of San Francisco.

But baseball transcended all other interests. Cronin was 18 when Joe Devine, a Pittsburgh scout, signed him for the Johnstown (Middle Atlantic) club. Three years later, the young shortstop was with Kansas City (American Association), having been sold outright by the Pirates, who were happy with shortstop Glenn Wright.

Enter Joe Engel, a scout for Washington. Kansas City's shortstop caught the scout's eye, and Engel arranged a deal with Blues Owner George Muehlebach to purchase the player for $7,500.

When Cronin joined the Senators, Owner Clark Griffith was not immediately impressed with the .242-hitting rookie. The Old Fox's personal choice for shortstop was Bobby Reeves, but every morning's paper revealed that Cronin was playing the position while the Nats were on the road.

Griffith wired his manager, Bucky Harris: "Reeves will never learn to play shortstop if you don't play him."

"Neither will Cronin," replied Bucky by return wire.

**Joe Cronin was a shortstop for the Washington Senators (above) in 1934 and the president of the American League (below) 25 years later.**

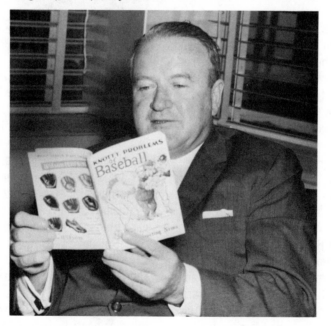

Harris admired Cronin's spirit, his willingness to take morning batting practice and field grounders by the hour.

By 1930, the Californian was regarded as the best all-around shortstop in the American League. With a batting average of .346 and 126 runs batted in, the 24-year-old Cronin was named the American League's Most Valuable Player.

At the close of the 1932 campaign, while he was recovering from a tonsillectomy in Washington, Joe was named manager of the Senators, succeeding Walter Johnson.

The next season, Cronin guided Washington to the American League pennant, although the Senators dropped a five-game World Series to the Giants.

After a seventh-place finish in injury-riddled 1934, Cronin was in his native San Francisco on his honeymoon when he received a call from Griffith. Tom Yawkey, young and wealthy owner of the Red Sox, had dazzled the Old Fox with his checkbook and offered $250,000, plus shortstop Lyn Lary, for Cronin, who would be named manager.

"Make the deal," said Cronin. "You can't afford not to."

Cronin was 36 in 1943 when he established an A.L. record with five pinch home runs, two with the bases loaded.

A fractured leg ended Cronin's playing career in April of 1945. He managed the Red Sox to a pennant in '46. In 1948, Joe was appointed the club's general manager, a position he held for 11 years, or until he was elected president of the American League. He occupied that chair until 1974 when, completing his Alger-like climb, he was named chairman of the A.L.

# Candy Cummings

Any youth walking along the beach in Brooklyn in the 1860s was apt to pick up a clam shell and give it a robust heave.

But young William Arthur Cummings, called Arthur by his family, was different from others his age. Watching the shells follow an irregular course as they flew across the water, Arthur grew curious. What accounted for the shells' unpredictable behavior, he wondered.

Curiosity led Cummings to the conclusion that a baseball could be made to act similarly if proper forces were applied.

Shortly, he was baffling players on neighborhood lots. Arthur's breaking pitch may have defied the laws of physics to his contemporaries, but they were unable to make contact with it while swinging wildly at the plate.

On the testimony of baseball historian Henry (Father) Chadwick, Arthur (Candy) Cummings invented the curveball and thereby earned a niche in the Hall of Fame.

Pitching in the face of the wind, Candy drove his catcher to distraction as the batterymate tried to corral the erratic pitches barehanded. To his dismay, Cummings learned his pitches were only routine tosses when the wind was at his back.

The young inventor's first recognition outside his hometown was gained in 1867 when the Excelsiors of Brooklyn visited New England where they opposed, among other teams, the "Harvards of Cambridge."

The Excelsiors' regular pitcher was indisposed, so Candy, a term of admiration in the 1860s, was nominated to pitch. The wind was again blowing toward the pitcher's mound, and Candy gave his new pitch a good workout.

After the game, the baffled Harvards asked Cummings: "What were you pitching us? It came at us and then it went away from us."

Candy's "horizontal whip of the wrist" soon found countless imitators. His secret was in the public domain.

Candy joined the "Stars of Brooklyn" in 1868, launching a four-year career with the aggregation that advertised itself as "the championship team of the United States and Canada." Cummings pitched the majority of the Stars' games, including a 24-12 victory over the Mutuals of New York, a professional organization like the Stars.

When Cummings defeated the Mutuals, 14-3, in an 1871 game, his reputation exceeded all bounds. Limiting an opponent to three runs in that era was exceedingly rare.

The prestigious Mutuals acquired Candy's services in 1872 when that club was a member of the National Association, forerunner of the National League. Player contracts were taken lightly in the 1870s, and Cummings signed with three other clubs before deciding that the Mutuals offered the best vehicle for his talents.

**Candy Cummings baffled many an opposing hitter after discovering how to make a baseball curve.**

Cummings was with Baltimore and Philadelphia the next two seasons before signing with the Hartford Dark Blues in the N.L.'s baptismal season of 1876. Inexplicably, Candy did not appear in any games from May through August, but compiled a 16-8 record in September and October. On September 9, the 120-pound righthander became the original "iron man" of baseball, hurling the Dark Blues to a doubleheader sweep over the Cincinnati Reds.

In 1877, Cummings was a member of the Cincinnati staff, but his touch was gone and the local journals blasted him unmercifully for his deficiencies. One paper editorialized: "This thing of examining scores of games in which the Cincinnati Reds play, and seeing from 18 to 25 hits each day being piled up against Cummings' record, is getting sickening. His presence on the team is demoralizing. Unless the evil is remedied, the club on its return will not attract 100 people to the games. No change could be for the worse."

Cummings' career ended in 1878 with the Forest City club of Cleveland. Candy returned to his native Massachusetts where, in the town of Athol, he opened a paint and wallpaper business in 1902. He sold the store in 1920, four years before his death.

# Kiki Cuyler

In the opinion of one highly respected scout, he was "a righthanded Ty Cobb . . . but more gentlemanly."

He could do more things with his glove than Cobb, could throw better, could pick up ground balls better and was one of the most graceful players of all time.

Kiki Cuyler's double won the deciding game of the 1925 World Series against Washington, yet two years later Kiki remained on the bench as the Pirates lost the Series to the Yankees in four games.

The mystery of Cuyler's absence in the Series was never discussed publicly by Cuyler or Manager Donie Bush, but many years later Paul Waner, a member of the 1927 Bucs, revealed the circumstances leading up to the strange treatment.

It all started when Bush promoted Cuyler from the No. 3 spot in the batting order to the No. 2 position, according to Waner. Cuyler seethed over the change, maintaining that—as an undisciplined hitter—he was ill-suited to bat second.

After a Pittsburgh victory in which Cuyler went hitless, Bush tried to console his outfielder. "Tough luck, Kiki," he said, "but don't worry about going hitless. We won and you'll start finding the holes."

"The hell with winning," Cuyler exploded. "I didn't get a hit and that's what counts."

Bush waited 30 seconds, then declared: "Cuyler, you have played your last game for this club as long as I'm manager."

Bush was as good as his word. While fans chanted "We want Cuyler" and banners bearing the same message fluttered around Forbes Field, Bush never glanced in Cuyler's direction, not even to pinch-hit. Shortly after the '27 season, Owner Barney Dreyfuss traded Cuyler to Chicago for Sparky Adams and Floyd Scott.

A native of Harrisville, Mich., Cuyler attended the United States Military Academy during World War I. He gained instant acclaim on the football field, but withdrew from the academy at the close of hostilities in Europe.

He obtained a job at the Buick plant in Flint, Mich., but when he was reduced to part-time work in the postwar recession, Cuyler turned to professional baseball and

**Kiki Cuyler was as graceful afield as he was devastating with his bat.**

joined the Bay City club in the Michigan-Ontario League.

In a 1921 doubleheader, Cuyler drove a ball over the left-field fence and batted in virtually all his team's runs. Still, a Detroit scout turned thumbs down on Cuyler because he reported—and Cuyler later confirmed—Kiki could not hit a curveball.

A Pittsburgh scout detected no such weakness and recommended his purchase. Two years later, while playing for Nashville, Cuyler mastered the curve. He also won an automobile as the most valuable player in the Southern Association and acquired the nickname that followed him the remainder of his life.

For years he had answered to the name of "Cuy." At Nashville, when a fly ball was hit toward center field, the shortstop, and then the second baseman, would cry "Cuy," signifying that Cuyler was to make the catch.

In turn, the spectators picked up the cry until a sportswriter tagged him phonetically with Kiki.

Cuyler was a full-fledged star by 1925, his second full major league season. He batted .357 and scored 144 runs, then a league record, to finish second to Rogers Hornsby in the National League's Most Valuable Player voting. Ten of his 220 hits came in succession.

In the '25 World Series, Kiki's home run clinched Game 2. And in Game 7, Cuyler made a spectacular catch before hitting a bases-loaded double off Walter Johnson that drove in the deciding runs.

In 1928, his first season with the Cubs, Cuyler ran into the wall and for weeks was unable to grip a bat properly.

But he was the Cuyler of old in 1929 when he batted .360 and drove in 102 runs to help the Cubs beat Bush's Pirates for the pennant.

Stints at Cincinnati and Brooklyn closed out Kiki's career. Cuyler became a successful minor league manager and he was a coach for the Red Sox under Joe McCarthy, his old Chicago boss, in 1949.

An ardent outdoorsman, Cuyler suffered a heart attack while ice fishing near Harrisville the following winter. Ten days later, while en route to a hospital in Ann Arbor, Mich., he was stricken fatally.

# Dizzy Dean

**Dizzy Dean (seated left) and brother Paul (right) were popular figures in 1935 when they accounted for 47 victories as members of St. Louis' Gashouse Gang.**

Almost every story told about Dizzy Dean, incredible as it may sound, contains an element of truth.

The "Great One" did nothing to discourage the legends that sprouted in his footsteps. Frequently, the stories were embroidered, but they were told in such a folksy, good-old-boy fashion that everyone subscribed willingly.

Like the day Dean stopped in front of the Boston dugout and proclaimed: "No curves today, fellas, just hard ones." He then shut out the Braves on three hits.

Or the day he wagered he could strike out Vince DiMaggio four times. He fanned the eldest DiMaggio three times and had a two-strike count on the batter when DiMaggio lifted a high pop foul. As the catcher prepared to make the catch, Dean raced in from the mound, shouting, "Drop it! Drop it!"

The catcher did as ordered, whereupon Dean fanned DiMaggio. He won the bet—all of one dollar.

Before the start of the 1934 season, Dean announced that "me 'n' Paul's gonna win 45 games." He erred slightly. They totaled 49 victories, with Diz accounting for 30.

When the Cardinals arrived in Detroit for the start of the '34 World Series, Dean, still in street clothes, strolled into the batting cage while the Tigers were taking practice. Grabbing the bat from Mickey Cochrane, the Tigers' catcher-manager, Diz clouted a pitch over the fence, then informed the flabbergasted Cochrane, "I'm the worst hitter on our club."

In Game 4 of the Series, Dean was inserted as a pinch-runner. It was an ill-advised action. Dean was knocked unconscious when struck on the head by an infielder's throw. But he was back in form for Game 7 when he blanked the Tigers, 11-0.

A native of Arkansas with only a fourth-grade education, Dean served in the United States Army where he learned the rudiments of pitching. At a Cardinals tryout camp in Texas, he dazzled the supervisors by striking out three batters on nine pitches. He was called back for a second look and repeated his earlier feat to earn a contract with St. Joseph (Western).

Dean progressed rapidly—about as speedily as the fastball he fogged past bewildered batters. On July 30, 1933, en route to 20 wins and 199 strikeouts, he set a major league record by striking out 17 Cubs.

But 1934 was the year of years for the big righthander. His 30-7 record, with 195 strikeouts, earned him the National League's Most Valuable Player award. Only Denny McLain, in 1968, matched Dean's victory total in the next half-century.

Ol' Diz was a constant thorn to Manager Frankie Frisch in that pennant-winning season of '34. He staged a brief strike because brother Paul was earning only $5,000 as a rookie. He missed exhibition games and was in headlines constantly with other capers, on and off the field.

But Frisch was not blind to Dean's superb talents.

"Dean was a natural," the manager declared. "He was the best fielding pitcher I ever saw. He could run the bases and when he was right, you didn't have to give him instructions, just the ball."

Dean, pinch-running in Game 4 of the 1934 World Series, goes down after being hit in the head by a throw from Detroit shortstop Billy Rogell. Dean was carried off on a stretcher. Broadcaster Dean (above) amused listeners with his peculiar use of the English language.

Dean wanted to bypass the 1937 All-Star Game because of fatigue, but yielded to Owner Sam Breadon's importunities and reported to Griffith Stadium in Washington. A line drive off the bat of Earl Averill struck and fractured Dean's toe in the third inning of the N.L.'s 8-3 loss.

Trying to pitch before his toe healed, Diz put an unnatural strain on his arm. He was pitching in Boston when something snapped. His arm was dead. In April of 1938, he was traded to the Cubs for three players and $185,000.

Dead-armed Diz enjoyed one last moment in the sun during the 1938 World Series. Pitching with nothing more than his old craftiness, Dean held a 3-2 lead over the Yankees until Frank Crosetti and Joe DiMaggio tagged him for late-inning home runs that gave New York a 2-0 edge in their World Series sweep.

Dean hung on for two more seasons before switching to the radio booth. He was broadcasting St. Louis Browns games in 1947 and criticizing pitchers regularly when management, as a promotional stunt, signed Dean for the last game of the season. In typical Dean manner, he blanked the Chicago White Sox for four innings.

Dean's peculiar use of the mother tongue sorely distressed the nation's English teachers. Fractured syntax was bad enough, but his past-tense forms were even worse, like slud for slid and throwed for threw.

After retiring from broadcasting, Dean made his home in Wiggins, Miss. He was in Reno, Nev., in 1974 when he suffered a fatal heart attack at age 63.

Dean's powerful right arm produced 150 wins against only 83 losses.

# Ed Delahanty

One of five brothers to play in the major leagues, Ed Delahanty is the only player in big-league history to lead both majors in hitting. Big Ed injected a lot of life into the dead ball.

Delahanty made his professional debut with Mansfield (Ohio State) in 1887. After his purchase for $1,900, considered a record at that time, he batted ninth and went hitless when he made his major league debut as a second baseman for the Phillies one year later.

Big Ed rapped his first single off George Borchers of Chicago, May 23, 1888; his first double off John Clarkson of Boston, on May 25; his first home run off Sam Moffet of Indianapolis on June 13, and his first triple off Frank Gilmore of Washington on June 19.

Delahanty enjoyed his most productive day at the plate in the Chicago White Stockings' old West Side Park on July 13, 1896. In the first inning, against Adonis Bill Terry, Delahanty lined a home run into the left-field bleachers.

In his second at-bat, he homered to right field. The next time, he lined a single. On his fourth trip, he homered to dead center.

With Terry still on the mound, and the Chicago fans cheering wildly, Big Ed homered to the clubhouse roof, thereby matching Bobby Lowe's four-homer record for one game.

Delahanty's demonstration was hardly an inspiration to his teammates, who collected only three additional hits in losing, 9-8.

Twice, Delahanty enjoyed 6-for-6 performances. He first accomplished the feat with Cleveland in the Players League on June 2, 1890. He belted a triple, a double and four singles off Marcus Baldwin of Chicago.

He repeated the feat on June 16, 1894, with the Phillies, rapping a double and five singles against Cincinnati.

Delahanty was one of eight players to achieve a .400 batting mark in two seasons. Curiously, in one such year (1894), his .400 average was good for only fourth place. He trailed Hugh Duffy, Tuck Turner and Sam Thompson. Turner and Thompson were Delahanty's teammates on a club that compiled a season average of .349.

Delahanty, a righthanded slugger, gained his first batting title in 1899 when he posted a .408 mark. Three years later, after jumping to the new American League, he batted a league-leading .376 for Washington.

Along the way, Big Ed clouted four doubles in one game and also reeled off 10 consecutive hits in two days, July 13-14, 1897.

For several years, Delahanty earned $2,400 annually, the maximum allowed by the National League, but in 1901 he was earning $3,000.

As an inducement to jump to Washington's A.L. club, Delahanty was offered $4,000, which he accepted. But

**Big Ed Delahanty is the only man in major league history to lead both the American and National leagues in hitting.**

disenchantment quickly set in when John McGraw made overtures from New York and advanced Ed $4,500 to return to the National League as a member of the Giants.

Peace between the two leagues before the 1903 season locked Delahanty to the Washington club, which only added to his discontentment. He was batting .338 when Washington played in Cleveland on June 25. Ed did not show up for the game.

Delahanty continued to travel with the team, then disappeared again on July 2. For nearly a week there was no word of his whereabouts. Eventually, the district superintendent of the Pullman Company reported that a man answering Delahanty's description had created a disturbance aboard a Michigan Central train the night of July 2.

The man, it was reported, had five drinks, then brandished an open razor in terrifying passengers on the sleeping car. When the train reached Bridgeburg on the Canadian side of Niagara Falls, the conductor put the man off the train.

A night watchman on the International Bridge spotted Delahanty trying to walk across the span, exchanged angry words with him and ordered him back to shore. Big Ed never made it.

The player's body was discovered on July 9, about 20 miles from the bridge. Money and jewelry worth $2,000 that Delahanty reportedly carried were never found.

# Bill Dickey

While Babe Ruth and Lou Gehrig earned bolder headlines and compiled more impressive home run and runs-batted-in statistics, the one Yankee of the late 1920s and early '30s whom many opposing pitchers feared the most was a durable catcher whose bat always seemed hottest in the clutch.

Bill Dickey was quiet, courteous and possessed a memory as long as some of his hunting treks across the hills of Arkansas.

For 13 consecutive years—1929 through 1941—Dickey caught 100 or more games a season, an accomplishment that has been matched only by Johnny Bench.

Dickey forgot his manners only once while in uniform. That lapse occurred on July 4, 1932, when the Yankees and Senators were embroiled in a typical donnybrook of that era. When Carl Reynolds, husky Washington outfielder, barreled across the plate and then started back to be certain that he touched the plate, Dickey mistook his actions as a signal for a fight. Bill got in the first punch, and Reynolds went down with a fractured jaw. Dickey received a $1,000 fine—out of his $14,000 salary—and a 30-day suspension.

At no time thereafter was Dickey able to explain his blowup.

But Bill had his moments to cherish against the Senators, too. There was the day that Walter Johnson, Nats manager, twice moved his center fielder as Dickey approached the plate. In each instance, Bill sliced a triple to left-center field.

When Dickey batted a third time, Johnson repeated his move, and Bill belted what should have been a record-tying third triple. But the humor of the occasion got to Dickey first. Laughing heartily, he was unable to get past second base.

Dickey possessed a steel-trap memory bank for the right way to pitch opposing batters. In 1943, a few hours after his two-run homer had wrapped up the five-game World Series against the Cardinals, Dickey stepped onto an

Bill Dickey was the first of two No. 8s to handle Yankee catching chores with Hall of Fame distinction.

As a catcher, Dickey had an uncanny memory for the weaknesses of opposing hitters.

As a hitter, Dickey was at his best when the game was on the line.

elevator in a St. Louis hotel.

A serviceman was already aboard the lift. Turning to Dickey, he said: "I'll bet you don't remember me."

Dickey studied the soldier for a moment, then confessed: "I don't recall your name, but I remember we pitched you inside and high."

The man was Joe Gantenbein, who had played two seasons with the Philadelphia Athletics.

A native of Bastrop, La., Dickey spent his early years in Arkansas where he attended Little Rock College. He was a member of an athletic family that included older brother Gus, a semipro player, and younger brother George, or Skeets, who played with the Red Sox and White Sox.

Signed by the local Southern Association club, Dickey was performing for Jackson (Cotton States) when Yankee scout Johnny Nee crossed his path.

"If this boy doesn't make it," Nee wired the New York front office, "I'll quit scouting."

Dickey had played in his eighth World Series and had batted .351 in limited service during the regular season when, at age 36, he enrolled in the Navy's officers candidate school late in 1943. After serving for two years in the Pacific, he returned to New York in 1946, only to find that the organization had undergone a drastic transformation.

Larry MacPhail was in command and while Joe McCarthy still was manager, the atmosphere was totally different. The season was young when Dickey, who had been approached about managerial jobs with the Phillies and the Boston Braves, was named to replace McCarthy.

Before the season ended, Dickey himself was succeeded by Johnny Neun. Bill's record as pilot was 57-48. Dickey tried his hand at managing the hometown Little Rock (Southern) club in 1947, but when the Travelers finished last with a 51-103 record, he washed his hands of further managerial chores.

In the spring of 1949, Dickey took a leave from his job with an investment banking firm in Little Rock to spend time with the Yankees again. His assignment was to refine the catching skills of his young successor, Yogi Berra.

"Do you think you can help Berra?" Bill was asked when he arrived for the start of spring training.

"If I didn't think so, I wouldn't be here," he replied.

Dickey's success was obvious. Not only are Dickey and Berra both in the Hall of Fame, but in 1972 the Yankees retired uniform No. 8—the numeral that Bill and Yogi had worn with distinction through their extraordinary careers.

# Martin Dihigo

Of all the players who could perform capably at more than one position, there was none, according to qualified observers, who could match Martin Dihigo.

John McGraw, a regular off-season visitor to Cuba, termed Dihigo the greatest natural player he had seen in his long and storied career.

Buck Leonard, who preceded Dihigo into the Hall of Fame, paid the following tribute to the big fellow who could play every position except catcher:

"He was the greatest all-around player I know. I say he was the best ballplayer of all time, black or white. He could do it all. He is my ideal ballplayer, makes no difference what race either. If he isn't the greatest, I don't know who is. You take your Ruths, Cobbs or DiMaggios. Give me Dihigo. Bet I'd beat you almost every time."

Renowed for his powerful arm, the 6-foot-3 Dihigo was credited with the first no-hitter in the Mexican League, was the first Cuban named to the Cooperstown Hall of Fame and the first player to be honored in the baseball shrines of Cuba, Mexico and the United States.

Dihigo made his initial appearance in the States as a second baseman in 1923, performing with the touring Cuban Stars. He had difficulty with the curveball at that time.

Two years later, however, he hit .307 in Negro league competition and in 1927, when he tied for the league lead in homers with 18, Dihigo posted a .331 mark. As a pitcher that year, he won four games and lost two.

Despite Martin's success as a pitcher, he would have been an even greater outfielder if he had concentrated on that position, according to many of his admirers. Ted Page of Pittsburgh, a Negro league outfielder whose opinions are respected universally, asserted: "He might have been an outfielder like Oscar Charleston (the Willie Mays of his day). And he had perhaps the finest throwing arm in baseball. As much as I liked Roberto Clemente, I liked Dihigo better."

As Dihigo matured, his statistics shot upward. In his homeland, his winter batting average skyrocketed from .179 to .300 to .344 to .415 to .450.

One year the league batting race between Willie Wells and Dihigo went down to the final day. Wells, batting third, went 4-for-4. Dihigo, batting behind him, went 5-for-5, including a home run in his final at-bat, to edge his teammate.

Dihigo's pitching performances were equally spectacular. In his heyday in Cuba, Dihigo posted marks of 11-2, 14-10, 11-5 and 14-2. In Mexico, in 1938, his record was 18-2. In 1942, Martin went 22-7, led the league in strikeouts and earned-run average and batted .319.

Dihigo enjoyed his top season in 1935 when he managed the New York Cubans to their best record, batted

**Martin Dihigo, the first Cuban in the Hall of Fame, was one of the best all-round players in history.**

.372 and won two of three pitching decisions.

Dihigo also was the leading vote-getter for the All-Star Game in which he played the outfield and pitched.

In the championship series between the Cubans and the Pittsburgh Crawfords, headed by Josh Gibson, Oscar Charleston and Cool Papa Bell, the Cubans won three of the first five games and enjoyed a substantial lead in the late innings of the sixth game. Unaccountably, Dihigo substituted himself for the starting hurler.

Underneath the stands, Cubans Owner Alex Pompoz was counting the receipts and estimating the winners' shares when the crowd roar tipped him off that the Crawfords had tied the score. Infuriated, Pompoz fired a roll of $500 bills across the room. His ire was not lessened when the Crawfords won and clinched the title the next day.

An easy-going individual with a gentle sense of humor and a penchant for practical jokes, Dihigo mastered the English language quickly and was extremely popular with American players.

Dihigo was living in Cuba when Fidel Castro came into power, and a mystery surrounds his last years. Whether he opposed or supported the Castro regime is unclear. It is generally believed, however, that Dihigo held the post of minister of sports at the time of his death at Cienfuegos in 1971.

# Joe DiMaggio

**DiMaggio was a superstar by 1950, when his 10th-inning homer beat the Phillies in Game 2 of the World Series.**

**Joe DiMaggio was a young outfielder for the San Francisco Seals in 1934.**

Few players, if any, earned the admiration and respect of all levels of society—and retained the popularity longer —than Joe DiMaggio, the son of a San Francisco fisherman.

In Yankee pinstripes or in retirement decades later, the Clipper was the cynosure of eyes and the symbol of professional class.

If fans were not reciting his miraculous catches in center field or warbling the catchy lyrics to "Jolting Joe DiMaggio," they were reminiscing about his incomparable batting streaks.

Joe was 17 when he broke in at shortstop with the San Francisco Seals of the Pacific Coast League in 1932, and he was still shy of his 19th birthday when he unreeled his 61-game batting streak one year later.

An outfielder at this point, DiMaggio launched his string with a single on May 28 and was stopped on July 25 by Ed Walsh, son of the White Sox immortal, who was pitching for Oakland. During the PCL streak, Joe went 104-for-257 for a .405 average.

In 1941, the Yankee Clipper posted an even higher average, .408, during his 56-game American League streak that caught the attention of the entire nation.

Again he started with a single, against the White Sox on

The DiMaggio brothers, Vince, Joe and Dom (left to right), reunited at a PCL old timers game in 1956.

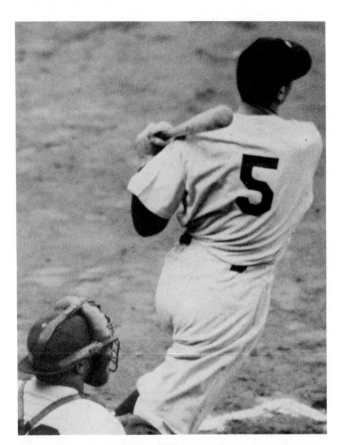

The grace and style exhibited by No. 5 earned him a special niche in the hearts of Yankee fans.

May 15. After rapping 91 hits in 223 at-bats, DiMaggio was halted at Cleveland by Al Smith and Jim Bagby, pitchers who received assistance from third baseman Ken Keltner (who made two fine plays on DiMaggio). After the streak, DiMaggio hit safely in the next 17 games. Mainly on the strength of the record streak, DiMaggio won a second Most Valuable Player award (he also was honored in 1939), beating out Ted Williams, who had hit .406.

Despite Joe's lofty batting averages as a minor leaguer, scouts were cool to him as a prospect. A knee injury created doubts and when the Pirates and Red Sox lost interest, the Yankees bought DiMaggio for $25,000 and assigned him back to San Francisco, where he tuned up with a .398 average in 1935.

DiMaggio, or Joe D. as he came to be known shortly thereafter, was not in the Yankees' lineup on opening day, 1936. He suffered a burn from a heat lamp while undergoing treatment on a twisted ankle and did not make his debut until May 3, when he appeared in right field.

Joe, who was joined in the majors by older brother Vince and younger brother Dominic, starred on world champion clubs during his first four years with the Yankees. He was the popular successor to Babe Ruth and a favorite of the Italian community.

After three years of military service in World War II, DiMag rejoined the Yankees in 1946. His average dipped below .300 that season, but he rebounded for a third MVP trophy in another world-championship season of '47.

For several years, Joe had suffered from a bone spur on his right heel. The condition worsened after the 1948 season and the gifted outfielder was forced to miss the first two months of the 1949 race. He played his first games under Manager Casey Stengel at Boston in mid-June and demonstrated his ability to rise to the occasion. In a three-game series, the Jolter socked four homers in what he later designated as his most satisfying experience.

With another young star, Mickey Mantle, about to blossom, DiMaggio announced his retirement after the Yankees clinched the 1951 World Series title, Joe's ninth.

In 1968, Charlie Finley, owner of the Oakland A's, talked Joe out of retirement. The old star served for two years as batting instructor and vice president.

DiMaggio was married twice, each time to an actress. His first wife was Dorothy Arnold, his second Marilyn Monroe. The second marriage collapsed in less than a year, but the pair remained close friends. For 20 years after Miss Monroe's death, Joe arranged for red roses to be placed at her grave twice weekly.

# Hugh Duffy

Ted Williams took one glance at the 5-foot-7 septuagenarian and asked, "How did such a little fellow hit .438? Bases on balls must have counted as hits."

Williams was even more perplexed when he was assured that walks did not count as hits in 1894 when Hugh Duffy, an undersized outfielder, registered his all-time major league record for a season batting average.

Duffy was 27 and in his seventh major league season when he established his record as a member of the Boston Nationals. Until his death in 1954, he expressed the hope that he would live to see Williams surpass his record. Ted's best effort fell 32 points short in 1941.

Williams would have been even more amazed to know that Hugh had hit four major league homers before he rapped a double or a triple. Playing for Cap Anson's Chicago White Stockings in 1888, Duffy walloped his first homer off Hank O'Day of Washington on July 11; another off Lady Baldwin of Detroit, July 28; a third off Ed Morris of Pittsburgh, July 30, and his fourth off Jim Galvin of Pittsburgh, August 1.

Duffy explained his failure to break into the Chicago lineup at an earlier date.

When he reported to the club, Anson sized him up and snarled, "Where's the rest of you?"

"This is all there is," replied Duffy. Anson, who favored big outfielders, was so incensed he did not speak to the rookie for two months.

During his 124-game season of 1894, Duffy went hitless in only 17 games. He rapped five hits in two games, four hits in 12, three hits in 19, two hits in 47 and one hit in 27.

He opened the season with three hits in six tries, but fell into the .260 range in early May. He regained the .300 plateau on May 19 and never looked back. He zoomed past .400 with a 5-for-6 performance on July 5 and attained a .441 mark before a slight decline at the finish.

As a reward for his brilliant season, Duffy's salary was raised $12.50 a week, to $2,700 annually. For this added compensation, he also had to serve as team captain and make certain that the bats and baseballs were returned to the clubhouse at the completion of the day's activities.

"No one thought much of averages in those days," the little fellow recalled 50 years later. "I didn't realize I had hit that much until the official averages were published four months later."

Although noted primarily for his hitting, Duffy made a catch in 1897 that drew the admiration of even the opposing players.

In a game against Baltimore, Duffy played shallow left field when Joe Corbett drove a pitch to deep left field. Turning with the crack of the bat, Duffy raced within two feet of the fence, leaped and caught the ball barehanded.

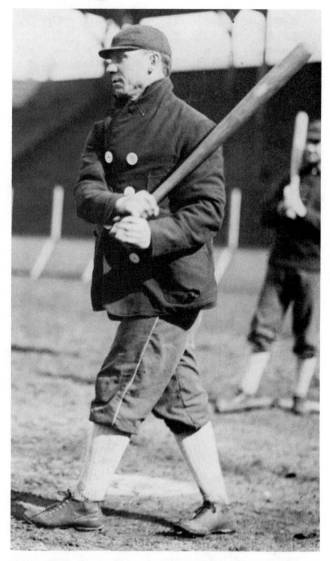

**Hugh Duffy was manager of the White Sox in 1910, 16 years after hitting a record .438.**

While still in midair, it was reported, Duffy turned and fired to the third baseman to complete a double play.

"So miraculous were the catch and throw," it was written, "that even the Baltimore players tossed their caps into the air and joined in cheering which lasted 15 minutes —probably the longest demonstration inspired by a play."

After his playing career ended in 1908, Duffy turned to managing and scouting. He piloted the White Sox and Red Sox before signing to scout for the Red Sox in 1924.

Annually thereafter, he signed a contract as a scout. Hugh directed tryout camps throughout New England, including sessions at Fenway Park when the Red Sox were on the road.

Duffy had been ill for several months before he died at his home in Allston, Mass., 60 years after his remarkable achievements in the batter's box.

# Billy Evans

The Youngstown, Ohio, semipro team was ready to begin a game in 1903 when it was discovered that the umpire had failed to show up.

The managers huddled, trying to agree on a substitute, when it was suggested that Billy Evans, an $18-a-week sportswriter for the Youngstown Vindicator, would be a fine choice inasmuch as his stories reflected fairness and honesty.

Evans was reluctant to leave the press box until somebody reminded him that the job paid $15. That was the origin of a career that carried Evans to the American League for 22 years, to the presidency of the Southern Association, to the general manager's chair of the Indians and Tigers and the farm director's position with the Red Sox.

Billy entered Organized Baseball in the Ohio-Pennsylvania League in 1905 and was umpiring a Niles-Youngstown game when a decision on the final pitch precipitated a riot. Billy was accorded a police escort, but his courage in making an unpopular decision against the home team impressed a spectator, Manager Jimmy McAleer of the St. Louis Browns. McAleer recommended Evans to A.L. President Ban Johnson.

Billy, who was forced to withdraw from Cornell University after his sophomore year because of the death of his father, joined the A.L. staff when he was 22, the youngest umpire in major league history and the only one to jump from Class C to the majors.

Evans worked behind the plate when Walter Johnson made his major league debut, he was there when Babe Ruth hit his 60th home run and he was present for six no-hitters. He was the A.L. answer to Bill Klem of the National League.

Billy was in his second A.L. season when he was knocked unconscious by a thrown pop bottle in St. Louis. Working before an overflow crowd, Evans was conferring with Detroit Manager Hugh Jennings and left fielder Davey Jones when he was struck on the head by the bottle. He collapsed in Jones' arms and was rushed to a hospital, where he hovered near death for several weeks.

After recovery, Ban Johnson asked Billy to press charges against the culprit, but the umpire refused, saying that the 17-year-old clerk "has apologized to me one hundred times for throwing the bottle."

Evans never backed down from a challenge and when Ty Cobb invited Billy to meet him under the grandstand at Washington in 1921 to settle a dispute, the umpire accepted. "It was like fighting Joe Louis and a wildcat at the same time," Evans admitted later after a sound whipping.

Evans was quick with a soft word and a witticism. Once, when Joe Cantillon was managing Washington and coaching at third base, Billy called the first pitch of the

Billy Evans went from sportswriting to an illustrious career as an umpire and baseball executive.

game a ball.

From third base came Cantillon's cry: "Let's not start the game like that."

Jerking off his mask, Evans thumbed Joe.

"You've taken on too big a job," Evans told Cantillon. "You simply can't manage and umpire at the same time."

Evans was instrumental in the assignment of four umpires to World Series games. In 1909, working with Klem, Billy was required to ask bleacherites if a ball landed fair or foul. The next game, four men were on the job.

Evans was an excellent story teller and never tired of relating an anecdote involving Washington's Walter Johnson. In a close game with Detroit, Johnson permitted two ninth-inning baserunners and fired two fastballs past Sam Crawford.

"Then the most beautiful fastball I ever saw came across the plate," Billy recalled. "Unfortunately, I called it a ball. Johnson only shrugged his shoulders.

"For the only time in my life I pulled for one team, praying that Crawford would make an out, which he did on a long drive to center field."

When Johnson walked off the mound, he said to Evans, "Where was that next-to-last pitch?"

"Where do you think?" asked Billy.

"Well, it may have been a trifle low."

Evans was 71 when he suffered a fatal heart attack while visiting his son in Miami.

# Johnny Evers

At 5-foot-9 and 140 pounds, the youngster scarcely resembled a major league player, and when he was asked to wear a uniform designed for a much-larger man, the dissemblance was even more pronounced.

Moreover, the kid's former manager at Troy in the New York State League had forwarded a message to the Chicago Cubs: "If you keep him, you can send me $500. If not, send him back."

Johnny Evers shunned all thoughts of going back. Only six months earlier he was working in a collar factory in his native Troy. When he was laid off, he wangled a tryout with the local baseball club, and he hung on. Now he was in the majors at age 21.

His prominent jaw proclaimed Evers a fighter from the start. He fought veterans for a chance to take batting practice. He swapped insults with teammates and opponents and even took on the Giants' John McGraw.

Before long he was a member of baseball's most celebrated double-play combination, Tinker to Evers to Chance, and he became an authority on the playing rules. In 1908, when a Pittsburgh runner failed to touch the next base on a game-winning hit in the ninth inning, Evers called the oversight to the attention of Hank O'Day.

The umpire maintained that players had been doing the same thing for years. Why change?

Later, on reflection, O'Day conceded the point to the Cub infielder. Thereafter, he said, he would call the runner out.

Fortunately for Evers and the Cubs, O'Day was umpiring at the Polo Grounds on September 23, when Fred Merkle of the Giants ran from first base to the clubhouse on what should have been a game-winning hit. Merkle was forever censured for his action; Evers, who called for the ball and forced out Merkle at second, was ever after lauded for his nimble intellect.

When the game was declared a tie, and the Cubs won the replay, Evers was credited with winning a pennant.

In 1914, Johnny provided the spark that carried the Boston Braves to the pennant. They faced the powerful Philadelphia A's, American League champions for the fourth time in five years, in the World Series.

At the instigation of Evers, the underdog Braves taunted the A's from the moment they appeared on the field. Unaccustomed to such treatment, the A's first grew angry, then disintegrated.

Before the fourth and final game, a Philadelphian told Evers, "You fellows have done a great job, you deserve a lot of credit."

Evers spat at the feet of his opponent and snarled: "We don't take praise from yellow dogs."

Johnny was too old for service in World War I, but he went to Europe as an athletic director for the Knights of

The middle man of the "Tinker to Evers to Chance" refrain was Johnny Evers, the Cubs' scrappy second baseman.

Columbus.

Evers managed the Cubs in 1913 and again in 1921, and piloted the White Sox in 1924. McGraw, once a bitter enemy, hired him as a coach in 1920, and Evers served as assistant manager for the Braves from 1929 through 1932.

For years Evers was a regular spectator at the World Series. He was in Chicago when the Cubs played the Yankees in 1938. Unknown to him or to Joe Tinker, the old double-play mates—who had not spoken to each other as players and had not seen each other for years—were scheduled to appear on the same broadcast. When they spotted each other, they fell into a clinch.

"Both of us could hardly keep from crying," related Evers.

After retiring from baseball, Johnny operated a sporting goods store in Albany, N.Y., and was superintendent of city-owned Bleeker Stadium.

In 1942, Evers suffered a paralytic stroke and for a while was confined to a chair in his home, from where he could gaze out the window at his store. He recovered sufficiently to go to Cooperstown in 1946 when he, Tinker and Chance were enshrined as a unit.

A second stroke paralyzed the old warrior further before a cerebral hemorrhage proved fatal to Evers in 1947.

# Buck Ewing

In 1932, when Mickey Cochrane was in his eighth season with the Philadelphia Athletics, John B. Foster, highly respected editor of the Spalding Baseball Guide, declared unequivocally that Buck Ewing was the No. 1 catcher in 56 years of major league baseball.

Foster fortified his thesis with the fact that Connie Mack, Cochrane's manager at the time, voted for Ewing as the game's foremost receiver.

"Buck could throw from any position," wrote Foster of the New York catcher of the 1880s. "It was not by accident that he threw fearlessly and unswervingly when he squatted down behind the batter, but because he chose to throw that way, because he knew he could and did catch runners with the same easy skill that he would have caught them if he were standing.

"Ewing could juggle the ball and still throw out the runner, and they had some fast men circling the bases in the days when he caught. He might have a 'half' passed ball and the runner on first would leave the base. . . to think that at last he had something on Ewing, only to come within two feet of second and find the baseman there with the ball."

The secret of Ewing's rifle throws was a sharp forearm snap that sent the ball with extraordinary speed to its objective, Foster stated.

Despite the speed of Buck's throws, the ball was reputed to be soft and easy to handle.

Ewing also was a diplomat behind the plate, according to Foster, who wrote: "Seldom was he critical of the umpires. He was what is known in these days as a good jollier. He had the friendship of umpires because he made life easy for them."

Ewing, nicknamed Buck by boyhood pals and credited by some historians as the first catcher to crouch behind the plate, made his major league debut with Troy on September 9, 1880, collecting a single in a 1-0 loss to Providence.

Ewing possessed only ordinary speed, but through a constant study of pitchers, he was able to achieve impressive stolen base totals. He was, said batterymate Mickey Welch, "a thinking man's player."

In one game, Ewing stole second and third base and then shouted for everyone to hear, "Now, I'm stealing home," which he accomplished with a hard slide.

The play was captured on a lithograph and became a popular novelty item among Giants fans.

When the Players League was formed in 1890, Ewing joined many others in deserting the National League. He was named manager of the New York outlaw club. The Giants sued for the return of their players but the courts ruled in favor of the jumpers, maintaining there was no "mutuality" in the contracts.

**Rifle-arm catcher Buck Ewing was a member of the New York Giants in 1887.**

Back with the Giants, after the Players League collapsed at the end of one season, Ewing injured his arm in 1892, but shifted to first base and continued to hit effectively.

At the end of the '92 season he was traded to Cleveland for shortstop George Davis. Ewing was released after two seasons and signed as player-manager of the Red Stockings in his native Cincinnati. He managed Cincinnati through 1899 before returning to the Giants as manager for part of the 1900 season.

Ewing was considered a wealthy man, the result of land holdings in the West, when he retired from baseball. He was living in Cincinnati with his wife and two daughters when he died of diabetes and paralysis a week before his 47th birthday.

# Red Faber

The 1917 World Series was both the best and the worst of times for Red Faber, the 29-year-old spitball pitcher from Cascade, Ia.

The White Sox righthander won three games, one of a handful of hurlers to turn the trick in Series play. He also suffered his greatest embarrassment in his 20 years with the Sox. It occurred in Game 2 which, fortunately for Faber, the American Leaguers won, 7-2, over the Giants en route to the Series title.

Buck Weaver was the runner at second base when Faber belted an infrequent hit, a two-out single. When the throw went to the plate, Faber continued to second, assuming Weaver had scored on the play.

When the pitcher took a long windup, Faber took off for third, only to find Weaver sliding in from the other side.

"Where in the hell do you think you're going?" Weaver asked.

"I'm goin' back to pitch," Faber replied red-faced.

When the White Sox won the pennant again in 1919, Faber was unable to pitch in the World Series because of an ankle injury. Years after the Sox lost the stained Series to the Cincinnati Reds, Faber's longtime batterymate, Ray Schalk, asserted: "If Red had been able to pitch, I'm sure there would have been no Black Sox scandal."

Faber was a student at St. Joseph College in Dubuque, Ia., when he pitched so impressively against the local Three-I League team that he was offered $100 monthly to turn pro.

On August 18, 1910, Red pitched a perfect game against Davenport. It was one of his 18 victories that season. The Pittsburgh Pirates acquired his contract after the Three-I season, but Faber never appeared in a game and was sold to Minneapolis. He was purchased by Chicago for $3,500 after he won 20 games for Des Moines (Western) in 1913.

At the close of that season, Faber was asked to join the Sox for the first stage of their world tour with the Giants. He was scheduled to remain with them only as far as

**Spitballer Red Faber is pictured in 1917, the year in which he won three World Series games for the White Sox.**

Seattle, point of embarkation for the two clubs, so that management could appraise his talents.

When the clubs reached Seattle, however, Christy Mathewson decided not to accompany the tour overseas. John McGraw needed a pitcher. "Why not take Faber?" inquired Chicago Owner Charles Comiskey.

McGraw accepted the suggestion and the young righthander wore a Giants uniform the remainder of the trip, defeating the Sox in Hong Kong, Brisbane, Melbourne and Cairo.

After the players were at sea, it was discovered that, in the frenzied activity in Seattle, Faber was traveling without a passport.

Faber won 10 games for the White Sox in 1914 and totaled 57 victories in the next three seasons.

After a year's service in the United States Navy in World War I, Faber rejoined the Sox in 1919, weak and underweight. He captured only 11 of 20 decisions.

When the spitball was outlawed in 1920 for all pitchers except established major leaguers, Faber was one of the favored 17 and he continued to baffle A.L. batters with the pitch he learned at Dubuque. He threw only the spitter and fastball, asserting that a curveball "is too hard on the arm."

After 1920, the Sox finished in the second division for the remainder of Faber's career, yet he posted 254 career victories.

"We were a lousy team in those years," said Schalk, "otherwise Red would have won 300 games easily."

When the Philadelphia A's sold Jack Quinn to Brooklyn in 1931, Faber was the only spitball pitcher remaining in the American League. He continued until the fall of 1933, pitching mainly in relief. In his final appearance, he hurled a five-hit shutout against the Cubs in the second game of the 1933 City Series. He was 44 at the time.

Thirteen years later, Faber donned a White Sox uniform again at the invitation of his old pitching colleague, Ted Lyons, the new manager. Red served as pitching coach for three years before going into retirement again.

Death came to the old spitball master at his home in Chicago at age 88.

# Bob Feller

In 1948, 29-year-old Bob Feller won 19 games for the Indians, but was a two-time loser in his only World Series appearance.

During the war years, Feller pitched for the Great Lakes Navy team.

He burst upon baseball like a bombshell. From out of nowhere, he appeared suddenly, firing a baseball—it was said by some—with a greater velocity than it had ever been thrown previously.

The nation took its first notice of the Van Meter, la., farmboy in 1936 when, as a 17-year-old, he struck out eight members of the St. Louis Cardinals in three innings of an exhibition game. Bob Feller was headline news thereafter, first as a Cleveland pitcher, then as a baseball ambassador who never feared to speak his mind.

The hard-throwing youngster was a cause celebre at the very beginning. The Indians, it developed, had signed Feller to a Fargo-Moorhead (Northern) contract. This, in itself, violated an existing regulation forbidding major league clubs from signing free agents other than college players.

In order to complete high school, Feller was advised to seek voluntary retirement in 1936, at which time his contract was transferred to New Orleans, another Cleveland farm, in the Southern Association.

When the youth subsequently appeared in a semipro tournament and scouts of other clubs learned that the phenom was unavailable because of his ties with Cleveland, Commissioner K.M. Landis conducted an investigation into the contract manipulations.

In time, Landis awarded Feller to the Indians, but they were ordered to pay $7,500 to the Des Moines (Western) club, whose owner, Lee Keyser, had charged the Tribe with violating the Major-Minor League Agreement.

A major factor in Landis' decision was the assurance by

Bob and his father Bill that they were pleased with their association with the Indians.

Following his explosive debut against the Cardinals, Feller appeared a couple times in relief before receiving his first starting assignment in mid-August. The righthander turned it into a memorable occasion with a 4-1 victory over the St. Louis Browns in which he struck out 15 batters.

In September, he established an American League record and matched the big-league mark by fanning 17 Philadelphia batters. When the season ended, he returned to Van Meter to complete his high school education.

Feller won 107 games before he was 23 and was on a 300-victory course for his career when, at the close of the 1941 season, he enlisted in the United States Navy and missed virtually all of the next four seasons. He earned six battle citations as a gun crew chief.

Although he pitched a no-hitter against Chicago on opening day of 1940 (and threw two other no-hitters in his career), Feller treasured even more his season inaugu-

Feller receives congratulations from his teammates after throwing the third no-hitter of his illustrious career on July 1, 1951, in the first game of a doubleheader against the Detroit Tigers.

ral against the White Sox in 1946. It was a 1-0 three-hitter, preserved when Bob Lemon, playing center field, made a spectacular catch of a short fly ball and doubled a runner off second base in the ninth inning.

As his salary skyrocketed in the late 1940s, Feller found it advantageous to incorporate as Ro-Fel Inc. In 1947, his income was reported to be $150,000, a combination of his player's salary, personal endorsements and a barnstorming tour in which his own major league all-stars opposed black all-stars.

With a slider, developed during his military career, to supplement his curve and blistering fastball, Feller posted 26 and 20 victories in his first two years following his postwar return to the Indians, but dropped to 19 in the pennant-winning season of 1948.

Bob opened the World Series in Boston and suffered his most crushing defeat when an umpire's questionable decision on a pickoff attempt led to a 1-0 loss.

He also started Game 5 before 86,000 Cleveland fans, but yielded eight hits in less than seven innings and was tagged with a second setback.

In 1954, when the Indians set a league record with 111 victories, Feller wasn't used in the World Series as the Giants swept Cleveland.

Feller appeared in five mid-summer classics, allowing five hits and one run in 12⅓ innings.

When Feller returned to Van Meter, Ia., in 1948, local batters were just as helpless as before.

78

# Elmer Flick

Members of the Phillies had difficulty concealing their mirth when the rookie arrived at their Cape May, N.J., training camp carrying a canvas bag that contained a thick-handled bat he had turned on a lathe back home in Ohio.

But their snickers turned to smiles when Elmer Flick started drilling the ball to all corners of the field on that day early in 1898.

Initially, Flick's chances of crashing the Phils' outfield were less than favorable. Ed Delahanty, Duff Cooley and Sam Thompson were firmly entrenched. One journalist, however, was impressed with the rookie, describing Flick as "the fastest and most promising youngster the Phillies ever had."

Flick opened the season on the bench, but when recurring back problems sidelined Thompson in April, Flick stepped in and rapped two singles against Boston. Thompson returned briefly, then called it quits in May and Flick returned to the lineup as a regular.

By mid-season, fans had virtually forgotten Thompson, a .400 hitter only four years earlier. Flick's productive bat and sharp fielding made him popular, even in opposing cities.

One afternoon Flick made a catch that was described in the press as the most spectacular ever seen in Pittsburgh. It was a leaping, one-handed grab that was rewarded by a shower of silver from the appreciative bleacherites.

By 1900, Elmer was a .378 hitter, but that figure failed to win a batting title because Honus Wagner compiled a .381 average.

When the American League started to raid National League clubs in 1901, several members of the Phillies, including Napoleon Lajoie, jumped to the Athletics. Flick followed a year later. His stay with the A's was brief, however. The Pennsylvania Supreme Court ruled that defectors could perform only with the Phillies as long as they remained within the state. Elmer was sold to Cleveland.

In 1905, Flick won the batting championship with a mark of .308, the lowest title-winning average in the majors until Carl Yastrzemski won with a .301 figure in 1968.

In the spring of 1907, Hughey Jennings, manager of the

It didn't take long for Elmer Flick to win over Phillies fans upon arrival in 1898.

Tigers, proposed a trade to Owner Charles Somers of the Indians. In exchange for Flick, the Bengals offered a young firebrand who had just engaged in a brawl before an exhibition game. Jennings was weary of his rabble rouser and wished to unload him.

Somers made a counterproposal that was rejected. Jennings offered the outfielder to two or three other clubs, none of which made satisfactory proposals. As a result, Ty Cobb remained with the Tigers until after the 1927 season.

And Flick remained with the Indians. For three consecutive years he led the A.L. in triples, a record that was matched later by only three players.

He also walloped a bases-loaded home run against Rube Waddell, the A's eccentric lefthander. "The center fielder misjudged the ball and got so mad he quit the team for a few days," Flick recalled.

In the spring of 1908, while the Indians were in New Orleans, Flick was stricken by a mysterious stomach ailment. Somers attributed the malady to drinking water, although no other players suffered similarly. Doctors were baffled. Elmer's weight dropped from 160 to 135 and he missed virtually the entire season.

When Flick came back in 1909, his speed was gone. He was only a shadow of his former self and retired from the majors after the 1910 campaign.

For years Flick was almost forgotten as he hobbled about his Warnersville Heights, O., home with a cane, the result of a broken hip. He did some scouting for the Indians.

When word arrived in 1963 that Elmer had been elected to the Hall of Fame, he was 87 years old, the senior living member of the shrine.

Accompanied by 17 members of his clan, Flick made it to Cooperstown in a three-car caravan and told the audience "what was in my heart."

Flick declared: "This is a bigger day than I've ever had before. And to think that this plaque will hang here until the end of time."

A lengthy illness preceded Flick's death before his 95th birthday.

# Whitey Ford

In 1950, Edward Ford arrived in New York and promptly won nine of his first 10 decisions.

By the end of 1964, Whitey Ford was the Yankee ace and a veteran of 11 World Series.

The blocky strawberry blond had a quip for every occasion and a pitch for every situation. To him, it made little sense to pitch if you couldn't have fun while doing it.

From the time he came off the sandlots of Astoria, Queens, Whitey Ford was smart beyond his years. His twinkling blue eyes and choirboy innocence masked the guile of a veteran. With excellent reason, Casey Stengel christened him "Slick." He dominated his profession so convincingly that batterymate Elston Howard referred to him respectfully as the "Chairman of the Board."

To his last breath, Stengel insisted—although Ford denied it—that it was Whitey who telephoned the Yankees' manager and announced early in 1950: "If you want to win the pennant, you'd better call up that kid Ford from Kansas City."

Whatever the motivation, Ford was a Yankee by mid-season and won nine consecutive games before a home run by Sam Chapman of Philadelphia inflicted the only blemish on his rookie record.

After beating the Phillies in the fourth and final game of the World Series, Ford encountered Dizzy Dean in the victors' clubhouse. Dean was then a broadcaster, but 16 years earlier he had won 30 games for the Cardinals.

"No wonder you won 30 games pitching in that crummy National League," Ford saluted Ol' Diz. "I could win 40 in that league myself."

For once, Dean was speechless.

Even as a rookie, Whitey demonstrated a delightful irreverence for tradition. After defeating the Tigers in a critical game, Ford was asked if it had been the most important game of his life.

"Not really," he deadpanned. "I remember pitching the Maspeth Ramblers to a 16 to 11 victory over the Astoria Indians. That was a big one, too."

Yogi Berra and Mickey Mantle (right, left photo) share a laugh with Ford and wife Joan during ceremonies to retire

Ford's No. 16 in 1974. Ford was 21 (right) when he posed with Binghamton teammate Tom Gorman in 1949.

On the same trip, Stengel notified Ford several days in advance that the rookie would open a series in Chicago, hopeful that Ford and roommate Yogi Berra would devote some hours discussing the proper way to pitch to White Sox batters.

The Yankees completed their pregame workout at Comiskey Park on the day of the game before it was discovered that Ford was absent. A frantic call to the hotel roused the towhead from deep slumber. He arrived at the park barely in time to warm up—and he pitched a three-hitter.

Rival managers were quick to marvel at the gifted left-hander. "No one is better in big ball games," said one.

"He'll beat you, never beats himself," added another.

"When he's got it, the ball game's over," offered a third.

Whitey had it through most of his career, which was interrupted by a military hitch (1951-52) and blighted in the latter stages by surgery to correct a circulatory problem in his shoulder.

But other times, Ford was superb. His .690 winning percentage was the best among modern pitchers with 200 or more victories. His 33⅔ consecutive scoreless innings broke a World Series record held previously by Babe Ruth when he was with the Red Sox.

Few of Whitey's 236 career victories were registered in Boston, where Fenway Park's left-field wall and the Red Sox's predominately righthanded lineup frequently spelled

misfortune for a lefthanded pitcher.

"I'd like to pitch here more," Ford once said with a mischievous air, recalling, no doubt, that he was only a .500 pitcher in Fenway.

Less than a year after Ford became a Yankee, he was joined by another blithe spirit, Mickey Mantle. Together they missed planes, were late for trains and celebrated (too well) Billy Martin's birthday at the Copacabana night club in New York.

While in San Francisco for the 1961 All-Star Game, the pair accepted an offer from Horace Stoneham to use the Giant owner's membership at a local country club. Before they were aware of it, Ford and Mantle had indebted Stoneham to the amount of $400.

An offer to pay met with a counterproposal. "We'll forget it," said Stoneham to Ford, "if you can strike out Willie Mays tomorrow."

In the first inning, Ford got two strikes on Mays, then "loaded up" a pitch that started at Willie's shoulders and wound up at his belt for the third strike. From center field, Mantle raced to the infield, where he pounded Ford violently on the back.

After his retirement in 1967, and his election to the Hall of Fame in 1974, Whitey revealed how, in moments of extreme stress, he had doctored a baseball with a sticky homemade substance and a specially made rasp ring, which, he informed an inquisitive umpire, is "my wedding ring."

# Rube Foster

When the 22-year-old son of a Methodist minister defeated Rube Waddell, 5-2, in the spring of 1902, his teammates agreed that the best compliment they could pay the young pitcher was to give him the same nickname as the promising Philadelphia lefthander. For the 29 years remaining to him, Andrew Foster was known as Rube.

In those nearly three decades, Rube Foster was an outstanding pitcher. He managed and owned teams, organized leagues and served as commissioner. More than any other, he deserved the title of "Father of black baseball."

A native of Calvert, Tex., Foster threw batting practice for major league clubs training in Texas while still a teenager. He pitched for the Fort Worth Yellow Jackets and in 1902, when he was credited with 51 victories, Foster was a member of E.B. Lamar's Cuban Giants (actually a team of American blacks playing out of Philadelphia).

Rube's salary was $40 a month.

By 1906, Rube was at the peak of his career, mixing his overpowering fastball with a tantalizing change-up. Honus Wagner called him "the smoothest pitcher I've ever seen." John McGraw, lamenting that the color barrier prevented him from signing Foster for the New York Giants, hired him as a pitching coach of sorts. Foster is reputed to have taught his screwball to Christy Mathewson. Big Six popularized the delivery as his fadeaway.

When Foster, a 6-foot-4, 240-pounder, joined the Leland Giants of Chicago in the first decade of the century, his first act was to rename the team the American Giants. The team played in the White Sox's old park at 39th and Wentworth. Regularly, the Giants attracted 11,000 fans on Sunday in competition with the Sox, who would draw 9,000, and the Cubs, who would play to 6,000.

One year the Giants played a three-game postseason series against the Cubs, second-place finishers in the National League. Although the Giants lost each game by one run, a writer for the Chicago Defender wrote that "fans made fun at the way officials deliberately favored the Cubs just enough to assure victory."

Frank Chance, Cubs manager in that era, termed Foster "the most finished product I've ever seen in the pitcher's box." In Cleveland, the Post proclaimed: "There have been but two real pitchers who have put their feet in the Cleveland ball yard. They are Addie Joss and Rube Foster."

Foster, who addressed everyone as "Darling," except his wife, whom he called "Smoothie," managed the American Giants into the most powerful black team in the country. While operating out of Chicago, the Giants traveled widely, generally in a private Pullman car. The 1910 team won 123 of 129 games.

In the winter of 1919, Foster convened the owners of leading Negro teams and organized the Negro National League. Quickly, player salaries that had totaled about $30,000 a year rose to $275,000.

In 1920, Rube organized the team that dominated Midwest black baseball for the next decade. The team was built on speed and bunting. In one game, eight consecutive batters bunted safely for hits.

Foster not only operated the Giants in the early 1920s, but the league as well. At his own expense, he placed a team in Dayton, O. When the club faltered at the gate, he shifted it to Columbus.

Wherever he traveled, Rube Foster attracted large crowds. He would reminisce at length when the Giants arrived in Kansas City, then predict what his club would do to the hometown Monarchs. On the day of the game, extra patrolmen were necessary to handle traffic en route to the ball park. Rube's showmanship guaranteed sellouts.

Foster died in 1930 at Kankakee, Ill., at age 51.

# Jimmie Foxx

Generally, those who knew him best discussed his genial personality or his unfortunate bankruptcy or the explosive power generated by his massive muscles when swinging a bat at a pitched ball.

Bill Dickey, longtime Yankee catcher, once remarked: "If I were catching blindfolded, I'd always know when it was Jimmie Foxx who connected. He hit the ball harder than anybody else."

Onetime teammate Moe Berg asserted that Foxx "had the greatest right arm ever hung on a human being."

Jimmie's bulging biceps bespoke a superhuman power. Prodigious wallops were his trademark. One such blow, against Lefty Gomez, landed in the last section of the third tier in left field at Yankee Stadium—and had enough force to break the back of a seat.

In Chicago, Double X drove a pitch out of double-decked Comiskey Park, onto a playground, an estimated 600 feet from home plate.

Another blast, which Jimmie regarded as one of his longest, was hit at Sportsman's Park in St. Louis in Game 5 of the 1930 World Series. In the first game of the Series, Burleigh Grimes had slipped a third-strike curve past a confused Foxx, who had been led to believe that Old Stubblebeard threw only a spitter.

In the ninth inning of the scoreless fifth game, with Mickey Cochrane on base via a walk, a smarter Foxx looked for a curve—and got it. The ball went over the fence in deep left-center field.

Later, Grimes conceded that the two curveballs to Foxx were the only ones he had thrown in the Series.

Sportsman's Park held other memories for Jimmie. On July 2, 1933, Foxx clouted two homers in the first game of a doubleheader, then came back with another pair in the nightcap, plus a triple and a double. The two lesser extra-base hits, it was said, missed the top of the wall by a total of one foot. He was that close to six homers for the day.

When Jimmie was pursuing Babe Ruth's 60-homer record in 1932, Sportsman's Park was a major deterrent in limiting his season total to 58. Jimmie socked five drives against a screen in front of the right-field pavilion. There was no screen there during Ruth's big season of 1927.

Also in '32, the Indians erected a screen in front of the left-field stands at League Park. Foxx bounced three drives off that screen. Had he played under conditions that prevailed in '27, Double X would have swatted more than 60 home runs in 1932.

A product of Sudlersville, Md., where he was discovered by Frank (Home Run) Baker, Foxx was 16 when he entered Organized Ball as a catcher. He was only 17 when, in 1925, he played 10 games with the A's and collected his first major league hit. Pinch-hitting for Lefty Grove, he singled against Vean Gregg at Washington on May 1.

When Jimmie won his second consecutive Most Valuable Player honor in 1933, he was asked to take a pay cut, from $16,333 to $12,000, because of the hard times. After a vigorous argument, Foxx agreed to a $16,000 contract. At Boston several years later, Foxx's top salary was about $32,000, including attendance bonuses.

When Foxx was at the peak of his game, everyone shared in his opulence. Johnny Peacock, a roommate of the Maryland strong boy with the Red Sox and Phillies, once said: "Jimmie always used to pay the whole room bill no matter who his roommate was. He'd pay all telephone, valet, room service—whatever. But when we roomed together on the Phils, he let me pay my own bills."

**Jimmie Foxx (sitting, second from right) was 13 when this picture was taken during the early 1920s.**

**When he joined the A's in 1925, Foxx was a catcher. Foxx (above right) was greeted by Bob Johnson after hitting a two-run homer in the 1935 All-Star Game in Cleveland. Foxx (below right) is pictured in 1932, the year he hit 58 home runs and drove in 169 for the A's.**

Jimmie closed out his major league career with the Phils in 1945.

During the twilight of his career, Foxx suffered from a sinus condition. In retirement, he suffered an acute heart ailment. Trying to move a trunk, he fell down a flight of stairs and fractured a spinal disc that caused partial paralysis to his left side.

In 1963, he made an appearance in Cleveland, where he had clouted a home run and a single to help the American League win the 1935 All-Star Game. This time, he announced that he was broke, and applied for unemployment benefits.

Foxx accepted a job selling sporting goods in a downtown department store. He also served as a front man at a restaurant in Galesburg, Ill.

The old slugger, who lost $100,000 on a golf course venture in St. Petersburg, Fla., and was in the habit of tipping $50 on a $150 tailor-made suit, never complained of any misfortunes, but said, "If I had it to do all over, I'd invest differently and not live so freely."

Jimmie choked to death in Miami in 1967 when a piece of meat lodged in his throat.

# Ford Frick

**National League President Ford Frick (right) gets a handshake from President Franklin D. Roosevelt as baseball**

**Commissioner Kenesaw Mountain Landis (center) looks on prior to the 1937 All-Star Game at Griffith Stadium.**

Of his countless contributions to baseball in 17 years as National League president and 14 years as commissioner, no achievement inspired greater pride in Ford Frick than his role in the founding of the Hall of Fame.

The city fathers of Cooperstown, N.Y., planned a celebration to mark the community's part in the origins of baseball and sent a representative to the N.L. office in New York to seek Frick's cooperation. The emissary suggested that major league all-star teams play a game there to focus attention on the game's reputed birthplace.

"Why do that?" replied Frick. "Why not start a baseball museum and have something that will last?"

Cooperstown accepted Frick's suggestion, and the Baseball Hall of Fame and Museum was dedicated on June 12, 1939 (three years after the first election of inductees).

A native of Indiana, Frick graduated from DePauw University and was writing sports for the Colorado Springs Gazette as well as teaching English courses at Colorado College when one of his sports articles came to the attention of Arthur Brisbane, New York editor for the Hearst newspapers.

Frick accepted an offer to join the New York American, and for a number of years he covered the Giants. Later he switched to the Journal and traveled with the Yankees.

He pioneered in radio sports shows and "ghosted" for Babe Ruth. Frick and the Bambino were golfing and bridge partners. Because of the close friendship, Frick found himself in one of his major controversies in 1961 when Roger Maris broke the Babe's season homer record. When the commissioner announced that an asterisk would be placed beside Maris' name to designate a 162-game schedule, as

compared with the 154 games in which Babe clouted his 60 homers, sportswriters accused him of favoritism toward his old crony.

In 1934, Frick became publicity director for the N.L. He held the post for less than one year before being elected league president, succeeding John Heydler (who was in failing health).

Frick survived his most critical moment in 1947 when Jackie Robinson broke the color line in baseball. Reacting to the epithets and threats against the Brooklyn rookie by rival players, Frick declared: "The National League will go down the line with Robinson and I don't care if it wrecks the league for five years." He said he would ban forever anyone who tried to halt the integration process.

When A.B. (Happy) Chandler was named to succeed Judge K.M. Landis as commissioner in 1945, Frick's name was entered as a candidate, although Frick did not campaign for the office. After Chandler resigned in 1951, Frick again was a candidate, along with Warren Giles, president of the Cincinnati Reds.

The 16 club owners balloted 20 times in an effort to obtain the necessary 16 votes. When the situation seemed hopelessly deadlocked, Giles withdrew from the race and Frick was elected the third commissioner of baseball.

Frick staunchly defended the reserve clause when it came under attack, but favored players earning hefty salaries. On a number of occasions, he was assailed by the press for his "That's a league matter" refrain, which was regarded as an effort to evade a decision.

Frick retired from what he described as "a lonely job" in 1965 to his Bronxville, N.Y., home, where he died in 1978 at age 83.

# Frank Frisch

**Frank Frisch (left and above) was an infielder for John McGraw's Giants upon arrival in the big leagues in 1919.**

John McGraw could either sign the collegian to a Giants contract, as the youngster requested, or the prospect would enter business with his father, a wealthy linen manufacturer in New York.

Unaccustomed as he was to acting against his will, the crusty manager acceded in this case, thereby giving baseball one of its most colorful individuals, Frank Francis Frisch.

Frisch had captained the baseball, football and basketball teams at Fordham University and was a second-team All-America halfback before he joined the Giants in 1919.

McGraw determined early that Frisch did not have the range nor the sure hands to remain at shortstop, his college position. The young switch-hitter also needed batting tips and guidance on how to slide properly. McGraw worked endless hours in polishing his prodigy, who quickly became the manager's pet.

When Frisch made his first start in September, playing third base against the pennant-bound Reds, a bad-hop smash caromed off his chest. Pouncing adroitly in pursuit, Frisch collared the ball and nipped the batter with a rifle throw to first.

"That was all I had to see," McGraw remarked. "The average youngster, nervous anyhow at making his first start, would have given up on the play."

The Flash performed at third and second

Player-Manager Frisch hit .305 and guided the Cardinals to a World Series title in 1934.

Cubs Manager Frisch got the thumb from umpire Augie Donatelli in 1951, only a few days before losing his job.

base for the pennant-winning Giants of 1921 through 1924, but when the Giants slipped the next two seasons and Frisch, as captain, received a lot of verbal abuse from his frustrated manager, he packed his bags when the team arrived in St. Louis and returned home.

A breach developed between McGraw and Frisch. Two months after the close of the 1926 season, Frisch was traded with pitcher Jimmy Ring to the world champion Cardinals for Rogers Hornsby.

Frankie was not enamored with the prospect of leaving his native city, but he spent the winter at Lake Placid, N.Y., skating, skiing and walking the rugged terrain to strengthen his legs. The program paid off handsomely. Frisch handled more than 1,000 chances at second base and batted .337 for the 1927 Cardinals, but missed the Most Valuable Player award by one vote to Paul Waner of Pittsburgh.

Frisch sparked the Cardinals to pennants in 1928, 1930 and 1931 and to a world title the last year, when he also was the National League's MVP.

He homered and singled in the first All-Star Game in Chicago and a year later, in '34, when the game was played at the Polo Grounds, the Old Flash announced: "I see that I'm leading off, and Lefty Gomez is starting for the American League. He likes to throw smoke on the first pitch and if he does, I'll hit it out."

Gomez was true to form and Frisch, batting right-handed, sliced a home run to right field.

Appointed manager of the Cardinals in mid-1933, Frisch drove the Gas House Gang to the pennant the following year. In the World Series against Detroit, the Old Flash enjoyed his biggest thrill when, in Game 7, the Tigers walked the previous batter to load the bases, giving Frankie an opportunity to rap a three-run double.

"It should have been a triple," he contended. "I was so fascinated watching the three runners score, I couldn't get past second. If anyone else had done the same thing, I'd have fined him."

Frisch's escapades with umpires were legion. He would draw the thumb from Beans Reardon in the afternoon, then swill beer with him at night. Once he went into a mock faint in protest of a Bill Klem decision. Running to the prostrate form, Klem barked, "Frisch, if you ain't dead, you're out of the game."

At other times, Frankie carried an open umbrella onto the field in protest of a game continuing in a drizzle. He was ejected. He made a low salaam to George Magerkurth when the umpire cleared the bench during Frank's managerial career in Pittsburgh.

But when an umpire's job was in jeopardy as the result of a Pittsburgh protest, the Old Flash withdrew his protest. "No game is worth an umpire's job," he said.

Frisch died at age 74 in Wilmington, Del., a month after suffering injuries in an automobile accident in 1973.

# Pud Galvin

His was not a household name, yet only five major league pitchers won more games in their careers than James (Pud) Galvin. He was the Walter Johnson of his time, blazing fastballs past bewildered batters.

Galvin hurled more innings—5,959—than any other pitcher except Cy Young.

He pitched two no-hitters for Buffalo, against Worcester and Detroit, and his gem against Detroit followed a one-hitter against the same club.

Galvin accounted for the first two victories scored by the Pittsburgh club in the National League, beating John Clarkson of Chicago, 6-2, and Lady Baldwin of Detroit, 8-3, in 1887.

After the powerful Providence team won 20 straight games in 1884, he shut out the Grays, beating Old Hoss Radbourn, 2-0.

Still, with his convincing credentials, it required the passage of 63 years after his death for Galvin to be elected to the Hall of Fame.

Sometimes he was called "Gentle James," in tribute to his personality. Other times he was known as "Pud," as in pudding, which, it was said, he made of opposing batters.

Galvin placed little stock in the curve as a pitching weapon, relying on his fastball and control to register 46 victories in both 1883 and 1884. In '83, he worked a staggering 656 innings.

Buck Ewing, incomparable New York catcher, insisted that "If I had Galvin to catch, no one would ever steal a base on me. That fellow keeps 'em glued to the base, and he also has the best control of any pitcher in the league."

Galvin's control was short of Ewing's high praise during one game in 1886 as he walked three consecutive batters. But to the baserunners' chagrin, they learned about Pud's knack of keeping runners "glued." Each was picked off base.

Gentle James was all but invincible for Buffalo during a six-day period in 1884. On August 2, he pitched a one-hitter. Two days later, he hurled a three-hit shutout and the next day he worked 11 scoreless innings before bowing, 1-0.

Late in the 1885 season, Pud was sold to the Allegheny (Pittsburgh) club of the American Association for $2,500, a princely sum of that day. He was given $700 from that amount, and handed a $1,000 raise by his new bosses, placing him in the $3,000 bracket.

The Buffalo owners' cash-gift generosity was in sharp contrast to their earlier treatment of Galvin. Infuriated that he was given no raise after a 46-22 campaign in '84, Galvin went to San Francisco and joined an independent club. Tales of his magnificent feats filtered back to Buffalo, where the Bisons were slumping dismally. On May 11, the Buffalo Express carried the welcome news: "There is

**Pud Galvin's blazing fastball made him the Walter Johnson of the 19th Century.**

great rejoicing on the baseball front. Negotiations have been opened with Gentle James."

Galvin rejoined the Buffalo club and posted a 13-19 record before being sold to Allegheny.

Although his lifetime batting average was barely above .200, Galvin played the outfield and once performed at shortstop.

An eye injury, suffered when struck by a pitched ball, made Gentle James gun-shy in later years, and a fractured leg, suffered in a collision with Cap Anson of Chicago, created idle time that boosted Pud's weight over 200 pounds by the time he retired in 1894.

Galvin umpired for one season in the National League before returning to Pittsburgh, where he opened one of the largest cafes in the city.

The father of 11—he once wisecracked that he should organize a family team and call it the "Galvinized Nine"—Galvin went broke. And, on Thanksgiving Day, 1901, he was taken sick with a stomach ailment. Less than four months later, at age 45, Galvin died.

Galvin, a friend of President Grover Cleveland, lived his final months in a rooming house on Pittsburgh's lower north side.

# Lou Gehrig

In an age when colorful nicknames were sprinkled liberally among the nation's sports heroes, no sobriquet was better suited than that of "The Iron Horse."

It symbolized durability and reliability in heat and cold, fair weather and foul, sickness and health. Yankee first baseman Lou Gehrig was every bit of that as he accumulated an almost incredible total of 2,130 consecutive games.

Then, as the locomotive yielded to more popular modes of transportation, the seemingly indestructible Gehrig yielded to an ailment that came to be known as "Lou Gehrig's disease," as incurable today as it was the day he died.

The derailment of baseball's Iron Horse occurred on May 2, 1939, in Detroit. Before heading west on the Yankees' first trip of the season, Gehrig had made a play at Yankee Stadium that, in his mind, was strickly routine. Yet, when he struggled back to first base to take a throw from Johnny Murphy, the pitcher had said, "Nice play, Lou."

May 1 was an off day, which Larruping Lou spent in his hotel room pondering his problem. The next day he confronted Manager Joe McCarthy and announced his decision: "I'm taking myself out of the lineup."

The pilot offered no resistance, but replied: "All right, but remember that first base is your position and it is there when you want it back."

But the Iron Horse never played another game.

Gehrig's first brush with fame occurred on June 26, 1920, when his Commerce High School team of New York visited Chicago to oppose Lane Tech at Wrigley Field. With the bases loaded in the ninth inning, the 17-year-old slugger walloped a home run onto Sheffield Avenue.

While at Columbia University, the son of German immi-

**At age 13, little did Lou Gehrig suspect the impact he would have on the baseball world.**

grants was scouted by Paul Krichell and when the Yankee scout offered Lou a $1,500 bonus, he pounced on it like a fastball down the middle.

After three stints with Hartford of the Eastern League, Gehrig had a hammer lock on the Yankee first-base job by June of 1925. His consecutive-game streak started with a pinch-hitting appearance on June 1. He took over at first base the next day when Wally Pipp complained of a splitting headache and was told by Manager Miller Huggins to "take the day off." The bag was Lou's for 14 years.

During that period Gehrig became Babe Ruth's running mate, laboring in the shadows of the Bambino but frequently eclipsing his luminous achievements.

In his own evaluation, Gehrig's top accomplishments were a home run off Carl Hubbell, famed Giants lefthander, in the 1936 World Series; a homer off Dizzy Dean in the 1937 All-Star Game after the great right-hander had waved off a curve-ball and insisted on throwing a fastball, and his four-homer day in Philadelphia on June 3, 1932.

In 1931, when Lou set an American League record with 184 runs batted in, he missed out on an outright home run leadership through the blunder of a teammate. When Gehrig hit a ball into the bleachers at Washington, baserunner Lyn Lary looked up in time to see the center fielder holding the ball. Thinking that the fielder had caught the ball, rather than fielding a rebound off a bleacher seat, Lary headed for the dugout after reaching third base. Unaware of Lary's mistake, Gehrig was called out for passing a baserunner. The blow should have given Gehrig 47 homers for the season. Instead, he tied Ruth at 46.

Nobody, Gehrig least of all, grew suspicious in 1938

On July 4, 1939, more than 61,000 fans jammed Yankee Stadium (above) to hear the terminally ill Gehrig bid them a tearful farewell. The occasion also called for an embrace (below) from former teammate Babe Ruth.

Gehrig was a star for the Columbia University team when discovered by the Yankees.

when Lou's home run production fell to 29 and his batting average to .295. He still drove in 114 runs and his 212-pound frame appeared as robust as ever. In the Yanks' four-game World Series sweep over the Cubs, however, Lou's four hits were singles and he had no home runs or RBIs.

Seven months later, Gehrig and a grieving public heard the sad news from the Mayo Clinic. Gehrig was suffering from lateral sclerosis, insidious and deadly.

The Yankees quickly arranged for a gigantic tribute to their stricken captain. On July 4, 1939, more than 61,000 fans jammed Yankee Stadium to pay homage. As members of the 1927 and 1939 Yankee teams looked on, Lou assured the world that "Today I consider myself the luckiest man on the face of the earth."

Gehrig was appointed to the New York City Police Commission and worked diligently with youth groups until one month before his death in June of 1941.

# Charley Gehringer

Teammates poked fun at his Sphinx-like demeanor, but nobody overlooked the easy manner and stylish grace that made Charley Gehringer one of the premier second basemen of all time.

Mickey Cochrane, Gehringer's manager with the world champion Detroit Tigers of 1935, said: "He says hello on opening day and goodbye on closing day, and in between he hits .350."

Roger (Doc) Cramer quipped: "You wind him up on opening day and forget about him."

Gehringer was not flamboyant, but he handled his position with long strides, soft hands and an unerring arm. A .320 lifetime batting average contributed to his reputation as a ballplayer's ballplayer.

A native of Fowlerville, Mich., Gehringer entered baseball over parental objections. His father thought the farm afforded a good livelihood and that his youngest son should appreciate the advantage of soil, crops and livestock.

Charley felt differently and drifted onto a town team that performed at the local fair grounds. Gehringer's natural ability caught the eye of a hunting partner of Bobby Veach. "Take a look at this kid before some other club grabs him," the friend told the old Tiger outfielder.

Veach took a look and was impressed. His words to the Tigers were "Grab him." By 1925, Gehringer was a Tiger for keeps, eased into his position by manager Ty Cobb.

Gehringer's aptitude was as good for major league baseball as it had been for baseball at the country fair level. By 1929 he led the American League in stolen bases and had rapped three triples in one game.

Although he went 0-for-3 in the first All-Star Game in 1933, Charley finished with a .500 average (10-for-20) in six mid-summer classics. Seven times he collected 200 or more hits in one season, and he posted his top average of .371 in 1937 when he captured the A.L. batting title along with the Most Valuable Player award.

In a 14-year span, Charley's average sank below .300 only once. Gehringer explained: "That was the year I was going to be like Babe Ruth. I think I had eight (home runs) before he had any and I began going for the fences. I wound up getting not many homers—and not many hits either." Actually, he had 184 hits that season (1932) and a .298 average.

"I honestly believe," noted his onetime manager, Del Baker, "Charley could spot a pitcher two strikes all season and still hit within 15 points of his regular average."

With all his sterling accomplishments, Gehringer regarded a day in which he was honored by hometown admirers as his most memorable event of a distinguished career.

The occasion was scheduled for a New York-Detroit game. Such events generally produce a hitless perfor-

**Charley Gehringer's personality was not as flamboyant as the numbers he put on the board.**

The always reliable Gehringer shows his form as he delivers a single during action in the first game of the 1934 World Series in Detroit. The Cardinals' catcher is Bill De-Lancey.

mance for the honored athlete, or perhaps a poor demonstration on the field. Gehringer was different.

Charley hit the first pitch to him over the right-field wall. He collected three other hits and won the game for the Tigers when he stole home.

After such a performance, the lefthanded hitter could forgive his Fowlerville friends for presenting him a set of golf clubs made for a righthander.

"I just turned around and learned to play righthanded and have been playing that way ever since," he explained matter of factly.

At the close of the 1940 World Series, which the Tigers lost to Cincinnati in seven games, Charley confessed that the entire season had been torture for him and that "some days I couldn't get out of bed until noon."

He disclosed that during a spring exhibition, he had raced in for a ground ball, fielded it and was about to throw to first base when he noticed a young player had run into his line of fire.

"In motion and off-balance, I checked my throw at the last minute, lurched and had misery thereafter," he revealed.

After the 1942 season, in which he batted only 45 times and hit .267, Gehringer was commissioned a lieutenant and served in the Navy fitness program for the remainder of the war.

Returning to civilian life, Charley became a highly successful manufacturers agent in Detroit.

Gehringer came out of retirement in 1951 to serve as Detroit general manager at the invitation of Tigers Owner Walter Briggs. He held the post two years, then remained as a club vice president until his retirement in 1959.

# Josh Gibson

A popular story around Griffith Stadium in Washington in the early 1930s concerned the time that Walter Johnson attended a game played by the Homestead Grays. The Big Train sat transfixed as he watched a muscular black catcher in action. At length, he turned to Clark Griffith, owner of the Senators, and said, "That boy is worth a quarter of a million dollars."

Even in those depressed times, more than a few major league clubs would have been happy to scrape up $250,000 if the unwritten rules of the day would have permitted the signing of black players.

Josh Gibson never had an opportunity to play in Organized Baseball as did Roy Campanella, Elston Howard and other black catchers of the integrated era.

A native of Buena Vista, Ga., Gibson moved to Pittsburgh at an early age. He was an 18-year-old member of the Grays in 1930 when he made his professional debut.

"It was the first night game ever played at Forbes Field," recalled his manager, Judy Johnson. "A bus in center field contained a generator and lights were placed on high extension ladders."

When the regular catcher was injured, Josh was asked if he could catch. "Yes, sir," he answered, giving birth to one of baseball's most fabulous careers.

The number of home runs that boomed off Gibson's bat never will be known. Haphazard scheduling could produce 200 games a season, some against non-league opposition. James (Cool Papa) Bell asserted once that Josh collected 72 homers in one year.

In the beginning, the 6-foot-1, 215-pound Gibson was a crude catcher, and did not learn the finer points of the position until he played winter ball, which he did regularly.

Homestead teammates referred to him as "Boxer" because, they said, he caught foul pops as though he were wearing boxing gloves. Gibson mastered this craft eventually, handling every type of pitch from the spitter to the shine ball.

Josh required no practice in his throwing. He possessed a strong, accurate arm and had the sort of speed seldom found in one his size.

In 1933, almost all of the Grays jumped to the Crawfords team of Pittsburgh. There Gibson teamed up with the legendary Satchel Paige and it became a common practice for the Crawfords to advertise that Satch would strike out the first nine batters in a forthcoming game and that Gibson would clout a home run.

After the '34 season, the Crawfords barnstormed with a team of major league all-stars featuring Dizzy and Paul Dean. The Crawfords won seven of the nine games in a series dominated by Gibson's prodigious blasts.

When the Crawfords disbanded in 1936, Paige joined the Kansas City Monarchs and Gibson returned to the

**Josh Gibson's home run accomplishments were legendary throughout the Negro leagues.**

Grays, setting up classic confrontations between the formidable pitcher and catcher. Once, it was said, Satchel walked two batters intentionally to bring up Gibson, whom he then struck out on three pitches.

Another time, Josh rocketed a drive off the clock on the center-field wall at Chicago's Comiskey Park.

By 1946, Josh had started his descent, although he still batted .331 and led the Negro National League in homers. His weight had ballooned to 230 pounds and he took to drinking heavily. Friends detected a personality change. Some said it was due to the breakup of his marriage.

On a Saturday night in January of 1947, Josh encountered friends on a Pittsburgh street corner.

"He was like always, full of fun and kidding around," an old pal reported, but Gibson complained of a headache, went home, had a drink and went to bed.

The next morning, Josh still complained of a headache. A doctor was summoned. He gave Gibson a shot and he fell into a sleep from which he never awakened.

# Bob Gibson

**Bob Gibson strikes out Detroit's Norm Cash (left) en route to a World Series-record 17 in Game 1 of the 1968** **classic. One of two Gibson leg fractures occurred in 1967 (right), courtesy of a Roberto Clemente line drive.**

The first batter in the ninth inning had struck out and more than 54,000 throats had turned Busch Memorial Stadium into a cavern of cacophony when the message board announced that the pitcher had tied a World Series record with his 15th strikeout of the game.

From behind home plate, St. Louis catcher Tim McCarver gestured to his batterymate, suggesting that he glance at the board and learn the reason for the thunderous ovation.

The pitcher resisted. Over the din, he shouted, "Gimme the damn ball."

Bob Gibson would savor that moment later in privacy. For now, he had to retire two more Detroit batters to sew up Game 1 of the 1968 Series, which he did in the same way he had dispatched 15 other batters—via strikeouts.

Intensity was Gibson's hallmark. A psychological tunnel vision directed all his energies toward the business at hand. The opponents were his enemies and were not to be engaged in chitchat before a game. To him, such conduct was traitorous.

The attitude paid off for the righthander during his 17 years with the Cardinals. In addition to the 17 strikeouts in a Series game, other highlights included more than 3,000 career strikeouts and 13 shutouts and a 1.12 earned-run average in 1968. During one 95-inning span, Gibson surrendered only two runs.

Gibson's success as a pitcher contrasted with his hum- ble origins in Omaha, Neb. His father died when he was 3 months old. As a child, Bob suffered from rickets and asthma and at one stage was not expected to live.

As a youngster, Gibson was a switch-hitting catcher and shortstop on a YMCA team. When he was in high school, he grew so rapidly that he needed a doctor's permission to compete in athletics because of a heart murmur.

Gibson won a scholarship to Creighton University, where he became the first member of the school's sports hall of fame. In basketball, he amazed spectators with his leaping ability by which he could touch the basket with his elbow.

Bob accepted a $4,000 bonus from the Cardinals to sign with their Omaha farm club in 1957.

Gibby's major league career was interrupted by two leg fractures. In 1962, he suffered a fracture when his spikes caught in the batter's box. In 1967, he was pitching against the Pirates when a Roberto Clemente smash struck Gibson on the left leg. Result—another fracture.

Weeks later in '67, when he returned to the clubhouse on crutches, Bob wearied quickly of answering questions. In self-defense, he erected a sign reading: "Yes, it's off (the cast). No, it doesn't hurt. I'm not supposed to walk on it for one week. I don't know how much longer. Ask Doc Bauman (trainer). Ask Doc Middleman (team surgeon)."

Gibson returned to action in time to lead the Cardinals

In 1981, at the urging of old teammate Joe Torre, Gibson came out of retirement to serve as pitching coach for Torre's New York Mets.

to a World Series victory over the Red Sox. His three victories were part of his record seven complete-game Series triumphs.

Gibson pitched his last major league game in early September of 1975, giving up a bases-loaded homer to Pete LaCock of the Cubs. "That was humiliating," Bob remembered years later. "He had never hit a foul ball—well, maybe a foul ball—off me before. I said, 'That's it, I'm finished.'"

At season's end—after 251 big-league victories—Gibson stepped into his $30,000 mobile home, a going-away gift from the Cardinals, and returned to Omaha. After 20 years in athletics, including intercollegiate play, one year with the Harlem Globetrotters and his career with the Cardinals, he was ready for an easier lifestyle. He was a network sportscaster for a time, had an interest in a radio station (which he sold), became chairman of the board of a bank and opened a restaurant-bar.

The old competitor discovered after years of retirement that he was still a coveted commodity in baseball, and he accepted a coaching position with the Mets under his old teammate, Joe Torre. He later accompanied Torre to Atlanta.

Torre was confident Gibson was the man for the job. When asked what had made Gibson a great pitcher, the former catcher-first baseman replied: "Try pride, intensity, talent, respect, dedication. . . . you need 'em all."

The competitive juices already were flowing when Gibson spent part of the 1960 season with the Cardinals.

# Warren Giles

In August of 1923, the president of the St. Joseph club of the Western Association telephoned the offices of the St. Louis Cardinals. He had some disturbing news. The option agreement on outfielder Taylor Douthit had elapsed and, under baseball law, the minor league club was entitled to sell the St. Louis farmhand to whomever it wished.

Branch Rickey, the Redbirds' front-office chief, admitted he had forgotten about Douthit. Nor were his feelings assuaged when he learned that the Pirates had offered $10,000 for the prospect. He knew the St. Joseph club could use 10 grand, strapped for funds as it was.

But Rickey felt greatly relieved when the caller added: "I know it was an honest oversight and you can have Douthit for nothing."

Two years later, Warren Giles was rewarded for his integrity, landing the general manager's post of the Cardinals' top farm club, Syracuse of the International League.

Giles, a native of Tiskilwa, Ill., and a three-sport athlete in high school, gained his foothold in the administrative phase of baseball in 1919 when, as a recent Army officer, he attended a meeting of the stockholders of the Moline (Three-I) club. His enthusiasm and generous advice on how the club should be operated caught the ear of the others.

"In effect," he recalled many years later, "they told me that if I knew so much, why didn't I run the club. They elected me president and there I was, suddenly, totally and happily, in baseball for life."

In 1928, the Syracuse franchise was transferred to Rochester, where it won four successive pennants. By the mid-1930s, Giles was the front-office boss of the Cincinnati Reds, succeeding Larry MacPhail. One of Giles' first moves there was to lure his old Rochester pilot, Bill McKechnie, away from the Boston Braves. By 1939, the Reds were National League champions and a year later they were world champions.

In his years as Cincinnati chief, Giles frequently found fault with the quality of umpiring, but when he succeeded Ford Frick as league president in 1951, he became a staunch defender of the arbiters.

When Giles moved into the N.L. office, he was replaced at the Reds' helm by longtime lieutenant Gabe Paul.

Before long, Giles was asked to rule on a rhubarb. One umpire had overruled another, creating a donnybrook in which Reds Manager Birdie Tebbetts was ejected. Tebbets was fined $50. Irate, Gabe fired off a telegram to his old boss.

Giles was criticized for penalizing the manager, and not the umpire, who provoked the incident.

When Giles and Paul met weeks later, Giles suggested that a phone call or private letter would have been more

National League President Warren Giles does the honors for the Pirates' 1961 opener at Forbes Field.

advisable than a telegram that was read by the entire office force.

Sweetly, Gabe reminded Giles of a wire Warren had sent Frick some years earlier.

"All I did was dig into the files for YOUR message," said Paul, "check off Frick's name, substitute yours and sign mine. Where is your sense of humor?"

"You dirty dog," was Giles' smiling response.

Unlike the American League system, which provides for a supervisor of umpires, Giles, with the aid of Fred Fleig, supervised the N.L. arbiters. As an old official, Giles had a feel for decision makers in athletic events. He had officiated in old Missouri Valley Conference football games.

In 18 years as N.L. president, Giles upheld only one protest. Frick, in 16 years, upheld five. Giles overruled his umpires in a Cincinnati-Milwaukee game. In the replay, the Braves won the contest, just as they had originally, but under different circumstances.

Giles retired as N.L. president in 1969 and was named president emeritus. For the next 10 years, he was "just a fan," trying to be neutral in a city (Cincinnati) that claimed his heart many years earlier, and keeping an eye on the adventures of his only child, Bill, general manager of the Phillies.

He was 83 when he died in February of 1979 after a lengthy illness and a few weeks before he was elected to the Hall of Fame.

# Lefty Gomez

As great as Vernon (Lefty) Gomez was—he was the only pitcher to win six World Series games without a loss, among other distinctions—the angular lefthander would have deserved a pedestal in the Hall of Fame if only for his Spanish-Irish wit that brightened baseball for more than half a century.

Known as the Gay Caballero because of his jolly and carefree manner, Gomez also was called El Goofy. He was so proud of the latter monicker that his license plates read "GOOF."

Gomez kept his teammates loose. He joked about the lordly and the lowly, a court jester in a profession that too often tended toward stodginess.

In a tense moment of a World Series he could stand in back of the mound and watch an airplane circling overhead. When he was censured by Tony Lazzeri, Lefty told the second baseman, "You take care of second base and spaghetti, I'll take care of pitching and aviation."

On another occasion, when the Yankees enjoyed a sizable lead at Detroit, Lefty fielded a hard smash by Hank Greenberg. Instead of throwing to shortstop Frank Crosetti covering second for a forceout, Gomez fired to Lazzeri, who was standing 20 feet from the base.

To a dumbfounded Lazzeri, Lefty explained, "I'd heard that you were such a smart player, I just wanted to see what you'd do with it."

A notoriously weak hitter, Gomez had an annual wager with Babe Ruth, betting $50 against the Babe's $500 that Lefty would collect 10 hits for the season. One year, swinging wildly, Lefty went 4-for-4 on opening day and, he said, "Babe's eyes were big as hubcaps."

From that point, however, "I went on a 42-game batting slump."

Once he attempted to take on the appearance of a hitter. Gomez swung his bat lustily as he approached the plate, gave a vigorous tug on the bill of his cap, tapped his spikes with his bat—and cracked an ankle.

There was another time when Lefty was swinging where the pitcher was pitching and he sliced a double to left field. He was promptly picked off base. "What happened out there?" Manager Joe McCarthy wondered.

"I don't know," quipped Gomez. "It was the first time I was ever out there."

But there was one hit that Gomez cherished above all others. In 1933, his single drove in the first run in All-Star Game history. The Yankee star pitched in five All-Star classics and was the winning hurler in three (1933, '35 and '37), while losing one (1938).

When Lou Gehrig's consecutive-game streak ended on May 2, 1939, and the durable first baseman and other

**Fun-loving Lefty Gomez got his baseball kicks in more ways than one.**

97

The 1939 All-Star Game was a fitting occasion for former great Walter Johnson to visit with current great Gomez.

A youthful Gomez (below) took the American League by storm, winning 21 and 24 games in his first two full seasons. When Gomez reached the twilight of his career (above), he was a veteran of five World Series.

players shed tears in the dugout, Gomez broke the tension. Laying a hand on Gehrig's shoulder, he cracked: "It took 'em 15 years to get you out of the lineup. They get me out of there in 15 minutes."

When Lefty walked off the field after beating the Giants in Game 2 of the 1936 World Series, Colonel Jake Ruppert beckoned him to his box. "Can you pitch tomorrow, too?" asked the owner.

"If the manager wants me to," said Lefty.

He didn't, of course, but when Ruppert again signaled to him after the third game, Gomez strolled to the owner's box and shook hands. Relaxing his grip, Gomez found a check for $1,000, the amount he had been cut in salary that year.

Gomez was a prankster as well as a humorist. On a dark, dreary day in Cleveland, he walked to the plate and struck a match before facing Bob Feller.

"What's the matter, can't you see Feller?" asked umpire Bill Summers.

"Oh, I can see him," came the reply, "I just want to be sure he can see me."

When Lefty joined the sales promotion department of a sporting goods company in 1948, a question on his employment form was: "Why did you leave your last job?"

He wrote: "I couldn't get anybody out."

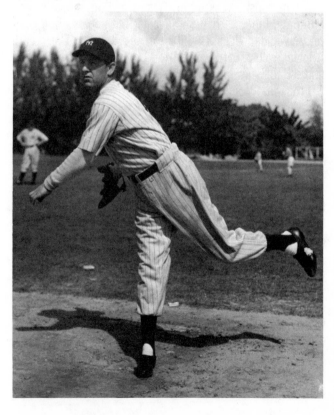

# Goose Goslin

In the spring of 1928, the Washington Senators trained at the Fair Grounds in Tampa, Fla. While the players worked out at one end of the field, a high school track team practiced at the other.

One morning, the Senators' left fielder strolled into the track team's area, picked up a 16-pound shot and started to throw it as if it were a baseball. The next day his arm was dead.

But there was no way that Manager Bucky Harris could bench Goose Goslin—his bat was too important to the Washington attack. Every time a ball was hit safely to left field, the shortstop raced into the area and took a lob from Goslin and relayed it to the infield.

Keeping Goslin in the lineup paid off in a batting championship. As the season dwindled down to the last day, Goslin led Heinie Manush of St. Louis by one point and, as fate would have it, the Nats and Browns met in the final game.

Manush rapped two hits, and so did Goslin. In his final at-bat, Goose needed a hit, a walk or an ejection from the game. The first two pitches were called strikes, eliciting howls of anguish from Goslin. He stepped on umpire Bill Guthrie's toes, hoping for banishment, but the arbiter, aware of the stakes, did not accept the bait.

**Goose Goslin always tempted fate by fearlessly crowding the plate.**

Ultimately, Goslin singled to right field and clinched the title by one point.

Goose, raised on a New Jersey farm, had been a glass blower and elevator mechanic before Bill McGowan, later a top-flight American League umpire, told the youngster he was good enough for professional ball.

Two years later, in 1921, Goose was the batting champion of the Sally League. Clark Griffith became interested in the lefthanded slugger when Jack Dunn, owner of the minor league Baltimore Orioles, revealed that he was about to bid $5,000 for Goslin.

Griffith promptly raised the ante to $6,000 and won the young prize.

In his first game for the Senators, Goslin socked a late-inning, bases-loaded triple to defeat Chicago. After the game, first baseman Joe Judge remarked idly, "I never thought we'd beat Red Faber today."

"Was that Faber?" the rookie replied innocently.

In appreciation for McGowan's good turn, Goslin asked Griffith to use his influence in acquiring McGowan for the A.L. As a result, the league benefited from 20 years of McGowan's umpiring talents.

Goslin feared no pitcher. He constantly crowded the plate until umpires threatened him with ejection unless he desisted. He swung with a gusto not unlike that of Babe Ruth and when he missed, he usually wound up on the seat of his pants.

Goose never conceded that he hit a ball with all his power. Once, when he was congratulated for hitting a line drive into the center-field bleachers at Boston, he responded, "I wish I had really gotten a hold of that ball, it really would have gone places."

Goslin hit three homers in both the 1924 and 1925 World Series and another in the '33 classic. Traded to Detroit in December of 1933, he sparked the Tigers to pennants the next two years and became a Motor City hero in 1935 when his ninth-inning single drove home Mickey Cochrane to give the Bengals the world championship over the Cubs.

His last association with Organized Ball was in 1941 when he managed the Trenton (Inter-State) club.

For years, Goslin operated a successful fishing and crabbing business out of Bayside, N.J.

Goslin made it to the Hall in 1968, three years before his death on May 15, 1971. Manush had died three days earlier.

# Hank Greenberg

Hank Greenberg gets a big reception after hitting a game-winning homer in Game 2 of the 1945 World Series.

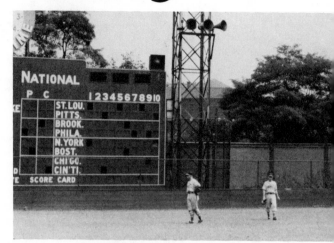

After obtaining Greenberg in 1947, the Pirates built a left-field bullpen in Forbes Field (above) and dubbed it Greenberg Gardens.

With five games remaining in the 1938 season, Detroit first baseman Hank Greenberg had 58 home runs. Two more would match the major league record established by Babe Ruth 11 years earlier.

The first of the five contests was played at home against St. Louis. The Tigers bombed Lefty Mills, 12-0, but the best the Detroit slugger could manage was two walks in five trips to the plate.

The next day, the record-seeking slugger again failed to hit a homer. He singled once in four at-bats.

It was on to Cleveland, where Denny Galehouse beat the Tigers without tossing a gopher pitch. A closing doubleheader the next day held the last hope for Greenberg. Bob Feller pitched the opener and struck out 18 batters. The best the Detroit muscle man could do was a double off the wall.

With shadows creeping across the field, Cleveland's Johnny Humphries and Clay Smith were holding the slugger at bay in the nightcap. After seven innings, umpire George Moriarty told Greenberg, "I'm sorry, Hank, this is as far as I can go."

"That's all right," replied Greenberg, "this is as far as I can go, too."

The son of Romanian immigrants who was raised in the Bronx, Hank might have been a Yankee but he rejected the Bombers' offer because common sense dictated that his development would be stymied as long as Lou Gehrig guarded first base.

Three years after graduating from James Monroe High School, Greenberg was a major leaguer to stay. In his second season with the Tigers, he was on a league championship team that bowed to the Cardinals in the 1934 World Series.

In 1935, after 170 runs batted in and 36 homers earned a Most Valuable Player award for the 24-year-old slugger, Hank played only the first two games of the World Series against the Cubs. He suffered a broken wrist in the second game and sat out the last four games.

After driving in 112 runs and hitting 33 homers in

Greenberg slides past Cardinal catcher Bill DeLancey (below) with the final run of Detroit's 10-4 win in Game 4 of the 1934 Series.

Greenberg and winning pitcher Virgil Trucks celebrate after the Tigers' Game 2 win over the Cubs in the '45 Series.

1939, Greenberg was stunned that winter to discover a $10,000 pay cut on his 1940 contract. When he confronted General Manager Jack Zeller, he was told that the only way to avoid the cut was to shift to left field so that a young powerhouse named Rudy York could play first base.

Recalling the years of toil and dedication that were necessary to make him a polished first baseman, Hank suggested that a new position be found for York. The notion was dismissed instantly.

Ultimately, it was agreed that if Greenberg opened the 1940 season in left field he would not only escape the $10,000 pay cut, but would receive a raise of an equal amount, to $50,000.

Hank mastered the intricacies of outfield play to earn the raise. He also won a second MVP, but the season came to a disappointing finish when the Tigers lost the seven-game World Series to Cincinnati.

In early May of 1941, after playing in only 19 games, Greenberg enlisted as a private in the United States Army. He was gone four years. When he returned in July of 1945, he found the Tigers in a pennant scramble again. The race was undecided until the final day when Greenberg hit a bases-loaded homer in St. Louis to clinch the flag.

One year after listening to the World Series via radio in India, Greenberg socked two homers in the fall classic to help beat the Cubs in seven games.

Sold to the Pirates in January of 1947, Hank considered retirement but a $100,000 salary offer coaxed him into a Pirate uniform for a final fling. Moreover, Pittsburgh provided an inviting homer target, constructing a bullpen in left field that was christened Greenberg Gardens. Twenty-five home runs and 74 RBIs later, Greenberg closed the book.

Hank joined Bill Veeck at Cleveland, serving as a vice president and eventually as general manager of the Indians. When he sold his stock years later, Greenberg discovered that his original $50-a-share investment had grown to $100 per share. Later, he was a White Sox vice president (also under Veeck).

# Clark Griffith

When Ban Johnson and Charles Comiskey fathered the American League, their most urgent need for credibility was a dominant player who could raid established National League clubs.

They found their man in Clark Griffith, a pitcher who had been a leading winner for Cap Anson's Chicago Colts in the 1890s and was willing to play a leading role in the formation of the new league.

Griffith had been a fighter all of his 31 years. He had spent his childhood in untamed western Missouri, where his father had been killed accidentally while hunting deer. He had battled malaria until his widowed mother, seeking a more healthful climate, moved her brood to Bloomington, Ill. There the youngster met the famed Hoss Radbourn, who taught Griffith his pitching secrets.

On May 1, 1888, Griffith made his debut in professional ball, pitching the Bloomington (Central Interstate) team to a 3-2 victory over Danville.

The 5-foot-8, 175-pounder was on his way, subduing muscular hitters with cunning and guile that led to his popular nickname of "Old Fox."

During the winter of 1900-01, the well-known Colts pitcher traipsed over the country, inducing big-name athletes to leave their N.L. clubs for more lucrative salaries. In return for his services, he was named manager of the Chicago White Sox, whom he led to the first A.L. championship in 1901.

Without Griffith, the American League would not have attained the quick success that it did.

After two years, the Johnson-Comiskey combine determined that a New York franchise was vital to the success of the league. Chicago's Comiskey agreed to release Griffith, his manager, so that Clark could oversee the New York operation and once more Griffith had a fight on his hands.

The Giants, a National League fixture in the city, took a

**Clark Griffith (pictured in 1903) won 240 games and was instrumental in the success of the American League.**

dim view of Hilltop Park, a facility that the new club was building in the upper Bronx. The N.L. club announced it would use its influence to halt construction of subway and streetcar lines short of the site.

But Griffith, proving he was indeed an "Old Fox," arranged for some Tammany Hall chiefs to invest in his club. The transportation lines were extended to the ball park.

When an opportunity arose to buy into the Washington club in 1912, Griffith mortgaged his Montana ranch to raise the necessary funds. In time, he became the intimate of Presidents. He conceived of a chief executive tossing the first pitch to open a new season, and it was his accessibility to the White House that helped baseball operate through two world wars.

And Griffith fought on. In the 1890s, he had engaged in many skirmishes with John McGraw and the Baltimore Orioles. Once, McGraw singled off Griffith, then taunted the pitcher and umpire Joe Cantillon (standing behind the mound) with his customary invective.

"Pick him off," Cantillon whispered to the Old Fox.

"How?" asked Griff, noting McGraw's small lead.

"Balk him off."

With an outrageous balk move, Griffith fired to first and the umpire waved McGraw out. The squawk that followed was loud and profane and led to McGraw's ejection.

Griffith tried the same move on the next runner, whereupon Cantillon yelled "Balk." How come, the Old Fox wondered. "Balks only work with McGraw," said the umpire.

As an owner with meager finances, Griffith resented clubs with bottomless coffers. In the 1930s, he pushed through legislation—aimed at the Yankees—forbidding champions to trade. The regulation lasted one year.

Griffith was approaching his 86th birthday when he suffered a massive stomach hemorrhage on October 22, 1955, and died five days later.

# Burleigh Grimes

Old headlines tell the story best: "Facing Grimes Was a Terrifying Thing" and "Grimes Called Toughest Loser" and "Old Stubblebeard Was a Mean One."

There was nothing gentlemanly about Burleigh Grimes. He fought with opponents, teammates, managers and reporters. In the 1920s, when he was with the Dodgers, he did not speak to Wilbert Robinson, his manager. When Robinson decided it was Grimes' turn to pitch, he notified him via the clubhouse boy.

In 1930, Bill Terry batted .401 to win the National League batting crown. The first time Grimes faced Terry in 1931, he strolled off the mound and asked the Giants' first baseman, "What did you hit last year?"

"Four-oh-one," replied Terry.

"Well, you won't be hitting .400 this year," snorted Grimes, who fired the first pitch at Terry's head.

As a Wisconsin farm boy, Grimes worked in a lumber camp from dawn to dusk for $1 a day. Once while driving four horses hitched to a sled, he was buried under seven tiers of 10-foot logs when a horse tripped over a stump. Lumberjacks extricated Grimes, who was unhurt.

Burleigh was 16 when his father handed him $25 with the advice, "Son, go out into the world and make something of yourself."

Grimes reached the majors in 1916 and stayed around for 19 years, winning 270 games with a fearless determination, a fine repertoire of pitches and a one-day growth of beard that enhanced his sinister appearance.

Of the 17 established pitchers who were licensed to pitch the spitball when it was outlawed in 1920, Old Stubblebeard stayed the longest in the majors. He did not throw the moist pitch as regularly as was generally thought, but only Art Fletcher of the Phillies was able to determine when Grimes was actually loading up a baseball or when he was faking.

Grimes wore a cap a half size too small. Before every pitch, Grimes held his glove in front of his mouth to shield his true intentions. One afternoon, eagle-eyed Fletcher detected a telltale signal. When Burleigh moved his jaws to generate saliva for a genuine spitter, the muscles in his head made his cap bobble. On the fake spitter, no muscles moved. Grimes solved the problem by wearing a larger cap, and his secret was safe once more.

When Grimes was on the mound, he recognized everybody as an enemy, even a callow rookie. In 1924, when the Dodgers and Giants were embroiled in a sizzling pennant race, Grimes called the starting nine for that day's game into a huddle. "Anyone who doesn't want to play today's game to win," he started, "let me know right now."

Nobody dissented. When the Cubs, who had defeated Dazzy Vance the previous day, came to bat in the first

**The prospect of facing Burleigh Grimes terrified many major league hitters.**

inning, Grimes' first pitch sent Art Weis, just up from the Texas League, sprawling from a head-hunter pitch. The pattern never changed. Burleigh won in the best way he knew, but the Giants won the flag.

Once, when the Cubs prepared to alight from a train in New York, a porter attempted to brush off Gabby Hartnett. "Never mind," said the catcher, "Burleigh Grimes will dust me off this afternoon."

Before he joined the Cardinals in 1930 and became a teammate of Frank Frisch, Old Stubblebeard conducted a running feud with the Old Flash. Invariably, Frankie would wind up in the dust as the first pitch sailed at his jaw.

"You have three shots at me," Frisch warned Grimes, "then you gotta pitch." Usually, Frisch drilled one of the pitches safely.

Grimes never changed, not even as a baseball old-timer. He was 40 and a Yankee when Goose Goslin hit a homer off him. Innings later, when Goose was in the on-deck circle, Grimes low-bridged him with a pitch.

Grimes' colorful major league career ended where it had started, with the Pirates. Burleigh claimed the last of his 1,512 strikeouts on September 20, 1934, when he fanned Brooklyn's Joe Stripp.

# Lefty Grove

**By 1935, Lefty Grove was pitching for Boston and just warming up for his run at 300 victories.**

The locker room at Sportsman's Park in St. Louis had been torn apart, locker-by-locker, by a man no one had dared to challenge.

In August of 1931, Lefty Grove, a tall lefthander from the coal-mining country of West Virginia, had a 25-2 record for the Philadelphia A's (who were en route to their third consecutive American League flag). He had won 16 straight games. One more would surpass the American League record shared by Joe Wood and Walter Johnson.

On the afternoon that the hard-throwing Grove tried for the record, the A's were not at full strength. Al Simmons, the regular left fielder, took the day off to seek medical treatment in Milwaukee. His place was taken by a rookie, Jimmy Moore.

In the third inning of the first game of a doubleheader, Fred Schulte singled off Grove and Oscar Melillo hit a line drive to left field. Moore misjudged the ball, which sailed over his head and permitted Schulte to score.

That was all Browns pitcher Dick Coffman needed to win the game. The A's collected only three hits and one walk, losing, 1-0.

Infuriated (not at Moore, but at Simmons), Grove exploded. His fury was heightened by the knowledge that his teammates were trampling the Browns, 10-0, behind Waite Hoyt in the nightcap.

Grove, who maintained a monastic silence for several days, compiled a 31-4 record for the season. His defeats were by scores of 7-5, 4-3, 2-1 and 1-0.

"Groves," as he was called by A's Manager Connie Mack, saved some of his most devastating performances for the Yankees when they were Murderers Row. There was the day when Grove held a 1-0 lead entering the last of the ninth inning at Yankee Stadium. Mark Koenig led off with a single, whereupon Grove struck out Babe Ruth, Lou Gehrig and Bob Meusel on nine pitches. Meusel fouled off one pitch.

"Another time in Philadelphia I replaced Jack Quinn with the bases loaded," Grove recalled in the twilight of his career. "And I struck out Ruth, Gehrig and Tony Lazzeri on 10 pitches."

Again, in Chicago, he found runners on second and third and none out when he came on in relief. He fanned the side on 10 pitches.

"The way Johnny Heving froze when he caught the last pitch, I knew he didn't see the ball," Grove said.

When the Yankees' streak of 308 games without a shutout was snapped in August of 1933, it was Grove who turned the trick, 7-0. Ruth, who socked only nine home runs in 10 years against Grove, struck out three times, Gehrig twice.

For years, Grove was content to let the public regard him as an ill-tempered prima donna. It wasn't until years after Grove retired that a onetime employee of a sporting goods company revealed that Lefty had visited the plant frequently in the early 1930s, buying the best grade of baseballs in four- and five-dozen lots and uniforms tailored to size for a kids team that he frequently stopped to watch on his way to the ball park.

Grove was 25 when he made his debut with the A's following five seasons—the last two 27-victory campaigns —with the International League's Baltimore Orioles. He was 27 when he blossomed as a 20-game winner in 1927, launching a spectacular seven-year period in which he compiled a 172-54 record. In 1930-31, his figures were 59-9.

Traded to the Red Sox in 1934 as part of the mass exodus from Philadelphia in the Great Depression, Lefty won 20 games only once the remainder of his career.

Grove had won 286 games after his 15-4 mark led the A.L. in

Grove (right) visits with the Giants' Carl Hubbell before the first All-Star Game at Comiskey Park in 1933.

percentage in 1939, but it required two more seasons of cunning, rather than the blazing fastball of old, for him to reach the coveted 300-victory mark. His two-year record was 14-13, and his ERA each season topped 4.00.

The talented Grove compiled his best seasons in 1930 (above) and 1931 (left) when he won 59 and lost only 9 for the Philadelphia A's.

# Chick Hafey

How good he might have been if he had been blessed with normal vision and good health will never be known, but it is generally agreed that bespectacled Californian Chick Hafey would have posted a lifetime average considerably higher than his .317.

Branch Rickey, who discovered Hafey and observed him throughout his major league career, asserted: "If Hafey had had good eyesight and good health he might have been the finest righthanded hitter baseball has ever known."

Jim Bottomley, who was a teammate of Hafey and Rogers Hornsby, declared, "Hafey hit harder than Rog. He hit with his arms and wrists. He used a long-handled bat and when he leaned on the ball you could hear the seams crack."

Hafey was a pitcher when he reported to his first Cardinals camp in 1923, but when Rickey got a glimpse of him in the batting cage, he said, "You hit the ball pretty well. I think you should be an outfielder."

Hafey was one of the first players in the original farm system as designed by Rickey. By 1925, he was with the Cardinals, running the bases instinctively, driving the ball with power and fielding his position impressively.

But Chick was hampered by frequent sinus attacks. During his career he underwent four operations, two in one season.

A shy and retiring individual, Hafey was, however, no pushover at the bargaining table. Prior to the 1928 season, Chick signed a three-year contract that paid him $7,000, $8,000 and $9,000. In that three-year period, he batted .337 overall, clouted 82 home runs, batted in 343 runs and scored 310. He demanded $15,000 for 1931.

After considerable haggling, Hafey signed for $12,500, with the understanding that, because he had missed much of spring training, the new contract would not take effect until the front office decided he was in condition to play. As a result, the Redbirds saved $2,100 and Hafey played for $10,400.

Despite this disappointment, Hafey produced one of his finest campaigns in 1931, winning the National League batting championship in a three-way battle with teammate Bottomley and Bill Terry of the Giants. Final figures showed Hafey with a mark of .3489, Terry .3486 and Bottomley .3482.

The following spring, Hafey and his wife drove to Florida to negotiate a new contract. The outfielder proposed a $17,000 salary that would include the $2,100 that was deducted from his 1931 pay. Rickey, general manager of the defending world champions, countered with a $13,000 offer, an increase of $500.

Infuriated, the Hafeys jumped into their car and headed westward. "I was so mad," said Hafey, "I drove 90 miles an hour across the desert."

**Chick Hafey compiled a .317 career average, despite being handicapped by poor eyesight.**

On April 11, he was notified that he had been traded to Cincinnati, a last-place club that paid him $15,000.

Handicapped by the flu and his old sinus problem, Hafey played only 83 games in 1932 but batted .344. He was the leftfielder for the National League in the first All-Star Game in 1933, in which he went 1-for-4, and batted .303 in the regular season.

Early in the 1935 season, the Reds and Giants played a game at the Polo Grounds in a steady drizzle. When the Reds arrived in Philadelphia that evening, Hafey got a chill that developed into the flu. Physicians were unable to cure him in the East, and he returned to his home in Walnut Creek, Calif., where he spent the remainder of the season convalescing.

But Hafey's strength did not return and he sat out the 1936 campaign. Hafey gave the game another whirl in 1937. He batted .261 in 89 games for the Reds, then called it a career.

# Jesse Haines

The righthanded knuckleballer was such a gentle person that observers found it difficult to picture him as a hard loser.

But there was the afternoon in Cincinnati when Jesse Haines tore apart the locker room at Crosley Field, even knocking over the ancient potbellied stove, because errors had cost him a victory.

And there was an earlier day when his catcher, Pickles Dillhoefer, threw wildly to a base and permitted the deciding run to score. Afterward, Haines had to be restrained by teammates from attacking his batterymate.

On the pitching mound, however, Haines was a relatively composed competitor. In his distinguished career with the Cardinals, he was ejected only twice.

Haines had a cup of coffee with the Tigers—but no pitching record—in 1915. Jesse had better fortune with Cincinnati in 1918. He appeared in one game. During the 1919 season, while winning 21 games for Kansas City (American Association), Jesse was a popular item on the playing market. Cardinals Manager Branch Rickey was among the interested parties.

The $10,000 sale price was a bit beyond the reach of the impecunious Cardinals, but Rickey turned on all of his forensic charm and talked the club's directors into investing ten grand on the 26-year-old hurler. The Redbirds never made a better investment.

Along his major league route, Haines acquired a knuckleball from Ed Rommel, an American League hurler and later an umpire in the same league. However, unlike later-day exponents who gripped the ball with their fingernails, Haines clasped the ball with his knuckles.

That pitch, mixed with a crackling fastball—and thrown in rapid sequence to intimidate the batters—helped Pop toss a no-hitter against the Boston Braves in 1924.

In 1926, Haines appeared in the first of four World Series. He relieved in the opener, hurled a 4-0 victory in Game 3 and started the seventh contest. He pitched until the seventh inning in the finale when the knuckler raised a blister and he gave way to Grover Cleveland Alexander, who preserved the 3-2 lead.

Neither the no-hitter nor the '26 Series victories produced Haines' greatest thrill. That occurred in the 1930 Series when he outpitched Lefty Grove, a 28-game winner in the regular season, 3-1, on a four-hitter.

Jesse did not pitch in the 1931 Series, having suffered a broken wrist when struck by a line drive off the bat of Babe Herman, but he was a member of the world champion Gas House Gang of 1934 at age 41.

When Dizzy Dean went on his famous sit-down strike in the Polo Grounds clubhouse, sending Cardinals Manager Frank Frisch into a purple rage, it was Haines who asked permission to speak to the young righthander.

Jesse Haines (pictured in 1930) combined a knuckleball and sizzling fastball to win 210 games for the Cardinals.

Frisch gave his okay and Jesse met with Diz.

"I keep thinking that Ol' Pop has one more chance at a World Series," Haines began, "but he can't do it without you."

Dean softened at the fatherly words and said, "All right, Pop, I'll do it for you, but not for that Frisch."

The Cardinals made it into the Series. The Dean brothers won two games apiece, and Ol' Pop pitched two-thirds of an inning in relief as the Cards defeated the Tigers in seven games.

Haines was 44 when he retired at the close of the 1937 season and he accepted a position as Dodgers pitching coach. When he ran as Republican candidate for the auditor's post in Montgomery Count, O., he won and was re-elected for six consecutive four-year terms before retiring.

Haines underwent surgery for the removal of a kidney in 1970, but recovered sufficiently to attend his Hall of Fame induction that summer. He was in ill health for several years preceding his death in 1978 at age 85.

# Billy Hamilton

The stocky Philadelphia baserunner had been a headache to the Cleveland Spiders all afternoon, running the bases almost at will as fielders tried in vain to head him off at the next base.

In frustration, the Cleveland third baseman introduced a new measure. Grabbing the runner as he approached third base, he carried him to the edge of the field and dumped him unceremoniously into the grandstand.

Fortunately, the runner suffered no bodily harm; only his composure was scarred.

For 14 major league seasons, Billy Hamilton drove opponents to the brink of distraction. In 1,578 games, he stole 937 bases. Ty Cobb, by comparison, swiped 892 bases in the 3,033 games that made up his 24-year career.

A lefthanded hitter, Hamilton broke into the majors with Kansas City (American Association) in 1888. The day was a tough one for the entire K.C. club—which was held hitless and scoreless by Gus Weyhing of the Athletics.

Hamilton stole his first base as a big leaguer on August 3, 1888, at the expense of Chris Fulmer, catching for Baltimore. There was no stopping him thereafter. On September 18, he scored five runs and swiped four bases against Cleveland.

When Matt Kilroy of Baltimore picked the youngster off base three times in one game, however, Manager Dave Rowe threw reins on Billy, who had been a 10.75 sprinter in high school.

Conditions were more favorable under a new manager, however, and Hamilton stole 117 bases while batting .301 in 1889.

When the Kansas City franchise was transferred to Syracuse in 1890, Hamilton joined the Philadelphia Nationals under Harry Wright. Among Billy's teammates was Billy Sunday, who set a torrid stolen base pace for Pittsburgh at the start of the campaign before joining Philadelphia. Hamilton overhauled Sunday by August 1 and posted 102 steals for the year; the future evangelist finished with 91.

In 1894, the season he scored 196 runs in 131 games, Hamilton batted .399, but it wasn't good enough to win the batting title. He was fourth best, trailing teammates Ed Delahanty (.400) and Sam Thompson (.404) and Boston's Hugh Duffy (.438).

That same season, Billy enjoyed his best day on the basepaths. Catcher Deacon Jim McGuire of Washington watched helplessly as Hamilton stole seven bases, tying a record set by George Gore of Chicago in 1881.

After the 1895 season, Hamilton was traded to Boston, where he replaced the aging Tommy McCarthy in an outfield of Tom Bannon and Hugh Duffy. Hamilton was an instant sensation with the Beaneaters, stealing a club-record 93 bases and batting a team-leading .363.

By 1900, Sliding Billy Hamilton already had spent 12 seasons driving opposing defenses crazy.

The following season, Billy scored 153 runs for his fourth and last big-league title in that department and batted .344 on a team that averaged .319. The Beaneaters won the '97 pennant by two games in a battle with Ned Hanlon's Baltimore Orioles.

Baltimore defeated Boston in the Temple Cup Series that followed the regular campaign. Billy did not play in the fifth and deciding game; his error on a routine fly ball in Game 4 earned him a seat on the bench for the finale.

A knee injury limited Hamilton to 109 games in 1898 and another knee injury held him to 81 games in 1899. He stole 59 bases in '98, but only 19 in '99.

After scoring more than 100 runs for the 11th time in his career in 1900, Billy rejected an offer from the Red Sox in the new American League and closed out his major league career with the Beaneaters in 1901.

Hamilton remained active for another decade, however, performing for Haverhill and Lynn of the New England League and Harrisburg of the Tri-State League. In 1904, he led all of Organized Baseball with a .412 average for Haverhill.

Hamilton scouted for the Red Sox in 1911 and 1912 and ended his baseball affiliation in 1916 when he was manager and part-owner of the Eastern League club in his home town of Worcester.

# Will Harridge

The young ticket agent for the Wabash railroad was dumbstruck when his superior informed him, "You have worked your last day for the railroad."

The agent's fears of dismissal were quickly allayed however. "You are not being fired," he was assured. "Next week you will start working as private secretary to Ban Johnson."

"But I don't know anything about baseball," protested Will Harridge, who had been handling the American League's ticket requirements on the Wabash for a number of years.

Harridge succeeded Robert McRoy, who had resigned as secretary to the A.L. president to join the Boston Red Sox.

"What made matters worse," Harridge recollected in later life, "was that McRoy had promised to stay on and teach me the ropes. He left the day I arrived."

Harridge's early weeks on the job were almost total chaos.

"Mr. Johnson would call for something out of the files and I wouldn't know where to look," said Harridge. "I was scared to death. But I had just been married and I needed the money. That gave me the courage to see it through."

Will had been earning $90 a month. His starting salary with Johnson was $50 a week.

Harridge was well-established and highly respected when Johnson, climaxing a series of clashes with club owners, resigned in 1927. Ernest Barnard of Cleveland was elected successor to the league founder.

Barnard died suddenly in March of 1931 and the presidency was offered to Harridge, who demurred briefly.

"I told the owners I'd continue as acting president for a year," He said, "and then, if they felt I had done a good job, they could consider me for the job."

The suggestion fell on deaf ears. Charles (Old Roman) Comiskey, owner of the White Sox, proposed that Will be elected immediately. On March 27, 1931, Harridge was elected president for a three-year term.

Dignified and soft-spoken in contrast to the stormy Johnson, Harridge faced his first crisis in 1932 when Bill Dickey broke Carl Reynolds' jaw in an altercation at Washington.

Harridge fined Dickey $1,000 and suspended him for a month in the heat of a pennant race. The action enraged Yankees Owner Jake Ruppert, who did not speak to Harridge for nearly a year.

Gentle Will also demonstrated early that he could be firm with umpires. He fined and suspended George Moriarty after the umpire engaged in fisticuffs with Chicago players after a game.

As much as he liked Jimmie Dykes, Harridge fined the manager more than any other individual. In his career, Dykes was fined 37 times by Harridge.

A.L. President Will Harridge (left) enjoys a light moment with Commissioner Happy Chandler in the late 1940s.

Will also was a persuasive salesman. In 1933, when Arch Ward proposed a major league all-star game as an adjunct to the Century of Progress Exposition in Chicago, Will convinced his club owners that the extravaganza would be beneficial to baseball.

Harridge possessed inordinate pride in his league, but generally concealed his emotions during his reign (when the A.L. dominated the World Series and All-Star Games).

One exception occurred in 1941 after Ted Williams' ninth-inning homer gave the A.L. All-Stars a 7-5 victory at Detroit. As the ball sailed out of the park, Harridge leaped to his feet and stumbled over chairs in a hasty exit from his box. Once he fell and had to be helped to his feet. In the clubhouse, he and Williams embraced jubilantly.

"I would have kissed him," Will confessed, "if there hadn't been so many people around."

Harridge was 75 when he resigned on December 3, 1958. He still enjoyed good health, but he had seen how owners demanded Johnson's resignation when Ban's health failed in 1927, and he resolved the same would not happen to him.

Harridge, succeeded by Joe Cronin, was named to the newly created post of chairman of the board. He was 87 when he died at an Evanston, Ill., nursing home on April 9, 1971.

# Bucky Harris

Few opponents could boast of outsmarting John McGraw, but the young manager of the Washington Senators earned the privilege of bragging—if he had wished—on October 10, 1924.

In an effort to chill the hot bat of the Giants' lefthanded-hitting Bill Terry, who had gone 6-for-12 in the World Series, Nats skipper Bucky Harris developed a strategy to curb the New York player's effectiveness—and maybe even get him out of the game. (Terry hadn't started games 2, 4 and 6 against lefthanders.)

While nominating righthander Curly Ogden to start Game 7, Harris had lefthander George Mogridge warming up under the stands for the Senators. After Ogden pitched to two batters, Mogridge was waved into the game. Terry went hitless in two at-bats against Mogridge, and McGraw removed Terry in favor of righthanded-hitting Emil (Irish) Meusel (and Harris soon inserted another righthanded pitcher).

The Senators went on to win, 4-3, in 12 innings, to capture the world championship.

Harris had the baseball smarts. He was gentlemanly when the occasion required, but he also could go for blood when others set the pattern. When a Yankee pitcher started to dust off Washington batters during the 1924 season, Harris pushed a bunt along the first-base line, challenging the pitcher to cover the base. The hurler did not take the bait.

On the next pitch, Harris barreled into second with spikes gleaming. The shortstop backed off, and tempers cooled quickly.

Bucky learned to be tough in the Pennsylvania State Basketball League, a professional circuit. When action got out of hand in one game, the 5-foot-9½ Harris socked a 6-foot-4 opponent, and opened a gash from ear to chin.

Bucky was a four-year veteran when, at age 27, he was named manager of the Senators in 1924. The appointment of one so young created banner headlines. A world championship the same season made Harris the Boy Wonder.

**During his five seasons as Tigers manager, Bucky Harris played only when necessary.**

The news was less worthy when he rejoined the Nats in later years, twice as a manager and once as a scout.

Throughout his career, Harris was the epitome of honesty. His word was always his bond. In 1947, when he was offered what amounted to a lifetime contract as general manager of the Tigers, he declined because he had verbally agreed to manage the Yankees (although he hadn't signed with the Yanks).

Bucky, who left school at 16 to become a breaker boy in a Pennsylvania coal mine, managed Washington for five years in his first stint there before taking over at Detroit, where he also put in five seasons. After the 1933 season, he announced his decision to resign.

Owner Frank Navin was extremely fond of Bucky, but Harris made his case by saying: "The Tigers are a ballclub now. Maybe it's because I've taken so much time in putting them together. . . . I'm tired of looking at them, or they're tired of looking at me, because neither one of us is doing as well as we could. Get a new manager and they'll win."

Under Mickey Cochrane, the Tigers won pennants in 1934 and 1935.

Harris had a winning way with his players due, in part, to the manner in which he supported them.

Normally outspoken, Bucky determined on one occasion that silence was the best answer to a sticky situation.

During his first term in a Washington uniform, Harris married the daughter of a United States senator from West Virginia. After a game in which Bucky had been plunked by a pitch that forced in the winning run for the Nats, Harris had dinner with his in-laws.

"People are saying that you deliberately let yourself be hit by that pitch so the Senators would win," his bride reported.

"Stanley would never do a dishonest thing like that just to win a game, I'm sure," responded her father.

Bucky decided not to enter the conversation.

# Gabby Hartnett

Darkness was rapidly enveloping Wrigley Field on a late September afternoon in 1938. The visiting Pirates, one-half game ahead of the Cubs in the National League pennant race, were tied with the home club, 5-5. As umpires huddled and debated the wisdom of letting the game continue into the ninth inning, 34,000 fans squirmed, knowing that a tie would force a doubleheader the next day.

The go-ahead was given, and ancient Charlie Root retired the Bucs in order in the ninth. Mace Brown, Pittsburgh's redoubtable reliever, then trudged to the mound in the gathering twilight.

Brown retired Phil Cavarretta and Carl Reynolds before facing Gabby Hartnett. The catcher-manager, nearing 38, swung and missed Brown's first pitch, a curve. He swung at—and fouled off—his second serve, another curve. Ordinarily, under such circumstances, a pitcher would waste a pitch. But Brown had confidence that another curve, down and away, would end the game and necessitate a twin bill.

"I put it over the plate between the belt and knees," Brown lamented.

Hartnett made solid contact. The ball streaked into the left-field bleachers for the famous "homer in the gloamin' " and the Cubs were in first place—to stay.

Hartnett was 20 years old and working in a steel and wire mill in Worcester, Mass., when he was offered a contract to play for the town's Eastern League club. He reached for a pen without delay and caught 100 games before the year was out.

Reports on the hard-throwing catcher filtered into New York, where John McGraw reflected on the Giants' need for such a commodity. He instructed his scout, Jesse Burkett, to check out the prospect.

In due time, the old slugger filed a wire report: "Hartnett will never be a big-league catcher. His hands are too small."

The Cubs found no such fault with Hartnett. They bought the youngster for $2,500.

The rookie was no blushing violet when he reported to Catalina Island for his first major league training camp in 1922. He chirped constantly, until one newspaperman wondered "Who's that gabby kid I can hear no matter where I go on the island?"

Henceforth, Hartnett was known as Gabby, although teammates called him by his middle name, Leo, and to others he was "Old Tomato Face."

Gabby was in his prime when he went to training camp in 1929, but his early optimism faded when, in making one of his customary hard throws to an infielder, he felt something snap in his shoulder. He appeared in just 25 games and batted only .273 for the pennant-winning Cubs.

Gabby, who reportedly missed only three foul flies in 1,990 games behind the plate, was the N.L. catcher in the

It was generally agreed that Gabby Hartnett's only weakness was his slowness afoot.

first five All-Star Games, including the 1934 classic when Carl Hubbell fanned Babe Ruth, Lou Gehrig, Jimmie Foxx, Al Simmons and Joe Cronin in order.

Gabby had the "best seat in the house" in the 1932 World Series in which Ruth allegedly "called" a homer.

"Babe was just replying to our bench jockeys," explained Gabby. "He held up one finger and said, 'It only takes one to hit.' "

Hartnett's only weakness, it was generally agreed, was his slowness afoot. "If he had had the speed of a Mickey Cochrane, he would have hit .400," insisted Pie Traynor.

In his 19-year major league career, Hartnett seldom felt censure. One exception took place in the late 1920s when Gabby was king of the Cubs and Al Capone was Chicago's reigning underworld figure. Prior to a game, Gabby was called to a box seat, where Capone asked him to autograph a baseball for his nephew. An alert photographer snapped a picture, which Commissioner K.M. Landis saw in the next day's newspapers. A non-fraternization edict was issued from Landis' office the next day.

A liver ailment proved fatal to Hartnett in Park Ridge, Ill., on his 72nd birthday.

# Harry Heilmann

Even a faulty memory can lead to a distinguished career as a major league outfielder.

At noon on a Saturday in 1913, the young bookkeeper at a San Francisco biscuit company closed his ledgers and left his office, looking ahead to some free time.

After walking a few blocks, he remembered that he had left his topcoat in the office. Retracing his steps, he met an old friend who was managing the Hanford team in the San Joaquin Valley League. The friend had a problem: His third baseman was ill. Could the bookkeeper fill in for the next day's game at Bakersfield? He was promised $10 and expenses, and accepted.

In storybook fashion, bookkeeper Harry Heilmann hit an 11th-inning double to give Hanford a 4-2 victory. Exuberant Hanford fans showered the field with money and when the hero of the day counted his new wealth he totaled $150 which, with the promised $10, represented more than a month's salary at the biscuit company.

Among the spectators at the game was a scout for the Portland club of the Northwest League. The next day the scout visited the bookkeeper's home and signed him to his first professional contract. As a bonus, the youngster received a spaghetti dinner. Three years later, Heilmann was in the major leagues to stay as an outfielder with the Detroit Tigers.

In the next 15 years, Harry failed to play as many as 100 games in only one season (spending part of 1918 in the Navy quartermaster department).

The righthanded hitter, known to his teammates as "Slug," was not an immediate sensation with the Tigers. His emergence as one of the top all-time hitters coincided with the elevation of Ty Cobb as manager in 1921.

"Until that time, Cobb didn't care whether I hit or not, just figured it wasn't any of his business, I guess," Heilmann explained. Cobb taught Heilmann how to distribute his weight while batting, "with a little more weight on the front foot," and how to study pitchers.

**Harry Heilmann's 1927 batting form resulted in his fourth batting championship.**

The improvement was dramatic. A .296 hitter for the five previous years, Heilmann batted .394 in 1921 and captured the first of four batting titles. He also won hitting championships in 1923, '25 and '27, clinching the last two crowns in last-day doubleheaders.

In 1925, Heilmann came on with a rush, picking up nearly 50 points on Tris Speaker in the final month. In the opener of the last day's twin bill, Harry rapped three hits to move ahead of Speaker. Teammates urged him to go home and enjoy his newly won laurels. He refused. "I'm playing out the string," he insisted before going 3-for-3 in the nightcap and beating Speaker by four points.

In 1927, Heilmann battled Al Simmons down to the wire. Because of the time differential, Heilmann learned early in St. Louis that Simmons had gone 2-for-5 for Philadelphia and moved one point ahead of him.

Heilmann had four hits, including a home run, in the first game, lifting him one point in front of Bucketfoot Al, and again friends suggested he take off the rest of the day. Again he refused. He collected three hits in the second game, winning the title comfortably—and honorably.

Traded to Cincinnati in 1930, Harry batted .333, then was forced to sit out a year because of arthritis. He came back in '32, but gave up after 15 games.

His finances depleted by the stock market crash, Heilmann was hired by the Tigers to broadcast their games in 1933 and became an instant success.

During spring training in Lakeland, Fla., in 1951, Harry collapsed in his hotel room. He was hospitalized in Lakeland and then returned to Detroit where he made occasional visits to the radio booth.

Heilmann had been Commissioner A.B. (Happy) Chandler's first choice to broadcast the 1951 All-Star Game from Detroit, but he declined because of failing health.

Harry died July 9, 1951, of lung cancer at Henry Ford Hospital in his adopted city, the day before that game.

# Billy Herman

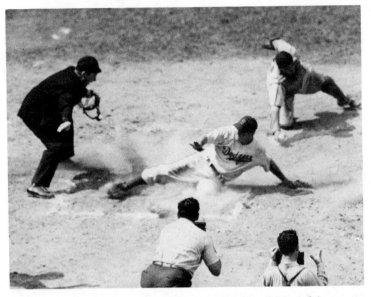

Casey Stengel called Billy Herman "one of the two or three smartest players ever to come into the National League."

Carl Hubbell, left-handed screwball artist of the Giants, was nothing more than "Cousin Carl" to the righthanded hitter after he started to use a longer, heavier bat and a delayed swing.

Herman was a marvel at stealing signs. Pee Wee Reese, his double-play partner at Brooklyn, recalled:

"It wouldn't take him long to break a code. As he took a lead off second base, he'd crouch to let a batter know a fastball was coming or stand straight up for a curve.

"When he coached at first or third base, it wouldn't take long before he'd tell you what the pitcher was throwing. If he yelled, 'Be ready,' you could expect a fastball. If he yelled, 'Come on,' it would be a breaking pitch."

Ruefully, Reese concluded, "Once we knew every pitch that Max Lanier (Cardinals) was throwing and he still shut us out."

Nobody ever questioned Herman's brains, although his mother may have had her doubts the day she sent Billy into town to make a mortgage payment on the family farm near New Albany, Ind. En route, the teen-ager spotted a game in progress and joined in. He played until nightfall, then retrieved the bag containing $250 in mortgage money that had been unattended during the game.

With his heady style of play, bat control and hit-and-run skills, Herman would have been an ideal player for John McGraw. And the Giants manager had a chance to buy Billy from Louisville, but rejected him as too small.

Billy was no more than a reserve infielder on his high school team, but he won some local acclaim after he pitched his church team to a league championship. He was 19 when he invested a dime in a round-trip fare to Louisville to sign with the American Association Colonels on the recommendation of Cap Neal, the club's colorful scout.

Neal's parting advice to Herman was, "You're an infielder, not a pitcher." Even after Neal saw infielder Herman commit five errors in a game while playing for Dayton (Central) a year later, he still insisted, "I'm not worried about that, son, and neither should you be. You're gonna

Billy Herman, traded to the Dodgers in 1941, slides safely across the plate in a game against St. Louis.

be one of the great ones."

By August of 1931, Billy had progressed so impressively that the Cubs shelled out $60,000 for his contract.

Billy, who grew into a solid 5-foot-11, 195-pounder, was a fearless batter. The first pitcher he faced in the majors was Si Johnson of Cincinnati. Herman greeted him with a single and on his second at-bat was struck behind the ear by a Johnson fastball.

Herman was trundled off the field, but the next time he faced Johnson he rapped three hits.

After he was traded to Brooklyn and sparked the Dodgers to a 1941 pennant, Herman was dusted off with a major league beanball by Paul Erickson of the Cubs in the heat of the 1942 race. Billy hit the next pitch into the left-field seats, one of only two homers he had that season.

When he was traded to the Braves in 1946, the old campaigner had the satisfaction of booming a double against his former Brooklyn teammates in a 4-0 Boston victory in the regular-season finale. The loss forced the Dodgers into a tie for the pennant. They lost the playoff to the Cardinals in two games.

Herman, a star on four pennant-winning clubs overall, saved his best performances for the All-Star Game. He performed in 10 contests, starting with the 1934 game, and batted a gaudy .433 (13-for-30).

When the Pittsburgh Pirates sought a manager in 1947, President Frank McKinney polled 12 highly respected baseball persons, seeking their recommendations. Herman's name topped 11 lists and ranked second on the other.

Billy got the job, but was fired as the Bucs tied for last place. Seventeen years later, he received a second managerial chance, this time with the Red Sox. Billy was in the second season of a two-year contract in 1966 and had just returned from a successful road swing when he strode into the front office and was greeted with the announcement, "We've decided to make a change."

Some minor league managerial jobs followed, as well as coaching positions with major league clubs that wished to capitalize on the talents of a super baseball intellect.

# Harry Hooper

The tourist was nearly 75 years old when he reminisced during a visit to the Baseball Hall of Fame in 1962, but he remembered in fine detail his memorable afternoon in a World Series game 47 years earlier.

Harry Hooper was a lefthanded batter who led off for the Red Sox in Game 5 at Baker Bowl in Philadelphia on October 13, 1915.

"In the third inning," he remembered, "I solved a pitch from Erskine Mayer and drove it over the wall. We were tied 4-4 in the ninth inning. Eppa Rixey, the lefthander, had replaced Mayer by that time. I realized it was no time to wait. I picked on the first pitch and that was it—another homer."

The ball flew past the outfielders, up a ramp and into the clubhouse where a teammate was taking a shower. He retrieved the ball and presented it to Hooper, who treasured it the rest of his life.

The second homer gave the Red Sox their second world championship in four years. They had defeated the Giants in the 1912 classic in which Hooper contributed an incredible barehand catch.

With the Giants leading, 1-0, in the fifth inning of the eighth and deciding game (one had been a tie), Larry Doyle walloped the ball toward the temporary bleachers in right-center field.

"I took off for the fence when the ball was hit," recalled the Red Sox captain, "saw the ball coming over my shoulder and stuck out my hand. I felt no impact.

"I knew I had the ball, but the fence was there and I was running into it. It was low, I jumped over and the crowd opened up.

"I can still see that instant, like everything was standing still, like a movie that is stopped. I can still see the ball—right there."

The Red Sox won the game, 3-2, in 10 innings.

Harry was in his fourth full season with the Sox at that time. A product of St. Mary's College in California, he joined the Alameda club in an outlaw California league in 1907. When he was sold to Sacramento (California State), Hooper pocketed $12.50, half of his sale price as per agreement with the club.

At the end of the 1908 season, Hooper was asked by Sacramento Manager Charley Graham how he'd like to join the Red Sox.

"I'd love it," replied the youngster.

Two years later, in 1910, Hooper was a member of one of baseball's greatest outfields, teaming up with Tris Speaker in center and Duffy Lewis in left.

As a fielder, Hooper specialized in the "rump slide." Instead of diving for a ball, Harry positioned himself feet first with one leg tucked under. It enabled him to come up instantly in position to throw.

**By 1910, Harry Hooper was part of a great Red Sox outfield that included Tris Speaker and Duffy Lewis.**

Harry cashed his last two Series checks, both winners' shares, in 1916 and 1918.

In 1919, Hooper suggested to Manager Ed Barrow that teammate Babe Ruth be converted from a pitcher to an outfielder to capitalize on his hitting prowess.

"They'd have me investigated if I did that to the best lefthander in the game," protested Barrow.

"But you've got $60,000 invested in the club," Hooper countered. "You're interested in bringing fans out. They come out when Ruth pitches, but they come to see him hit. Play him in the outfield and they can see him hit every day."

Barrow did—and the fans did.

When Harry held out for a $15,000 salary in 1921 he was traded to the White Sox, who gave him $13,250.

Hooper retired after the 1925 campaign but played one season with the Missions (Pacific Coast) before calling it quits.

He accepted a temporary appointment as postmaster of Capitola, Calif., but stayed on the job for 25 years. He was an expert bowler and spent a lot of time hunting and fishing, as well as watching the surf from his seaside home in Santa Cruz, Calif. He was the oldest member of the Hall of Fame when he died in 1974 at age 87.

# Rogers Hornsby

**Rogers Hornsby, manager of the St. Louis Browns in 1936, confined most of his hitting to practice sessions. The** **seven-time batting champion made only five plate appearances.**

Although the 19-year-old shortstop for Denison (Western Association) had batted only .277 and made 58 errors in his second pro season, Bob Connery decided he was worth a $500 investment.

Wiring news of the purchase of Rogers Hornsby to the home office, the Cardinals' scout said, "If the boy fails to make good, you can take the money out of my salary."

Before he died more than 50 years later, Connery had the satisfaction of seeing his discovery develop into the greatest righthanded hitter of all time.

Over a five-year span (1921 through 1925), Hornsby averaged .402 as a major league hitter. In 1924, he established a modern record by batting .424 in 143 games. He missed three games in May because of a dislocated thumb and eight late-season games because of a wrenched back.

In his remarkable season of '24, the Rajah hit safely one time in 44 contests, twice in 46, three times in 25 and four times in four. He was blanked only 24 times and, curiously, the pitcher who enjoyed the greatest success against Rog was a lefthander, Johnny Cooney of Boston who shut him out three times.

Hornsby, named St. Louis manager on June 1, 1925, attained his peak of popularity in 1926 when helped the Redbirds to their first pennant and a stunning upset of the Yankees in the seven-game World Series.

But success was not without its perils. An outspoken individual, Hornsby was openly critical of Owner Sam Breadon, calling him a money-grubbing cheapskate for scheduling a late-season exhibition game at New Haven, Conn., when, Rog insisted, a day of rest would have been more beneficial to the players.

Relations between the two men strained further when Hornsby demanded a three-year contract at $50,000 a season. Shortly before Christmas of 1926, an incensed St. Louis citizenry learned that the Rajah had been traded to the Giants for Frank Frisch and Jimmy Ring.

Hornsby's blunt manner never changed. With the Giants, he quarreled with Owner Charles Stoneham and others. One evening, while Rog was at dinner with shortstop Eddie (Doc) Farrell, a newspaperman asked Hornsby if the Giants had a chance to win the pennant. "Not as long as Farrell plays shortstop," was his unsmiling reply.

After one season in New York, the Rajah was traded in 1928 to Boston, where he was named manager in May. "Can this team win the pennant?" asked Owner Emil Fuchs. "Not with these humpty-dumpties," answered

**Hornsby began his career as a shortstop, but by 1920 he had found his niche at second base.**

Hornsby.

Rog wore out his Boston welcome in one year, too, and moved on to Chicago. By late-September of 1930, he was named Cubs' manager. One afternoon when the Cubs and Braves were locked in a tie, Rog inserted himself as a pinch-hitter for Rollie Hemsley and socked a game-winning, bases-loaded homer.

In the clubhouse, Bill Veeck Sr., Cubs' general manager, greeted him by saying, "You should not have put yourself on such a spot."

"I know I'm a better hitter than Hemsley," replied Hornsby, confident to the end.

In 1932, after Hornsby was replaced in mid-season as manager, the Cubs went on to win the flag under Charlie Grimm. The players demonstrated their feelings to their old boss by cutting him out of the World Series pool.

The Rajah neither drank nor smoked, nor understood players who did. He did not attend movies for fear of possible damage to his icy-blue eyes. His only acquaintance with a newspaper was to read the averages.

But he took kindly to outfielder Jim Rivera in 1952 when Rog managed the Browns. "Haven't you heard," asked Rivera, "movies stopped flickering long ago?"

Rog openly criticized Ted Williams for failure to hit to left field when opponents shifted to the right side. "He's not a great hitter," Hornsby reasoned.

In later years, when Hornsby scouted for the Mets, his evaluations were classics in brevity. On one report, he wrote "too fat." On another, "He didn't impress me." On a third, "Glasses."

For the many precautions that he exercised to guard his vision, it was ironic that Hornsby was in a Chicago hospital for removal of cataracts when a slight heart attack and a blood clot proved fatal in 1963.

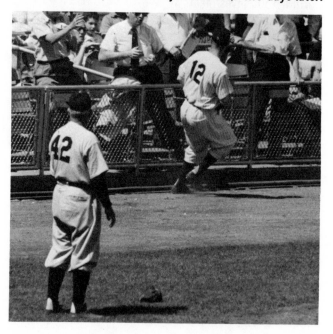

**Hornsby's best season was 1924 (above) when he hit .424. Hornsby (below, No. 42) was St. Louis Browns manager in 1952 when a controversial play occurred that might have cost him his job. Yankee Gil McDougald (12) missed connections with a foul pop (the ball is behind him), but the umpires ruled the batter out because of fan interference. Hornsby's mild reaction to the call angered Owner Bill Veeck, and The Rajah was fired two days later.**

# Waite Hoyt

The 15-year-old youngster had pitched batting practice for the Giants for a few weeks and had grown weary of the long, round-trip ride from his Brooklyn home. Fearlessly, he approached crusty John McGraw and explained the disadvantages under which he was working.

"Get this boy a contract," the New York manager told an aide. The youngster, Waite Hoyt, was dumbfounded. All he really wanted was a raise. When he and his father signed a contract the next day, the Giants slipped Waite $5 to seal the deal.

The teen-ager touched the fin briefly. Outside the Polo Grounds, his father said, "Five dollars is too much for you. I'll keep it."

Hoyt, who made one relief appearance for the Giants in 1918 after three seasons in the minors, wore a Red Sox uniform when he made his first major league start in 1919 against Ty Cobb, Harry Heilmann, Bobby Veach and company. Cobb, Detroit's third batter in the first inning, screamed imprecations at the youngster from the bench before he walked to the batter's box. Hoping to unnerve Hoyt, the Georgia Peach stood at the plate for 5 minutes, with his back to the mound.

When Cobb finally stepped in, Hoyt turned around on the mound and gave Cobb 5 minutes of his own medicine. Eventually, the two squared off and Hoyt, after running the count to 2-and-2, fanned Cobb on a changeup.

Hoyt proved particularly effective against Cobb throughout their American League careers. And he was in top form in World Series competition as well, winning six games for the Yankees.

Hoyt regarded his performance in the second game of the '21 Series as his superlative effort. The game was played at the Polo Grounds, where the Yankees were tenants of the Giants.

As Waite warmed up, he heard a raucous voice inquiring, "Is this the young punk who's gonna beat us?" It was Giants outfielder Ross Youngs talking to Frank Frisch.

Hoyt held the Giants to two hits in posting a 3-0 victory. Late in the game, his old benefactor, McGraw, tossed a piece of soap at Hoyt's feet as the pitcher walked by the dugout after grounding out.

Unshaken, Waite fired the soap back with considerable speed. The missle grazed McGraw's ear.

The son of a minstrel man, Hoyt mastered the act of self expression at an early age. He could be caustic or cute as the situation demanded.

He was at his best on an afternoon that produced a sharp exchange with umpire George Moriarty. In his last outburst at the umpire, Hoyt seethed, "You should be a traffic cop so you could stand in the middle of the street

**Waite Hoyt collected 19 victories in 1921, his first season with the Yankees.**

with a badge on your chest and insult people with impunity."

Waite, a 237-game winner in the majors, once sought a raise from Yankees Owner Jake Ruppert, whose wealth was estimated conservatively at $10 million.

"Can't do it," retorted the Colonel. "Ruth wants a raise, Meusel wants a raise. What do you fellows think I am, a millionaire?"

Once, while pitching as a National Leaguer at Wrigley Field late in his career, Hoyt was subjected to a savage riding from the Cubs' bench. It was after the Yankees had beaten the Cubs four straight in the 1932 World Series.

Hoyt tolerated the abuse for awhile, then silenced his hecklers by yelling, "If you don't shut up I'll put on my old Yankee uniform and scare you to death."

As a pal of Babe Ruth and an all-night reveler, Hoyt knew that the Bambino would have approved a remark made on a hot day when Waite and former teammate Joe Dugan stood by Babe's grave.

"I'd give anything for a cold beer," muttered Dugan.

"So would the Babe," said Hoyt.

# Cal Hubbard

To be a good umpire, Cal Hubbard once commented, it is necessary to maintain discipline and know the rules. He could have added that 265 pounds on a 6-foot-2½ frame also was desirable.

With such dimensions, the hulking Hubbard had little difficulty keeping order. Neither players nor managers saw fit to engage Cal in prolonged dispute, although Yogi Berra once went about as far as he dared.

For several innings, the Yankee catcher found fault with Hubbard's ball-and-strike decisions until Cal yanked off his mask and addressed his critic.

"There's just no sense in both of us umpiring this game," he told Berra. "The unfortunate part of the situation from your standpoint is that I'm being paid to stand behind the plate and umpire. You're not. You're only being paid to catch. One of us is obviously unnecessary and has to go. It breaks my heart to say so, but the guy who's gonna go is you."

"C'mon, Cal," screamed a suddenly contrite Yogi, "I'll be quiet, I promise." Hubbard let him stay.

Another catcher who got Cal's message was Mike Tresh of the White Sox. Hubbard lectured the carping catcher thusly: "If you don't shut up, I'm gonna hit you so hard on the top of your head it'll take a derrick to get you back to ground level."

Another catcher, Gene Desautels of the Red Sox, was responsible for Cal's most embarrassing moment. Desautels bickered frequently with Hubbard in spring exhibitions, but Cal held his temper, figuring his chance would come to crush the receiver.

In a regular-season game at Detroit, Desautels doubled. The next batter smashed a hard liner that second baseman Charley Gehringer caught with a spectacular leap. His throw to shortstop Billy Rogell arrived just as Desautels slid back into the base in a cloud of dust. "Yer out," shouted Cal as the runner came up beefing.

"So you want to give me trouble again," growled Hubbard. "Okay, I'll call it again. 'Yer out.'"

"But," yelled the runner, "I've got the ball."

A native of Missouri, Hubbard was a nationally known sports figure long before he became a major league um-

**Big Cal Hubbard is a two-sport Hall of Famer.**

pire. He was an outstanding football lineman at Centenary College under Bo McMillin. When Bo transferred to Geneva College in Beaver Falls, Pa., Cal followed. "I followed my heart," explained the big fellow.

At Geneva, Hubbard earned All-America honors while starring on a team that, among other achievements, upset Harvard.

Even then, Hubbard knew the rule book. "I've seen him hold up games three and four times while he corrected officials," recalled McMillin. "He knew more about rules than the officials because he spent more time studying them."

After leaving Geneva, Cal played two seasons with football's New York Giants and then was traded to Green Bay, where his size, strength and speed earned him all-league recognition.

While most pro players were earning $50 or $75 a game, Hubbard was drawing $175, and ultimately $200, as the highest-paid player in the National Football League.

Cal began his umpiring career while still in his prime as a football player. He began in the Piedmont League in 1928 and called 'em in the Southeastern and Sally leagues and the Western Association before joining the International League in 1931.

When he joined the A.L. in 1936, veteran arbiters said he was the best freshman umpire in league history. He had studied the baseball rules book as avidly as he had the football book.

Hubbard umpired in four All-Star Games and three World Series until he was forced to retire after the 1951 season. While Cal was hunting, a shotgun pellet ricocheted off a rock into his left eye. Blurred vision forced him to retire. He accepted a position as assistant to Tommy Connolly, supervisor of American League umpires. When Connolly stepped down in 1954, Cal stepped up. In turn, he yielded the post to Dick Butler in 1970.

When Hubbard was elected to the baseball Hall of Fame in 1976, it gave him the distinction of being the only man elected to the college and pro football and the baseball shrines.

Cal was 76 when he died of cancer on October 17, 1977, at St. Petersburg, Fla.

# Carl Hubbell

Dick Kinsella, a Giants scout, was an Illinois delegate to the Democratic national convention at Houston in 1928. One humid afternoon, when convention business dragged on endlessly, Kinsella forsook the political arena for the baseball arena and visited the local Texas League park where the Buffs were playing Beaumont.

The Beaumont pitcher, an angular lefthander, quickly drew the scout's attention. When Kinsella returned to his hotel, he telephoned New York and told John McGraw, "This afternoon I saw another Art Nehf. He beat Houston, 1-0, in extra innings."

The comparison to the Giants' lefthanded pitching star of earlier championship years was sufficient recommendation for McGraw, who bought Carl Hubbell for $30,000, a record price for a Texas League player.

Hubbell had been the property of the Detroit Tigers, but in two spring camps with the American League club he had pitched only one inning, in a "B" game against the University of Texas. When he was optioned to Beaumont, Carl told his manager that he would not return to Detroit. If he was not sold to another major league club, he would quit professional baseball and work for an oil firm that offered an opportunity for year-round employment and a chance to pitch for the company team.

The screwball that was to be his trademark with the Giants was not a part of Hubbell's repertoire in 1928. As Tiger property, he had experimented with the delivery and had attained proficiency with it before coach George McBride warned him of possible damage to his elbow.

Hubbell did not throw the pitch again until one afternoon while facing the Cardinals. With two runners on base and a count of 3-and-1 on righthanded slugger Chick Hafey, Carl's batterymate, Shanty Hogan, signaled for a fastball. "I threw a screwball," reported Hubbell, "and it fooled Hafey. Hogan called for another fastball and I threw another screwball and Hafey struck out."

"I don't know what that pitch was," Hogan said, "but keep throwing it."

From then on the screwball was Hub's bread-and-butter pitch, and Carl was the "Meal Ticket" of the Giants.

Control was one of Hubbell's major assets. In July of 1933, before 50,000 fans at the Polo Grounds, he defeated the Cardinals, 1-0, in 18 innings. In what amounted to two nine-inning shutouts, Hubbell did not walk a batter, struck out 12 and allowed only six hits. In his 16 years with the Giants, he averaged fewer than two bases on balls per nine innings.

The long shutout game was not his finest effort, contended Hub. Nor was his no-hitter against the Pirates in 1929, nor any of his 24 consecutive victories over a two-year period. It was a one-hitter against the Dodgers at Ebbets Field in 1940. The only Dodger hit was a single by

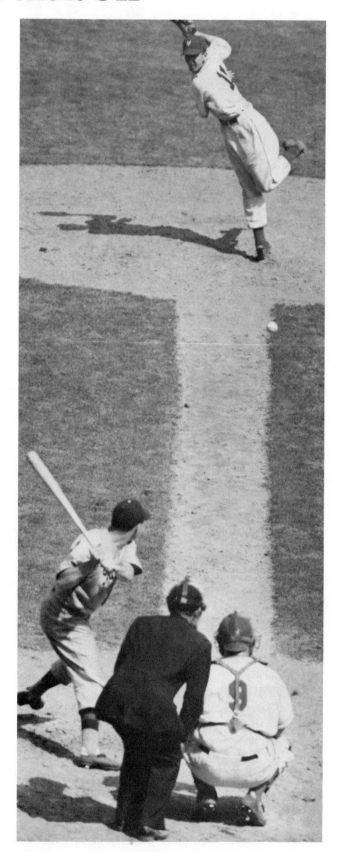

**After five seasons in the minors, Carl Hubbell brought his screwball to New York and dazzled N.L. hitters.**

In 1935, Hubbell won 23 games and was just one season away from his career-best 26-6 mark.

Hubbell gets a handshake and a gold watch from crosstown great Babe Ruth in 1930.

Johnny Hudson, who was retired on a double play.

"Control made that the most memorable game for me," said Hubbell. "Every pitch went just where I wanted it to go. I never had such control before or afterward. I can't explain it. I made only 81 pitches. I faced only 27 batters and only three balls were hit to the outfield."

In the 1933 World Series, King Carl pitched 20 innings without allowing an earned run. In the opening game, he struck out the first three batters—Buddy Myer, Goose Goslin and Heinie Manush—and beat the Washington Senators, 4-2. He won the fourth game, 2-1, in 11 innings. That same season he had hurled 46 consecutive shutout innings.

Carl launched his 24-game unbeaten streak with a 6-0 victory over the Pirates on July 17, 1936. It was the only shutout of his streak, which was snapped by the Dodgers, 10-3, on Memorial Day of 1937.

For all his glittering efforts in championship play, Hubbell always will be remembered best for his spectacular pitching in the second All-Star Game played at the Polo

Grounds in 1934. After the first two batters reached base, catcher Gabby Hartnett instructed Hubbell, "Just throw that 'thing.' It'll get 'em out. It always gets me out."

Carl followed orders, striking out Babe Ruth, Lou Gehrig and Jimmie Foxx to end the inning. Only Foxx made contact, hitting a harmless foul.

In the second inning, the Meal Ticket fanned Al Simmons and Joe Cronin, yielded a single to Bill Dickey and then struck out Lefty Gomez.

Throughout his 535 major league games, the two-time Most Valuable Player never forgot his manners. Veteran umpire Babe Pinelli recalled: "Only once did he complain and then I don't think the fans realized it. With the count 2-and-2 on the batter he threw a pitch he thought was a strike. I called it a ball and on the next pitch the batter hit a home run. As he walked by me at the end of the inning he said, 'Babe, I thought that third ball was a pretty good pitch.' I answered, 'Carl, I thought it was a little inside.' "

After retiring in 1943, Hubbell was named farm director of the Giants.

# Miller Huggins

The diminutive Miller Huggins, manager of the great Yankee teams of the 1920s, is flanked, and dwarfed, by his two great sluggers, Babe Ruth (left) and Lou Gehrig, during spring training in 1928.

At 5-foot-4 and 146 pounds, he had to be a scrapper. And he spent many of his 49 years proving he belonged and that he could hold his own among those who were better endowed physically.

Miller Huggins battled for an opportunity to gain a foothold as a major league second baseman, and succeeded admirably. He battled as manager of the Cardinals, fought an owner's prejudice against men who wore caps and fought the likes of Babe Ruth, Joe Dugan and Joe Bush to demonstrate his ability to manage the strong-willed Yankee players of the 1920s.

Hug, an excellent leadoff batter during his 13 years in the majors, was named successor to Roger Bresnahan as the Cardinals' manager in 1913 and led the club to two third-place finishes in five years.

All the while, American League President Ban Johnson was squirming in his Chicago swivel chair as the Yankees lagged in the second division. He was convinced that a strong New York franchise was necessary to take the play away from the solidly entrenched Giants.

On a visit to St. Louis, Johnson asked his friend, J.G. Taylor Spink, publisher of The Sporting News, to sound out Huggins. Would Hug be interested in managing the Yankees? The answer was affirmative. Miller was instructed to visit the Yankees' offices on his next visit to New York to negotiate with club President Jacob Ruppert.

After numerous delays, which included time to convince Ruppert that cap-wearing gentlemen could be managerial giants, Huggins was offered the job. But now he imposed a condition. He demanded that Bob Connery, the Cardinal scout who discovered Rogers Hornsby, accompany him to the Yankees.

Eventually, that issue was resolved and, in January of 1918, Little Hug was signed for the position that produced his greatest fame.

He won his first pennant in 1921 and followed with five in the next seven seasons.

A native of Cincinnati, Huggins graduated from the University of Cincinnati Law School. Although he was admitted to the bar, he never practiced law.

Huggins poses with big Frank Chance, manager of the Red Sox, during the 1923 season.

Despite his size, Huggins achieved respectability as a second baseman before becoming Cardinals manager in 1913.

While attending college, Miller played for Mansfield (Inter-State) under the name of Proctor and in the summer performed as a second baseman for the team that yeast king Julius Fleischmann ran for his own amusement in the Catskills. The catcher on the team was Red Dooin, later manager of the Phillies. A pitcher was Doc White, later an outstanding lefthander with the White Sox.

Still using the alias, Huggins played for St. Paul (Western Association) in 1901. After a successful season, he notified his father that baseball—not law—was to be his profession. Thereafter he played baseball under his legal name.

Miller joined the Reds in 1904 and scored 96 runs his first year before tallying a career-high 117 in his second season. A sore arm and batting slump limited Hug to 46 games in 1909, after which Manager Clark Griffith traded him to St. Louis.

In 1913, Schuyler P. Britton, owner of the Cardinals, named Huggins manager.

By the time Huggins led the Yankees to their first world championship in 1923, Ruppert had dropped his bias against caps. After saluting Ruth and all his teammates at the victory celebration, the Colonel declared: "And lastly, I give credit where credit is mostly due, to that great manager of a great team, little Hug."

Huggins finished in the second division only once as a Yankee skipper. In 1925, the year Ruth suffered his spring collapse and later was fined $5,000 after a run-in with Hug, the Yanks finished seventh.

The Yankees were running second to the Philadelphia A's in September of 1929 when Huggins arrived at Yankee Stadium for the last time. Instructing coach Art Fletcher to take over for him, Little Hug entered a hospital, where he died of crysipelas five days later. He was buried in his native Cincinnati.

At his death, Huggins was worth approximately $400,000. He frequently had advised players on investments. In his later years he and Connery owned the controlling interest in the St. Paul (American Association) club.

# Monte Irvin

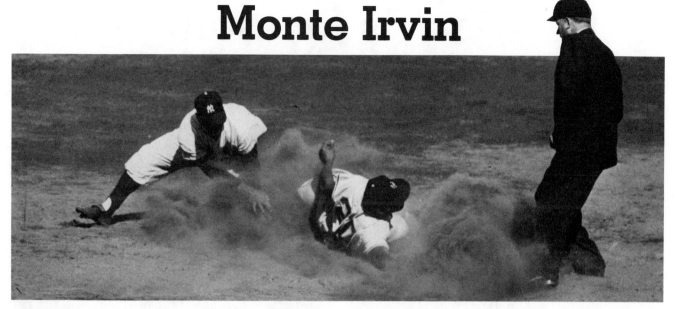

The outfielder for the Newark Eagles was dejected. It was 1948, and his contemporaries in the Negro National League were entering Organized Baseball while he was being ignored.

Jackie Robinson, the first modern black in the white man's game, was still at UCLA in the early 1940s when the Newark slugger batted .432 and hit 41 home runs. Those who knew the Eagles player and his accomplishments were as puzzled as he.

Eventually, said Monte Irvin, "I made up my mind to forget that they'd overlooked me. I was in good physical shape and saw no reason why I couldn't play my kind of ball."

Twenty-five years later, when Irvin was enshrined at Cooperstown, his former adversary, Roy Campanella, asserted, "Monte was the best all-round player I ever saw. As great as he was in 1951 (at age 32) when the Giants won the pennant, he was twice that good 10 years earlier in the Negro league."

Irvin almost became a Brooklyn teammate of Campanella. While playing in the Cuban Winter League, Monte was scouted by Fresco Thompson of the Dodgers and signed a St. Paul (American Association) contract.

When Mrs. Effa Manley, owner of the Eagles, reminded the Dodgers that the player was under contract to her team, the Dodgers offered to buy him for $2,500. The offer was rejected as inadequate. He was purchased by the Giants in 1949 on the recommendation of scout Hank DeBerry.

One of 10 children of an Alabama farm couple who moved north in the 1920s, Monte was a four-sport high school star in Orange, N.J., before he turned pro at 17. In the next decade, he estimated, he averaged .350 at bat. One year, he batted .397 and was named the Most Valuable Player in the Mexican League.

Irvin was in his first full season with the Giants when he sparked them to the 1951 pennant in "The Little Mira-

**Yankee shortstop Phil Rizzuto is late with the tag as the Giants' Monte Irvin steals second base during Game 2 of the 1951 World Series in Yankee Stadium.**

cle of Coogan's Bluff." When the Giants and Dodgers ended the 154-game race in a tie, Monte was encountered by a newsman.

"How ya feeling?" he was asked.

"I feel so good," came the reply, "that I've a mind to give a month's rent free to my neighbors if we lick Brooklyn."

Bobby Thomson's ninth-inning home run in the third playoff game took a sizable slice from Monte's paycheck, but during the World Series with the Yankees—after Irvin went 4-for-5 in the first game and 3-for-4 in the second— Monte found time to pose for a newspaper photo with his neighbors, who were cheering their benefactor.

Soft-spoken, modest Monte batted .458 in the Series and drove in two runs to go with the 121 that he amassed to lead the National League in the regular season.

Irvin was 33 when he went to training camp in 1952. As was their annual custom, the Giants barnstormed eastward with the Cleveland Indians. On April 2, the teams stopped at Denver for a game. In the second inning, Monte led off with a walk, then sped to third when Willie Mays lined a single to right-center field. The throw from the outfield went to second base, but Irvin slid needlessly into third and "something popped like a paper bag."

Irvin's spikes had caught in the dirt. His right ankle was fractured. Monte did not return to action until late July, but he rebounded in 1953 to bat .329.

He was still a solid man for the world champion Giants of 1954, but he was 35 at the time and retired after the '56 season (which he spent with the Cubs).

Monte accepted a position as a special assistant to Commissioner Bowie Kuhn. In 1973, his boss introduced him to the media as a new member of the Hall of Fame.

# Travis Jackson

John McGraw was enjoying the comforts of his Memphis hotel suite in 1922 when he received a visitor, Kid Elberfeld, who had been a shortstop for New York's American League club years earlier when Little Napoleon was winning pennants with the Giants.

McGraw was in Memphis because the Giants made an annual stopover there en route from their training camp in San Antonio to New York. Elberfeld was there to promote an 18-year-old shortstop performing for the Little Rock (Southern Association) club that he managed.

"You'd like him," said the Kid. "He's skinny with not much power at the plate just now, but he'll get better as he goes along. But he can hound the ball, and you never saw a shortstop with a better arm. Have somebody look at him. He should be ready for you after one more year in this league."

. "If anyone should know a shortstop, you should," McGraw replied. The reports that McGraw received from Dick Kinsella, his one-man scouting board, were as flattering as Elberfeld's and before the season was out Travis Jackson had played three games for the Giants.

Elberfeld saw Jackson for the first time when the native of Waldo, Ark., was 14 years old. Jackson's uncle, a Little Rock druggist and a friend of Elberfeld, introduced the youth to Kid. Four or five times a summer, Jackson visited Little Rock, where Elberfeld batted ground balls at him by the hour. "There wasn't anything about playing shortstop that Elberfeld didn't teach me," Jackson remembered. "And when I got to the Giants at 18, John McGraw never had a criticism of my fielding."

In June of 1923, Dave Bancroft, the Giants' regular shortstop, was stricken with pneumonia and missed nearly two months of the season. During his absence, Jackson filled in with a steady glove and an active bat that was good for a .275 average.

At the end of the season, Bancroft was traded to Boston, where he was appointed manager of the Braves.

"Who's gonna play shortstop next season, Jackson?" a reporter asked McGraw, who only smiled.

"Do you think that such a young fellow is ready for such a big job?"

"Do you think," replied McGraw, "that I would have let Bancroft go if I thought he wasn't ready?"

Throughout his career, Jackson was hindered by injury. At Little Rock, he collied with the center fielder while they were chasing a Texas Leaguer at full tilt. Both were knocked unconscious and were hospitalized. Jackson suffered a deep gash on his foreheaded. The center fielder lost an eye.

Early in his major league career, Jackson injured his knee while running the bases and was periodically handicapped thereafter. In 1932 and 1933, he appeared in

Travis Jackson (right) with Manager John McGraw in 1932, McGraw's last season with the Giants.

barely over 50 games each season, but a Memphis surgeon rebuilt his knee during the winter and Travis gave it a rugged workout the next spring. Cautioned by teammates, he responded, "If the knee holds up, fine; If not, I'll go back to Waldo."

The knee not only held up in 1934, but Jackson played 137 games, drove in 101 runs and was the starting shortstop in the All-Star Game at the Polo Grounds.

Jackson was named captain of the Giants in the spring of 1928 when he motored to Hot Springs, Ark., to see the batterymen work out in advance of the regulars. On arriving at the camp, Jax was greeted by McGraw's announcement: "From now on, you're captain of this club."

After concluding his career as a third baseman in the 1936 World Series, Jackson managed minor league clubs for many years and served at other times as a coach for the Giants. He retired from baseball after managing Davenport (Midwest) in 1960. "I just got tired of the bus rides," he explained.

When he was elected to the Hall of Fame in 1982, Jackson joined the three other members of the 1927 Giants' starting infield—Bill Terry, Fred Lindstrom and Hornsby.

# Hughey Jennings

A former breaker boy from the hard-coal mines of Pennsylvania, he was red-haired, freckled, smiling, cocky and tough, a candidate for immortality among the old Baltimore Orioles who terrorized the National League in the 1890s.

Hughey Jennings was so tough that he survived three skull fractures. But above all, Jennings was intelligent. He earned a law degree from Cornell, coached baseball at Cornell and Georgia and managed the Tigers to three consecutive pennants at a time when they were less intent on winning than they were on abusing a young firebrand named Ty Cobb.

The son of Scotch-Irish parentage, Jennings was a catcher for a semipro team in Lehighton, Pa., in 1890 when his 15 putouts, four assists and five hits in one game caught the eye of the manager of the Allentown club of the Eastern Interstate League. After 13 games, the league collapsed and Hughey rejoined Lehighton.

At Louisville the following season, Jennings started out as a first baseman, switched to third base on June 30 and to shortstop on July 4. He became a major leaguer in 1892 when Louisville entered the National League. Following a trade, he made his Oriole debut on Independence Day in 1893, after which he developed rapidly under the tutelage of Ned Hanlon.

After three pennants and one Temple Cup championship in the mid-1890s, Jennings, Hanlon, Willie Keeler and Joe Kelley transferred to the Brooklyn Superbas, who were under the same ownership as the Orioles, in 1899. The quartet formed the nucleus of the team that won pennants in 1899 and 1900.

After obtaining his law degree, Jennings retired from professional baseball for a short while. However, when the Phillies offered him the opportunity to captain their club in 1901, he jumped at the chance to return to the diamond.

Hughey was playing with Baltimore, now in the Eastern League, in 1906 when the Tigers sought to buy him. Hanlon demanded $5,000. Frank Navin, secretary of the

**"Ee-yah" was the battle cry of Hughey Jennings, whose greatest fame came as Tigers manager.**

Tigers, politely declined, then drafted Jennings for $1,000.

Jennings' foremost asset and most painful headache at Detroit was Cobb, then in his second full season. Driven by a fierce determination to succeed, Cobb engaged in clubhouse brawls almost daily. The Georgian was no boxer and bore numerous bruises and scars from his escapades. No matter how badly he had been beaten up the previous day, Cobb kept coming back for more until Jennings stepped in.

"This has gone far enough," Hughey told the Tiger veterans. "I'm convinced that the kid has as much guts as I thought he had. By this time he should have proved it to you. Now let him alone. He's not going to be driven off this club if I have to fire everybody else. The next guy who taunts him or lays a hand on him will have to answer to me."

The warning restored order, and with Jennings plucking grass from the coaching box and shouting his mysterious "Ee-yah" at his players, the Tigers won flags in 1907, '08 and '09. Each year, however, they were beaten in the World Series.

Jennings remained on the job until 1920 when he stepped down in favor of Cobb. He rejoined his old buddy, John McGraw, as a coach for the Giants and enjoyed four consecutive pennants all the more because of the light responsibilities that he carried.

In the winter of 1923, Hughey and his wife accompanied the McGraws on a tour of Europe, and a year later Jennings visited the continent as a member of the Giants-White Sox tour.

In 1925, when McGraw was taken ill, he turned the reins over to Hughey, who brought the club home in second place.

After the season, Jennings, a Scranton lawyer, suffered a nervous breakdown. He recovered in Asheville, N.C.

The old Oriole suffered an attack of spinal meningitis in January of 1928 and died the next month at age 57.

# Ban Johnson

The son of a Cincinnati educator, descended from old New England stock, Byron Bancroft Johnson was the premier organizer in baseball.

Johnson organized the American League, numbering among the foremost planks in his platform the elimination of rowdyism and staunch support of his umpires. Within a few years, he had built his circuit into such a powerful force that the National League was forced to recognize it and accept it as an equal.

Barely a quarter of a century later, Johnson locked his desk in his Chicago office and closed the door for the last time, broken in health and spirit and nearly blind.

Johnson was targeted early in life for the ministry, but that parental hope was abandoned when Ban rebelled against compulsory chapel attendance at Oberlin College and transferred to Marietta College. As a collegian, he was said to have been so outstanding a catcher that he was offered a contract by Cleveland of the National League.

Johnson graduated from the University of Cincinnati Law School and practiced the legal profession for a while. Inadequate compensation left him to forsake law in favor of a reporter's job with the Cincinnati Commercial-Gazette that paid $25 a week.

He advanced to city editor, but when the sports editor's job became available, he eagerly sought—and obtained—that position. Ban was serving in that capacity when Charles (Old Roman) Comiskey arrived in town to take over as manager of the Reds.

Johnson and Comiskey developed a close friendship, from which was born the Western League in 1894 and the American League a few years later.

Johnson, Comiskey and allies changed the league's name from Western to American in 1899, and operated as a minor circuit in 1900. The following year, with strong franchises in Chicago, Boston, Detroit, Philadelphia, Baltimore, Cleveland, Washington and Milwaukee, the league fathers announced they were ready to operate as a second major loop and would raid established N.L. clubs for playing talent.

Johnson was elected president for a 10-year term. With the club owners' approval, he barred the sale of liquor in ball parks. Profanity on the field was forbidden. Umpires were vested with total authority. And there was no $2,400 salary limit such as prevailed in the N.L. In that infant season of 1901, more than half of the new league's players were former National Leaguers.

By 1903, the N.L. was ready to sue for peace. Johnson helped to forge the National Agreement that brought the two leagues into harmony and provided for the National Commission, the ruling board that consisted of the two league presidents and Garry Herrmann, president of the Cincinnati Reds.

Ban Johnson was the prime force behind the organization and success of the American League.

With the transfer of the Milwaukee franchise to St. Louis in 1902 and the Baltimore franchise to New York in 1903, Johnson's organization flourished instantly. With the lure of former N.L. stars and the advent of young players such as Ty Cobb, the league not only attained equality but superiority.

But success took its toll on the Johnson-Comiskey friendship. The old drinking cronies who had organized the league in a room off the bar-lounge in the Fisher Building drifted apart for reasons never fully explained.

The estrangement deepened with the Black Sox scandal of 1919. Comiskey accused Johnson of negligence in not canceling the World Series after the first two games aroused suspicions of a fix.

The election of Judge K.M. Landis as the first commissioner terminated the National Commission and eliminated much of Johnson's traditional power. Ban started to quarrel with club owners. He rejected a suggestion by Clark Griffith of Washington and Jake Ruppert of New York that he take a leave of absence. But, on October 17, 1927, the rugged individualist, accompanied by a coterie of newsmen, walked from the Fisher Building for the last time.

Johnson retired with his wife to Spencer, Ind., and died of diabetes in St. Louis at age 67.

# Walter Johnson

The different looks of Walter Johnson: During his third season with the Senators (left), before his fastball began taking its toll on A.L. hitters; with catcher Gabby Street (above right) in 1917 when the righthander won 23 games, and late in his career (right), when he was closing in on 400 victories.

In the summer of 1908, the Washington Senators arrived in New York for a series with the Highlanders at Hilltop Park.

The visitors were among the weakest teams in the league and would finish seventh, 22½ games behind the pennant-winning Tigers.

But the Senators did have one magnificent asset, a 6-foot-1, 200-pound righthander from Coffeyville, Kan., who had been discovered a year earlier in an Idaho semi-pro league.

On Friday, the 20-year-old pitched a four-hit shutout. The next day astonished spectators watched him hurl a three-hit shutout. Because Sunday baseball had not been legalized in New York, the next game was played Monday. The script was changed only slightly, as the phenom charged to the pitching mound again and blanked the home club on a two-hitter.

Joe Cantillon, Washington manager, was tipped off to Walter Johnson in 1907. A friend in Idaho wrote to Pongo

Joe extolling the talents of the pitcher who neither smoked nor drank, but threw a blinding fastball.

The Senators had no scouts, but Cantillon had an injured catcher-first baseman, Cliff Blankenship, who could serve in that capacity.

Cantillon instructed Blankenship to go to Wichita and check on a swift young outfielder, Clyde Milan, later a Senators star.

"And while you're out there," Cantillon added, "you might as well run up to Idaho and see about that young pitcher."

Blankenship recommended the acquisition of both players. Before Johnson signed, however, he made one stipulation. If he failed to make the grade, the Senators would have to pay his transportation back to Idaho. The condition was met immediately.

Johnson won five games for the Nats in his first season, including the first two shutouts of his record total of 110. The youngster pitched a five-hitter in his debut on August

Johnson, who had just shut out the Pirates in Game 4 of the 1925 World Series, gets a handshake from brother

Leslie (left). Before he was finished, Johnson had struck out 3,508 major league hitters.

2, but lost to the Tigers, 3-2.

Before long, Johnson was christened "Big Train" and opponents stood awestruck at the plate as his fastball shot past.

Ping Bodie of New York, a good fastball hitter, stood motionless as three pitches rocketed through the strike zone.

"You can't hit what you can't see," he moaned.

In his 21 major league seasons, the Big Train suffered only one sore arm, yet, curiously, it was during that time that he pitched his only no-hitter, against the Red Sox in 1920.

On at least two occasions, Johnson fanned the side on nine pitches with the bases loaded. He performed the feat against Ty Cobb, Sam Crawford and Bobby Veach of Detroit and Tris Speaker, Chick Gandil and Elmer Smith of Cleveland.

They were just six of his 3,508 major league strikeouts, all for Washington.

In 1913, Johnson hurled 55⅔ consecutive scoreless

innings, a record that stood until Don Drysdale of the Dodgers surpassed it in 1968. Johnson's streak would have ended 20 innings earlier except that Tris Speaker was struck by a batted ball for the third out of the inning.

Annually, Johnson pitched the season opener at Griffith Stadium. In 14 inaugurals, most of them before the President of the United States, he won nine times, seven of them by shutouts.

After 18 major league seasons, Johnson pitched in his first World Series in 1924. Walter lost two games in the Series and won one, but the victory came in the seventh and deciding contest. He pitched the final four innings of the Senators' 12-inning, 4-3 triumph over the Giants.

The Big Train defeated the Pirates twice in the 1925 Series, but lost the seventh game.

After managerial stops at Newark (International), Washington and Cleveland, Johnson retired to his 550-acre farm near Germantown, Md. A stroke, caused by a brain tumor, paralyzed his left side in April of 1946, eight months before his death at age 59.

**Willie Mays**

Casey Stengel

Sandy Koufax

Warren Spahn

Frank Robinson

Juan Marichal

Al Kaline

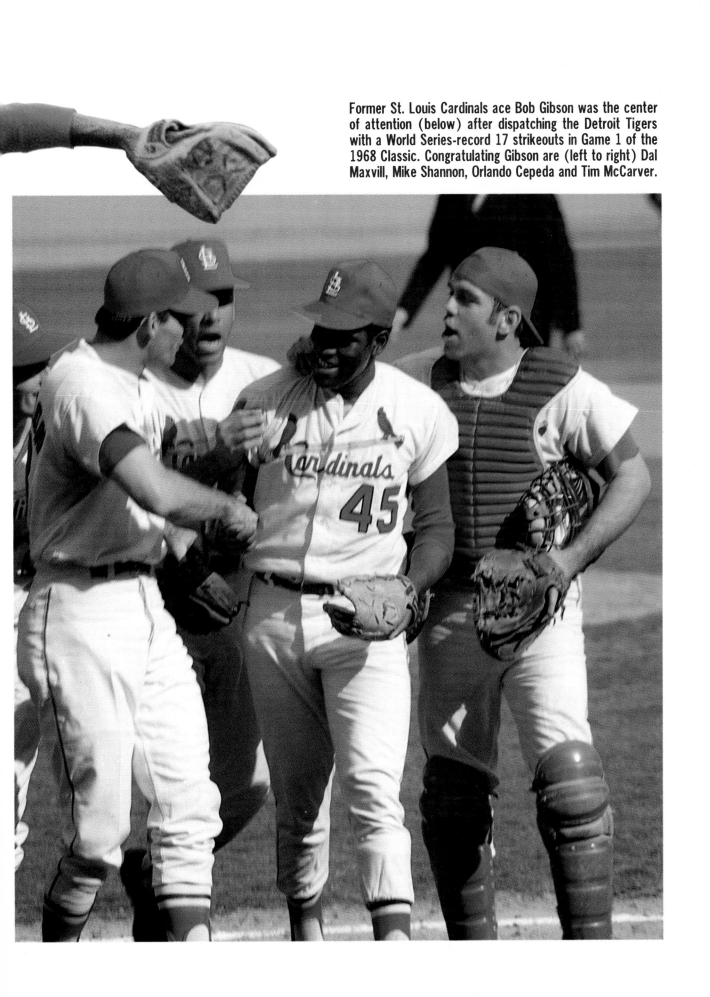

Former St. Louis Cardinals ace Bob Gibson was the center of attention (below) after dispatching the Detroit Tigers with a World Series-record 17 strikeouts in Game 1 of the 1968 Classic. Congratulating Gibson are (left to right) Dal Maxvill, Mike Shannon, Orlando Cepeda and Tim McCarver.

Brooks Robinson

rnie Banks

Mickey Mantle

Hank Aaron

Whitey Ford

**Roberto Clemente**

# William (Judy) Johnson

Connie Mack observed the black third baseman for several years, dreaming of what he might mean to the fortunes of the Philadelphia Athletics.

Asked for his opinion of the extraordinary fielder, .350 hitter and fleet runner, Mack replied, "If Judy Johnson was white, he could name his own price."

Johnson, son of a seaman who moved his family from Snow Hill, Md., to Wilmington, Del., in the early 1900s, was known as Billy in his younger years. He was in his early 20s when teammates started to call him Judy because, they said, he resembled Judy Gans, a veteran player.

The elder Johnson had hoped that his son would develop into a boxer. When Billy was 8, his father bought him a pair of boxing gloves, and a second pair for his 12-year-old sister, Mary Emma, the neighborhood tomboy.

Obediently, Billy went along with his dad's program until he grew tired of his sister's thrashings and turned to less strenuous activities.

Billy performed for integrated baseball and football teams in Wilmington. At Howard High School, however, there was no sports program, so Billy terminated his formal education after his freshman year and took a job on a loading dock in Deepwater Point, N.J. He returned home after World War I and caught on with the Chester Giants in Pennsylvania. His pay was $5 a game, plus transportation.

Johnson then performed for the Bacharach Giants, still for $5 a game, but by 1920 he was with the Philadelphia All-Stars.

In 1921 he was sold to the Hilldale team, a powerful Philadelphia club, for $100. Suddenly, Judy was enjoying the affluence of $100 a month.

At this point in Judy's career, according to veteran observer Cool Papa Bell, Johnson "was the best hitter among the four top third basemen in Negro baseball. Although someone else might hit as high as Judy, no one would drive in as many clutch runs as he. He was a solid player, real smart, and the kind of player who would get the job done. He was dependable, quiet, not flashy at all, but could handle anything that came up.

"And above all, he was a gentleman on and off the field. Oh, nobody could push him around, but his quiet, easy, down-to-business manner made him a standout as a player and as a man."

Johnson was a key figure for the Hilldale club that participated in the first Negro World Series in 1924. He led all hitters in that series with a .341 mark.

The following year, although suffering a fractured arm while playing shortstop, Johnson batted .392, which he believed was his all-time high.

Judy joined the Homestead Grays as player-manager in 1929, receiving $500 a month, his top baseball salary.

**By 1925, Judy Johnson was among the best third basemen in Negro league history.**

Two years later, he joined the Darby Daisies, formerly the Hilldale team, and then moved again in 1932, becoming player-manager of the powerful Pittsburgh Crawfords and a teammate of Satchel Paige, Josh Gibson and Cool Papa Bell.

Johnson led the Crawfords to the league title in 1935 and the second-half championship in 1936.

Judy retired from the playing field after the 1937 season and took a job as a supervisor with the Continental Can Company in Wilmington. In 1940, he and his brother opened a general store, but a few years later Judy returned to Continental Can, where he remained until 1951 when he joined the Philadelphia A's as an instructor and scout. One of his major assignments was to ease the entry of Bob Trice and Vic Power, young blacks, into the majors. As a scout, Judy recommended the purchase of Hank Aaron from the Indianapolis Clowns for $3,500, but the financially strapped A's vetoed the suggestion.

When John Quinn, general manager of the Milwaukee Braves, switched to the Phillies in 1959, Johnson joined him and helped with the acquisition of Richie Allen.

In 1973, Judy retired to his home in Marshallton, Del.

# Addie Joss

To many, it was the most extraordinary game ever pitched, better than the Vaughn-Toney double no-hitter, better than the Oeschger-Cadore marathon.

What made the game of October 2, 1908, extra special was that it was pitched in the heat of a pennant race. The Cleveland Naps and the Chicago White Sox were in frenzied pursuit of the Detroit Tigers in a race that would go to the Bengals by a half-game over Cleveland and 1½ games over Chicago.

Addie Joss was seeking his 24th victory for Cleveland, Ed Walsh his 41st for the visiting Chicago team. Walsh already had hurled more than 400 innings for the Sox.

In the third inning, the Naps solved Walsh for a run. Joe Birmingham singled, went to second on a delayed steal and took third when the throw struck him on the shoulder and bounced away. A wild pitch permitted him to score.

Birmingham's single was one of four hits yielded by Walsh, who struck out 15. On this day it was Big Ed's misfortune to hook up with a pitcher who was letter perfect. Only four balls were hit to the outfield.

Joss received some sparkling help from Nap Lajoie at second base. The Frenchman raced behind the mound on several occasions to field slow-hopping balls and throw out the batter.

Pat Dougherty, leading off the eighth inning, accounted for the only hard-hit ball against Addie. The ball was a ground smash toward right field, but graceful, gliding Lajoie gloved the ball and threw out the runner.

In the seventh inning, Fielder Jones of Chicago worked the count to 3-and-2. As the next pitch crossed the plate, Jones dropped his bat and started toward first base. Umpire Tom Connolly, however, called the pitch strike three.

Jones sent in three pinch-hitters in the ninth inning in an effort to break Joss' spell. The first was retired on a grounder to Lajoie, the second on strikes. At that point, one reporter noted, "A mouse working his way along the grandstand floor would have sounded like a shovel scraping over concrete."

The third pinch-hitter was big John Anderson, powerful but slow afoot. Anderson lined the first pitch to left field, where the ball curved foul at the last instant. On the second pitch, Anderson hit a smash over third base, but Bill Bradley, who had no previous chances, collared the ball and fired toward first. The throw was low, but George Stovall scooped it up and umpire Silk O'Loughlin waved the batter out on a bang-bang play to complete the perfect game.

Joss was discovered while pitching for Toledo (Western Association) in 1901 and made his major league debut in St. Louis on April 26, 1902. He was superb on that date, too, holding the Browns to one hit in a 3-0 victory.

The only safety was a single by Jesse Burkett on a drive

**Addie Joss is pictured in 1910, his final season before dying at age 31.**

that the right fielder insisted he caught. Umpire Bob Caruthers ruled otherwise.

On June 12, 1903, Joss engaged Rube Waddell in another masterful performance. The Philadelphia lefthander edged Joss, 2-1, in a 14-inning thriller reeled off in 2 hours, 10 minutes.

Joss, a former University of Wisconsin athlete, attained the 20-victory mark in four consecutive seasons, starting in 1905. He hurled a second no-hitter, also against the White Sox, on April 20, 1910, but there were a few flaws in the performance. He issued two bases on balls and one batter reached base on an error. Only five balls were hit to the outfield.

After slipping to 14-13 and 5-5 records in 1909 and 1910, Joss reported to training camp in 1911. During an exhibition game at Chattanooga, Tenn., he fainted on the bench, but dismissed the incident as insignificant after treatment at a local hospital. He maintained that he had only "pulled a baby trick."

When the team reached Cincinnati, Joss was taken ill. Doctors diagnosed his ailment as pleurisy and ordered him to his home in Toledo. On April 14, two days after the Naps opened the season in St. Louis, Joss died of tubercular meningitis. He was 31.

The funeral, at which evangelist Billy Sunday preached, was said to be the largest in Toledo history. Among the mourners were all of Joss' teammates.

# Al Kaline

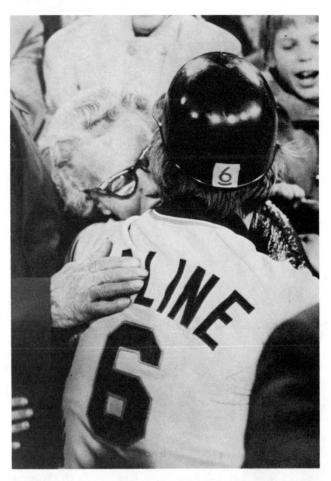

In 1955, 20-year-old Al Kaline (left) became the young-est player ever to win a batting championship. Nineteen years later, Kaline received a big hug from his mother after rapping out hit No. 3,000.

When the skinny youngster, obviously ill at ease, stepped into the batting cage and hit a few pitches weakly past the infield, veteran Detroit players looked quizzically at one another as if to say, "Is this the kind of kid they're giving $30,000 bonuses these days?"

Manager Fred Hutchinson, however, had no reserva-tions about 18-year-old Al Kaline, who was just out of Southern High School in Baltimore. "He'll be all right," said Hutch. "He has fine wrist action."

Ed Katalinas' scouting report was much more exciting. Among the points he emphasized were: "Showed outstand-ing arm, has good speed, excellent body control, is the best player I ever scouted."

Kaline was groomed by his father for a professional baseball career. At 14, he played on an iron and metal company team that competed against clubs whose pitch-ers had minor league experience. "As a result," Kaline said, "I learned to hit the curve and change of pace."

In three seasons of high school competition, Al batted

.353, .418 and .469.

Kaline would have preferred to sign with the Washing-ton Senators, but they did not reciprocate his affection. He could have opted for the Yankees, but chose the Tigers because of Katalinas' four-year interest in him and be-cause the Bengals were in a youth program that had already snatched Harvey Kuenn and Billy Hoeft.

Kaline made his major league debut on June 25, 1953, one day after joining the Tigers. He relieved center fielder Jim Delsing in the eighth inning of a game at Philadelphia and flied to center field on the first pitch from Harry Byrd in the ninth inning.

Al recorded his first hit on July 8. It was a single off Luis Aloma at Chicago. His initial home run was hit on September 26. It was a ninth-inning bases-empty clout off Dave Hoskins in a 12-3 Tiger loss at Cleveland.

When Steve Souchock suffered a fractured wrist while playing winter ball in Cuba and was unable to start in right field the next spring, Hutchinson gave the job to Kaline.

**The strong bat and golden glove made Kaline (pictured in 1972 above and 1973 right) one of the best all-round players during his 22 seasons with the Tigers.**

Spurred by a couple of nine-game batting streaks, Kaline's average shot above the .300 mark in early May. However, a pulled thigh muscle and water on the knee that resulted from a collision with the outfield wall restricted Al to 138 games and contributed to his season-ending .276 batting average.

During the season Hutchinson introduced Kaline to Ted Williams and asked the Red Sox slugger to give the youngster some batting tips. Williams stressed exercises to develop shoulders and arms and suggested that Kaline swing a bat daily through the winter to accelerate his wrist action.

Kaline put the advice to quick advantage. He reported to spring training with 20 more pounds, up to 175, and staged one of his lustiest hitting exhibitions at Briggs Stadium on April 17, 1955. Al lashed four hits in five at-bats, including three homers, two in one inning. It marked the first time that an American Leaguer had homered twice in one inning since Joe DiMaggio in 1936. Only two other American League batters had ever accomplished the feat, Ken Williams of St. Louis in 1922 and Bill Regan of Boston in 1928.

Throughout the season, Kaline demonstrated increased power. From one homer as a rookie and four the next year, he exploded for 27 in '55. Only three A.L. players had more.

Kaline's emergence as a hitter led Casey Stengel to exclaim: "That feller has picked up five years of experience in two."

Al collected 200 hits in 1955, but more important, he won the league batting championship with a .340 average. He was only 20 years old, the youngest batting king in history.

Kaline became the 12th player to register 3,000 career hits on September 24, 1974. The milestone hit was a double down the right-field line against Dave McNally in Baltimore. Al was the first American Leaguer to attain that plateau since Eddie Collins of Chicago in June of 1925, nearly half a century earlier.

Kaline's final safety, on October 1, 1974, was a single off Jim Palmer of Baltimore that gave the Tiger star 3,007 career hits.

# Tim Keefe

Buck Ewing had no idea when he yanked his starting pitcher on July 16, 1888, that he would create a 20th Century controversy.

His strategy was perfectly sound. New York held a 9-0 lead in the second inning and Ewing's best hurler was on the mound for the Giants. Why not switch the pitcher with the right fielder, a part-time hurler, and save the starter for another day since the game was virtually won anyway?

Tim Keefe, the starter, had won eight consecutive games previously and he would win 10 straight after July 16. By 20th Century scoring rules, a pitcher must work at least five innings to receive credit for a victory. There was no such provision in the code of the 1880s, so Keefe was awarded the July 16 victory over the Chicago White Stockings for an overall 19 consecutive triumphs.

Almost from the time that Rube Marquard won 19 consecutive games for the Giants in 1912, there has been a question as to whether he tied Keefe's mark or set a record. Most authorities give Keefe credit for 19 straight inasmuch as he achieved the mark under existing rules.

Chicago snapped Tim's streak on August 14. A Polo Grounds crowd of 10,000 watched the White Stockings score two unearned runs in the fifth inning and pull out a 4-2 decision.

The next day a correspondent wrote: "After 19 victories, Keefe officiated in a losing game."

Keefe, the son of Irish immigrants, grew up in Cambridge, Mass. His father, Patrick, was a builder who was working in the South at the outbreak of the Civil War. Rather than serve in the Confederate Army, Patrick spent three years in prison manufacturing bullets for the Rebels. Two of Patrick's brothers were killed fighting for the Union.

When he returned home, Patrick found his son, then 9 years old, already deeply interested in baseball. Despite parental objections, Tim continued to pitch, firing his fastball and curve and pioneering in the development of a change of pace.

At 29, Keefe was a mainstay of the New York staff, teaming with Smiling Mickey Welch to form one of the most potent mound duos of the day.

The righthander was a quiet, gentle man off the field who, at the peak of his career, studied shorthand so he would have a skill if his arm should fail him.

In 1887, Tim missed several weeks of the season as the result of a nervous breakdown, suffered after one of his fastballs struck Boston second baseman John Burdock on the temple.

But Keefe came back strong the next year, which he climaxed by winning four games in a postseason series as the Giants defeated the St. Louis Browns of the American Association.

**Tim Keefe was a pioneer in the use of a change of pace to complement his fastball and curve.**

Keefe, who had held out for $2,100 when he was with Troy some years earlier, demanded $4,500 after his 1888 performance and got it. He was the highest-salaried Giant, followed by pitcher Ed Crane at $3,800 and first baseman Roger Connor at $3,500.

After closing his pitching career with the Phillies in 1893, Keefe applied to N.L. President Nick Young for a job as an umpire. He was hired, but his term was brief. The man who never complained about an umpire's decision as a player made a few unpopular calls in a game at the Polo Grounds, scene of his greatest triumphs. Branded a thief and a robber, Keefe was bombarded with dust and pebbles as he was escorted to safety by gendarmes. That night he telegraphed is resignation to league headquarters.

Keefe returned to Cambridge where he became a real-estate man. He also coached baseball at Harvard, Tufts and Princeton and attended games at Fenway Park and Braves Field on the average of once a week.

After Keefe died at age 76, Welch declared, "I never saw a pitcher better than Keefe. It is true that he did his greatest work at the old distance of 50 feet. But if he had been a modern pitcher at 60 feet, 6 inches, he would have had no superior. He was a master strategist who knew the weakness of every batter in the league. I'd put him in the class of Hoss Radbourn and John Clarkson."

# Willie Keeler

On opening day of the 1897 season, the diminutive Baltimore outfielder lashed a single and double in five at-bats against Boston. The two hits set a pattern that was to endure for nearly two months, from April 22 through June 18. In 44 consecutive games, Willie Keeler hit safely at least once. For 44 years the old Oriole held the major league record—until Joe DiMaggio broke it in 1941.

Willie was stopped by Pittsburgh lefthander Frank Killen, after Keeler had registered one four-hit game, eight three-hit games, 19 two-hit contests and 16 in which he was held to a single safety.

The son of a Brooklyn trolley switchman, Keeler broke into professional ball with Binghamton of the Eastern League in 1892. Although a lefthanded thrower, Willie made his debut at shortstop. He handled eight of nine chances afield and contributed a single in three tries.

Late that season, Keeler was purchased by the New York Giants and made his debut at the Polo Grounds on September

**Willie Keeler is best remembered for his 44-game hitting streak that was a record for 44 years.**

30 as a third baseman. His single off Tim Keefe of the Phillies was the first of nearly 3,000 hits he would collect during his illustrious career.

Willie fractured his ankle early the next season and was sold to Brooklyn for $800 by Manager John Montgomery Ward, who maintained that the 5-foot-4½ sprite was incapable of withstanding big-league punishment.

Before the 1894 season, Keeler and first baseman Dan Brouthers were traded to Baltimore, where Ned Hanlon converted Willie into an outfielder. With his natural speed and reliable glove, Willie was in his element in right field, but it was as a batter that he gained his greatest distinction.

With Keeler batting first and John McGraw second, the Orioles became proficient in the hit-and-run play. And they perfected the "Baltimore chop," the slick maneuver in which batters drove the ball into the ground and then sprinted to first base as infielders waited helplessly for the high bounder to descend.

Bat control was Willie's specialty. If infielders played deep, he would bunt for a single. If they played shallow, he would loop the ball over their head. He was so dexterous that when he was asked the secret of his success, he replied, "Keep your eye clear and hit 'em where they ain't." Ever after, batters attempted to imitate his "hit 'em where they ain't" style.

Wee Willie also scampered wildly on the bases. He stole 30 in 1894, raised his total to 57 the next season and 73 in '96. Attempting to lead the Orioles to a fourth consecutive flag in 1897 (the Orioles finished two games back), Keeler batted .432, second only to Hugh Duffy's record .438, and stole 63 bases. His 243 hits were a record until Ty Cobb topped the mark in 1911 with 248. Keeler won another batting title in 1898 with an average of .379, then moved to Brooklyn with his manager, Ned Hanlon, and a few teammates for the 1899 season.

Willie played on championship clubs in Brooklyn in 1899 and 1900, giving him the distinction of performing for five pennant winners and two runners-up in his first seven years as a regular.

When American League clubs raided the N.L. in 1901 and '02, Willie remained loyal to the senior league. However, Frank Farrell and Bill Devery, owners of the New York A.L. club, made Willie an offer he could not refuse prior to the 1903 campaign. Limited for years by the N.L.'s $2,400 salary ceiling, Keeler jumped to the Highlanders and became baseball's first $10,000 player.

When Clark Griffith resigned as manager of the Highlanders in the 1908 season, the owners wanted to offer the job to Keeler. Willie got wind of the plan, however, and went into hiding.

Keeler was a pinch-hitter for the Giants under old pal McGraw in 1910, coached for the Brooklyn Federal League team in 1914 and scouted for the Boston Braves in '15.

He was 50 when death came in a lonely shack in Brooklyn on New Year's Day, 1923.

# George Kell

Andy High, a scout for the Brooklyn Dodgers, took the stocky, sandy-haired kid aside one day in the early 1940s and said, "You'll never be a major leaguer until you know the disappointment of being released by some club."

Larry MacPhail, majordomo of the Dodgers, was even more negative. "Get rid of him," snapped MacPhail after watching the kid struggle at third base. "He'll never be a ballplayer."

The player was set to take a construction job at an attractive salary when his new wife stepped in and said, "Don't quit."

The advice kept George Kell on the baseball trail. Cut loose as a Brooklyn farmhand, he applied for a job with the Lancaster club of the Inter-State League.

"Can you play second base?" asked Manager Tom Oliver.

"Sure," replied Kell with more confidence than honesty.

"You're on," said Oliver in the spring of 1942. Kell did not impress at second base, or shortstop, or the outfield, but an injury to the Red Roses' third baseman created a vacancy that George filled handsomely. By the end of the 1943 season, Kell was a member of the Philadelphia A's. His .396 average for Lancaster that year was the highest in Organized Ball.

Connie Mack scouted George personally. "How would you like to come to Philadelphia?" he asked Kell.

The native of Swifton, Ark., answered in the affirmative. But he was with the A's only a short while when Mack cautioned him, and coach Al Simmons concurred, "You'll never be a major league hitter."

After his earlier discouragements, not even Mack's opinion could deflate Kell. Through courage, concentration and persistence, George developed not only into an All-Star third baseman but a Hall of Famer as well.

One factor in Kell's ascent to the majors that Mack ignored was that he was jumping from Class B, and even though he made the leap during World War II, it still was a big climb. In 1946, Mack traded George to Detroit. The deal, Connie acknowledged later, was a mistake.

Kell suffered from weak knees throughout his career. As a toddler, he would pitch headlong for no apparent reason. After playing a doubleheader for Lancaster, he found that his knees would not support his weight and

**Slick-fielding third baseman George Kell compiled nine .300-plus seasons.**

wife Charlene spent long hours massaging his knees with hot water to relieve the pain that prevented sleep.

Despite his handicap, Kell was surprisingly agile on the basepaths and drove pitchers to distraction with false starts off the bag.

He also was a mystery to pitchers while in the batters' box, changing positions as often as four times in one at-bat. By noting the alignment of the fielders and using one of the lightest bats in the game, George learned to drive the ball to open areas.

In 1949, the Tiger third baseman—who, according to Mack, would never be a good hitter—won the American League batting championship on the final day of the season. With one game to go, Kell trailed Boston's Ted Williams by three points. A phone call from Charlene in Arkansas inspired him.

"Two hits today will win it for you," said his wife. "Get 'em."

A double and a single in three at-bats raised Kell's average to .3429. Williams, hitless, finished at .3428.

George learned how to play in pain. In May of 1948 at Yankee Stadium, he threw up his hand to deflect a Vic Raschi fastball hurtling toward his head. The sound of breaking bone—Kell's wrist was fractured—was heard in the bullpen, and doctors predicted a long recuperation for George. In 10 days, though, he was back throwing—accurately, but with intense pain.

In August of the same year, again in New York, a savage drive off the bat of Joe DiMaggio struck a pebble and smashed into Kell's jaw. Instinctively, George groped for the ball, picked it up and stepped on the base for a forceout. He then staggered to the dugout, where he collapsed in the arms of the trainer. Having suffered a jaw fracture, Kell missed the rest of the season.

Although only 35, Kell retired after the 1957 season and was hired by CBS to conduct pregame interviews on Game of the Week telecasts. In 1959, the off-season high school teacher in Swifton joined the Detroit broadcasting team as a replacement for the late Mel Ott.

George resigned his $50,000-a-year job after the 1963 season. He was quitting, Kell said, to be with his wife, son and daughter in Swifton. However, after only a year away from the game, Kell was lured back to Detroit in 1965 as a telecaster for weekend games.

# Joe Kelley

The left fielder for Ned Hanlon's fabled Baltimore Orioles of the 1890s was a mite different from most left fielders. In fact, he was unlike any other major leaguer.

The dissimilarity stemmed from a mirror that the outfielder carried with him at all times. Between pitches, it was not unusual for Joe Kelley to withdraw the mirror from his pocket and preen himself in full view of the customers.

But the spectactors loved Kelley. He had a rare personal magnetism, and he could inspire the fans to heights of emotion with his behavior on the diamond.

One afternoon, Kelley stirred the fans and players to paroxysms of laughter. It had been his habit to hide a baseball in the tall outfield grass to be used when the proper moment presented itself.

On this particular day, he chased a drive in the alley, picked up the ball and fired it to the infield at the same time that center fielder Steve Brodie snatched the hidden ball and threw it to a baseman. That ended the outfielder's "hidden ball" trick.

A native of Cambridge, Mass., Kelley entertained a youthful dream of pitching for the powerful Boston club of the National League. At 19, he signed with Lowell of the New England League as a pitcher. He performed satisfactorily, too, winning 10 of 13 decisions. But he also played the outfield and batted .331. In addition, he stole 21 bases in 57 games. Such everyday talent was not to be wasted on the pitching mound. Thereafter, Joe was a full-time outfielder.

During the 1891 season, Kelley wore Boston and Pittsburgh uniforms for a total of 14 games. However, at the start of the 1892 campaign he was with Omaha (Western), where he played so well that he was sold to Pittsburgh in June. In September, he was traded to Baltimore for George Van Haltren and played 10 games before the end of the season.

Under the influence of Hanlon, Kelley became a polished player quickly. Regularly each morning when the Orioles were at home, Kelley and Hanlon reported to the park, where the manager worked on the player's bunting and baserunning. In 1893, Joe batted over .300 for the first of 12 consecutive seasons.

In 1894, when the Orioles completed their two-year

**By 1908, Joe Kelley was nearing the end of a career that produced 2,245 hits.**

leap from last place in the 12-team National League to first, Kelley swiped 45 bases and batted .391.

On September 3, Kelley performed a feat unequalled before or since. He went 9-for-9 in a doubleheader. In the opener, he rapped three singles and a triple. He blasted four doubles and a single in the nightcap.

During his heyday with the Orioles, Kelley spent the off-season as superintendent of a drayage business in Baltimore. On the same day that teammate Hughey Jennings took a bride, Kelley married Margaret Mahon, daughter of James Mahon, part-owner of the Orioles and a leading politician in Maryland.

Joe accompanied Hanlon and several teammates to Brooklyn in 1899 and, as team captain, batted .330 in the first of two pennant-winning seasons.

Kelley jumped to the American League in 1902, returning to Baltimore where his old crony, John McGraw, was now manager. In midseason, however, McGraw went to New York to pilot the Giants and Kelley, with Mike Donlin and Cy Seymour, defected to Cincinnati. Two weeks later, Kelley was named manager of the Reds. His 33-26 record in his first managerial effort helped the team finish fourth.

Joe managed the Reds through 1905, but stayed on as a player in 1906 when his old skipper, Hanlon, replaced him as a pilot.

A stint as manager at Toronto followed and in 1908 Kelley was back in Boston as skipper of the N.L. club. Differences with catcher Frank Bowerman and Owner George Dovey led to Joe's dismissal.

Kelley managed Toronto for six more years and then scouted for the Yankees in 1915-16. As a ivory hunter, Kelley earned the thanks of the club's frugal co-owner, Colonel Til Huston, for not recommending the purchase of a single player in an entire season. His negative reports saved the club $150,000.

When Kelley quit scouting, he took a job with the Maryland Racing Commission. His last baseball connection was as a coach with Brooklyn in 1926.

The last survivor of the old Orioles had been ill for a year when death came in 1943 in his adopted city of Baltimore.

# High Pockets Kelly

The tall, righthanded first baseman never could understand why John McGraw demonstrated uncommon patience with him. The 19-year-old kid out of San Francisco went hitless in his first 19 at-bats for the Giants, and often was a strikeout victim.

One journalist wrote that he would retire when the youngster got a hit "because there was nothing more to see."

After a slow start, first baseman George Kelly won the hearts of skeptical New York Giants fans.

But McGraw never wavered on George Kelly. His confidence in the player may have stemmed from the fact that the youth was the nephew of Bill (Little Eva) Lange, a star outfielder with the Chicago Colts of the 1890s. Or maybe it was because scout Dick Kinsella had filed a favorable report on the kid. What McGraw didn't know was that Kinsella fell asleep in a Victoria, B.C., hotel room and didn't see the player before sending in a report based entirely on hearsay.

The long drought ended for Kelly on his 20th trip to the plate. He connected with a fastball in St. Louis and smacked a triple. In any other park, it was said, it would have been a home run.

High Pockets Kelly became the Giants' regular first baseman in 1920, and there were distressful overtones to that move.

Since Kelly had succeeded Hal Chase, one of the most graceful of all first basemen, the most myopic spectators could spot the difference and were quick to let Kelly know of his inadequacies.

McGraw took the 6-foot-3 Kelly aside.

"Don't listen to what they yell or what you read in the papers," he counseled. "I put you in there because I thought you could do the job. Stick in there and soon those people who are yelling will be cheering you."

By the spring of 1921, Kelly had found himself as a major league hitter. When he socked seven homers in April, New York newspapers printed daily comparisons between Kelly and Babe Ruth, who had clouted a record 54 homers for the Yankees in 1920.

The comparisons were not published long. Ruth went on to hit 59 homers; Kelly finished with 23 (but led the N.L. that season).

George drove in 122 runs during the '21 season, four coming on an August afternoon at the Polo Grounds. The Pirates arrived in New York with a 7½-game lead and were in high spirits as they opened a five-game series against the second-place club.

Pittsburgh led by three runs in the seventh inning when the Giants loaded the bases against Babe Adams. In previous trips to the plate, Kelly had been baffled by Adams' curveball and as he batted with the bases loaded, he received three straight "take" signs from McGraw. The three curves broke out of the strike zone.

On a 3-and-0 count, Kelly was given the hit sign. Startled by the unlikely development, Kelly looked again. The sign still indicated hit, and when Adams laid a fastball across the middle of the plate, Kelly hammered it into the stands for a grand-slam.

McGraw, smug over his correct call, announced in the clubhouse, "If my brains hold out, we'll win this thing." The brains did and the Giants did.

Constantly that year, McGraw had challenged Kelly to "pull a good play." The chance to muzzle Little Napoleon came in the ninth inning of the last World Series game. With Aaron Ward of the Yankees on first base with one out, Frank Baker slashed a grounder toward right field. Second baseman Johnny Rawlings made a spectacular stop and throw to nip Baker, but Ward—confident the ball would go through—turned second and raced for third, only to be cut down on Kelly's bullet throw to Frank Frisch. The Series was over and so was McGraw's needling about "pulling a good play."

Kelly enjoyed his biggest day as a major league batter at Wrigley Field in September of 1923, hitting a single, double and three home runs.

In 1924, Kelly divided his time between first base and the outfield so that Bill Terry could add lefthanded power to the lineup. George also filled in at second base before he was traded to Cincinnati in 1927. He was acquired by the Cubs to help out in their unsuccessful pennant bid in 1930, and concluded his major league career with Brooklyn in 1932 after playing with Minneapolis.

George toured Japan with major league all-stars in 1931 and '34. He coached the Reds and Braves, managed Wenatchee to a last-place finish in the Western International League and also coached at Oakland where, among other things, he taught Billy Martin how to throw accurately to first base.

# Mike Kelly

There was nobody quite like Michael Joseph (King) Kelly, an intelligent, handsome, mustachioed Irishman from Troy, N.Y.

"King Kel," 5-foot-10½, 185-pounder, could surpass any man going from base to base or bar to bar.

He could drink any two men under the table, arise from his perch and with top hat cocked at a rakish angle, welcome the morning sun.

Kelly also could play baseball in a singular style. He could score six runs in a game (as he did while playing for Boston against Pittsburgh on August 27, 1887), and he could steal six bases in a game (as he did for Boston of the Players League against Cleveland on May 19, 1890).

In the days of the one-umpire system, Mike was not above scoring from second base without benefit of tagging third. What the umpire did not see he could not call.

When a batter lifted a pop foul beyond the reach of the catcher and first baseman, Kelly jumped out of the dugout, shouted, "Kelly now catching for Boston," and made the grab barehanded. No rule said it couldn't be done.

Another time, he duped Jesse Burkett into a putout at the plate. With the St. Louis star on third base, the batter grounded to the shortstop, whose throw to first arrived too late to retire the hitter. Seeing Burkett approach the plate, catcher Kelly dropped his mitt and Burkett slowed down, convinced the third out had been made at first base. However, in a flash, Kelly caught the throw from the first baseman barehanded and tagged out an astonished Burkett.

Kelly was a multi-position player, but it was as a catcher that he became "The $10,000 Beauty" when, in 1887, he was traded by Chicago to Boston for that unheard of sum.

Kelly paid immediate dividends for his new team. In his first five games he made more hits, scored more runs and stole more bases than the rest of the team. The famous cry of "Slide, Kelly, slide" rang loud and often across the Boston Commons.

In Chicago, meanwhile, fans mourned the absence of their favorite. The White Stockings were virtually boycotted except on days when Boston was in town, when the fans thronged the park to cheer for the visitors and hiss the home club.

The King, who earned $3 a week as a paper mill laborer in Paterson, N.J., in his early years, earned $4,000 a season from 1887 through 1889. He supplemented that income with off-season stage appearances, once touring one of the major circuits with Billy Jerome, a leading parodist of the era.

The King also was an author.

He wrote a book, "Play Ball," which sold for 25 cents and was dedicated to the players and fans of America.

**King Kelly was as colorful both on and off the field as anybody in baseball.**

If Kelly had a weakness, it was in "stepping on himself." Chicago journalist O.P. Caylor wrote: "His only fault was a seemingly lasting weakness to fall down without any terrestrial cause, and often while actually waiting to catch a ball, his feet seemed to go into a panic and throw him."

Once Kelly eagerly wagered $100 on himself in a foot race with a notorious slowpoke. Mike took an early lead, then sprawled ignominiously on the ground as his adversary lumbered on to victory. "I knew he couldn't run that far without falling at least once," said the smiling winner.

Kelly's lifetime desire to play for a New York team was realized in 1893 when he was 35. He was just a shadow of the athlete that Cap Anson once called "as great a hitter as anyone and as great a thrower, both from the catcher's position and the field, more men being thrown out by him than any other man."

Mike played a handful of games for the Giants, then drifted to the minors.

Kelly opened a saloon in New York with umpire John Kelly (no relation) and then received a call to appear in the Palace Theater in Boston. En route by boat, he contracted a cold that developed into pneumonia.

As Kelly was being carried into a Boston Hospital, the litter bearers stumbled and he slid to the floor. "That's my last slide," cracked the once-great base stealer, who died at age 36 on November 8, 1894.

# Ralph Kiner

Ralph Kiner, a nine-year slugger in the National League, hits his first American League home run in April of 1955 as a member of the Cleveland Indians. It was the first of 18 in his final season.

As a rookie in 1946, the handsome youngster from Alhambra, Calif., led the National League in home runs with 23. There was no question that his future was assured, but it would be even more luminous if he could reduce his strikeouts.

The cure arrived on January 8, 1947, when the Pirates acquired Hank Greenberg, former American League home run king, from Detroit. Greenberg asked to room with the muscular mauler, thereby affording endless hours for teacher-pupil discussions that paid off at the ball park.

Ralph Kiner listened intently as Greenberg imparted the knowledge gained from years of major league experience. Gradually, a finished ballplayer emerged. At season's end, the sophomore slugger had tied Johnny Mize of the Giants for the majors' home run championship at 51.

Greenberg not only impressed on Kiner the value of sleep as a success factor, but discussed at length on the science of hitting. He suggested that Ralph spread his feet, stand closer to the plate and, above all, relax.

"In 1946," Kiner explained, "I was afraid that when the pitcher got two strikes on me, the next pitch would come at me. I'd bite at the pitch and strike out. With Hank's coaching, I learned to swing only when the ball was over the plate."

Before long, Kiner clouted 15 homers with the count of two strikes.

In his youth, Kiner performed for a West Coast team known as the Yankee Juniors, and it was generally assumed that he was headed for the South Bronx. New York scouts dallied however, and Pittsburgh scout Hollis Thurston beat them to the prize. Thurston delivered Kiner to the Pirates for a $3,000 bonus and a $5,000 salary.

Ralph was 17 in the spring of 1940 when Pirates Manager Frank Frisch inserted him as a pinch-hitter against the White Sox in an exhibition game at Pasadena, Calif. The prodigy blasted a 450-foot homer off Bill Dietrich, one of Chicago's better pitchers.

Kiner performed for Albany (Eastern) and Toronto (International) before enlisting in the Navy in 1943. He was a patrol bomber pilot, "but never got into action, never even saw a whale."

Ralph was ticketed for Hollywood (Pacific Coast) in

1946, but his 13 preseason homers and a batting average of well over .400 convinced the Pirates that Kiner deserved a varsity berth.

For the first six weeks of the N.L. season, he struggled badly, batting under .100. Once he found the range, however, home runs followed and his batting average climbed near .250.

Ralph exploded in 1947. He clouted home runs on four consecutive trips to the plate. He slugged five in two games, six in three and seven in four.

In his first four seasons, Kiner clouted 168 homers, more than any previous big-league hitter.

The handsome, wealthy bachelor became the first citizen of Pittsburgh. Groupies virtually demolished his convertible in their uncontrolled adulation. He received 1,000 letters a week.

"He's the franchise," acknowledged General Manager Roy Hamey.

The Pirates were a mediocre team at the time, but fans were loyal, at least until Kiner had his last at-bat of the game, after which they swarmed toward the exits.

Tales of his prodigious accomplishments sprouted around him. One afternoon the Pirates trailed the Cubs, 12-9, in the eighth inning. Kiner, with a temperature of 103, was on the rubbing table in the trainer's room when the call came, asking if he was in condition to pinch-hit. Weak and trembling, he managed to get to the plate and hit a game-winning grand slam.

At Boston, he powered a homer that knocked the neon tubing off the new scoreboard, nearly 500 feet distant.

Kiner captured the fourth of his seven successive (outright or shared) home run titles in 1949 with 54, two short of Hack Wilson's N.L. record.

By 1952, Kiner's big bat had earned the respect of the Giants (above), who employed a shift during a game at the Polo Grounds. The Pirate slugger gets a handshake from Stan Musial (below) after hitting a ninth-inning homer to send the 1950 All-Star Game into extra innings.

After brief terms with the Cubs and Indians, Kiner retired in 1955 and served as general manager of the San Diego (Pacific Coast) Padres.

In 1961, the articulate former slugger joined the White Sox broadcasting team. A year later he was behind the microphones for the New York Mets.

# Chuck Klein

Chuck Klein, Philadelphia Phillies slugger, watches the flight of the ball along with Boston catcher Rick Ferrell during action in baseball's first All-Star Game at Chicago's Comiskey Park in 1933.

One year he was working in an Indianapolis steel mill, stripped to the waist and catching white-hot ingots through an eight-hour shift with no time off for lunch.

Four years later, Chuck Klein was the Most Valuable Player in the National League, the toast of Philadelphia and recognized as the premier slugger in the N.L.

Klein, an Indiana farm boy, was playing for the Keystones Athletic Club in Indianapolis when a Prohibition agent spotted him and recommended Chuck to the owner of the Evansville club in the Three-I League.

Klein stayed with the team through the 13-day training period, but was released on opening day with the managerial admonition: "Kid, you can't time the ball right. You hit too many fouls."

Later, however, a player shortage won Klein a second chance with Evansville. He played only 14 games the remainder of the 1927 season, the result of a leg fracture suffered while sliding into second base. That winter he was sold to Fort Wayne (Central) for $200.

The 1928 season was barely half over when Burt Shotton arrived in Fort Wayne to evaluate the young slugger who had hit 26 home runs and was batting around .330.

The Phillies' manager needed only one glimpse of Klein, who propelled a 400-foot homer. The Phils bought Klein for $7,500.

Barely an hour after alighting from the train, Chuck reported to Baker Bowl, where the Phillies were playing the Cardinals. He was greeted by Shotton, who informed the rookie, "You'll room with Pinky Whitney (third baseman). Now suit up."

Klein rode the bench until late in the game. Shotton then sent him up as a pinch-hitter for pitcher Augie Walsh, and Chuck popped out to infielder Wattie Holm. But the Phils won the 16-inning contest, 7-6. The date was July 30, 1928.

The next day Klein was installed as the regular right fielder, replacing 40-year-old Cy Williams. To mark the occasion, Klein socked a double and single off Grover Cleveland Alexander, but Old Pete won handily.

The Hoosier Hammerer turned on a full burst of power in 1929 when he belted 43 home runs, an N.L. record. The final clout, which bounced off the right-field foul pole, was

Klein and Phillies teammate Lefty O'Doul take some time away from the batting cage to pose during the 1930 season.

Klein, who played in his only World Series as a member of the Cubs in 1935, scored the tying run (right) on Augie Galan's ninth-inning fly ball during Game 3 against Detroit.

off Carl Hubbell of the Giants.

After being named the No. 1 N.L. player by The Sporting News in 1931 and 1932, Klein enjoyed a Triple Crown season in 1933 when he drove in 120 runs, hit 28 homers and batted .368.

Chuck, who played the outfield in the first two All-Star games, was sold by the financially strapped Phils to the Cubs after the 1933 season and was with the Bruins when they unleashed their 21-game winning streak that clinched the 1935 pennant.

Klein rode the bench for the majority of those victories. However, when outfielder Fred Lindstrom injured an ankle in the World Series against Detroit, Chuck returned to action and batted .333 with a home run among his four hits.

Subsequently, Klein was traded back to the Phillies, then went to the Pirates. A third stint with the Phils—which lasted five seasons—rounded out his career.

Chuck staged the loudest hitting show of his 17 years in the majors in 1936 when he hit four home runs for the Phils in a 10-inning game at Pittsburgh, two off Jim Weav-er and two off Mace Brown.

In his later years, when it was suggested he had amassed impressive statistics because of the favorable dimensions of Baker Bowl with its high wall only 280 feet from the plate, Chuck rebutted: "Those four home runs weren't hit at Baker Bowl. And while I did get some homers on high flies over the fence, I also lost a lot because line drives that would have cleared the fence in other parks ricocheted off the wall at Baker Bowl."

After retiring as a Phillies coach in 1945, Klein briefly operated a tavern in Philadelphia. An unhappy marriage led him back to Indianapolis. Due to excessive drinking and malnutrition, he suffered from a disease that affected his central nervous system and left one leg partially paralyzed.

The last game he was known to have attended was at Cincinnati in the late 1940s. Chuck spent the evening reminiscing with veteran writers.

Klein was washing his hands after working in the yard in March of 1958 when he was fatally stricken by a cerebral hemorrhage. He was 52.

# Bill Klem

In 1904, a young American Association umpire was officiating a game by himself and receiving a steady verbal abuse from a rowdy outfielder.

The umpire had just called a runner safe at second base and was returning to his position behind the plate when, out of the corner of his eye, he saw the bully running toward him. By this time the umpire was at the batters' box, where he calmly drew a line in the dirt with his spikes, turned his back on the player and walked away.

**When discussion centers on good umpires, past or present, the name Bill Klem always is mentioned first.**

Recognizing the mark as his "dead line," the outfielder drew up quickly and retreated.

The line that Bill Klem drew as a minor league umpire became his trademark and proved effective against the National League's saltiest characters.

Klem was a native of Rochester, N.Y., as was Silk O'Loughlin, an American League umpire who gave young Bill a letter of introduction to President Jim O'Rourke of the Connecticut State League. Orator Jim, former National League outfielder, also was owner, manager and catcher of the Bridgeport club.

In the heat of one game, Klem ejected the Bridgeport shortstop, bringing a torrent of abuse from O'Rourke. "You'll never umpire another game in this league," he shouted.

"Maybe so," said Bill soothingly, "but I'll umpire this one."

Klem joined the National League staff in 1905 and called 'em for 37 years, after which he became chief of staff for the final 10 years of his life.

By common agreement, managers, players, writers and executives rated Bill the best umpire in the N.L. Klem's vote made the decision unanimous.

The scoreboard at the Polo Grounds in Klem's early years was partly in fair territory, partly in foul. The right-field foul line started at the base of the wall, leaped over the scoreboard and then continued upward. One day a New York batter bounced a long drive off the board that Bill ruled foul, bringing an enraged John McGraw from the dugout.

Entering the park the next day, Klem was met by the groundskeeper who told him, "Mr. McGraw asked me to check where that ball hit yesterday. And would you believe it, I could tell by the dent in the board that it was three inches foul."

"Naturally," replied Bill. "I've never missed one in my life."

The legend that was born on that spot was softened years later when the Old Arbitrator elaborated, "I never missed one in my heart."

Klem umpired in 18 World Series, and from 1908 to 1918 he missed only two fall classics. In the 1934 Series, Detroit outfielder Goose Goslin made the mistake of calling Klem "Catfish," the one name that Klem despised.

The next day a contrite Goslin sought to apologize to Bill in a Detroit hotel elevator, but the umpire would not let him off that easily. Calling on all his purple prose, Klem berated Goslin in the packed elevator and then doggedly pursued him through the lobby—shouting invectives all the while.

When word of the incident reached Commissioner K.M. Landis, Klem was fined $50. The money was deducted from Bill's Series check.

Maintaining that he was innocent of any wrongdoing, Klem returned the check. Landis sent it back, and for nearly a year the pair played their little game until Klem cashed the check.

While working a Chicago series, Klem visited Landis' office. As he was about to leave, the commissioner remarked, "I understand you play the horses." Most baseball personalities would have trembled and melted in the face of the Judge's withering gaze, but not the Old Arbitrator.

Approaching the Judge's desk, he declared, "Yes, sir, for 35 years . . . and I've always paid 100 cents on the dollar." The subject was never broached again.

Because of the Series incident and his admission that he wagered on the ponies, Klem did not receive a Series assignment from 1935 through 1939. In 1940, though, N.L. President Ford Frick interceded with Landis, asking that Bill be allowed to work the Detroit-Cincinnati classic as a fitting climax to his illustrious career. The request was granted.

Klem made his home in Miami where, after a month's hospitalization, he died in 1951 of a heart ailment at age 77.

# Sandy Koufax

**By 1965, Koufax was dominant and on his way to a shutout over Minnesota in Game 7 of the World Series.**

How great he might have been—and what records he might have established—had not an arthritic elbow intervened will remain a subject of speculation for decades.

He was only 30, had won 27 games and led the National League in earned-run average for the fifth consecutive season when he called a press conference and revealed that he had decided to retire rather than risk permanent damage to the arm that had made him one of baseball's all-time pitching masters.

Sandy Koufax could have accepted another fat contract from the Dodgers and made some token appearances. But, as a man of principle, he informed the world that his brilliant career was at an end. The 1966 announcement produced shock waves throughout baseball, for even though his elbow ailment was common knowledge, Koufax had pitched in pain for several years and was expected to continue in the same manner until his fastball no longer left a blue trail and his curveball no longer snapped.

"The arm is more important than any amount of money," Sandy explained.

Koufax was born Sanford Braun, but took his stepfather's name when his mother remarried following a divorce. He earned a baseball scholarship to the University of Cincinnati, where his talents drew the attention of major league scouts.

As a native of Brooklyn, Sandy would have been a

**As a second-year Dodger in 1956, Sandy Koufax was far from the dominant pitcher of later years.**

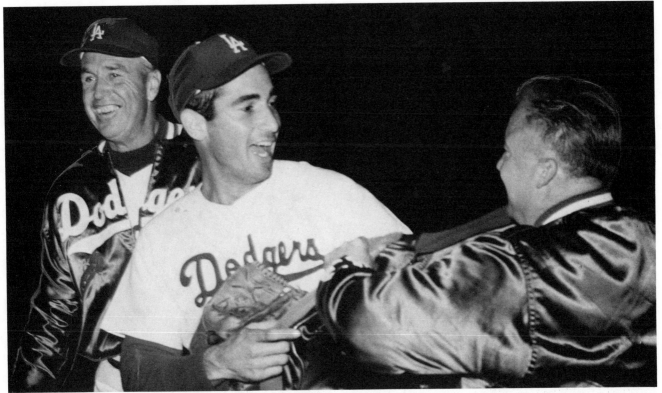

**Koufax is greeted by Manager Walter Alston (left) and trainer Wayne Anderson after throwing his second career** **no-hitter, an 8-0 victory over San Francisco, on May 11, 1963.**

natural as a gate attraction for any of the three major league clubs in Greater New York at the time. He worked out at the Polo Grounds, but, he said, "nobody seemed to care, so I left."

The Yankees displayed interest, but backed away when the youngster asked for a bonus. "I felt," Sandy said, "that if I was going to leave college and give up my scholarship to play ball, then I needed money so that if I decided to return to college, I could pay my way."

The Dodgers agreed to the bonus, signing Koufax in 1955 and paying him $14,000. As Sandy left the Dodger office, a Pittsburgh scout met him and revealed that Pirates General Manager Branch Rickey would top any offer by $5,000. Sandy had not signed a contract, but he rejected the offer. He even declined when the proposal was raised by $10,000.

Success was slow in arriving for Koufax. Wildness was a constant companion. According to pitching coach Joe Becker, the kid with the powerful shoulders "needed a loose wrist to get snap in the ball at the point of release, not more muscular tension that he was already creating. But it was hard to get that point across."

After six seasons, Koufax's record was 36-40.

Sandy's turn toward greatness occurred at an unlikely time in an unexpected place. He was with the "B" squad heading out of Vero Beach, Fla., for an exhibition game in

the spring of 1961 when catcher Norm Sherry, said, "Why not have some fun today? Don't try to throw so hard and use more curves and change-ups."

The seed took root. In the next six seasons, Koufax won 129 games and lost only 47. He pitched four no-hitters, including a perfect game. He became the first pitcher to strike out 300 batters in three seasons, achieving a record 382 in 1965, and he twice struck out 18 in one game.

The traumatic arthritis that terminated Koufax's career was discovered in 1964 when, after falling on his elbow while making a pickoff throw to second base, Sandy found his elbow so badly swelled that he could neither straighten his arm nor bend it beyond the hooked position it had taken.

"I had to drag my arm out of bed like a log," Koufax reported. "I could actually hear liquid squishing round in my elbow, like there was a sponge in it."

Sandy made his final pitching appearance in the second game of the 1966 World Series, yielding six hits and four runs in six innings against the Orioles, who swept the Dodgers in four games.

Exceedingly poised and articulate, Sandy accepted a 10-year contract, at a reported $100,000 a year, to broadcast Saturday games for NBC. He fulfilled six years of the contract, then retired to the privacy he had treasured throughout his public life.

# Nap Lajoie

The crunching bat of Cleveland's Nap Lajoie produced 3,252 hits in a marvelous career.

Because the 1910 batting race was so close, both Ty Cobb and Lajoie received the traditional Chalmers car.

From the time he stepped down off his hack in Woonsocket, R.I., to sign his first contract, Napoleon Lajoie was the epitome of grace on a baseball diamond. To him, every play was easy, whether he glided to his left or right, or raced in to make a pickup and throw on a slow, tricky ground ball.

At bat, the big Frenchman swung with crunching force and any third baseman who played shallow in anticipation of a bunt was inviting disfigurement from a blistering smash off the righthanded hitter's bat.

Lajoie did not insist on a pitch being over the plate. Once, on a hit-and-run play, he threw his bat at the ball and singled into right field.

Nap was with Fall River of the New England League in 1896 when a Phillies scout arrived in town to check on outfielder Phil Geier. When the Phils offered $1,500 for Geier, Manager Charles Marston was so smitten by their generosity that he tossed Lajoie into the deal.

Marston's gesture indicates he was unaware of the prize property he was discarding, but the manager wasn't alone. Boston player Tommy McCarthy, sent by Manager Frank Selee to pass judgment on Lajoie, offered this report: "He'll never learn to hit."

Lajoie remained a Phil until 1901, when the promise of a salary far in excess of the National League's $2,400

In 1912, Cleveland fans presented the popular Lajoie with a giant horseshoe festooned with more than 1,000 silver dollars.

limit lured Larry to the Athletics of the new American League. He promptly batted .422, which stands as the record A.L. average and ranks second in the modern majors only to Rogers Hornsby's .424.

For a number of years, record books based Larry's .422 mark on 220 hits in 543 at-bats. When an eagle-eyed mathematician notified the record keepers that the numbers figured out to .405, the average was revised without regard to the hits or at-bats. Further research revealed that a typesetter in the early century had set "220" instead of "229," so another change was authorized restoring Lajoie's missing 17 points.

The Phils sued for the return of their star second baseman, and the State Supreme Court ruled that Lajoie could not play for any Pennsylvania team other than the Phillies.

As a consequence, the Athletics traded Lajoie to Cleveland midway through the 1902 season.

Larry was appointed manager of the Cleveland club in 1905. In his honor, the team was called the "Naps," a name it retained until Lajoie departed in 1915 (when Cleveland became the Indians).

Lajoie was a participant in one of the hottest and most controversial batting races in history in 1910. Several days before the end of the season, Ty Cobb left the Detroit Tigers, confident that his average was high enough to win the championship. He did not figure on Lajoie going 8-for-8 in the final day's doubleheader at St. Louis.

Seven of Nap's hits were bunts, dropped in front of rookie third baseman Red Corriden, who had been told to "play deep" rather than run the risk of being maimed.

Because Lajoie was popular among his peers and Cobb was fiercely disliked, A.L. President Ban Johnson suspected collusion between Cleveland and St. Louis. But an investigation, in which umpire Billy Evans defended the Browns, cleared everybody's good name. Even with his final flourish, Lajoie just barely lost the batting title.

One of Larry's proudest moments occurred in 1912 when Cleveland fans presented him with a giant horseshoe festooned with more than 1,000 silver dollars. Earlier, he had been awarded a Chalmers car by the manufacturer after his near-miss batting race with Cobb.

Lajoie collected his 3,000th lifetime hit against the Yankees in 1914. Two years later, he closed his big-league career with a triple, hit No. 3,252.

Larry managed Toronto and Indianapolis before retiring to Daytona Beach, Fla., where he died of pneumonia in 1959 at age 83.

# Kenesaw Mountain Landis

Baseball's first commissioner, Judge Kenesaw Mountain Landis, acted quickly and with authority.

In the 1934 World Series, Cardinal left fielder Joe Medwick was showered with debris by irate Tiger fans. Landis

In the 1920s, Will Rogers entertained audiences with his own account of how baseball came to name Kenesaw Mountain Landis as its first commissioner.

"The game needed a touch of class and distinction," drawled the Oklahoma philosopher, "and somebody said, 'Get that old guy who sits behind first base all the time. He's out here everyday anyway.'

"So," concluded Will, "they offered him a season pass and he grabbed at it."

It was true that Landis was a frequent spectator at Cubs and White Sox games and had been a baseball fan since his early years in Logansport, Ind. And he was not unknown at the time. In 1907, the federal judge had fined the Standard Oil Company $29 million in a freight rebate case.

Landis accepted an offer of $50,000 to become the commissioner of baseball, replacing the three-man National Commission that had governed the game for years. He served from 1921 to 1944.

A native of Millville, O., Landis was the son of Abraham Landis, a Union Army surgeon who had lost a leg at the Battle of Kenesaw Mountain in Georgia. For unknown reasons, the parents dropped an "n" in their son's name.

Dropping out of high school after two years, Landis dreamed of becoming a railroad brakeman. But when the Vandalia and Southern rejected his application, Kenesaw turned his attention to bicycle riding and gained a reputation for speed at the Indiana county fairs.

He operated a roller rink with a conspicuous lack of success and eventually mastered shorthand and took a job in the South Bend, Ind., courthouse where he decided on a law career. Landis attended the Cincinnati Law School before earning his degree at Union Law School (later called Northwestern University).

In 1905, President Theodore Roosevelt appointed Landis a United States Judge for the Northern District of Illinois. During World War I, Landis imprisoned 94 members of the International Workers of the World. Weeks later, his office was bombed, but he was absent at the time.

Landis violently opposed gambling, horse racing and baseball officials who attempted to operate on the fringe of baseball law. His first decision as commissioner freed Phil Todt, a young first baseman who, Landis contended, had been "covered up" for two years by Branch Rickey of the Cardinals. Todt later signed with the St. Louis Browns.

conferred (above) with Medwick (center) and Manager Frank Frisch and had Medwick removed from the game.

Landis (above) officially opens the 1928 World Series between St. Louis and the Yankees at Yankee Stadium.

Functioning in an era when the game was trying to recover from the Black Sox scandal, Landis banned pitcher Phil Douglas of the Giants for suggesting that he go AWOL so another club could win the pennant.

Jimmy O'Connell, a Giants outfielder, and coach Cozy Dolan were similarly banished for life for telling Phillies shortstop Heinie Sand, "It will be worth $500 to you if you don't bear down too hard against us today."

Babe Ruth and Bob Meusel of the Yankees were suspended for 40 days at the start of a season for defying the Judge's edict against barnstorming tours the preceding fall, and Landis fined Bill Klem a substantial amount when the veteran umpire loudly and profanely berated a player in the elevator and lobby of a Detroit hotel during the 1934 World Series.

In that same Cardinal-Tiger classic, Landis removed St. Louis outfielder Joe Medwick from the seventh game "for his own safety." Medwick had been the target of fruit showers from the left-field bleacherites after a spiking incident at third base.

Landis was an implacable opponent of the farm system and the hiding of players. In March of 1938, he liberated 91 Cardinal farmhands and fined minor league affiliates

Sacramento (Pacific Coast), Cedar Rapids (Western) and Springfield (Western Association) amounts ranging up to $1,000. Moreover, none of the 91 players was permitted to sign with a St. Louis farm for at least three years. One of the freed players was Pete Reiser, who went on to stardom with the Brooklyn Dodgers.

On January 14, 1940, the Landis ax fell again. Once more scores of farmhands were set free, this time the property of the Detroit Tigers. Landis also ordered payments totaling more than $40,000 to a number of other players with whom the Tigers had dealt.

One player whom Landis did not free was Bob Feller. Feller's contract had been owned by several minor league clubs—none of whom he ever joined—before the pitcher broke in with the Indians. Landis based his decision on the fact that Feller and his father "zealously sought" validation of the Cleveland contract.

Landis, who voluntarily cut his salary $10,000 during the Depression, earned $65,000 during his final years as commissioner.

One of the judge's final rulings prior to his death in 1944 at age 78 was to banish Phillies Owner Bill Cox from baseball for betting on his own team.

# Bob Lemon

Cleveland's Bob Lemon (center) is flanked by teammates Jim Hegan (right) and Dale Mitchell after his June 30, 1948, no-hitter against Detroit.

Lemon came to the Indians in 1941 as an infielder before moving to the mound permanently in 1948.

Cleveland and Detroit players were warming up for an exhibition game at Lakeland, Fla., in 1946 when Birdie Tebbetts of the Tigers addressed a newspaperman covering the Indians.

"What's the idea, why third base?" wondered Tebbetts, nodding to a former Navy man working out at that spot for Cleveland.

There was no special reason, Birdie was told, except that the player was a third baseman.

"You may think he's a third baseman," replied shrewd Birdie, "but I know he's a pitcher. I hit against him during the war in the Pacific and if I never have to bat against him again it will be too soon."

Cleveland Manager Lou Boudreau received more glowing reports, and by midseason Bob Lemon was given his first starting assignment. Two years later, when the Tribe won the World Series, Lemon was a 20-game winner and en route to the Hall of Fame.

Lemon's education as a pitcher was entrusted to coach Bill McKechnie. The canny Scot was not unfamiliar with conversion projects. As manager of the Boston Braves and Cincinnati Reds, he had been instrumental in transforming Bucky Walters from an ordinary third baseman into a superlative hurler.

In 1948, his first season as a full-time pitcher, Lemon

joined the ranks of no-hit artists. The righthander, who for years refused to wear a toeplate as a symbol of his distaste for pitching, blanked Detroit, 2-0.

Lemon retired the first 21 batters in a 1951 game against Detroit, then grooved a slider that Vic Wertz slammed into the right-field seats. Lemon retired the next six batters in order.

As a youth in Long Beach, Calif., Lemon was a teammate of Vern Stephens, later an American League shortstop. The legion team was managed by Stephens' father.

Lemon's own father, who had played professionally, groomed his offspring for a baseball career. At 17, Bob was signed to a $100-a-month contract by John Angel, a Cleveland scout. In five seasons, he bounced around the minor leagues with only year-end glimpses of Cleveland. Three years in the Navy and competition against service teams on Pacific islands prepared Lemon for his introduction to major league pitching.

Lemon, one of a select group of pitchers to win 20 games or more seven times, did not enjoy the publicity of more colorful hurlers, but he was highly respected by opposing batters. He was incapable of throwing a straight fastball. His pitches would dip or take off horizontally, even when he threw from third base.

Also, because of his infield experience, Bob was a su-

In the 1950s, Lemon became one of a select group of pitchers to compile seven 20-victory seasons.

perb fielder on the mound and could contribute as well from the batter's box. He hit 37 homers for the Indians.

Lemon appeared in four World Series games, beating the Boston Braves twice in 1948 and losing twice in 1954 when the New York Giants swept the Indians.

In the '54 opener, Lemon held the Giants to two runs in nine innings at the Polo Grounds. But Dusty Rhodes' 260-foot fly, a routine out most everywhere else, found the home run range in right field and pinned Lemon with a 5-2 loss. He lasted only four innings in the finale.

Lemon suffered a leg injury in 1957 and an elbow injury the following season. He concluded his career with San Diego (Pacific Coast) in 1958.

Because of his talents as a pitching instructor, Lemon was never jobless after his pitching days. He scouted, coached and managed at the minor and major league levels. In the majors, he piloted the Royals, White Sox and Yankees (getting two stints with the Yanks). He produced a world championship in his initial New York regime (1978), then lost to the Dodgers in the 1981 World Series.

Lemon managed the Yankees to a World Series title in 1978, but lost to the Dodgers in 1981.

# Buck Leonard

A salary of $125 a month in the Depression year of 1933 was better than unemployment, but it did not excite a working man's visions of the finer things in life. It required a lot of skimping and a bit of conniving if you were performing in the Negro leagues that functioned in the eastern portion of the United States at that time.

"The thing to do," recalled Walter (Buck) Leonard, "was to borrow enough from the club so you'd be in debt at the end of the season. Then you could be sure they'd have you back next season. But they got wise to that, too, so after a while it didn't work."

Leonard's salary did not remain at $125, of course, but neither did it soar into the stratosphere. By 1942, Buck was earning $500 a month—for a 4½-month season—plus 75 cents-a-day meal money. In 1942, his salary was doubled to $1,000 a month, and he hit the top in 1948 when he earned $10,000 for summer and winter play.

That was the pay scale for the Negro League's top hitter (.391) in 1948 and one of the leading home run hitters (42) in 1942.

Leonard, nicknamed Buck by a brother who could not pronounce Buddy (the family's pet name for Walter), left his Rocky Mount, N.C., home in 1933 to join the Portsmouth Firefighters. In August, he joined the Baltimore Stars and a month later was with the Brooklyn Royal Giants.

The next season Buck was the first baseman for the Homestead Grays, with whom he remained for 17 seasons.

The Grays originally were based in Pittsburgh, but starting in 1937 they were a two-city club, playing in Pittsburgh when the Pirates were on the road and in Washington when the Senators were out of town. In the course of a year, the Grays played 200-210 games.

"We'd play a semipro team, say, in Rockville, Md.," Buck once recalled, "and then a league game at Griffith Stadium at night. Or we'd play semipro teams around Pittsburgh. We'd start around 6:30 and get in as many innings as we could before dark. The Grays would get $75-$100 a game. But weekends was when you were really expected to make enough money to pay off your players. These were the games you played in Forbes Field, Griffith Stadium or Yankee Stadium. They were called 'Getting-Out-of-the-Hole-Days.' "

Frequently, the Grays departed by bus from Pittsburgh early on a Sunday morning, drove 220 miles to Washington and reported to the park by 11:30. If the players weren't there at the appointed hour, the gates would not be opened.

After a doubleheader—one game lasting seven innings—the Grays returned to their three hotel rooms for showers, then grabbed a bite to eat and boarded the bus to doze as well as they could until they tumbled into bed in

**By 1946, Buck Leonard was an aging first baseman for the Homestead Grays.**

Pittsburgh at 7:30 a.m.

Playing under such unfavorable conditions, Leonard teamed with Josh Gibson and others to lead the Grays to Negro League titles from 1937 to '45.

"If he (Leonard) batted fourth, behind Gibson," Roy Campanella once noted, "we could pitch around him and make him hit an outside off-speed pitch. He had a real quick bat, and you couldn't get a fastball by him. He was strictly a pull hitter with tremendous power."

Buck was selected for 12 all-star games in which he batted .273 and hit three home runs.

With the young black stars entering Organized Baseball, the Grays succumbed at the end of the 1950 season. Buck was offered a job by Bill Veeck with the St. Louis Browns, but he was in his 40s and declined the invitation.

Instead, the slugger (who had spent his winters playing in Cuba, Puerto Rico and Venezuela) joined the Obregon club of the Mexican League. He also performed for Jalapa in the same circuit. At 48, Buck closed out his career in 1955 with Durango of the Mexican Central League two years after playing 10 games for Portsmouth of the Class B Piedmont League.

Leonard returned to Rocky Mount, where he served as a truant officer and physical education instructor in an elementary school. He also was a director of the Rocky Mount club in the Carolina League and was president of the Buck Leonard Realty Agency.

# Fred Lindstrom

One evening in the 1920s, John McGraw visited a New York hospital to cheer up his outfielder-third baseman who had suffered a broken leg.

The conversation commenced on a friendly tone. Then the Giants' manager berated Fred Lindstrom for his carelessness.

"I hope you break YOUR leg," replied the athlete.

Blind with rage, McGraw raced from the hospital into the path of a taxi and, true to his player's wish, suffered a broken leg.

Lindstrom's relations with his boss were not always acrimonious. There was one occasion when the Giants trailed Pittsburgh by two runs in extra innings. When Lindstrom came to bat, runners were on first and second with none out. Looking at the coach for a sign, Lindstrom caught no hint of whether to bunt or hit. He strolled to the dugout and asked for instructions.

"Hit a homer on the first pitch," said McGraw.

And that's what Freddie did, slicing a Babe Adams pitch into the right-field seats. Ordinarily, McGraw would have awaited the day's hero in the runway. This time, he raced onto the field to extend congratulations.

A native of Chicago, Lindstrom was an outstanding shortstop at Loyola High School. A workout with the Cubs was arranged, but at the conclusion he was told that the club was not interested. Later, Freddie learned that Manager Bill Killefer had been playing cards in the clubhouse and had not seen the workout.

"Just suppose he'd seen me," Freddie mused in later life. "I might have been a Cub instead of a Giant."

A month after the workout, Lindstrom joined Toledo (American Association). The manager was George Whitted and the club president was Roger Bresnahan, onetime catching great of the Giants.

"I was only 16, so young that Bresnahan wouldn't let me sit on the bench during a game," recalled Lindstrom. "The team was going so badly, however, that Whitted had to do something. 'That kid's doing us no good in the bleachers,' he told Bresnahan, 'so I'm gonna stick him in the game whether you like it or not.' "

Two years later, Lindstrom was playing third base for

**Fred Lindstrom's first big season was 1928, when he hit .358 with 107 RBIs for the Giants.**

the Giants and batting .333 in the World Series against the Senators.

Freddie was best remembered in that 1924 classic as the third baseman who watched helplessly as a ground ball hit by Earl McNeely struck a pebble and bounced over his head, driving in the winning run in Game 7 of the Series.

A handsome blond with a delightful sense of humor, Lindstrom was the only non-complainer at one time when his teammates lamented loud and long about food and services at a hotel. Asked why he did not join the chorus, Freddie explained, "When a fellow is hitting .240, whatever he gets is much too good for him."

But Lindstrom could show displeasure, too. When the Giants purchased Johnny Vergez in the winter of 1930-31 and McGraw announced that Fred would be shifted to the outfield to make way for the young third baseman, he responded: "Taking me out and moving me to a strange position to make room for a busher . . . I don't like it."

But, just as McGraw had predicted, Lindstrom became an excellent outfielder, with speed and an unerring glove.

Lindstrom's displeasure grew in June of 1932 when McGraw resigned and Bill Terry was named to succeed him. Owner Charles Stoneham had led Freddie to believe that he would be McGraw's successor.

Outspoken as usual, Lindstrom announced to his former roommate Terry, "I'm sorry, Bill, but I can't play for you. Trade me."

Against his wishes, Memphis Bill traded Lindy to Pittsburgh. In 1935, Freddie was peddled to the Cubs, for whom he might have started his career except for Killefer's card game.

Lindstrom appeared with the Cubs in the 1935 World Series and finished his career with the Dodgers the next year. He was only 30.

Lindstrom served for years as baseball coach at Northwestern University and later was postmaster at Evanston, Ill.

He retired from the postal position in 1964 and lived in New Port Richey, Fla., prior to his death in Chicago in 1981 at age 75.

# John Henry Lloyd

In a game at Augusta, Ga., in 1905, the visiting Macon team, too poor to afford proper equipment, presented the unusual sight of a catcher working behind the plate without a mask.

In the third inning, the 21-year-old player's left eye was struck by a foul tip. In the seventh, another tip closed his right eye. Unable to see, he calmly announced, "Gentlemen, I guess I'll have to quit."

The next day the wounded warrior showed up with a wire basket that he strapped over his face to finish the series. The next year, John Henry (Pop) Lloyd showed up in Philadelphia as an infielder. Before long he was performing such extraordinary feats at shortstop and at bat that he gained the sobriquet of "the black Honus Wagner."

A native of Palatka, Fla., and an elementary school dropout, Lloyd arrived in Philadephia with $1.50 and a pocket watch among his few earthly possessions. He joined the Cuban X Giants in 1906 and gained an early following by hitting a game-winning, ninth-inning double in the season opener.

In 1910, Lloyd and several teammates joined the Leland Giants of Chicago, an affiliation that lasted one season. In 1911, Pop was in the East once more, playing with the new Lincoln Giants of New York.

For three years, Lloyd starred under his old Philadelphia manager, Sol White, fielding spectacularly and posting impressive statistics at the plate.

One of the highlights of Pop's career with the Lincoln Giants was a game with the Philadelphia Phillies in 1913. The Giants pounded out 14 hits in a 9-2 victory over Grover Cleveland Alexander, a 22-game winner that season.

Explaining that "wherever the money was, that's where I was," Lloyd moved westward again in 1914, joining Rube Foster's Chicago American Giants, with whom he remained through 1917.

During the winter of 1917-18, Lloyd worked in the Army Quartermaster's depot in Chicago and refused to accompany the Giants to Florida for winter ball. Shortly, he learned he had been displaced as shortstop by Bobby Williams. Lloyd was named manager of the Brooklyn Royal Giants and frequently played first base, hinting that, perhaps, at 34, he had slowed too much to perform adequately at his old position.

From 1918 until his retirement from pro ball in 1931, Pop managed and played for the Royal Giants, the Columbus (O.) Buckeyes, the Bacharach Giants, the Hilldale club of Philadelphia and the Lincoln Giants.

Lloyd topped the .400 batting mark three times. In 1911, at 27, he batted .475 for the Lincoln Giants. Twelve years later, pushing 40, he batted .415 for the Hilldales and bettered that average at .422 the following season.

John Henry Lloyd poses with fellow Hall of Famer Jimmie Foxx well after his 1931 retirement.

Although Pop retired from professional ball in 1931, he did not hang up his spikes. He continued to play with semipro teams around Atlantic City, N.J., until he was 58.

"Pop never got mad at anything, like when people would yell things at him," said a sportswriter who knew him well. "One day a loudmouth guy was yelling at him from the stands and his manager asked him why he didn't yell back. 'Well,' said Lloyd, 'the Lord gave us two ears and one mouth, so I think he wanted us to listen more than we talked. So that's what I do.' "

Lloyd accepted a janitorial job in the post office and for years served as Atlantic City's Little League commissioner.

His adopted city honored Lloyd on October 2, 1949, by renaming the municipal athletic field "Pop Lloyd Stadium." In an emotion-packed ceremony, congratulatory telegrams were read from Jackie Robinson, Roy Campanella, Don Newcombe, Larry Doby and Satchel Paige.

After a two-year illness, Pop died of arteriosclerosis on March 19, 1965, at age 80. In 1974, he was inducted posthumously into the Black Athletic Hall of Fame at Las Vegas, Nev., together with Campanella and Roberto Clemente.

# Al Lopez

Wilbert Robinson was partial to big catchers and when the Brooklyn manager spotted newcomer Al Lopez in 1928, he exclaimed, "They're sending me midgets. This Cuban ain't never gonna make a catcher. He's too small and skinny."

Uncle Robbie, it turned out, was wrong on two scores. Lopez was not a Cuban, but a Floridian of Spanish ancestry. And, for all his unimposing dimensions, Al developed into an excellent catcher and an even more outstanding major league manager.

Robbie might have looked more kindly on Lopez had he known that four years earlier, when he was a high school student of 16, the Senor had caught Walter Johnson in a barnstorming game at Tampa, Fla.

Lopez was something of a schoolboy celebrity at the time, and was selected to catch the Big Train as a means of drawing the local citizenry to the game. The gimmick worked and the youngster handled the old master with consummate ease.

Johnson's pregame conversation with Lopez consisted of: "Kid, it'll be all fastballs today except some curves that I'm saving for Ike Boone (Red Sox) and Jacques Fournier (Dodgers)."

Johnson set up both players with fastballs and struck them out with curves.

Six years earlier, at age 10, Lopez received a rough baptism to baseball. He was knocked unconscious when struck in the face by a ball. After hospital treatment to repair broken bones, he was given trolley fare to his home, where he was soundly thrashed by his father for playing hooky.

With the Dodgers, Al's start was less painful. On September 27, 1928, the final day of the season, Lopez caught a doubleheader (after appearing in one earlier contest). He went hitless in both games, but was thrilled the next day to read a quote in the newspaper by Jess Petty, Brooklyn's first-game pitcher.

"Al Lopez caught two fine contests. He knows what it's all about," Petty said.

By the time Lopez caught his last major league game, he had set a record by working more than 1,900 contests.

In 1935, the Senor was traded to the Boston Braves in an effort by the Dodgers to obtain pitching help. Al's skill behind the plate was instrumental in lifting the Braves from eighth place to sixth, one rung above the Dodgers.

But the Braves were no turnstile match for the Red Sox, who were flourishing as the "Gold Sox," and on June 14, 1940, Bob Quinn, president of the struggling National Leaguers, called a press conference, at which he announced: "I've just sold Lopez to Pittsburgh. It was the toughest job I've had to do in 50 years in baseball."

Al closed his major league playing career with Cleveland

In 1930, Brooklyn's Al Lopez was just beginning his march toward a career-record 1,918 games behind the plate.

in 1947 before beginning his illustrious managerial career at Indianapolis.

Graduating to the major leagues, Lopez was an immediate success with the Indians. Drawing from his experiences under Casey Stengel at Brooklyn and Bill McKechnie at Boston, the Senor produced a pennant winner in Cleveland in 1954 and another American League champion with the Chicago White Sox in 1959. Each year he snapped a string of pennants by his old pal, Stengel. Casey had won five consecutive flags before the Indians won in '54 and four straight titles before the Sox triumphed five years later.

Lopez was the complete manager. He knew when to gamble and when to play the percentages. His clubs consistently had the best pitching in the A.L.

He was kind, considerate and understanding. His work with pitchers was exceptional, each being treated as an individual. He was a father confessor to young players, always available to listen to their problems.

Reporters never departed from Lopez with an empty notebook. His patience and charm made him one of the most popular managers. After the White Sox lost the 1959 World Series to Los Angeles, Lopez sat in his office in full uniform, long after his players had left the clubhouse, until the last newsman's questions were answered.

Health problems led to Al's retirement to his Tampa home after the 1965 season. He was back as the White Sox manager for a brief period in 1968-69.

# Ted Lyons

In 1922, when the Philadelphia Athletics trained at Lake Charles, La., coach Harry Davis visited the home of a young pitcher who was compiling an impressive record at Baylor University.

A contract was offered —"and it was a good one," said the hurler— but Ted Lyons rejected it in favor of one tendered by the Chicago White Sox.

Seven years later, A's Manager Connie Mack encountered Lyons in the lobby of a Chicago hotel just before the A's opened the World Series against the Cubs.

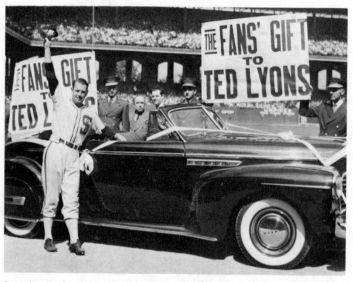

Popular Ted Lyons salutes the White Sox fans who chipped in to buy their star a new automobile in 1940.

"Young man," said Mack, shaking a finger at the big one that got away, "you see what would have happened if you had signed with us. You'd now be with a championship team."

Pitching in rotation with Lefty Grove, George Earnshaw and Rube Walberg, Lyons may have made the A's invincible for years. As it was, he never appeared in a World Series while serving as the backbone of the Chicago staff for nearly 20 years.

Lyons was directed to the White Sox by his college coach, Frank Bridges. In 1923, the White Sox trained in Waco, Tex., site of Baylor University. Bridges invited Chicago catcher Ray Schalk to drop by the campus and catch some pitches from Lyons. Schalk was immediately impressed and recommended Ted to Kid Gleason, his manager.

Ted made his major league debut in St. Louis, pitching one inning of relief in which he retired Urban Shocker, Johnny Tobin and Wally Gerber in order.

Although the White Sox finished in the second division more often than not during Lyons' career, Ted won 260 games. How many he might have won with a contender has long been a subject for speculation.

A gentleman off the field, Lyons was a fiery competitor on the diamond—even when he opposed a close friend. When Moe Berg, erudite Princeton alumnus, was with the White Sox, he and Lyons were the best of cronies. Traded to Washington, Berg singled in his first at-bat against Lyons, driving in the winning run. Berg touched first base, then accelerated his pace in leaving the field because Lyons, with eyes blazing, was in hot pursuit. Ted overhauled Moe in the clubhouse, where he pounded his pal

over the head with a glove and shouted, "A fine friend you are."

Lyons pitched a no-hitter against the Boston Red Sox in 1926—and it was more unusual than most no-hitters.

He walked the first Boston batter on four pitches. The next hitter smacked a vicious line drive on which outfielder Johnny Mostil made a circus catch and threw to first base for a double play. Thereafter, Ted retired every batter in order.

Another time, Lyons went the distance in a 21-inning marathon in which his mound opponent, George Uhle of the Tigers, started Ted on his way to a 6-5 loss with an infield hit.

Lyons' overall record might have been even more remarkable except for a damp and raw night in Houston in 1931.

In a spring exhibition under the lights against the Giants, Lyons suffered a shoulder injury while breaking off a curve. A 73-game winner in the four preceding seasons, Ted won only 35 in the next four.

In his last full major league season, 1942, the 41-year-old hurler started and finished 20 games, posted a 14-6 record and led the American League in earned-run average with 2.10.

Although he could have escaped military service in World War II, Lyons entered the Marine Corps and saw duty in the Pacific.

Twenty-three years after he made his major league debut, Lyons closed his active career in 1946 with one victory in five decisions.

On May 25, 1946, Lyons was appointed manager of the White Sox, replacing Jimmie Dykes. The team that had gone 10-20 under Dykes fashioned a 64-60 record under Lyons to finish fifth.

Ted guided the Sox to sixth place in 1947, but was dismissed after the White Sox dropped to the basement in 1948.

From 1949 through 1953, Ted coached the Detroit pitchers.

He coached for the Dodgers in 1954 and scouted for his old Chicago team for 12 years before retiring to a 750-acre rice farm in Vinton, La.

# Connie Mack

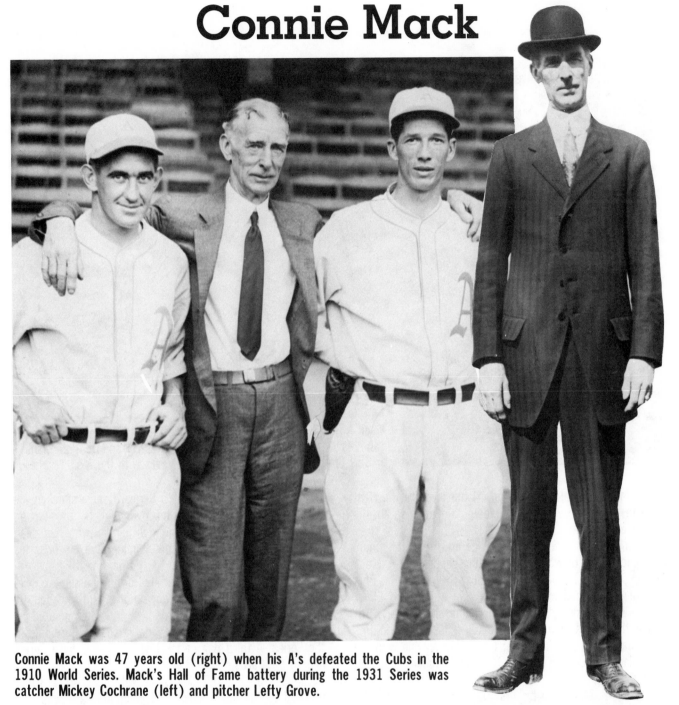

Connie Mack was 47 years old (right) when his A's defeated the Cubs in the 1910 World Series. Mack's Hall of Fame battery during the 1931 Series was catcher Mickey Cochrane (left) and pitcher Lefty Grove.

In light of his gentle and gracious manner in later years, it seemed unlikely—even impossible—for the manager of the Philadelphia Athletics to have been ejected from a game and fined $100 for his vehement protest of a play at second base in 1895.

What was said to umpire Hank O'Day to draw a banishment and such a healthy fine was not revealed, but, yes, Connie Mack conceded, he was a bit fiery in his youth.

As a catcher for Pittsburgh, the tall and gaunt Mack was not above tipping the bat with his glove on occasion. And if a pitch came near the bat, Connie at times would smack his tongue against the roof of his mouth, deceiving the umpire into believing that the ball ticked the bat.

Mack was born Cornelius McGillicuddy in East Brookfield, Mass., but changed his name so it would fit into a box score. He made his major league debut with Washington on October 7, 1886, hitting a triple and single in a 12-3 romp over Kansas City.

Mack was playing manager of the Pittsburgh club in 1896 when he was dismissed by Owner William W. Kerr, who insisted on interfering with strategy on the field. The move proved a stroke of fortune for the 33-year-old Connie. He was invited to Chicago to meet with Ban Johnson, already envisioning a second major league.

Johnson offered Connie the managerial job with Milwaukee in the Western League. Mack accepted and a few

Mack was a 39-year-old "youngster" (left) in 1902, and 87 years old (above) when A.L. President Will Harridge (left) and Dodgers Manager Burt Shotton honored him for his 50 years with the A's.

years later was told by Johnson, "I think you're the right person to take over the Philadelphia franchise in the American League."

Again Connie accepted the advice and, with the financial backing of Ben Shibe, a sporting goods dealer, Mack established the Philadelphia Athletics. By raiding the Phillies of established stars, such as Nap Lajoie and Elmer Flick, Mack produced a contending club immediately. But when the Pennsylvania Supreme Court issued an injunction that prevented the former Phils from playing with the A's, Mack traded the onetime National Leaguers to Cleveland.

By 1902, Mack had his first flag winner. By 1905, he had another league champion. But the '05 season ended on a sour note when the A's lost the World Series to Christy Mathewson and the Giants, four shutouts to one.

By 1910, the A's were riding high behind their "$100,000 Infield" of Stuffy McInnis, Eddie Collins, Jack Barry and Frank Baker, and a pitching staff that featured Chief Bender, Eddie Plank and Jack Coombs.

Philadelphia beat the Cubs in the 1910 Series, defeated the Giants in 1911 and 1913 and lost to the Miracle Braves in a four-game upset in 1914.

Crushed by the '14 collapse, Mack disposed of most of his stars in 1915 and suffered through a 15-year dry spell until he reached the top again in 1929.

In the first game of the '29 Series, Connie shocked the baseball world, particularly his own players, by starting Howard Ehmke, a 35-year-old righthander who had seen little action late in the season. Ehmke gave his boss his greatest thrill by striking out 13 and beating the Cubs.

Behind a powerful offense featuring Jimmie Foxx, Al Simmons and Mickey Cochrane and a staff headed by Lefty Grove and George Earnshaw, the A's repeated as champions in 1930 when they defeated the Cardinals in the Series. A third flag in 1931 was followed by a Series loss to the Cards.

In his straw hat and high collar, with his scorecard that he used to wig-wag players into position, Mack was now the Grand Old Man of baseball. But the Great Depression was taking a heavy toll at the turnstiles and Connie was forced to sell his high-priced stars for a second time. The A's plunged to the bottom of the league and Mack never again enjoyed a championship.

Connie managed the American League team in the first All-Star Game in 1933 and completed a half century at the A's helm in 1950.

The 87-year-old gentleman was saluted on his final swing around the circuit, including a ticker-tape parade in New York.

A fractured hip, which Connie suffered while getting out of bed, led to Mack's death in 1956 at age 93.

# Larry MacPhail

He was abrasive and bombastic, but he also was base-ball-smart, with a healing touch for dying franchises and the skill to make healthy clubs even healthier.

In his relatively brief time in the major leagues, Larry MacPhail made enemies, but none was a stockholder in a club that he raised from the death bed. Last rites had been performed on the Cincinnati Reds and Brooklyn Dodgers when MacPhail burst upon the scene and administered his magic potions. And he was the chief executive officer of the Yankees at the birth of a new dynasty following World War II.

MacPhail's most memorable achievement, though, was the introduction of night baseball to the major leagues. The old guard opposed the move vigorously, but MacPhail was not accustomed to defeat. He persisted in his crusade until, reluctantly, National League club owners granted permission for arc contests in Cincinnati, one against each rival.

When the landmark game was played in 1935 and the fiscal benefits became apparent, resistance melted and the onetime Big Ten Conference football official was hailed as a Moses in baseball's wilderness.

MacPhail, a native of Cass City, Mich., attended Staunton Military Academy in Virginia, where he distinguished himself in the classroom as well as in baseball and football.

At 16, he passed the entrance exams to the United States Naval Academy. On the advice of his father and because of his youth, however, he passed up Annapolis in favor of Beloit College in Wisconsin.

Two years later, he entered the University of Michigan Law School. After another year, he transferred to the George Washington University Law School where he obtained his law degree at the age of 20.

MacPhail joined a Chicago law firm, then resigned within six months because the firm refused to make him a partner. He joined another firm, reorganized a tool company and then resigned from the law firm to join the tool company. At 24, he was president of a large department store in Nashville, Tenn.

MacPhail served in the 114th Field Artillery during World War I and participated in the abortive attempt to kidnap the Kaiser after the Armistice. However, he did obtain one of the Kaiser's bronze ash trays, which he treasured the remainder of his life.

Returning to civilian life, MacPhail settled in Columbus, O., where he practiced law, owned an automobile agency and dealt in real estate. In 1930, he bought Columbus' debt-ridden American Association club and immediately pumped new vitality into it. The team was said to be the first in Organized Ball to travel by air.

In the fall of 1933, the Central Trust Co. of Cincinnati

**Larry MacPhail (right) poses with Yankee slugger Joe DiMaggio (left) and Manager Joe McCarthy in 1946.**

asked MacPhail to revitalize the nearly bankrupt Reds.

With the aid of night ball, a refurbished Crosley Field and shrewd player deals, MacPhail revived baseball interest and put the Reds on the road to success that produced pennants in 1939 and 1940.

By that time, however, MacPhail had moved on to Brooklyn, where he breathed new life into a moribund franchise. The team was $1.2 million in debt and had lost $500,000 from 1933 to 1937 when Larry arrived on the scene at the invitation of the Brooklyn Trust Co. Using his old formulas, MacPhail turned the Dodgers into contenders in a few years and had a pennant winner by 1941.

MacPhail's manager at the time was Leo Durocher, equally as volatile as the Redhead. "He fired me 66 times," the Lip once reported. "It was only six," Larry replied.

Before the close of the 1942 season, MacPhail resigned as president and general manager of the Dodgers to become a lieutenant colonel in the Army Services of Supply.

At the end of the year, Larry and partners Dan Topping and Del Webb bought the Yankees from the estate of Jake Ruppert. For less than $2 million, they acquired the Yankees, Yankee Stadium, four minor league clubs and the rights to 400 players. At a cost of nearly $1 million, MacPhail modernized the park with new and more comfortable seats and organized the swank Yankee Stadium Club.

Amid the Yankees' victory celebration after the 1947 World Series, MacPhail bade a teary farewell and retired to his farm in Bel Air, Md. He was 85 when he died in Miami in 1975 after a lengthy illness.

# Mickey Mantle

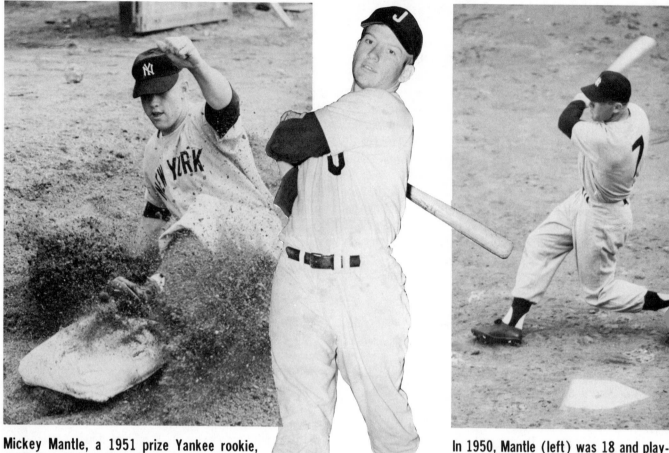

Mickey Mantle, a 1951 prize Yankee rookie, works in a sliding pit during spring training.

In 1950, Mantle (left) was 18 and playing for Class C Joplin. In 1953, Mantle

Before the arrival of the Oklahoma Kid, nobody expended the time or effort to measure prodigious home runs. When a batter unloaded an extraordinary clout, witnesses could only gape in amazement, chatter excitedly and speculate on the approximate distance.

But that all changed in 1953 when a young superstar of the Yankees bludgeoned a pitch out of Griffith Stadium in Washington. By mathematical calculations and some leg work, an enterprising New York publicist determined that Mickey Mantle's blast had carried 565 feet. From that point, "tape measure homers" were part of baseball's lexicon.

Nobody had ever socked a fair ball out of Yankee Stadium, but Mantle came the closest. One drive struck the facade of the right-field stands, 106 feet above ground level and 390 feet from the plate.

On July 23, 1957, Mantle drove a pitch from Bob Keegan of the White Sox against a seat only two rows from the top of the right-field bleachers.

"I thought it was gone," admitted Mantle, who added a single, double and triple for his only major league "cycle."

Mickey smacked a 550-foot drive at Comiskey Park,

and in an exhibition game at Forbes Field in Pittsburgh he cleared the right-field stands. Only Babe Ruth and Ted Beard had performed the Forbes Field feat earlier. At the same park in the 1960 World Series, the Yankee standout became the first to clear the wall in right-center field.

The son of an Oklahoma lead and zinc miner, Mantle was coached to be a switch-hitter from age 5. With his father pitching to him from one side and his grandfather from the other, Mickey mastered the art of swinging from either side of the plate and became the most powerful turn-around hitter in the history of the game.

In a high school football game, Mickey suffered a leg bruise that developed into osteomyelitis. He overcame that handicap, as well as surgery on both knees, a shoulder operation, a broken foot and an ankle so weak that it buckled under him when he batted lefthanded.

Mantle arrived at Yankee Stadium in 1951, fresh from Joplin of the Class C Western Association. After being sent to Class AAA Kansas City during the season and then recalled, Mickey was the Yankees' starting right fielder and leadoff man as the '51 Yankees-Giants World Series connected (above) for a grand slam against the Dodgers in the World Series.

Mantle abhorred speeches, but took his turn at the microphone in September of 1965 to thank Yankee fans for their support on "Mickey Mantle Day."

got under way. However, he tripped over a drain pipe in right field in Game 2 at Yankee Stadium, suffered torn knee cartilage and missed the rest of the Series.

The youngster's father, Elvin, or Mutt, was a spectator at the Series. The day after his son's injury, Mutt was taken ill and joined Mickey in the hospital. The next summer Mickey's father died of Hodgkin's disease.

Mantle roamed the outfield through 1966, after which he switched to first base for his last two years as a concession to his aching legs.

Winner of one Triple Crown and three Most Valuable Player awards, Mantle performed in 12 World Series in his first 14 seasons as a Yankee. His bases-loaded home run in the 1953 classic against Brooklyn rated as his foremost thrill.

The grand slam was hit at Ebbets Field in Brooklyn just after Dodgers Manager Charley Dressen lifted Johnny Podres, a lefthander, and brought in righthander Russ Meyer.

Mickey's second most cherished moment occurred in the 1964 Series when his ninth-inning homer off Barney Schultz gave the Bronx Bombers a 2-1 victory over the Cardinals.

When he wasn't hammering baseballs to distant points, the Commerce Comet was burning baselines with the speed that carried him from home plate to first base in 3.1 seconds. He would steal bases at the risk of permanent injury to his legs.

A shy, reticent type, Mickey was never completely at ease among strangers, or even some media people. His happiest hours were spent in the company of Whitey Ford and Billy Martin, who shared Mantle's penchant for late-hour fun.

Mickey retired in 1969, after testing his legs in spring training. At a hastily called press conference in Fort Lauderdale, Fla., he announced simply, "I'm not going to play any more baseball."

In his last official at-bat the previous September 28, he had popped up against Jim Lonborg at Fenway Park. Mickey's last hit was a single against Luis Tiant of Boston at Yankee Stadium, September 25, and his final homer came off Lonborg on September 20.

Mantle abhorred speeches, but at the retirement of his uniform No. 7, he told 60,000 Yankee Stadium fans, "Playing 18 years for you folks has to be the best thing that ever happened to a ballplayer."

# Heinie Manush

In the sixth inning of Game 4 of the 1933 World Series, a Washington player was called out on a close play at first base.

A heated argument between player and umpire Charley Moran ensued and eventually the player was ejected. Many thought the banishment resulted from the player brushing against Moran after crossing the bag. It wasn't until 31 years later, when he entered the Hall of Fame, that Heinie Manush revealed the real story behind his ejection.

"I was too smart to lay a hand on Moran when I came back to argue the call," said the former outfielder. "But when he bellied up to me and asked what I was gonna do about it, there was temptation that was too much.

"Like all other umpires of that day, Moran was wearing a little black, leather bow tie, the kind that comes ready-made with elastic around the neck. I didn't lay a hand on Moran, but I did pull the tie two feet away from his neck and let it snap back against his throat."

Manush was the last player thrown out of a Series game by an umpire because Judge K.M. Landis, who fined Manush $50 for his conduct, ruled that henceforth only a commissioner would be empowered to take such action.

The loss of Manush conceivably cost the Senators the game. With Heinie gone, Goose Goslin shifted to left field and Dave Harris took over in right field. Harris was the Nats' premier righthanded pinch-hitter and would have been called on in the 11th inning when the Senators loaded the bases with one out.

Instead, the call went to Cliff Bolton, a painfully slow runner who grounded into a game-ending double play. The Nats lost the game, 2-1, and were beaten by the Giants again the next day on a Mel Ott home run.

Manush, the seventh son of a family of eight, was a 17-year-old student at the Massey Military Academy in Pulaski, Tenn., when he decided to strike out on his own. He went to Burlington, Ia., where he worked in his brother George's plumbing business. Tired of digging ditches, he drifted westward to Salt Lake City and ultimately to Portland.

Heinie was let go before he got into a Pacific Coast

**Heinie Manush played in his only All-Star Game as a member of the Senators.**

League game and didn't make his professional debut until he joined the Edmonton (Western Canada) club in 1921. After playing at Omaha (Western) in 1922, Manush joined the Tigers in 1923 for the start of a 17-year major league career. He was only 21.

Conditions on the Tigers were not ideal for a rookie. "Ty Cobb (manager) wouldn't even let me bat," Manush once recalled. "Every time I'd go to the plate, Cobb would yell, 'Get outta there, kid.' Finally, Harry Heilmann felt sorry for me and said, 'You can take my turn at bat.'"

Gradually, Cobb softened his attitude toward Heinie, who batted .334 in 1923 to go along with Heilmann's league-leading .403 and Cobb's .340.

"You had to get your hits to stay in there," Manush remembered. "Two hitless games in a row and you were on the bench." Waiting on the bench were Bobby Veach and Bob Fothergill, both .300 hitters.

Manush won the American League batting title in 1926, beating out Babe Ruth with six hits in nine at-bats in the closing day's doubleheader for a .378 average. After his average dipped below .300 in 1927, Heinie was traded to the St. Louis Browns.

In 1928, Heinie again hit .378, only to lose out to Goslin in a batting race that was unresolved until the last day of the season.

A lengthy salary hassle with Browns Owner Phil Ball in the spring of 1930 hastened Heinie's departure to the Senators. Manush played in his only All-Star Game (1934) as a member of the Nats.

After his trade to the Red Sox in December of 1935, Manush closed his big-league career with the Dodgers and Pirates. He managed numerous minor league clubs.

At his Hall of Fame induction in 1964, Heinie encounted Bill Terry, the Giants' first baseman in 1933 when Manush was ejected from the Series game.

"Hey, Bill," Manush said, "wasn't I safe?"

"It was very close," replied Terry.

"You haven't been telling the truth for 31 years," snorted Heinie.

A lengthy bout with cancer that cost Manush the power of speech led to Heinie's death in 1971 at age 69.

# Rabbit Maranville

Aside from the fact that he had more names than most major league players, James Walter Vincent Maranville was different from his contemporaries in other ways as well.

In 23 National League seasons, he created a legend of wild nights and zany stunts, of incredible escapades on and off the field.

The Rabbit, named for his large ears and small build (5-foot-5 and 155 pounds), led a fabled and charmed life from the time the Boston Braves bought him from New Bedford of the New England League for $1,000.

He was the shortstop of the 1914 Miracle Braves team that beat the powerful Philadelphia A's in four straight games in the World Series. Afterward, Rabbit and several teammates went on a vaudeville tour. In Lewiston, Me., Maranville croaked through a few songs, related a few anecdotes and then announced: "I will now demonstrate how I stole second base against Bullet Joe Bush in the Series."

Sprinting nimbly, he went into a picture slide. But he had miscalculated the distance. Flying over the footlights, he landed on a drum in the orchestra pit and broke his leg.

This was the free spirit of whom Manager George Stallings had said at the end of the Series, "I consider Maranville the greatest player to come into the game since Ty Cobb."

One afternoon, Maranville slid between the legs of umpire Hank O'Day on a steal of second base. Stuffily, the dignified umpire checked the rules book for a possible violation. Finding none, he begrudgingly ruled Maranville safe at second.

In New York, Rabbit arranged with pitcher Jack Scott to chase him through Times Square shouting "Stop, thief!"

A crowd took up the pursuit, until a breathless Maranville ducked into a saloon that, he knew from experience, had a rear exit.

In St. Louis, Rabbit dived fully clothed into a shallow pool and emerged with a goldfish between his teeth. "There's a mean fish down there that bit me," he reported.

"What did you do?" he was asked.

"I bit him right back," Maranville replied mischievously.

In Philadelphia, Maranville returned from a night on the town to find his hotel room locked and a card game in

**Aside from baseball, Rabbit Maranville was known best for his legendary off-field escapades.**

progress on the inside. Rabbit did not seek admittance by conventional methods. Moments later a card player heard a tapping on the window. Maranville's face was pressed tightly against the pane.

Rabbit had gone to an adjoining room and climbed along a narrow ledge, 20 floors above the sidewalk.

Another time, teammates heard screams coming from Rabbit's room. There were sounds of breaking glass, some gunfire and then Maranville shouting, "Eddie, you're killing me."

When the door was broken down, Rabbit and two accomplices paraded past the astonished teammates, greeting them airily with "Hiya fellas."

Thrown out of a game in Brooklyn by Bill Klem, Rabbit was observed later in full uniform hawking newspapers outside Ebbets Field and shouting, "Read all about it, Maranville and that big baboon Klem."

When Maranville was fined $100 for drunken driving and $25 for refusing to obey a patrolman's order the same evening, a judge in a Boston suburb commented, "It must have been quite a night. I observe from the record that you played baseball all the next day. Congratulations."

Maranville had one managerial experience, and it was brief. In July of 1925, he was named skipper of the Cubs. A few nights later, he marched through the Pullman car, pouring ice water on sleeping players and shouting, "No sleeping under Maranville's management, especially at night." In early September, he was fired.

The master of the vest-pocket catch was sent to the minors in 1927. The demotion had a sobering effect on Maranville—literally. He took the pledge on May 24, 1927, and never touched another drop.

In 1927, he was acquired by the Cardinals from their Rochester farm and the following season batted more than .300 in the World Series against the Yankees.

By the spring of 1934, Rabbit, now a second baseman, was back with the Braves. Maranville played his last big-league game in 1935, managed a few years in the minors, then served as director of the sandlot baseball program for the New York Journal-American.

On January 5, 1954, Maranville suffered a heart attack at Woodside, N.Y., and died at age 62, a short time before his election to the Hall of Fame.

# Juan Marichal

The blemish on Juan Marichal's career came in 1965 when he attacked catcher John Roseboro with a bat. Sandy Koufax (right) tried to intercede.

From the moment he joined the Michigan City club of the Midwest League in 1958, it was apparent that the high-kicking righthander was mature beyond his years.

Juan Marichal was only 19, but he pitched overhand, three-quarter sidearm, sidearm and underhand. He possessed above-average speed and his control was almost flawless. He struck out 246 batters, walked only 50 and compiled an earned-run average of 1.87.

After one season at Springfield (Eastern) and 18 games at Tacoma (Pacific Coast), the "Dominican Dandy" made his major league debut with the Giants on July 19, 1960, hurling a one-hit, 2-0 victory against the Phillies. The losers' only hit was an eighth-inning single by Clay Dalrymple.

Twelve years earlier, Marichal was manufacturing his own baseball from a piece of rubber, threads unwound from an old silk stocking and adhesive tape. The ball was crude, even lopsided, but it provided the first essential of the deprived youngster's education in the art of pitching in the Dominican Republic.

In 1958, Juan accepted a $500 bonus from San Francisco scouts Horacio Martinez and Alex Pompez.

Marichal's features generally were creased in a smile, and to many he was known as "Laughing Boy."

In the mid-1960s, former Phillies catcher Gus Triandos noted, "The thing that I hated about him was that it seemed so easy for him. It was one thing to go hitless against pitchers like Sandy Koufax or Don Drysdale; at least you could look out there and see the cords standing out on their neck. They look like they're working—and worried. Marichal just stands there laughing at you."

During his prime, when he was winning 20 or more games from 1963 through 1966, Marichal was the dominant righthanded pitcher in the game. Some considered him a superior pitcher to the Dodgers' Koufax.

A two-time National League leader in complete games and shutouts, the Dominican enjoyed his greatest success against the Dodgers. At Candlestick Park, Juan compiled a 24-1 record against Los Angeles. Overall, he was 37-18.

The most serious blemish against Marichal's record occurred at Candlestick Park on August 22, 1965, when he swung a bat at the head of Los Angeles catcher John Roseboro. The third-inning incident followed an earlier pitch that brushed Marichal back from the plate. "You

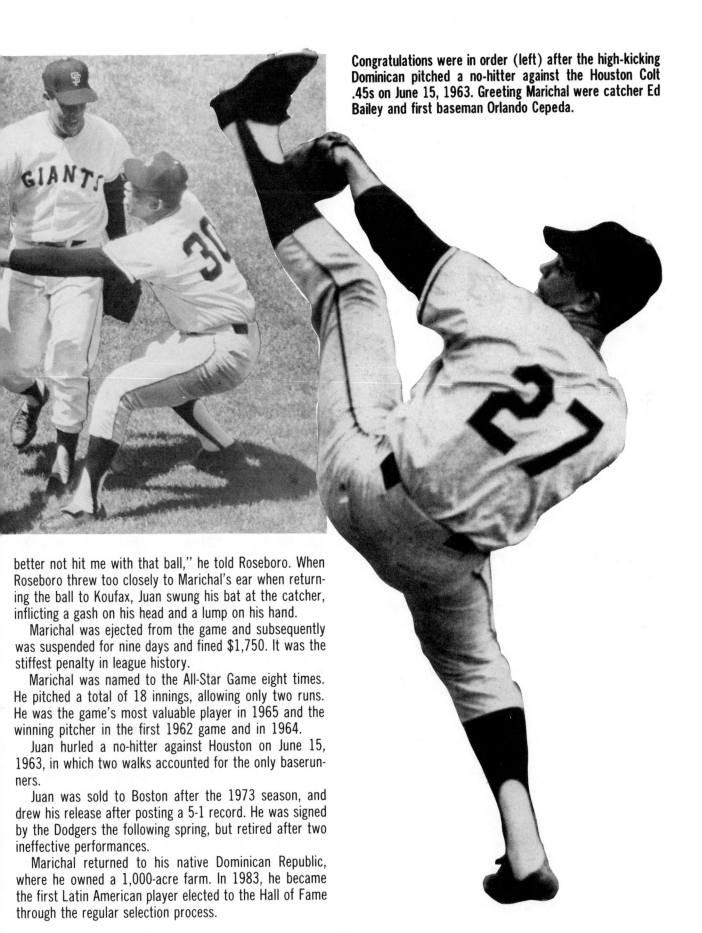

Congratulations were in order (left) after the high-kicking Dominican pitched a no-hitter against the Houston Colt .45s on June 15, 1963. Greeting Marichal were catcher Ed Bailey and first baseman Orlando Cepeda.

better not hit me with that ball," he told Roseboro. When Roseboro threw too closely to Marichal's ear when returning the ball to Koufax, Juan swung his bat at the catcher, inflicting a gash on his head and a lump on his hand.

Marichal was ejected from the game and subsequently was suspended for nine days and fined $1,750. It was the stiffest penalty in league history.

Marichal was named to the All-Star Game eight times. He pitched a total of 18 innings, allowing only two runs. He was the game's most valuable player in 1965 and the winning pitcher in the first 1962 game and in 1964.

Juan hurled a no-hitter against Houston on June 15, 1963, in which two walks accounted for the only baserunners.

Juan was sold to Boston after the 1973 season, and drew his release after posting a 5-1 record. He was signed by the Dodgers the following spring, but retired after two ineffective performances.

Marichal returned to his native Dominican Republic, where he owned a 1,000-acre farm. In 1983, he became the first Latin American player elected to the Hall of Fame through the regular selection process.

# Rube Marquard

The season of 1912 was a notable year for pitchers. In the American League, Walter Johnson won 16 consecutive games for the Senators and Joe Wood won the same number in succession for the Red Sox.

But the No. 1 achievement was credited to a slim lefthander of the Giants. A few years earlier, he had been ridiculed as "the $11,000 lemon." By 1912, he had blossomed as "the $11,000 beauty."

Richard LeMarquis, a Cleveland native who was better known as Rube Marquard, won his first start of the season, beating the Dodgers, 18-3, in Brooklyn. Marquard pieced together 19 consecutive victories until, on July 8, he lost to the Cubs, 7-2, in Chicago.

"I should have had 20," Rube stoutly maintained the rest of his days. In a game against Brooklyn, Marquard relieved Jeff Tesreau with the bases loaded and none out in the eighth inning. He struck out Jake Daubert and Zack Wheat and retired a third batter on an infield grounder.

When the Giants scored a ninth-inning run to win the game, the official scorer, following the practice of the times, awarded the victory to Tesreau because he had pitched more innings than Marquard.

In the more than seven decades that followed, Marquard's winning streak withstood the onslaughts of countless other hurlers.

The lefthander's surname was changed by an unknown baseball writer for a long-forgotten reason. And Richard was christened Rube because an Indianapolis newspaperman discerned a resemblance to Rube Waddell, the great and eccentric lefthander of the Philadelphia Athletics.

In 1908, Marquard was on his way to 367 innings pitched and 28 victories for Indianapolis when major league scouts picked up the scent. Just about every club was represented on September 5 when Rube took the mound at Columbus. It was announced that the Indianapolis club would accept offers at the end of the game. After the lefthander hurled a no-hitter, his hometown Cleveland club (which had been shut out by Rube, 2-0, in a spring exhibition) bid $10,500. The Giants, however, won the prize with a bid of $11,000.

Several days later, Marquard arrived at the Polo Grounds and knocked on the clubhouse door, which was opened by Cy Seymour.

"Who the hell are you?" asked the tough-talking outfielder.

"Marquard," was the answer.

"Hey, fellows," yelled Mike Donlin, "look at the bum John McGraw paid $11,000 for."

In his first start, against Cincinnati, jittery Rube hit the first batter and walked the next two.

Marquard beckoned to his catcher. "Maybe I'm trying too hard," he said. "Maybe I should take something off the

**Giants pitcher Rube Marquard is pictured in 1910, the year before his first 20-win season.**

next pitch."

"Okay," replied Roger Bresnahan, "but don't take off too much or this guy will bust one."

Bresnahan was correct. Hans Lobert drove a pitch to the old car barns on Eighth Avenue.

By 1912, Marquard was the idol of Broadway with 26 victories. After his winning streak, in which his teammates supported him with 139 runs while he yielded only 49, the lefthander won only seven games the balance of the year. But he won twice in the World Series, which the Giants lost to the Red Sox.

Rube's popularity was at an all-time peak. Hearts fluttered wherever the 23-year-old celebrity appeared. He made a movie, and he married Blossom Seely, star of the musical comedy stage. He toured with his wife during the winter, doing dance routines with Miss Seely. The marriage was one of three for the pitcher.

After winning 23 games in 1913—for a three-year total of 73—and participating in his third successive World Series, Rube dipped below the 20-victory total. During the 1915 season he was waived to Brooklyn.

Marquard fractured a leg while sliding in 1919 and won only three games, but he came back to help the team win the pennant in 1920, just as he had done in 1916.

One season with Cincinnati and four with the Boston Braves concluded Rube's major league career. Marquard umpired one season in the Eastern League and pitched his final game with Atlanta (Southern) at age 43.

Marquard later worked as a mutuels clerk at various race tracks. He died in 1980 at age 90.

# Eddie Mathews

**Boston Braves rookie Eddie Mathews signs autographs before the team's 1952 home opener.**

In 1949, when it was mandatory for a major league club to retain on its roster for two years any free agent who was paid more than $6,000, Brooklyn's Branch Rickey offered a young California slugger a $10,000 bonus, plus an additional $30,000 for his family, which the family could have used.

So it was more than surprising, and highly suspicious, when scout Johnny Moore of the Boston Braves obtained the youngster's signature, as well as that of his father, for $6,000.

Moore had been a fine—but not great—major league outfielder. However, the speed with which he grabbed the prodigy was of Hall of Fame quality.

Eddie Mathews was at his high school graduation dance in Santa Barbara, Calif., when, at 12:01 a.m., the first possible moment the youth could be signed, Moore arrived on the scene. The formalities were quickly completed and Mathews was headed for baseball prominence, the seventh player to sock 500 career homers.

Explaining their choice of the Boston offer, the father and son revealed they had studied major league rosters and decided that the Braves offered the best opportunity for a young aspirant inasmuch as third baseman Bob Elliott was in the twilight of his career. Moreover, Eddie had no desire to ride a bench for two years without a chance to develop.

Mathews was a triple-threat football player in high school and had dazzled college scouts in the California championship game. However, baseball was his primary interest, an interest that had been nurtured by his grandfather and father, a Western Union operator who transmitted Pacific Coast League box scores.

By the end of the 1951 season, Eddie was with Milwaukee, then in the American Association. In his first at-bat, Mathews, just weeks short of his 20th birthday, slugged a bases-loaded home run.

Eddie's first major league homer was off Phillies left-hander Ken Heintzelman and the ball sailed over the high, distant wall in right-centerfield at Shibe Park in Philadelphia.

Prodigious homers became an early Mathews trademark. He socked one past the scoreboard in center field at Wrigley Field, and another far over the right-field pavilion in St. Louis. But Eddie always felt that his most powerful blow was struck at Crosley Field in Cincinnati where the ball landed three rows from the top of the center-field bleachers and still was rising at impact.

As a rookie in 1952, Mathews rapped 25 homers, beating Ralph Kiner's freshman record set six years earlier. On the next-to-last day of the season, Eddie belted three at

**By 1959, Mathews and Hank Aaron provided the Braves with the most awesome left-right punch in baseball.**

In 1959, Mathews (above) produced 46 home runs and 114 RBIs. Nine years later, Mathews was in St. Louis (below) for Game 2 of the 1968 World Series as a member of the Tigers. He retired at the end of the season.

Ebbets Field, one off Joe Black and two off Ben Wade, to become the first rookie to hit three homers in one game.

When the Braves transferred to Milwaukee in 1953, Mathews was caught up in the civic enthusiasm that helped sweep the team to a pennant four years later. Eddie started slowly in the 1957 World Series, but his home run produced a victory in Game 4 and his high-hopping infield single led to the only run of Game 5.

In the ninth inning of Game 7, when the Yankees loaded the bases with one out, Eddie dived to his right for a backhand stab of Moose Skowron's smash and stepped on third base for a Series-ending force play.

As a thrill, said Mathews, "that play ranked right up there with breaking the 500-homer barrier. I'd made better plays, but that big one in the spotlight stamped me the way I wanted to be remembered."

Eddie was a first baseman for the Houston Astros in July of 1967 when he clouted homer No. 500. The wallop came at the expense of Juan Marichal in Candlestick Park.

Mathews hit 30 homers or more nine straight seasons before he fell one short of that total in 1962. Eddie explained the decline: "One day against Turk Farrell of Houston I took a tremendous swing, missed the ball completely, and tore all the ligaments and tendons in my shoulder. The injury was slow to heal, and even after it did, I became a defensive hitter and developed some bad batting habits. I didn't hit over 30 homers again until 1965."

Mathews finished his playing career as a part-time performer with the 1968 world champion Detroit Tigers.

Eddie managed the Atlanta Braves for part of the 1972 season, all of 1973 and a portion of 1974, until replaced by Clyde King on July 21.

# Christy Mathewson

**Christy Mathewson, known as "Gun Boots" during his collegiate days at Bucknell, was positioned in the back row,** **second from the right, when this 1899 team picture was taken.**

When a 21-year-old pitcher wins 20 games for a seventh-place team, it is generally agreed that he is an artisan of inordinate skill.

But that was not the case in 1902 when the New York Giants attempted to convert Christy Mathewson into a first baseman, and then a shortstop.

The architect of this transformation was Horace Fogel, a gentleman of questionable intellect, who was ushered into the front office early in the year to make way for George Smith as manager.

In July, Smith was replaced by John McGraw, newly arrived from Baltimore. "You can get rid of Fogel," McGraw notified Owner Andrew Freedman. "Anybody who doesn't know any more about baseball than that doesn't have a right to the ball park."

Thus Mathewson was saved for the pitching mound, where he performed so creditably that he was the first pitcher elected to the Hall of Fame.

"There is no doubt that Matty was the greatest pitcher of all time," insisted longtime batterymate Roger Bresnahan. "He was the perfect pitcher. He always pitched to the batter's weakness. He had all kinds of stuff and he knew just where to use it."

During his collegiate days at Bucknell, Mathewson was known as "Gun Boots" because of his proficiency in drop-kicking a football.

Matty broke into pro ball on July 21, 1899, when, pitching for Taunton, he lost to Manchester, 6-5, in a New England League game. The next season, with Norfolk (Virginia), Matty compiled a 20-2 record by July, when he was purchased by the Giants for $2,000.

In addition to a curve and pinpoint control, Mathewson featured a fadeaway (the modern screwball) that he threw about a dozen times a game. The fadeaway, which exerted an excessive strain on his arm, broke into a right-handed batter and, naturally, away from a lefthander.

According to Grover Hartley, a contemporary of Mathewson, the righthander had such magnificent control of all his pitches that he could throw them into an area the size of a grapefruit. One season, Matty hurled 391 innings and walked only 42 batters.

If Christy had a weakness, it was in his habit of coasting with a big lead. On one such occasion, he loaded the bases with none out, bringing McGraw from the dugout. Little Napoleon raved and ranted, but Matty soothed his friend and manager by saying: "Take it easy, it's more fun this way." He then proceeded to strike out the side.

Early in his New York years, Mathewson was nicknamed Big Six after the city's most punctual and efficient fire company. Sam Crane, baseball writer for the Journal,

Mathewson (right) in 1912 with fellow Hall of Famers John McGraw (center), Giants manager, and Wilbert Robinson, a Giants coach.

attached the name to Matty when he wrote: "Mathewson is certainly the Big Six of pitchers."

In 1903, Matty beat the powerful, pennant-winning Pittsburgh Pirates eight times in as many tries, but his best performance came in 1905 when he shut out the Philadelphia A's three times in the World Series.

Mathewson's most heart-breaking game was the final contest of the 1912 World Series against the Red Sox. With the Giants leading by a run, Boston's leadoff batter in the 10th inning hit an easy fly to center field where Fred Snodgrass muffed the ball, allowing the runner to take second. One out later, a walk put runners on first and third with Tris Speaker at the plate.

Again it appeared the Giants were world champions when the Gray Eagle lifted a foul between first and the plate. First baseman Fred Merkle and catcher Chief Meyers converged, pulled up short and let the ball drop.

Speaker then singled to tie the game and the next batter drove home the winning run with a sacrifice fly.

When his arm went dead in 1916, Big Six was traded to Cincinnati, where he was appointed manager. He pitched his final game on September 4, ending the season with 373 victories, high in the National League.

Matty was an Army officer in World War I. He coached the Giants for three seasons and served as president of the Boston Braves from 1923 to 1925 before he died of tuberculosis at age 45.

By 1909, Mathewson was in the midst of one of the greatest baseball careers in history.

# Willie Mays

**Willie Mays was well known for his fielding artistry, but one of his real masterpieces was unveiled in Game 1 of** the 1954 World Series at the Polo Grounds when he made his famous catch to rob Cleveland's Vic Wertz.

Unquestionably, it was the most spectacular getaway in the history of the minor leagues—a .477 average in 35 games, eight home runs, 30 runs batted in, breathtaking speed and outfield catches that challenged the eye of man.

The Minneapolis Millers' 20-year-old center fielder was the rage of the American Association. Nobody doubted that he was programmed for the major leagues.

Once, in a game against Louisville, the phenom raced to the wall in right-center field, dug his spikes into the fence, leaped and somehow came down with the baseball. The batter, Taft Wright, was so confident he had hit a double that he remained glued to second until Manager Pinky Higgins trotted from the dugout to relay the sad tidings.

The prodigy was at the movies in Sioux City, Ia., where the Millers had stopped for an exhibition game, when a phone call came from New York: "Have Willie Mays join the Giants immediately."

Willie did not find immediate success in the National League. In his first 26 times at bat, he made only one hit, a mammoth home run off Warren Spahn.

"Boss man," Willie sobbed to Manager Leo Durocher in the depths of his slump. "I'm hurtin' this team. You'd better bench me or send me back to the minors."

"Don't worry," replied the Lip. "You aren't going anywhere. Just keep swinging because you're my center fielder if you don't get another hit the rest of the year."

Willie's drives soon started to find open spaces. For several weeks he batted at a .360 clip and his average climbed. He was on his way to becoming the Rookie of the Year, finishing with a .274 average and 20 homers.

A native of Westfield, Ala., Willie was playing for the Birmingham Black Barons when he was discovered by Giant scouts Ed Montague and Bill Harris. The Boston Braves had offered $7,500 for Mays, with another $7,500 if he made good, but the Barons' financially pressed owner needed immediate aid, and he accepted the Giants' $10,000 bid. Mays also was given a $5,000 bonus.

Two years later, Willie was a fixture in the New York outfield. Constantly, he would run out from beneath his cap and would make two catches on the same play, spearing the ball with his glove, his cap with his right hand.

Mays' miraculous fielding plays were the talk of the league. Willie made a diving catch against the left-field wall at Ebbets Field to rob Bobby Morgan of extra bases. He held a Del Ennis "triple" to a single. And he threw out Joe Adcock at second base on a sure double.

But the super deluxe production was a catch and throw at the Polo Grounds against the Dodgers.

With Billy Cox on third base, Carl Furillo smacked a drive to right-center field. Just making the catch would have been all that anyone could have asked. But Mays caught the ball, spun in mid-air and uncorked a line throw

**Mays (left) connects for one of his four home runs during a 1961 game against the Milwaukee Braves. Mays (right)** salutes the New York fans who came out to pay tribute to their former star in May of 1963.

to catcher Wes Westrum, who tagged out Cox.

Willie was part of the "Little Miracle of Coogan's Bluff" in 1951 before spending nearly two years in military service. When ne returned, the Giants captured another pennant, in 1954, when Mays won the first of two Most Valuable Player awards.

Wonderful Willie moved west with the Giants in 1958, but he never enjoyed the immense popularity in San Francisco that had been his in Gotham. In the City by the Bay, fans had vivid memories of Joe DiMaggio and, said Willie, "I was just a visitor from New York."

But Mays' sterling qualities as the complete ballplayer never suffered. The man who never had hit more than two homers in a game socked four at Milwaukee—two off Lew Burdette, one off Seth Morehead and one off Don McMahon—on April 30, 1961. On September 22, 1969, he rapped his 600th homer, joining Babe Ruth in that select group, and on July 18, 1970, he singled for his 3,000th hit, becoming only the 10th player to reach that milestone.

Willie appeared in 24 All-Star Games, compiling a .307 average. His foremost thrill was not one of his several homers, but a catch he made on a Ted Williams drive just as it was about to leave Milwaukee's County Stadium in the 1955 All-Star contest.

Mays closed his career where it had started, in New York, with the Mets in 1973. And, as he had started in 1951, he appeared in a World Series. But, at 42, he was only a shadow of the effervescent youth that brought excitement and joy to baseball fans everywhere.

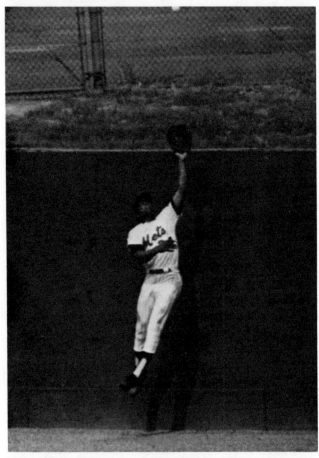

**Mays still had his moments as a Met in 1973, such as this catch that robbed Atlanta's Darrell Evans of a home run.**

# Joe McCarthy

Joe McCarthy (left) made his major league managerial debut with the Cubs, but by the 1939 All-Star Game,

Gabby Hartnett was Chicago's manager and McCarthy was leading the Yankees.

In the winter of 1915-16, Ed Barrow, president of the International League, recommended a Buffalo infielder to the New York Yankees.

A deal was in negotiation when the player decided to sign with Brooklyn of the Federal League. When that outlaw league collapsed, however, the infielder signed with Louisville of the American Association.

By that curious happenstance, Joe McCarthy missed an opportunity to wear a major league uniform a decade before he took over as manager of the Chicago Cubs.

McCarthy possessed only average playing talents, but his keen mind and ability to handle players made him a superlative manager. Many superstars who were in a position to know flatly declared that Joe was the No. 1 skipper.

A native of the Germantown section of Philadelphia, McCarthy attended Niagara University for two years before launching his professional baseball career. Managerial experience at Wilkes-Barre (New York State) and Louisville prepared him for the major league call that came in 1926 from the Cubs.

Marse Joe—he was nicknamed by a Chicago writer—took over an eighth-place club and produced a pennant winner in his fourth season. In his rookie year, McCarthy

demonstrated his strength as a pilot by firing Grover Cleveland Alexander after the pitcher strayed once too often.

The dismissal occurred in Philadelphia. McCarthy received quick support for his actions. A telegram from Owner William Wrigley informed McCarthy: "Congratulations. I've been looking for a manager with enough nerve to do that."

After the Cubs lost the 1929 World Series to the A's, Marse Joe was given another year to avenge the embarrassment, but when he failed in that mission in 1930, he was fired by Wrigley.

One of the Cubs' brightest stars during the McCarthy regime was Hack Wilson, a patron of night spots and John Barleycorn. Under Joe's tactful discipline, Hack batted .356 in 1930, set a major league record by driving in 190 runs and established a National League mark with 56 homers.

Under another manager in 1931, the slugging outfielder's average plunged to .261 and his homer and RBI outputs dwindled to 13 and 61, respectively.

McCarthy took over the Yankees in 1931, inheriting another touchy situation in the person of Babe Ruth, who had applied for the managerial post and was rebuffed with

**McCarthy had taken over the Red Sox by 1949, with Casey Stengel handling his old duties in New York.**

the statement, "You can't manage yourself, how can you manage others?"

But McCarthy had only one request of the Bambino. "Be prompt," Marse Joe requested, and Ruth generally was.

When Joe won a flag with the Cubs in 1929, he became the first pennant-winning pilot without major league playing experience. When he won with the Yankees in 1932, he became the first to produce a champion in both leagues.

While it was not in McCarthy's nature to gloat, he derived a deep sense of satisfaction when the Yanks swept the Cubs in the 1932 Series.

The square-jawed Irishman won seven more titles with the Yankees and won six world championships. He frequently expressed his success formula as "get the players and keep them happy."

Marse Joe had his share of top-flight players who appreciated McCarthy's talents as a leader. "There wasn't a day," said Joe DiMaggio, "that someone on the Yankees didn't learn something from McCarthy."

Phil Rizzuto added, "He would never say anything behind a player's back and he would never second-guess his men."

Marse Joe seldom displayed irritation, but he bristled during his Yankee heyday when Jimmie Dykes of the White Sox referred to him as "a push-button manager."

Marse Joe also flared when it was suggested that differences with Yankees President Larry MacPhail led to his resignation in 1946. It was strictly a matter of ill health, the skipper insisted.

With improved health, McCarthy accepted the managerial post with the Red Sox in 1948.

McCarthy was 90 when he died of pneumonia in 1978 at his farm in suburban Buffalo.

**As Yankee manager, McCarthy cornered eight American League pennants and seven World Series titles.**

# Tommy McCarthy

Of all the colorful nicknames applied to professional baseball players, especially those of the 19th Century, few can equal the designation attached to two outfielders with the Boston Nationals.

With their innovative style of play and lofty batting marks, two sons of the Ould Sod were christened the "Heavenly Twins."

Tommy McCarthy and Hugh Duffy were naturals for adulation in Boston, the seat of Irish culture in America. McCarthy, from South Boston, and Duffy, from small-town Rhode Island, were among the first practitioners of the hit-and-run play.

In addition, McCarthy pioneered in the trap play. He would race in from his outfield position, grab a line drive on the shorthop and throw out a baserunner standing flatfooted. One season, McCarthy was credited with 53 assists, many of them on the trap-play maneuver.

As a player on the diamonds of Boston, McCarthy caught the attention of Tim Murnane, a prominent pitcher of the day and later a sportswriter.

Tommy received his first notice in public print in the Sporting Life in July of 1884: "The Boston Unions are trying a new local player of promise named McCarthy."

In his debut with the Union Association club, Tommy batted ninth and played right field in a 2-1 loss to Chicago. The Boston team collected only one hit off Hugh (One-Armed) Daily and committed nine errors, none by McCarthy.

A righthander, McCarthy also tried his luck at pitching that season but failed to post a victory in seven decisions. His best efforts came in a 2-1 loss to Kansas City and a 2-0 defeat to Milwaukee.

After seeing action with Boston and Philadelphia (both National League clubs) in the next three years, Tommy joined the St. Louis Browns of the American Association, a major league, in 1888. Under the guidance of Charles (Old Roman) Comiskey, Tommy batted .276 in 131 games and stole 109 bases in helping the Browns to their fourth consecutive pennant.

In 1890, when Comiskey jumped to the Players League, McCarthy was appointed manager of the Browns. But the experiment was short-lived, Tommy resigning with a 13-13 record.

Although the A.A. folded after the 1891 season, Browns Owner Chris Von der Ahe maintained that he still owned the rights to his players. The beer baron hired a break-and-entry artist to vandalize McCarthy's hotel room. The escapade netted $19 in cash and a watch, which Chris regarded as a debt paid in full.

Back with Boston (National), McCarthy registered his best batting averages and scoring statistics as he shared the spotlight with other top names like King Kelly, Bobby

**Tommy McCarthy's mastery of the trap play led to later adoption of the infield fly rule.**

Lowe, Fred Tenney and Herman Long.

By this time Tommy was recognized as the master of the trap play, a tactic that umpire Bill Klem noted many years later, led to the adoption of the infield fly rule.

Tommy also was credited with being one of the first to steal a catcher's signs.

After retiring from the game, McCarthy opened a bowling alley and saloon with his "Heavenly Twin" partner. The establishment was known as "Duffy and McCarthy" and was located on Washington Street in Boston. The business prospered until Bostonians developed new Irish heroes.

Tommy scouted for Cincinnati from 1909 to 1912 and for the Boston Braves in 1914 and 1917. In 1918 he managed Newark (International), where one of his players was Ed Rommel, later an outstanding American League pitcher and umpire.

At various times, McCarthy coached baseball at Dartmouth, Holy Cross and Boston College. At Holy Cross, he converted Bill Carrigan from an outfielder into a catcher, the position Carrigan occupied when he starred for the Boston Red Sox.

Another McCarthy product at Holy Cross was Jack Barry, who entertained ideas of being a pitcher until Tommy switched him to shortstop, which Barry played as a member of the Philadelphia A's "$100,000 Infield" in the 1910-14 period.

# Joe McGinnity

Even before he pitched his first doubleheader, the husky righthander from Illinois was known as the "Iron Man."

When he joined the Brooklyn Superbas in 1900, the pitcher was asked by a sportswriter, "What do you do during the off-season?"

"I work in my father-in-law's iron foundry in Oklahoma; I'm an iron man," replied Joe McGinnity who, in at least one journalist's accounts, was referred to as "Iron Man Joe."

McGinnity gained immortality as the iron man of the pitching mound in 1903 when he hurled three doubleheaders in one month.

Joe was on his way to a 31-victory season for the Giants when he staked his claim to superior stamina and durability. He won a twin bill in Boston, 4-1 and 5-2, on August 1.

A week later, Iron Man Joe repeated the stunt at the Polo Grounds, defeating Brooklyn, 6-1 and 4-3. An excellent runner for a man his size, McGinnity stole home for the Giants' first run in the nightcap and also contributed two singles to the victory.

On August 31, Joe beat the Phillies twice at the Polo Grounds, 4-1 and 9-2.

Two other times in his career, McGinnity pitched both ends of doubleheaders, which he split.

McGinnity broke into Organized Ball with Montgomery (Southern). After pitching for Kansas City (Western), McGinnity dropped out of the professional ranks for three seasons. The nation was in the throes of a financial panic and Joe found that semipro ball in Decatur, Ill., was more profitable, especially for a newlywed.

One season with Peoria (Western Association) led to Joe's acquisition by the Baltimore Orioles in 1899. The following year, McGinnity accompanied his manager, Ned Hanlon, and several teammates to Brooklyn. He returned to Baltimore in the early days of the American League, then moved to the Giants with John McGraw in 1902.

Despite his outstanding achievements, McGinnity appeared in only one World Series. He might have added a second, except that McGraw refused to take on the A.L. champion Red Sox in 1904.

Giants pitcher Joe McGinnity, pictured in 1908, was known for his stamina.

The following season, McGinnity faced the Philadelphia A's twice in the Series. He lost to Chief Bender, 3-0, in the second game, but defeated Eddie Plank, 1-0, in the fourth.

Iron Man Joe played a key role in the famous Fred Merkle incident of 1908. McGinnity was coaching at third base when Al Bridwell singled home what appeared to be the winning run against the Cubs. But Merkle, the runner at first base, followed the practice of the day and did not touch second. The omission was spotted by second baseman Johnny Evers, who shouted for the baseball. On the throw from the outfield, McGinnity scuffled with Chicago players. He stoutly maintained that he recovered the game ball and threw it into the stands. The ball that Cub teammates threw to Evers, who stepped on the bag for the forceout of Merkle, was, according to Joe, an extra ball supplied from the Cubs' bench.

McGinnity's departure from the majors after the 1908 season did not mean the end of pitching for Joe. As a pitcher and manager, he roamed the minor leagues and won more than 200 games in the bushes. At 52, he won 15 games for Dubuque (Mississippi Valley). He was 54 when he compiled a 6-6 record for Dubuque in 1925.

The following seasons, McGinnity returned to the Dodgers as a coach. He was stationed in the first-base box, his legs crossed and his hands shoved deep in the pockets of his sweater (which players wore in the days before windbreakers). Within weeks after the start of the season, Joe's sweater had been stretched to his knees.

When he got a sign from the bench, Joe sprang into action, uncrossing his legs and slapping his hands on his knees. His gestures brought a droll observation from his manager, easy-going Wilbert Robinson:

"Every time I give Joe a sign, it's like ringing a fire alarm. I don't know if any players are gettin' the sign, but I know everybody in the park is, including the peanut vendor."

McGinnity was an assistant coach at Williams College before he succumbed to cancer in 1929 at age 58.

# John McGraw

John McGraw was a 17-year-old first-year player (left) for Olean of the New York-Pennsylvania League in 1890.

By 1902, he was the player-manager of the New York Giants.

Honus Wagner was the runner at second base when the next Louisville batter stroked a single to the outfield on which the speedy Dutchman seemed certain to score. When Wagner reached the vicinity of third base, however, the fielder thrust out his hip and knocked Wagner off stride. Honus was out at the plate.

That was the way the fielder, John McGraw, played baseball. His antics could go unnoticed because the attention of the single umpire working the game was directed elsewhere.

When a runner tagged up, intent on scoring on a sacrifice fly, McGraw would slip his finger around the unsuspecting fellow's belt, delaying his start just long enough to produce a putout at the plate.

That trick worked only until Pete Browning unbuckled his belt, leaving it dangling in McGraw's hand as Pete scored.

Despite his size (5-foot-7, 155 pounds), McGraw was a scrapper from the very beginning. In his first day with the Baltimore Orioles, he was referred to as "the batboy." Veteran players crowded onto the bench until the rookie, sitting at the end, was shoved onto the ground. He came up with fists flailing and thereafter was an accepted member of the rough and rowdy crew.

The Truxton, N.Y., Irishman joined the Orioles in 1892 and was a leading actor in baseball drama for 40 years. His first Baltimore contract called for $1,500 a year, uncommonly high for a rookie.

McGraw sparked the Orioles to three pennants in the 1890s. He was as fast on his feet as he was with his fists. He was expert on the hit-and-run play and he could foul pitches off almost at will. Once he fouled off 15 consecutive pitches from Clark Griffith of Chicago. At the time, fouls were not considered strikes.

At another time against Griffith, McGraw maneuvered his knee over the plate and was struck by the ball. Umpire Hank O'Day called, "Strike one." Griffith threw again, another nick on the knee. "Strike two." The Old Fox threw again and McGraw took a third pitch off his knee. "Yer out," shouted O'Day as McGraw walked away boiling.

When Manager Ned Hanlon and several key players shifted to Brooklyn in 1899, McGraw stayed behind. He and catcher Wilbert Robinson owned a saloon-bowling alley called "The Diamond" that needed attention and, for a second reason, John was named manager of the Orioles.

Little Napoleon played for St. Louis in 1900, then ac-

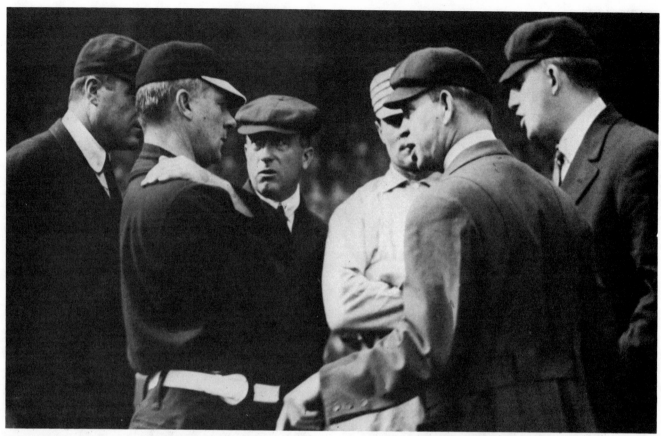

Manager John McGraw came decked out in his special black uniform for the 1911 World Series against the A's. The Giants discarded their regular uniforms because black was what they wore in their last Series triumph in 1905. Also pictured are (from left) Bill Dinneen, Tommy Connolly, the A's Harry Davis, Bill Klem and Bill Brennan.

cepted Ban Johnson's suggestion that he take over the Baltimore franchise in the American League, a new major league.

But in July of 1902, the accomplished umpire baiter grew disenchanted with Johnson for the manner in which the league president backed his arbiters. McGraw accepted an offer to manage the New York Giants. His release was purchased for $10,000, which represented a dividend to McGraw, who was a Baltimore stockholder.

McGraw made his New York debut on July 19, 1902, and the Giants lost to Philadelphia, 4-3. Four days later, he posted his initial victory, 4-1, at Brooklyn.

In 30 years as the Giants' manager, McGraw won 10 pennants and three World Series. He finished out of the first division only twice.

One sure method of infuriating McGraw was to call him "Muggsy," a fact unknown to Brooklyn's Tommy McMillan. Passing McGraw during pregame activities, the rookie called out airily, "Hiya, Muggsy." McGraw unleashed a torrent of oaths on the kid, who apologized the next day after learning the seriousness of his offense. McGraw was so affected by the apology that he escorted McMillan to shortstop where he gave him pointers on playing the position.

McGraw was earning about $75,000 late in his career and also received dividends as a stockholder in the Giants. The first modern manager to win four consecutive pennants, he was a soft touch for old players, generally finding jobs for them in the organization.

He also was free with his money. When the Florida land boom burst in the 1920s—a promotion to which McGraw had lent his name—and a number of former players went broke in their investments, John gave up nearly all his salary for six years to rectify the financial setbacks.

On June 3, 1932, McGraw summoned Bill Terry into his office and offered him the managerial post. The manager and first baseman—who accepted the job—had not talked for two years after Terry openly criticized his boss' harassment of a player.

Doctors had ordered McGraw to retire as manager, but permitted him to remain as a club vice-president.

John made his last public appearance in early February of 1934 when he attended a dinner given by Giants Owner Charles Stoneham for National League club owners.

McGraw died of internal hemorrhaging at New Rochelle Hospital later that month and was buried in Baltimore.

# Bill McKechnie

Pittsburgh Manager Bill McKechnie and Senators Manager Bucky Harris join in festivities before the start of the 1925 World Series.

In the days before World War I, Frank Chance was asked why his constant off-the-field companion was a .200 hitter.

"Because he's the only guy on this club," explained the manager of the New York Highlanders, "who knows what the game is all about. He can't hit worth a hoot, but he has something under his cap."

For more than 40 years, Bill McKechnie was regarded as one of the keenest intellects in baseball. He knew how the game should be played and detected things that escaped the attention of others. He knew the capabilities of his players without expecting too much from them.

He was the only manager to win pennants with three franchises, a distinction that would have eluded him if he had won a political contest in 1929.

McKechnie won a flag with the St. Louis Cardinals in 1928, but lost the World Series to the Yankees in four games and was demoted to Rochester (International). He was crushed.

Bill sought and won the Republican nomination for tax collector in his native Wilkinsburg, Pa., promising the electorate that he would retire from baseball if he won the post.

Deacon Bill lost the race and remained in the game for another 20 years. He piloted Boston's National League club for eight seasons, winning Manager of the Year honors in 1937 for guiding a supposedly dismal team to a 79-73 record and fifth place.

A master handler of pitchers, McKechnie turned aging minor leaguers Jim Turner and Lou Fette into 20-game winners for Boston. But the club's future was bleak; Judge Emil Fuchs, the owner, was in financial straits constantly. When the call came to take over the Cincinnati Reds under wealthy Owner Powel Crosley, McKechnie accepted. In two years he converted an eighth-place team into a pennant winner. In 1940, he again won managerial honors by man-

ufacturing another world championship to go with one he had produced at Pittsburgh in 1925.

The Deacon received his initial managerial opportunity as a player-manager in the summer of 1915 when he replaced Bill Phillips at the helm of the Newark club in the Federal League. The Federal League died at the end of the season and McKechnie didn't manage again until 1922, when he became the Pirates' skipper. Three years later, the N.L. champion Bucs beat Washington in the World Series.

Ordinarily, Bill was a soft-spoken, affable individual, but he was an unchained demon in Game 3 of the '25 Series when umpire Cy Rigler's decision went against Pittsburgh.

In the eighth inning, with the Senators leading by one run, Earl Smith of the Bucs hit a deep fly to right-center field where Sam Rice leaped against the low fence, tumbled into the Griffith Stadium bleachers and, after a tantalizing delay, emerged with the ball. Rigler allowed the catch. The Deacon protested vehemently—but in vain.

In later years, the weight of evidence indicated that a bleacherite had slipped the ball into Rice's glove.

The incident did not influence the outcome of the Series, the Pirates winning in a dramatic seventh game.

After his second world title in 1940, when the Reds defeated the Tigers, Bill remained on the job in Cincinnati through 1946.

McKechnie accepted the role as pitching coach under Lou Boudreau at Cleveland and polished up a world championship staff in 1948. The Deacon had opportunities to manage the Chicago Cubs and White Sox, the St. Louis Browns and the Pirates, but declined the offers.

McKechnie retired after the 1949 season and several years later moved to Bradenton, Fla. The canny Scot had no financial worries. He owned oil wells, a meat-saw factory, half of a rock-bearing mountain, parcels of real estate in Pittsburgh and a tomato farm in Florida. He was 78 at the time of his death in 1965.

# Joe Medwick

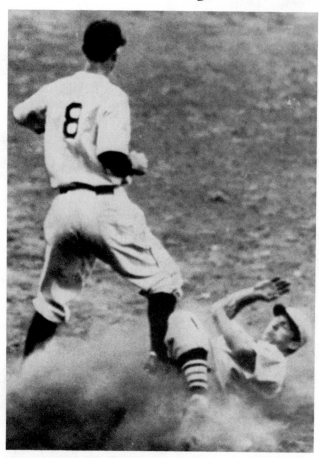

The Joe Medwick controversy in Game 7 of the 1934 Series began with a hard slide into Detroit's Marv Owen.

When Medwick (7) returned to his left-field position, irate Tiger fans showered debris onto the field, delaying the game

The 1934 World Series had just ended disastrously for the Detroit Tigers and Manager Mickey Cochrane was in the clubhouse following his club's 11-0 loss in Game 7. Reflecting on the 23-year-old left fielder of the St. Louis Cardinals, Cochrane exclaimed, "Where, oh where, do they grow fellows like that?"

Black Mike had ample cause to be impressed with Joe (Muscles) Medwick, who rapped four hits in Game 1 and 11 for the Series in which he batted .379.

Barrel-chested Joe was the son of Hungarian immigrants and a three-sport star at Carteret (N.J.) High School, where he was discovered by Charles (Pop) Kelchner, a scout for the Cardinals.

Medwick had visions of a college football career and hesitated to sign a professional baseball contract until it was suggested that he play under an alias to protect his amateur status.

As Mickey King, he broke into Organized Ball in 1930 with Scottdale of the Middle Atlantic League and batted .419 in 75 games.

A two-year stint in the Texas League was all the additional seasoning that Joe needed before joining the Cardi-

nals in late 1932. Nicknamed Ducky because a fan thought his walking style resembled that of a waterfowl, Medwick met instantaneous success as the left fielder on the rough-and-tumble club known as the Gas House Gang.

Joe contributed generously to the National League team's reputation as a brawling aggregation. He was quick with his fists, so quick that teammate Dizzy Dean observed; "You try to argue with him and before you can say a doggone word, he bops you."

Cardinal players learned early the folly of talking impolitely to the swaggering outfielder. One day pitcher Ed Heusser censured Joe for failing to hustle after a fly ball. A punch to the jaw sent Ed to the dugout floor.

Another time, pitcher Tex Carleton, scheduled to start for the Redbirds, reported to Manager Frank Frisch with a black eye. Tex had made the mistake of walking in front of Medwick once too often as Joe posed for a photographer. "Do that once more," snarled Joe, "and I'll smack you."

Once, in Pittsburgh, a dispute arose between Dizzy and Paul Dean on one side and Medwick on the other. The brothers decided to teach their teammate a lesson and started for him. Grabbing a bat, Ducky announced, "One

Commissioner Kenesaw Mountain Landis finally ordered Medwick removed from the game for his own safety.

Medwick was the last National Leaguer to win the Triple Crown, accomplishing the feat in 1937.

at a time, and I'll kill you both. But if you're comin' together, I'll separate you." The Deans revised their plans.

At the plate, Medwick was oblivious to the strike zone. Leo Durocher remembered that the first time he saw Joe, the kid clouted a double, two home runs and a single— "and he had to reach for every pitch."

Eldon Auker, who was victimized by Joe's hitting in the 1934 Series, lamented, "You throw him a strike and he ignores it. Throw the ball over his head and he hits a home run."

More than anything, Joe loved his base hits. At a time when Pepper Martin was in a slump, a newspaperman scattered hairpins in a hotel lobby, hoping that Martin would find the pins (each one was regarded as a base hit by superstitious ballplayers).

But Medwick came along first and started to scoop up the pieces of luck.

"Hey," said the newsman, "those are for Pepper."

"The hell with Martin," snapped Medwick, "let him find his own hairpins."

Medwick was not on the premises when the Cardinals wrapped up the 1934 World Series. In running out a triple,

he had engaged in a kicking match with third baseman Marv Owen. On returning to his left-field position, Joe was bombarded with over-ripe fruit and vegetables by the bleacherites. When the fans would not desist, Medwick was removed from the game "for your own safety," according to Commissioner K.M. Landis.

At the time, Medwick had 11 hits and would have batted once more in quest of a record 12th hit. Chick Fullis, who replaced Joe, got the last at-bat—and singled.

Medwick, a Triple Crown winner and N.L. Most Valuable Player with the Cardinals in 1937, was traded to Brooklyn in June of 1940. A few days later, the Cardinals visited Ebbets Field where Bob Bowman, who had some heated words with Joe in a hotel elevator, beaned Ducky and sent him to the hospital with a concussion.

Although only 28 when the beaning occurred, Medwick never regained the savage batting style of other years.

The onetime firebrand mellowed in his later years and was welcomed affectionately at baseball gatherings. He was serving as a minor league batting instructor for the Cardinals in 1975 when he suffered a fatal heart attack at St. Petersburg, Fla., at age 63.

# Johnny Mize

By 1939, Johnny Mize was a bona fide slugger for the St. Louis Cardinals. Ten years later, Mize was wearing the

same uniform as another slugging great, Joe DiMaggio, and nearing the end of his career.

Cincinnati Manager Charley Dressen was ecstatic about the graceful first baseman, calling him "the greatest rookie I've ever seen." It was the spring of 1935 and the kid carried a $55,000 price tag that the Reds would have to pay if they decided to keep the Cardinal prospect.

"I was willing to gamble on him," said General Manager Larry MacPhail, "but the board of directors wasn't."

The Cardinals shipped the prospect, Johnny Mize, to Rochester where, in midseason, he suffered another in a series of Charley horses that had blighted his career.

Mize was recalled by the Cards and turned over to Dr. Robert F. Hyland, famed "Surgeon General of Baseball," who discovered a growth on the player's pelvis. The doctor leveled with Mize, informing him that even if an operation were successful, it would not necessarily enable him to return to baseball. There was a possibility, too, that he could be crippled for life.

"Get the knives ready," said the big Georgian.

"He never batted an eye," reported Hyland. "I'm as proud of the results as anything I've ever done in the operating room."

Hyland's skill and Mize's determination to succeed combined to produce one of the foremost performers in the history of the Cardinals, Giants and Yankees.

Mize made his debut with St. Louis in the spring of 1936, dividing his time between the outfield and first base. Of Johnny's first 28 hits, five were home runs, four were triples and eight were doubles. Mize went on to Rookie of the Year honors with an average of .329.

By 1938, reports were circulating around the National League that Mize could be handled by a change-of-pace curve. His .250 average lent substance to the notion until the Boston Bees visited St. Louis. Jim Turner tried the slow treatment on Big John and watched three home runs sail out of Sportsman's Park.

A week later, the Giants repeated the slow-curve approach. Again, three home runs. Mize finished the season with a .337 average.

In addition to his hitting achievements, Mize was a fielding artist, a quality that won him his nickname of "Big Cat." One afternoon, while John was catching low throws and stopping wicked bouncers at first base, teammate Joe

**Mize gets a warm reception from Yogi Berra after hitting a home run in the fourth game of the 1952 World Series against the Dodgers. Mize played in five Series, all with the Yankees.**

Orengo exclaimed, "Ain't he a wonder? Why, he's a big cat."

During his Cardinal career, Mize made two unassisted double plays in one game and set a record for first basemen by playing 61 consecutive games without making an error.

After the 1941 season, Mize was swapped to the Giants in a multi-player trade. He performed admirably in his first season at the Polo Grounds, then spent three years in the Navy in the Pacific.

When peace rumors started to circulate, Big John, who was larger than when he left the States, embarked on a major weight-loss program that returned him to the Giants at a svelte 220 pounds.

Mize slugged 51 home runs in 1947 (when the Giants socked 221), but he found himself a discard two seasons later when the Giants sold him to the Yankees because, Leo Durocher said, the slowed-down slugger did not fit into the manager's plans for a running team at the Polo Grounds.

As a Yankee, the big fellow participated in five World Series in as many years. He was devastating in the seven-game 1952 classic against the Brooklyn Dodgers.

In the ninth inning of Game 3, Mize pinch-hit for pitcher Tom Gorman and crashed a homer into the right-field seats.

The next day, in Game 4, he took over at first base for slumping Joe Collins and clouted a fourth-inning homer in Allie Reynolds' 2-0 victory.

John smacked a third homer in as many days in an 11-inning loss in Game 5, then contributed two singles in the deciding triumph in Game 7. At 39, Mize led all Series players with a .400 average.

The superlative performance earned Mize another contract with the Yankees, but he pinch-hit only three times in the 1953 Series and failed to hit safely.

When Dodgers catcher Roy Campanella was asked if John's 0-for-3 performance meant the Dodgers had finally learned how to pitch to the aging slugger, he quipped: "We always did know how to pitch to him, but some days when you're squatting behind the plate Mr. Mize's bat swells up."

# Stan Musial

**Stan Musial wore a Rochester uniform for 54 games in 1941 before making the jump to St. Louis.**

In August of 1940 at Orlando, Fla., the 19-year-old center fielder for the Daytona Beach team made a diving catch of a line drive and landed heavily and painfully on his left shoulder.

A lump formed and the lefthander, who had compiled an 18-5 pitching record while not playing the outfield, saw hopes for a mound career evaporate in the months that followed.

But there was one redeeming factor. While he may have been unable to pitch, Stan Musial retained a sharp batting eye. And when it came time to distribute the wealth of talent in the St. Louis Cardinals' farm system the next spring, the fleet-footed youngster was assigned to Springfield of the Western Association.

Before the 1941 season had run its course, the dead-armed pitcher of a year earlier had batted .379 in the Class C league, .326 for Rochester (International) and .426 in 12 games for the Cardinals.

Musial was in the National League to stay for 22 seasons. On the last day of the 1963 campaign, Commissioner Ford Frick saluted the nearly 43-year-old grandfather as "baseball's perfect warrior. . . . baseball's perfect knight."

Between arrival and departure, Musial ingratiated himself to millions with his qualities as a player and as a person. He wore a perpetual smile and when he wasn't driving baseballs to every corner of National League parks, he was greeting folks with his trademark salutation: "Waddya say! Waddya say!"

The son of a Polish immigrant who settled in the indus-

**By 1942, Musial was a Cardinal regular and well on the road to greatness.**

**Musial connected for hit No. 3,000 on May 13, 1958, off Cubs pitcher Moe Drabowsky during a game at Wrigley** **Field. Musial played five more seasons and collected 630 more hits.**

trial town of Donora, Pa., Stan passed up a basketball scholarship at the University of Pittsburgh to cast his lot with professional baseball.

He registered his first major league hit on September 17, 1941. It was the first of his 725 doubles and was struck against Jim Tobin, knuckleball pitcher of the Boston Braves.

In the first game of a doubleheader against Chicago that same year, Musial doubled twice and singled twice. In the ninth inning, while the Cubs' first baseman argued over a close play, Stan raced home from second base with the winning run. In the second game, he rapped two more hits and made two diving catches, leading Chicago Manager Jimmy Wilson to comment: "Nobody, but nobody, can be that good."

Musial's batting crouch was unique. It was described as resembling a small boy peeking around a corner looking for the cops. When Ted Williams imitated the stance, he hit himself on his leg with the bat when he swung.

Musial was not easily intimidated. In a game against Brooklyn, he was knocked down on the first two pitches from Van Lingle Mungo. On the third pitch, Musial tripled. As umpire Larry Goetz brushed off the plate, he yelled to the mound, "Hey, Van, you sure scared the hell out of that kid, didn't you!"

When the Pasquel brothers of Mexico raided major league clubs for talent in 1946, Musial was a prime objec-

tive. Stan, earning $12,500 at the time, was offered a $75,000 bonus and a five-year contract for $125,000. He turned it down to honor his contract with the Cardinals.

Stan could play hurt, too. In Boston, he abruptly ripped tape off his injured wrists and rapped five hits off Warren Spahn and relievers. It was his fourth five-hit game of the season, tying a record set by Ty Cobb.

Musial enjoyed his finest season in 1948 when he led the N.L. in all major offensive departments except home runs—and he missed in that department by only one rained-out homer.

Stan clouted six homers in 24 All-Star Games. His most notable drives occurred in Milwaukee in 1955 when his 12th-inning blow produced an N.L. victory, and at Yankee Stadium in 1960 when he socked a pinch homer into the third tier of the right-field stands to evoke a standing ovation.

May 2, 1954, proved a home run bonanza for Stan. Facing the Giants on an overcast Sunday at St. Louis, Musial belted three home runs in the first game of a doubleheader and two in the second.

Musial collected his 3,000th major league hit—a double—at Chicago on May 13, 1958, and closed his career with 3,630 safeties (1,815 at home, 1,815 on the road).

In lasting admiration for a superstar, the baseball writers of St. Louis erected a statue of Musial outside Busch Memorial Stadium.

# Kid Nichols

Although not an imposing figure at 5-foot-10½ and 180 pounds, Kid Nichols had a fastball that reportedly was the equal of that thrown by Amos Rusie, famed righthander of the New York Giants.

Nichols was one of baseball's all-time bargains. He was sold by Omaha of the Western Association for $3,000 and won 20 or more games in each of his first 10 seasons with Boston's National League team. In nine consecutive years, the pitcher topped the 25-victory mark.

Nichols was a workhorse. In his first five major league seasons, his innings-pitched totals were 424, 423, 454, 414 and 417. In six of the next seven years he registered more than 300 innings.

Although he never pitched a no-hitter, Kid (so called early in his career because of his size) came as close as possible on a number of occasions. His most memorable performance occurred in his rookie season when he hooked up with Rusie at the Polo Grounds. The teams battled in a scoreless tie in the 1890 game until, with two out in the 13th inning, outfielder Mike Tiernan tagged Nichols for a home run.

It was the year of the Players League and after one of that circuit's games at a nearby park, fans swarmed into the Polo Grounds to watch the conclusion of the Nichols-Rusie struggle.

Kid pitched the Beaneaters to pennants in 1897 and 1898. He was already earning the top salary permitted by the league, $2,400. He demanded a raise for 1899 and finally accepted a $235 bonus for winning the pennant the previous year.

By this time the press was referring to Nichols as "Nervy Nick." He had defeated the Baltimore Orioles two out of three times to clinch the flag for Boston.

After three more seasons in Boston, Nichols bought a part interest in the Kansas City (Western) club. He managed the team in 1902 and 1903 and pitched Kansas City to a total of 48 victories.

Nichols was pitcher-manager for the St. Louis Cardinals

**Fastballer Kid Nichols put together his final 20-victory season in 1904 for the Cardinals.**

in 1904. Although he won 21 games, the club suffered from a shortage of talent and finished fifth.

Conditions did not improve appreciably the next season and the Cardinals won only 19 of their first 48 games before Nichols was ousted as manager in mid-June.

Frank DeHaas Robinson had hired Nichols, but Kid was dismissed by Frank's brother, Stanley.

"Somehow, I always felt that Stanley had it in for me," explained Kid. "But firing me as manager was only the beginning of my troubles. In Cincinnati one day—I think I had pitched the day before—Stanley ordered me to work on one of the gates. Players had to make themselves useful in more ways than one in those days and he wanted me to keep an eye on the tickets to see that we got an honest count.

"Anyhow, I told Stanley I wasn't going to work any gate, that I was going to the Latonia race track. He fired me off the club."

Kid joined Philadelphia and, in his first appearance, defeated the Cardinals, 2-1. "That gave me a lot of personal satisfaction," he said.

Nichols retired from the game after the 1906 season and opened bowling alleys in Kansas City. In partnership with Joe Tinker, former Cub shortstop, he entered the motion picture business. He also sold movie film in outlying areas and dabbled in real estate.

Kid also managed a 34-alley bowling emporium, one of the largest in Missouri, and he was recognized as one of the finest bowlers in Kansas City. At age 64, he won the Class A championship.

For a while, Kid coached the baseball team at Missouri Valley College in Marshall, Mo.

Nichols' finest hour came in 1949 when he went to Cooperstown to see his name enshrined in the Hall of Fame. It was an honor denied him for many years, although he always was among the leading candidates.

Nichols died in Kansas City in 1953 at age 83.

# Jim O'Rourke

As a player for the Buffalo club of the National League in 1881, John Peters compiled an undistinguished record. But he did acquire a measure of distinction for the answer he received when he asked for a pay raise.

"I'm sorry," the team manager replied, "but the exigencies of the occasion and the condition of our exchequer will not permit anything of the sort at this period of our existence. Subsequent developments in the field of finance may remove the present gloom and we may emerge into a condition where we may see fit to reply in the affirmative to your exceedingly modest request."

Not surprisingly, Peters did not renew his request. One confrontation with Orator Jim O'Rourke convinced him that his present salary was altogether adequate.

Unquestionably, O'Rourke had a way with words. Once, when he was president of the Connecticut League and also catcher for Bridgeport in the same circuit, he became embroiled in a heated dispute with the umpire. After using profanity, O'Rourke recognized the seriousness of his offense and whipped off his mask. Addressing the crowd, he said: "As president of the Connecticut League, I hereby fine player James O'Rourke $10 for swearing at the umpire." He then resumed his position.

O'Rourke, the son of a Bridgeport, Conn., farmer, was left fatherless at a young age and played ball only when farm chores would allow. Before his mother would permit him to sign a professional contract, she insisted that the team management provide a farm laborer to pinch-hit for her son.

When the N.L. opened for business in 1876, Jim was a member of the Boston team that inaugurated the season in Philadelphia on April 22. With two outs in the first inning, O'Rourke singled to left off Lon Knight, thereby rapping the first hit in big-league history.

O'Rourke had arrived in Boston in 1873, playing for the city's team in the National Association (a professional league). Because the Irish were held in low regard at that point in Boston history, Manager Harry Wright asked Jim if he would change his surname to conceal his Gaelic origins. The suggested alias was Rourke, a poorly veiled pseudo-

**Orator Jim O'Rourke (pictured in 1887) had a way with words and bat.**

nym, but it made no difference to Jim, who replied, "Mr. Wright, I would rather die than give up my father's name. A million dollars would not tempt me."

In 1874, Jim was a member of the first missionary group to visit England. The Red Stockings and Philadelphia Athletics played 14 games in the United Kingdom, Boston winning eight contests.

O'Rourke played three seasons with the Boston Nationals and became a local favorite. When the team sought to deduct $20 from his 1878 salary to pay for his uniform, Jim resisted adamantly. The impasse was resolved only when the fans passed the hat and raised the required amount.

Orator Jim moved on to Providence for one season, back to Boston for another, and then to Buffalo for four years before going to New York. In 1888, he played on the Giants' first flag winner.

After five more years as a big-league player, O'Rourke tried his hand at umpiring in the N.L. in 1894, but gave it up after one season.

Back in Bridgeport, he organized the Victor League, forerunner of the Connecticut League. Jim managed and caught for the local club, which played its games on a diamond constructed on the old O'Rourke farm.

In 1904, O'Rourke longed to play once more with the team for which he helped win pennants in 1888 and 1889. Manager John McGraw gave his consent and allowed the 52-year-old man to catch the Giants' pennant-clinching game. O'Rourke singled once in four at-bats.

O'Rourke sold the Bridgeport club after the 1908 season and devoted his remaining years to the practice of law. He earlier had earned his degree from the Yale Law School.

He was a member of the fire commission and the paving and street commission in Bridgeport, and he served as a director of the National League and the Arbitration Board of the minors.

On New Year's Day of 1919—"a very cold day," according to his daughter—Orator Jim walked into Bridgeport to see a client. He contracted a cold that developed into pneumonia, which claimed his life seven days later.

# Mel Ott

The rise of Mel Ott's right foot usually spelled trouble for opposing pitchers.

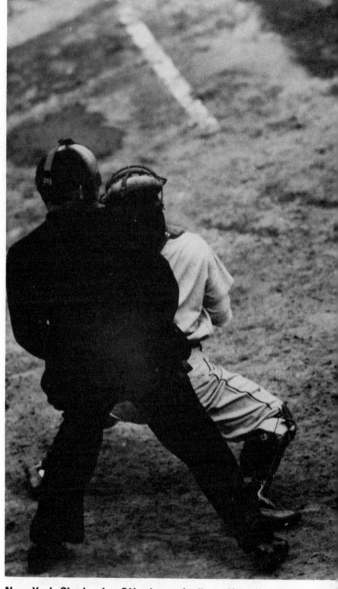

New York Giants star Ott, shown fouling off a pitch in the 194? All-Star Game, hit four home runs in his three World Series, bu~

The 16-year-old catcher from Gretna (La.) High School was heartbroken. He and his batterymate had tried out for the New Orleans (Southern) team. The pitcher had received a contract, but the catcher had not.

"You're too young," the catcher was told.

Years later, Mel Ott recalled that "I must have blubbered something in my disapointment because the owner said to me, 'If you want to play semipro ball in the country, I can fix you up with a team that plays three or four games a week. It's in a little town called Patterson, about 90 miles from here. Just tell Harry Williams that I sent you.' "

The sadness over his failure to make the New Orleans team evaporated when Ott learned that Williams, a wealthy lumber baron, would pay him $150 a month plus expenses, including haircuts, movies and sodas. "And whenever somebody did well," said Mel, "they passed the hat so that I was earning more in extras than I was in salary."

Before the summer was spent, Williams dispatched a telegram to his friend, John McGraw, telling the manager of the New York Giants, "I think I have a real prize for you."

"Have your prize report to me at the Polo Grounds,"

McGraw replied. After quieting maternal fears about his safety in the big city, the teen-ager boarded a train and arrived in Penn Station on schedule.

Getting to the Polo Grounds presented more of a problem. "I must have changed subway trains 12 times in the two hours it took me to get to the Polo Grounds, but I finally made it," he remembered.

McGraw's first decision after watching the prodigy was that he was not a catcher. Ott's stocky legs were not intended to do a lot of crouching; Mel was designed to be an outfielder.

McGraw's second decision was that Ott would remain on the bench with him, that his development would not be entrusted to a minor league manager, not even Casey ever connected in any of the 11 midseason classics in which he participated.

Stengel.

"I could help you develop that kid Ott if you let me have him for a year at Toledo," said Stengel.

McGraw exploded. "Ott stays with me!" he bellowed in red-faced rage. "No minor league manager is going to ruin him."

McGraw feared that somebody would tamper with Ott's unique batting style, in which he lifted his right foot before striding into the pitch.

The manager took a fatherly interest in the youngster, even fining him for playing poker with Bill Terry and other veterans. "I don't want you playing cards with the men," McGraw advised.

Ott played in 35 games as a 17-year-old, 82 at age 18,

During his illustrious career with the Giants, Ott hit 511 home runs and produced 2,876 hits.

124 at 19 and 150 (all but one of the Giants' games) when he was 20.

Ott smacked the first of his 511 major league home runs on July 18, 1927. It was an inside-the-park blow on which Chicago center fielder Hack Wilson missed a shoestring catch.

Ott's last homer was hit at New York on opening day, April 16, 1946, when he connected against Oscar Judd of the Phillies.

For 22 seasons, Ott patrolled right field for the Giants, delivering crucial hits, throwing out baserunners with his rifle arm and ingratiating himself to everyone with his pleasant manner and constant smile.

He set records in wholesale lots and for many years his 511 home runs represented a National League record. He socked four home runs in three World Series, but never connected in 11 All-Star Games.

Ott succeeded teammate Terry as manager in 1942 and remained on the job until midseason of 1948 when he was replaced by Leo Durocher. Mel was too easy-going, it was generally agreed, to get the most out of his players.

He broadcast Detroit Tigers games for a while and managed Oakland (Pacific Coast) in 1951-52.

Ott was in the contracting business in New Orleans when, on the night of November 14, 1958, he was involved in a head-on automobile collision near Bay St. Louis, La.

The former home run king suffered fractures of both legs and multiple internal injuries. After emergency treatment at Gulfport, Miss., he was moved to New Orleans, where he died on November 21 at age 49.

# Satchel Paige

Future teammates Bob Feller and Satchel Paige got together in 1946 (left) during an Indians-Kansas City Mon-

archs barnstorming tour. Two years later, Paige (right) was ready to make his major league debut for Cleveland.

His age was never clearly determined, but he insisted—usually when all other research failed—that he was born in Mobile, Ala., in 1906.

But his age was of little consequence when Leroy (Satchel) Paige started to throw a baseball. His control was phenomenal and stories of his accuracy mushroomed along his pathway as he meandered with his oversized feet through the Negro Leagues and, in the final stages, into the white man's major leagues.

When Bill Veeck brought him into the major leagues with Cleveland in 1948, the question arose if Satch still could thread a needle with his pitches.

"Jim Hegan grabbed a towel to brush off the plate," Paige remembered later. "I told him there wasn't any use for that and gave him a gum wrapper and told him to lay it lengthwise on the plate. After I split that wrapper a few times with my fastball, they decided I still had my control."

The life story of the rubber-armed righthander is told best in anecdotes. In 1948, when the Yankees were challenging the pennant-bound Indians for the league lead, Satch was summoned with none out in the ninth inning and Phil Rizzuto dancing off third base. As Paige passed the Scooter on his way to the mound, he told him: "Don't get nervous, little man, you ain't goin' nowhere."

After the hurler retired the next three batters on 10 pitches, Veeck accosted him in feigned disgust. "Leroy," he said, "What about that 10th pitch? Why did you waste one?"

"Don't you worry none about ol' Satch," came the reply. "He won't let you down."

That same year, when Paige would read in the bullpen before a game, fellow pitchers would chide him lightly with, "Ain't you gonna run, ain't you gonna get in shape?"

His response invariably was: "No, where I come from we throw the ball across the plate, we don't carry it

Paige, a man of many windups, was pitching for the St. Louis Browns in 1952 (left) and came back for one final appearance in 1965, at age 59, as a member of the Kansas City A's.

across.''

Paige was well known for his homespun humor and his admonition, "Don't look back. Something might be gaining on you.''

He declared that "there never was a man on earth who pitched more than me. The more I pitched, the stronger my arm would get.''

Satchel once started 29 games in a month in Bismarck, N.D., and insisted that he won 104 of the 105 games he pitched in 1934.

The tall, slender Paige was at his best as a member of the Pittsburgh Crawfords in 1933. Using an assortment of pitches, including a unique delivery called the hesitation pitch that was banned in the major leagues, he won 31 games and lost four. He won 21 consecutive games and registered 62 straight scoreless innings.

Satchel's family name originally was spelled without the ''i,'' but the ballplayer explained, "The family added the extra letter to sound more high-toned.''

Paige acquired his nickname, he explained, while working as a 7-year-old porter in the Mobile railroad depot.

"I rigged up ropes around my shoulders and waist,'' he said. "I carried a satchel in each hand an one under each arm. I carried so many satchels that all you could see was satchels. You couldn't see Leroy Paige.''

In 1924, Satchel obtained a trial with the Mobile Tigers, a semipro team, and fired 10 fastballs past the manager. He had a job, and the start of an exceptional career.

In succeeding years, Paige pitched in the Negro leagues during the summer and Caribbean leagues in the winter. He faced major league barnstorming teams almost annually. Once he outpitched Dizzy Dean, 1-0. Another time he struck out Rogers Hornsby five times in one game. Joe DiMaggio called him "the best and the fastest pitcher I've ever faced.''

Paige died of a heart attack in Kansas City in 1982.

# Herb Pennock

Miller Huggins, who did not express opinions carelessly, called the slender pitcher "the greatest lefthander in the history of baseball."

There were other expressions of varying shades, but nobody disputed the fact that Herb Pennock exhibited style and class during his more than 10 years in the American League.

At his peak, Pennock threw with a free and easy manner so that batters yearned to bat against him. To their chagrin, the ball never arrived at the plate when or where they expected it.

Bucky Harris, when he was managing and playing for the Washington Senators, said of Pennock, "Nicest fellow in the world, off the field. On the field, he just stands out there and looks at you and tugs on the bill of his cap . . . and winds up and lets go. The ball is never where you think it's going to be. When you swing at it the best you get is a piece of it. You fuss and fume and sweat and holler and he stands out there and looks at you . . . and tugs at the bill of his cap and—aw, what's the use?"

A native of Kennet Square, Pa., and as comfortable riding to the hounds as he was on the pitching mound, Pennock attended Friends School in West Town, Pa., but the sports program there was inadequate for Herb so he transferred to Cedar Croft school.

Instead of matriculating at the University of Pennsylvania, as his parents wished, Herb accepted a contract with the Philadelphia Athletics. "Just sit on the bench," Connie Mack told the 18-year-old. "I won't ask you to do any pitching for a long time."

Two days later (May 14, 1912), however, when Jack Coombs was treated roughly by the White Sox, Mack called on Pennock, who allowed only one hit in four innings.

Herb registered his first of 240 major league victories on June 28 when, pitching the last two innings, he received credit for a 10-inning victory over Walter Johnson and the Senators.

Waived to the Red Sox in 1915, Pennock considered retirement from the game because of his chronic wildness. He was dissuaded, though, by Manager Ed Barrow and embarked on an intensive program to develop control.

In later years, when he was asked by young pitchers how he gained control, Pennock would explain, "When I was struggling, I pitched in games, in batting practice, before games, in morning games and during the off-season. When I couldn't get anybody to catch me, I'd throw against a stone wall or a barn door. It wasn't always fun, but I kept plugging away because it meant so much to me."

Herb discovered early that speed was not essential to success. His pitches floated to the plate, causing Gee

Former Yankee Manager Miller Huggins called Herb Pennock the greatest lefthander in baseball history.

Walker of the Tigers to observe, "The only comforting thing about hitting against him is that you don't have to be afraid of getting hurt. Even if he hits you on the head with his fastball, he won't knock your hat off."

Pennock gained his greatest fame after being acquired by the Yankees on January 30, 1923, exactly 25 years before his death. He won five World Series games without a loss, compiling an earned-run average of 1.95.

His foremost performance occurred in Game 3 of the 1927 Series. Facing the Pittsburgh Pirates, who were tough on N.L. lefthanders, Pennock retired the first 22 batters en route to a three-hit victory.

Although not much of a hitter himself, Herb was frequently consulted by Babe Ruth, Lou Gehrig, Bob Meusel and Tony Lazzeri when they went into slumps.

Pennock hit one home run he always cherished. It was stroked in Fenway Park when he was with the Red Sox. The Yankees' Ruth had difficulty picking up the ball in the tall right-field grass and Herb swan-dived into the plate with an inside-the-park homer.

"It was the only time I was photographed with a bat in my hand," he beamed after cameramen snapped the hero of the day.

Pennock was vice president and general manager of the Phillies and was attending an N.L. meeting in New York when he died of a cerebral hemorrhage in 1948.

# Eddie Plank

By majority opinion, he was the king of dawdlers on the pitching mound. He fidgeted so long between pitches and his games consumed so much time that commuters, it was maintained, would shun the ball park on days he worked for fear of missing their trains home.

Eddie Collins, who played second base behind Eddie Plank for a number of years on the Philadelphia Athletics, once summarized the lefthander's modus operandi as follows:

"To some he would pitch without fussing. To others he would throw the ball only when the umpire warned him against delay.

"Plank's favorite situation was two men on and a slugger up. The better the hitter, the better Eddie liked it. For, if the man had a reputation to uphold, the fans would urge him on and he would be aching to hit.

"Plank would fuss and fiddle with the ball, with his shoes, then try to talk to the umpire.

"His motion was enough to give the batter nervous indigestion. He'd dish up something the batter couldn't reach with two bats, would follow that with an equally wild pitch—inside. Probably, the next would be a twister that the batter could reach, but could not straighten out. A couple

**Eddie Plank (pictured in 1905) often was called king of the dawdlers.**

of fouls, and he would wink knowingly at me.

"Then he would attempt to pick off the baserunners, which he frequently did.

"Then, suddenly, Plank would turn his attention to the fretting batter who would, in all probability, pop up in disgust."

A native of Gettysburg, Pa., where he worked as a battlefield guide in the off-season, Plank enrolled at Gettysburg College when he was 21. Eddie had played little, if any, baseball in his youth on the family farm, but at the suggestion of Coach Frank Foreman, he tried out for the college team. Four years later, Foreman recommended Plank to Connie Mack of the Athletics.

Plank, who threw with a three-quarter motion as well as a sidearm crossfire, made his big-league debut on May 13, 1901, at Baltimore, yielding three runs in a four-inning relief stint. He registered the first of his 305 victories five days later, an 11-6 decision over Washington.

A humorless individual, Eddie suffered from a nasal condition that impaired his breathing. He also complained frequently of a sore arm, but teammates noticed that he pitched most effectively when the alleged pain was most severe.

Plank pitched on six pennant-winning teams, but appeared in only four World Series. There was no inter-league classic in 1902 when Mack's team won its first flag; in 1910, when the A's faced the Cubs for the world title, Mack entrusted the pitching to righthanders Chief Bender and Colby Jack Coombs.

In 1905, Eddie opposed the New York Giants twice, losing to Christy Mathewson, 3-0, in Game 1 and to Joe McGinnity, 1-0, in Game 4.

He split two decisions with the Giants in 1911, beating Rube Marquard on a five-hitter in Game 2 and losing in relief in Game 5 on Fred Merkle's sacrifice fly in the 10th inning.

Plank faced Mathewson twice in the 1913 Series. He lost, 3-0, in Game 2 before coming back in the fifth and final game to pitch what many regarded as his finest game ever. He outdueled Mathewson, 3-1, on a two-hitter. The only safeties were singles by Matty and catcher Larry McLean.

In his final Series effort, Eddie suffered his fifth setback. It was a 1-0 decision to Bill James of the Boston Braves in 1914.

After the A's were upset by the Miracle Braves, Plank, Bender and Coombs were released by Mack, who was unable to compete with salaries offered by the outlaw Federal League. Coombs went to the Dodgers, Bender to the Baltimore Feds and Plank, at age 39, to St. Louis' Federal League club.

When the Federal League died after the 1915 season, Plank stayed in St. Louis as a member of the Browns.

Along with Del Pratt and $15,000, Eddie was traded to the Yankees for five players in January of 1918. He refused to report, however, choosing instead to pitch in the Bethlehem Steel League.

Plank returned to his home in Gettysburg where, on February 22, 1926, he suffered a stroke that led to his death two days later. He was 50.

# Charles Radbourn

Why Charley Sweeney quit the Providence Grays in July of 1884 has never been determined conclusively. The cause for his precipitate action may have been his removal from a game while he was ahead, or it may have stemmed from the manager's insistence that he play the outfield when not pitching, a not uncommon practice in that era.

Anyhow, Sweeney bolted the club, leaving a squad of eight players, plus Charley (Old Hoss) Radbourn, who was under suspension for cursing his catcher and firing the baseball at him and knocking him flat on his back. The catcher's offense was dropping a third strike.

As the manager convened his players and discussed the necessity of disbanding the club, Radbourn spoke up.

"Do you want to win the pennant?" he asked.

"Of course, I do," the skipper replied.

"I'll pitch every game," Radbourn volunteered. "And don't worry about my being able to do it."

In return for his Herculean performance, the Providence righthander asked some extra compensation and his free agency at the close of the National League season.

Between August 7 and September 6, the Grays won 20 straight games, with Old Hoss accounting for 18 of the victories. Providence won the flag and then polished off the New York Metropolitans, champions of the American Association, in the first fully sanctioned big-league playoff as Radbourn won all three games, 6-0, 3-1 and 11-2.

Radbourn's compensation for the extraordinary season —he posted a 60-12 record, worked 679 innings and struck out 411 batters—was $3,000.

The excessive labors took a heavy toll on the pitcher's arm. He was unable to raise his hand to his ear "even if you held a $5 bill up there." He would apply hot towels to his protesting muscles for an hour or two, then toss an iron ball underhand for several minutes. Gradually, he would toss a baseball at ever-lengthening distances until he felt ready to throw at the regulation distance, at which point the game would begin.

Radbourn, whose name for years was spelled mistakenly with a final "e," learned to pitch on the family farm in Bloomington, Ill., although, strangely, he played right field for Buffalo when he made his debut in the National League on May 5, 1880. Batting sixth, Charley hit safely once and did not commit any of the Bisons' 17 errors in a 22-3 loss to Cleveland. Radbourn was released after six games.

Old Hoss made his pitching bow on May 5, 1881, when he hurled Providence to a 4-2 victory over Boston.

Although not renowned as a hitter, Radbourn enjoyed one brief moment in the spotlight because of his slugging. On April 17, 1882, he clouted an 18th-inning home run to give John Montgomery Ward a 1-0 victory over Detroit.

Radbourn did not exercise his option to join another

**Charley Radbourn won 60 games in 1884 while working 679 innings and striking out 411.**

club after his taxing performance of 1884, but returned to Providence to win 26 games in 1885. When the franchise folded at the close of that season, Charley joined Boston, where he posted three more 20-victory seasons. He closed his career with a 12-12 record for Cincinnati in 1891.

With his wife and stepson, Old Hoss returned to Bloomington, where he opened a saloon and pool hall. An avid outdoorsman, he hunted regularly until an accident disfigured his face. He lost an eye and suffered partial paralysis and the loss of speech. Embarrassed to face the public, Radbourn spent his final years in a darkened rear room of his establishment. The once tireless pitcher was only 43 when he died.

In 1940, more than four decades after Radbourn's death, Clark Griffith, president of the Washington Senators and also a product of the Bloomington sandlots, unveiled a plaque in the city's cemetery that recounted the achievements of Old Hoss.

In his dedicatory speech, Griffith, who learned to throw a curve on instructions from Radbourn, said, "Charley . . . I hope your spirit is hovering near so that it may be witness to the tribute paid this day to the memory of you, the greatest pitcher of all time. . . . You gave me many lessons in how to pitch and above all instilled in me the spirit of determination and courage—to you, my dear friend, thanks."

# Sam Rice

One afternoon in 1915, Clark Griffith announced to the Washington press that the Senators had acquired a player by the name of Rice from the Petersburg club of the Virginia League, which had just folded.

"What's Rice's first name?" a journalist wondered.

Without hesitation and hiding the fact he had no idea of the correct answer, the president-manager of the Nats blurted, "Sam."

In such fashion was born a nickname that Edgar Charles Rice carried for the remainder of his days.

Rice was a pitcher with an 11-12 record and a .301 batting average when he was acquired by the Senators for a $500 loan that Griffith had extended to the Petersburg club to meet a payroll. The preceding year, Rice bought his way out of the Navy where he had gained some success as an off-duty pitcher.

Eddie Foster, a Washington outfielder, suggested to Griffith that Rice be converted into an outfielder, a move that the Old Fox adopted after Sam collected seven pinch-hits in nine at-bats. Rice became a complete player, fast afoot with a sure glove and sharp batting eye.

A lefthanded batter, Rice hit Lefty Grove with consummate ease.

"If I can't nick Grove for a couple of hits a game," Sam once remarked, "I think something's wrong."

A native of Indiana, Rice worked in the wheat fields of the Dakotas and Minnesota, served as a railroad section hand and bottled whiskey at the Green River distillery in Louisville before drifting to Norfolk, Va., and a short-lived Navy life.

Two questions stood out about Rice's career: (1) Why did he retire with 2,987 hits when he had an opportunity to become the seventh player with 3,000? (2) Did he really catch Earl Smith's long fly while tumbling into the bleachers in the 1925 World Series?

Rice was released by the Senators at the end of the 1933 season and signed with the Cleveland Indians, whose general manager, Billy Evans, told him he could play only

Senators great Sam Rice finished his career 13 hits short of the magic 3,000 level.

when Evans felt like it.

Later, Sam regretted his failure to stick around long enough to collect 13 more hits, but explained, "You must remember, there wasn't much emphasis on 3,000 hits when I quit. And to tell the truth, I didn't know how many hits I had when I retired." Another factor, of course, was his age. Rice was 44 when he retired.

Sam's controversial catch occurred in the eighth inning of Game 3 of the 1925 World Series at Griffith Stadium, where temporary bleachers were erected in center field to handle the overflow from the crowd of more than 36,000.

With the Senators leading, 4-3, Smith whacked a Fred Marberry pitch to deepest right-center field. From his position in right field, Rice raced to the spot, leaped, extended his glove and tumbled into the stands.

At least 10 seconds elapsed before Rice crawled into view holding the baseball aloft. Cy Rigler, who was umpiring at second base, ruled it a legitimate catch.

The Pirates stormed the field protesting the call. Eventually, they appealed to Commissioner K.M. Landis, who tried to pry the truth from Rice. The outfielder's only comment was: "The umpire said I caught the ball." That was his stock answer to the question until the day he died.

More than 1,600 bleacherites filed affidavits and had them notorized, giving varying views on the play. Some maintained that Rice struggled with a fan for possession of the ball, others said that a fan had picked up the ball and stuck it in Sam's glove.

After Sam's death, his widow reported that her husband had shown her a letter, to be opened after his death, which he mailed to the Hall of Fame.

After considerable searching, the missing letter was found. In the letter, Rice revealed that he indeed had made the catch, adding that "at no time did I lose possession of the ball."

The whole matter would have been much more weighty if the Bucs, after losing the game, 4-3, had not gone on to win the Series in seven games.

# Branch Rickey

In 1948, Branch Rickey officiated at Jackie Robinson's second signing, a year after he broke the color barrier.

Two baseball heavyweights, Larry Ma Phail (left) and Rickey, are pictured

In 1905, Rickey played his first major league game as a member of the St. Louis Browns.

Without much doubt, nobody exercised as profound an influence on baseball for an extended period as the Ohio farm boy who invented the farm system, broke the color barrier and, through the founding of a third major league, forced the existing big leagues to expand.

A mediocre player himself but possessed of enormous enthusiasm, Branch Rickey left his imprint on baseball with his fertile brain and active imagination. He was, said a newspaperman, "a man of many facets—all turned on."

Rickey was a superb orator who delighted in blackboard lectures to players, some of whom comprehended his message. He was a master phrase-maker. Among his best remembered adages was "luck is the residue of design."

He invented the sliding pit, originated Ladies Days and organized the Knot-Hole Gang so school children could see major league games at a moderate price.

Rickey was an indefatigable worker with a highly developed eye for raw baseball talent. At a tryout camp, he spotted a graceful prospect who walked with an unnatural stride. Investigation revealed that the youngster had nailed spikes to his badly worn street shoes.

"Judas Priest!" exclaimed Rickey, then manager of the Cardinals, "let me get you a decent pair of shoes."

The player was Sunny Jim Bottomley, longtime Redbird first baseman and a Hall of Fame selection.

The son of devout Methodist parents, Rickey promised his mother while still a young man that he would not attend a ball game on Sunday. He never violated his promise. His first major league opportunity was ended before

ether during their prime as top-level ex-
cutives.

**Rickey shares a laugh with Cardinal Manager Frank Frisch (right) and Dizzy Dean in spring training of 1935.**

he had a chance to play a game for Cincinnati in 1904 because he refused to play on the Sabbath.

The product of a little red schoolhouse education, Rickey earned a law degree from the University of Michigan in 1911, paying for his tuition by coaching the baseball team. By that stage of his career, he had caught for the St. Louis Browns and New York Highlanders, for whom he permitted 13 stolen bases in one game.

Rickey managed the Browns for two seasons and was vice president-business manager of the Cardinals before starting a 6½-year term as field boss of the National League team in 1919.

While with the Cards, Rickey was offered the general manager's post at Detroit because, said Tigers President Frank Navin, "He's the smartest man in baseball and also he's baseball's best salesman. He'll earn two or three times his salary in the sale of surplus players."

The deal fell through, however, when Navin was unable to match Rickey's $40,000 salary with the Redbirds.

The founding of the farm system, Rickey always said, "was not a stroke of genius, it was necessity." As the operating chief of an impoverished Cardinal club, Rickey was unable to compete with wealthier clubs on the open player market. By leaving their ball park, Robison Field, and moving into Sportsman's Park as tenants of the Browns, the Cards obtained capital to buy a half interest in the Fort Smith (Western Association) and Syracuse (International) clubs.

From those two affiliates, the Cardinal farm system

grew into a productive supply source for pennant winners in 1926, 1928, 1930, 1931, 1934 and 1942.

Because of Rickey's differences with club President Sam Breadon, Branch's contract—which netted him between $75,000 and $100,000 annually—was not renewed after December 1, 1942.

Rickey joined the Brooklyn Dodgers as president-general manager and three years later announced that he had signed Jackie Robinson, a black shortstop from the Kansas City Monarchs, to a Montreal (International) contract. Robinson's success in 1946 (with the Class AAA team) and in 1947 (when he won N.L. Rookie of the Year honors with the Dodgers) paved the way for countless other blacks to achieve distinction in the major leagues.

When his co-owners protested his heavy overhead, Rickey sold them his Brooklyn stock for a reported $875,000 profit in October of 1950. Known as "The Mahatma," he moved on to Pittsburgh, where he directed Pirate operations for five years.

When the National and American leagues refused to entertain bids for new franchises in the late 1950s, Rickey and wealthy sportsmen in major league-hungry cities organized the Continental League as a third major loop. The circuit never functioned, however, as the majors began to enact expansion measures in 1960.

At age 80, Rickey was named senior consultant for the Cardinals in 1962, an office he held for three years.

Rickey suffered a heart attack on November 13, 1965, that proved fatal less than a month later.

# Eppa Rixey

Charley (Cy) Rigler, a longtime National League umpire, was studying law and coaching the baseball team at the University of Virginia in the early months of 1912 when he spotted a tall, gangling lefthander with a blazing fastball.

"You've got a future in professional baseball," Rigler informed the big fellow out of Culpeper, Va.

"I plan to be a chemist," the youth replied.

"I'll make a deal with you," said Rigler. "I'll arrange for the Phillies to give you a $2,000 bonus and we'll split it."

The proposition appealed to Eppa Rixey and he signed a Philadelphia contract. However, Rixey never received a cent of the promised compensation because the National League adopted a rule that an umpire could not scout for one particular team.

While Rixey got nothing, the Phils got a superb pitcher whose 266 career victories represented a record for an N.L. lefthander until the arrival of Warren Spahn.

For much of his career and through no fault of his own, the pitcher was known as Eppa Jeptha Rixey. The middle name, it developed, was the creation of Bill Phelon, a Cincinnati writer who found pleasure in bizarre nomenclature.

Easy-going Eppa Rixey never objected to the added cognomen. "It sounds," he said, "like a cross between a Greek letter fraternity and a college yell."

Although he possessed a fastball, Rixey was not a strikeout pitcher. The 6-foot-5 hurler preferred to "work" on batters and force them to swing at bad pitches. He appeared to have an unusually large number of 3-and-2 counts, yet did not issue many bases on balls. In 22 major league campaigns, he averaged only 2.1 walks per nine innings.

Eppa was not an especially good hitter. "I usually hit my weight," the 210-pounder said. But there was one day in St. Louis in 1924 that Rixey treasured forever. Batting against Jesse Haines, another future Hall of Famer, Cincinnati's Rixey clouted a home run, double and two singles. That evening he telephoned the good news to his fiancee, Dorothy Meyers, in Cincinnati.

Lefthander Eppa Rixey recorded 266 career victories for the Phillies and Reds (above).

"Goodness," she exclaimed. "Something dreadful is about to happen in St. Louis if you hit a home run."

The next day a tornado struck the Mound City.

The homer was one of three Eppa hit during his career. He belted one as a Phillie in 1920 and his last for the Reds at Boston in 1928.

Three years after joining the Phillies, Rixey appeared in his only World Series. Replacing Erskine Mayer in the fifth and final game against the Red Sox in 1915, he allowed four hits in 6⅔ innings and was tagged with a 5-4 defeat when Harry Hooper hit a home run in the ninth inning.

Eppa served overseas in the Chemical Warfare Division in World War I. He pitched two more years for the Phils after his return to the States before he was traded to Cincinnati.

With the Reds, Rixey formed a battery with Bubbles Hargrave. Together, they represented perhaps the slowest runners in the game, so it was something of a major accomplishment when they executed a double steal against the Cubs.

"Gabby Hartnett, the best thrower in the game, couldn't believe it," related Eppa. "He just stood there open-mouthed and forgot to throw."

Eppa's finest moment as a pitcher, he often remarked, occurred in 1920 in Cincinnati when he was with the Phillies.

After Edd Roush tripled to lead off the ninth inning of a tie game, Rixey walked the next two batters, then induced Greasy Neale to bounce back to the mound for the start of a double play. Eppa retired the next batter and the Phils won in the 15th inning.

Another career highlight came when Rixey hurled a two-hitter against the Giants, facing only the minimum 27 batters.

Rixey retired after recording his final six victories during the 1933 season and developed a lucrative insurance business in Cincinnati. He died of a heart attack at age 71 in 1963, one month after he was elected to the Hall of Fame.

# Robin Roberts

As a star at Michigan State, Robin Roberts (above) was only a year away from the major leagues. After signing with the Phils, Roberts joined the parent club in 1948 (above right) after a 9-1 stint with Wilmington.

A pitching staff built around Warren Spahn and Robin Roberts most certainly would have produced more than two pennants for the Milwaukee Braves in the 1950s and '60s. However, Roberts got away because the Philadelphia Phillies' agents talked fast—and acted even faster.

Roberts' potential as a major league hurler was no secret in 1947. Robin had pitched in a Vermont summer league and was coveted by six major league clubs, including the Phils and Braves, then located in Boston.

Both clubs arranged workouts for Robin at Wrigley Field in Chicago, but, fortunately for Philadelphia, the schedule called for the Phillies to arrive first. The right-hander worked out and the Phils were deeply impressed. Roberts was offered a $25,000 bonus.

Robin liked the offer, but demurred on signing because the Braves had offered his parents, living in Springfield, Ill., an expense-paid week's vacation to Chicago.

The Phils could not afford the risk, so an executive suggested that Roberts phone his father in Springfield and discuss the matter. The elder Roberts recommended that Robin wait. His offspring countered with a promise to pay

**Roberts was sky high on the final day of the 1950 season when his 20th victory gave the Phillies their first pennant in 35 years.**

for the week-long Chicago vacation from his bonus. That clinched the matter and Robin signed with the Phils.

In his first appearance in a spring exhibition, Roberts struck out Joe DiMaggio for openers, then repeated against Phil Rizzuto.

"Did that kid throw you a fastball?" the Clipper asked the Scooter.

"I'll say he did," answered Rizzuto. "It almost flew up and hit me."

Roberts threw with an effortless motion that betrayed his fastball. The pitch arrived at the plate with deceptive swiftness, frequently freezing the bat on the hitter's shoulder.

Cardinal second baseman Red Schoendienst said the "ball seemed to skid across the strike zone as though it were on a piece of ice."

Control was never a problem for Roberts, a Michigan State graduate. He said it was a mystery to him why he had pinpoint accuracy. "I can neither understand it nor explain it," he said. "I can't comprehend why other pitchers are wild."

Robbie's chief problem after joining the Phils from a 9-1 performance at Wilmington (Inter-State) in 1948 was a needless haste between pitches. To cure the habit, coach Bennie Bengough suggested a tedious routine in which Roberts would fondle the ball in his glove, hitch up his belt, adjust his trouser leg, tug at the bill of his cap, wipe his brow, take off his glove and maybe then take the catcher's sign.

**Roberts was sold to the Yankees after the 1961 season but appeared in a New York uniform only during spring training of 1962 before being released.**

In the 1950 National League pennant race, Manager Eddie Sawyer called on Robbie three times in the last five days. On the closing day, with everything on the line at Ebbets Field, Roberts outpitched Don Newcombe in a 10-inning struggle. Dick Sisler's homer gave Robbie his 20th victory of the year and the Phils their first flag since 1915.

Roberts pitched Game 2 of the World Series and battled Allie Reynolds into the 10th inning before DiMaggio's homer gave the Yankees a 2-1 triumph.

For six consecutive seasons, Roberts registered 20 or more victories with his explosive fastball and almost impeccable control.

He was at the crest of his career when a new manager, Mayo Smith, advised him: "You have to develop a new pitch, perhaps a sinker or a slider. You can't get by forever with just a fastball."

"I don't agree," the hurler responded. "I've gotta pitch the only way I know how."

When Roberts' speed started to fade, there was no backup pitch. Robin drifted around the majors for several years trying to win with a slowed-down fastball. But time ran out on the once-powerful righthander. He finished with 286 victories, 14 shy of the goal he might have attained with the extra pitch that he rejected.

# Brooks Robinson

Paul Richards never dreamed when he opened his mail on a February morning in 1955 that a new era was about to dawn for the Baltimore Orioles.

Among the manager's communications was a letter from a former minor league opponent, Lindsay Deal, a resident of Little Rock, Ark.

The letter trumpeted the talents of an 18-year-old high school senior who "measures up to having a good chance in major league baseball . . . he is a natural third baseman . . . his physique is outstanding for a boy his age . . . he is not a speed demon but neither is he a truck horse . . . he has a lot of baseball savvy and always is cool when the chips are down . . . seven other clubs are definitely interested in him."

Baltimore scouts followed up on the tip and confirmed Deal's judgment. For a $4,000 bonus, the Orioles acquired Brooks Robinson, an all-time great as a third baseman and as a person.

Robinson, the son of a Little Rock fireman, made his debut with the Orioles late in the 1955 season. In his first game, he rapped two singles against Washington. One of the hits, off Vibert Clarke, produced his first run batted in.

In the buoyancy of youth, Brooks told himself, "This sport was made for me."

That attitude was quickly shattered. Brooks did not get another hit in 18 remaining at-bats that season. In his 22 official at-bats in '55, Robinson struck out 10 times.

"That opened my eyes," he admitted. "I knew from then on I was going to have to work like blazes."

To improve all segments of his game Robbie

Brooks Robinson in 1955, his first season with the Orioles.

By 1966, Robinson's bat was complementing his magic glove and combining with the big bat of teammate and future Hall of Famer Frank Robinson to drive the Orioles to new heights.

Robinson's glove was always at its magical best during World Series, such as this 1970 diving catch against the Reds and Johnny Bench that helped the O's prevail in Game 3.

worked in good times and bad, even through excruciating pain. Chasing a foul fly in Detroit one day, he crashed into a concrete ledge that laid open his lower jaw and chipped off parts of five teeth. In a semi-conscious state, he heard the trainer say, "Call the ambulance."

The youngster leaped to his feet and demanded, "Give me my glove and let's get on with the game. Didn't you ever see anyone shaken up before?"

Almost overnight, Robbie was an accomplished third baseman.

Pie Traynor, acknowledged king of third basemen, said, "He has exceptional reflexes and the strongest pull hitters can't get the ball by him."

Casey Stengel contributed, "Traynor was the best, but Robinson is nearly up there with him."

Brooks was at his unbelievable best in the 1970 World Series, a five-game victory for the Orioles. "Robinson beat us," groaned Manager Sparky Anderson of the losing Cincinnati Reds after Brooks batted .429 with nine hits and set a record of 17 total bases.

But Robinson's performance in the field was even more implausible. The Oriole star dived to his left and to his right, robbing Reds of sure hits. One disgruntled loser moaned, "He can field a ball with a pair of pliers."

Robinson's defense was so consistently spectacular that Cincinnati cleanup hitter Johnny Bench, a frequent victim, was incapable of anger.

"I walked back to the dugout appreciating his play for what it was—a thing of beauty," said the catcher.

While Robbie dazzled on the field, he sparkled just as brightly off it. One observer said, "Other stars had fans, Robbie made friends."

At the All-Star Game in California in 1967, Red Ruffing, the newest member of the Hall of Fame, was congratulated by only one player from the two squads. It was Brooks Robinson.

During spring training in Florida, a lady asked Brooks to pose for a photo, pure drudgery for most players. When it was discovered that the camera was out of order, Robinson took it from the lady, adjusted the mechanism, handed it back and said, "Now, see if it works."

The shutter clicked and the two parted, each smiling.

Then, too quickly, the long honeymoon was over. On September 18, 1977, Baltimore threw open its heart on "Thanks Brooks Day." A throng of 51,798, the largest regular-season crowd in the history of the franchise, jammed Memorial Stadium to say farewell to everybody's favorite player.

Gifts were few because that was the way Brooks wanted it. But there was an overflow of emotion as Robbie expressed gratitude to his wife, his parents and "to Almighty God for giving me the health and the talent."

# Frank Robinson

By 1956, Frank Robinson (left) was just beginning the trek that would carry him to MVP honors for the Reds in

1961. Robinson was even better in 1966 (right) when he won a Triple Crown and MVP as an Oriole.

Shrewd as he was as a baseball executive, Bill DeWitt was not immune to human frailties, such as errors of judgment in assessing the future of a 10-year major league veteran.

When the president of the Cincinnati Reds was asked in December of 1965 why he had traded a 30-year-old outfielder who had smashed 324 home runs and driven in 1,009 runs in 10 seasons with the club, DeWitt replied, "because he's an old 30."

The Baltimore Orioles entertained no such qualms. And in six seasons with the Birds, discarded slugger Frank Robinson dominated four pennant winners and two world-championship clubs.

When he retired as an active player at age 41, Robinson left behind a 21-year big-league career that produced Most Valuable Player awards in both major leagues (the only player so distinguished), 586 homers (fourth highest), a Triple Crown, a World Series MVP honor and the distinction of being the majors' first black manager.

One of 10 children, Robinson played for the Bill Erwin Legion Post team of Oakland, Calif., at a time when catcher J.W. Porter was the most coveted young player in the country. The Reds failed to land Porter, who accepted a $65,000 bonus from the White Sox and played parts of only six big-league seasons, but they did sign Porter's teammate, Robinson, for $3,000—and he was a major leaguer from 1956 to 1976.

Robinson's capabilities as a teen-ager were common knowledge. In 1953, when the Reds were offering five players for infielder Danny O'Connell, Branch Rickey, front-office chief of the Pirates, remarked casually, "How about throwing in that kid Robinson at Ogden?" Ogden was in the Class C Pioneer League.

The suggestion was quickly quashed by Gabe Paul, Rickey's counterpart at Cincinnati. "No way," retorted Gabe. "Robinson is the type of player you dream about. He stays."

For a fleeting moment there was some question if Robby would remain with the Reds. During spring training of 1960, irritated over Manager Fred Hutchinson's plan to make him into a first baseman, the slugger was within one step of bolting the team when Paul reminded him of the seriousness of walking out while under contract.

After his trade to Baltimore, Frank arrived at the 1966

In 1972, Robinson (left) returned to the National League as a Dodger. On opening day in 1975, player-manager

Robinson led the Indians to victory with his first-inning homer. He was greeted (right) by John Lowenstein.

training camp two days late. He leaped into his uniform and, without batting practice, rapped a first-pitch double in an intra-squad game.

"Hey," shouted second baseman Dave Johnson, "this guy is gonna help us."

He sure did.

The season was barely a month old when Robinson walloped the first home run ever hit out of Memorial Stadium. The historic drive, off Luis Tiant of Cleveland, carried more than 500 feet.

Another time, during a tie game in Boston's Fenway Park, Robinson crashed into the right-field railing while making a catch that deprived slugger George Scott of a home run.

As the leadoff batter in the next inning, Frank cleverly laid down a bunt that the third baseman fielded—and nothing more.

Robinson eventually scored the winning run, but why, he was asked, did he select that spot to deliver his first bunt in 12 years.

Simple, explained Frank. He had damaged his ribs in crashing into the wall and could scarcely breathe, let alone

take a full swing.

For years, Robinson spent his winters managing in the Caribbean leagues in preparation for the day when he might be tapped as the majors' first black pilot. His credentials were favorable and he got his opportunity in 1975 when he was named the player-manager of the Cleveland Indians. On opening day, the manager-designated hitter clouted a first-inning home run to help defeat the Yankees, 5-3.

But the Indians were not of contending quality and on June 19, 1977, Robby was released. Some reported he was too tough on black players, others that he was too lenient.

"I did the best I could," he commented without bitterness. "Race was not a factor."

Robinson then served as a coach with the Angels and Orioles and as manager for Rochester (International) before being appointed manager of the San Francisco Giants in 1981.

He was named the National League's Manager of the Year by United Press International in 1982 after leading the Giants to a third-place finish.

# Jackie Robinson

Jackie Robinson (left) was a three-sport star at UCLA before joining the Kansas City Monarchs (center, 1944) as a shortstop. By 1948, Robinson (right) had weathered his first major league season.

In the aftermath of World War II, Branch Rickey decided that the social climate of the United States was at last favorable for implementing a plan that he had held in abeyance for a number of years.

The Mahatma of Brooklyn determined that the time was ripe for all-white major league baseball to admit a black player. That pioneer could not be just any black athlete, but one who measured up to the standards established by the Dodgers' president.

The player had to be a college product, a competitor, an intelligent individual with baseball talent who had the moral and physical courage to shrug off the on-field insults with remarkable displays of self-control.

Rickey's search for this extraordinary person ended with Jackie Robinson, a former three-sport star at UCLA and an Army lieutenant in World War II before joining the Kansas City Monarchs of the Negro League as a shortstop.

Rickey subjected Robinson to withering blasts of profanity and obscenity before he was convinced that the athlete possessed the discipline to hold his tongue. Only then was Jackie signed to a 1946 contract with the Montreal farm club.

Robinson won the batting championship of the International League, which ordinarily was enough of a credential for a cordial major league welcome. But the major leagues were unprepared for a social upheaval. Club owners voted 15 to 1 against the pioneering venture before Commissioner A. B. (Happy) Chandler gave his overriding approval.

Acceptance was a different matter. Once, in infield practice, Jackie was taking a blistering salvo from the opposing dugout when shortstop-captain Pee Wee Reese, a Kentuckian, laid a consoling hand on Robinson's shoulder as if to warn opponents, "He's my teammate, lay off."

Reports were circulated that the Cardinals were plotting to strike their games with the Dodgers, until National League President Ford Frick threatened lifetime banishment for anyone guilty of such actions.

Nor did all the Dodgers greet Jackie warmly. Outfielder Dixie Walker, a Georgian, was noticeably cool until he determined that Robinson was an asset to the team, at which point he gave the newcomer batting tips.

"I had to fight hard against loneliness, abuse and the knowledge that any mistake I made would be magnified because I was the only black man out there," Robinson wrote in his autobiography.

But Jackie fought fiercely, and the Dodgers won because of him. In Robinson's 10 seasons with Brooklyn, the Dodgers won six pennants and one world championship. Jackie was the Rookie of the Year in 1947 and the N.L.'s Most Valuable Player two years later when he won the batting championship.

Robinson was a pressure player of the highest order. On the last day of the regular season in 1951, when the Giants had already won and assured themselves of a pennant tie, the Dodgers were locked in an extra-inning game at Philadelphia. The Phillies loaded the bases with two outs in the 12th inning when Jackie made a diving catch of a wicked line drive. In doing so, however, he jammed an elbow into his stomach and was knocked unconscious.

Two innings later Robinson socked a game-winning homer that created a pennant tie (which was resolved in the historic playoff with the Giants).

If it had not been for Rickey, Jackie was set to quit baseball. "It was too dificult in the black league," he declared. "The travel was brutal. Financially, there was no reward. It took everything you made to live off."

Had he quit baseball, Robinson said, he probably "would have gone to coach baseball at Sam Houston College (in Texas). My minister had gone there. That was about the only thing a black had left then, a chance to coach somewhere at a small black college."

After the 1956 season Jackie, then 37, was traded to the Giants. Rather than report, however, he announced his retirement in a bylined article in Look magazine.

Robinson went on to hold numerous executive positions within the business community. He was chairman of the board of the Freedom National Bank.

Less than two weeks after Jackie was honored at the 1972 World Series, he suffered his second heart attack at his Stamford, Conn., home and died at age 53.

Daring baserunning was a Robinson trademark, such as his steal of home (above) in Game 1 of the 1955 World Series against the Yankees and catcher Yogi Berra. Robinson (below) forces out Yankee pitcher Allie Reynolds on a double-play attempt during the 1949 Series.

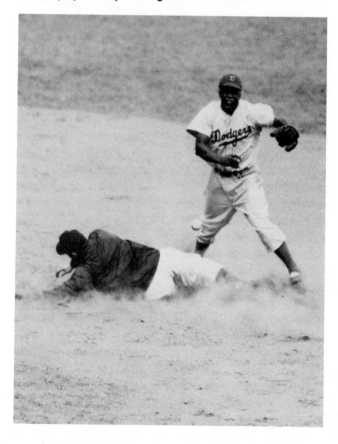

# Wilbert Robinson

He was legendary in his own time, a Falstaffian figure with sound baseball instincts but renowned chiefly for anecdotes presenting him as an amiable leader of less gifted athletes.

When three Brooklyn players wound up on third base, he muttered, "That's the first time they've been together all season."

When Zack Taylor tripled to lead off the ninth inning of a tie game, his manager, coaching at third base, extended his hand. "Great going, kid," he bubbled. "Put 'er there." Taylor did as he ordered, stepped off the bag and was tagged out.

When the Brooklyn Daffiness Boys of the 1920s became unbearably zany, the pilot announced the formation of a Bonehead Club.

Wilbert Robinson, best known for his years as Brooklyn Dodgers manager, was a catcher for the National League Baltimore franchise in the 1890s.

Anyone guilty of a mental misadventure would be fined $10. He then gave the umpires an old batting order, costing the Dodgers some runs and the game.

Wilbert Robinson, known universally as Uncle Robbie, was like that, lovable but certainly not loony.

As a youth in Massachusetts, Robbie drove a fishmonger's wagon, earning him his first nickname as Billy Fish. His formal education was limited, and spelling was a constant puzzle to him.

On a day when he wished to start Oscar Roettger at first base instead of Claude Hendricks, Robinson started to fill out the lineup card. Coming to Roettger's name, he began R-o-t, then erased it. He gave it another try . . . R-e-o. In frustration he cried out "Hendricks, you play first base."

From the beginning, it appeared that Uncle Robbie's career would be different from most. While playing for the Baltimore Orioles on June 10, 1892, Robbie collected seven hits in as many at-bats and drove in 11 runs in a 25-4 victory over St. Louis. The record achievement went unnoticed in the daily newspapers the next day and remained undetected for 20 years until Heywood Broun unearthed it in a casual conversation with Robinson.

While with the Orioles, Robbie became a fast friend of John McGraw. They opened a cafe and bowling establishment known as The Diamond, where duckpins were invented. The business flourished, but it was dissolved when McGraw moved to New York as manager of the Giants in 1902.

Robbie was named player-manager of the Orioles upon McGraw's departure. A broken finger in July of 1904 led to his quitting the game in favor of a saloon enterprise. He also operated a butcher shop and was extremely proud of his skills in that business. Many years later, when the Dodgers were given a tour of the Chicago stockyards, Robbie, on invitation, picked up an executioner's hammer and slew a steer with one well-aimed blow to the head.

Robinson returned to baseball in 1911 as a coach under McGraw. In that role, he was credited with the development of Rube Marquard and Jeff Tesreau as top-flight pitchers.

Old cronies Robinson and McGraw fell out over strategy in the 1913 World Series and Robbie moved to Brooklyn the next season where he began an 18-year reign as manager. In tribute to the new pilot, the team was renamed the Robins.

The club won two pennants under Robbie, but lost the 1916 World Series to the Red Sox and the 1920 Series to the Indians.

For the first 11 years in Brooklyn, Robinson enjoyed a pleasant relationship with Charles Ebbets. When the club president died in 1925, however, and Vice-President Ed McKeever passed away a short time later, heirs battled fiercely for control of the club and, as a compromise, Robbie added the presidential duties to his managerial responsibilities. It was an impossible situation.

During spring training of 1927, the Giants threw a big party in Venice, Fla., to mark McGraw's 25 years as manager. Dodger officials were invited, but Uncle Robbie flatly refused to attend. At the last minute, he yielded to vigorous persuasion and healed old wounds.

In his later years, Robbie made his winter home at Dover Hall, Ga., where he loved to hunt and fish and sit before a roaring fire quaffing choice viands. Having undergone major surgery, he asked his doctor if he were permitted alcohol. "No more than a mouthful a day," he was told. Thereafter he would pour himself a water tumbler full. When he was queried about the excessive amount, he would reply, "That's a mouthful—a cow's mouth."

Robinson's death at 70 was followed by burial at Sea Island, Ga., in close proximity to the graves of his beloved hunting, fishing and drinking buddies, Col. Til Huston, former co-owner of the Yankees, and Bill McGeehan, noted New York sportswriter.

# Edd Roush

The atmosphere on the Giants' bench was tense as John McGraw picked up a bat that had been flicked away by a batter. "Whose is this?" he snarled.

"Don't say anything," coach Hans Lobert advised the guilty party.

"That's my bat," said the kid from Indiana, ignoring the advice.

"Don't ever let me catch you using that bat again," growled the manager.

"Sh-h-h-h," Lobert advised again.

"This is the first damn league I ever played in where the manager picked the bat for you," came the rejoinder.

"What league did you ever hit .300 in?" McGraw wanted to know.

"Every league I ever played in," replied the not-quite-honest rookie, Edd Roush, "and I'd do it in this league, too, if I'd play regularly."

Roush was an original. Nobody, not even the belligerent McGraw, intimidated him. Edd detested spring training and he knew his value as a player, even if it meant holding out all season in defense of a principle.

Edd's initial "J" did not stand for a name. Roush's grandfather's were named Jim and Joe and so not to show favoritism, his parents settled on the initial.

Shortly after his clash with McGraw in 1916, Roush was traded to Cincinnati, and McGraw spent the next decade trying to buy him back.

In Roush's opinion, the lengthy spring training periods were unnecessary. When he was asked when he could be expected to join his teammates, Edd would reply, "Just before you break camp." Generally, he did not sign his contract until he reached camp. There was one exception and it was, said Roush, "my biggest mistake."

That was in his first year with the Giants when McGraw invited Edd to Mineral Wells, Tex., the Giants' training site, to "talk it over." Roush complied. When the manager would not budge, Edd realized that a return home would be at his own expense, so he signed. Thereafter he held out in his hometown of Oakland City, Ind.

His first day in camp, Edd would take batting practice to sharpen his eye. The next day he would field infield grounders to flex some muscles. The third day he would field flies in the outfield, and by then he was ready to go. One year he did not report until July, then banged three hits in his first game.

Roush swung a 48-ounce bat, the heaviest manufactured by the makers of Louisville Sluggers. He insisted he never broke a bat. He ordered six at the start of each season. By closing day they were gone, given away by Edd or the clubhouse boy.

The Giants reacquired Roush in January of 1927 and, as customary, the player held out. McGraw wired an invi-

In 1920, Edd Roush was coming off one of his two batting championships as a member of the Cincinnati Reds.

tation to meet him in Chattanooga—at the manager's expense.

"Don't you want to play for me?" asked McGraw.

"Hell, no," shot back Roush.

"I won't climb over you or call you names," McGraw promised. "I'll leave you alone. I can't pay the $30,000 you demand, but I'll give you a three-year contract for $70,000." Roush accepted.

When the Giants sought to cut his pay $7,500 in 1930, Edd stoutly resisted, announcing, "I never got a $7,500 raise, so I ain't taking a $7,500 cut." He stayed out of the game that year.

Back with Cincinnati in 1931, he played 101 games, then retired.

During his big-money days, Roush was not a spendthrift. While others were buying drinks for the house, Roush went to a local brewery "where I could drink as much beer as was good for me."

Out of his relatively high earnings, and with a frugal lifestyle, Edd invested heavily in General Motors, Procter and Gamble and Sears & Roebuck, as well as in government bonds. As a result, he was able to live and travel as he pleased during his retirement.

# Red Ruffing

One afternoon in 1929, a Boston Red Sox pitcher was hitting fungoes to outfielders in pregame drills when the Yankees' manager called him aside.

"I understand," said Miller Huggins, "they are trying to make an outfielder out of you. Don't let 'em do it. Someday you may be with us."

The next season Red Ruffing was with the Yankees. Huggins, though, had died in September of 1929.

Ruffing remained a pitcher for the remainder of his career. The absence of four toes from his left foot, the result of a mine accident, restricted his running speed. His productive bat was limited to pinch-hitting appearances and to those days when he was wheeling his fastball and sharp curve from the mound.

At age 15, Ruffing played first base on a mine company team managed by his father in Nokomis, Ill. After the mine mishap cost him his toes, the youngster just about abandoned hopes for a major league career.

"I couldn't run a lick," he remembered, "but one day our team was to play against another mine team which was loaded with ringers and our pitcher developed a sore arm.

"Everybody on the team said I should pitch and I only lost the game, 3-2, in the 10th inning because our left fielder dropped a fly ball. In my next game I struck out 16.

"The foot bothered me the rest of my career and I had to land on the side of my left foot in my follow-through."

The youngster's success with the mine team caught the attention of the owner of a Nokomis semipro team.

Asked how much his father paid him per game, Ruffing said, "My dad doesn't pay any of his players."

"I'll give you $75 to play three games next week," the club owner told Ruffing. "My dad just lost a pitcher," the redhead replied.

By the time he was 19, Red was with the Red Sox, who were struggling to attain respectability after a previous owner disposed of the club's stars. In a little more than five seasons, Ruffing won only 39 games and lost 96. He lost 25 games one year and 12 straight the following season while en route to 22 defeats for the campaign.

Ruffing's fortunes improved dramatically with the Yankees. In time, Bill Dickey would say, "If I were asked to choose the best pitcher I've ever caught, I would have to say Ruffing."

Red topped the 20-victory mark four times. And generally, the big righthander opened the World Series for the Yankees, as he did in 1942 against the Cardinals in St. Louis. It was Red's most memorable Series performance although, strangely, he was not around for the finish of the game.

Ruffing issued two walks in the first inning, but then mowed down the Redbirds with regularity until, after six

In 1936, Red Ruffing embarked on a string of four 20-victory seasons for the Yankees.

innings, he said to a teammate, "You guys don't have to be so damn quiet. I know I've got a no-hitter, and if I get through the eighth I'll keep it."

But, with two out in the eighth, Terry Moore broke the spell with a single. Ruffing had a 7-0 lead with one out in the ninth, but the Cards scored four runs and Spud Chandler came on to preserve the lead.

Overall, Ruffing posted a 7-2 Series record.

After two years in military service, Ruffing rejoined the Yankees in 1945.

In 1946, he had a 5-1 record when he suffered a broken kneecap when struck by a line drive and was sidelined for the remainder of the year. He concluded his active career with the White Sox in 1947.

The winner of 273 games scouted for the White Sox and Indians and also managed several minor league clubs before his appointment as the first pitching coach for the Mets in 1962.

In September of 1973, Ruffing suffered a stroke that confined him to a wheelchair. Despite his handicap, Red still managed to travel from his Cleveland home to Cooperstown, N.Y., for the Hall of Fame installation ceremonies.

# Amos Rusie

The powerful righthander came out of Indiana in 1890 and because of his blinding speed he was immediately nicknamed the "Hoosier Thunderbolt."

Amos Rusie was the first genuine sports idol of New York City. Actress Lillian Russell asked to be introduced to him. Comedians Weber and Fields wrote a skit in his honor. A hotel bar concocted a cocktail that bore his name, and small boys everywhere saved their pennies—25 of them—so they could buy a paperback titled "Secrets of Amos Rusie, the World's Greatest Pitcher, How He Obtained His Incredible Speed on Ball."

Whether Rusie's fastball attained greater velocity than those of later pitchers in problematical, but in the 1890s it was regarded as second only to the speed of sound.

One of Amos' pitches struck Hughey Jennings on the head, knocking the Baltimore shortstop unconscious for four days. Another of Rusie's fastballs was lined back to the mound where it struck the pitcher on the ear and damaged his hearing permanently.

Partly because of Rusie's speed, the pitching distance was increased from 50 feet to 60 feet, 6 inches. The change was not only a safety measure for batters, but was an aid to Amos as well, inasmuch as it provided the extra distance needed to put the break on his overpowering curveball.

Rusie, who quit school at an early age to work in a lounge factory, made his baseball debut as an outfielder with a team in the Indianapolis City League. When the regular pitcher was knocked out of a game, teammates suggested that Amos replace him. Rusie never again played the outfield.

The hard-throwing pitcher's reputation led to a contract with the Indianapolis (National) club. In his first appearance, Amos opposed the New York Giants. It was, observers agreed, an unfair test for the young hurler, but Amos took it in stride. He struck out the first batter on three pitches (none of which, the victim said, he saw).

Rusie himself became a Giant in 1890 when the Indianapolis franchise was transferred to New York, where he became an instant hero.

Differences between Rusie and Owner Andrew Freedman created a sticky situation, though. When Rusie rejected a young pupil because "he was a smart aleck" and unwilling to learn, Freedman fined the pitcher $100.

**Amos Rusie was the first genuine sports idol of New York City.**

Later, when Amos insisted he was in bed at 11 p.m., the owner accused him of being out all night. A second $100 fine resulted.

When he received his 1896 contract, which did not restore what he considered unjust fines, Rusie refused to sign. Freedman stood firm. The pitcher sat out the entire season, after which he sued Freedman for $5,000.

Rather than have the case come to trial, other N.L. owners, in a meeting at Indianapolis, voted to make up the amount of the suit. As a consequence, Rusie earned $2,000 more by remaining idle than if he had pitched.

Rusie signed his 1897 contract, but then it was Freedman's turn. He issued orders that Amos should not be issued a uniform.

Shortly, the owner relented to the point that Rusie was given a uniform and ordered to sit in the bullpen. When the Giants lost a number of games—and fans started to cry for Freedman's scalp—the owner yielded and Amos came on to snap the losing streak.

In 1898, after compiling a 20-10 record, Rusie attempted to pick off Chicago's Bill Lange without first moving his foot toward first base. Something "like a jolt of electricity" shot through his arm. The pain was blinding. He did not know that Lange had been called out, nor was he able to catch the ball when it was returned to the mound.

Amos finished the game, however, throwing "floating curves." The next day he commenced a series of visits to doctors, none of whom could diagnose his problem.

Rusie remained out of baseball for two years, then was traded to Cincinnati in a deal that sent Christy Mathewson to the Giants. Amos pitched three games for the Reds in 1901 and was kayoed each time. At 30 he was washed up.

Rusie worked in a Muncie, Ind., paper and pulp mill for three years until it closed. He moved to Vincennes, Ind., and engaged in fresh water pearling in the Wabash River.

In 1911, Amos got a job as a steamfitter in Seattle, working in that capacity for 10 years and eventually becoming foreman. In 1921, John McGraw, learning of Rusie's whereabouts, offered him a job as superintendent of the Polo Grounds.

He resigned in 1929 and returned to the Northwest, where he bought a small ranch and raised chickens and engaged in farming on a small scale. in 1934, he suffered multiple injuries in a car accident that handicapped him until his death in 1942 at age 71.

# Babe Ruth

A young Babe Ruth, standing (left) with the catcher's mitt and mask, poses with his teammates at St. Mary's Industrial School, where he learned the rudiments of baseball.

In the after-stench of the Black Sox scandal, when baseball urgently needed a magnetic personality to restore public confidence in the game, there emerged a bulbous figure with an explosive bat who, more than any other player, set the game soaring to unprecedented popularity.

On and off the playing field, Babe Ruth was a man of gargantuan achievements. He was a symbol of that deliriously wacky age known as the "Roaring Twenties," and he roared louder than his contemporaries.

When he wasn't setting home run records, Ruth was shattering all known gastronomic marks. A quart of chocolate ice cream and pickled eels were standard fare between games of a doubleheader. A breakfast might consist of a pint of bourbon and ginger ale, a porterhouse steak, four fried eggs, fried potatoes and a pot of coffee.

Ruth did everything in a style unknown to lesser mortals. He could party all night, drive cars at break-neck speed, consume enormous portions of food and drink and then perform as the demigod of the diamond.

Babe was in a class by himself as a gate attraction. After establishing records as a lefthanded pitcher, he became a symbol for majestic, dramatic home runs and for equally majestic, dramatic strikeouts, all of which earned him adulation from the spectators.

A Baltimore waterfront waif who learned to sip beer and chew tobacco before he was 7, George Herman Ruth entered St. Mary's Industrial School, where he learned a degree of discipline and the rudiments of baseball.

When Ruth was 18, his tutor, Brother Mathias, recommended him to Jack Dunn of the Baltimore (International) Orioles. The owner was impressed and signed the kid, immediately named Babe, as a pitcher. By the end of the 1914 season, Ruth was purchased by the Boston Red Sox.

For five years he was a mainstay of the Sox's pitching staff, appearing in three World Series. Gradually, however, as his batting talent became apparent, he saw more action as an outfielder. By the time he was traded to the Yankees in 1920, Babe's days as a pitcher were virtually ended.

Aided by a new, lively ball, the Bambino won a nation's heart by slugging 60 home runs in 1927 and a career total of 714. At other times, he flouted the authority of club management as well as the commissioner of baseball.

When he collapsed on the Asheville, N.C., railroad platform in 1925, suffering from "the world's largest belly ache," Babe was fined $5,000 by the Yankees for breaking training rules and curfew.

Another time, he ignored Commissioner K.M. Landis' edict against postseason barnstorming and drew a 30-day suspension as well as a fine.

Meanwhile, home runs flew in abundance. Ruth swatted

Ruth (center) was a strong-armed lefthanded pitcher for the Red Sox during his early years. By 1926, Ruth was making headlines with his bat (left) and colorful off-field exercises (right).

three in one World Series game against the Cardinals in 1926 and duplicated the feat against the same team in 1928. In his 10th and last Series, against the Cubs in 1932, the Babe walloped two homers, including a controversial shot that may, or may not, have been called.

As Ruth's homer totals soared, so did his salary—until it reached $80,000 annually. During Herbert Hoover's administration, Ruth once was a holdout. Seeking to break the impasse, a writer friend reminded Ruth that he was already earning more than the President.

"I had a better year than he did," grunted Ruth.

Several years earlier, while all the Yankees were being introduced to Calvin Coolidge at a Washington opener, Babe broke the routine with: "Geez, it sure is hot, ain't it, Prez."

The Babe eagerly sought the Yankees' managerial job before the appointment of Joe McCarthy in 1931, but Owner Jake Ruppert passed him by.

The Sultan of Swat was released after the 1934 season and joined the Boston Braves as vice president, assistant manager and outfielder. Babe socked six homers in the National League, the final three in a May 25, 1935, game at Pittsburgh. He retired after appearing in 28 games.

His once-powerful frame shriveled by cancer, Ruth died in 1948 at age 53.

Ruth watches the flight of his 60th home run in 1927, the homer that stood as a baseball standard until 1961.

# Ray Schalk

When the Milwaukee team of the American Association needed a catcher immediately in 1911, the Detroit Tigers agreed to let the Brewers have a teen-ager on whom they had acquired an option for $750.

The young player was with Taylorville in the Illinois-Missouri League. The following season he joined the White Sox, starting a 17-year career with Chicago that earned him recognition as one of the game's all-time best catchers.

Ray Schalk was one day short of his 20th birthday when he reported to the White Sox at Comiskey Park on August 11, 1912. Schalk arrived a few hours before the start of a Sunday doubleheader and was greeted by Manager Jimmy Callahan, who told him, "Here's your pitcher, Doc White. You're catching the first game."

**By 1920, White Sox catcher Ray Schalk had developed into one of the premier receivers in baseball history.**

The youth handled White like an old pro and rapped a single off Chief Bender, but the Sox lost to the Athletics, 3-1.

When and how Schalk obtained the nickname of Cracker was never determined satisfactorily. One version insisted it stemmed from a remark of a veteran player who, seeing Schalk, asked, "Who's that little cracker?"

Another explanation traced the name to the fact that Ray cracked the whip over the Chicago pitchers. The catcher could shed no light on the matter.

Fast for a catcher and ever alert, Schalk generally was credited with being the first catcher to run to first base behind the batter to guard against an overthrow.

At the suggestion of first baseman Hal Chase, Schalk also covered third base to make putouts and once surprised a runner with a putout at second.

"One day," Schalk related, "a ball was hit over the infield and in front of the center fielder. I had a hunch it would fall safely, so I ran out over the pitcher's mound and when the ball dropped in I yelled to Eddie Collins, who threw the ball to me in time to tag the runner as he slid in (at second). We worked the play two or three more times."

Schalk also was credited with making a catcher out of Moe Berg, who was a shortstop when he graduated from Princeton.

Cracker was managing the White Sox at the time and was incapacitated by a fractured thumb when a foul tip split the hand of Buck Crouse, the No. 2 catcher.

"Any one of you fellows ever a catcher?" asked Ray, surveying the bench.

"I thought I was once," said Berg, "but somebody told me I wasn't."

"Who was that?" asked Schalk.

"My high school coach in Newark," replied Moe.

"Well, as long as he isn't around, how about getting in there and trying it again?" suggested the manager.

"If you can stand it, I can," answered Moe, a catcher thereafter.

Schalk received a winner's share in the White Sox' World Series victory over the Giants in 1917 and also appeared in the 1919 Series when he was believed to be the first to sense that some teammates were not making an all-out effort to defeat the Reds.

While he flatly refused to discuss the Black Sox scandal in subsequent years, Ray did declare that "we could have won if Red Faber had not been sick."

Schalk caught four no-hitters in his tenure with the White Sox, including Charley Robinson's perfect game at Detroit in 1922.

Ray ended his affiliation with the White Sox midway through the 1928 season. He had managed the club for 1½ years and the team had compiled a 32-42 record in '28 when he stepped down from his $25,000-a-year job. He had expected to remain as a player for $15,000, but when Owner Charles Comiskey offered approximately half that amount, the Cracker severed his Chicago connection.

For years Schalk operated a Chicago bowling establishment and served as an assistant baseball coach at Purdue University.

He succumbed to a long siege of cancer in 1970 at age 77.

# Joe Sewell

The University of Alabama graduate had played fewer than 100 games with New Orleans of the Southern Association when he was ordered to join the Cleveland Indians. It was an emergency. Shortstop Ray Chapman had just been killed by a pitched ball.

It was not the ideal spot for a 21-year-old kid to break into the majors, but the 5-foot-7 infielder not only held up in the pressure spot, he batted .329 in the 22 games remaining in the Indians' pennant-winning 1920 season.

Joseph Wheeler Sewell—he was named for the Confederate cavalry officer—stayed in the majors for 13 more seasons, earning a reputation for durability and a sharp eye at the plate.

Joe played in 1,103 consecutive games before being sidelined because of the flu. The streak would have been longer except that, in an early year with Cleveland, Sewell sat out two games while Manager Tris Speaker experimented with another infield alignment.

Sewell's primary claim to fame, however, was in laying the bat on the ball. In 7,132 major league at-bats, Joe struck out only 113 times, an average of once every 63 trips to the plate.

Swinging a 40-ounce bat that he christened Black Betsy, Sewell once played 115 consecutive games without striking out. The most troublesome pitchers for the left-handed-batting Sewell were lefthanders Hubert (Dutch) Leonard and Pat Caraway.

Leonard, who pitched for the Red Sox and Tigers, threw a spitball that Sewell found bothersome. Caraway, a 6-4 Chicago stringbean who compiled a 22-40 lifetime record, "couldn't throw hard enough to blacken my eye," Sewell said, "but he had a floppy-armed delivery with that soft stuff and when he threw it from a white-shirted background, I had trouble picking it up. Struck me out twice in one game."

The only other hurler to strike out Joe twice in a game

**Cleveland infielder Joe Sewell's primary claim to fame was his ability to get his bat on the ball.**

was Wally Warmoth, a rookie lefthander with Washington who accomplished the feat on May 13, 1923. In 1925 and 1929, Sewell struck out only four times.

Sewell enjoyed perhaps his biggest day against the Philadelphia A's Lefty Grove in New York in 1932, Joe's second season with the Yankees.

"I got five hits in five times up," Joe recalled, "and the last one was a home run into the right-field bleachers. When I hit it, Grove threw his glove in the air and followed me around the bases yelling at me."

Sewell recalled one of his strikeouts against George Blaeholder of St. Louis.

"Bill McGowan was the umpire and the count went to 3-and-2," he said. "The next pitch was a fastball right even with my cap. McGowan hollered, 'Strike three, oh my God I missed it' all in one breath. I looked at him, but did not say a word. The next day he apologized for missing the third strike. He was a good umpire, very capable, and I never held it against him."

Joe, who had two brothers in the majors (Tommy appeared in one game for the Cubs in 1927 and Luke was a longtime American League catcher), was released by Cleveland after the 1930 season. He signed with the Yankees and played three more seasons as a third baseman.

After retiring, Sewell coached the Alabama baseball team, worked as a good-will ambassador for a diary and entered the hardware business, which he sold "because I wasn't too good a businessman," he explained.

"I'd upset my store manager by scooping cash out of the drawer to go fishing or hunting. Finally, I agreed to leave a note on how much money I took so he could balance the books, but doggone it, I'd forget.

"Oh, I'd remember to leave the note, all right. But my store manager was still mystified when, in my haste, I wrote only, 'I took it all.'"

# Al Simmons

**As an A's rookie in 1924, Al Simmons hit .308, a portent of things to come.**

**Simmons' career ended in 1944 back in Philadelphia, with the career .334 hitter 73 hits short of 3,000.**

The husky Polish kid from the south side of Milwaukee had a longtime ambition to play for the powerful New York Giants and their dynamic manager, John McGraw.

The most direct route to the Polo Grounds, the outfielder decided, was to write to Roger Bresnahan, manager of the Giants' American Association farm team at Toledo, and offer his services. He was available, Bresnahan was informed, for $150 in expenses. The youth never received a reply, so Al Simmons—he was christened Aloysius Harry Syzmanski—performed conspicuously for the Philadelphia Athletics.

"Can you imagine what I'd have hit in the Polo Grounds with those short fences?" Simmons mused frequently. But then he frequently added, "I'm not sure I'd have enjoyed playing for McGraw. We were both hotheads and I'm afraid we'd have clashed."

Probably no great hitter looked less like a hitter than Simmons. A righthanded batter, he stood with his left foot pointed toward third base. When Al reported to his first major league training camp, veterans ridiculed his style.

"Let that young man alone," A's Manager Connie Mack advised. "He hit .398 at Milwaukee and .360 at Shreveport, and if he can hit like that it's all right with me if he stands on his head at the plate."

Simmons resented the "Bucketfoot Al" tag that was tacked on him and explained scientifically how he could hit outside pitches despite his unorthodox style.

"I've studied movies of myself batting," he said. "Although my left foot stabbed out toward third base, the rest of me, from the belt up, especially my wrists, arms and shoulders, was swinging in a proper line over the

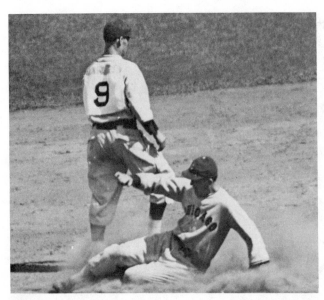

Simmons, shown sliding into second base with one of his two doubles in the 1934 All-Star Game, was one of the five A.L. sluggers who struck out consecutively against Carl Hubbell in the same game.

plate.''

Simmons never swung better than he did on Memorial Day of 1930 when the A's played a morning-afternoon doubleheader against the first-place Washington Senators. The A's were losing the first game, 6-3, with two out in the ninth inning at Shibe Park when Spencer Harris and Dib Williams singled. Simmons homered to tie the score and eventually tallied the deciding run in the 13th inning.

Moments before crossing the plate, Al had dived back into third base and felt something snap in his knee. By the time Simmons reached the clubhouse, the knee was badly swollen. The doctor informed him a blood vessel was ruptured and that, while he might be able to pinch-hit in the second game, he should not consider running.

The Nats led, 7-5, in the fourth inning of the second game when the A's loaded the bases and Mack beckoned to Simmons to pinch-hit. With a count of 2-and-0, pitcher Bump Hadley threw a change-up that Al caught just right. The ball landed in the left-field seats for a grand-slam. The A's won the game, 15-11.

Months later, after the A's captured their second consecutive pennant, Washington Owner Clark Griffith told Mack, "I checked up on Simmons this year. He hit 14 homers in the eighth and ninth innings and every one figured in the ball game. We were never the same after he licked us in that doubleheader."

In the 1929 World Series, when the A's were losing to the Cubs, 8-0, in the seventh inning of Game 4, it was Simmons who spoiled Charlie Root's shutout with a homer. "What a way to waste a homer," Al said to himself.

In 1937, Simmons became a member of the Washington Senators, his fourth American League team.

Before the inning was over, Simmons also singled and scored again as the A's tallied 10 times in the most productive of World Series innings.

Simmons, who batted .329 in four World Series and .462 in three All-Star Games, was sold along with Jimmie Dykes and Mule Haas to the White Sox after the 1932 season as Mack dismembered his second great club. He had two more stints with the A's, though, finishing his playing career with Mack's team in 1944.

Al died of a heart attack in 1956, four days after his 54th birthday.

# George Sisler

During his .420 season in 1922, slick-fielding first base-man George Sisler was dazzling St. Louis fans with his bat and glove and was mentioned in the same breath with such heavyweight contemporaries as Yankee slugger Babe Ruth (left).

When a player bats .420, as George Sisler did for the St. Louis Browns in 1922, it is inconceivable that he could have had a superior season.

Sisler, though, regarded his 1920 performance as more satisfying. In '20, the first baseman played every inning of 154 games, established a major league record with 257 hits, scored 137 runs, drove in 122, stole 42 bases and batted .407. He had 49 doubles, 18 triples and 19 home runs.

On the final day of the season, George got three hits, scored two runs, stole three bases and, although he hadn't pitched competitively in four seasons, hurled the final inning against the White Sox.

A graduate of the University of Michigan (where he played for Branch Rickey), Sisler was a cause celebre after it was discovered that he had signed contracts with the Browns and the Pirates. The National Commission, ruling body of baseball at the time, awarded him to St. Louis, where he immediately blossomed into stardom.

Sisler's career started downhill in 1927, when the Browns sold him to the Washington Senators.

Sisler entered the majors in 1915 (Rickey was his first big-league manager), breaking in as a pitcher. In one of his early games, George was matched against Walter Johnson, his boyhood idol. Sleepless the night before and nervous to a fault before the game, Sisler settled down quickly after the game started and defeated the Big Train, 2-1.

By 1918, Gorgeous George, then 25, was a full-time first baseman, dazzling with his agility afield and his skill at bat.

Sisler was mannerly and gentle, but no weakling, as pitcher Bob Groom discovered. Groom berated Sisler unmercifully on the bench for failing to catch a high throw, where upon George walked over to Groom and decked him.

Generally, his temper was in tight control, but Sisler once slapped umpire George Hildebrand with his glove and drew a short suspension.

Reports of Sisler's genius with the glove staggered the imagination, but creditable witnesses vouched for the feats. Once, George made a superlative stop of a hard smash and lobbed gently toward first base in the expectation that the pitcher would cover the bag. When the pitcher failed to arrive, Sisler raced to the base and caught his own throw for the putout.

Another time, Hal Janvrin of the Red Sox was on third base and Tris Speaker on first when the batter hit a line drive to Burt Shotton in left field. Feeling that he had no chance to get Janvrin at home plate, Shotton fired to Sisler, who tagged out Speaker and then whirled and caught Janvrin at the plate.

On a third occasion, George raced in to field a squeeze bunt, tagged out the batter and then dived for the plate to nip the runner trying to score.

After his great year of 1922, Sisler suffered a violent sinus attack that caused double vision and sidelined him for the entire 1923 season. He rejoined the Browns in 1924 and although he batted .345 one year and .340 another, he was never again—by his own admission—the same player he had been before his illness.

Sisler was appointed manager of the Browns in 1924 and held the position for three years although he was poorly suited for the job.

The Sisler name remained in the public eye. Three of the Hall of Famer's sons had ties to the game—George Jr. as a longtime minor league executive, Dick as a first baseman-outfielder for three major league clubs and Dave as a big-league pitcher.

After retiring from the game in 1932, George entered the sporting goods business in St. Louis. He returned to baseball when Rickey, then with Brooklyn, offered him a job as a scout. Sisler accompanied the Mahatma to Pittsburgh and remained active until a few years before his death at age 80.

# Duke Snider

Snider celebrates after the final out of the Dodgers' win over the Yankees in Game 1 of the 1952 Series.

In 1949, Duke Snider (left) spent his first full season in a Brooklyn uniform. He was producing homers with regular-

ity by 1955, hitting four in the World Series (including two in Game 5, right) against the Yankees.

The Pittsburgh scout was deeply impressed with the 17-year-old who was hitting and fielding spectacularly with a Navy team during World War II.

"I'll give you $20,000 to sign with the Pirates," Babe Herman told the teen-ager, who replied, "I'm sorry, Mr. Herman, but I've already signed with the Dodgers for a $750 bonus and $250 a month."

As an all-round sports star at Compton High School in California, Duke Snider was trailed by scouts of the Reds, Cardinals and Dodgers. He chose the Brooklyn club because it "had a couple of players named Pee Wee Reese and Pete Reiser when it won the pennant in 1941 and I

was a great admirer of them."

Edwin Donald Snider, nicknamed by his father when still a tyke, earned 10 letters in baseball, football, basketball and track while in junior high school and four more monograms in 1½ years at Compton High.

After graduation in February of 1944, Duke took off for Bear Mountain, N.Y., where the Dodgers did their wartime training. One season at Newport News (Piedmont) and a Navy hitch preceded stints at Fort Worth (Texas) and St. Paul (American Association) before Snider was ready for the Dodgers.

Even then, however, he was not fully prepared for the

When the Dodgers moved to Los Angeles in 1958, Snider's prolific slugging days were nearing an end.

National League. He had one serious flaw—ignorance of the strike zone.

Inventive Branch Rickey devised a cure. He sent Duke to Vero Beach, Fla., with a special coach, George Sisler. The cure consisted of Snider standing at the plate, bat on shoulder, with an umpire on hand.

"After the ball was delivered," Duke recalled, "the ump would call it a strike or ball and then Sisler would ask my opinion. I wasn't permitted to swing even if it was right down the gut. At first we were far apart—and then I began to notice that I was calling more of 'em right. Moreover, when I got into a game I didn't lunge for pitches so much."

Snider was justifiably proud of his arm. In high school, he had tossed a football 70 yards in a throwing contest. In a game, he threw a 63-yard pass to pull out a victory in the last 15 seconds.

Once, in a pregame discussion, the subject of how far Snider could throw a baseball was raised. While the groundkeepers were tidying up Ebbets Field, and while bewildered spectators looked on, Snider stood at home plate and let fly. His first throw struck the scoreboard in right-center field. His second cleared the right-field fence, 40 feet high and at least 350 feet from home plate.

Snider insisted that his arm was even stronger when he played at Newport News in 1944. "In 1947 I didn't warm up properly during a damp night in St. Paul and my arm hasn't been the same since," he said.

After the Dodgers moved to Los Angeles, Duke attempted to throw a baseball out of Memorial Coliseum. He strained his arm and was unable to play for one game. He was fined one day's pay, approximately $245.

Duke had brilliant and dismal World Series experiences. He struck out eight times and collected only three hits in the 1949 classic. However, Snider rapped 10 hits in the 1952 Series and walloped four home runs in both the '52 and 1955 Series.

En route to more than 2,000 hits and 400 homers in the majors, Snider enjoyed many unforgettable moments and days, but none to equal a game against the Phillies when he smashed three consecutive homers and a fourth drive that missed by only a foot or two of clearing the wall.

Perhaps his most notable defensive play also was at the expense of the Phillies in Philadelphia. Snider dug his spikes into the fence in left-center field and made a leaping, one-handed catch of a Willie Jones drive as the potential winning run headed for the plate.

After completing his active career with the Giants, the onetime Major League Player of the Year scouted and managed in the minors before turning his talents to the radio booth with the Montreal Expos.

# Warren Spahn

A 19-year-old Warren Spahn (right, left photo) played his first professional season for Bradford of the Pony League in 1940. In 1948, Spahn was congratulated by catcher Bill Salkeld (right) after winning Game 5 of the 1948 World Series with a scoreless relief stint.

Ordinarily, three years of military service when a professional athlete is in his early 20s would be regarded as unfortunate, but the shrewd pitcher who won more games than any lefthander in big-league history never regarded it as a tough break.

"People say that my absence from the major leagues may have cost me a chance to win 400 games," said Warren Spahn. "But I don't know about that. I matured a lot in three years and I think I was a lot better equipped to handle major league hitters at 25 than I was at 22. Also, I pitched until I was 44. Maybe I wouldn't have been able to do that otherwise."

Spahn was given a field commission as a first lieutenant for action in repairing the Remagen Bridge over the Rhine River. He was wounded in the same action, but shrugged it off as "only a scratch."

The native of Buffalo, N.Y., pitched for the Braves in four games in the 1942 season—two at the beginning and two at the end. The rest of the season he pitched for Hartford (Eastern). In his big-league debut, Spahn retired both batters to face him in a relief appearance against the Giants.

In his second year back from the war, Spahn was a 21-game winner. It was his first of 13 seasons in the 20-victory circle. Only Cy Young, with 16, had achieved it more frequently.

Warren missed the 20 mark in 1948, but he helped pitch the Braves to their first pennant since 1914. Down the stretch, he and Johnny Sain seemed to pitch almost daily and New Englanders pinned flag hopes on "Spahn and Sain and pray for rain."

Spahn split two decisions in the World Series against the Cleveland Indians, then notched victory totals of 21, 21 and 22 before dropping to 14 in 1952. Boston attendance fell alarmingly in the last two years, and Spahn was asked to take a $5,000 pay cut (down from $25,000).

The pitcher refused to sign, and Braves President Lou Perini countered with an offer of 10 cents on every admission for 1953. Spahn was adamant. He had to have $25,000 and Perini ultimately yielded.

How was Spahn to know that the Braves would transfer to Milwaukee for the '53 season? Had he accepted the

During his final major league season (1965), Spahn was a teammate of fellow Hall of Famer Willie Mays.

Spahn delivers a ninth-inning pitch (above) en route to a September 16, 1960, no-hitter against Philadelphia, the first of two in his career. Victory No. 300 came in 1961 and earned Spahn handshakes from Hank Aaron (below right) and catcher Joe Torre.

10-cent proposal, he would have earned more than $150,000 from the outpouring of Milwaukee fans.

With a wide assortment of pitches, plus cunning control and a bat that smacked a total of 35 homers, Spahn piled victory upon victory. He notched two no-hitters and 63 career shutouts. He was, said Charley Dressen, his manager in 1960 and most of '61, "my go-to-sleep pitcher." Translated, that meant Charley could "go to bed the night before Spahn pitches and get a good night's sleep."

Whitlow Wyatt, a Dodger pitcher when Spahn came up, was pitching coach for Milwaukee when Spahn was the club's foremost hurler.

"I pitched against him in 1942," recounted Wyatt, "and 15 years later he reminded me that the first time I faced him I threw him a fastball, then a curve, then another fastball that he hit to the shortstop. He not only remembered the hitters, but the pitchers, too."

Spahn won his 100th game on August 15, 1951, by beating the Phillies. He gained his 200th, also over the Phils, on September 13, 1956. He reached the 300 milestone on August 11, 1961, when he defeated the Cubs. Curiously, Richie Ashburn was a member of the losing club in each game, although he did not play in the latter contest.

Spahn, who underwent three knee operations during his career, remained in shape during the off-season by swimming and working on his ranch in Hartshoren, Okla. He was 42 when he posted a 23-7 mark for Milwaukee in 1963. He was sold to the Mets after the 1964 season and finished the '65 campaign with San Francisco.

The stylish old master won his last major league game on September 12, 1965 beating Chicago, 9-2, in the second game of a twin bill. It was Warren's 363rd lifetime victory, the highest total by a lefthander and the fifth-best mark in history.

# Albert Spalding

The $5-a-week grocery clerk in Rockford, Ill., was dazzled by the offers that poured in from professional baseball clubs seeking his services in 1867.

He was only 17 when the National Baseball club of Washington made an extended tour of the Midwest. The Nationals were regarded as the strongest club in the land and readily accepted the challenge of the Forest City team of Rockford.

When the young pitcher defeated the Nationals, he became a national celebrity and salary offers up to $2,500 were received from teams in New York, Cleveland and Washington. He resisted the blandishments to remain with Forest City, but four years later the righthander succumbed to the inducements of Harry Wright, then organizing a team in Boston.

For Albert Goodwill Spalding, the die was cast. For the remainder of his life he was recognized internationally as a premier pitcher, manager, club president, founder of a worldwide sporting goods business and high-ranking counselor in the inner chambers of baseball.

Spalding was the only pitcher on the Boston roster during his first season, when he posted a 20-10 mark in 1871. He was the pitcher of record in all but one contest. Thereafter, Spalding pitched the Red Stockings to four consecutive National Association flags, climaxing the string with a 56-4 record in 1875.

During the '75 season, Spalding was approached by William A. Hulbert, a Chicago businessman who had been offered the presidency of the White Stockings, a mediocre team. Before acting on the offer, Hulbert told the Boston pitcher:

"Spalding, you've no business playing in Boston. You're a western boy . . . If you come to Chicago to play and manage next season, I'll accept the presidency of the club and we'll give those easterners a fight for their lives."

The season was only half over, but Spalding and Boston teammates Ross Barnes, Cal McVey and Deacon Jim White signed contracts secretly to play the following season for Chicago.

News of their undercover actions leaked out, however, and the quartet played out the season listening to cries of—among other things—"Your White Stockings will turn gray."

In the meantime, Hulbert grew disgusted with the way in which gamblers had infiltrated the National Association and, eyeing reform, he instituted plans to organize the National League, which made its debut the following year.

Al contributed 47 victories to Chicago's total of 52 in the N.L. pennant-winning season of 1876. In '77, he played first and second base as the White Stockings dropped to fifth place.

Spalding made his final Rockford appearance in uniform

**Albert Spalding's baseball career started on the mound and eventually wound through the game's inner chambers.**

on Harry Wright Day, April 13, 1896, when he pitched in an old-timers' game.

In 1888, Spalding led two teams on a worldwide tour, one club named "Chicago" and the other "All-America." After launching the trip at Chicago on October 20, the travelers headed westward via San Francisco. They visited 14 countries in an effort to popularize baseball before returning in April of 1889.

Because his sporting goods company, founded on capital of $500, was demanding more of his time, Spalding severed his baseball connections in 1891 and moved to Point Loma, Calif.

In 1900, President William McKinley appointed Spalding a U.S. commissioner to the Olympic Games in Paris. In tribute to his work in behalf of international sport, the government of France made him a member of the Legion of Honor.

Spalding was called eastward in 1901 when the National League was at war with the American. Through his efforts, the old and the new leagues signed a Major League Agreement.

Spalding wrote "America's National Game," an illuminating review of baseball's early years.

Two strokes took a heavy toll on his mobility before his death in 1915 at age 65.

# Tris Speaker

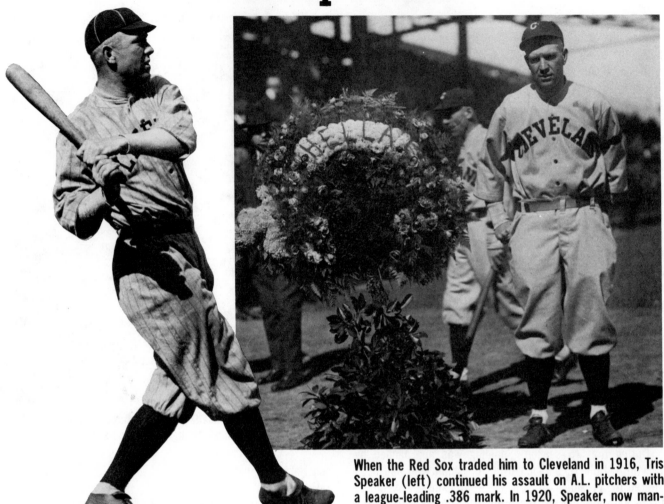

When the Red Sox traded him to Cleveland in 1916, Tris Speaker (left) continued his assault on A.L. pitchers with a league-leading .386 mark. In 1920, Speaker, now managing the Indians, posed with a floral piece prior to Game 1 of the World Series against Brooklyn.

If John McGraw's memory on October 16, 1912, extended to the spring of 1908, he could only condemn the quirks of history that made him a loser in his third World Series.

In 1908, a young outfielder offered his services to McGraw while the Giants were training in Marlin, Tex. Little Napoleon explained that he already had an abundance of outfielders in camp and could not give the newcomer a fair trial.

Maybe McGraw recalled that incident in the fall of 1912 when the same rejected player, now a brilliant performer for the Red Sox, drove in the tying run in the 10th inning of the final Series game that was won by Boston.

Speaker had played briefly with Boston in 1907, but did not receive a 1908 contract before the deadline. Realizing he was a free agent, he traveled 40 miles from his native Hubbard, Tex., to the Giants' camp.

At age 16, Speaker was a lefthanded pitcher for a semipro team when he was spotted by the owner of the Cleburne club of the North Texas League. Signed to a

$50-a-month contract, Tris was told to report to the Cleburne team, then playing in Waco. The brash youngster awakened the manager, Benny Shelton, at 6:30 a.m. and was told to wait in the hotel lobby until a more respectable hour.

At the ball park, Speaker was ordered to warm up. He did, for 30 minutes. "Must have made 300 pitches," he recalled years later. Then Shelton ordered: "Shag flies." The kid did, throughout batting practice of both clubs. As game time approached, Shelton barked, "You're pitching today, warm up."

"Warm up," cried Speaker, "what the hell do you think I've been doing?"

Speaker allowed only two hits, but was a 3-2 loser when Shelton, playing first base, argued a ninth-inning decision as two runners crossed the plate.

Some time later, when Cleburne's right fielder suffered a cheek fracture, Speaker announced that he also was an outfielder. He never pitched another game.

The Senators and Pirates also had opportunities to ac-

As the 1927 season began, fellow greats Speaker (right, left photo) and Rogers Hornsby were wearing unfamiliar uniforms. Speaker, long retired by the 1939 All-Star Game, poses (right) with Yankee great Joe DiMaggio.

quire Speaker, but the Red Sox, having passed him up once, bought him from Little Rock for $750 after the 1908 season. In quick order, Tris was recognized as the premier center fielder in the major leagues.

The Gray Eagle—Speaker was prematurely gray—played an uncommonly shallow center field which enabled him to catch many balls that ordinarily would fall in for hits. It also enabled him to cover second base on sacrifices and in one season, 1918, to pull two unassisted double plays. He also turned one in the 1912 Series against the Giants.

Speaker, or Spoke as he was known in the dugout, credited Cy Young with helping to make him a superb outfielder.

"Cy used to hit fungoes to me every day when I joined the Red Sox," Spoke said. "He always tried to hit the ball just one step beyond me so that I couldn't catch it unless I hustled.

"I watched him and in a few days I knew just by the way he swung whether the ball would go to my right or left. Then I figured that if I could do that with a fungo hitter I could do it in a ball game. I asked our pitchers how they pitched to each batter. I also studied the batters and

when he started his swing, I knew if he would hit to my left or right and I was on my way."

Speaker played with the Red Sox through 1915, a Boston pennant season, but balked when Owner Joe Lannin asked him to take a 50 percent slash in pay, from $18,000 to $9,000, for 1916.

Tris was traded to Cleveland in April of 1916. With about two months left in the 1919 season, he was named manager of the Indians.

Speaker resigned after the 1926 season when he and Ty Cobb were under investigation by Commissioner K.M. Landis for allegedly conspiring to fix a late-season game several years earlier. Both received a clean bill of health.

After completing his major league career with the Philadelphia Athletics in 1928, Speaker managed Newark (International) for two seasons. He broadcast major league games in Chicago for two years, after which he joined comedian Joe E. Brown in ownership of the minor league Kansas City Blues. A couple of years later, he sold his interest and returned to Cleveland as a broadcaster of Indians games.

The Gray Eagle was 70 when a coronary attack proved fatal in 1958.

# Casey Stengel

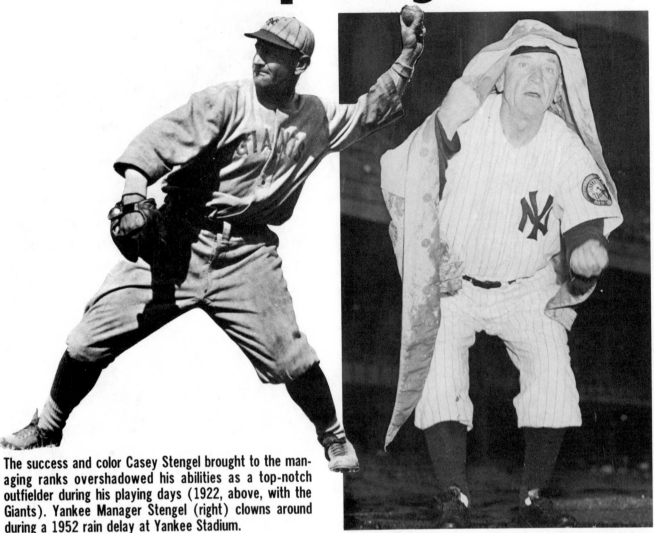

The success and color Casey Stengel brought to the managing ranks overshadowed his abilities as a top-notch outfielder during his playing days (1922, above, with the Giants). Yankee Manager Stengel (right) clowns around during a 1952 rain delay at Yankee Stadium.

They called him the "Old Perfessor," probably because his fractured syntax, mixed metaphors and non sequiturs were totally unlike what was heard in a college classroom.

For years he was recognized chiefly for his comical behavior on a baseball field. He was 60 when the world suddenly realized that beneath his clownish veneer lay a baseball intellect capable of establishing managerial records.

His name wasn't even Casey. He was born in Kansas City, the initials of which were slurred into the world-famed nickname of Charles Dillon Stengel.

Because of his success as a manager, Stengel's playing skill was frequently overlooked. But Casey qualified as a top-notch outfielder with the Dodgers, Pirates, Phillies, Giants and Braves.

Before entering baseball, Stengel was a dentist in his native city. "I was not very good at pulling teeth," he confessed, "but my mother loved my work."

Casey's comic art was developed before he reached the majors. While playing for Montgomery (Southern), Stengel spied a manhole in the outfield. While the spectators' attention was directed elsewhere, he slipped off the cover and lowered himself into the hole, leaving just enough space to observe the progress of the game.

When a ball was hit in that direction, Stengel arose majestically from the depths, circled under the ball and made the catch.

"Boy, was the manager mad," he said.

Ol' Case probably was remembered best for his stunt at Brooklyn after he had been traded to the Pirates. Jeered lustily on his first at-bat, Stengel made a grand, sweeping bow and doffed his cap as a liberated bird soared out of Ebbets Field.

Casey played in three World Series. His last was in 1923, when he socked two home runs in the Giants' losing cause to the Yankees. On Stengel's second homer a syndicated writer described how the 33-year-old outfielder limped and hobbled around the bases. In California, the parents of Casey's fiancee wondered what sort of antique their daughter was about to marry.

By 1963, Stengel (left) was pulling the strings for the hapless Mets. Former Yankee stars Whitey Ford (center, right photo) and Yogi Berra were on hand in 1970 when the Yankees retired Stengel's number.

Edna Lawson Stengel was her husband's loyal companion for more than half a century, tolerating his escapades and furnishing a steadying influence.

Casey began his managerial career at Worcester (Eastern) in 1925, also serving as club president and right fielder. It was not an auspicious season. On the final day, Stengel, as manager, released Stengel the player. As president he fired Stengel the manager, and then resigned as president.

Ol' Case managed Brooklyn and Boston from 1934 to '43, never finishing higher than fifth in the National League. When he was struck by a cab in Boston and suffered a broken leg, it appeared Stengel was ready to call it a career. He was wealthy from oil holdings in Texas and real estate and banking interests in California.

In 1944, however, he managed the Milwaukee (American Association) club as a favor to a friend. It was the turning point of his career. A year at Kansas City and three at Oakland prepared him for his appointment, in 1949, as skipper of the Yankees.

Casey might have earned the Yankee position earlier except that Ed Barrow, then front-office chief, recalled how Stengel, in his home run hobble of 1923, had thumbed his nose at the heckling Yanks before more than 62,000 Yankee Stadium spectators.

Stengel lost no time in convincing doubters that his clowning days were far behind. He won a world championship his first year in New York, and extended the World Series title string to five straight. He introduced the platoon system to baseball, a highly unpopular move with the players but a popular strategy with his bosses.

After 10 pennants in 12 years—he was beaten only by his oil partner, Al Lopez, in 1954 at Cleveland and in 1959 at Chicago—Casey was retired by the Yankees at age 71.

Stengel was unemployed only one season. When his old boss, George Weiss, took charge of the expansion Mets in 1962, he tapped his former sidekick, then 72, as the franchise's manager. Not even Casey was up to this challenge. His first three Met teams compiled 40-120, 51-111 and 53-109 records and the '65 club was on the way to 112 losses when Stengel stepped down at mid-season.

The Old Perfessor died in 1975 at age 86.

# Bill Terry

By 1930, Bill Terry was a bona fide Giants star, both with bat and glove (left and center). Terry and Yankees Manager Joe McCarthy posed together (above) prior to a World Series game in 1936, Terry's final season.

Progress had been frustratingly slow for the young left-hander, so when he and his wife sat down to breakfast in a Shreveport, La., coffee shop in 1917 they made a decision. If the major leagues did not beckon at the end of the coming season, pitcher Bill Terry would return to Memphis, Tenn., and enter a more rewarding business.

Terry won 14 games in the Texas League during the ensuing months. Still, no scouts gave him an offer and he returned to Memphis where, as a 15-year-old school dropout, he had worked in a railroad yard.

This time, Bill entered the oil business. Prospects were encouraging, and when he wasn't at work he was playing first base for a semipro team.

A few years later, when the Giants made their annual spring stop in Memphis, a friend tipped off John McGraw to the young oil man.

McGraw invited the local hero to meet him at the Peabody Hotel. For several hours the Giants' manager expounded on the honor of playing for the Giants under his leadership, finally suggesting that his guest sign a contract with the Toledo farm club.

"For how much?" Terry asked.

After McGraw recovered from the shock caused by such monumental ingratitude, he and Terry haggled for a time before Bill agreed to play for $5,000.

Memphis Bill put in two seasons in the American Association and, although only 24, managed the Mud Hens for a portion of the 1923 campaign.

Terry was not a complete first baseman when he joined the Giants in 1924. His chief flaws were in making the first-to-shortstop-to-first double play and throwing to the plate. Through diligent morning practice, however, the weaknesses became strengths and Terry evolved into one of baseball's all-time great first basemen.

Bill played only half the schedule in 1924, being platooned with righthanded-hitting George Kelly, but he was a regular in 1925.

Annually, his salary wrangles with McGraw were explosive affairs. One year, the exasperated manager told Bill to make a deal for himself.

In 1939, Terry was managing the Giants and Leo Durocher (left, left photo) the Brooklyn Dodgers. Ten years later,

Terry was hitting coach for the Cincinnati Reds as spring training began.

"Make your own deals," shot back Terry. "I have enough trouble playing first base."

A shrewd businessman who had come up the hard way, Terry knew his own value and did not mind expressing his views even to McGraw, who inspired only fear in others.

During a McGraw clubhouse diatribe against a player whose misplay had resulted in defeat, Terry bristled and told Little Napoleon publicly, "You've been blaming other people for the mistakes you've been making for 20 years."

Another time, Terry and Irish Meusel were three minutes late for the 11:30 p.m. curfew. A movie, Terry explained, had run longer than they had anticipated. But McGraw made no exception. Bill was fined $50, and was not in the starting lineup the next day.

Taking a seat at the end of the dugout, Terry removed his shoes and was in sweet repose when, late in the game, a teammate whispered that McGraw wanted him to pinch-hit. Stirring slowly, Terry shuffled to a spot in front of the manager, leisurely put on his shoes and then strode to the plate, leaving behind an infuriated skipper.

Terry responded with a game-winning homer. That eve-

ning McGraw refunded his fine and invited Bill to his suite for some Prohibition beer.

Terry won the 1930 batting title with a .401 mark—he is the last National Leaguer to achieve that plateau—and finished second in a three-way battle with Chick Hafey and Jim Bottomley in 1931.

McGraw and Terry had not spoken for two years when, on June 3, 1932, Muggsy summoned Terry into his office. "I was expecting to be notified I was traded," Bill said.

Instead, Bill was offered the managerial job—and he accepted. Almost immediately, he earned unpopularity with some writers for refusing to give out his private telephone number. He also denied permission for a newspaper to photograph his family, maintaining it was an invasion of privacy.

Terry managed the Giants to three pennants before turning over his job to Mel Ott in 1942. Memphis Bill remained with the club as farm director for one year, then resigned to devote his energies to an automobile agency in Memphis. Later, he moved to Florida, where he eventually operated three lucrative dealerships.

# Sam Thompson

Carpenters in Danville, Ind., were earning $2.50 a day in 1883 when the Detroit Wolverines of the National League arrived for an exhibition against the town team.

Scurrying about the village to round up all the players, the manager discovered an outfielder perched on a house roof making repairs. The 23-year-old was interested in playing, but first he wanted a full day's pay for a half day's work. He got it. He also received an encouraging appraisal that earned him a shot at minor league ball in 1884.

By July of 1885, Sam Thompson was in a Detroit uniform. He replaced the regular right fielder, who had been injured. In two at-bats, Thompson collected one hit and scored a run.

The lefthanded hitter used

Big Sam Thompson was a power hitter in an era when such players were looked down upon.

a unique batting style. From a crouch, he would leap up when the pitch was delivered and lash out viciously at the ball. Because of the small, lightly padded gloves of the time, infielders were reluctant to stand in the direct path of his savage smashes.

The first time Thompson faced Boston, he found second baseman John (Black Jack) Burdock in a shallow position. From behind the plate, the Boston catcher yelled to his teammate: "Better play back, Birdie."

Burdock would have none of it, replying, "Nobody can knock 'em through Birdie."

Seconds later, Birdie jacknifed to the turf to escape decapitation by Big Sam's rifle shot.

At 6-2 and 207 pounds, Thompson was the game's foremost slugger in an era when power hitters were regarded as untalented players.

The Spalding Guide of the 1890s asserted that Thompson "belongs to that rutty class of slugging batsmen who think of nothing else when they go to the bat but gaining the applause of the groundlings by the novice's hit to the outfield for a homer, one of the least difficult hits known to batting in baseball as it needs only muscle and not brains to do it."

Some folks' low opinion of the home run did not disturb Sam. According to one observer, "he took the fans' breath

away with his hitting and fielding." Thompson's throws from the outfield were strong and accurate. One source credited him with originating the one-hop throw to the catcher to head off baserunners attempting to score.

In the 1887 world championship playoff between Detroit, champion of the N.L., and the St. Louis Browns, American Association titlists, Thompson became the first player to hit two homers in one game in a postseason series.

In the first 11 games of the tournament, at which point Detroit won a decisive eighth time, Sam had 19 hits, including the two homers and two doubles. In Game 7, he saved a 3-1 victory by catching a long line drive with two on and two out.

Despite his build, Thompson was not particularly slow. He stole 33 bases one season and 235 during his career.

A sore arm limited Thompson to only 55 games in 1888 and he was sold to the Philadelphia Phillies at the end of the season. In Philadelphia, he teamed up with Billy Hamilton in center field and Ed Delahanty in left to form a future Hall of Fame outfield.

In his first season with the Phils, Thompson belted 20 home runs, a personal record. During his career, he socked 126.

Thompson played more than 100 games in 1896, but a back ailment sidelined the big slugger after only three games the following season. He attempted to play again in 1898, but was forced to retire after 14 games.

Sam made his home in Detroit, and he was on call in 1906 when Tigers Manager Bill Armour sought a temporary replacement for injured Sam Crawford. In his first game back, the 46-year-old Thompson was standing on the right-field foul line adjusting his sunglasses when the pitcher made his first delivery. The batter hit a drive down the line where Sam, far out of position, reached up to make the catch.

At various times in later life, Sam served as a U.S. Marshal, sold real estate and worked as a bailiff. He died of heart disease in 1922 at age 62.

# Joe Tinker

Most batters considered it cause for great rejoicing if they got a scratch single off Christy Mathewson, famous fadeaway pitcher of the New York Giants.

But Cubs shortstop Joe Tinker, who had a lifetime average of .264, batted over .350 against Matty in 1902 and topped .400 against the Giants' star in 1908.

Tinker earned his reputation as a steady shortstop for the Cubs under Peerless Leader Frank Chance in the first decade of the 20th century. To the Giants, however, he was cyanide—taken internally.

In 1908, the season that Fred Merkle's failure to touch second base forced the Giants and Cubs into a pennant-deciding makeup game, Tinker left his imprint on the Polo Grounders as follows:

May 25—Batted in the deciding run in a 10-inning, 8-7 victory.

July 17—Homered off Mathewson in a 1-0 triumph.

July 18—Drove in the deciding run in the ninth inning as the Cubs won, 5-4.

August 8—Saved the Cubs from a shutout with a sacrifice fly in 4-1 loss.

August 10—Rapped three hits off Mathewson and scored a run in a 3-2 Cub defeat.

August 11—Drove in half of the Cubs' runs in 4-0 victory.

August 30—Scored the deciding run in the fifth inning of 2-1 victory.

September 23—Homered for the Cubs' only run in the famous Merkle game, a 1-1 tie.

October 8—Led the assault on Matty with a triple as the Cubs defeated the Giants, 4-2, to win the pennant in a replay of the Merkle game.

Tinker's greatest renown, however, was earned as the front man of the Tinker-to-Evers-to-Chance doubleplay combination that was immortalized by Franklin P. Adams.

Tinker was a $35-a-month shortstop for a Coffeyville, Kan., team in 1899 when he played in an exhibition game against Kansas City. The 19-year-old performed so elegantly that the Kansas City manager recommended him to

**The Cubs' Joe Tinker usually saved his best for superstar pitcher Christy Mathewson and the Giants.**

Denver (Western), where his pay was $75 monthly. Two years later, Joe was a member of the Cubs.

After the 1912 season, Tinker was traded to Cincinnati, where he served one year as manager. Joe batted .317, his highest major league average, but the Reds finished seventh. The season was a series of confrontations between Tinker and club President Garry Herrmann, who allowed Tinker no voice in trade negotiations and sent a representative on team trips to keep an eye on the players.

At the end of the 1913 season, the Reds traded Tinker to Brooklyn, but the shortstop refused to report. Instead, he accepted the managerial position with the Chicago Whales of the Federal League. Tinker was the first player of note to join the new league.

A popular figure in Chicago, Joe led the Whales to a second-place finish in 1914 and to a pennant in '15. The team played its games in a park that in 1916 became the home of the Cubs.

After the Federal League folded Tinker remained in Chicago as manager of the Cubs in '16, but was released after a fifth-place finish. For several years he owned an interest in and managed the Columbus (American Association) club before migrating to Orlando, Fla., in the early 1920s.

Joe, who was associated with numerous minor league franchises in the decade that followed, acquired extensive land holdings during the Florida boom (during which his wealth was estimated at more than a million dollars). He was wiped out, however, when the boom collapsed.

In the depth of the Depression, Tinker operated a billiard parlor in Orlando. After the repeal of Prohibition, he opened the city's first barroom and the establishment became the popular headquarters for the local sporting gentry.

Joe suffered greatly in his last years from diabetes, which led to the amputation of his left leg. The old shortstop, for whom Orlando's ball park, Tinker Field, is named, died in 1948 on his 68th birthday.

# Pie Traynor

How he acquired his unusual nickname never was determined satisfactorily, but there never was any doubt that Harold Joseph (Pie) Traynor was one of the finest third basemen in major league history.

One version of the origin of his nickname dates to the long-ago day when he returned home after hours of vigorous activity, covered from head to foot with dirt and grime. His father, a printer, reportedly took one glance at his offspring and announced, "You look like pied type."

By another account, the youth played regularly on a local parish playground. At the end of the day, the priest, in recognition of cooperation and fair play, asked each youngster what he would like for a treat.

Invariably, the one who resembled pied type replied, "I'll take pie."

Regardless of the origin, Traynor imparted to his nickname superior quality as a gentleman and third baseman for the Pittsburgh Pirates.

A resident of Somerville, Mass., the youthful Traynor developed a deep affection for the Red Sox, but it was a Braves scout who found him and invited Pie to Braves Field for a tryout. Unfortunately, the scout failed to notify George Stallings. When the

**Pie Traynor was a slick-fielding third baseman for the Pittsburgh Pirates.**

miracle manager of 1914 spotted the unidentified teenager on the field, he ordered him off the premises.

"I ran halfway back to Somerville," Pie said.

Traynor was scouted by the Philadelphia A's and his favorite club, the Red Sox. When the manager of the Portsmouth club of the Virginia League wired Pie an offer, the youth showed it to Boston Manager Ed Barrow, who advised him, "Go ahead, we have a working agreement with Portsmouth and if you do well, we'll buy you."

Pie batted .270 in his first pro season, earning a glowing report from Pittsburgh scout Tom McNamara. Although other clubs were interested, Pie was sold to the high-bidding Pirates for $10,000.

Traynor made his major league debut on September 15, 1920, playing at shortstop. He had two assists in as many fielding chances and doubled once in two at-bats as the Pirates bowed to the Boston Braves, 4-1.

On July 22, 1937, he singled twice in five at-bats against the Dodgers for his last major league safeties. Pie

played his final game against the Cardinals on August 14, 1937, scoring in a pinch-running role in the ninth inning.

Between his first and last appearances, Traynor was regarded as the king of third basemen. His only serious competition as the all-time best at the hot corner was Jimmy Collins, who stood out for the Red Sox in the early 1900s.

Pie was particularly adept at fielding bunts and slow hoppers. He dived to either side with equal agility and speared hot smashes with a glove that contained a felt interior, rather than leather. "With the felt lining, a hard-hit ball, if not caught cleanly, will drop at your feet," he explained. "With a leather liner, it will glance off for a base hit."

Traynor did most of his hitting with discarded bats. In 1927, he and Paul Waner used a thick-handled bat cast away by a member of the San Francisco Seals. Waner batted .380 to win the league batting title and Traynor hit .342.

Gentlemanly Pie was ejected from only one game. "He said he was sick," reported umpire Pete McLaughlin, ". . . sick and tired of my lousy decisions." In truth, Traynor had thrown the ball to the ground in protest to a call and, said McLaughlin, umpires were "instructed to put out of the game any player who makes a gesture indicating disrespect."

Traynor never learned to drive a car. He was an inveterate walker. In the early 1950s, Pie ate breakfast at his New York hotel on 34th Street, then walked to Yankee Stadium, more than 100 blocks away, for a World Series game.

The saddest walk Traynor ever took was in Chicago in 1938 when, as manager of the Pirates, he strolled from Wrigley Field to the Bucs' downtown hotel after the Cubs had knocked Pittsburgh out of first place on Gabby Hartnett's historic homer. With him was the club trainer and a young writer. Not a word was spoken the entire route. "If either one had said a word, I'd have slugged him," Pie said.

A respiratory ailment took Traynor's life in 1972 while Pie was visiting a friend in Pittsburgh. He was 72.

# Dazzy Vance

Tales of the hard-throwing righthander are legion, but all attest to the fact that he was in a class by himself when it came to blinding speed.

He was pitching for a National League all-star team against American Leaguers in California one autumn when he broke off three explosive curveballs to Baby Doll Jacobson of the St. Louis Browns. On the third strike, Jacobson was flat on his back.

"Strike three, yer out," cried the umpire.

"And damn glad of it," replied Jacobson.

In St. Louis, the pitcher was informed by a writer before a game that "Rogers Hornsby hasn't struck out this season."

"That so? Well, save that story until after the game."

"Why?"

"Because I'm pitching."

That afternoon, Dazzy Vance fanned the Rajah three times and retired him the fourth time on a foul pop.

Vance, who gained his nickname in Nebraska from mimicking a cowboy's pronunciation of "Daisy," was a minor league vagabond for 10 years and reached the majors to stay only because the Dodgers were forced to take him. Brooklyn wanted Hank DeBerry from New Orleans, but the Pelicans refused to sell the catcher unless the National League club also took Vance. The Dodgers were easily coerced—and never regretted it.

When Dazzy arrived with DeBerry in his first training camp, he was greeted warmly by virtually everyone in sight. Curious about Vance's wide circle of acquaintances, DeBerry was told, "Why, my boy, these are old friends of mine. We've played with or against each other here, there, everywhere. I'd bet one hundred bucks that if I dropped in on every minor league camp in the country—and I wouldn't care how small the league—I would know at least three guys in every one of them."

Vance, who had pitched in a total of 11 big-league games for the Pirates and Yankees before joining the Dodgers in 1922 at age 31, led N.L. pitchers in strikeouts in '22 and repeated the next six years. In 1924, he registered a 28-6 record, which could have been 32-2 with a little more support.

**Dazzy Vance was a 10-year minor league veteran before he got a legitimate shot with Brooklyn.**

The following spring, the Dazzler held out until mid-March. Arriving at the Clearwater, Fla., camp in an aged touring car, he used the steering wheel for a desk and signed a three-year contract calling for $47,500.

Dazzy proceeded to win 22 games in 1925 and he pitched a no-hitter against the Phillies. He lost his shutout—Brooklyn won, 10-1—on an error.

By 1928, Vance was earning $20,000 and the next year the Dodgers' foremost gate attraction was earning $25,000 as the highest-paid pitcher in baseball at that time.

During Dazzy's heyday, the Brooklyn club was known as the Robins, in tribute to Manager Wilbert Robinson. But the team also was called the Daffiness Boys, acknowledging the bizarre events that frequently marked their style of play. It was Vance who was the lead man when three Brooklyn players wound up on third base. He also was the president of an off-hour group of revelers known as the "Night Prowlers," whose vice president was the inimitable Rabbit Maranville.

Vance took his pitching seriously, though.

When Wally Berger was a fine young outfielder with the Braves, Vance fanned him on his first at-bat with three curves. On Berger's second appearance, Dazzy fanned him on three fastballs.

"What kind of pitching is that?" grumbled Berger. "You learn how to strike me out one way and then you ignore what you've learned to strike me out another way. I don't understand it."

"Someday you will, my friend," said Vance. "The unexpected pitch is still the best pitch anyone can throw."

Dazzy threw the "unexpected pitch"—strike three—past 2,045 major league batters. But his hopes for 200 victories were dashed when, after two short hitches with the Cardinals and one with the Reds, he was released by the Dodgers in 1935, several months after appearing in his only World Series (with the Cards). He was 44 when he signed to pitch with the Bushwicks, a famed New York semipro team of that period.

For many years, Vance operated a hunting and fishing lodge in Homosassa Springs, Fla., where he died of a heart attack in 1961 shortly before his 70th birthday.

# Rube Waddell

Connie Mack always insisted that the finest pitcher in his experience was the one who gave him his biggest headaches.

Mack, who piloted the A's for 50 years, treasured the memory of the husky lefthander who pitched like a superman but whose child-like nature required infinite managerial patience and tact.

"The pitcher who had the best combination of speed and curve was Rube Waddell," said Mack, who managed the eccentric player around the turn of the century. "I saw Rube throw curves that came up waist-high and watched Nap Lajoie and Ty Cobb swing while the catcher dug the ball out of the dirt."

When Waddell was not pitching, he likely was fishing, chasing fire engines, shooting marbles with youngsters or enjoying himself at the local saloon.

His fascination with fire engines started when he was 3 years old. He ran away from home and was discovered asleep in the fire house.

Rube, known to his friends as Eddie, may have loved fishing even more than pitching. When Waddell was with Milwaukee playing minor league ball for Mack in 1900, the manager proposed to him, "If you pitch both games today, I'll give you three days off."

The opportunity to get away to his favorite fishing hole was too attractive for Waddell to pass up. Rube scattered 13 hits in the 17-inning opener, winning, 3-2, then allowed one hit in the 1-0 nightcap victory halted by darkness after five innings.

Demon rum, though, created many problems for Waddell. Usually without funds, Waddell would whisper to a bartender, "Give me a drink and I'll give you the ball I used to beat Cy Young in 20 innings."

The ruse worked regularly and hundreds of bartenders across the country displayed what they believed to be the historic souvenir.

On one occasion, the distraught pitcher told Mack, "I've lost my watch charm, the one I got for winning the pennant."

"Offer a reward for it," Mack told the penniless pitcher, "and if someone finds it, I'll pay the reward."

The next day, Rube phoned his boss from a nearby saloon. "A fellow found the watch charm," he reported. "Come over and give the guy his money."

**After the 1907 season, A's Manager Connie Mack traded Rube Waddell to the St. Louis Browns.**

Mack complied. He recognized the finder as a bartender. "As soon as my back was turned," said Connie, "the fellow turned the $10 over to Rube."

Rube might have had a long career with the Pirates except that Manager Fred Clarke was unable to handle him. In 1901, the Bucs traded Waddell to the Cubs. That fall, the lefthander accompanied an all-star tour to the West Coast and remained in Los Angeles to pitch the next year. Mack, who had moved from Milwaukee to Philadelphia, sent Rube a wire, early in 1902, inviting him to join the A's.

"Send $100 and transportation," the pitcher wired back.

Connie obliged—and waited. He learned that Waddell had boarded an eastbound train, but that a Californian had found him and delivered an impassioned speech focusing on Rube's "betrayal" of his loyal Los Angeles subjects. Waddell got off the train, weeping profusely.

Mack put Pinkerton detectives on his trail. The A's were in St. Louis when Mack received word that Waddell was in custody of the detectives, who were heading for Kansas City. Connie grabbed a train and met his elusive pitcher there.

In September of 1905, the playful hurler engaged in some horseplay with teammate Andy Coakley and fell on his left shoulder. The next morning Rube was unable to lift his arm high enough to attach his collar and missed the remainder of the season, including the World Series, which the A's lost to the Giants in five games.

Mack traded Waddell to St. Louis after the 1907 season. Rube made his first 1908 appearance against the A's in Philadelphia on May 19 and beat his old teammates. On July 29, in St. Louis, Rube boasted to the A's that he would set a strikeout record against them that afternoon; he fanned 16 to equal the existing modern record.

By 1911, Rube was pitching for Minneapolis (American Association). He was befriended by Manager Joe Cantillon and was at Joe's home in Hickman, Ky., in the spring of 1912 when the Mississippi River went on a rampage. Waddell responded to the emergency and stood for hours in icy water up to his armpits helping to place sandbags.

He contracted a severe cold and, although he pitched through 1913, he came down with tuberculosis that claimed his life in San Antonio in 1914 at age 37.

# Honus Wagner

Honus Wagner is considered by many the best shortstop of all time. Wagner was en route to a .329 averge in 1902 (above), the sixth in a string of 17 straight seasons in which he compiled a .300-plus mark. In 1909 (right), Wagner was working on his fourth consecutive batting championship.

While discussions may rage about the greatest all-time players at other positions, a unanimity prevails on the foremost shortstop in the first century of baseball.

He was thick-chested with massive shoulders. His legs were bowed like parentheses. A barrel, it was said, could be rolled through his legs, but a baseball, never. His arms were so long, cracked Lefty Gomez, that he was the only player who could tie his shoelaces without bending over.

Honus Wagner was colorful, quick and complete as a ballplayer. Awkward in appearance, he nevertheless performed with a speed that earned him the nickname of the "Flying Dutchman."

One of nine children born to a Bavarian immigrant, Wagner quit school at age 12 to work in the western Pennsylvania coal fields at $3 a week. When the opportunity arose at 21 to play baseball professionally, he leaped at the chance and performed for five teams in his first two seasons. A year later, however, Honus was in the majors, playing for Louisville of the National League.

The first time Wagner faced the Baltimore Orioles, the scourge of the league, he hit what should have been a stand-up triple. As Honus rounded first base, Jack Doyle gave him the hip. At second, Heinie Reitz "nearly killed

me," Wagner said. "Hughey Jennings tripped me at short and John McGraw was waiting for me with everything but a shotgun at third."

"Don't let 'em get away with that. Knock 'em over," bawled Manager Fred Clarke when Honus returned to the bench after being tagged out by McGraw.

The Dutchman heeded the advice. On his next triple against Baltimore, he toppled infielders like tenpins, knocking McGraw halfway to the dugout as he charged into third base. From that point, Wagner owned the respect of the Orioles. To his last breath, McGraw maintained that Honus was the greatest player he had ever seen.

When Barney Dreyfuss transferred the Louisville franchise to Pittsburgh in 1900, nobody was happier than Wagner. The shortstop was born in nearby Carnegie, Pa.

Wagner won the first of his eight batting titles in 1900 and he soon was coveted by the new, free-spending American League clubs. Clark Griffith, manager of New York Highlanders starting in 1903, placed a score of $1,000 bills before Honus, but he declined without even asking Dreyfuss for a raise.

The Pirates won pennants in 1901, 1902, 1903 and

**Though awkward in appearance, Wagner earned the nickname of "Flying Dutchman."**

1909. In '09, Wagner had his only confrontation with Ty Cobb.

The first time the Detroit star reached first base in the World Series, he cupped his hands and, after prefacing his remarks with a slur, shouted his base-stealing intentions at Wagner.

"I'll be waiting," replied the Dutchman who, a few seconds later, took the catcher's throw and applied a none-too-gentle tag on Cobb's lip that brought blood.

In his early major league seasons, Wagner earned $2,400 annually, the maximum allowed by the N.L. By 1909, his salary had escalated to $10,000. When contract-signing time arrived in subsequent years and Dreyfuss asked what Honus wanted in salary, the invariable answer was, "Same as last year." The owner would produce a blank contract, Wagner would sign and Dreyfuss would insert the figure.

As Honus' baseball stature increased, babies were named for Wagner, as well as a cigar and brands of beer. But the use of his photo with a cigarette advertisement was another matter.

A Pittsburgh sportswriter was offered $10 to obtain the Dutchman's permission to publish his picture with the product. Wagner's written answer was: "I don't want my picture with cigarettes, but I don't want you to lose the $10 either, so I'm sending you a check for the sum." The letter was never destroyed, nor the check cashed.

A line-drive hitter with power to all fields, Honus solved the great pitchers as well as the lesser breed. Against Nap

**Wagner and Ty Cobb (right) discuss hitting techniques at the 1909 World Series.**

Rucker, he batted over .350; against Christy Mathewson, Wagner hit over .300.

The Flying Dutchman ended his active career in 1917, the same season he managed the Pirates for four days. Named to succeed Jimmy Callahan on July 1, he turned the job over to Hugo Bezdek on July 4.

Wagner coached baseball and basketball at Carnegie Tech for a while, served as sergeant-at-arms for the Pennsylvania Legislature and, with Pie Traynor, owned a sporting goods store.

Honus was a coach for the Pirates from 1933 through 1951, during which time he amused younger folks with outrageously funny yarns of his superhuman accomplishments as a player.

Wagner was 81 when he died in 1955.

# Bobby Wallace

Connie Mack, who accepted congratulations graciously, also could chuckle when reminded of his failures.

When Bobby Wallace, a 5-foot-8 shortstop of the St. Louis Browns, crossed paths with Mack, the Philadelphia manager would grin and mutter, "Too small, huh?"

Mack's smile indicated that he remembered that day in 1893 when he was manager of the Pittsburgh club and an 18-year-old Scot obtained a tryout. At the conclusion, Mack issued his "too small" edict and promptly forgot about Wallace, who had earned recognition in western Pennsylvania semipro ranks as a pitcher.

Even so perceptive an individual as Mack was unable to detect shortstop possibilities in Wallace, who won 24 games for Cleveland before switching to third base and ultimately to shortstop, where he starred for many years.

The first American League shortstop to be elected to the Hall of Fame, Wallace was earning $45 a month, plus board and lodging, with the Franklin (Pa.) semipro club when the financial panic struck in 1893. The Franklin team folded and Bobby was considering returning to his brother-in-law's feed store—where he had once wrestled 100-pound sacks of corn and oats—when he received a wire from Pat Tebeau.

The manager of the Cleveland team was desperate for a righthanded pitcher. Would Bobby be interested?

The answer was yes, and Wallace made his major league debut on September 15, 1894. In a game shortened to six innings by rain, Bobby yielded 14 hits in suffering a 7-2 loss to Boston. He defeated Philadelphia in his second outing.

Bobby compiled a 12-13 record in 1895 and a 10-7 log in '96, when the Spiders qualified to meet the Baltimore Orioles in the Temple Cup Series, forerunner to the modern World Series. Bobby lost his only start, 7-2, and made two pinch-hitting appearances in the four-game Baltimore sweep, but at the completion he was richer by $117.

Although he had been a winning pitcher, Bobby was informed abruptly at Louisville in 1897 that "You're on third today." In 1899, after the Spiders had been moved to St. Louis, Wallace was shifted to shortstop, a position

**Connie Mack's evaluation of Bobby Wallace was way off the mark.**

he dominated for the next decade.

"We were in Philly when Tebeau shifted me," he recalled. "Right off, I knew I had found my dish."

Wallace was credited with pioneering the scoop-and-toss style of playing shortstop. Instead of fielding a ground ball, coming erect and throwing, as predecessors had done, Bobby fielded and threw in one continuous motion.

"I noticed more and more runners were beating out infield hoppers by a fraction of a second," he related. "It was apparent that I had to learn to throw from the ankle and off-balance as well."

When the American League opened for business in 1901, Wallace was a prime target for the agents raiding the established league.

On assurance that he was receiving top dollar, Wallace agreed to sign with the new league and received a dollar to seal the agreement. Later, on learning that other players were receiving four and five times the amount paid him, he abrogated the contract, returned the one dollar and stayed in the N.L. By 1902, though, Wallace had jumped to St. Louis' new American League team. He played more than 100 games in each of the next 10 seasons.

In 1911, Bobby was offered the managerial post and accepted reluctantly. However, after an eighth-place finish, and with the club in last place in June of 1912, he was relieved of his job.

A broken hand in 1912 and burns suffered in an accident in 1914 sharply limited Wallace's activity. Bobby regained his old position in 1915, but quit on June 1 to try his hand as an A.L. umpire. He was teamed with Billy Evans, premier umpire, but resigned on August 1, 1916. He rejoined the Browns and played 14 games the remainder of the season.

Wallace started the 1917 season as manager of Wichita (Western). By June, however, he had experienced enough and obtained his release to join the Cardinals. Bobby played eight games for St. Louis that year and 32 in 1918 before retiring for good.

Back in California, Wallace devoted his hours to golf, billiards and model sailing ships. He died in 1960, one day before his 86th birthday.

# Ed Walsh

In the closing days of the American League pennant race in 1908, one pitcher stood a head taller than the others. In fact, there may never have been another performance to match that of the Chicago righthander who hurled 41⅓ innings in an eight-day span in a futile effort to bring a pennant to the White Sox.

Ed Walsh started his incredible iron-man pitching on Tuesday, September 29, when he defeated Boston in both halves of a doubleheader. He allowed three hits in the first game and four in the second.

Big Ed returned to the mound on Friday, facing Cleveland which, like Chicago, was in the midst of a hectic flag race. Walsh drew Addie Joss as his mound opponent. Although Walsh struck out 15 batters and allowed only four singles, one hit was converted into a run on a stolen base, error and passed ball. Nothing more was needed by Joss, who pitched a perfect game.

Walsh, a spitball artist, returned to the mound on Saturday, October 3, relieving Frank Smith with one out and the bases full of Indians in the seventh inning. The first batter to face Walsh was Bill Hinchman, who grounded into a force-out at the plate.

Larry Lajoie, Cleveland's manager and hard-hitting second baseman, was up next. Years later, Walsh remembered what happened:

"Lajoie fouled off the first two spitters I threw him, one a screamer to left field, the other back into the stands. Billy Sullivan signaled for another spitter, but I just stared at him. Then Sully walked out to the mound. 'What's the matter?' Bill asked me. 'I'll give him a fast one,' I said, but Billy was dubious. Finally, he agreed. I threw a fastball and Larry watched it come over without even an offer. 'Strike three,' roared umpire Silk O'Louglin. Lajoie sort of grinned, tossed his bat toward the bench without even a word. That was the high spot of my baseball career, fanning Larry in the clutch without him swinging."

After finishing the Saturday game, Walsh rested for one day. He defeated the Tigers on a four-hitter on Monday, October 5, and followed with 3⅔ innings of relief the next day in a 7-0 loss to the Tigers, who thereby clinched the pennant.

**Ed Walsh gave his spitball and arm a severe test during the 1908 season.**

The victory in the Monday contest was the 40th of the year for Walsh. The final-game stint raised his season total of innings pitched to 464, a modern major league record.

Big Ed's salary for his remarkable season was $3,500. Later, when the White Sox were relaxing at the Wisconsin lodge of Charles Comiskey, the owner slipped Walsh a check for $3,500 in appreciation for his magnificent pitching. But when Ed opened the envelope containing his 1909 contract a few months later, he was distressed to find it called for the same figure as in '08.

Walsh boarded a train for Chicago and argued his case before Comiskey. The Old Roman was adamant and on opening day Ed, still unsigned, was about to catch a train for his Connecticut home when a messenger arrived with the news that Comiskey would pay him a $1,500 bonus for his signature. Walsh agreed, but at the end of the season he was hard-pressed to extract the promised bonus from his penny-pinching boss.

The youngest of 13 children born to Irish immigrants, Walsh worked in the coal fields of Pennsylvania before starting his professional career. By 1904, he was a rookie with the White Sox and drew Elmer Stricklett as his spring training roommate in Marlin, Tex. Stricklett, an early exponent of the spitball, taught the moist delivery to the youngster, but Walsh did not use it until 1906. That season, Big Ed won 17 games, 10 of them shutouts, as the Hitless Wonders won the flag and then upset the powerful Cubs in the World Series.

Walsh won two decisions in the six-game '06 Series. He captured Game 3, 3-0, on a two-hitter.

After his grueling 1908 season, Walsh slipped to 15 victories in 1909, engendering rumors that overwork had taken its toll. In 1911 and 1912, however, he posted 27-victory seasons.

Walsh concluded his active career with the Boston Braves in 1917, after which he briefly tried his hand at umpiring in the American League.

The Hall of Famer made his last appearance at Comiskey Park on Ed Walsh Day, June 22 1958. He died in 1959, at age 78.

# Lloyd Waner

Pirate third baseman Pie Traynor took one look at the Pittsburgh rookie in the spring of 1927 and immediately pronounced him "too small, too thin and too scrawny."

For years Lloyd Waner made a practice of confounding folks with his lack of size. When he joined the Pirates, Lloyd was a 132-pounder. But he scooted like a jackrabbit on the plains of his native Oklahoma.

"Oh, he was fast," Traynor remembered 40 years later. "He was the fastest man in the league and got a tremendous jump on balls hit to center field."

On his first at-bat in the major leagues, Waner grounded to the shortstop, who made a seemingly routine play only to discover that Waner was four steps past first base when the throw arrived.

Lloyd was three years younger than his Hall of Fame brother Paul, with whom he played in the Pittsburgh outfield for 14 years. But according to Lloyd, neither of the brothers was the best hitter in the family.

"Our sister Alma was the best," Lloyd acknowledged on the day he was enshrined at Cooperstown. "We used to soak corncobs in water so they wouldn't fly so far when we hit 'em. Alma was the first to hit one far enough to break a window in the barn."

Like Paul, Lloyd broke into professional baseball with San Francisco (Pacific Coast), but he was released after six games in 1926. The release puzzled Paul, then an established star with the Pirates, who interceded with Pittsburgh Owner Barney Dreyfuss. "He's a better player than I am," insisted Paul in a slight exaggeration.

Dreyfuss invited Lloyd to Pittsburgh and, despite the 20-year-old's unimpressive size, signed him to a Columbia (Sally) contract. A .345 batting average earned Lloyd a promotion to the Pirates, for whom he became an instant starter. He collected more than 200 hits in his rookie season and shared the National League lead in runs. He batted .355.

Although the Pirates lost the '27 World Series to the Yankees in four games, Lloyd batted .400 and Paul .333. Together they collected 11 hits.

After the Series, which was dominated by Babe Ruth and Lou Gehrig, the Waners embarked on a cross-country vaudeville tour, Paul playing the saxophone and Lloyd the violin. The act played 16 weeks in major theaters in New

**Though "too small, too thin and too scrawny," Lloyd Waner produced Hall of Fame numbers.**

York, Pittsburgh, St. Louis, Los Angeles and San Francisco. The brothers were paid $2,100 weekly, far in excess of their pay with the Pirates.

Part of their act that never failed to bring down the house consisted of Paul playing the sax and Lloyd arriving on the stage breathlessly. "Where ya been?" Paul would ask. "I've just finished chasing the last ball hit by Babe Ruth," cracked Lloyd.

Lloyd earned a $1,000 raise after his spectacular rookie season, but never made more than $13,500—even in his prime.

Early in his career Lloyd acquired the nickname of "Little Poison," while Paul was tagged "Big Poison."

The names traced to an afternoon in Brooklyn, Lloyd explained. A press-box habitue with a heavy accent referred to the pair as big and little person, but to others it sounded like poison, which the brothers were to the opposition.

Lloyd was extremely difficult to strike out, fanning only 173 times in the majors.

Although Lloyd did not share in Paul's reputation as an all-night creature, he could perform with distinction in the wee hours. Anyone encountering the brothers in a hotel lobby at 8 a.m., it was said, could not be sure if they were coming in or going out.

An appendectomy forced Lloyd to miss almost half of the 1930 season, but he bounced back to lead the N.L. in at-bats and hits the following year.

Little Poison was traded to Boston early in the 1941 season. Before the season ended he was acquired by the Reds. He was with the Phillies in 1942, then decided to retire when shipped to Brooklyn during spring training of 1943.

When the player pinch grew tighter during World War II, however, Waner had a change of heart and joined the Dodgers. He was released after 15 games and received an offer from his old club, the Pirates, the next day. A hero's welcome was accorded Little Poison when he was introduced at Forbes Field. Used primarily as a pinch-hitter, Waner batted .321 in 1944 and .263 in '45 before calling it a career.

Lloyd, who scouted for the Bucs and Orioles and then served as field clerk for the municipal government in Oklahoma City, died in 1982 at age 76.

# Paul Waner

**By 1928, Paul Waner was indeed "Big Poison" to opposing National League pitchers.**

**The Waner brothers, Paul (right) and Lloyd, patrolled the Pirates outfield together for 14 seasons.**

It was May 20, 1932, and the Pirates were in Chicago to play the Cubs at Wrigley Field. As the 29-year-old Pittsburgh outfielder wobbled to home plate, he said to catcher Gabby Hartnett, "I didn't get too much sleep last night and won't be able to follow the flight of the ball too well. Please see that the pitchers don't throw too close to my head."

Assured that Hartnett would signal for no pitches high and tight, Paul Waner lashed four doubles to tie a major league record.

Big Poison was not a temperance group's shining example on the evils of drink. He thrived on all-night conviviality and made no attempts to hide his habits. Once, as a favor

to his manager, he went on the wagon and promptly fell into a horrendous slump. A return to his old lifestyle seemingly restored his batting eye.

Paul's middle name was Glee, and no parents ever selected a more appropriate name for an offspring because fun was paramount to Waner. After an all-night tour of New York watering holes, he arrived at the Polo Grounds for a doubleheader with eyes glazed and head throbbing. In the first game, he clouted a double, homer and single; in the second contest, Paul hit two doubles, a homer and a single.

Fred Lindstrom, a teammate in the 1930s, once arrived at the Waner home for a morning golf date and was advised by Mrs. Waner: "Paul's gone to the store for a loaf of bread."

Lindstrom waited and waited. With patience all but exhausted, Lindstrom inquired, "When did he leave for the store?"

"Last night," replied Mrs. Waner, accustomed to her husband's antics.

Paul, a three-time National League batting champion, stood with his feet close together in the batter's box, about five inches from the back line. When attacking a pitch, he took a full stride, raising his right foot about four inches. Line drives rattled off his bat to all sectors of the field.

Power was not the forte of the 153-pounder. He hit only 113 home runs in his illustrious career, but he racked up large totals of doubles and triples because of his daz-

**Paul Waner's speed and strong left arm complemented his blazing bat and baserunning abilities.**

zling speed. Waner led the N.L. in triples in his first two seasons and, as a sophomore, topped the N.L. in hits, 237, and batting average, .380.

Paul, who was joined in the Pittsburgh outfield by younger brother Lloyd in 1927, possessed unusual eyesight. Uncle Wilbert Robinson, then managing Brooklyn, once remarked that the brothers ''have cats' eyes . . . probably can see in the dark.''

Yet a specialist recommended that Paul wear glasses because he was unable to read the scoreboard from home plate. But Waner wore spectacles for only a few days. ''With glasses,'' he said, ''the pitch appears the size of a baseball. Without them, it's as big as a grapefruit.''

Casey Stengel once suggested that Waner ''hits from memory,'' which seemed reasonable in that Big Poison piled up more than 3,000 hits. He was the seventh major leaguer to top that mark.

Waner was a member of the Boston Braves when he registered his 3,000th hit on June 19, 1942. Earlier in the series at Braves Field, Waner had signaled to the press box that he did not want credit for the milestone hit when he beat out an infield roller that could have been ruled a hit or an error.

The Braves were playing the Pirates when Paul reached No. 3,000. Old teammate Rip Sewell walked Waner on his first two at-bats, but in the fifth inning Big Poison rapped a clean, run-scoring single to center field.

Minutes later, a note was delivered to the Boston press corps. ''Let's have a party tonight,'' read the message,

**Paul Waner played with the Dodgers in 1943, the season after he collected his 3,000th hit.**

signed by the player who never tired of all-night parties.

Waner rapped 3,151 hits as a National Leaguer and one in the A.L., a single with the Yankees in 1944,

Waner tried his hand at managing, but one year convinced him he was not cut out for the job. He was hired as a batting instructor by the Milwaukee Braves and was credited with making superior hitters out of a number of key players on the World Series championship club of 1957. Later, he served in a similar capacity with the Cardinals and Phillies.

Paul was 62 when he died in 1975 of pulmonary emphysema, complicated by pneumonia, at his home in Sarasota, Fla.

# John Montgomery Ward

When the Penn State student forsook his education to try his hand in professional baseball, his hometown newspaper commented negatively. To the Bellefonte (Pa.) Democratic Watchman, John Montgomery Ward had violated the sacred memory of his forebears.

On July 13, 1877, the ever-vigilant Watchman observed: "Monte Ward, youngest son of the late, lamented James and Ruth Ward of this place, a young man of talent and whom we expected to see as scholar and statesman, perhaps, has become a hired baseball pitcher. There is no reason why a baseball pitcher should not become eventually a great man, but the chances for Monte's sake, we are sorry to say, are against it, and trust he will pause and reconsider.

**John Montgomery Ward, pictured in 1885, didn't restrict himself to pitching.**

Mr. Ward pitched a trial game for the Philadelphia Athletics on Saturday, last week, and won high praise, we believe. Nevertheless, Monte, quit it and go to your books again."

If Monte read the counsel, he did not heed it. His back was turned forever on his birthplace as he became one of the game's finest pitchers, a reliable hitter, a manager, union organizer, club owner and, after retirement, a highly respected attorney.

The Watchman later softened its attitude. "There is nothing WRONG in pitching ball any more than there is in making shoes or picking type," the paper said, "and when the motive is a good one as this is (earning money to complete his education), we think the individual is to be commended."

Ward, by this time, had moved westward to Wisconsin where he had received a $75 bonus and a $20-a-week contract.

In 1878, the 18-year-old righthander joined Providence of the National League. He made his debut on July 20, blanking Indianapolis, 4-0, on a two-hitter.

Monte played five seasons with the Grays, dividing his time between the mound, the infield and outfield. One of his most memorable performances took place on August 17, 1882, when he hurled an 18-inning, 1-0 victory over Detroit. The only run was scored on a homer by Hoss Radbourn, playing right field that day.

After Monte's trade to the Giants, the Watchman reported on August 3, 1883: "Ward . . . gets $3,000 for this season's work. They paid him $1,000 down when the

bargain was made, and $1,000 when he commenced work with them—the remainder to be paid when the season is about half over."

By 1884, Ward's arm was dead and he became a full-time infielder. When the manager was dismissed late in the season, Ward handled the Giants for the last two weeks.

Ward was not only adroit defensively, but was a jackrabbit on the bases. He led the N.L. three times in stolen bases, once swiping 111.

As a member of the Giants, Monte attended night law classes at Columbia University. At graduation exercises in 1885, he was awarded a $50 second prize in the department of political science.

In 1887, Ward authored a magazine article denouncing baseball's reserve clause. Shortly thereafter, he laid the groundwork for the Brotherhood of Professional Base Ball Players. In 1890, approximately 100 members formed the Players League, which operated one season in competition with the National League.

Ward managed Brooklyn for two years following the peace agreement. During this period, when betting was an accepted part of the game, he won 20 shares of Giant stock on a wager. It created the unusual situation of a Brooklyn player being a shareholder in a rival club.

After two years with Brooklyn (the club was in the N.L. in 1891), Ward wanted to return to the Giants. A deal was agreed upon, but the Giants lacked the necessary cash. As a result, Brooklyn agreed to take a portion of the Giants' gate in exchange for the player's contract.

In 1894, John Montgomery led the Giants to a sweep of the Baltimore Orioles in the Temple Cup Series. Cantankerous Owner Andrew Freedman fired the manager a short time later and although he was only 34, Ward retired from baseball to devote his energies to his law practice.

Much of his practice involved ballplayers' suits. Ward won a cash settlement for pitcher Fred Pfeffer, who had been suspended illegally by Freedman.

John Montgomery was a member of the triumvirate that purchased the Boston Braves in 1911. His partners bought out Ward in July of 1912.

Ward, who earlier had denounced the reserve clause, defended it frequently in later years and remained in close contact to the game as a member of the rules committee. He contracted pneumonia and died in 1925 at age 65.

# George Weiss

To some, he was cold and dispassionate, a heartless creature who never left his office without a briefcase and who lived by the maxim: "There are no hours in baseball."

In the opinion of others, he was a shy individual, a workaholic who could, in the proper environment, engage in delightful conversation while playing host in his 200-year-old Greenwich, Conn., home that overflowed with baseball nostalgia.

The spotlight was for others because George Weiss preferred it that way. He was content to stand in the shadows while others less deserving took the bows and uttered bits of wisdom about world championship teams designed by a master architect in the front office.

Weiss, the son of a New Haven storekeeper, engaged in baseball promotion while still a student at Yale. As head of a semipro team known as the Colonials, Weiss scheduled Sunday games with major league clubs who were prohibited from playing Sabbath contests in their own cities. The Colonials played in an island park known as Rocky Point.

When Sunday ball was legalized in New Haven in 1920, Weiss, with a $5,000 loan, bought an Eastern League franchise and was on the road that led to four Major League Executive of the Year Awards (including three in succession).

In 1922, Weiss and his manager, Bill Donovan, produced a championship New Haven team that defeated the Baltimore Orioles, International League champions, twice in a three-game series. When the Orioles went on to defeat St. Paul in the Junior World Series, Weiss claimed the minor league championship for his Class A club and invited a Pullman car full of New York writers to New Haven for a banquet to celebrate the fictional title.

More than a year later, Weiss and Donovan were in a sleeper bound for the winter meetings in Chicago. Weiss, 28, had the lower berth, but generously offered it to the older Donovan. A train wreck during the night killed Donovan.

In the winter of 1928-29, Weiss visited Baltimore to arrange spring exhibition dates with the Orioles. Legendary Jack Dunn had died some months earlier, leaving the club affairs in disarray. During the discussion on spring dates,

**One of George Weiss' first moves as Yankee G.M. was to hire Casey Stengel as manager.**

the attorney for the estate suddenly asked Weiss, "How'd you like to be general manager?"

George accepted, and for three years he conducted a profitable operation. His shrewd deals attracted attention among major leaguers, particularly Col. Jake Ruppert. The owner of the Yankees had differences with Weiss years earlier when the Yanks arrived in New Haven for an exhibition game without Babe Ruth, whose appearance had been advertised widely by the club president.

His promotion damaged, Weiss refused to pay the Yankees. Ruppert squawked, but developed a firm admiration for George. When the Colonel tired of paying exorbitant prices for minor league players on the open market and decided to build his own farm system, he turned to Weiss. Ruppert signed him secretly on December 31, 1931, and phoned Ed Barrow, telling his general manager, "I hope you fellows get along."

Although the two were never chummy, Weiss and Barrow were compatible professionally most of the time. One major clash occurred when Weiss proposed the purchase of Joe DiMaggio from San Francisco of the Pacific Coast League. Barrow objected to the deal, but Weiss took a carload of top Yankee scouts to French Lick, Ind., where Ruppert and Barrow were vacationing, and convinced the two that DiMaggio was a bargain at $25,000.

During Weiss' years as farm director, the Yanks won nine pennants and eight world championships. When Dan Topping, Del Webb and Larry MacPhail bought the club in 1945, Weiss was given high-sounding titles that pointed him toward the general managership that Barrow had relinquished earlier. In the hysteria that followed the 1947 World Series triumph, MacPhail fired Weiss, then offered his resignation to his partners, who promptly rehired Weiss as general manager. In that role, Weiss produced 10 pennants and seven world championships.

One of George's first moves after gaining complete control was to hire Casey Stengel.

Weiss and Stengel were pushed aside in the Yankees' youth movement following the 1960 season. After one year of unemployment, they surfaced with the Mets.

Weiss, associated with the Mets until December of 1971, died the next year at age 77.

# Mickey Welch

The little fellow standing watch at the bleacher entrance to the Polo Grounds in the second decade of the 20th century was a popular figure with fans who wanted to reminisce about the emerging years of baseball.

Smiling frequently, the old-timer recalled how he had won more than 300 major league games, pitching from distances of 45 and 50 feet.

Mickey Welch, an Independence Day baby in 1859, learned the rudiments of baseball on the streets and sandlots of his native Brooklyn before traveling up the Hudson River to play for the Poughkeepsie Volunteers in 1877. The 5-foot-7 righthander was 18 at the time.

After two seasons with Auburn and Holyoke, both of the National Association, Welch entered the National League as a member of the Troy (N.Y.) Haymakers in 1880. He was an instant sensation, winning 34 games in 574 innings of work. Mickey did not possess blinding speed, but he made the most of a good curve, a change of pace and an early version of the screwball popularized by Christy Mathewson and Carl Hubbell in the next century.

Welch, nicknamed Smiling Mickey by cartoonist E.V. Munkitrick, reduced his innings of work in 1882, but he completed all of his 40 starts for a two-year figure of 104 consecutive complete games. The string was snapped at 105 in 1883.

John B. Day, who had owned the New York club of the American Association, purchased the Troy franchise in '83 and transferred it to New York where, as the Maroons, the club played in the original Polo Grounds next to the northern edge of Central Park.

In '83, Mickey pitched more than 400 innings. Before signing for '84, he insisted that his contract contain a clause stipulating that he could pitch more frequently than every other day. For the remainder of his career, the clause was a standard part of his contract.

Welch completed 62 of 65 starts in '84 and struck out 349 batters. He also walked 141, tops in the league.

By 1885 the New York club was known as the Giants. The nickname stemmed from a cry by Jim Mutrie. After an especially sweet victory, the manager shouted, "My big fellows, my giants." The name caught on and Welch, de-

In his later years, Mickey Welch enjoyed reminiscing about his 307 career wins.

spite his lack of brawn, was a Goliath among them.

Welch once fanned the first nine Cleveland batters to face him, and between July 18 and September 4, 1885, Mickey won 17 straight games, including four shutouts and four one-run games. The string was snapped on September 5 when Welch, pitching out of turn because Tim Keefe was ill, lost to Charley Ferguson of Philadelphia, 3-1.

Although earned-run averages were not a part of statistics at the time, an examination of boxscores indicated that Mickey's ERA would have been around 1.70.

Asked after his 44-victory season of '85 to what he attributed his success, Welch cracked, "To drinking beer."

With Welch and Keefe accounting for 61 of the team's 84 victories, the Giants won their first pennant in 1888. The club boasted only one .300 hitter, Buck Ewing, and had a combined batting average of .242.

In a postseason series against the St. Louis Browns, champions of the American Association, the Giants won six of 10 games. Welch split two decisions, losing his first to Elton Chamberlain, 3-0, on October 17, and beating the same pitcher, 12-5, on a three-hitter, on October 22.

By winning 17 of their last 20 games, the Giants edged Boston for the 1889 pennant. In the postseason series against Brooklyn, New York prevailed—six games to three.

Smiling Mickey remained loyal to the Giants during the Brotherhood War of 1890, but he won only five of 14 decisions in 1891.

Because Ewing, his regular catcher of earlier years, was sidelined much of the '91 season, Welch was unable to develop a winning stride, creating friction with Manager Pat Powers (who took over the club in 1892). After one game in '92, Mickey was sent to the Giants' farm club at Troy, where he terminated his active career.

After retirement, Welch moved to Holyoke, Mass., where he served for a long time as steward of the Elks club. He returned to New York in 1912 when John McGraw offered him a job at the Polo Grounds.

Mickey was visiting a grandson in Nashua, N.H., in 1941 when he was taken sick. He died at age 82.

# Zack Wheat

Charles Ebbets was skeptical when Larry Sutton revealed that he had purchased a 21-year-old outfielder from Mobile of the Southern Association for $1,200.

"What did he hit?" asked the president of the Brooklyn Dodgers.

"He hit .246," answered the club's one-man scouting staff, "but he'll hit better."

"That's the trouble around here," grumbled Ebbets. "We have too many .246-hitting outfielders."

But Ebbets was smiling before the 1909 season ended. In 26 games, Zack Wheat batted .304 in launching a Brooklyn career that extended through 18 illustrious seasons. Zack finished his big-league career with the Philadelphia A's in 1927.

Wheat batted .312 during the Dodgers' championship season of 1916. Late in the year, he ran off a 29-game batting streak that was snapped by Fred Toney of Cincinnati.

In the World Series against Boston, however, the lefthanded batter collected only four hits and drove in only one run as Brooklyn lost in five games.

**Zack Wheat's popularity in New York transcended contemporary Babe Ruth.**

Wheat held out stubbornly the following spring. Even a visit by Ebbets to Zack's Missouri home failed to sway the outfielder. Later, when the team was in training, Zack showed up flashing a telegram signed by "C.H. Ebbets" and ordering him to report immediately.

Ebbets denied authorship. The two exchanged heated words before retiring to a room where they ironed out their differences and emerged smiling in due time.

Eventually, the telegram mystery was explained with the revelation that Brooklyn sports editor Abe Yager had sent the wire to provide his scoop of the day.

Wheat won his only batting championship in the war-shortened season of 1918, but it required an executive ruling to clinch the title.

Zack batted .335 in 105 games, Billy Southworth of Pittsburgh hit .341 in 64 games and Edd Roush of Cincinnati posted a .333 mark in 113 games.

National League President John Heydler eliminated Southworth because he had played too few games. He then awarded the crown to Wheat because he had hit for a higher average in only eight fewer games.

The quiet-spoken Wheat was willing to fight for his rights on the field, but he knew the limits of his dissent. He was never ejected from a game.

"I never could see any sense in cursing an umpire," he said of his good conduct. "Most of the time it means you're out of the game. And I came to play nine innings or longer."

Wheat was not only a hero in Brooklyn, but in all New York as well. At a time when Babe Ruth was socking homers for the Yankees and Frank Frisch was sparking the Giants to four straight pennants, Wheat was voted the most popular player in all of Gotham.

Wheat could handle curveballs as well as fastballs and for years John McGraw enforced a rule prohibiting Giants pitchers from feeding Zack curves at the Polo Grounds. McGraw feared that Wheat would pull the breaking pitch into the short right-field stands.

Once, however, Jess Barnes got two strikes on Zack, who sensed that the next pitch would be a curve.

"I hit the ball way up in the upper deck," Zack recalled. "I knew it was a homer when the ball was hit. As I was running to first base, I could hear McGraw shouting, 'Barnes, you blankety-blank pinhead, that'll cost you $500!'"

Zack hit his last National League home run at Ebbets Field in 1926. Rounding first base, he pulled a leg muscle so severely that he was forced to sit on second base for a full five minutes. For a time it was feared he would be unable to complete the trip around the bases, and Rabbit Maranville was suggested as a pinch-runner. Ultimately, however, Zack arose and completed the tour of the bases at a snail's pace.

After retirement, Zack was co-owner of a bowling alley in Kansas City and served on that city's police force for awhile.

Wheat later operated a hunting and fishing lodge at Sunrise Beach, Mo. Death came in Sedalia, Mo., at age 83.

# Ted Williams

In 1935, Ted Williams (left) was a member of the Herbert Hoover High School team in San Diego. Six years later, Williams was the toast of the American League after his ninth-inning homer ended the 1941 All-Star Game.

His mother had hoped that her tall, gangling son would follow in her footsteps and join the Salvation Army, but the kid with the picture-perfect batting stroke respectfully declined. His heart was set on baseball, and no one could deny his ambition.

His eyesight was phenomenal. Opthalmologists reported that they encountered his type of vision only once in 100,000 cases.

While it wasn't true that Ted Williams could read the label of a 78-rpm record while it was spinning, that was about all that exceeded his capabilities. When he returned to the Red Sox from the Korean War and stepped into the batters' box for the first time, Ted told General Manager Joe Cronin that the plate was out of line.

It was impossible, Cronin replied, but to humor the slugger he ordered a check of the alignment. It was off by a fraction of an inch.

A graduate of Herbert Hoover High School in San Diego, Williams was in the major leagues three years after turning professional with his hometown Padres of the Pacific Coast League. He reeked with confidence in his ability as a

hitter. When Ted joined the Red Sox and was told, "Wait till you see Jimmie Foxx hit," his instant response was: "Wait til Foxx sees me hit."

It didn't take long for The Kid, or the Splendid Splinter, to start his demonstration. In his first major league game, he struck out twice against Red Ruffing in Yankee Stadium before slamming a double off the right-field fence. That started the hit parade that did not end for 21 years with time out for World War II and the Korean conflict.

Williams gave Tiger fans an early look at his prodigious drives. He hit two homers on May 4, 1939, and on the second smash he became the first player to drive a ball over Detroit's double-decked right-field stands.

In his early major league seasons, Ted ran the emotional gamut. Once, when his line drives were zipping right into waiting gloves, he fumed, "Nuts to baseball, I'd rather be a fireman."

The quote found its way into public print, which gave pixyish Chicago Manager Jimmie Dykes the chance to equip his players with fire helmets and screaming sirens when Ted next visited Comiskey Park.

Williams' big 1941 season was capped by a .406 batting average, the last .400-plus mark in major league history. Williams' illustrious career was nearing its final stage in

1960 when the Red Sox slugger hit homer No. 500 (right) en route to career-ending totals of 2,654 hits and 521 home runs.

In the opinion of many, Williams' most dramatic homer occurred in the 1941 All-Star Game when, with two out in the ninth inning, he clouted a three-run homer to give the American League a 7-5 victory.

Entering the final day of the '41 season, Ted was batting .39955, or .400. No major leaguer had attained that magic level since Bill Terry in 1930. Williams was given the option of sitting out the closing doubleheader in Philadelphia to protect his average, but he refused. He rapped six hits in eight at-bats and finished with a .406 average.

When the Most Valuable Player ballots were tabulated at season's end, Ted was edged by Joe DiMaggio, whose .357 average was accompanied by his 56-game hitting streak and a league-leading 125 RBIs. Many regarded the vote as a reflection on Ted's poor relationship with some members of the press.

Williams captured the MVP in 1946, his first season back from a career as a Navy pilot. It also was the season in which Cleveland Manager Lou Boudreau devised the Williams Shift. The alignment invited Ted to try for an opposite-field single, but, proud hitter that he was, the

Splinter continued to pull every chance he got.

Williams' inside-the-park homer at Cleveland clinched a tie for the 1946 pennant for the Red Sox, who wrapped up the flag two hours later when the second-place Tigers lost to the Yankees. In the World Series, however, he was held to five singles and one RBI by the Cardinals.

Ted was sidelined for much of the 1950 season after fracturing his elbow in an All-Star Game mishap. Two years later, although he was nearly 34, he was called back to active military duty and missed most of two seasons.

Ted's playing career came to a close on a September afternoon in 1960 when, dramatically as always, Williams homered off Jack Fisher of Baltimore. It was No. 521 and was rapped on his final at-bat.

In 1969, Williams came out of retirement to manage the Washington Senators. He transferred to Texas with the franchise, but retired after a four-year term that produced one Manager of the Year citation.

After turning in his managerial portfolio, Williams went back to his stomping grounds, the Florida Keys, to match wits with the game fish.

# Hack Wilson

**Hack Wilson (pictured in 1931) was a physical oddity with massive shoulders and chest anchored by size-6 feet.**

**Wilson is pictured in 1932 with Max Carey, who retired in 1929 after a Hall of Fame career.**

Tales of the slugging outfielder range from extreme admiration to compassion to extreme sadness.

On the field or in all-night roistering, he dispatched high balls with a prowess unknown to lesser mortals. He was a physical oddity, with a size-18 collar, massive shoulders and chest, a protruding abdomen, oak-like legs and size-6 shoes. Nothing about the man conformed to pattern.

When the 5-foot-6, 195-pound player joined the New York Giants in 1923, the clubhouse man complained to John McGraw that he had no uniform to fit the original Mr. Five-by-Five.

Reaching into his locker, the manager extracted a uniform which he tossed to the youngster, saying, "Don't disgrace this uniform. It was once worn by a great player."

"Who?" asked the prospect.

"Me."

"Don't worry, a great player will wear it again," Hack Wilson assured Little Napoleon.

In some ways, Wilson was right. In 1930, playing for the Cubs, Hack set a National League record for home runs with 56 and a major league mark for runs batted in with 190. However, in the seventh inning of Game 4 of the previous year's World Series, he lost a fly ball in the sun and the misplay helped Philadelphia score 10 runs and erase an 8-0 Chicago lead.

The Giants lost Wilson through "a clerical error," as McGraw explained. Hack was optioned to Toledo in 1925. When the Giants failed to exercise the option in time, the Mud Hens sold him to the Cubs, for whom he enjoyed his most productive seasons under Manager Joe McCarthy.

A master handler of players, McCarthy knew when to pat Wilson on the back and when to censure him. And he constantly interceded for Wilson when his after-hours adventures offended Owner William Wrigley, an ardent prohibitionist.

McCarthy once tried to demonstrate the evils of liquor to his wayward star.

"If I drop a worm in a glass of water it just swims around," said Joe, fitting actions to his words. "But if I drop it in a glass of whiskey, the worm dies. What does

By 1933, Wilson was playing in Brooklyn and nearing the
end of his major league career.

that prove?"

"It proves," said Wilson brightly, "that if you drink
whiskey you'll never get worms."

The slugger, a onetime printer's devil who swung a
sledge hammer in a locomotive factory and also worked in
a shipyard after quitting school in the sixth grade, was
known as Lew Wilson until he joined the Giants. A New
York teammate observed, "You remind me of Hack Miller."

Miller, the son of a circus strongman, had been a big-
league outfielder some years earlier. The nickname stuck.

Wilson packed as much punch in his fists as in his bat.
One time he decked a teammate with one punch during a
card-game argument in the Giant clubhouse. He scored a
double knockout in Cincinnati. He dropped pitcher Ray
Klop during a game, and that evening—when the Reds and
Cubs were about to board a train out of Cincinnati—he
leveled Pete Donohue, another hurler.

When Hack sought to take his pugilistic talents into the
ring, Commissioner K.M. Landis vetoed the move.

Wilson's star went into decline after McCarthy left the
Cubs late in the '30 season. Hack became a Dodger in
1932 and a big press party was scheduled in Brooklyn at
the same time the major league owners were in town for

Wilson was awesome in 1930, when he hit 56 homers and
drove in a major league-record 190 runs.

the winter meetings. As Wilson was about to sign his
contract, he spied McCarthy. "I wish I were going to play
for you," Hack told Joe.

"I wish you were, too," said the new Yankee skipper.

After retiring from baseball, Hack held various jobs. He
was a master of ceremonies in a Chicago night club and
manager of the Druid Hills Park swimming pool in Baltimore, where he spent his last years.

In 1948, he appeared on a network radio show in which
he held himself up as an example of the negative effects of
demon rum. Shortly thereafter, friends found Hack suffering from a fall. He was 48 when he died of internal
hemorrhaging.

The onetime star, who had earned more than $200,000
during his career, died penniless. The hat was passed at a
Martinsburg, W. Va., saloon to help defray expenses for
internment in that city.

# George Wright

When Harry Wright launched a search for a shortstop on the first professional baseball team, he looked no farther than his immediate family. Brother George was a perfect choice.

George Wright was not a pure amateur when he was tapped by the Cincinnati Red Stockings of 1869. A native of the Harlem section of New York City, George attained local prominence in baseball circles before accepting an offer from the Washington Nationals in 1867. Allegedly, the Nationals were amateurs, but reason suggests that some inducement was necessary for George to travel so far afield.

A roster of the Washington players listing their occupations and business addresses showed George's occupation as "clerk." However, his address on Pennsylvania Avenue was a public park.

Wright returned to New York in 1868 where, as a member of the Morrisania club, he was recognized as the foremost player in the East.

The son of a onetime English cricket star, Wright was 22 when he heeded the call from Cincinnati in 1869. Brother Harry signed him for $1,400, which was $200 more than Harry was paid to manage the club. In later years, George revealed that his salary actually was $2,000.

As the star of the Red Stockings, George revolutionized shortstop play. Instead of playing on the basepath as had been the style, he played deep from where, with a rifle arm, he was able to retire batters with ease.

In addition, Wright would catch a ball directly in front of his body, with his heels close together, to prevent a batted ball from skipping through his legs. Also, instead of catching a ball stiff-armed, he would relax his arms to deaden the force of the blow.

In the 20th century, former teammate Deacon White said of Wright, "There isn't an infielder in the game today who has anything on George when it came to playing shortstop. George fielded hard-hit balls barehanded, and gathered them up or speared them when in the air with either hand. He was an expert and accurate thrower, being able to throw with either hand."

Wright accompanied his brother to Boston in 1871 and starred on four National Association champions (1872-75) before switching to that city's club in the new National League in 1876.

Boston's N.L. team won flags in 1877 and '78, after which George moved to Providence as shortstop-manager. The Grays captured the pennant in '79, meaning Wright had performed on seven title winners in eight years. After playing only 53 games in the next three years, the standout player retired.

Although primarily a shortstop, George could handle

George Wright (right), the man who revolutionized shortstop play in the 19th Century, poses with N.L. President Ford Frick at the 1936 All-Star Game.

other positions as well. One who observed him in his prime wrote that "while he called shortstop his home position, he was, when called upon, equally at home on any of the bases. He could catch as well as the best catchers of his day and was a fine emergency pitcher."

Wright became interested in the sporting goods business while playing in Washington and opened his own store in Boston in 1871. Later, with a partner, he started to manufacture athletic wear in Boston. The firm gained a worldwide reputation as Wright & Ditson. When the Union Association organized in 1884 as a third major league, it adopted the Wright & Ditson product as its official ball.

Wright became interested in tennis while touring England with two major league baseball teams in 1874 and introduced the game to America. He was a member of the Longwood Cricket Club in Boston. One year, he conducted a tour of young players to the West Coast to familiarize Californians with the game. One of the tour members was Dwight Davis, then a Harvard student and later donor of the Davis Cup, symbol of international tennis supremacy. Beals Wright, one of George's two sons, was a member of the United States Davis Cup team prior to World War I.

Another time, George displayed a set of golf clubs in his store window, strictly as a curiosity item. When a Scotsman stopped by and explained the game to Wright, he became fascinated and shortly thereafter obtained permission to lay out a nine-hole course in Franklin Park near Boston.

For years Wright held the No. 1 pass to National League ball parks. He never lost his enthusiasm for baseball and was a frequent spectator at games in Boston.

The last surviving member of the game's first pro team died in his Boston home in 1937 at age 90.

# Harry Wright

Unquestionably, nobody pioneered in more phases of baseball than Harry Wright, English-born son of a professional cricket player.

Wright was the first to be honored with a special day in all of Organized Baseball, and he was the first supervisor of umpires. As a manager, he was the first to outfit his team in knickers, introduce cooperative team play, take his team on a foreign tour, win four consecutive pennants and use hand signs in coaching.

Harry was a tyke when he came to America with his parents. His first love was cricket, and he gained proficiency as a member of the St. George Club on Long Island. The cricketers played on a field adjoining that of the New York Knickerbockers, baseball's foremost team of that day. Wright watched the Knickerbockers at play and was invited to join them.

Hooked on the game, Wright made his baseball debut in the fall of 1858, making three excellent catches in center field but going hitless against a Brooklyn team. The game also was noteworthy in that it was the first at which admission was charged.

When not engaged in his profession as a jeweler, Wright played with the Knickerbockers for five years before moving to Cincinnati as the pro of the Union Cricket Club. In July of 1866 he helped to organize the Cincinnati Red Stockings—who became a wholly professional team three years later—and dropped his affiliation with cricket.

In 1867, Wright achieved his most remarkable feat as a player. In a game against Newport, Ky., he slugged seven home runs. In June of the same year, he was named manager of the Red Stockings.

At the close of the '67 season, during which the Cincinnati team posted a 41-7 record, Harry was married. As a wedding gift, his players presented him a gold watch wrapped in a $100 government bond.

Wright gained national prominence in 1869 when he masterminded the Red Stockings to 56 consecutive victories. Touring the eastern half of the country, the team traveled more than 21,000 miles and played before more than 200,000 paying customers. The streak was extended to 130 games in 1870 before the team bowed to the Atlantics of Brooklyn, 8-7, in 11 innings.

When the Red Stockings disbanded at the close of the '70 season, Harry accepted an offer to manage the Boston club of the new National Association. He produced four successive pennants from 1872 to '75.

Harry constantly crusaded for the betterment of baseball and was particularly distressed when the Athletics displayed their championship flag of 1871 in a Philadelphia saloon. He expected his players to be gentlemanly and temperate at all times. In denying a player's request to report two days late for spring training, Wright wrote:

Harry Wright was one of major league baseball's foremost pioneers.

"Professional ballplaying is a business and, as such, I trust you will regard it while the season lasts."

When the National League was founded in February of 1876, Harry served as secretary of the meeting and was lauded highly for his contributions in drafting legislation for the new circuit.

Wright's Boston club failed to win the first N.L. pennant, but it finished No. 1 the next two years. After the 1881 season, Harry switched to Providence for two years and then to Philadelphia where he managed for a decade before failing eyesight forced his retirement. In appreciation for his countless contributions to baseball, the N.L. created the special post of supervisor of umpires for Wright.

After Harry's death from pneumonia in Atlantic City, the 1896 Reach Guide editorialized: "Every magnate in the country is indebted to this man for the establishment of baseball as a business, and every patron for fulfilling him with a systematic recreation. Every player is indebted to him for inaugurating an occupation in which he gains a livelihood, and the country at large for adding one more industry . . . to furnish employment."

On "Harry Wright Day" the following season, more than $3,000 was collected in ball parks throughout the country for a monument to the "Father of Professional Baseball" in West Laurel Hill Cemetery in Philadelphia.

# Early Wynn

**Early Wynn (left) was the 21-year-old ace for Springfield of the Eastern League when he got the call from Washington. Wynn (center, right photo) looks on during an early-** **career spring training session as coach Benny Bengough returns a throw to a pitcher. Standing to Wynn's left is Calvin Griffith, son of Senators Owner Clark Griffith.**

Late in 1936, a chunky kid, clad in overalls and with a battered baseball glove dangling at his side, walked into a Washington Senators tryout camp at Sanford, Fla., and announced that he was a pitcher.

"Let's see you throw some," said Clyde Milan, the camp director whose initial impression was less than favorable.

After a few pitches, however, Milan changed his mind. The kid had a whistling fastball, and his look of determination could not be discounted.

The youngster, uninvited and unscouted, was signed to a Class D contract for $100 a month and one dollar a day meal money.

Nearly 27 years later the same righthander, now 43, took the mound for the Cleveland Indians in the second game of a Saturday doubleheader at Kansas City. He pitched the first five innings, then departed with a 5-4 lead. Jerry Walker shut out the A's the remainder of the game and when the Indians clinched the 7-4 victory, Early Wynn was in the radio booth ready to be interviewed as baseball's newest 300-game winner.

The date was July 13, 1963, nearly 22 years after Wynn arrived in the majors to stay as a member of the Senators.

Wynn made his big-league debut in 1939, pitching three late-season games for the Senators. He knew he wouldn't be back the next season and explained why.

"In a game against Cleveland I was getting my ears pinned back," he said. "But Washington was making some runs for me and it was still close in the ninth inning. We had men on first and second with none out and they let me bat, to sacrifice. I bunted—into a triple play."

Wynn, nicknamed Gus because, somebody said, "he looks like a Gus," spent 1940 and most of 1941 in the minors. He then pitched for the Senators in six of the next seven seasons, missing only 1945—a year in which the usually also-ran Senators were in the American League pennant race until the last day of the season. Wynn was in the military service in '45.

Traded to Cleveland after the Tribe's world-championship season of 1948, Wynn learned the finer points of his craft from pitching coach Mel Harder. Previously, Early had tried to throw every pitch as hard as he could. Under Harder's guidance, he learned the value of changing speeds. Thanks, too, to Harder's advice, Wynn's control improved markedly.

One phase of his game that did not change however, was the fierce determination to win. The one-quarter Cherokee from Alabama dusted off many a batter who took liberties at the plate. He was especially rough on

In 1954, Wynn (left) was one of the moving forces of the pennant-winning Indians with 23 victories. Five seasons later, Wynn was on his way to 22 wins as a member of the Chicago White Sox.

hitters who drove hard smashes through the pitchers' box which, he maintained, "is my office."

In a 1956 game at Washington, Jose Valdivielso drilled the ball up the middle and it struck Wynn on the chin. As Valdivielso stood on base contemplating what might occur on his next at-bat, Al Lopez checked out his pitcher.

"Let me see," said the Cleveland manager.

"I'm fine," replied Gus through clenched jaws.

Lopez repeated the question and Wynn repeated the reply several times until Al said, "Let me see or I'll take you out without looking."

At that, Early yielded, revealing a gash on his chin that would require 16 stitches and a mouth so badly chopped that he would lose seven lower teeth. Under protest, Wynn left the mound—and Valdivielso heaved a sigh of relief.

Truly, Wynn was "the man you would least like to meet in a dark alley on a rainy night."

Gus won 20 or more games four times for the Indians before Bill Veeck, his old boss at Cleveland, acquired him for the White Sox during the winter meetings of 1957.

Wynn was nearly 38, but he had enough of the old cunning, pride and determination to win 14 games in 1958 and a league-leading 22 games for the A.L. champion White Sox of 1959.

At the start of the 1962 season, Wynn still was eight victories short of the coveted 300 mark. He had adopted a strict dietary regimen to prepare himself physically for the final assault. Using a high slider and a knuckleball extensively, he made an admirable effort, but fell one victory short with a 7-15 record. At the end of the season, the White Sox handed Early his release.

The old fighter stayed in shape, although there were no offers. At last, on June 21, 1963, he received a call from his old club. The Indians needed pitching help. Within a month, Wynn had scaled the final peak.

Wynn became a pitching coach for the Indians and Twins, scouted for the Twins and managed a number of minor league clubs. He returned to the scene of many conquests in the early 1980s as a broadcaster for the White Sox.

# Tom Yawkey

American League club owners were aghast in 1933 when the new owner of the Boston Red Sox arose at his first meeting and announced that he was prepared to pay handsome prices for established major leaguers.

"Would you be interested in Rick Ferrell and Lloyd Brown?" asked Phil Ball, owner of the St. Louis Browns.

"I would," answered the young millionaire, who started to write a check for a deal in which he gave up catcher Marvyn Shea and cash.

With the acquisition of catcher Ferrell and pitcher Brown, Tom Yawkey—born Thomas Austin—launched a career that carried him through more than four decades and millions of dollars. He built the Red Sox into solid contenders, sometimes known as "Gold Sox" and other times as "Millionaires" because of their owner's generosity in salaries and his free-spending practices in obtaining talent.

For all his efforts, however, Yawkey saw only three A.L. pennants fly from the Fenway Park flagpole—in 1946, 1967 and 1975. And on each occasion, the pennant was followed by a loss in a seven-game World Series.

Thomas Austin was born into a baseball atmosphere. His grandfather, William Clyman Yawkey, founded a lumber and iron-ore empire. He was negotiating for the purchase of the Detroit Tigers in 1904 when he was stricken fatally. His son, William Hoover Yawkey, completed the transaction.

As the brother of young Tom's mother, William Hoover Yawkey became Thomas Austin's foster father and eventually adopted the boy (and Tom took the name Yawkey). Throughout his life, Tom Yawkey always referred to his uncle as Dad.

The elder Yawkey died in 1917, leaving a sizable estate to Tom, who inherited additional millions when he came of age.

As a boy in Detroit, Tom had idolized Ty Cobb and maintained contacts with the old Tiger star into adulthood. At dinner one night, Cobb suggested that Yawkey invest in a major league club. The suggestion germinated until 1933 when Yawkey, then 30, purchased the Red Sox from Bob Quinn for $1.5 million.

A year later, Yawkey spent an identical sum to refur-

Tom Yawkey's lavish spending finally resulted in a Boston pennant in 1946.

bish Fenway Park, which had fallen into disrepair since the club's last pennant in 1918.

Yawkey's first move after acquiring the Red Sox was to install Eddie Collins as vice president. Both men had attended the Irving School in Tarrytown, N.Y. They were not contemporaries, but Yawkey formed a lasting admiration for the old second baseman (who had been a coach for the Philadelphia A's in 1932).

By that time Yawkey had earned a degree in the Sheffield Scientific School at Yale and was head of the business empire he had inherited.

With Collins supplying the expertise and Yawkey the money, the Red Sox bought lavishly, obtaining Lefty Grove, Jimmie Foxx, Max Bishop, Roger Cramer, Rube Walberg and John Marcum from the A's. Tom made his most newsworthy transaction in 1934 when he acquired Joe Cronin from the Washington Senators. He gave up $250,000 and shortstop Lyn Lary to get the Nats' manager-shortstop, who was installed as the Red Sox's pilot.

Yawkey never lost the willingness to spend large sums for proven players. Just weeks before his death, he agreed to a $2 million purchase of Rollie Fingers and Joe Rudi from Oakland. The deal was quashed later by Commissioner Bowie Kuhn.

A frustrated athlete himself, Yawkey was a crack shot with a rifle and in his late 30s was able to compete with national handball champions.

While he maintained suites at fashionable hotels in New York and Boston, Yawkey was not considered one of the social elite. He was most comfortable on his 40,000-acre estate in South Carolina where, in battered hat and clothes, he could spend hours hunting with plantation employees.

In his 43 years of club ownership, Tom developed his greatest affection for Ted Williams and Carl Yastrzemski. He cringed when either was booed. But neither was he blind to the faults of his players. He once fined Williams $5,000 for allegedly making an obscene gesture to the crowd.

The worthiest of owners—who spent millions of dollars without a whimper in an effort to produce championships —died of leukemia in 1976 in Boston at age 73.

# Cy Young

In 1891, Cy Young recorded his first 20-victory season for the Cleveland Spiders. By 1901, Young was pitching for Boston and well on his way to a major league-record 511 career victories.

On an August evening in 1890, Cap Anson, manager of the Chicago White Stockings, was relaxing with David Hawley, an official of the Cleveland Spiders, when the conversation turned to that afternoon's game, in which a young farmer had pitched Cleveland to an 8-1 victory in his major league debut.

"That big rube had a lot of luck beating us," said Anson. "He is too green to do your club much good, but I believe I might make a pitcher out of him in a couple of years. Anyway, I'm willing to give you $1,000 for him."

Hawley was not easily deluded.

"If I recall correctly," Hawley responded, "that big rube struck you out twice today, and I believe he can do it again. What's more, I believe he can do us as much good as Chicago, so keep your $1,000 and we'll keep the rube."

The 23-year-old pitcher, who had spaced three hits and did not walk a batter, was Cy Young, destined to be the biggest winner in big-league history. Young had just come off a farm in eastern Ohio and he was, as Anson noted, a rube. When the newcomer reported to the Spiders, Hawley took one glance at his ill-fitting and unfashionable attire and hustled him to a haberdasher before the veterans could crush the youngster's spirits with their ridicule.

When the pitcher left home he was known as Dent Young. Before long, however, he was nicknamed Cy, as in Cyclone, because of his blinding fastball. Or maybe, as some suggested, he got the name because it was a practice of the times to apply it to rural youths.

Young's first stop on the road to national acclaim was Canton in the Tri-State League. The rookie compiled a 15-15 record and soon was being offered to the majors for $500. Only the Spiders were willing to take the gamble. Before long a national sports weekly reported:

"Young, new pitcher of the Cleveland club, is a big, strong countryman who was a rail-splitter before he played ball. He is said to be speedier than Hutchison (Bill Hutchison of Chicago) and has a drop ball that is a killer."

Years later, Tris Speaker rated Young's fastball in the class of Walter Johnson's and Bob Feller's.

During a 22-year career that produced 511 triumphs, Cy reached or topped the 20-victory mark 16 times and exceeded the 30-win plateau five times. Three of his vic-

In 1895, Young (left) recorded the third of five 30-plus victory seasons. When Connie Mack (left, right photo) and Young posed in 1949, the former was 86 years old, the latter 82.

tories were no-hitters, the first a 6-0 decision over Cincinnati in 1897 in which Young walked one batter.

Cy's second no-hitter was a masterpiece. In 1904, he defeated Rube Waddell and the Philadelphia A's, 3-0, without permitting a baserunner. The righthander concentrated so intently on the job at hand that he did not realize he had pitched a perfect game until outfielder Chick Stahl presented him the last ball of the game.

Young was 41 when, in 1908, he hurled his third gem in an 8-0 triumph over New York. Young, who aided his own cause with three hits, allowed only one baserunner (on a walk).

Cy moved with the Spiders franchise to St. Louis in 1899. He was earning the National League's maximum salary of $2,400 a year and was in a receptive mood when Ban Johnson, forming the American League as a new major circuit, offered him a $600-a-year raise to jump to the Boston Red Sox in 1901. Cy accepted.

Young, who had defeated the Baltimore Orioles three times in a five-game Temple Cup Series in 1895, pitched in four games for the Red Sox during the first World Series in 1903. He won two decisions—both coming after the Pittsburgh Pirates had captured three of the first four contests —as Boston took the world championship.

For all his accomplishments, Young's most memorable day was August 13, 1908, when the Boston Post sponsored a "Cy Young Day" unlike any other celebration before or since. All American League activity was suspended for the day so that an all-star team could honor the veteran pitcher by meeting the Red Sox in an exhibition game at the old Huntington Avenue grounds.

The gates opened at 11:30 a.m. Within an hour, 20,000 fans had jammed the ancient park. Another 10,000 were turned away. Young's gifts included a traveling bag from the umpires, a cup from the American League, numerous floral arrangements and a cash donation of at least $6,000.

Young, who pitched the first two innings against the all-stars, was so overcome by emotion—according to the account of the day—that "he could make no response to the presentation speeches."

Cy was a member of the Braves in 1911 when, at 44, he pitched his last game, a loss to Eddie Dent of the Dodgers.

Young returned to his native eastern Ohio where, seated in his favorite armchair and gazing out across the familiar pasture lands, he suffered a fatal heart attack in 1955 at age 88.

# Ross Youngs

From the beginning, John McGraw recognized the kid's extraordinary talent. The 20-year-old player would require minor league polish, but the manager of the New York Giants wanted to be certain that nothing was done to harm the prospect's many skills.

The Giants had a working agreement with the Rochester club of the International League in 1917. The Red Wings' manager was Mickey Doolan, a longtime major leaguer.

"I'm going to give you a kid who is going to be a great player," McGraw told Doolan. "Take good care of him because if anything happens to him, I'll hold you responsible."

Doolan followed orders faithfully. Before the season ended, Ross Youngs—after batting .356—was with the Giants, ready for a brilliant career that ended in tragedy.

Youngs' career was still in its infancy when fans nicknamed him Pep. Frequently, the "s" was dropped from his surname.

As a youth, Youngs attended West Texas Military Academy, where he was better known as a halfback and track star than as a baseball player. Football teammate Joe Straus, who later was an outstanding player at Pennsylvania, said if Youngs had attended Penn "as I wanted him to, you never would have heard of me."

But Youngs' heart was set on baseball. He refused to be discouraged when the Austin (Texas) club released him after a lackluster 10-game stint in 1914, and he bounced around the Texas bush leagues for two seasons before he caught on with Sherman (Western Association), where New York scout Dick Kinsella discovered him in 1916.

While Youngs received a major league trial on the infield, McGraw concluded that his arm was not suited to the positions. Ross was switched to right field and almost immediately mastered the position. In all phases of outfield play, Youngs distinguished himself so that McGraw, in his declining years, declared: "He was the greatest outfielder I ever saw. He could do everything that a baseball player should do and do it better than most players. As an outfielder, he had no superiors. And he was the easiest man I ever knew to handle. In all his years with the Giants he never caused one moment's trouble for myself or the club. On top of all that, a gamer player than Youngs never played ball."

Youngs starred on the Giants' four consecutive pennant-winning clubs (1921-24), batting from .327 the first year to .356 the last. In the seventh inning of Game 3 of the 1921 World Series, he sparked an eight-run rally with a double and triple to become the first player to register two hits in a Series inning.

When the Giants slipped to second place in 1925, Ross' batting average dropped below .300, plummeting to .264, for the first time. When Youngs reported to training camp

**Giants star Ross Youngs was only 30 when he succumbed to Bright's disease.**

in 1926, a physical examination revealed that he was suffering from Bright's disease, a serious kidney ailment. Many observers contended that the disease stemmed from Youngs' habit of diving into bases.

McGraw hired a male nurse to accompany Youngs wherever the Giants went during the '26 season. The player referred to the nurse as "my keeper." Despite failing health, Ross maintained his high spirits throughout the campaign. He batted .306 and taught the fine points of outfield play to his successor, Mel Ott.

Youngs was bed-ridden during the entire 1927 season, and he died on October 22 that year at age 30.

Contemporaries were lavish in their praise of the talented Texan.

Waite Hoyt called Youngs "a smaller Ty Cobb." In the onetime pitcher's book, "he was built like Enos Slaughter, had the same hustle—but more ability."

When Ford Frick was asked for his personal all-time, all-star team, the father of the Hall of Fame selected the popular outfield choices of Babe Ruth, Ty Cobb and Tris Speaker. Then he added, "But somehow I've got to find a place for Pep Youngs.

"Don't ask me to take somebody out. I've just got to put Pep in there somewhere."

# Career Records of Hall of Famers
*Denotes led league. ●Denotes tied for league lead.

## HENRY LOUIS (HANK) AARON

| Year | Club | League | G. | AB. | R. | H. | HR. | RBI. | B.A. |
|------|------|--------|-----|------|------|------|------|------|------|
| 1952—Eau Claire | North. | | 87 | 345 | 79 | 116 | 9 | 61 | .336 |
| 1953—Jacksonville | Sally | | 137 | 574 | *115 | *208 | 22 | *125 | *.362 |
| 1954—Milwaukee | Nat. | | 122 | 468 | 58 | 131 | 13 | 69 | .280 |
| 1955—Milwaukee | Nat. | | 153 | 602 | 105 | 189 | 27 | 106 | .314 |
| 1956—Milwaukee | Nat. | | 153 | 609 | 106 | *200 | 26 | 92 | *.328 |
| 1957—Milwaukee | Nat. | | 151 | 615 | *118 | 198 | *44 | *132 | .322 |
| 1958—Milwaukee | Nat. | | 153 | 601 | 109 | 196 | 30 | 95 | .326 |
| 1959—Milwaukee | Nat. | | 154 | 629 | 116 | *223 | 39 | 123 | *.355 |
| 1960—Milwaukee | Nat. | | 153 | 590 | 102 | 172 | 40 | *126 | .292 |
| 1961—Milwaukee | Nat. | | *155 | 603 | 115 | 197 | 34 | 120 | .327 |
| 1962—Milwaukee | Nat. | | 156 | 592 | 127 | 191 | 45 | 128 | .323 |
| 1963—Milwaukee | Nat. | | 161 | 631 | *121 | 201 | ●44 | *130 | .319 |
| 1964—Milwaukee | Nat. | | 145 | 570 | 103 | 187 | 24 | 95 | .328 |
| 1965—Milwaukee | Nat. | | 150 | 570 | 109 | 181 | 32 | 89 | .318 |
| 1966—Atlanta | Nat. | | 158 | 603 | 117 | 168 | *44 | *127 | .279 |
| 1967—Atlanta | Nat. | | 155 | 600 | ●113 | 184 | *39 | 109 | .307 |
| 1968—Atlanta | Nat. | | 160 | 606 | 84 | 174 | 29 | 86 | .287 |
| 1969—Atlanta | Nat. | | 147 | 547 | 100 | 164 | 44 | 97 | .300 |
| 1970—Atlanta | Nat. | | 150 | 516 | 103 | 154 | 38 | 118 | .298 |
| 1971—Atlanta | Nat. | | 139 | 495 | 95 | 162 | 47 | 118 | .327 |
| 1972—Atlanta | Nat. | | 129 | 449 | 75 | 119 | 34 | 77 | .265 |
| 1973—Atlanta | Nat. | | 120 | 392 | 84 | 118 | 40 | 96 | .301 |
| 1974—Atlanta | Nat. | | 112 | 340 | 47 | 91 | 20 | 69 | .268 |
| 1975—Milwaukee | Amer. | | 137 | 465 | 45 | 109 | 12 | 60 | .234 |
| 1976—Milwaukee | Amer. | | 85 | 271 | 22 | 62 | 10 | 35 | .229 |
| American League Totals | | | 222 | 736 | 67 | 171 | 22 | 95 | .232 |
| National League Totals | | | 3076 | 11628 | 2107 | 3620 | 733 | 2202 | .310 |
| Major League Totals | | | 3298 | 12364 | 2174 | 3771 | 755 | 2297 | .305 |

### CHAMPIONSHIP SERIES RECORD

| Year | Club | League | G. | AB. | R. | H. | HR. | RBI. | B.A. |
|------|------|--------|-----|------|------|------|------|------|------|
| 1969—Atlanta | Nat. | | 3 | 14 | 3 | 5 | 3 | 7 | .357 |

### WORLD SERIES RECORD

| Year | Club | League | G. | AB. | R. | H. | HR. | RBI. | B.A. |
|------|------|--------|-----|------|------|------|------|------|------|
| 1957—Milwaukee | Nat. | | 7 | 28 | 5 | 11 | 3 | 7 | .393 |
| 1958—Milwaukee | Nat. | | 7 | 27 | 3 | 9 | 0 | 2 | .333 |
| World Series Totals | | | 14 | 55 | 8 | 20 | 3 | 9 | .364 |

## GROVER CLEVELAND (PETE) ALEXANDER

| Year | Club | League | G. | IP. | W. | L. | Pct. | ERA. |
|------|------|--------|-----|------|------|------|------|------|
| 1909—Galesburg | Ill.-Mo. | | 24 | 219 | 15 | 8 | .652 | ...... |
| 1910—Syracuse | N.Y. State | | *43 | 245 | *29 | 14 | .674 | ...... |
| 1911—Philadelphia | Nat. | | 48 | *366 | *28 | 13 | .683 | ...... |
| 1912—Philadelphia | Nat. | | 46 | ●310 | 19 | 17 | .528 | 2.81 |
| 1913—Philadelphia | Nat. | | 47 | 306 | 22 | 8 | .733 | 2.82 |
| 1914—Philadelphia | Nat. | | 46 | *355 | ●27 | 15 | .643 | 2.38 |
| 1915—Philadelphia | Nat. | | 49 | *376 | *31 | 10 | *.756 | *1.22 |
| 1916—Philadelphia | Nat. | | 48 | *390 | *33 | 12 | .733 | *1.55 |
| 1917—Philadelphia | Nat. | | 45 | *387 | *30 | 13 | .698 | *1.83 |
| 1918—Chicago | Nat. | | 3 | 26 | 2 | 1 | .667 | 1.73 |
| 1919—Chicago | Nat. | | 30 | 235 | 16 | 11 | .593 | *1.72 |
| 1920—Chicago | Nat. | | 46 | *363 | *27 | 14 | .659 | *1.91 |
| 1921—Chicago | Nat. | | 31 | 252 | 15 | 13 | .536 | 3.39 |
| 1922—Chicago | Nat. | | 33 | 246 | 16 | 13 | .552 | 3.39 |
| 1923—Chicago | Nat. | | 39 | 305 | 22 | 12 | .647 | 3.19 |
| 1924—Chicago | Nat. | | 21 | 169 | 12 | 5 | .706 | 3.03 |
| 1925—Chicago | Nat. | | 32 | 236 | 15 | 11 | .577 | 3.39 |
| 1926—Chicago-St. Louis | Nat. | | 30 | 200 | 12 | 10 | .545 | 3.06 |
| 1927—St. Louis | Nat. | | 37 | 268 | 21 | 10 | .677 | 2.52 |
| 1928—St. Louis | Nat. | | 34 | 244 | 16 | 9 | .640 | 3.36 |
| 1929—St. Louis | Nat. | | 22 | 132 | 9 | 8 | .529 | 3.89 |
| 1930—Philadelphia | Nat. | | 9 | 22 | 0 | 3 | .000 | 9.00 |
| 1930—Dallas | Texas | | 5 | 24 | 1 | 2 | .333 | 8.25 |
| Major League Totals | | | 696 | 5188 | 373 | 208 | .642 | 2.56 |

### WORLD SERIES RECORD

| Year | Club | League | G. | IP. | W. | L. | Pct. | ERA. |
|------|------|--------|-----|------|------|------|------|------|
| 1915—Philadelphia | National | | 2 | 17⅔ | 1 | 1 | .500 | 1.53 |
| 1926—St. Louis | National | | 3 | 20⅓ | 2 | 0 | 1.000 | 1.33 |
| 1928—St. Louis | National | | 2 | 5 | 0 | 1 | .000 | 19.80 |
| Major League Totals | | | 7 | 43 | 3 | 2 | .600 | 3.56 |

## WALTER EMMONS ALSTON
### RECORD AS MANAGER

| Year | Club | League | Position | W. | L. |
|------|------|--------|----------|------|------|
| 1940—Portsmouth | Mid. Atl. | | Sixth | 59 | 68 |
| 1941—Springfield | Mid. Atl. | | Fourth | 69 | 57 |
| 1942—Springfield | Mid. Atl. | | Fifth | 59 | 71 |
| 1944—Trenton | Int.-St. | | Sixth | 31 | 18 |
| 1945—Trenton | Int.-St. | | Third | 70 | 69 |
| 1946—Nashua | N. Eng. | | Second | 80 | 41 |
| 1947—Pueblo | West. | | Third | 70 | 58 |
| 1948—St. Paul | A. A. | | Third | 86 | 68 |
| 1949—St. Paul | A. A. | | First | 93 | 60 |
| 1950—Montreal | Int. | | Second | 86 | 67 |
| 1951—Montreal | Int. | | First | 95 | 59 |
| 1952—Montreal | Int. | | First | 95 | 56 |
| 1953—Montreal | Int. | | Second | 89 | 63 |
| 1954—Brooklyn | Nat. | | Second | 92 | 62 |
| 1955—Brooklyn | Nat. | | First | 98 | 55 |
| 1956—Brooklyn | Nat. | | First | 93 | 61 |
| 1957—Brooklyn | Nat. | | Third | 84 | 70 |
| 1958—Los Angeles | Nat. | | Seventh | 71 | 83 |
| 1959—Los Angeles | Nat. | | First | 88 | 68 |
| 1960—Los Angeles | Nat. | | Fourth | 82 | 72 |
| 1961—Los Angeles | Nat. | | Second | 89 | 65 |
| 1962—Los Angeles | Nat. | | Second | 102 | 63 |
| 1963—Los Angeles | Nat. | | First | 99 | 63 |
| 1964—Los Angeles | Nat. | | Sixth | 80 | 82 |
| 1965—Los Angeles | Nat. | | First | 97 | 65 |
| 1966—Los Angeles | Nat. | | First | 95 | 67 |
| 1967—Los Angeles | Nat. | | Eighth | 73 | 89 |
| 1968—Los Angeles | Nat. | | Seventh | 76 | 86 |
| 1969—Los Angeles | Nat. | | Fourth(W) | 85 | 77 |
| 1970—Los Angeles | Nat. | | Second(W) | 87 | 74 |
| 1971—Los Angeles | Nat. | | Second(W) | 89 | 73 |
| 1972—Los Angeles | Nat. | | Third(W) | 85 | 70 |
| 1973—Los Angeles | Nat. | | Second(W) | 95 | 66 |
| 1974—Los Angeles | Nat. | | First(W) | 102 | 60 |
| 1975—Los Angeles | Nat. | | Second(W) | 88 | 74 |
| 1976—Los Angeles | Nat. | | Second(W) | 90 | 68 |
| Major League Totals | | | | 2040 | 1613 |

### CHAMPIONSHIP SERIES RECORD

| Year | Club | League | W. | L. |
|------|------|--------|------|------|
| 1974—Los Angeles | National | | 3 | 1 |

### WORLD SERIES RECORD

| Year | Club | League | W. | L. |
|------|------|--------|------|------|
| 1955—Brooklyn | National | | 4 | 3 |
| 1956—Brooklyn | National | | 3 | 4 |
| 1959—Los Angeles | National | | 4 | 2 |
| 1963—Los Angeles | National | | 4 | 0 |
| 1965—Los Angeles | National | | 4 | 3 |
| 1966—Los Angeles | National | | 0 | 4 |
| 1974—Los Angeles | National | | 1 | 4 |

## ADRIAN CONSTANTINE (CAP) ANSON

| Year | Club | League | G. | AB. | R. | H. | HR. | SB. | B.A. |
|------|------|--------|-----|------|------|------|------|------|------|
| 1870—Marshalltown | Ind. | | ..... | | | | | | |
| 1871—Rockford | N.As'n | | 25 | 122 | 30 | 43 | ..... | ..... | .352 |
| 1872—Ath. of Phila. | N.As'n | | 45 | 231 | 60 | 88 | ..... | ..... | .381 |
| 1873—Ath. of Phila. | N.As'n | | 51 | | 52 | 103 | ..... | ..... | |
| 1874—Ath. of Phila. | N.As'n | | 55 | 267 | 51 | 98 | ..... | ..... | .367 |
| 1875—Ath. of Phila. | N.As'n | | 69 | 330 | 83 | 105 | ..... | ..... | .318 |
| 1876—Chicago | Nat. | | 66 | 321 | 63 | 110 | 2 | ..... | .343 |
| 1877—Chicago | Nat. | | 47 | 200 | 36 | 67 | 0 | ..... | .335 |
| 1878—Chicago | Nat. | | 59 | 256 | 54 | 86 | 0 | ..... | .336 |
| 1879—Chicago | Nat. | | 49 | 221 | 41 | 90 | 0 | ..... | *.407 |
| 1880—Chicago | Nat. | | 84 | 346 | 52 | 117 | 1 | ..... | .338 |
| 1881—Chicago | Nat. | | 84 | 343 | 66 | *137 | 1 | ..... | *.399 |
| 1882—Chicago | Nat. | | 82 | 348 | 69 | 126 | 1 | ..... | .362 |
| 1883—Chicago | Nat. | | 98 | 413 | 69 | 127 | 0 | ..... | .308 |
| 1884—Chicago | Nat. | | 111 | 471 | 108 | *159 | 19 | ..... | .338 |
| 1885—Chicago | Nat. | | 112 | 464 | 100 | 144 | 7 | ..... | .310 |
| 1886—Chicago | Nat. | | 125 | 504 | 117 | *187 | 10 | 29 | .371 |
| 1887—Chicago | Nat. | | 122 | 532 | 107 | 224 | 7 | 27 | *.421 |
| 1888—Chicago | Nat. | | 134 | 515 | 101 | 177 | 10 | 28 | *.344 |
| 1889—Chicago | Nat. | | 134 | 518 | 99 | 177 | 7 | 27 | .342 |
| 1890—Chicago | Nat. | | *139 | 504 | 102 | 157 | 6 | 29 | .312 |
| 1891—Chicago | Nat. | | 136 | 537 | 82 | 158 | 8 | 21 | .294 |
| 1892—Chicago | Nat. | | 147 | 561 | 62 | 154 | 1 | 15 | .275 |
| 1893—Chicago | Nat. | | 101 | 381 | 70 | 123 | 0 | 13 | .323 |
| 1894—Chicago | Nat. | | 83 | 347 | 87 | 137 | 5 | 17 | .395 |
| 1895—Chicago | Nat. | | 122 | 476 | 88 | 161 | 2 | 16 | .338 |
| 1896—Chicago | Nat. | | 106 | 403 | 72 | 135 | 2 | 28 | .335 |
| 1897—Chicago | Nat. | | 112 | 423 | 66 | 128 | 3 | 16 | .303 |
| Major League Totals | | | 2253 | 9084 | 1712 | 3081 | 92 | 266 | .339 |

### WORLD SERIES RECORD

| Year | Club | League | G. | AB. | R. | H. | SB. | B.A. |
|------|------|--------|-----|------|------|------|------|------|
| 1885—Chicago | Nat. | | 7 | 26 | 8 | 11 | 6 | .423 |
| 1886—Chicago | Nat. | | 6 | 20 | 3 | 5 | 1 | .250 |
| World Series Totals | | | 13 | 46 | 11 | 16 | 1 | .348 |

## LUCIUS BENJAMIN (LUKE) APPLING

| Year Club | League | G. | AB. | R. | H. | HR. | RBI. | B.A. |
|---|---|---|---|---|---|---|---|---|
| 1930—Atlanta | South. | 104 | 374 | 63 | 122 | 5 | 75 | .326 |
| 1930—Chicago | Amer. | 6 | 26 | 2 | 8 | 0 | 2 | .308 |
| 1931—Chicago | Amer. | 96 | 297 | 36 | 69 | 1 | 28 | .232 |
| 1932—Chicago | Amer. | 139 | 489 | 66 | 134 | 3 | 63 | .274 |
| 1933—Chicago | Amer. | 151 | 612 | 90 | 197 | 6 | 85 | .322 |
| 1934—Chicago | Amer. | 118 | 452 | 75 | 137 | 2 | 61 | .303 |
| 1935—Chicago | Amer. | 153 | 525 | 94 | 161 | 1 | 71 | .307 |
| 1936—Chicago | Amer. | 138 | 526 | 111 | 204 | 6 | 128 | ★.388 |
| 1937—Chicago | Amer. | 154 | 574 | 98 | 182 | 4 | 77 | .317 |
| 1938—Chicago | Amer. | 81 | 294 | 41 | 89 | 0 | 44 | .303 |
| 1939—Chicago | Amer. | 148 | 516 | 82 | 162 | 0 | 56 | .314 |
| 1940—Chicago | Amer. | 150 | 566 | 96 | 197 | 0 | 79 | .348 |
| 1941—Chicago | Amer. | 154 | 592 | 93 | 186 | 1 | 57 | .314 |
| 1942—Chicago | Amer. | 142 | 543 | 78 | 142 | 3 | 53 | .262 |
| 1943—Chicago | Amer. | ●155 | 585 | 63 | 192 | 3 | 80 | ★.328 |
| 1944— | | | | (In Military Service) | | | | |
| 1945—Chicago | Amer. | 18 | 57 | 12 | 21 | 1 | 10 | .368 |
| 1946—Chicago | Amer. | 149 | 582 | 59 | 180 | 1 | 55 | .309 |
| 1947—Chicago | Amer. | 139 | 503 | 67 | 154 | 8 | 49 | .306 |
| 1948—Chicago | Amer. | 139 | 497 | 63 | 156 | 0 | 47 | .314 |
| 1949—Chicago | Amer. | 142 | 492 | 82 | 148 | 5 | 58 | .301 |
| 1950—Chicago | Amer. | 50 | 128 | 11 | 30 | 0 | 13 | .234 |
| Major League Totals | | 2422 | 8856 | 1319 | 2749 | 45 | 1116 | .310 |

## HOWARD EARL (ROCK) AVERILL

| Year Club | League | G. | AB. | R. | H. | HR. | RBI. | B.A. |
|---|---|---|---|---|---|---|---|---|
| 1926—San Francisco | P. C. | 188 | 679 | 131 | 236 | 23 | 119 | .348 |
| 1927—San Francisco | P. C. | 183 | 754 | 134 | 244 | 20 | 116 | .324 |
| 1928—San Francisco | P. C. | 189 | 763 | ★178 | 270 | 36 | 173 | .354 |
| 1929—Cleveland | Amer. | 152 | 596 | 110 | 198 | 18 | 96 | .332 |
| 1930—Cleveland | Amer. | 139 | 534 | 102 | 181 | 19 | 119 | .339 |
| 1931—Cleveland | Amer. | 155 | ★627 | 140 | 209 | 32 | 143 | .333 |
| 1932—Cleveland | Amer. | 153 | 631 | 116 | 198 | 32 | 124 | .314 |
| 1933—Cleveland | Amer. | 151 | 599 | 83 | 180 | 11 | 92 | .301 |
| 1934—Cleveland | Amer. | ●154 | 598 | 128 | 187 | 31 | 113 | .313 |
| 1935—Cleveland | Amer. | 140 | 563 | 109 | 162 | 19 | 79 | .288 |
| 1936—Cleveland | Amer. | 152 | 614 | 136 | ★232 | 28 | 126 | .378 |
| 1937—Cleveland | Amer. | 156 | 609 | 121 | 182 | 21 | 92 | .299 |
| 1938—Cleveland | Amer. | 134 | 482 | 101 | 159 | 14 | 93 | .330 |
| 1939—Clev.-Detroit | Amer. | 111 | 364 | 66 | 96 | 11 | 65 | .264 |
| 1940—Detroit | Amer. | 64 | 118 | 10 | 33 | 2 | 20 | .280 |
| 1941—Boston | Nat. | 8 | 17 | 2 | 2 | 0 | 2 | .118 |
| 1941—Seattle | P. C. | 78 | 223 | 24 | 55 | 1 | 17 | .247 |
| American League Totals | | 1661 | 6335 | 1222 | 2017 | 238 | 1162 | .318 |
| National League Totals | | 8 | 17 | 2 | 2 | 0 | 2 | .118 |
| Major League Totals | | 1669 | 6352 | 1224 | 2019 | 238 | 1164 | .318 |

### WORLD SERIES RECORD

| Year Club | League | G. | AB. | R. | H. | HR. | RBI. | B.A. |
|---|---|---|---|---|---|---|---|---|
| 1940—Detroit | Amer. | 3 | 3 | 0 | 0 | 0 | 0 | .000 |

## JOHN FRANKLIN (HOME RUN) BAKER

| Year Club | League | G. | AB. | R. | H. | HR. | RBI. | B.A. |
|---|---|---|---|---|---|---|---|---|
| 1907—Baltimore | East. | 5 | 15 | 0 | 2 | 0 | .... | .133 |
| 1908—Reading | Tri-State | 119 | 451 | 65 | 135 | 6 | .... | .299 |
| 1908—Philadelphia | Amer. | 9 | 30 | 5 | 9 | 0 | 4 | .300 |
| 1909—Philadelphia | Amer. | 148 | 541 | 73 | 165 | 4 | 89 | .305 |
| 1910—Philadelphia | Amer. | 146 | 561 | 83 | 159 | 2 | 73 | .283 |
| 1911—Philadelphia | Amer. | 148 | 592 | 96 | 198 | ★11 | 115 | .334 |
| 1912—Philadelphia | Amer. | 149 | 577 | 116 | 200 | ●10 | ★133 | .347 |
| 1913—Philadelphia | Amer. | 149 | 564 | 116 | 190 | ★12 | ★126 | .337 |
| 1914—Philadelphia | Amer. | 150 | 570 | 84 | 182 | ★9 | 97 | .319 |
| 1915—Philadelphia | Amer. | | | (Refused to report; played with Upland, Pa.) | | | | |
| 1916—New York | Amer. | 100 | 360 | 46 | 97 | 10 | 52 | .269 |
| 1917—New York | Amer. | 146 | 553 | 57 | 156 | 6 | 70 | .282 |
| 1918—New York | Amer. | 126 | 504 | 65 | 154 | 6 | 68 | .306 |
| 1919—New York | Amer. | ●141 | 567 | 70 | 166 | 10 | 78 | .293 |
| 1920—New York | Amer. | | | (Voluntarily retired; played with Upland, Pa.) | | | | |
| 1921—New York | Amer. | 94 | 330 | 46 | 97 | 9 | 71 | .294 |
| 1922—New York | Amer. | 69 | 234 | 30 | 65 | 7 | 36 | .278 |
| 1924—Easton | Ea. Shore | 43 | 92 | 14 | 27 | 5 | .... | .293 |
| Major League Totals | | 1575 | 5983 | 887 | 1838 | 96 | 1012 | .307 |

### WORLD SERIES RECORD

| Year Club | League | G. | AB. | R. | H. | HR. | RBI. | B.A. |
|---|---|---|---|---|---|---|---|---|
| 1910—Philadelphia | Amer. | 5 | 22 | 6 | 9 | 0 | 4 | .409 |
| 1911—Philadelphia | Amer. | 6 | 24 | 7 | 9 | 2 | 5 | .375 |
| 1913—Philadelphia | Amer. | 5 | 20 | 2 | 9 | 1 | 7 | .450 |
| 1914—Philadelphia | Amer. | 4 | 16 | 0 | 4 | 0 | 2 | .250 |
| 1921—New York | Amer. | 4 | 8 | 0 | 2 | 0 | 0 | .250 |
| 1922—New York | Amer. | 1 | 1 | 0 | 0 | 0 | 0 | .000 |
| World Series Totals | | 25 | 91 | 15 | 33 | 3 | 18 | .363 |

## DAVID JAMES (BEAUTY) BANCROFT

| Year Club | League | G. | AB. | R. | H. | HR. | RBI. | B.A. |
|---|---|---|---|---|---|---|---|---|
| 1909—Duluth-Sup. | Wis.-Min. | 111 | 367 | 43 | 77 | 1 | .... | .210 |
| 1910—Superior | Wis.-Min. | ●127 | 438 | 55 | 117 | 1 | .... | .267 |
| 1911—Superior | Wis.-Min. | 122 | 524 | 73 | 143 | .... | .... | .273 |
| 1912—Portland | P. C. | 166 | 565 | 68 | 120 | 0 | .... | .213 |
| 1913—Portland | N. W. | 133 | 483 | 79 | 118 | 2 | .... | .244 |
| 1914—Portland | P. C. | 177 | 668 | 99 | 185 | 2 | .... | .277 |
| 1915—Philadelphia | Nat. | 153 | 563 | 85 | 143 | 7 | 33 | .254 |
| 1916—Philadelphia | Nat. | 142 | 477 | 53 | 101 | 3 | 27 | .212 |
| 1917—Philadelphia | Nat. | 127 | 478 | 56 | 116 | 4 | 38 | .243 |
| 1918—Philadelphia | Nat. | 125 | 499 | 69 | 132 | 0 | 18 | .265 |
| 1919—Philadelphia | Nat. | 92 | 335 | 45 | 91 | 0 | 29 | .272 |
| 1920—Phila.-N.Y. | Nat. | 150 | 613 | 102 | 183 | 0 | 36 | .299 |
| 1921—New York | Nat. | 153 | 606 | 121 | 193 | 6 | 67 | .318 |
| 1922—New York | Nat. | ●156 | 651 | 117 | 209 | 4 | 60 | .321 |
| 1923—New York | Nat. | 107 | 444 | 80 | 135 | 1 | 31 | .304 |
| 1924—Boston | Nat. | 79 | 319 | 49 | 89 | 2 | 21 | .279 |
| 1925—Boston | Nat. | 128 | 479 | 75 | 153 | 2 | 49 | .319 |
| 1926—Boston | Nat. | 127 | 453 | 70 | 141 | 1 | 44 | .311 |
| 1927—Boston | Nat. | 111 | 375 | 44 | 91 | 1 | 31 | .243 |
| 1928—Brooklyn | Nat. | 149 | 515 | 47 | 127 | 0 | 51 | .247 |
| 1929—Brooklyn | Nat. | 104 | 358 | 35 | 99 | 1 | 44 | .277 |
| 1930—New York | Nat. | 10 | 17 | 0 | 1 | 0 | 0 | .059 |
| 1936—Sioux City | West. | 1 | 4 | 1 | 1 | 0 | 0 | .250 |
| Major League Totals | | 1913 | 7182 | 1048 | 2004 | 32 | 579 | .279 |

### WORLD SERIES RECORD

| Year Club | League | G. | AB. | R. | H. | HR. | RBI. | B.A. |
|---|---|---|---|---|---|---|---|---|
| 1915—Philadelphia | Nat. | 5 | 17 | 2 | 5 | 0 | 1 | .294 |
| 1921—New York | Nat. | 8 | 33 | 3 | 5 | 0 | 3 | .152 |
| 1922—New York | Nat. | 5 | 19 | 4 | 4 | 0 | 2 | .211 |
| 1923—New York | Nat. | 6 | 24 | 1 | 2 | 0 | 1 | .083 |
| World Series Totals | | 24 | 93 | 10 | 16 | 0 | 7 | .172 |

## ERNEST BANKS

| Year Club | League | G. | AB. | R. | H. | HR. | RBI. | B.A. |
|---|---|---|---|---|---|---|---|---|
| 1953—Chicago | Nat. | 10 | 35 | 3 | 11 | 2 | 6 | .314 |
| 1954—Chicago | Nat. | ●154 | 593 | 70 | 163 | 19 | 79 | .275 |
| 1955—Chicago | Nat. | ●154 | 596 | 98 | 176 | 44 | 117 | .295 |
| 1956—Chicago | Nat. | 139 | 538 | 82 | 160 | 28 | 85 | .297 |
| 1957—Chicago | Nat. | ●156 | 594 | 113 | 169 | 43 | 102 | .285 |
| 1958—Chicago | Nat. | ★154 | ★617 | 119 | 193 | ★47 | ★129 | .313 |
| 1959—Chicago | Nat. | ●155 | 589 | 97 | 179 | 45 | ★143 | .304 |
| 1960—Chicago | Nat. | ★156 | 597 | 94 | 162 | ★41 | 117 | .271 |
| 1961—Chicago | Nat. | 138 | 511 | 75 | 142 | 29 | 80 | .278 |
| 1962—Chicago | Nat. | 154 | 610 | 87 | 164 | 37 | 104 | .269 |
| 1963—Chicago | Nat. | 130 | 432 | 41 | 98 | 18 | 64 | .227 |
| 1964—Chicago | Nat. | 157 | 591 | 67 | 156 | 23 | 95 | .264 |
| 1965—Chicago | Nat. | 163 | 612 | 79 | 162 | 28 | 106 | .265 |
| 1966—Chicago | Nat. | 141 | 511 | 52 | 139 | 15 | 75 | .272 |
| 1967—Chicago | Nat. | 151 | 573 | 68 | 158 | 23 | 95 | .276 |
| 1968—Chicago | Nat. | 150 | 552 | 71 | 136 | 32 | 83 | .246 |
| 1969—Chicago | Nat. | 155 | 565 | 60 | 143 | 23 | 106 | .253 |
| 1970—Chicago | Nat. | 72 | 222 | 25 | 56 | 12 | 44 | .252 |
| 1971—Chicago | Nat. | 39 | 83 | 4 | 16 | 3 | 6 | .193 |
| Major League Totals | | 2528 | 9421 | 1305 | 2583 | 512 | 1636 | .274 |

## JACOB PETER (JAKE) BECKLEY

| Year Club | League | G. | AB. | R. | H. | HR. | SB. | B.A. |
|---|---|---|---|---|---|---|---|---|
| 1886—Leavenworth | West. | .... | 305 | 65 | 104 | .... | .... | .341 |
| 1887—Leav.-Lincoln | West. | .... | 526 | .... | 211 | .... | .... | .401 |
| 1888—St. Louis | W. A. | 34 | 145 | 23 | 41 | .... | 17 | .283 |
| 1888—Pittsburgh | Nat. | 71 | 283 | 35 | 97 | 1 | 20 | .343 |
| 1889—Pittsburgh | Nat. | 123 | 522 | 92 | 157 | 9 | 11 | .301 |
| 1890—Pittsburgh | Play | 121 | 517 | 109 | 168 | 9 | 19 | .325 |
| 1891—Pittsburgh | Nat. | 129 | 535 | 91 | 156 | 4 | 17 | .292 |
| 1892—Pittsburgh | Nat. | 152 | 603 | 102 | 151 | 10 | 40 | .250 |
| 1893—Pittsburgh | Nat. | 131 | 497 | 108 | 161 | 5 | 24 | .324 |
| 1894—Pittsburgh | Nat. | 132 | 534 | 122 | 184 | 7 | 20 | .345 |
| 1895—Pittsburgh | Nat. | 131 | 536 | 105 | 174 | 5 | 19 | .325 |
| 1896—Pitts.-N.Y. | Nat. | 99 | 395 | 79 | 106 | 9 | 19 | .268 |
| 1897—N.Y.-Cinn. | Nat. | 114 | 437 | 84 | 142 | 8 | 22 | .325 |
| 1898—Cincinnati | Nat. | 116 | 458 | 86 | 137 | 3 | 7 | .299 |
| 1899—Cincinnati | Nat. | 135 | 519 | 87 | 173 | 3 | 18 | .333 |
| 1900—Cincinnati | Nat. | 138 | 559 | 99 | 192 | 2 | 22 | .343 |
| 1901—Cincinnati | Nat. | 140 | 590 | 80 | 177 | 3 | 6 | .300 |
| 1902—Cincinnati | Nat. | 129 | 532 | 82 | 176 | 5 | 16 | .331 |
| 1903—Cincinnati | Nat. | 119 | 459 | 85 | 150 | 2 | 23 | .327 |
| 1904—St. Louis | Nat. | 142 | 551 | 72 | 179 | 1 | 17 | .325 |
| 1905—St. Louis | Nat. | 134 | 514 | 48 | 147 | 1 | 12 | .286 |
| 1906—St. Louis | Nat. | 85 | 320 | 29 | 79 | 0 | 3 | .247 |
| 1907—St. Louis | Nat. | 32 | 115 | 6 | 24 | 0 | 0 | .209 |
| 1907—Kansas City | A. A. | 100 | 378 | 65 | 138 | 1 | 12 | .365 |
| 1908—Kansas City | A. A. | 136 | 496 | 66 | 134 | 1 | 13 | .270 |
| 1909—Kansas City | A. A. | 113 | 428 | 41 | 120 | 1 | 12 | .280 |
| 1910—Bartlesville | W. A. | 70 | 249 | 21 | 64 | 0 | 13 | .257 |
| 1910—Topeka | West. | 63 | 233 | 19 | 60 | 1 | 1 | .258 |
| 1911—Hannibal | C. A. | 98 | 355 | 50 | 100 | 0 | 22 | .282 |
| National League Totals | | 2252 | 8959 | 1492 | 2762 | 78 | 316 | .308 |
| Players' League Totals | | 121 | 517 | 109 | 168 | 9 | 19 | .325 |
| Major League Totals | | 2373 | 9476 | 1601 | 2930 | 87 | 335 | .309 |

## CHARLES ALBERT (CHIEF) BENDER

| Year | Club | League | G. | IP. | W. | L. | Pct. | ERA. |
|---|---|---|---|---|---|---|---|---|
| 1903—Philadelphia | Amer. | 36 | 270 | 17 | 15 | .531 | ...... |
| 1904—Philadelphia | Amer. | 29 | 205 | 10 | 11 | .476 | ...... |
| 1905—Philadelphia | Amer. | 35 | 230 | 18 | 11 | .621 | ...... |
| 1906—Philadelphia | Amer. | 36 | 240 | 15 | 10 | .600 | ...... |
| 1907—Philadelphia | Amer. | 33 | 222 | 16 | 8 | .667 | ...... |
| 1908—Philadelphia | Amer. | 18 | 139 | 8 | 9 | .471 | ...... |
| 1909—Philadephia | Amer. | 34 | 250 | 18 | 8 | .692 | ...... |
| 1910—Philadelphia | Amer. | 30 | 250 | 23 | 5 | ★.821 | ...... |
| 1911—Philadelphia | Amer. | 31 | 216 | 17 | 5 | ★.773 | ...... |
| 1912—Philadelphia | Amer. | 27 | 171 | 13 | 8 | .619 | ...... |
| 1913—Philadelphia | Amer. | 48 | 238 | 21 | 10 | .667 | 2.19 |
| 1914—Philadelphia | Amer. | 28 | 179 | 17 | 3 | ★.850 | 2.26 |
| 1915—Baltimore | Federal | 26 | 179 | 4 | 16 | .200 | 4.27 |
| 1916—Philadelphia | Nat. | 27 | 123 | 7 | 7 | .500 | 3.73 |
| 1917—Philadelphia | Nat. | 20 | 113 | 8 | 2 | .800 | 1.67 |
| 1918— | (Voluntarily retired—worked in shipyards) | | | | | | |
| 1919—Richmond | Va. | 34 | ★280 | ★29 | 2 | ★.935 | ...... |
| 1920—New Haven | East. | ★47 | ★324 | ★25 | 12 | .676 | 1.94 |
| 1921—New Haven | East. | 36 | 196 | 13 | 7 | .650 | 1.93 |
| 1922—Reading | Inter. | 30 | 183 | 8 | 13 | .381 | 2.42 |
| 1923—Baltimore | Inter. | 18 | 93 | 6 | 3 | .667 | 5.03 |
| 1924—New Haven | East. | 12 | 91 | 6 | 4 | .600 | 3.07 |
| 1925—Chicago | Amer. | 1 | 1 | 0 | 0 | .000 | 18.00 |
| 1927—Johnstown | Mid. Atl. | 18 | 108 | 7 | 3 | .700 | 1.33 |
| American League Totals | | 386 | 2611 | 193 | 103 | .652 | ...... |
| National League Totals | | 47 | 236 | 15 | 9 | .625 | 2.75 |
| Major League Totals | | 433 | 2847 | 208 | 112 | .650 | ...... |

### WORLD SERIES RECORD

| Year | Club | League | G. | IP. | W. | L. | Pct. | ERA. |
|---|---|---|---|---|---|---|---|---|
| 1905—Philadelphia | Amer. | 2 | 17 | 1 | 1 | .500 | 1.06 |
| 1910—Philadelphia | Amer. | 2 | 18⅔ | 1 | 1 | .500 | 1.93 |
| 1911—Philadelphia | Amer. | 3 | 26 | 2 | 1 | .667 | 1.04 |
| 1913—Philadelphia | Amer. | 2 | 18 | 2 | 0 | 1.000 | 4.00 |
| 1914—Philadelphia | Amer. | 1 | 5⅓ | 0 | 1 | .000 | 10.13 |
| World Series Totals | | 10 | 85 | 6 | 4 | .600 | 2.44 |

## LAWRENCE PETER (YOGI) BERRA

| Year | Club | League | G. | AB. | R. | H. | HR. | RBI. | B.A. |
|---|---|---|---|---|---|---|---|---|---|
| 1943—Norfolk | Pied. | 111 | 376 | 52 | 95 | 7 | 56 | .253 |
| 1944-45—Kansas City | A. A. | (In Military Service) | | | | | | |
| 1946—Newark | Int. | 77 | 277 | 41 | 87 | 15 | 59 | .314 |
| 1946—New York | Amer. | 7 | 22 | 3 | 8 | 2 | 4 | .364 |
| 1947—New York | Amer. | 83 | 293 | 41 | 82 | 11 | 54 | .280 |
| 1948—New York | Amer. | 125 | 469 | 70 | 143 | 14 | 98 | .305 |
| 1949—New York | Amer. | 116 | 415 | 59 | 115 | 20 | 91 | .277 |
| 1950—New York | Amer. | 151 | 597 | 116 | 192 | 28 | 124 | .322 |
| 1951—New York | Amer. | 141 | 547 | 92 | 161 | 27 | 88 | .294 |
| 1952—New York | Amer. | 142 | 534 | 97 | 146 | 30 | 98 | .273 |
| 1953—New York | Amer. | 137 | 503 | 80 | 149 | 27 | 108 | .296 |
| 1954—New York | Amer. | 151 | 584 | 88 | 179 | 22 | 125 | .307 |
| 1955—New York | Amer. | 147 | 541 | 84 | 147 | 27 | 108 | .272 |
| 1956—New York | Amer. | 140 | 521 | 93 | 155 | 30 | 105 | .298 |
| 1957—New York | Amer. | 134 | 482 | 74 | 121 | 24 | 82 | .251 |
| 1958—New York | Amer. | 122 | 433 | 60 | 115 | 22 | 90 | .266 |
| 1959—New York | Amer. | 131 | 472 | 64 | 134 | 19 | 69 | .284 |
| 1960—New York | Amer. | 120 | 359 | 46 | 99 | 15 | 62 | .276 |
| 1961—New York | Amer. | 119 | 395 | 62 | 107 | 22 | 61 | .271 |
| 1962—New York | Amer. | 86 | 232 | 25 | 52 | 10 | 35 | .224 |
| 1963—New York | Amer. | 64 | 147 | 20 | 43 | 8 | 28 | .293 |
| 1964—New York | Amer. | (Did not play—served as manager.) | | | | | | |
| 1965—New York | Nat. | 4 | 9 | 1 | 2 | 0 | 0 | .222 |
| American League Totals | | 2116 | 7546 | 1174 | 2148 | 358 | 1430 | .285 |
| National League Totals | | 4 | 9 | 1 | 2 | 0 | 0 | .222 |
| Major League Totals | | 2120 | 7555 | 1175 | 2150 | 358 | 1430 | .285 |

### WORLD SERIES RECORD

| Year | Club | League | G. | AB. | R. | H. | HR. | RBI. | B.A. |
|---|---|---|---|---|---|---|---|---|---|
| 1947—New York | Amer. | 6 | 19 | 2 | 3 | 1 | 2 | .158 |
| 1949—New York | Amer. | 4 | 16 | 2 | 1 | 0 | 1 | .063 |
| 1950—New York | Amer. | 4 | 15 | 2 | 3 | 1 | 2 | .200 |
| 1951—New York | Amer. | 6 | 23 | 4 | 6 | 0 | 0 | .261 |
| 1952—New York | Amer. | 7 | 28 | 2 | 6 | 2 | 3 | .214 |
| 1953—New York | Amer. | 6 | 21 | 3 | 9 | 1 | 4 | .429 |
| 1955—New York | Amer. | 7 | 24 | 5 | 10 | 1 | 2 | .417 |
| 1956—New York | Amer. | 7 | 25 | 5 | 9 | 3 | 10 | .360 |
| 1957—New York | Amer. | 7 | 25 | 5 | 8 | 1 | 2 | .320 |
| 1958—New York | Amer. | 7 | 27 | 3 | 6 | 0 | 2 | .222 |
| 1960—New York | Amer. | 7 | 22 | 6 | 7 | 1 | 8 | .318 |
| 1961—New York | Amer. | 4 | 11 | 2 | 3 | 1 | 3 | .273 |
| 1962—New York | Amer. | 2 | 2 | 0 | 0 | 0 | 0 | .000 |
| 1963—New York | Amer. | 1 | 1 | 0 | 0 | 0 | 0 | .000 |
| World Series Totals | | 75 | 259 | 41 | 71 | 12 | 39 | .274 |

## JAMES LEROY (SUNNY JIM) BOTTOMLEY

| Year | Club | League | G. | AB. | R. | H. | HR. | RBI. | B.A. |
|---|---|---|---|---|---|---|---|---|---|
| 1920—Sioux City | West. | 6 | 14 | 0 | 1 | 0 | 0 | .071 |
| 1920—Mitchell | S. Dak. | ●97 | 378 | 69 | 118 | 7 | ...... | .312 |
| 1921—Houston | Tex. | 130 | 459 | 50 | 104 | 4 | 62 | .227 |
| 1922—Syracuse | Int. | 119 | 460 | 78 | 160 | 14 | 94 | .348 |
| 1922—St. Louis | Nat. | 37 | 151 | 29 | 49 | 5 | 35 | .325 |
| 1923—St. Louis | Nat. | 134 | 523 | 79 | 194 | 8 | 94 | .371 |
| 1924—St. Louis | Nat. | 137 | 528 | 87 | 167 | 14 | 111 | .316 |
| 1925—St. Louis | Nat. | ●153 | 619 | 92 | ★227 | 21 | 128 | .367 |
| 1926—St. Louis | Nat. | 154 | 603 | 98 | 180 | 19 | ★120 | .299 |
| 1927—St. Louis | Nat. | 152 | 574 | 95 | 174 | 19 | 124 | .303 |
| 1928—St. Louis | Nat. | 149 | 576 | 123 | 187 | ●31 | ★136 | .325 |
| 1929—St. Louis | Nat. | 146 | 560 | 108 | 176 | 29 | 137 | .314 |
| 1930—St. Louis | Nat. | 131 | 487 | 92 | 148 | 15 | 97 | .304 |
| 1931—St. Louis | Nat. | 108 | 382 | 73 | 133 | 9 | 75 | .348 |
| 1932—St. Louis | Nat. | 91 | 311 | 45 | 92 | 11 | 48 | .296 |
| 1933—Cincinnati | Nat. | 145 | 549 | 57 | 137 | 13 | 83 | .250 |
| 1934—Cincinnati | Nat. | 142 | 556 | 72 | 158 | 11 | 78 | .284 |
| 1935—Cincinnati | Nat. | 107 | 399 | 44 | 103 | 1 | 49 | .258 |
| 1936—St. Louis | Amer. | 140 | 544 | 72 | 162 | 12 | 95 | .298 |
| 1937—St. Louis | Amer. | 65 | 109 | 11 | 26 | 1 | 12 | .239 |
| 1938—Syracuse | Int. | 7 | 14 | 0 | 1 | 0 | 0 | .071 |
| American League Totals | | 205 | 653 | 83 | 188 | 13 | 107 | .288 |
| National League Totals | | 1786 | 6818 | 1094 | 2125 | 206 | 1315 | .312 |
| Major League Totals | | 1991 | 7471 | 1177 | 2313 | 219 | 1422 | .310 |

### WORLD SERIES RECORD

| Year | Club | League | G. | AB. | R. | H. | HR. | RBI. | B.A. |
|---|---|---|---|---|---|---|---|---|---|
| 1926—St. Louis | National | 7 | 29 | 4 | 10 | 0 | 5 | .345 |
| 1928—St. Louis | National | 4 | 14 | 1 | 3 | 1 | 3 | .214 |
| 1930—St. Louis | National | 6 | 22 | 1 | 1 | 0 | 0 | .045 |
| 1931—St. Louis | National | 7 | 25 | 2 | 4 | 0 | 2 | .160 |
| World Series Totals | | 24 | 90 | 8 | 18 | 1 | 10 | .200 |

## LOUIS BOUDREAU

| Year | Club | League | G. | AB. | R. | H. | HR. | RBI. | B.A. |
|---|---|---|---|---|---|---|---|---|---|
| 1938—Cedar Rapids | I.I.I. | 60 | 231 | 56 | 67 | 3 | 29 | .290 |
| 1938—Cleveland | Amer. | 1 | 1 | 0 | 0 | 0 | 0 | .000 |
| 1939—Buffalo | Int. | 115 | 481 | 88 | 159 | 17 | 57 | .331 |
| 1939—Cleveland | Amer. | 53 | 225 | 42 | 58 | 0 | 19 | .258 |
| 1940—Cleveland | Amer. | 155 | 627 | 97 | 185 | 9 | 101 | .295 |
| 1941—Cleveland | Amer. | 148 | 579 | 95 | 149 | 10 | 56 | .257 |
| 1942—Cleveland | Amer. | 147 | 506 | 57 | 143 | 2 | 58 | .283 |
| 1943—Cleveland | Amer. | 152 | 539 | 69 | 154 | 3 | 67 | .286 |
| 1944—Cleveland | Amer. | 150 | 584 | 91 | 191 | 3 | 67 | ★.327 |
| 1945—Cleveland | Amer. | 97 | 345 | 50 | 106 | 3 | 48 | .307 |
| 1946—Cleveland | Amer. | 140 | 515 | 51 | 151 | 6 | 62 | .293 |
| 1947—Cleveland | Amer. | 150 | 538 | 79 | 165 | 4 | 67 | .307 |
| 1948—Cleveland | Amer. | 152 | 560 | 116 | 199 | 18 | 106 | .355 |
| 1949—Cleveland | Amer. | 134 | 475 | 53 | 135 | 4 | 60 | .284 |
| 1950—Cleveland | Amer. | 81 | 260 | 23 | 70 | 1 | 29 | .269 |
| 1951—Boston | Amer. | 82 | 273 | 37 | 73 | 5 | 47 | .267 |
| 1952—Boston | Amer. | 4 | 2 | 1 | 0 | 0 | 2 | .000 |
| Major League Totals | | 1646 | 6029 | 861 | 1779 | 68 | 789 | .295 |

### WORLD SERIES RECORD

| Year | Club | League | G. | AB. | R. | H. | HR. | RBI. | B.A. |
|---|---|---|---|---|---|---|---|---|---|
| 1948—Cleveland | Amer. | 6 | 22 | 1 | 6 | 0 | 0 | .273 |

### RECORD AS MANAGER

| Year | Club | League | Position | W. | L. |
|---|---|---|---|---|---|
| 1942—Cleveland | American | Fourth | 75 | 79 |
| 1943—Cleveland | American | Third | 82 | 71 |
| 1944—Cleveland | American | Fifth | 72 | 82 |
| 1945—Cleveland | American | Fifth | 73 | 72 |
| 1946—Cleveland | American | Sixth | 68 | 86 |
| 1947—Cleveland | American | Fourth | 80 | 74 |
| 1948—Cleveland | American | First | 97 | 58 |
| 1949—Cleveland | American | Third | 89 | 65 |
| 1950—Cleveland | American | Fourth | 92 | 62 |
| 1952—Boston | American | Sixth | 76 | 78 |
| 1953—Boston | American | Fourth | 84 | 69 |
| 1954—Boston | American | Fourth | 69 | 85 |
| 1955—Kansas City | American | Sixth | 63 | 91 |
| 1956—Kansas City | American | Eighth | 52 | 102 |
| 1957—Kansas City | American | Eighth | 36 | 67 |
| 1960—Chicago | National | Seventh | 54 | 83 |
| Major League Totals | | | 1162 | 1224 |

### WORLD SERIES RECORD

| Year | Club | League | W. | L. |
|---|---|---|---|---|
| 1948—Cleveland | American | 4 | 2 |

## ROGER PHILLIP (DUKE) BRESNAHAN

| Year | Club | League | G. | AB. | R. | H. | HR. | SB. | B.A. |
|---|---|---|---|---|---|---|---|---|---|
| 1897—Washington | Nat. | 7 | 18 | 2 | 6 | 0 | 0 | .333 |
| 1898—Toledo | Int.-State | 4 | 12 | 0 | 5 | 0 | 0 | .417 |
| 1899—Minneapolis | West. | 3 | 1 | 0 | 1 | 0 | 0 | 1.000 |

| Year | Club | League | G. | AB. | R. | H. | HR. | SB. | B.A. |
|---|---|---|---|---|---|---|---|---|---|
| 1900—Chicago | Nat. | 1 | 2 | 0 | 0 | 0 | 0 | .000 | |
| 1901—Baltimore | Amer. | 86 | 293 | 40 | 77 | 1 | 10 | .263 | |
| 1902—Baltimore | Amer. | 66 | 234 | 31 | 64 | 4 | 11 | .274 | |
| 1902—New York | Nat. | 50 | 178 | 16 | 52 | 1 | 6 | .292 | |
| 1903—New York | Nat. | 111 | 406 | 87 | 142 | 4 | 34 | .350 | |
| 1904—New York | Nat. | 107 | 402 | 81 | 114 | 5 | 13 | .284 | |
| 1905—New York | Nat. | 95 | 331 | 58 | 100 | 0 | 11 | .302 | |
| 1906—New York | Nat. | 124 | 405 | 69 | 114 | 0 | 25 | .281 | |
| 1907—New York | Nat. | 104 | 328 | 57 | 83 | 4 | 15 | .253 | |
| 1908—New York | Nat. | 139 | 449 | 70 | 127 | 1 | 14 | .283 | |
| 1909—St. Louis | Nat. | 69 | 234 | 27 | 57 | 0 | 11 | .244 | |
| 1910—St. Louis | Nat. | 78 | 234 | 35 | 65 | 0 | 13 | .278 | |
| 1911—St. Louis | Nat. | 78 | 227 | 22 | 63 | 3 | 4 | .278 | |
| 1912—St. Louis | Nat. | 48 | 108 | 8 | 36 | 1 | 4 | .333 | |
| 1913—Chicago | Nat. | 69 | 162 | 20 | 37 | 1 | 7 | .228 | |
| 1914—Chicago | Nat. | 101 | 248 | 42 | 69 | 0 | 14 | .278 | |
| 1915—Chicago | Nat. | 77 | 221 | 19 | 45 | 1 | 19 | .204 | |
| 1916—Toledo | A. A. | 44 | 120 | 19 | 29 | 2 | 4 | .242 | |
| 1917—Toledo | A. A. | 40 | 80 | 10 | 22 | 0 | 1 | .275 | |
| 1918—Toledo | A. A. | 19 | 52 | 4 | 12 | 1 | 0 | .231 | |
| National League Totals | | 1258 | 3953 | 613 | 1110 | 21 | 190 | .281 | |
| American League Totals | | 152 | 527 | 71 | 141 | 5 | 21 | .268 | |
| Major League Totals | | 1410 | 4480 | 684 | 1251 | 26 | 211 | .279 | |

### PITCHING RECORD

| Year | Club | League | G. | W. | L. | Pct. |
|---|---|---|---|---|---|---|
| 1897—Washington | National | 7 | 4 | 0 | 1.000 | |
| 1898—Toledo | Inter-State | 4 | 2 | 2 | .500 | |
| 1899—Minneapolis | Western | 3 | 0 | 2 | .000 | |
| 1901—Baltimore | American | 1 | 0 | 0 | .000 | |
| 1910—St. Louis | National | 1 | 0 | 0 | .000 | |
| American League Totals | | 1 | 0 | 0 | .000 | |
| National League Totals | | 8 | 4 | 0 | 1.000 | |
| Major League Totals | | 9 | 4 | 0 | 1.000 | |

### WORLD SERIES RECORD

| Year | Club | League | G. | AB. | R. | H. | HR. | SB. | B.A. |
|---|---|---|---|---|---|---|---|---|---|
| 1905—New York | Nat. | 5 | 16 | 3 | 5 | 0 | 1 | .313 | |

## DENNIS (DAN) BROUTHERS

| Year | Club | League | G. | AB. | R. | H. | HR. | SB. | B.A. |
|---|---|---|---|---|---|---|---|---|---|
| 1879—Troy | Nat. | 39 | 168 | 17 | 46 | 4 | ..... | .274 | |
| 1880—Troy | Nat. | 3 | 13 | 0 | 2 | 0 | ..... | .154 | |
| 1881—Buffalo | Nat. | 65 | 270 | 60 | 86 | *8 | ..... | .319 | |
| 1882—Buffalo | Nat. | 84 | 351 | 71 | *129 | 6 | ..... | *.368 | |
| 1883—Buffalo | Nat. | 97 | 420 | 83 | *156 | 2 | ..... | *.371 | |
| 1884—Buffalo | Nat. | 90 | 381 | 80 | 124 | 14 | ..... | .325 | |
| 1885—Buffalo | Nat. | 98 | 407 | 87 | 146 | 7 | ..... | .359 | |
| 1886—Detroit | Nat. | 121 | 489 | 139 | 181 | 10 | 21 | .370 | |
| 1887—Detroit | Nat. | 122 | 570 | *153 | *239 | 13 | 34 | .419 | |
| 1888—Detroit | Nat. | 129 | 522 | *118 | 160 | 10 | 34 | .306 | |
| 1889—Boston | Nat. | 126 | 485 | 105 | 181 | 6 | 22 | *.373 | |
| 1890—Boston | Players | 123 | 464 | 116 | 160 | 1 | 26 | .345 | |
| 1891—Boston | A. A. | 123 | 458 | 111 | *160 | 5 | 33 | .349 | |
| 1892—Brooklyn | Nat. | 152 | 588 | 121 | *197 | 3 | 36 | ●.335 | |
| 1893—Brooklyn | Nat. | 75 | 267 | 53 | 93 | 2 | 8 | .348 | |
| 1894—Baltimore | Nat. | 123 | 528 | 137 | 182 | 9 | 40 | .345 | |
| 1895—Balt.-L'ville. | Nat. | 29 | 121 | 15 | 35 | 2 | 1 | .289 | |
| 1896—Philadelphia | Nat. | 57 | 218 | 41 | 72 | 1 | 8 | .330 | |
| 1896—Springfield | East. | 51 | 205 | 42 | 82 | .... | 9 | .400 | |
| 1897—Springfield | East. | 126 | 501 | 112 | *208 | 14 | 21 | *.415 | |
| 1898—Spring.-Toronto | East. | 50 | 189 | 42 | 63 | 4 | 2 | .333 | |
| 1899—Spring.-Roch. | East. | 45 | 170 | 27 | 40 | 3 | 2 | .235 | |
| 1904—New York | Nat. | 2 | 5 | 0 | 0 | 0 | 0 | .000 | |
| 1904—Poughkeepsie | Hudson R. | ..... | 424 | ..... | 158 | .... | ... | .373 | |
| 1905—Poughkeepsie | Hudson R. | ..... | 308 | ..... | 91 | .... | ... | .295 | |
| American Association Totals | | 123 | 458 | 111 | 160 | 5 | 33 | .349 | |
| National League Totals | | 1412 | 5803 | 1280 | 2029 | 97 | 204 | .350 | |
| Players League Totals | | 123 | 464 | 116 | 160 | 1 | 26 | .345 | |
| Major League Totals | | 1658 | 6725 | 1507 | 2349 | 103 | 263 | .349 | |

## MORDECAI PETER CENTENNIAL (THREE FINGER) BROWN

| Year | Club | League | G. | IP. | W. | L. | Pct. | ERA. |
|---|---|---|---|---|---|---|---|---|
| 1901—Terre Haute | I.I.I. | 31 | .... | *23 | 8 | *.742 | ...... | |
| 1902—Omaha | Western | ●43 | 352 | 27 | 15 | .643 | ...... | |
| 1903—St. Louis | National | 26 | 201 | 9 | 13 | .409 | ...... | |
| 1904—Chicago | National | 26 | 212 | 15 | 10 | .600 | ...... | |
| 1905—Chicago | National | 30 | 249 | 18 | 12 | .600 | ...... | |
| 1906—Chicago | National | 36 | 278 | 26 | 6 | .813 | ...... | |
| 1907—Chicago | National | 34 | 233 | 20 | 6 | .769 | ...... | |
| 1908—Chicago | National | 44 | 312 | 29 | 9 | .763 | ...... | |
| 1909—Chicago | National | *50 | *343 | *27 | 9 | .750 | ...... | |
| 1910—Chicago | National | 46 | 295 | 25 | 14 | .641 | ...... | |
| 1911—Chicago | National | *53 | 270 | 21 | 11 | .656 | ...... | |
| 1912—Chicago | National | 15 | 89 | 5 | 6 | .455 | 2.63 | |
| 1913—Cincinnati | National | 39 | 167 | 11 | 12 | .478 | 3.02 | |
| 1914—St.L.-Brooklyn | Federal | 35 | 233 | 14 | 11 | .560 | 3.09 | |

| Year | Club | League | G. | IP. | W. | L. | Pct. | ERA. |
|---|---|---|---|---|---|---|---|---|
| 1915—Chicago | Federal | 35 | 238 | 17 | 8 | .680 | 2.12 | |
| 1916—Chicago | National | 12 | 48 | 2 | 3 | .400 | 3.94 | |
| 1917—Columbus | Am. Assoc. | 30 | 185 | 10 | 12 | .455 | 2.77 | |
| 1918—Columbus | Am. Assoc. | 12 | 50 | 3 | 2 | .600 | 2.70 | |
| 1919—Terre Haute | I.I.I. | 33 | 175 | 16 | 6 | .727 | 2.88 | |
| 1919—Indianapolis | Am. Assoc. | 6 | 34 | 0 | 3 | .000 | ...... | |
| 1920—Terre Haute | I.I.I. | 13 | 80 | 4 | 6 | .400 | 2.59 | |
| Federal League Totals | | 70 | 471 | 31 | 19 | .620 | 2.60 | |
| National League Totals | | 411 | 2697 | 208 | 111 | .652 | ...... | |
| Major League Totals | | 411 | 2697 | 208 | 111 | .652 | ...... | |

### WORLD SERIES RECORD

| Year | Club | League | G. | IP. | W. | L. | Pct. | ERA. |
|---|---|---|---|---|---|---|---|---|
| 1906—Chicago | National | 3 | 19⅔ | 1 | 2 | .333 | 3.20 | |
| 1907—Chicago | National | 1 | 9 | 1 | 0 | 1.000 | 0.00 | |
| 1908—Chicago | National | 2 | 11 | 2 | 0 | 1.000 | 0.00 | |
| 1910—Chicago | National | 3 | 18 | 1 | 2 | .333 | 5.50 | |
| World Series Totals | | 9 | 57⅔ | 5 | 4 | .556 | 2.81 | |

## JESSE CAIL (CRAB) BURKETT

| Year | Club | League | G. | AB. | R. | H. | HR. | RBI. | B.A. |
|---|---|---|---|---|---|---|---|---|---|
| 1888—Scranton | Cent. | 35 | 115 | 25 | 26 | 0 | ..... | .226 | |
| 1889—Worcester | Atl. A. | 49 | 175 | 31 | 49 | 3 | 16 | .280 | |
| 1890—New York | Nat. | 101 | 401 | 67 | 124 | 4 | 14 | .309 | |
| 1891—Lincoln | W. A. | 93 | 395 | 78 | 138 | 3 | ..... | .349 | |
| 1891—Cleveland | Nat. | 40 | 166 | 30 | 45 | 0 | 2 | .271 | |
| 1892—Cleveland | Nat. | 145 | 605 | 117 | 168 | 3 | 36 | .278 | |
| 1893—Cleveland | Nat. | 124 | 480 | 144 | 179 | 6 | 39 | .373 | |
| 1894—Cleveland | Nat. | 124 | 518 | 134 | 185 | 8 | 32 | .357 | |
| 1895—Cleveland | Nat. | 132 | 555 | 149 | *235 | 5 | 47 | *.423 | |
| 1896—Cleveland | Nat. | ●133 | *585 | *159 | *240 | 6 | 32 | *.410 | |
| 1897—Cleveland | Nat. | 128 | 519 | 128 | 199 | 2 | 27 | .383 | |
| 1898—Cleveland | Nat. | 148 | 624 | 115 | *215 | 0 | 20 | .345 | |
| 1899—St. Louis | Nat. | 138 | 567 | 115 | 228 | 7 | 22 | .402 | |
| 1900—St. Louis | Nat | ●142 | 560 | 88 | 202 | 7 | 31 | .361 | |
| 1901—St. Louis | Nat. | ●142 | *597 | *139 | *228 | 10 | 27 | *.382 | |
| 1902—St. Louis | Amer. | 137 | 549 | 99 | 168 | 5 | 22 | .306 | |
| 1903—St. Louis | Amer. | 133 | 514 | 74 | 152 | 3 | 16 | .296 | |
| 1904—St. Louis | Amer. | 147 | 576 | 72 | 157 | 2 | 12 | .273 | |
| 1905—Boston | Amer. | 149 | 573 | 78 | 147 | 4 | 13 | .257 | |
| 1906—Worcester | N. Eng. | 98 | 363 | 59 | 125 | 1 | ..... | *.344 | |
| 1907—Worcester | N. Eng. | 52 | 195 | 23 | 66 | 1 | 9 | .338 | |
| 1908—Worcester | N. Eng. | 97 | 375 | 49 | 110 | 1 | 8 | .293 | |
| 1909—Worcester | N. Eng. | 75 | 218 | 30 | 71 | 1 | 6 | .326 | |
| 1910—Worcester | N. Eng. | 38 | 72 | 3 | 24 | 0 | 1 | .333 | |
| 1911—Worcester | N. Eng. | 76 | 243 | 42 | 83 | 1 | 1 | .342 | |
| 1912—Worcester | N. Eng. | 28 | 60 | 6 | 21 | 0 | 1 | .350 | |
| 1913—Worcester | N. Eng. | 19 | 42 | 4 | 10 | 0 | 0 | .238 | |
| 1916—Low.-Law.-Hart. | East. | 24 | 38 | 5 | 8 | .... | 0 | .211 | |
| American League Totals | | 566 | 2212 | 323 | 624 | 14 | 63 | .282 | |
| National League Totals | | 1497 | 6177 | 1385 | 2248 | 58 | 329 | .364 | |
| Major League Totals | | 2063 | 8389 | 1708 | 2872 | 72 | 392 | .342 | |

### PITCHING RECORD

| Year | Club | League | G. | IP. | W. | L. | Pct. |
|---|---|---|---|---|---|---|---|
| 1890—New York | National | 21 | 6 | 116 | 1 | 11 | |
| 1894—Cleveland | National | 1 | 0 | 4 | 0 | 0 | |
| 1902—St. Louis | American | 1 | 0 | 1 | 0 | 1 | |
| National League Totals | | 22 | 6 | 120 | 1 | 11 | |
| American League Totals | | 1 | 0 | 1 | 0 | 1 | |
| Major League Totals | | 23 | 6 | 121 | 1 | 12 | |

## ROY CAMPANELLA

| Year | Club | League | G. | AB. | R. | H. | HR. | RBI. | B.A. |
|---|---|---|---|---|---|---|---|---|---|
| 1946—Nashua | New Eng. | 113 | 396 | 75 | 115 | 13 | 96 | .290 | |
| 1947—Montreal | Int. | 135 | 440 | 64 | 120 | 13 | 75 | .273 | |
| 1948—St. Paul | A.A. | 35 | 123 | 31 | 40 | 13 | 39 | .325 | |
| 1948—Brooklyn | Nat. | 83 | 279 | 32 | 72 | 9 | 45 | .258 | |
| 1949—Brooklyn | Nat. | 130 | 436 | 65 | 125 | 22 | 82 | .287 | |
| 1950—Brooklyn | Nat. | 126 | 437 | 70 | 123 | 31 | 89 | .281 | |
| 1951—Brooklyn | Nat. | 143 | 505 | 90 | 164 | 33 | 108 | .325 | |
| 1952—Brooklyn | Nat. | 128 | 468 | 73 | 126 | 22 | 97 | .269 | |
| 1953—Brooklyn | Nat. | 144 | 519 | 103 | 162 | 41 | *142 | .312 | |
| 1954—Brooklyn | Nat. | 111 | 397 | 43 | 82 | 19 | 51 | .207 | |
| 1955—Brooklyn | Nat. | 123 | 446 | 81 | 142 | 32 | 107 | .318 | |
| 1956—Brooklyn | Nat. | 124 | 388 | 39 | 85 | 20 | 73 | .219 | |
| 1957—Brooklyn | Nat. | 103 | 330 | 31 | 80 | 13 | 62 | .242 | |
| Major League Totals | | 1215 | 4205 | 627 | 1161 | 242 | 856 | .276 | |

### WORLD SERIES RECORD

| Year | Club | League | G. | AB. | R. | H. | HR. | RBI. | B.A. |
|---|---|---|---|---|---|---|---|---|---|
| 1949—Brooklyn | Nat. | 5 | 15 | 2 | 4 | 1 | 2 | .267 | |
| 1952—Brooklyn | Nat. | 7 | 28 | 0 | 6 | 0 | 1 | .214 | |
| 1953—Brooklyn | Nat. | 6 | 22 | 6 | 6 | 1 | 2 | .273 | |
| 1955—Brooklyn | Nat. | 7 | 27 | 4 | 7 | 2 | 4 | .259 | |
| 1956—Brooklyn | Nat. | 7 | 22 | 2 | 4 | 0 | 3 | .182 | |
| World Series Totals | | 32 | 114 | 14 | 27 | 4 | 12 | .237 | |

## MAX GEORGE (SCOOPS) CAREY

| Year | Club | League | G. | AB. | R. | H. | HR. | RBI. | B.A. |
|---|---|---|---|---|---|---|---|---|---|
| 1909—South Bend | Cent. | | 48 | 158 | 5 | 25 | 0 | ..... | .158 |
| 1910—South Bend | Cent. | | 96 | 327 | 39 | 96 | 2 | ..... | .293 |
| 1910—Pittsburgh | Nat. | | 2 | 6 | 2 | 3 | 0 | 2 | .500 |
| 1911—Pittsburgh | Nat. | | 122 | 427 | 77 | 110 | 5 | 41 | .258 |
| 1912—Pittsburgh | Nat. | | 150 | 587 | 114 | 177 | 5 | 61 | .302 |
| 1913—Pittsburgh | Nat. | | 154 | ★620 | ●99 | 172 | 5 | 53 | .277 |
| 1914—Pittsburgh | Nat. | | ●156 | ★593 | 76 | 144 | 1 | 32 | .243 |
| 1915—Pittsburgh | Nat. | | 140 | 564 | 76 | 143 | 3 | 28 | .254 |
| 1916—Pittsburgh | Nat. | | 154 | 599 | 90 | 158 | 7 | 42 | .264 |
| 1917—Pittsburgh | Nat. | | 155 | 588 | 82 | 174 | 1 | 53 | .296 |
| 1918—Pittsburgh | Nat. | | 126 | 468 | 70 | 128 | 3 | 44 | .274 |
| 1919—Pittsburgh | Nat. | | 66 | 244 | 41 | 75 | 0 | 9 | .307 |
| 1920—Pittsburgh | Nat. | | 130 | 485 | 74 | 140 | 1 | 35 | .289 |
| 1921—Pittsburgh | Nat. | | 140 | 521 | 85 | 161 | 7 | 56 | .309 |
| 1922—Pittsburgh | Nat. | | 155 | 629 | 140 | 207 | 10 | 70 | .329 |
| 1923—Pittsburgh | Nat. | | 153 | 610 | 120 | 188 | 6 | 63 | .308 |
| 1924—Pittsburgh | Nat. | | 149 | 599 | 113 | 178 | 7 | 55 | .297 |
| 1925—Pittsburgh | Nat. | | 133 | 542 | 109 | 186 | 5 | 44 | .343 |
| 1926—Pitts.-Brook. | Nat. | | 113 | 424 | 64 | 98 | 0 | 35 | .231 |
| 1927—Brooklyn | Nat. | | 144 | 538 | 70 | 143 | 1 | 54 | .266 |
| 1928—Brooklyn | Nat. | | 108 | 296 | 41 | 73 | 2 | 19 | .247 |
| 1929—Brooklyn | Nat. | | 19 | 23 | 2 | 7 | 0 | 1 | .304 |
| Major League Totals | | | 2469 | 9363 | 1545 | 2665 | 69 | 797 | .285 |

### WORLD SERIES RECORD

| Year | Club | League | G. | AB. | R. | H. | HR. | RBI. | B.A. |
|---|---|---|---|---|---|---|---|---|---|
| 1925—Pittsburgh | Nat. | | 7 | 24 | 6 | 11 | 0 | 2 | .458 |

## FRANK LEROY (HUSK) CHANCE

| Year | Club | League | G. | AB. | R. | H. | HR. | SB. | B.A. |
|---|---|---|---|---|---|---|---|---|---|
| 1898—Chicago | Nat. | | 42 | 146 | 32 | 42 | 1 | 5 | .288 |
| 1899—Chicago | Nat. | | 57 | 190 | 36 | 55 | 1 | 11 | .289 |
| 1900—Chicago | Nat. | | 48 | 151 | 26 | 46 | 0 | 9 | .305 |
| 1901—Chicago | Nat. | | 63 | 228 | 37 | 66 | 1 | 30 | .289 |
| 1902—Chicago | Nat. | | 67 | 236 | 40 | 67 | 1 | 28 | .284 |
| 1903—Chicago | Nat. | | 123 | 441 | 83 | 144 | 2 | ★67 | .327 |
| 1904—Chicago | Nat. | | 124 | 451 | 89 | 140 | 6 | 42 | .310 |
| 1905—Chicago | Nat. | | 115 | 392 | 92 | 124 | 2 | 38 | .316 |
| 1906—Chicago | Nat. | | 136 | 474 | ●103 | 151 | 3 | ★57 | .319 |
| 1907—Chicago | Nat. | | 109 | 382 | 58 | 112 | 1 | 35 | .293 |
| 1908—Chicago | Nat. | | 126 | 452 | 65 | 123 | 2 | 27 | .272 |
| 1909—Chicago | Nat. | | 92 | 324 | 53 | 88 | 0 | 29 | .272 |
| 1910—Chicago | Nat. | | 87 | 295 | 54 | 88 | 0 | 16 | .298 |
| 1911—Chicago | Nat. | | 29 | 88 | 23 | 21 | 1 | 9 | .239 |
| 1912—Chicago | Nat. | | 2 | 5 | 2 | 1 | 0 | 1 | .200 |
| 1913—New York | Amer. | | 11 | 24 | 3 | 5 | 0 | 1 | .208 |
| 1914—New York | Amer. | | 1 | 0 | 0 | 0 | 0 | 0 | .000 |
| American League Totals | | | 12 | 24 | 3 | 5 | 0 | 1 | .208 |
| National League Totals | | | 1220 | 4255 | 793 | 1268 | 20 | 404 | .298 |
| Major League Totals | | | 1232 | 4279 | 796 | 1273 | 20 | 405 | .297 |

### WORLD SERIES RECORD

| Year | Club | League | G. | AB. | R. | H. | HR. | RBI. | B.A. |
|---|---|---|---|---|---|---|---|---|---|
| 1906—Chicago | Nat. | | 6 | 21 | 3 | 5 | 0 | 2 | .238 |
| 1907—Chicago | Nat. | | 4 | 14 | 3 | 3 | 0 | 3 | .214 |
| 1908—Chicago | Nat. | | 5 | 19 | 4 | 8 | 0 | 5 | .421 |
| 1910—Chicago | Nat. | | 5 | 17 | 1 | 6 | 0 | 0 | .353 |
| World Series Totals | | | 20 | 71 | 11 | 22 | 0 | 10 | .310 |

## JOHN DWIGHT (HAPPY JACK) CHESBRO

| Year | Club | League | G. | IP. | W. | L. | Pct. |
|---|---|---|---|---|---|---|---|
| 1895—Albany-Johnstown | N.Y.L. | | 19 | 156 | 7 | 10 | .412 |
| 1895—Springfield | Eastern | | 7 | 33 | 3 | 0 | 1.000 |
| 1896—Roanoke | Virginia | | 20 | 156 | 7 | 11 | .389 |
| 1897—Richmond | Atlantic | | 38 | 283 | 16 | 18 | .471 |
| 1898—Richmond | Atlantic | | 40 | 351 | 23 | 15 | .605 |
| 1899—Richmond | Atlantic | | 21 | 192 | 17 | 4 | .810 |
| 1899—Pittsburgh | National | | 19 | 141 | 6 | 10 | .375 |
| 1900—Pittsburgh | National | | 32 | 213 | 14 | 12 | .538 |
| 1901—Pittsburgh | National | | 36 | 289 | 21 | 9 | ★.700 |
| 1902—Pittsburgh | National | | 35 | 286 | ★28 | 6 | ★.824 |
| 1903—New York | American | | 40 | 325 | 21 | 15 | .583 |
| 1904—New York | American | | ●55 | ★454 | ★41 | 13 | ★.759 |
| 1905—New York | American | | 41 | 302 | 19 | 13 | .594 |
| 1906—New York | American | | ★49 | 326 | 24 | 16 | .600 |
| 1907—New York | American | | 30 | 206 | 10 | 10 | .500 |
| 1908—New York | American | | 45 | 289 | 14 | 20 | .412 |
| 1909—New York-Boston | American | | 10 | 55 | 0 | 4 | .000 |
| American League Totals | | | 270 | 1957 | 129 | 91 | .586 |
| National League Totals | | | 122 | 929 | 69 | 37 | .651 |
| Major League Totals | | | 392 | 2886 | 198 | 128 | .607 |

## FRED CLIFFORD CLARKE

| Year | Club | League | G. | AB. | R. | H. | HR. | SB. | B.A. |
|---|---|---|---|---|---|---|---|---|---|
| 1892—Hastings | Neb. St. | | (No Records Available) | | | | | | |
| 1893—St. Joseph | W. Ass'n | | (No Records Available) | | | | | | |

| Year | Club | League | G. | AB. | R. | H. | HR. | RBI. | B.A. |
|---|---|---|---|---|---|---|---|---|---|
| 1893—Montgomery | South. | | 32 | 120 | 21 | 35 | 0 | 1 | .292 |
| 1894—Savannah | South. | | 54 | 219 | 60 | 68 | 2 | 20 | .311 |
| 1894—Louisville | Nat. | | 76 | 316 | 55 | 87 | 7 | 24 | .275 |
| 1895—Louisville | Nat. | | 132 | 556 | 94 | 197 | 3 | 36 | .354 |
| 1896—Louisville | Nat. | | 131 | 517 | 93 | 169 | 9 | 32 | .327 |
| 1897—Louisville | Nat. | | 129 | 525 | 122 | 213 | 6 | 60 | .406 |
| 1898—Louisville | Nat. | | 147 | 598 | 115 | 190 | 2 | ★66 | .318 |
| 1899—Louisville | Nat. | | 147 | 601 | 124 | 209 | 5 | 47 | .348 |
| 1900—Pittsburgh | Nat. | | 103 | 398 | 85 | 112 | 3 | 18 | .281 |
| 1901—Pittsburgh | Nat. | | 128 | 525 | 118 | 166 | 6 | 22 | .316 |
| 1902—Pittsburgh | Nat. | | 114 | 461 | 104 | 148 | 2 | 34 | .321 |
| 1903—Pittsburgh | Nat. | | 102 | 427 | 88 | 150 | 5 | 21 | .351 |
| 1904—Pittsburgh | Nat. | | 70 | 278 | 51 | 85 | 0 | 11 | .306 |
| 1905—Pittsburgh | Nat. | | 137 | 525 | 95 | 157 | 2 | 24 | .299 |
| 1906—Pittsburgh | Nat. | | 110 | 417 | 69 | 129 | 1 | 18 | .309 |
| 1907—Pittsburgh | Nat. | | 144 | 501 | 97 | 145 | 2 | 37 | .289 |
| 1908—Pittsburgh | Nat. | | 151 | 551 | 83 | 146 | 2 | 24 | .265 |
| 1909—Pittsburgh | Nat. | | 152 | 550 | 97 | 158 | 3 | 31 | .287 |
| 1910—Pittsburgh | Nat. | | 118 | 429 | 57 | 113 | 2 | 12 | .263 |
| 1911—Pittsburgh | Nat. | | 101 | 392 | 73 | 127 | 5 | 10 | .324 |
| 1913—Pittsburgh | Nat. | | 9 | 13 | 0 | 1 | 0 | 0 | .077 |
| 1914—Pittsburgh | Nat. | | 2 | 2 | 0 | 0 | 0 | 0 | .000 |
| 1915—Pittsburgh | Nat. | | 1 | 2 | 0 | 1 | 0 | 0 | .500 |
| Major League Totals | | | 2204 | 8584 | 1620 | 2703 | 65 | 527 | .315 |

### WORLD SERIES RECORD

| Year | Club | League | G. | AB. | R. | H. | HR. | SB. | B.A. |
|---|---|---|---|---|---|---|---|---|---|
| 1903—Pittsburgh | Nat. | | 8 | 34 | 3 | 9 | 0 | 1 | .265 |
| 1909—Pittsburgh | Nat. | | 7 | 19 | 7 | 4 | 2 | 3 | .211 |
| World Series Totals | | | 15 | 53 | 10 | 13 | 2 | 4 | .245 |

## JOHN GIBSON CLARKSON

| Year | Club | League | G. | IP. | W. | L. | Pct. |
|---|---|---|---|---|---|---|---|
| 1882—Worcester | National | | 3 | 24 | 1 | 2 | .333 |
| 1883—Saginaw | Northwestern | | 23 | .... | .... | .... | .... |
| 1884—Saginaw | Northwestern | | 42 | 357 | 31 | 8 | .795 |
| 1884—Chicago | National | | 14 | 109 | 10 | 3 | .769 |
| 1885—Chicago | National | | ★70 | ★622 | ★53 | 16 | .768 |
| 1886—Chicago | National | | 53 | 469 | 35 | 17 | .673 |
| 1887—Chicago | National | | ★60 | ★496 | ★38 | 21 | .644 |
| 1888—Boston | National | | 53 | ★485 | 33 | 20 | .623 |
| 1889—Boston | National | | ★72 | ★629 | ★49 | 19 | ★.721 |
| 1890—Boston | National | | 44 | 383 | 26 | 18 | .591 |
| 1891—Boston | National | | 52 | 465 | 34 | 18 | .654 |
| 1892—Boston-Cleveland | National | | 42 | 386 | 24 | 16 | .600 |
| 1893—Cleveland | National | | 34 | 296 | 16 | 18 | .471 |
| 1894—Cleveland | National | | 22 | 150 | 8 | 8 | .500 |
| Major League Totals | | | 519 | 4514 | 327 | 176 | .650 |

## ROBERTO WALKER CLEMENTE

| Year | Club | League | G. | AB. | R. | H. | HR. | RBI. | B.A. |
|---|---|---|---|---|---|---|---|---|---|
| 1954—Montreal | Int. | | 87 | 148 | 27 | 38 | 2 | 12 | .257 |
| 1955—Pittsburgh | Nat. | | 124 | 474 | 48 | 121 | 5 | 47 | .255 |
| 1956—Pittsburgh | Nat. | | 147 | 543 | 66 | 169 | 7 | 60 | .311 |
| 1957—Pittsburgh | Nat. | | 111 | 451 | 42 | 114 | 4 | 30 | .253 |
| 1958—Pittsburgh | Nat. | | 140 | 519 | 69 | 150 | 6 | 50 | .289 |
| 1959—Pittsburgh | Nat. | | 105 | 432 | 60 | 128 | 4 | 50 | .296 |
| 1960—Pittsburgh | Nat. | | 144 | 570 | 89 | 179 | 16 | 94 | .314 |
| 1961—Pittsburgh | Nat. | | 146 | 572 | 100 | 201 | 23 | 89 | ★.351 |
| 1962—Pittsburgh | Nat. | | 144 | 538 | 95 | 168 | 10 | 74 | .312 |
| 1963—Pittsburgh | Nat. | | 152 | 600 | 77 | 192 | 17 | 76 | .320 |
| 1964—Pittsburgh | Nat. | | 155 | 622 | 95 | ●211 | 12 | 87 | ★.339 |
| 1965—Pittsburgh | Nat. | | 152 | 589 | 91 | 194 | 10 | 65 | ★.329 |
| 1966—Pittsburgh | Nat. | | 154 | 638 | 105 | 202 | 29 | 119 | .317 |
| 1967—Pittsburgh | Nat. | | 147 | 585 | 103 | ★209 | 23 | 110 | ★.357 |
| 1968—Pittsburgh | Nat. | | 132 | 502 | 74 | 146 | 18 | 57 | .291 |
| 1969—Pittsburgh | Nat. | | 138 | 507 | 87 | 175 | 19 | 91 | .345 |
| 1970—Pittsburgh | Nat. | | 108 | 412 | 65 | 145 | 14 | 60 | .352 |
| 1971—Pittsburgh | Nat. | | 132 | 522 | 82 | 178 | 13 | 86 | .341 |
| 1972—Pittsburgh | Nat. | | 102 | 378 | 68 | 118 | 10 | 60 | .312 |
| Major League Totals | | | 2433 | 9454 | 1416 | 3000 | 240 | 1305 | .317 |

### CHAMPIONSHIP SERIES RECORD

| Year | Club | League | G. | AB. | R. | H. | HR. | RBI. | B.A. |
|---|---|---|---|---|---|---|---|---|---|
| 1970—Pittsburgh | Nat. | | 3 | 14 | 1 | 3 | 0 | 1 | .214 |
| 1971—Pittsburgh | Nat. | | 4 | 18 | 2 | 6 | 0 | 4 | .333 |
| 1972—Pittsburgh | Nat. | | 5 | 17 | 1 | 4 | 1 | 2 | .235 |
| Championship Series Totals | | | 12 | 49 | 4 | 13 | 1 | 7 | .265 |

### WORLD SERIES RECORD

| Year | Club | League | G. | AB. | R. | H. | HR. | RBI. | B.A. |
|---|---|---|---|---|---|---|---|---|---|
| 1960—Pittsburgh | Nat. | | 7 | 29 | 1 | 9 | 0 | 3 | .310 |
| 1971—Pittsburgh | Nat. | | 7 | 29 | 3 | 12 | 2 | 4 | .414 |
| World Series Totals | | | 14 | 58 | 4 | 21 | 2 | 7 | .362 |

## TYRUS RAYMOND (GEORGIA PEACH) COBB

| Year | Club | League | G. | AB. | R. | H. | HR. | RBI. | B.A. |
|---|---|---|---|---|---|---|---|---|---|
| 1904—Augusta | | Sally | 37 | 135 | 14 | 32 | 1 | .... | .237 |
| 1904—Ann.-Shef. | | Tn.-Ala. | 32 | 128 | 22 | 40 | 0 | .... | .313 |
| 1905—Augusta | | Sally | 103 | 411 | 60 | 134 | 1 | .... | ★.326 |
| 1905—Detroit | | Amer. | 41 | 150 | 19 | 36 | 1 | 12 | .240 |
| 1906—Detroit | | Amer. | 98 | 350 | 45 | 112 | 1 | 41 | .320 |
| 1907—Detroit | | Amer. | 150 | 605 | 97 | ★212 | 5 | ★116 | ★.350 |
| 1908—Detroit | | Amer. | 150 | 581 | 88 | ★188 | 4 | ★101 | .324 |
| 1909—Detroit | | Amer. | 156 | 573 | ★116 | ★216 | ★9 | ★115 | ★.377 |
| 1910—Detroit | | Amer. | 140 | 509 | ★106 | 196 | 8 | 88 | ★.385 |
| 1911—Detroit | | Amer. | 146 | 591 | ★147 | ★248 | 8 | ★144 | ★.420 |
| 1912—Detroit | | Amer. | 140 | 553 | 119 | ★227 | 7 | 90 | ★.410 |
| 1913—Detroit | | Amer. | 122 | 428 | 70 | 167 | 4 | 65 | ★.390 |
| 1914—Detroit | | Amer. | 97 | 345 | 69 | 127 | 2 | 57 | .368 |
| 1915—Detroit | | Amer. | 156 | 563 | ★144 | ★208 | 3 | 95 | .369 |
| 1916—Detroit | | Amer. | 145 | 542 | ★113 | 201 | 5 | 67 | .371 |
| 1917—Detroit | | Amer. | 152 | ★588 | 107 | ★225 | 6 | 108 | ★.383 |
| 1918—Detroit | | Amer. | 111 | 421 | 83 | 161 | 3 | 64 | ★.382 |
| 1919—Detroit | | Amer. | 124 | 497 | 92 | ●191 | 1 | 69 | ★.384 |
| 1920—Detroit | | Amer. | 112 | 428 | 86 | 143 | 2 | 63 | .334 |
| 1921—Detroit | | Amer. | 128 | 507 | 124 | 197 | 12 | 101 | .389 |
| 1922—Detroit | | Amer. | 137 | 526 | 99 | 211 | 4 | 99 | .401 |
| 1923—Detroit | | Amer. | 145 | 556 | 103 | 189 | 6 | 88 | .340 |
| 1924—Detroit | | Amer. | ●155 | 625 | 115 | 211 | 4 | 79 | .338 |
| 1925—Detroit | | Amer. | 121 | 415 | 97 | 157 | 12 | 62 | .378 |
| 1926—Detroit | | Amer. | 79 | 233 | 48 | 79 | 4 | 62 | .339 |
| 1927—Philadelphia | | Amer. | 133 | 490 | 104 | 175 | 5 | 94 | .357 |
| 1928—Philadelphia | | Amer. | 95 | 353 | 54 | 114 | 1 | 40 | .323 |
| Major League Totals | | | 3033 | 11429 | 2245 | 4191 | 117 | 1960 | .367 |

### WORLD SERIES RECORD

| Year | Club | League | G. | AB. | R. | H. | HR. | RBI. | B.A. |
|---|---|---|---|---|---|---|---|---|---|
| 1907—Detroit | | Amer. | 5 | 20 | 1 | 4 | 0 | 0 | .200 |
| 1908—Detroit | | Amer. | 5 | 19 | 3 | 7 | 0 | 4 | .368 |
| 1909—Detroit | | Amer. | 7 | 26 | 3 | 6 | 0 | 6 | .231 |
| World Series Totals | | | 17 | 65 | 7 | 17 | 0 | 10 | .262 |

## GORDON STANLEY (MICKEY) COCHRANE

| Year | Club | League | G. | AB. | R. | H. | HR. | RBI. | B.A. |
|---|---|---|---|---|---|---|---|---|---|
| 1923—Dover | | East. Sh. | 65 | 245 | 56 | 79 | 5 | ..... | .322 |
| 1924—Portland | | P. C. | 99 | 300 | 43 | 100 | 7 | 56 | .333 |
| 1925—Philadelphia | | Amer. | 134 | 420 | 69 | 139 | 6 | 55 | .331 |
| 1926—Philadelphia | | Amer. | 120 | 370 | 50 | 101 | 8 | 47 | .273 |
| 1927—Philadelphia | | Amer. | 126 | 432 | 80 | 146 | 12 | 80 | .338 |
| 1928—Philadelphia | | Amer. | 131 | 468 | 92 | 137 | 10 | 57 | .293 |
| 1929—Philadelphia | | Amer. | 135 | 514 | 113 | 170 | 7 | 95 | .331 |
| 1930—Philadelphia | | Amer. | 130 | 487 | 110 | 174 | 10 | 85 | .357 |
| 1931—Philadelphia | | Amer. | 122 | 459 | 87 | 160 | 17 | 89 | .349 |
| 1932—Philadelphia | | Amer. | 139 | 518 | 118 | 152 | 23 | 112 | .293 |
| 1933—Philadelphia | | Amer. | 130 | 429 | 104 | 138 | 15 | 60 | .322 |
| 1934—Detroit | | Amer. | 129 | 437 | 74 | 140 | 2 | 76 | .320 |
| 1935—Detroit | | Amer. | 115 | 411 | 93 | 131 | 5 | 47 | .319 |
| 1936—Detroit | | Amer. | 44 | 126 | 24 | 34 | 2 | 17 | .270 |
| 1937—Detroit | | Amer. | 27 | 98 | 27 | 30 | 2 | 12 | .306 |
| Major League Totals | | | 1482 | 5169 | 1041 | 1652 | 119 | 832 | .320 |

### WORLD SERIES RECORD

| Year | Club | League | G. | AB. | R. | H. | HR. | RBI. | B.A. |
|---|---|---|---|---|---|---|---|---|---|
| 1929—Philadelphia | | Amer. | 5 | 15 | 5 | 6 | 0 | 0 | .400 |
| 1930—Philadelphia | | Amer. | 6 | 18 | 5 | 4 | 2 | 4 | .222 |
| 1931—Philadelphia | | Amer. | 7 | 25 | 2 | 4 | 0 | 1 | .160 |
| 1934—Detroit | | Amer. | 7 | 28 | 2 | 6 | 0 | 1 | .214 |
| 1935—Detroit | | Amer. | 6 | 24 | 3 | 7 | 0 | 1 | .292 |
| World Series Totals | | | 31 | 110 | 17 | 27 | 2 | 7 | .245 |

## EDWARD TROWBRIDGE (COCKY) COLLINS

| Year | Club | League | G. | AB. | R. | H. | HR. | RBI. | B.A. |
|---|---|---|---|---|---|---|---|---|---|
| 1906—Philadelphia | | Amer. | 6 | 17 | 1 | 4 | 0 | 0 | .235 |
| 1907—Philadelphia | | Amer. | 14 | 20 | 0 | 5 | 0 | 3 | .250 |
| 1907—Newark | | East. | 4 | 16 | 6 | 7 | 0 | .... | .438 |
| 1908—Philadelphia | | Amer. | 102 | 330 | 39 | 90 | 1 | 27 | .273 |
| 1909—Philadelphia | | Amer. | 153 | 571 | 104 | 198 | 3 | 69 | .346 |
| 1910—Philadelphia | | Amer. | 153 | 581 | 81 | 188 | 3 | 80 | .322 |
| 1911—Philadelphia | | Amer. | 132 | 493 | 92 | 180 | 3 | 71 | .365 |
| 1912—Philadelphia | | Amer. | 153 | 543 | ★137 | 189 | 0 | 66 | .348 |
| 1913—Philadelphia | | Amer. | 148 | 534 | ★125 | 184 | 3 | 75 | .345 |
| 1914—Philadelphia | | Amer. | 152 | 526 | ★122 | 181 | 2 | 81 | .344 |
| 1915—Chicago | | Amer. | 155 | 521 | 118 | 173 | 4 | 78 | .332 |
| 1916—Chicago | | Amer. | 155 | 545 | 87 | 168 | 0 | 56 | .308 |
| 1917—Chicago | | Amer. | 156 | 564 | 91 | 163 | 0 | 67 | .289 |
| 1918—Chicago | | Amer. | 97 | 330 | 51 | 91 | 2 | 32 | .276 |
| 1919—Chicago | | Amer. | 140 | 518 | 87 | 165 | 4 | 73 | .319 |
| 1920—Chicago | | Amer. | 153 | 600 | 113 | 220 | 3 | 75 | .369 |
| 1921—Chicago | | Amer. | 139 | 526 | 79 | 177 | 2 | 58 | .337 |
| 1922—Chicago | | Amer. | 154 | 598 | 92 | 194 | 1 | 69 | .324 |
| 1923—Chicago | | Amer. | 145 | 505 | 89 | 182 | 5 | 67 | .360 |
| 1924—Chicago | | Amer. | 152 | 556 | 108 | 194 | 6 | 86 | .349 |
| 1925—Chicago | | Amer. | 118 | 425 | 80 | 147 | 3 | 80 | .346 |

| Year | Club | League | G. | AB. | R. | H. | HR. | SB. | B.A. |
|---|---|---|---|---|---|---|---|---|---|
| 1926—Chicago | | Amer. | 106 | 375 | 66 | 129 | 1 | 62 | .344 |
| 1927—Philadelphia | | Amer. | 95 | 226 | 50 | 76 | 1 | 15 | .338 |
| 1928—Philadelphia | | Amer. | 36 | 33 | 3 | 10 | 0 | 7 | .303 |
| 1929—Philadelphia | | Amer. | 9 | 7 | 0 | 0 | 0 | 0 | .000 |
| 1930—Philadelphia | | Amer. | 3 | 2 | 1 | 1 | 0 | 0 | .500 |
| Major League Totals | | | 2826 | 9946 | 1816 | 3309 | 47 | 1307 | .333 |

### WORLD SERIES RECORD

| Year | Club | League | G. | AB. | R. | H. | HR. | RBI. | B.A. |
|---|---|---|---|---|---|---|---|---|---|
| 1910—Philadelphia | | Amer. | 5 | 21 | 5 | 9 | 0 | 3 | .429 |
| 1911—Philadelphia | | Amer. | 6 | 21 | 4 | 6 | 0 | 0 | .286 |
| 1913—Philadelphia | | Amer. | 5 | 19 | 5 | 8 | 0 | 3 | .421 |
| 1914—Philadelphia | | Amer. | 4 | 14 | 0 | 3 | 0 | 1 | .214 |
| 1917—Chicago | | Amer. | 6 | 22 | 4 | 9 | 0 | 2 | .409 |
| 1919—Chicago | | Amer. | 8 | 31 | 2 | 7 | 0 | 1 | .226 |
| World Series Totals | | | 34 | 128 | 20 | 42 | 0 | 10 | .328 |

## JAMES JOSEPH (JIMMY) COLLINS

| Year | Club | League | G. | AB. | R. | H. | HR. | SB. | B.A. |
|---|---|---|---|---|---|---|---|---|---|
| 1893—Buffalo | | East. | 76 | 297 | 49 | 85 | 2 | 10 | .286 |
| 1894—Buffalo | | East. | 125 | 562 | 126 | ★198 | 8 | 18 | .352 |
| 1895—Bos.-L'ville | | Nat. | 104 | 410 | 75 | 114 | 7 | 14 | .278 |
| 1896—Boston | | Nat. | 83 | 303 | 52 | 91 | 1 | 10 | .300 |
| 1897—Boston | | Nat. | 133 | 529 | 102 | 183 | 6 | 16 | .346 |
| 1898—Boston | | Nat. | 152 | 600 | 106 | 202 | ★14 | 10 | .337 |
| 1899—Boston | | Nat. | 151 | 597 | 98 | 164 | 4 | 16 | .275 |
| 1900—Boston | | Nat. | ●142 | ★585 | 104 | 175 | 6 | 20 | .299 |
| 1901—Boston | | Amer. | 138 | 563 | 109 | 185 | 5 | 18 | .329 |
| 1902—Boston | | Amer. | 105 | 425 | 71 | 138 | 6 | 11 | .325 |
| 1903—Boston | | Amer. | 130 | 541 | 87 | 160 | 5 | 22 | .296 |
| 1904—Boston | | Amer. | 156 | 633 | 85 | 168 | 3 | 19 | .265 |
| 1905—Boston | | Amer. | 131 | 508 | 66 | 140 | 4 | 18 | .276 |
| 1906—Boston | | Amer. | 37 | 142 | 17 | 39 | 1 | 1 | .275 |
| 1907—Bos.-Phila. | | Amer. | 141 | 523 | 51 | 146 | 0 | 8 | .279 |
| 1908—Philadelphia | | Amer. | 115 | 433 | 34 | 94 | 0 | 5 | .217 |
| 1909—Minneapolis | | A. A. | 153 | 556 | 61 | 152 | 2 | 13 | .273 |
| 1910—Providence | | East. | 121 | 438 | 35 | 98 | 1 | 12 | .224 |
| 1911—Providence | | East. | 8 | 23 | 3 | 4 | 0 | 0 | .174 |
| American League Totals | | | 953 | 3768 | 520 | 1070 | 24 | 102 | .284 |
| National League Totals | | | 765 | 3024 | 537 | 929 | 38 | 86 | .307 |
| Major League Totals | | | 1718 | 6792 | 1057 | 1999 | 62 | 188 | .294 |

### WORLD SERIES RECORD

| Year | Club | League | G. | AB. | R. | H. | HR. | SB. | B.A. |
|---|---|---|---|---|---|---|---|---|---|
| 1903—Boston | | Amer. | 8 | 36 | 5 | 9 | 0 | 3 | .250 |

## EARLE BRYAN COMBS

| Year | Club | League | G. | AB. | R. | H. | HR. | RBI. | B.A. |
|---|---|---|---|---|---|---|---|---|---|
| 1922—Louisville | | A.A. | 130 | 485 | 86 | 167 | 4 | 55 | .344 |
| 1923—Louisville | | A.A. | 166 | 634 | 127 | ★241 | 14 | 145 | .380 |
| 1924—New York | | Amer. | 24 | 35 | 10 | 14 | 0 | 2 | .400 |
| 1925—New York | | Amer. | 150 | 593 | 117 | 203 | 3 | 61 | .342 |
| 1926—New York | | Amer. | 145 | 606 | 113 | 181 | 8 | 56 | .299 |
| 1927—New York | | Amer. | 152 | ★648 | 137 | ★231 | 6 | 64 | .356 |
| 1928—New York | | Amer. | 149 | 626 | 118 | 194 | 7 | 56 | .310 |
| 1929—New York | | Amer. | 142 | 586 | 119 | 202 | 3 | 65 | .345 |
| 1930—New York | | Amer. | 137 | 532 | 129 | 183 | 7 | 82 | .344 |
| 1931—New York | | Amer. | 138 | 563 | 120 | 179 | 5 | 58 | .318 |
| 1932—New York | | Amer. | 144 | 591 | 143 | 190 | 9 | 65 | .321 |
| 1933—New York | | Amer. | 122 | 417 | 86 | 125 | 5 | 60 | .300 |
| 1934—New York | | Amer. | 63 | 251 | 47 | 80 | 2 | 25 | .319 |
| 1935—New York | | Amer. | 89 | 298 | 47 | 84 | 3 | 35 | .282 |
| Major League Totals | | | 1455 | 5746 | 1186 | 1866 | 58 | 629 | .325 |

### WORLD SERIES RECORD

| Year | Club | League | G. | AB. | R. | H. | HR. | RBI. | B.A. |
|---|---|---|---|---|---|---|---|---|---|
| 1926—New York | | Amer. | 7 | 28 | 3 | 10 | 0 | 2 | .357 |
| 1927—New York | | Amer. | 4 | 16 | 6 | 5 | 0 | 2 | .313 |
| 1928—New York | | Amer. | 1 | 0 | 0 | 0 | 0 | 1 | .000 |
| 1932—New York | | Amer. | 4 | 16 | 8 | 6 | 1 | 4 | .375 |
| World Series Totals | | | 16 | 60 | 17 | 21 | 1 | 9 | .350 |

## CHARLES ALBERT (OLD ROMAN) COMISKEY

| Year | Club | League | G. | AB. | R. | H. | HR. | SB. | B.A. |
|---|---|---|---|---|---|---|---|---|---|
| 1877—Elgin | | Ind. | .... | .... | .... | .... | .... | .... | ...... |
| 1878—Dubuque | | Ind. | 21 | .... | .... | .... | .... | .... | .282 |
| 1879—Dubuque | | N.W. | 45 | .... | .... | .... | .... | .... | .235 |
| 1880—Dubuque | | Ind. | .... | .... | .... | .... | .... | .... | ...... |
| 1881—Dubuque | | Ind. | .... | .... | .... | .... | .... | .... | ...... |
| 1882—St. Louis | | A.A. | 78 | 327 | 58 | 80 | 1 | .... | .245 |
| 1883—St. Louis | | A.A. | 96 | 404 | 76 | 120 | 2 | .... | .297 |
| 1884—St. Louis | | A.A. | 108 | 461 | 86 | 111 | 2 | .... | .241 |
| 1885—St. Louis | | A.A. | 83 | 342 | 66 | 89 | 2 | .... | .260 |
| 1886—St. Louis | | A.A. | 131 | 577 | 94 | 150 | 3 | 47 | .260 |
| 1887—St. Louis | | A.A. | 125 | 563 | 136 | 207 | 4 | 122 | .368 |
| 1888—St. Louis | | A.A. | 137 | 576 | 101 | 156 | 5 | 77 | .271 |
| 1889—St. Louis | | A.A. | 137 | 586 | 105 | 169 | 3 | 71 | .288 |

| Year  Club | League | G. | AB. | R. | H. | HR. | RBI. | B.A. |
|---|---|---|---|---|---|---|---|---|
| 1890—Chicago | Players | 88 | 375 | 53 | 93 | 0 | 35 | .248 |
| 1891—St. Louis | A.A. | 130 | 532 | 82 | 141 | 3 | 39 | .265 |
| 1892—Cincinnati | Nat. | 140 | 554 | 60 | 124 | 4 | 28 | .224 |
| 1893—Cincinnati | Nat. | 62 | 253 | 38 | 58 | 0 | 12 | .229 |
| 1894—Cincinnati | Nat. | 59 | 230 | 26 | 61 | 0 | 9 | .265 |
| 1895—St. Paul | West. | 17 | 67 | 15 | 23 | .... | 3 | .343 |
| American Association Totals | | 1025 | 4368 | 804 | 1223 | 25 | 356 | .280 |
| National League Totals | | 261 | 1037 | 124 | 243 | 4 | 49 | .234 |
| Players League Totals | | 88 | 375 | 53 | 93 | 0 | 35 | .248 |
| Major League Totals | | 1374 | 5780 | 981 | 1559 | 29 | 440 | .270 |

### WORLD SERIES RECORD

| Year  Club | League | G. | AB. | R. | H. | HR. | SB. | B.A. |
|---|---|---|---|---|---|---|---|---|
| 1885—St. Louis | A.A. | 7 | 24 | 6 | 6 | 0 | 0 | .250 |
| 1886—St. Louis | A.A. | 6 | 23 | 1 | 6 | 0 | 0 | .261 |
| 1887—St. Louis | A.A. | 15 | 62 | 8 | 20 | 0 | 4 | .323 |
| 1888—St. Louis | A.A. | 10 | 41 | 6 | 11 | 0 | 5 | .268 |
| World Series Totals | | 38 | 150 | 21 | 43 | 0 | 9 | .287 |

### ROGER CONNOR

| Year  Club | League | G. | AB. | R. | H. | HR. | SB. | B.A. |
|---|---|---|---|---|---|---|---|---|
| 1880—Troy | Nat. | 83 | 340 | 53 | 113 | 3 | .... | .332 |
| 1881—Troy | Nat. | 84 | 361 | 54 | 104 | 2 | .... | .288 |
| 1882—Troy | Nat. | 79 | 339 | 63 | 111 | 4 | .... | .327 |
| 1883—New York | Nat. | 96 | 401 | 80 | 145 | 1 | .... | .362 |
| 1884—New York | Nat. | 112 | 462 | 93 | 146 | 4 | .... | .316 |
| 1885—New York | Nat. | 110 | 455 | 102 | *169 | 1 | .... | *.371 |
| 1886—New York | Nat. | 118 | 485 | 105 | 172 | 7 | 17 | .355 |
| 1887—New York | Nat. | 127 | 546 | 113 | 209 | 17 | 43 | .383 |
| 1888—New York | Nat. | 134 | 481 | 98 | 140 | 14 | 27 | .291 |
| 1889—New York | Nat. | 131 | 496 | 117 | 157 | 13 | 21 | .317 |
| 1890—New York | Players | 123 | 484 | 134 | 180 | 14 | 23 | .372 |
| 1891—New York | Nat. | 129 | 477 | 110 | 140 | 7 | 32 | .293 |
| 1892—Philadelphia | Nat. | 153 | 558 | 122 | 159 | 11 | 20 | .285 |
| 1893—New York | Nat. | ●135 | 490 | 111 | 158 | 11 | 29 | .322 |
| 1894—N.Y.-St. Louis | Nat. | 121 | 462 | 93 | 145 | 8 | 15 | .313 |
| 1895—St. Louis | Nat. | 104 | 402 | 78 | 131 | 6 | 8 | .326 |
| 1896—St. Louis | Nat. | 126 | 485 | 68 | 137 | 8 | 14 | .282 |
| 1897—St. Louis | Nat. | 22 | 83 | 13 | 19 | 1 | 3 | .229 |
| 1987—Fall River | N. Eng. | 47 | 171 | 32 | 49 | .... | 9 | .287 |
| 1898—Waterbury | Conn. | 95 | .... | .... | .... | .... | .... | .319 |
| 1899—Waterbury | Conn. | 92 | 347 | 79 | 136 | 5 | 18 | *.392 |
| 1900—Waterbury | Conn. | 83 | 286 | 54 | 82 | 2 | 20 | .287 |
| 1901—Water.-N. Hav. | Conn. | 107 | 411 | 58 | 123 | .... | .... | .299 |
| 1902—Springfield | Conn. | 62 | 224 | 25 | 58 | 1 | 15 | .259 |
| 1903—Springfield | Conn. | 75 | 279 | 28 | 76 | 0 | 12 | .272 |
| National League Totals | | 1864 | 7323 | 1473 | 2355 | 118 | 229 | .322 |
| Players League Totals | | 123 | 484 | 134 | 180 | 14 | 23 | .372 |
| Major League Totals | | 1987 | 7807 | 1607 | 2535 | 132 | 252 | .325 |

### WORLD SERIES RECORD

| Year  Club | League | G. | AB. | R. | H. | HR. | B.A. |
|---|---|---|---|---|---|---|---|
| 1888—New York | National | 7 | 23 | 7 | 6 | 0 | .261 |
| 1889—New York | National | 9 | 36 | 9 | 12 | 0 | .333 |
| World Series Totals | | 16 | 59 | 16 | 18 | 0 | .305 |

### STANLEY COVELESKI

| Year  Club | League | G. | IP. | W. | L. | Pct. | ERA. |
|---|---|---|---|---|---|---|---|
| 1908—Shamokin | Atlantic | 12 | .... | 6 | 2 | .750 | ...... |
| 1909—Lancaster | Tri-State | 43 | 272 | *23 | 11 | .676 | ...... |
| 1910—Lancaster | Tri-State | 30 | .... | 15 | 8 | .652 | ...... |
| 1911—Lancaster | Tri-State | 36 | 272 | 15 | ●19 | .441 | ...... |
| 1912—Atlantic City | Tri-State | 39 | .... | 20 | 13 | .606 | ...... |
| 1912—Philadelphia | American | 5 | 21 | 2 | 1 | .667 | ...... |
| 1913—Spokane | N. W. | 48 | 316 | 17 | *20 | .459 | ...... |
| 1914—Spokane | N. W. | 43 | 314 | 20 | 15 | .571 | ...... |
| 1915—Portland | P. C. | ●64 | 293 | 17 | 17 | .500 | 2.67 |
| 1916—Cleveland | American | 45 | 232 | 15 | 12 | .556 | 3.41 |
| 1917—Cleveland | American | 45 | 297 | 19 | 14 | .576 | 1.81 |
| 1918—Cleveland | American | 38 | 311 | 22 | 13 | .629 | 1.82 |
| 1919—Cleveland | American | 43 | 286 | 24 | 12 | .667 | 2.52 |
| 1920—Cleveland | American | 41 | 315 | 24 | 14 | .632 | 2.49 |
| 1921—Cleveland | American | 43 | 316 | 23 | 13 | .639 | 3.36 |
| 1922—Cleveland | American | 35 | 277 | 17 | 14 | .548 | 3.31 |
| 1923—Cleveland | American | 33 | 228 | 13 | 14 | .481 | *2.76 |
| 1924—Cleveland | American | 37 | 240 | 15 | 16 | .484 | 4.05 |
| 1925—Washington | American | 32 | 241 | 20 | 5 | *.800 | *2.84 |
| 1926—Washington | American | 36 | 245 | 14 | 11 | .560 | 3.12 |
| 1927—Washington | American | 5 | 14 | 2 | 1 | .667 | 3.21 |
| 1928—New York | American | 12 | 58 | 5 | 1 | .833 | 5.74 |
| Major League Totals | | 450 | 3081 | 215 | 141 | .604 | 2.88 |

### WORLD SERIES RECORD

| Year  Club | League | G. | IP. | W. | L. | Pct. | ERA. |
|---|---|---|---|---|---|---|---|
| 1920—Cleveland | Amer. | 3 | 27 | 3 | 0 | 1.000 | 0.67 |
| 1925—Washington | Amer. | 2 | 14⅓ | 0 | 2 | .000 | 3.77 |
| World Series Totals | | 5 | 41⅓ | 3 | 2 | .600 | 1.74 |

### SAMUEL EARL (WAHOO SAM) CRAWFORD

| Year  Club | League | G. | AB. | R. | H. | HR. | SB. | B.A. |
|---|---|---|---|---|---|---|---|---|
| 1899—Chatham | Canadian | 43 | 173 | 34 | 64 | 0 | 7 | .370 |
| 1899—Col.-Gr. Rapids | Western | 60 | 261 | 46 | 87 | 5 | 3 | .333 |
| 1899—Cincinnati | Nat. | 31 | 127 | 25 | 39 | 0 | 3 | .307 |
| 1900—Cincinnati | Nat. | 96 | 385 | 67 | 104 | 6 | 15 | .270 |
| 1901—Cincinnati | Nat. | 124 | 523 | 89 | 175 | *16 | 12 | .335 |
| 1902—Cincinnati | Nat. | ●140 | 555 | 94 | 185 | 3 | 15 | .333 |
| 1903—Detroit | Amer. | 137 | 545 | 93 | 181 | 4 | 23 | .332 |
| 1904—Detroit | Amer. | 150 | 571 | 46 | 141 | 2 | 20 | .247 |
| 1905—Detroit | Amer. | 154 | 575 | 73 | 171 | 6 | 22 | .297 |
| 1906—Detroit | Amer. | 145 | 563 | 65 | 166 | 2 | 24 | .295 |
| 1907—Detroit | Amer. | 144 | 582 | *102 | 188 | 4 | 18 | .323 |
| 1908—Detroit | Amer. | 152 | *591 | 102 | 184 | *7 | 15 | .311 |
| 1909—Detroit | Amer. | 156 | 589 | 83 | 185 | 6 | 30 | .314 |
| 1910—Detroit | Amer. | 154 | 588 | 83 | 170 | 5 | 20 | .289 |
| 1911—Detroit | Amer. | 146 | 574 | 109 | 217 | 7 | 37 | .378 |
| 1912—Detroit | Amer. | 149 | 581 | 81 | 189 | 4 | 41 | .325 |
| 1913—Detroit | Amer. | 153 | *610 | 78 | 193 | 9 | 13 | .316 |
| 1914—Detroit | Amer. | 157 | 582 | 74 | 183 | 8 | 25 | .314 |
| 1915—Detroit | Amer. | 156 | 612 | 81 | 183 | 4 | 24 | .299 |
| 1916—Detroit | Amer. | 100 | 322 | 41 | 92 | 0 | 10 | .286 |
| 1917—Detroit | Amer. | 61 | 104 | 6 | 18 | 2 | 0 | .173 |
| 1918—Los Angeles | P.C. | 96 | 356 | 38 | 104 | 1 | 8 | .292 |
| 1919—Los Angeles | P.C. | 173 | 664 | 103 | *239 | 14 | 14 | .360 |
| 1920—Los Angeles | P.C. | 187 | 719 | 99 | 239 | 12 | 3 | .332 |
| 1921—Los Angeles | P.C. | 175 | 626 | 92 | 199 | 9 | 10 | .318 |
| American League Totals | | 2114 | 7989 | 1117 | 2461 | 70 | 322 | .308 |
| National League Totals | | 391 | 1590 | 275 | 503 | 25 | 45 | .316 |
| Major League Totals | | 2505 | 9579 | 1392 | 2964 | 95 | 367 | .309 |

### WORLD SERIES RECORD

| Year  Club | League | G. | AB. | R. | H. | HR. | SB. | B.A. |
|---|---|---|---|---|---|---|---|---|
| 1907—Detroit | Amer. | 5 | 21 | 1 | 5 | 0 | 0 | .238 |
| 1908—Detroit | Amer. | 5 | 21 | 2 | 5 | 0 | 0 | .238 |
| 1909—Detroit | Amer. | 7 | 28 | 4 | 7 | 1 | 1 | .250 |
| World Series Totals | | 17 | 70 | 7 | 17 | 1 | 1 | .243 |

### JOSEPH EDWARD CRONIN

| Year  Club | League | G. | AB. | R. | H. | HR. | RBI. | B.A. |
|---|---|---|---|---|---|---|---|---|
| 1925—Johnstown | Mid.-Atl. | 99 | 352 | 64 | 110 | 3 | .... | .313 |
| 1926—Pittsburgh | Nat. | 38 | 83 | 9 | 22 | 0 | 11 | .265 |
| 1926—New Haven | East. | 66 | 244 | 61 | 78 | 2 | .... | .320 |
| 1927—Pittsburgh | Nat. | 12 | 22 | 2 | 5 | 0 | 3 | .227 |
| 1928—Kansas City | A.A. | 74 | 241 | 34 | 59 | 0 | 32 | .245 |
| 1928—Washington | Amer. | 63 | 227 | 23 | 55 | 0 | 25 | .242 |
| 1929—Washington | Amer. | 145 | 494 | 72 | 139 | 8 | 60 | .281 |
| 1930—Washington | Amer. | ●154 | 587 | 127 | 203 | 13 | 126 | .346 |
| 1931—Washington | Amer. | *156 | 611 | 103 | 187 | 12 | 126 | .306 |
| 1932—Washington | Amer. | 143 | 557 | 95 | 177 | 6 | 116 | .318 |
| 1933—Washington | Amer. | 152 | 602 | 89 | 186 | 5 | 118 | .309 |
| 1934—Washington | Amer. | 127 | 504 | 68 | 143 | 7 | 101 | .284 |
| 1935—Boston | Amer. | 144 | 556 | 70 | 164 | 9 | 95 | .295 |
| 1936—Boston | Amer. | 81 | 295 | 36 | 83 | 2 | 43 | .281 |
| 1937—Boston | Amer. | 148 | 570 | 102 | 175 | 18 | 110 | .307 |
| 1938—Boston | Amer. | 143 | 530 | 98 | 172 | 17 | 94 | .325 |
| 1939—Boston | Amer. | 143 | 520 | 97 | 160 | 19 | 107 | .308 |
| 1940—Boston | Amer. | 149 | 548 | 104 | 156 | 24 | 111 | .285 |
| 1941—Boston | Amer. | 143 | 518 | 98 | 161 | 6 | 95 | .311 |
| 1942—Boston | Amer. | 45 | 79 | 7 | 24 | 4 | 24 | .304 |
| 1943—Boston | Amer. | 59 | 77 | 8 | 24 | 5 | 29 | .312 |
| 1944—Boston | Amer. | 76 | 191 | 24 | 46 | 5 | 28 | .241 |
| 1945—Boston | Amer. | 3 | 8 | 1 | 3 | 0 | 1 | .375 |
| American League Totals | | 2074 | 7474 | 1222 | 2258 | 170 | 1409 | .302 |
| National League Totals | | 50 | 105 | 11 | 27 | 0 | 14 | .257 |
| Major League Totals | | 2124 | 7579 | 1233 | 2285 | 170 | 1423 | .301 |

### WORLD SERIES RECORD

| Year  Club | League | G. | AB. | R. | H. | HR. | RBI. | B.A. |
|---|---|---|---|---|---|---|---|---|
| 1933—Washington | Amer. | 5 | 22 | 1 | 7 | 0 | 2 | .318 |

### HAZEN SHIRLEY (KIKI) CUYLER

| Year  Club | League | G. | AB. | R. | H. | HR. | RBI. | B.A. |
|---|---|---|---|---|---|---|---|---|
| 1920—Bay City | Mich.-Ont. | 69 | 240 | 24 | 62 | 1 | 26 | .258 |
| 1921—Bay City | Mich.-Ont. | 116 | 417 | 79 | 132 | 8 | 82 | .317 |
| 1921—Pittsburgh | Nat. | 1 | 3 | 0 | 0 | 0 | 0 | .000 |
| 1922—Charleston | Sally | 131 | 489 | 84 | 151 | 12 | 46 | .309 |
| 1922—Pittsburgh | Nat. | 1 | 0 | 0 | 0 | 0 | 0 | .000 |
| 1923—Nashville | Southern | 149 | 574 | 114 | 195 | 9 | 108 | .340 |
| 1923—Pittsburgh | Nat. | 11 | 40 | 4 | 10 | 0 | 2 | .250 |
| 1924—Pittsburgh | Nat. | 117 | 466 | 94 | 165 | 9 | 85 | .354 |
| 1925—Pittsburgh | Nat. | ●153 | 617 | *144 | 220 | 18 | 102 | .357 |
| 1926—Pittsburgh | Nat. | *157 | 614 | *113 | 197 | 8 | 92 | .321 |
| 1927—Pittsburgh | Nat. | 85 | 285 | 60 | 88 | 3 | 31 | .309 |
| 1928—Chicago | Nat. | 133 | 499 | 92 | 142 | 17 | 79 | .285 |
| 1929—Chicago | Nat. | 139 | 509 | 111 | 183 | 15 | 102 | .360 |
| 1930—Chicago | Nat. | ●156 | 642 | 155 | 228 | 13 | 134 | .355 |
| 1931—Chicago | Nat. | 154 | 613 | 110 | 202 | 9 | 88 | .330 |

| Year Club | League | G. | AB. | R. | H. | HR. | RBI. | B.A. |
|---|---|---|---|---|---|---|---|---|
| 1932—Chicago | Nat. | 110 | 446 | 58 | 130 | 10 | 77 | .291 |
| 1933—Chicago | Nat. | 70 | 262 | 37 | 83 | 5 | 35 | .317 |
| 1934—Chicago | Nat. | 142 | 559 | 80 | 189 | 6 | 69 | .338 |
| 1935—Chi.-Cinc. | Nat. | 107 | 380 | 58 | 98 | 6 | 40 | .258 |
| 1936—Cincinnati | Nat. | 144 | 567 | 96 | 185 | 7 | 74 | .326 |
| 1937—Cincinnati | Nat. | 117 | 406 | 48 | 110 | 0 | 32 | .271 |
| 1938—Brooklyn | Nat. | 82 | 253 | 45 | 69 | 2 | 23 | .273 |
| 1939—Chattanooga | Southern | 58 | 159 | 19 | 43 | 0 | 18 | .270 |
| 1940—Chattanooga | Southern | 1 | 1 | 1 | 1 | 0 | 0 | 1.000 |
| Major League Totals | | 1879 | 7161 | 1305 | 2299 | 128 | 1065 | .321 |

### WORLD SERIES RECORD

| Year Club | League | G. | AB. | R. | H. | HR. | RBI. | B.A. |
|---|---|---|---|---|---|---|---|---|
| 1925—Pittsburgh | Nat. | 7 | 26 | 3 | 7 | 1 | 6 | .269 |
| 1929—Chicago | Nat. | 5 | 20 | 4 | 6 | 0 | 4 | .300 |
| 1932—Chicago | Nat. | 4 | 18 | 2 | 5 | 1 | 2 | .278 |
| World Series Totals | | 16 | 64 | 9 | 18 | 2 | 12 | .281 |

## JAY HANNA (DIZZY) DEAN

| Year Club | League | G. | IP. | W. | L. | Pct. | ERA. |
|---|---|---|---|---|---|---|---|
| 1930—St. Joseph | Western | 32 | 217 | 17 | 8 | .680 | 3.69 |
| 1930—Houston | Texas | 14 | 85 | 8 | 2 | .800 | 2.86 |
| 1930—St. Louis | National | 1 | 9 | 1 | 0 | 1.000 | 1.00 |
| 1931—Houston | Texas | 41 | 304 | ★26 | 10 | .722 | ★1.57 |
| 1932—St. Louis | National | 46 | ★286 | 18 | 15 | .545 | 3.30 |
| 1933—St. Louis | National | ★48 | 293 | 20 | 18 | .526 | 3.04 |
| 1934—St. Louis | National | 50 | 312 | ★30 | 7 | ★.811 | 2.65 |
| 1935—St. Louis | National | 50 | ★324 | ★28 | 12 | .700 | 3.11 |
| 1936—St. Louis | National | ●51 | ★315 | 24 | 13 | .649 | 3.17 |
| 1937—St. Louis | National | 27 | 197 | 13 | 10 | .565 | 2.70 |
| 1938—Chicago | National | 13 | 75 | 7 | 1 | .875 | 1.80 |
| 1939—Chicago | National | 19 | 96 | 6 | 4 | .600 | 3.38 |
| 1940—Chicago | National | 10 | 54 | 3 | 3 | .500 | 5.17 |
| 1940—Tulsa | Texas | 21 | 142 | 8 | 8 | .500 | 3.17 |
| 1941—Chicago | National | 1 | 1 | 0 | 0 | .000 | 18.00 |
| 1947—St. Louis | American | 1 | 4 | 0 | 0 | .000 | 0.00 |
| American League Totals | | 1 | 4 | 0 | 0 | .000 | 0.00 |
| National League Totals | | 316 | 1962 | 150 | 83 | .644 | 3.04 |
| Major League Totals | | 317 | 1966 | 150 | 83 | .644 | 3.04 |

### WORLD SERIES RECORD

| Year Club | League | G. | IP. | W. | L. | Pct. | ERA. |
|---|---|---|---|---|---|---|---|
| 1934—St. Louis | National | 3 | 26 | 2 | 1 | .667 | 1.73 |
| 1938—Chicago | National | 2 | 8⅓ | 0 | 1 | .000 | 6.48 |
| World Series Totals | | 5 | 34⅓ | 2 | 2 | .500 | 2.88 |

## EDWARD JAMES (BIG ED) DELAHANTY

| Year Club | League | G. | AB. | R. | H. | HR. | SB. | B.A. |
|---|---|---|---|---|---|---|---|---|
| 1887—Mansfield | Ohio St. | 73 | 366 | 90 | 130 | 5 | ..... | .355 |
| 1888—Wheeling | Tri. St. | 21 | 98 | 20 | 40 | 5 | 15 | .408 |
| 1888—Philadelphia | Nat. | 74 | 290 | 40 | 66 | 1 | 38 | .228 |
| 1889—Philadelphia | Nat. | 54 | 246 | 37 | 72 | 0 | 19 | .293 |
| 1890—Cleveland | Play. | 115 | 513 | 106 | 152 | 3 | 24 | .296 |
| 1891—Philadelphia | Nat. | 128 | 545 | 92 | 136 | 5 | 27 | .250 |
| 1892—Philadelphia | Nat. | 120 | 470 | 78 | 147 | 6 | 35 | .313 |
| 1893—Philadelphia | Nat. | 132 | ★588 | 145 | 218 | ★19 | 36 | .371 |
| 1894—Philadelphia | Nat. | 114 | 497 | 149 | 199 | 4 | 29 | .400 |
| 1895—Philadelphia | Nat. | 116 | 481 | 148 | 192 | 11 | 46 | .399 |
| 1896—Philadelphia | Nat. | 122 | 505 | 131 | 199 | ●13 | 37 | .394 |
| 1897—Philadelphia | Nat. | 129 | 530 | 110 | 200 | 4 | 28 | .377 |
| 1898—Philadelphia | Nat. | 142 | 547 | 114 | 183 | 3 | 62 | .335 |
| 1899—Philadelphia | Nat. | 145 | 573 | 133 | ★234 | 9 | 38 | ★.408 |
| 1900—Philadelphia | Nat. | 130 | 542 | 82 | 173 | 1 | 14 | .319 |
| 1901—Philadelphia | Nat. | 138 | 538 | 106 | 192 | 8 | 28 | .357 |
| 1902—Washington | Amer. | 123 | 474 | 103 | 178 | 10 | 14 | ★.376 |
| 1903—Washington | Amer. | 43 | 154 | 22 | 52 | 1 | 3 | .338 |
| American League Totals | | 166 | 628 | 125 | 230 | 11 | 17 | .366 |
| National League Totals | | 1544 | 6352 | 1365 | 2211 | 84 | 437 | .348 |
| Players League Totals | | 115 | 513 | 106 | 152 | 3 | 24 | .296 |
| Major League Totals | | 1825 | 7493 | 1596 | 2593 | 98 | 478 | .346 |

## WILLIAM MALCOLM DICKEY

| Year Club | League | G. | AB. | R. | H. | HR. | RBI. | B.A. |
|---|---|---|---|---|---|---|---|---|
| 1925—Little Rock | South. | 3 | 10 | 1 | 3 | 0 | ..... | .300 |
| 1926—Muskogee | W.A. | 61 | 212 | 27 | 60 | 7 | ..... | .283 |
| 1926—Little Rock | South. | 21 | 46 | 6 | 18 | 0 | 8 | .391 |
| 1927—Jackson | Cot. St. | 101 | 364 | 46 | 108 | 3 | ..... | .297 |
| 1928—Little Rock | South. | 60 | 203 | 22 | 61 | 4 | 32 | .300 |
| 1928—Buffalo | Int. | 3 | 8 | 0 | 1 | 0 | 0 | .125 |
| 1928—New York | Amer. | 10 | 15 | 1 | 3 | 0 | 2 | .200 |
| 1929—New York | Amer. | 130 | 447 | 60 | 145 | 10 | 65 | .324 |
| 1930—New York | Amer. | 109 | 366 | 55 | 124 | 5 | 65 | .339 |
| 1931—New York | Amer. | 130 | 477 | 65 | 156 | 6 | 78 | .327 |
| 1932—New York | Amer. | 108 | 423 | 66 | 131 | 15 | 84 | .310 |
| 1933—New York | Amer. | 130 | 478 | 58 | 152 | 14 | 97 | .318 |
| 1934—New York | Amer. | 104 | 395 | 56 | 127 | 12 | 72 | .322 |
| 1935—New York | Amer. | 120 | 448 | 54 | 125 | 14 | 81 | .279 |
| 1936—New York | Amer. | 112 | 423 | 99 | 153 | 22 | 107 | .362 |

| Year Club | League | G. | AB. | R. | H. | HR. | RBI. | B.A. |
|---|---|---|---|---|---|---|---|---|
| 1937—New York | Amer. | 140 | 530 | 87 | 176 | 29 | 133 | .332 |
| 1938—New York | Amer. | 132 | 454 | 84 | 142 | 27 | 115 | .313 |
| 1939—New York | Amer. | 128 | 480 | 98 | 145 | 24 | 105 | .302 |
| 1940—New York | Amer. | 106 | 372 | 45 | 92 | 9 | 54 | .247 |
| 1941—New York | Amer. | 109 | 348 | 35 | 99 | 7 | 71 | .284 |
| 1942—New York | Amer. | 82 | 268 | 28 | 79 | 2 | 37 | .295 |
| 1943—New York | Amer. | 85 | 242 | 29 | 85 | 4 | 33 | .351 |
| 1944-45—New York | Amer. | (In Military Service) | | | | | | |
| 1946—New York | Amer. | 54 | 134 | 10 | 35 | 2 | 10 | .261 |
| 1947—Little Rock | South. | 8 | 12 | 2 | 4 | 1 | 2 | .333 |
| Major League Totals | | 1789 | 6300 | 930 | 1969 | 202 | 1209 | .313 |

### WORLD SERIES RECORD

| Year Club | League | G. | AB. | R. | H. | HR. | RBI. | B.A. |
|---|---|---|---|---|---|---|---|---|
| 1932—New York | Amer. | 4 | 16 | 2 | 7 | 0 | 4 | .438 |
| 1936—New York | Amer. | 6 | 25 | 5 | 3 | 1 | 5 | .120 |
| 1937—New York | Amer. | 5 | 19 | 3 | 4 | 0 | 3 | .211 |
| 1938—New York | Amer. | 4 | 15 | 2 | 6 | 1 | 2 | .400 |
| 1939—New York | Amer. | 4 | 15 | 2 | 4 | 2 | 5 | .267 |
| 1941—New York | Amer. | 5 | 18 | 3 | 3 | 0 | 1 | .167 |
| 1942—New York | Amer. | 5 | 19 | 1 | 5 | 0 | 0 | .263 |
| 1943—New York | Amer. | 5 | 18 | 1 | 5 | 1 | 4 | .278 |
| World Series Totals | | 38 | 145 | 19 | 37 | 5 | 24 | .255 |

## JOSEPH PAUL (YANKEE CLIPPER) DI MAGGIO

| Year Club | League | G. | AB. | R. | H. | HR. | RBI. | B.A. |
|---|---|---|---|---|---|---|---|---|
| 1932—San Francisco | P. C. | 3 | 9 | 2 | 2 | 0 | 2 | .222 |
| 1933—San Francisco | P. C. | 187 | 762 | 129 | 259 | 28 | ★169 | .340 |
| 1934—San Francisco | P. C. | 101 | 375 | 58 | 128 | 12 | 69 | .341 |
| 1935—San Francisco | P. C. | 172 | 679 | ★173 | 270 | 34 | ★154 | .398 |
| 1936—New York | Amer. | 138 | 637 | 132 | 206 | 29 | 125 | .323 |
| 1937—New York | Amer. | 151 | 621 | ★151 | 215 | ★46 | 167 | .346 |
| 1938—New York | Amer. | 145 | 599 | 129 | 194 | 32 | 140 | .324 |
| 1939—New York | Amer. | 120 | 462 | 108 | 176 | 30 | 126 | ★.381 |
| 1940—New York | Amer. | 132 | 508 | 93 | 179 | 31 | 133 | ★.352 |
| 1941—New York | Amer. | 139 | 541 | 122 | 193 | 30 | ★125 | .357 |
| 1942—New York | Amer. | 154 | 610 | 123 | 186 | 21 | 114 | .305 |
| 1943-44-45—New York | | (In Military Service) | | | | | | |
| 1946—New York | Amer. | 132 | 503 | 81 | 146 | 25 | 95 | .290 |
| 1947—New York | Amer. | 141 | 534 | 97 | 168 | 20 | 97 | .315 |
| 1948—New York | Amer. | 153 | 594 | 110 | 190 | ★39 | ★155 | .320 |
| 1949—New York | Amer. | 76 | 272 | 58 | 94 | 14 | 67 | .346 |
| 1950—New York | Amer. | 139 | 525 | 114 | 158 | 32 | 122 | .301 |
| 1951—New York | Amer. | 116 | 415 | 72 | 109 | 12 | 71 | .263 |
| Major League Totals | | 1736 | 6821 | 1390 | 2214 | 361 | 1537 | .325 |

### WORLD SERIES RECORD

| Year Club | League | G. | AB. | R. | H. | HR. | RBI. | B.A. |
|---|---|---|---|---|---|---|---|---|
| 1936—New York | Amer. | 6 | 26 | 3 | 9 | 0 | 3 | .346 |
| 1937—New York | Amer. | 5 | 22 | 2 | 6 | 1 | 4 | .273 |
| 1938—New York | Amer. | 4 | 15 | 4 | 4 | 1 | 2 | .267 |
| 1939—New York | Amer. | 4 | 16 | 3 | 5 | 1 | 3 | .313 |
| 1941—New York | Amer. | 5 | 19 | 1 | 5 | 0 | 1 | .263 |
| 1942—New York | Amer. | 5 | 21 | 3 | 7 | 0 | 3 | .333 |
| 1947—New York | Amer. | 7 | 26 | 4 | 6 | 2 | 5 | .231 |
| 1949—New York | Amer. | 5 | 18 | 2 | 2 | 1 | 2 | .111 |
| 1950—New York | Amer. | 4 | 13 | 2 | 4 | 1 | 2 | .308 |
| 1951—New York | Amer. | 6 | 23 | 3 | 6 | 1 | 5 | .261 |
| World Series Totals | | 51 | 199 | 27 | 54 | 8 | 30 | .271 |

## HUGH DUFFY

| Year Club | League | G. | AB. | R. | H. | HR. | RBI. | B.A. |
|---|---|---|---|---|---|---|---|---|
| 1886—Hartford | East. | 7 | 18 | 3 | 5 | 0 | 1 | .278 |
| 1887—Springfield | East. | 17 | 80 | 20 | 28 | 1 | 17 | .350 |
| 1887—Salem-Lowell | N. Eng. | 78 | 325 | 103 | 139 | 16 | 16 | .428 |
| 1888—Chicago | Nat. | 71 | 298 | 60 | 84 | 7 | 13 | .282 |
| 1889—Chicago | Nat. | ●136 | ★584 | 144 | 182 | 12 | 52 | .312 |
| 1890—Chicago | Play. | 137 | 591 | ★161 | 194 | 7 | 79 | .328 |
| 1891—Boston | A. A. | 121 | 511 | 124 | 174 | 10 | 83 | .341 |
| 1892—Boston | Nat. | 146 | 609 | 125 | 184 | 5 | 61 | .302 |
| 1893—Boston | Nat. | 131 | 537 | ●149 | 203 | 6 | 50 | ★.378 |
| 1894—Boston | Nat. | 124 | 539 | 160 | ★236 | ●18 | 49 | ★.438 |
| 1895—Boston | Nat. | 131 | 540 | 113 | 190 | 8 | 42 | .352 |
| 1896—Boston | Nat. | 131 | 533 | 93 | 161 | 5 | 45 | .302 |
| 1897—Boston | Nat. | 134 | 554 | 131 | 189 | 8 | 45 | .341 |
| 1898—Boston | Nat. | 151 | 561 | 97 | 179 | 8 | 32 | .319 |
| 1899—Boston | Nat. | 147 | 588 | 102 | 164 | 5 | 18 | .279 |
| 1900—Boston | Nat. | 50 | 181 | 28 | 54 | 2 | 12 | .298 |
| 1901—Milwaukee | Amer. | 78 | 286 | 41 | 88 | 2 | 13 | .308 |
| 1902—Milwaukee | West. | 140 | 505 | 79 | 147 | 2 | 37 | .291 |
| 1903—Milwaukee | West. | 71 | 257 | 45 | 77 | 0 | 30 | .300 |
| 1904—Philadelphia | Nat. | 18 | 46 | 10 | 13 | 0 | 3 | .283 |
| 1905—Philadelphia | Nat. | 15 | 40 | 7 | 12 | 0 | 0 | .300 |
| 1906—Philadelphia | Nat. | 1 | 1 | 0 | 0 | 0 | 0 | .000 |
| 1907—Providence | East. | 35 | 73 | 9 | 22 | 0 | 5 | .301 |
| 1908—Providence | East. | 37 | 57 | 10 | 19 | 1 | 5 | .333 |

| | G. | AB. | R. | H. | HR. | RBI. | B.A. |
|---|---|---|---|---|---|---|---|
| American Association Totals | 121 | 511 | 124 | 174 | 10 | 83 | .340 |
| American League Totals | 78 | 286 | 41 | 88 | 2 | 13 | .308 |
| National League Totals | 1386 | 5611 | 1219 | 1851 | 84 | 422 | .330 |
| Players League Totals | 137 | 591 | 161 | 194 | 7 | 79 | .328 |
| Major League Totals | 1722 | 6999 | 1545 | 2307 | 103 | 597 | .330 |

## JOHN JOSEPH (CRAB) EVERS

| Year | Club | League | G. | AB. | R. | H. | HR. | RBI. | B.A. |
|---|---|---|---|---|---|---|---|---|---|
| 1902—Troy | N.Y.S. | | 84 | 333 | 50 | 95 | 10 | | .285 |
| 1902—Chicago | Nat. | | 25 | 89 | 7 | 20 | 0 | | .225 |
| 1903—Chicago | Nat. | | 123 | 464 | 70 | 136 | 0 | | .293 |
| 1904—Chicago | Nat. | | 152 | 532 | 49 | 141 | 0 | | .265 |
| 1905—Chicago | Nat. | | 99 | 340 | 44 | 94 | 1 | | .276 |
| 1906—Chicago | Nat. | | 154 | 533 | 65 | 136 | 1 | | .255 |
| 1907—Chicago | Nat. | | 151 | 508 | 66 | 127 | 2 | 55 | .250 |
| 1908—Chicago | Nat. | | 123 | 416 | 83 | 125 | 0 | 35 | .300 |
| 1909—Chicago | Nat. | | 126 | 463 | 88 | 122 | 1 | 20 | .263 |
| 1910—Chicago | Nat. | | 125 | 433 | 87 | 114 | 0 | 25 | .263 |
| 1911—Chicago | Nat. | | 44 | 155 | 29 | 35 | 0 | 9 | .226 |
| 1912—Chicago | Nat. | | 143 | 478 | 73 | 163 | 1 | 56 | .341 |
| 1913—Chicago | Nat. | | 136 | 446 | 81 | 127 | 3 | 48 | .285 |
| 1914—Boston | Nat. | | 139 | 491 | 81 | 137 | 1 | 33 | .279 |
| 1915—Boston | Nat. | | 83 | 278 | 38 | 73 | 1 | 23 | .263 |
| 1916—Boston | Nat. | | 71 | 241 | 33 | 52 | 0 | 15 | .216 |
| 1917—Bos.-Phila. | Nat. | | 80 | 266 | 25 | 57 | 1 | 11 | .214 |
| 1922—Chicago | Amer. | | 1 | 3 | 0 | 0 | 0 | 1 | .000 |
| 1929—Boston | Nat. | | 1 | 0 | 0 | 0 | 0 | 0 | .000 |
| Major League Totals | | | 1776 | 6136 | 919 | 1659 | 12 | | .270 |

### WORLD SERIES RECORD

| Year | Club | League | G. | AB. | R. | H. | HR. | RBI. | B.A. |
|---|---|---|---|---|---|---|---|---|---|
| 1906—Chicago | Nat. | | 6 | 20 | 2 | 3 | 0 | 1 | .150 |
| 1907—Chicago | Nat. | | 5 | 20 | 2 | 7 | 0 | 1 | .350 |
| 1908—Chicago | Nat. | | 5 | 20 | 5 | 7 | 0 | 2 | .350 |
| 1914—Boston | Nat. | | 4 | 16 | 2 | 7 | 0 | 2 | .438 |
| World Series Totals | | | 20 | 76 | 11 | 24 | 0 | 6 | .316 |

## WILLIAM BUCKINGHAM (BUCK) EWING

| Year | Club | League | G. | AB. | R. | H. | HR. | RBI. | B.A. |
|---|---|---|---|---|---|---|---|---|---|
| 1878—Mohawk Browns | Ind. | | | | | | | | |
| 1879—Mohawk Browns | Ind. | | | | | | | | |
| 1880—Cin. Buckeyes | Ind. | | | | | | | | |
| 1880—Rochester | N. Assn. | | 13 | | | | | | .148 |
| 1880—Troy | Nat. | | 13 | 46 | 1 | 8 | 0 | | .174 |
| 1881—Troy | Nat. | | 65 | 267 | 38 | 65 | 0 | | .243 |
| 1882—Troy | Nat. | | 72 | 318 | 65 | 87 | 2 | | .274 |
| 1883—New York | Nat. | | 85 | 369 | 88 | 113 | *10 | | .306 |
| 1884—New York | Nat. | | 88 | 374 | 87 | 104 | 3 | | .278 |
| 1885—New York | Nat. | | 81 | 342 | 81 | 104 | 6 | | .304 |
| 1886—New York | Nat. | | 70 | 275 | 59 | 85 | 4 | 18 | .309 |
| 1887—New York | Nat. | | 76 | 348 | 81 | 127 | 6 | 53 | .365 |
| 1888—New York | Nat. | | 103 | 415 | 83 | 127 | 5 | 53 | .306 |
| 1889—New York | Nat. | | 96 | 407 | 91 | 133 | 3 | 34 | .327 |
| 1890—New York | Play. | | 83 | 349 | 99 | 122 | 7 | 39 | .350 |
| 1891—New York | Nat. | | 14 | 49 | 8 | 17 | 0 | 3 | .347 |
| 1892—New York | Nat. | | 97 | 394 | 58 | 126 | 8 | 53 | .320 |
| 1893—Cleveland | Nat. | | 114 | 477 | 116 | 177 | 6 | 53 | .371 |
| 1894—Cleveland | Nat. | | 53 | 212 | 32 | 54 | 2 | 19 | .255 |
| 1895—Cincinnati | Nat. | | 103 | 439 | 90 | 139 | 3 | 34 | .317 |
| 1896—Cincinnati | Nat. | | 67 | 266 | 41 | 75 | 1 | 47 | .282 |
| 1897—Cincinnati | Nat. | | 1 | 1 | 0 | 0 | 0 | 0 | .000 |
| National League Totals | | | 1198 | 4999 | 1019 | 1541 | 59 | | .308 |
| Players League Totals | | | 83 | 349 | 99 | 122 | 7 | 39 | .350 |
| Major League Totals | | | 1281 | 5348 | 1118 | 1663 | 66 | | .311 |

### WORLD SERIES RECORD

| Year | Club | League | G. | AB. | R. | H. | HR. | RBI. | B.A. |
|---|---|---|---|---|---|---|---|---|---|
| 1888—New York | Nat. | | 7 | 26 | 5 | 9 | 1 | 5 | .346 |
| 1889—New York | Nat. | | 8 | 36 | 5 | 9 | 0 | 2 | .250 |
| World Series Totals | | | 15 | 62 | 10 | 18 | 1 | 7 | .290 |

## URBAN CLARENCE (RED) FABER

| Year | Club | League | G. | IP. | W. | L. | Pct. | ERA. |
|---|---|---|---|---|---|---|---|---|
| 1909—Dubuque | I.I.I. | 15 | 114 | 7 | 6 | .538 | |
| 1910—Dubuque | I.I.I. | 44 | 334 | 18 | 19 | .486 | |
| 1911—Minneapolis | Amer. Assn. | 2 | 6 | 0 | 0 | .000 | |
| 1911—Pueblo | Western | 29 | 180 | 12 | 8 | .600 | |
| 1912—Des Moines | Western | 43 | 304 | 21 | 14 | .600 | |
| 1913—Des Moines | Western | 50 | *373 | 20 | 17 | .541 | 2.49 |
| 1914—Chicago | American | 40 | 181 | 10 | 9 | .526 | 2.69 |
| 1915—Chicago | American | ●50 | 300 | 24 | 14 | .632 | 2.55 |
| 1916—Chicago | American | 35 | 205 | 17 | 9 | .654 | 2.02 |
| 1917—Chicago | American | 41 | 248 | 16 | 13 | .552 | 1.92 |
| 1918—Chicago | American | 11 | 81 | 4 | 1 | .800 | 1.22 |
| 1919—Chicago | American | 25 | 162 | 11 | 9 | .550 | 3.83 |
| 1920—Chicago | American | 40 | 319 | 23 | 13 | .639 | 2.99 |
| 1921—Chicago | American | 43 | 331 | 25 | 15 | .625 | *2.47 |
| 1922—Chicago | American | 43 | *353 | 21 | 17 | .553 | *2.80 |

| Year | Club | League | G. | IP. | W. | L. | Pct. | ERA. |
|---|---|---|---|---|---|---|---|---|
| 1923—Chicago | American | 32 | 234 | 14 | 11 | .560 | 3.41 |
| 1924—Chicago | American | 21 | 161 | 9 | 11 | .450 | 3.86 |
| 1925—Chicago | American | 34 | 238 | 12 | 11 | .522 | 3.78 |
| 1926—Chicago | American | 27 | 185 | 15 | 8 | .652 | 3.55 |
| 1927—Chicago | American | 18 | 111 | 4 | 7 | .364 | 4.54 |
| 1928—Chicago | American | 27 | 201 | 13 | 9 | .591 | 3.76 |
| 1929—Chicago | American | 31 | 234 | 13 | 13 | .500 | 3.88 |
| 1930—Chicago | American | 29 | 169 | 8 | 13 | .381 | 4.21 |
| 1931—Chicago | American | 44 | 184 | 10 | 14 | .417 | 3.82 |
| 1932—Chicago | American | 42 | 106 | 2 | 11 | .154 | 3.74 |
| 1933—Chicago | American | 36 | 86 | 3 | 4 | .429 | 3.45 |
| Major League Totals | | 669 | 4089 | 254 | 212 | .545 | 3.15 |

### WORLD SERIES RECORD

| Year | Club | League | G. | IP. | W. | L. | Pct. | ERA. |
|---|---|---|---|---|---|---|---|---|
| 1917—Chicago | American | 4 | 27 | 3 | 1 | .750 | 2.33 |

## ROBERT WILLIAM ANDREW FELLER

| Year | Club | League | G. | IP. | W. | L. | Pct. | ERA. |
|---|---|---|---|---|---|---|---|---|
| 1936—Cleveland | American | 14 | 62 | 5 | 3 | .625 | 3.34 |
| 1937—Cleveland | American | 26 | 149 | 9 | 7 | .563 | 3.38 |
| 1938—Cleveland | American | 39 | 278 | 17 | 11 | .607 | 4.08 |
| 1939—Cleveland | American | 39 | *297 | *24 | 9 | .727 | 2.85 |
| 1940—Cleveland | American | *43 | *320 | *27 | 11 | .711 | *2.62 |
| 1941—Cleveland | American | *44 | *343 | *25 | 13 | .658 | 3.15 |
| 1942-43-44—Cleveland | American | (In Military Service) | | | | | |
| 1945—Cleveland | American | 9 | 72 | 5 | 3 | .625 | 2.50 |
| 1946—Cleveland | American | *48 | *371 | ●26 | 15 | .634 | 2.18 |
| 1947—Cleveland | American | 42 | *299 | *20 | 11 | .645 | 2.68 |
| 1948—Cleveland | American | 44 | 280 | 19 | 15 | .559 | 3.57 |
| 1949—Cleveland | American | 36 | 211 | 15 | 14 | .517 | 3.75 |
| 1950—Cleveland | American | 35 | 247 | 16 | 11 | .593 | 3.43 |
| 1951—Cleveland | American | 33 | 250 | *22 | 8 | *.733 | 3.49 |
| 1952—Cleveland | American | 30 | 192 | 9 | 13 | .409 | 4.73 |
| 1953—Cleveland | American | 25 | 176 | 10 | 7 | .588 | 3.58 |
| 1954—Cleveland | American | 19 | 140 | 13 | 3 | .813 | 3.09 |
| 1955—Cleveland | American | 25 | 83 | 4 | 4 | .500 | 3.47 |
| 1956—Cleveland | American | 19 | 58 | 0 | 4 | .000 | 4.97 |
| Major League Totals | | 570 | 3828 | 266 | 162 | .621 | 3.25 |

### WORLD SERIES RECORD

| Year | Club | League | G. | IP. | W. | L. | Pct. | ERA. |
|---|---|---|---|---|---|---|---|---|
| 1948—Cleveland | American | 2 | 14⅓ | 0 | 2 | .000 | 5.02 |

## ELMER HARRISON FLICK

| Year | Club | League | G. | AB. | R. | H. | HR. | SB. | B.A. |
|---|---|---|---|---|---|---|---|---|---|
| 1896—Youngstown | Int. St. | | 31 | 130 | 34 | 57 | | | .438 |
| 1897—Dayton | Int. St. | | 126 | 474 | 135 | 183 | | | .386 |
| 1898—Philadelphia | Nat. | | 133 | 447 | 84 | 142 | 7 | 29 | .318 |
| 1899—Philadelphia | Nat. | | 125 | 486 | 101 | 167 | 2 | 31 | .344 |
| 1900—Philadelphia | Nat. | | 138 | 547 | 106 | 207 | 11 | 37 | .378 |
| 1901—Philadelphia | Nat. | | 138 | 542 | 111 | 182 | 8 | 26 | .336 |
| 1902—Phil.-Cleve. | Amer. | | 121 | 464 | 83 | 137 | 2 | 24 | .295 |
| 1903—Cleveland | Amer. | | *142 | 529 | 84 | 158 | 2 | 27 | .299 |
| 1904—Cleveland | Amer. | | 149 | 575 | 95 | 174 | 6 | ●42 | .303 |
| 1905—Cleveland | Amer. | | 131 | 500 | 72 | 154 | 4 | 35 | *.308 |
| 1906—Cleveland | Amer. | | *157 | *624 | *98 | 194 | 1 | ●39 | .311 |
| 1907—Cleveland | Amer. | | 147 | 549 | 80 | 166 | 3 | 41 | .302 |
| 1908—Cleveland | Amer. | | 9 | 35 | 4 | 8 | 0 | 0 | .229 |
| 1909—Cleveland | Amer. | | 66 | 235 | 28 | 60 | 0 | 9 | .255 |
| 1910—Cleveland | Amer. | | 24 | 68 | 5 | 18 | 1 | 1 | .265 |
| 1911—Toledo | A. A. | | 84 | 313 | 63 | 102 | 3 | 10 | .326 |
| 1912—Toledo | A. A. | | 115 | 382 | 60 | 100 | 2 | 28 | .262 |
| American League Totals | | | 946 | 3579 | 549 | 1069 | 18 | 218 | .299 |
| National League Totals | | | 534 | 2022 | 402 | 698 | 28 | 123 | .345 |
| Major League Totals | | | 1480 | 5601 | 951 | 1767 | 46 | 341 | .315 |

## EDWARD CHARLES (WHITEY) FORD

| Year | Club | League | G. | IP. | W. | L. | Pct. | ERA. |
|---|---|---|---|---|---|---|---|---|
| 1947—Butler | Mid. Atl. | 24 | 157 | 13 | 4 | .765 | 3.84 |
| 1948—Norfolk | Pied. | 30 | 216 | 16 | 8 | .667 | 2.58 |
| 1949—Binghamton | East. | 26 | 168 | 16 | 5 | .762 | *1.61 |
| 1950—Kansas City | A. A. | 12 | 95 | 6 | 3 | .667 | 3.22 |
| 1950—New York | Amer. | 20 | 112 | 9 | 1 | .900 | 2.81 |
| 1951-52—New York | Amer. | (In Military Service) | | | | | |
| 1953—New York | Amer. | 32 | 207 | 18 | 6 | .750 | 3.00 |
| 1954—New York | Amer. | 34 | 211 | 16 | 8 | .667 | 2.82 |
| 1955—New York | Amer. | 39 | 254 | ●18 | 7 | .720 | 2.62 |
| 1956—New York | Amer. | 31 | 226 | 19 | 6 | *.760 | *2.47 |
| 1957—New York | Amer. | 24 | 129 | 11 | 5 | .688 | 2.58 |
| 1958—New York | Amer. | 30 | 219 | 14 | 7 | .667 | *2.01 |
| 1959—New York | Amer. | 35 | 204 | 16 | 10 | .615 | 3.04 |
| 1960—New York | Amer. | 33 | 193 | 12 | 9 | .571 | 3.08 |
| 1961—New York | Amer. | 39 | *283 | *25 | 4 | *.862 | 3.21 |
| 1962—New York | Amer. | 38 | 258 | 17 | 8 | .680 | 2.90 |
| 1963—New York | Amer. | 38 | *269 | *24 | 7 | *.774 | 2.74 |
| 1964—New York | Amer. | 39 | 245 | 17 | 6 | .739 | 2.13 |

| Year Club | League | G. | IP. | W. | L. | Pct. | ERA. |
|---|---|---|---|---|---|---|---|
| 1965—New York | Amer. | 37 | 244 | 16 | 13 | .552 | 3.25 |
| 1966—New York | Amer. | 22 | 73 | 2 | 5 | .286 | 2.47 |
| 1967—New York | Amer. | 7 | 44 | 2 | 4 | .333 | 1.64 |
| Major League Totals | | 498 | 3171 | 236 | 106 | .690 | 2.74 |

### WORLD SERIES RECORD

| Year Club | League | G. | IP. | W. | L. | Pct. | ERA. |
|---|---|---|---|---|---|---|---|
| 1950—New York | Amer. | 1 | 8⅔ | 1 | 0 | 1.000 | 0.00 |
| 1953—New York | Amer. | 2 | 8 | 0 | 1 | .000 | 4.50 |
| 1955—New York | Amer. | 2 | 17 | 2 | 0 | 1.000 | 2.12 |
| 1956—New York | Amer. | 2 | 12 | 1 | 1 | .500 | 5.25 |
| 1957—New York | Amer. | 2 | 16 | 1 | 1 | .500 | 1.13 |
| 1958—New York | Amer. | 3 | 15⅓ | 1 | 0 | 1.000 | 4.11 |
| 1960—New York | Amer. | 2 | 18 | 2 | 0 | 1.000 | 0.00 |
| 1961—New York | Amer. | 2 | 14 | 2 | 0 | 1.000 | 0.00 |
| 1962—New York | Amer. | 3 | 19⅔ | 1 | 1 | .500 | 4.12 |
| 1963—New York | Amer. | 2 | 12 | 0 | 2 | .000 | 4.50 |
| 1964—New York | Amer. | 1 | 5⅓ | 0 | 1 | .000 | 8.44 |
| World Series Totals | | 22 | 146 | 10 | 8 | .556 | 2.71 |

### JAMES EMORY (JIMMIE) FOXX

| Year Club | League | G. | AB. | R. | H. | HR. | RBI. | B.A. |
|---|---|---|---|---|---|---|---|---|
| 1924—Easton | East. Sh. | 76 | 260 | 33 | 77 | 10 | .... | .296 |
| 1925—Philadelphia | Amer. | 10 | 9 | 2 | 6 | 0 | 0 | .667 |
| 1925—Providence | Int. | 41 | 101 | 12 | 33 | 1 | 15 | .327 |
| 1926—Philadelphia | Amer. | 26 | 32 | 8 | 10 | 0 | 5 | .313 |
| 1927—Philadelphia | Amer. | 61 | 130 | 23 | 42 | 3 | 20 | .323 |
| 1928—Philadelphia | Amer. | 118 | 400 | 85 | 131 | 13 | 79 | .328 |
| 1929—Philadelphia | Amer. | 149 | 517 | 123 | 183 | 33 | 117 | .354 |
| 1930—Philadelphia | Amer. | 153 | 562 | 127 | 188 | 37 | 156 | .335 |
| 1931—Philadelphia | Amer. | 139 | 515 | 93 | 150 | 30 | 120 | .291 |
| 1932—Philadelphia | Amer. | 154 | 585 | ★151 | 213 | ★58 | ★169 | .364 |
| 1933—Philadelphia | Amer. | 149 | 573 | 125 | 204 | ★48 | ★163 | .356 |
| 1934—Philadelphia | Amer. | 150 | 539 | 120 | 180 | 44 | 130 | .334 |
| 1935—Philadelphia | Amer. | 147 | 535 | 118 | 185 | ●36 | 115 | .346 |
| 1936—Boston | Amer. | ●155 | 585 | 130 | 198 | 41 | 143 | .338 |
| 1937—Boston | Amer. | 150 | 569 | 111 | 162 | 36 | 127 | .285 |
| 1938—Boston | Amer. | 149 | 565 | 139 | 197 | 50 | ★175 | .349 |
| 1939—Boston | Amer. | 124 | 467 | 130 | 168 | ★35 | 105 | .360 |
| 1940—Boston | Amer. | 144 | 515 | 106 | 153 | 36 | 119 | .297 |
| 1941—Boston | Amer. | 135 | 487 | 87 | 146 | 19 | 105 | .300 |
| 1942—Boston | Amer. | 30 | 100 | 18 | 27 | 5 | 14 | .270 |
| 1942—Chicago | Nat. | 70 | 205 | 25 | 42 | 3 | 19 | .205 |
| 1943—Chicago | Nat. | (Did not play) | | | | | | |
| 1944—Chicago | Nat. | 15 | 20 | 0 | 1 | 0 | 2 | .050 |
| 1944—Portsmouth | Pied. | 5 | 2 | 0 | 0 | 0 | 0 | .000 |
| 1945—Philadelphia | Nat. | 89 | 224 | 30 | 60 | 7 | 38 | .268 |
| 1946— | | (Out of Organized Ball) | | | | | | |
| 1947—St. Petersburg | Fla. Int. | 6 | 6 | 0 | 1 | .... | .... | .167 |
| American League Totals | | 2143 | 7685 | 1696 | 2543 | 524 | 1862 | .331 |
| National League Totals | | 174 | 449 | 55 | 103 | 10 | 59 | .229 |
| Major League Totals | | 2317 | 8134 | 1751 | 2646 | 534 | 1921 | .325 |

### PITCHING RECORD

| Year Club | League | G. | IP. | W. | L. | Pct. | ERA. |
|---|---|---|---|---|---|---|---|
| 1939—Boston | Amer. | 1 | 1 | 0 | 0 | .000 | 0.00 |
| 1945—Philadelphia | Nat. | 9 | 23 | 1 | 0 | 1.000 | 1.57 |
| Major League Totals | | 10 | 24 | 1 | 0 | 1.000 | 1.50 |

### WORLD SERIES RECORD

| Year Club | League | G. | AB. | R. | H. | HR. | RBI. | B.A. |
|---|---|---|---|---|---|---|---|---|
| 1929—Philadelphia | Amer. | 5 | 20 | 5 | 7 | 2 | 5 | .350 |
| 1930—Philadelphia | Amer. | 6 | 21 | 3 | 7 | 1 | 3 | .333 |
| 1931—Philadelphia | Amer. | 7 | 23 | 3 | 8 | 1 | 3 | .348 |
| World Series Totals | | 18 | 64 | 11 | 22 | 4 | 11 | .344 |

### FRANK FRANCIS (FORDHAM FLASH) FRISCH

| Year Club | League | G. | AB. | R. | H. | HR. | RBI. | B.A. |
|---|---|---|---|---|---|---|---|---|
| 1919—New York | Nat. | 54 | 190 | 21 | 43 | 2 | 22 | .226 |
| 1920—New York | Nat. | 110 | 440 | 57 | 123 | 4 | 77 | .280 |
| 1921—New York | Nat. | 153 | 618 | 121 | 211 | 8 | 100 | .341 |
| 1922—New York | Nat. | 132 | 514 | 101 | 168 | 5 | 51 | .327 |
| 1923—New York | Nat. | 151 | 641 | 116 | ★223 | 12 | 111 | .348 |
| 1924—New York | Nat. | 145 | 603 | ●121 | 198 | 7 | 69 | .328 |
| 1925—New York | Nat. | 120 | 502 | 89 | 166 | 11 | 48 | .331 |
| 1926—New York | Nat. | 135 | 535 | 75 | 171 | 5 | 44 | .314 |
| 1927—St. Louis | Nat. | 153 | 617 | 112 | 208 | 10 | 78 | .337 |
| 1928—St. Louis | Nat. | 141 | 547 | 107 | 164 | 10 | 86 | .300 |
| 1929—St. Louis | Nat. | 138 | 527 | 93 | 176 | 5 | 74 | .334 |
| 1930—St. Louis | Nat. | 133 | 540 | 121 | 187 | 10 | 114 | .346 |
| 1931—St. Louis | Nat. | 131 | 518 | 96 | 161 | 4 | 82 | .311 |
| 1932—St. Louis | Nat. | 115 | 486 | 59 | 142 | 3 | 60 | .292 |
| 1933—St. Louis | Nat. | 147 | 585 | 74 | 177 | 4 | 66 | .303 |
| 1934—St. Louis | Nat. | 140 | 550 | 74 | 168 | 3 | 75 | .305 |
| 1935—St. Louis | Nat. | 103 | 354 | 52 | 104 | 1 | 55 | .294 |
| 1936—St. Louis | Nat. | 93 | 303 | 40 | 83 | 1 | 26 | .274 |
| 1937—St. Louis | Nat. | 17 | 32 | 3 | 7 | 0 | 4 | .219 |
| Major League Totals | | 2311 | 9112 | 1532 | 2880 | 105 | 1242 | .316 |

### WORLD SERIES RECORD

| Year Club | League | G. | AB. | R. | H. | HR. | RBI. | B.A. |
|---|---|---|---|---|---|---|---|---|
| 1921—New York | Nat. | 8 | 30 | 5 | 9 | 0 | 1 | .300 |
| 1922—New York | Nat. | 5 | 17 | 3 | 8 | 0 | 2 | .471 |
| 1923—New York | Nat. | 6 | 25 | 2 | 10 | 0 | 1 | .400 |
| 1924—New York | Nat. | 7 | 30 | 1 | 10 | 0 | 0 | .333 |
| 1928—St. Louis | Nat. | 4 | 13 | 1 | 3 | 0 | 1 | .231 |
| 1930—St. Louis | Nat. | 6 | 24 | 0 | 5 | 0 | 0 | .208 |
| 1931—St. Louis | Nat. | 7 | 27 | 2 | 7 | 0 | 1 | .259 |
| 1934—St. Louis | Nat. | 7 | 31 | 2 | 6 | 0 | 4 | .194 |
| World Series Totals | | 50 | 197 | 16 | 58 | 0 | 10 | .294 |

### JAMES F. (PUD or GENTLE JAMES) GALVIN

| Year Club | League | G. | IP. | W. | L. | Pct. | ShO. |
|---|---|---|---|---|---|---|---|
| 1875—St. Louis | National Assn. | 9 | .... | 4 | 2 | .... | .... |
| 1876—St. Louis Red Stockings | | (Independent Ball) | | | | | |
| 1877—Allegheny | Int. Assn. | 19 | .... | .... | .... | 96 | 4 |
| 1878—Buffalo | Int. Assn. | 38 | .... | .... | .... | .... | .... |
| 1879—Buffalo | National | 66 | 592 | 37 | 27 | .578 | 6 |
| 1880—Buffalo | National | 58 | 462 | 20 | 37 | .351 | 5 |
| 1881—Buffalo | National | 56 | 470 | 29 | 24 | .547 | 5 |
| 1882—Buffalo | National | 52 | 437 | 28 | 22 | .560 | 3 |
| 1883—Buffalo | National | 76 | ★656 | 46 | 29 | .613 | ●5 |
| 1884—Buffalo | National | 72 | 636 | 46 | 22 | .676 | ★12 |
| 1885—Buffalo | National | 33 | 287 | 13 | 19 | .406 | 3 |
| 1885—Allegheny | American Assn. | 11 | 89 | 3 | 7 | .300 | 0 |
| 1886—Allegheny | American Assn. | 50 | 443 | 29 | 21 | .580 | 2 |
| 1887—Pittsburgh | National | 49 | 440 | 28 | 21 | .571 | 3 |
| 1888—Pittsburgh | National | 50 | 436 | 23 | 25 | .479 | 6 |
| 1889—Pittsburgh | National | 41 | 347 | 23 | 16 | .590 | 4 |
| 1890—Pittsburgh | Players | 26 | 216 | 12 | 13 | .480 | 1 |
| 1891—Pittsburgh | National | 33 | 260 | 14 | 13 | .519 | 2 |
| 1892—Pitt. -St. L. | National | 24 | 188 | 10 | 13 | .435 | 0 |
| 1894—Buffalo | Eastern | 2 | .... | 0 | 2 | .000 | .... |
| National League Totals | | 610 | 5211 | 317 | 268 | .542 | 54 |
| American Association Totals | | 61 | 532 | 32 | 28 | .533 | 2 |
| Players League Totals | | 26 | 216 | 12 | 13 | .480 | 1 |
| Major League Totals | | 697 | 5959 | 361 | 309 | .539 | 57 |

### HENRY LOUIS (LOU or IRON HORSE) GEHRIG

| Year Club | League | G. | AB. | R. | H. | HR. | RBI. | B.A. |
|---|---|---|---|---|---|---|---|---|
| 1921—Hartford | East. | 12 | 46 | 5 | 12 | 0 | .... | .261 |
| 1922— | | (Not in Organized Ball) | | | | | | |
| 1923—New York | Amer. | 13 | 26 | 6 | 11 | 1 | 9 | .423 |
| 1923—Hartford | East. | 59 | 227 | 54 | 69 | 24 | .... | .304 |
| 1924—New York | Amer. | 10 | 12 | 2 | 6 | 0 | 5 | .500 |
| 1924—Hartford | East. | 134 | 504 | 111 | 186 | 37 | .... | .369 |
| 1925—New York | Amer. | 126 | 437 | 73 | 129 | 20 | 68 | .295 |
| 1926—New York | Amer. | 155 | 572 | 135 | 179 | 16 | 107 | .313 |
| 1927—New York | Amer. | ★155 | 584 | 149 | 218 | 47 | ★175 | .373 |
| 1928—New York | Amer. | 154 | 562 | 139 | 210 | 27 | ●142 | .374 |
| 1929—New York | Amer. | 154 | 553 | 127 | 166 | 35 | 126 | .300 |
| 1930—New York | Amer. | ●154 | 581 | 143 | 220 | 41 | ★174 | .379 |
| 1931—New York | Amer. | 155 | 619 | ●163 | ★211 | 46 | ★184 | .341 |
| 1932—New York | Amer. | ★156 | 596 | 138 | 208 | 34 | 151 | .349 |
| 1933—New York | Amer. | 152 | 593 | ★138 | 198 | 32 | 139 | .334 |
| 1934—New York | Amer. | ●154 | 579 | 128 | 210 | ★49 | ★165 | ★.363 |
| 1935—New York | Amer. | 149 | 535 | ★125 | 176 | 30 | 119 | .329 |
| 1936—New York | Amer. | ●155 | 579 | ★167 | 205 | ★49 | 152 | .354 |
| 1937—New York | Amer. | ★157 | 569 | 138 | 200 | 37 | 159 | .351 |
| 1938—New York | Amer. | ●157 | 576 | 115 | 170 | 29 | 114 | .295 |
| 1939—New York | Amer. | 8 | 28 | 2 | 4 | 0 | 1 | .143 |
| Major League Totals | | 2164 | 8001 | 1888 | 2721 | 493 | 1990 | .340 |

### WORLD SERIES RECORD

| Year Club | League | G. | AB. | R. | H. | HR. | RBI. | B.A. |
|---|---|---|---|---|---|---|---|---|
| 1926—New York | Amer. | 7 | 23 | 1 | 8 | 0 | 3 | .348 |
| 1927—New York | Amer. | 4 | 13 | 2 | 4 | 0 | 4 | .308 |
| 1928—New York | Amer. | 4 | 11 | 5 | 6 | 4 | 9 | .545 |
| 1932—New York | Amer. | 4 | 17 | 9 | 9 | 3 | 8 | .529 |
| 1936—New York | Amer. | 6 | 24 | 5 | 7 | 2 | 7 | .292 |
| 1937—New York | Amer. | 5 | 17 | 4 | 5 | 1 | 3 | .294 |
| 1938—New York | Amer. | 4 | 14 | 4 | 4 | 0 | 0 | .286 |
| World Series Totals | | 34 | 119 | 30 | 43 | 10 | 34 | .361 |

### CHARLES LEONARD (MECHANICAL MAN) GEHRINGER

| Year Club | League | G. | AB. | R. | H. | HR. | RBI. | B.A. |
|---|---|---|---|---|---|---|---|---|
| 1924—London | Mich.-Ont. | 112 | 401 | 60 | 117 | 3 | 60 | .292 |
| 1924—Detroit | Amer. | 5 | 13 | 2 | 6 | 0 | 1 | .462 |
| 1925—Toronto | Int. | 155 | 633 | 128 | 206 | 25 | 108 | .325 |
| 1925—Detroit | Amer. | 8 | 18 | 3 | 3 | 0 | 0 | .167 |
| 1926—Detroit | Amer. | 123 | 459 | 62 | 127 | 1 | 48 | .277 |
| 1927—Detroit | Amer. | 133 | 508 | 110 | 161 | 4 | 61 | .317 |
| 1928—Detroit | Amer. | 154 | 603 | 108 | 193 | 6 | 74 | .320 |
| 1929—Detroit | Amer. | ●155 | 634 | ★131 | ●215 | 13 | 106 | .339 |
| 1930—Detroit | Amer. | ●154 | 610 | 144 | 201 | 16 | 98 | .330 |
| 1931—Detroit | Amer. | 101 | 383 | 67 | 119 | 4 | 53 | .311 |
| 1932—Detroit | Amer. | 152 | 618 | 112 | 184 | 19 | 107 | .298 |
| 1933—Detroit | Amer. | ●155 | 628 | 103 | 204 | 12 | 105 | .325 |

| Year Club | League | G. | AB. | R. | H. | HR. | RBI. | B.A. |
|---|---|---|---|---|---|---|---|---|
| 1934—Detroit | Amer. | ●154 | 601 | *134 | *214 | 11 | 127 | .356 |
| 1935—Detroit | Amer. | 150 | 610 | 123 | 201 | 19 | 108 | .330 |
| 1936—Detroit | Amer. | 154 | 641 | 144 | 227 | 15 | 116 | .354 |
| 1937—Detroit | Amer. | 144 | 564 | 133 | 209 | 14 | 96 | *.371 |
| 1938—Detroit | Amer. | 152 | 568 | 133 | 174 | 20 | 107 | .306 |
| 1939—Detroit | Amer. | 118 | 406 | 86 | 132 | 16 | 86 | .325 |
| 1940—Detroit | Amer. | 139 | 515 | 108 | 161 | 10 | 81 | .313 |
| 1941—Detroit | Amer. | 127 | 436 | 65 | 96 | 3 | 46 | .220 |
| 1942—Detroit | Amer. | 45 | 45 | 6 | 12 | 1 | 7 | .267 |
| Major League Totals | | 2323 | 8860 | 1774 | 2839 | 184 | 1427 | .320 |

### WORLD SERIES RECORD

| Year Club | League | G. | AB. | R. | H. | HR. | RBI. | B.A. |
|---|---|---|---|---|---|---|---|---|
| 1934—Detroit | Amer. | 7 | 29 | 5 | 11 | 1 | 2 | .379 |
| 1935—Detroit | Amer. | 6 | 24 | 4 | 9 | 0 | 4 | .375 |
| 1940—Detroit | Amer. | 7 | 28 | 3 | 6 | 0 | 1 | .214 |
| World Series Totals | | 20 | 81 | 12 | 26 | 1 | 7 | .321 |

## ROBERT GIBSON

| Year Club | League | G. | IP. | W. | L. | Pct. | ERA. |
|---|---|---|---|---|---|---|---|
| 1957—Omaha | Amer. Assoc. | 10 | 42 | 2 | 1 | .667 | 4.29 |
| 1957—Columbus | Sally | 8 | 43 | 4 | 3 | .571 | 3.77 |
| 1958—Omaha | Amer. Assoc. | 13 | 87 | 3 | 4 | .429 | 3.31 |
| 1958—Rochester | International | 20 | 103 | 5 | 5 | .500 | 2.45 |
| 1959—Omaha | Amer. Assoc. | 24 | 135 | 9 | 9 | .500 | 3.07 |
| 1959—St. Louis | National | 13 | 76 | 3 | 5 | .375 | 3.32 |
| 1960—St. Louis | National | 27 | 87 | 3 | 6 | .333 | 5.59 |
| 1960—Rochester | International | 6 | 41 | 2 | 3 | .400 | 2.85 |
| 1961—St. Louis | National | 35 | 211 | 13 | 12 | .520 | 3.24 |
| 1962—St. Louis | National | 32 | 234 | 15 | 13 | .536 | 2.85 |
| 1963—St. Louis | National | 36 | 255 | 18 | 9 | .667 | 3.39 |
| 1964—St. Louis | National | 40 | 287 | 19 | 12 | .613 | 3.01 |
| 1965—St. Louis | National | 38 | 299 | 20 | 12 | .625 | 3.07 |
| 1966—St. Louis | National | 35 | 280 | 21 | 12 | .636 | 2.44 |
| 1967—St. Louis | National | 24 | 175 | 13 | 7 | .650 | 2.98 |
| 1968—St. Louis | National | 34 | 305 | 22 | 9 | .710 | *1.12 |
| 1969—St. Louis | National | 35 | 314 | 20 | 13 | .606 | 2.18 |
| 1970—St. Louis | National | 34 | 294 | ●23 | 7 | .767 | 3.12 |
| 1971—St. Louis | National | 31 | 246 | 16 | 13 | .552 | 3.04 |
| 1972—St. Louis | National | 34 | 278 | 19 | 11 | .633 | 2.46 |
| 1973—St. Louis | National | 25 | 195 | 12 | 10 | .545 | 2.77 |
| 1974—St. Louis | National | 33 | 240 | 11 | 13 | .458 | 3.83 |
| 1975—St. Louis | National | 22 | 109 | 3 | 10 | .231 | 5.04 |
| Major League Totals | | 528 | 3885 | 251 | 174 | .591 | 2.91 |

### WORLD SERIES RECORD

| Year Club | League | G. | IP. | W. | L. | Pct. | ERA. |
|---|---|---|---|---|---|---|---|
| 1964—St. Louis | National | 3 | 27 | 2 | 1 | .667 | 3.00 |
| 1967—St. Louis | National | 3 | 27 | 3 | 0 | 1.000 | 1.00 |
| 1968—St. Louis | National | 3 | 27 | 2 | 1 | .667 | 1.67 |
| World Series Totals | | 9 | 81 | 7 | 2 | .778 | 1.89 |

## VERNON (LEFTY) GOMEZ

| Year Club | League | G. | IP. | W. | L. | Pct. | ERA. |
|---|---|---|---|---|---|---|---|
| 1928—Salt Lake | Utah-Idaho | *39 | 194 | 12 | *14 | .462 | 3.48 |
| 1929—San Francisco | Pacific Coast | 41 | 267 | 18 | 11 | .621 | *3.44 |
| 1930—New York | American | 15 | 60 | 2 | 5 | .286 | 5.55 |
| 1930—St. Paul | Amer. Assn. | 17 | 86 | 8 | 4 | .667 | 4.08 |
| 1931—New York | American | 40 | 243 | 21 | 9 | .700 | 2.63 |
| 1932—New York | American | 37 | 265 | 24 | 7 | .774 | 4.21 |
| 1933—New York | American | 35 | 235 | 16 | 10 | .615 | 3.18 |
| 1934—New York | American | 38 | *282 | *26 | 5 | *.839 | *2.33 |
| 1935—New York | American | 34 | 246 | 12 | 15 | .444 | 3.18 |
| 1936—New York | American | 31 | 189 | 13 | 7 | .650 | 4.39 |
| 1937—New York | American | 34 | 278 | *21 | 11 | .656 | *2.33 |
| 1938—New York | American | 32 | 239 | 18 | 12 | .600 | 3.35 |
| 1939—New York | American | 26 | 198 | 12 | 8 | .600 | 3.41 |
| 1940—New York | American | 9 | 27 | 3 | 3 | .500 | 6.67 |
| 1941—New York | American | 23 | 156 | 15 | 5 | *.750 | 3.75 |
| 1942—New York | American | 13 | 80 | 6 | 4 | .600 | 4.28 |
| 1943—Washington | American | 1 | 5 | 0 | 1 | .000 | 5.40 |
| 1946—Binghamton | Eastern | 1 | 3 | 0 | 0 | .000 | 9.00 |
| 1947—Binghamton | Eastern | 1 | 1 | 0 | 0 | .000 | 0.00 |
| Major League Totals | | 368 | 2503 | 189 | 102 | .649 | 3.34 |

### WORLD SERIES RECORD

| Year Club | League | G. | IP. | W. | L. | Pct. | ERA. |
|---|---|---|---|---|---|---|---|
| 1932—New York | American | 1 | 9 | 1 | 0 | 1.000 | 1.00 |
| 1936—New York | American | 2 | 15⅓ | 2 | 0 | 1.000 | 4.70 |
| 1937—New York | American | 2 | 18 | 2 | 0 | 1.000 | 1.50 |
| 1938—New York | American | 1 | 7 | 1 | 0 | 1.000 | 3.86 |
| 1939—New York | American | 1 | 1 | 0 | 0 | .000 | 9.00 |
| World Series Totals | | 7 | 50⅓ | 6 | 0 | 1.000 | 2.86 |

## LEON ALLEN (GOOSE) GOSLIN

| Year Club | League | G. | AB. | R. | H. | HR. | RBI. | B.A. |
|---|---|---|---|---|---|---|---|---|
| 1920—Columbia | Sally | 90 | 319 | 52 | 101 | 4 | 65 | .317 |
| 1921—Columbia | Sally | 142 | 549 | *124 | *214 | 16 | *131 | *.390 |
| 1921—Washington | Amer. | 14 | 50 | 8 | 13 | 1 | 6 | .260 |

| Year Club | League | G. | AB. | R. | H. | HR. | RBI. | B.A. |
|---|---|---|---|---|---|---|---|---|
| 1922—Washington | Amer. | 101 | 358 | 44 | 116 | 3 | 53 | .324 |
| 1923—Washington | Amer. | 150 | 600 | 86 | 180 | 9 | 99 | .300 |
| 1924—Washington | Amer. | 154 | 579 | 100 | 199 | 12 | *129 | .344 |
| 1925—Washington | Amer. | 150 | 601 | 116 | 201 | 18 | 113 | .334 |
| 1926—Washington | Amer. | 147 | 568 | 105 | 201 | 17 | 108 | .354 |
| 1927—Washington | Amer. | 148 | 581 | 96 | 194 | 13 | 120 | .334 |
| 1928—Washington | Amer. | 135 | 456 | 80 | 173 | 17 | 102 | *.379 |
| 1929—Washington | Amer. | 145 | 553 | 82 | 159 | 18 | 91 | .288 |
| 1930—Wash.-St.L. | Amer. | 148 | 584 | 115 | 180 | 37 | 138 | .308 |
| 1931—St. Louis | Amer. | 151 | 591 | 114 | 194 | 24 | 105 | .328 |
| 1932—St. Louis | Amer. | 150 | 572 | 88 | 171 | 17 | 104 | .299 |
| 1933—Washington | Amer. | 132 | 549 | 97 | 163 | 10 | 64 | .297 |
| 1934—Detroit | Amer. | 151 | 614 | 106 | 187 | 13 | 100 | .305 |
| 1935—Detroit | Amer. | 147 | 590 | 88 | 172 | 9 | 109 | .292 |
| 1936—Detroit | Amer. | 147 | 572 | 122 | 180 | 24 | 125 | .315 |
| 1937—Detroit | Amer. | 79 | 181 | 30 | 43 | 4 | 35 | .238 |
| 1938—Washington | Amer. | 38 | 57 | 6 | 9 | 2 | 8 | .158 |
| 1939—Trenton | Int.-St. | 99 | 349 | 65 | 113 | 3 | 58 | .324 |
| 1940—Trenton | Int.-St. | 49 | 128 | 24 | 32 | 1 | 16 | .250 |
| Major League Totals | | 2287 | 8656 | 1483 | 2735 | 248 | 1609 | .316 |

### WORLD SERIES RECORD

| Year Club | League | G. | AB. | R. | H. | HR. | RBI. | B.A. |
|---|---|---|---|---|---|---|---|---|
| 1924—Washington | Amer. | 7 | 32 | 4 | 11 | 3 | 7 | .344 |
| 1925—Washington | Amer. | 7 | 26 | 6 | 8 | 3 | 6 | .308 |
| 1933—Washington | Amer. | 5 | 20 | 2 | 5 | 1 | 1 | .250 |
| 1934—Detroit | Amer. | 7 | 29 | 2 | 7 | 0 | 2 | .241 |
| 1935—Detroit | Amer. | 6 | 22 | 2 | 6 | 0 | 3 | .273 |
| World Series Totals | | 32 | 129 | 16 | 37 | 7 | 19 | .287 |

## HENRY BENJAMIN (HANK) GREENBERG

| Year Club | League | G. | AB. | R. | H. | HR. | RBI. | B.A. |
|---|---|---|---|---|---|---|---|---|
| 1930—Hartford | East. | 17 | 56 | 10 | 12 | 2 | 6 | .214 |
| 1930—Raleigh | Pied. | 122 | 452 | 88 | 142 | 19 | 93 | .314 |
| 1930—Detroit | Amer. | 1 | 1 | 0 | 0 | 0 | 0 | .000 |
| 1931—Evansville | I.I.I. | ●126 | 487 | 88 | 155 | 15 | 85 | .318 |
| 1931—Beaumont | Texas | 3 | 2 | 0 | 0 | 0 | 0 | .000 |
| 1932—Beaumont | Texas | 154 | 600 | *123 | 174 | *39 | 131 | .290 |
| 1933—Detroit | Amer. | 117 | 449 | 59 | 135 | 12 | 87 | .301 |
| 1934—Detroit | Amer. | 153 | 593 | 118 | 201 | 26 | 139 | .339 |
| 1935—Detroit | Amer. | 152 | 619 | 121 | 203 | ●36 | *170 | .328 |
| 1936—Detroit | Amer. | 12 | 46 | 10 | 16 | 1 | 16 | .348 |
| 1937—Detroit | Amer. | 154 | 594 | 137 | 200 | 40 | *183 | .337 |
| 1938—Detroit | Amer. | 155 | 556 | *144 | 175 | *58 | 146 | .315 |
| 1939—Detroit | Amer. | 138 | 500 | 112 | 156 | 33 | 112 | .312 |
| 1940—Detroit | Amer. | 148 | 573 | 129 | 195 | *41 | *150 | .340 |
| 1941—Detroit | Amer. | 19 | 67 | 12 | 18 | 2 | 12 | .269 |
| 1942-43-44—Detroit | Amer. | | (In Military Service) | | | | | |
| 1945—Detroit | Amer. | 78 | 270 | 47 | 84 | 13 | 60 | .311 |
| 1946—Detroit | Amer. | 142 | 523 | 91 | 145 | *44 | *127 | .277 |
| 1947—Pittsburgh | Nat. | 125 | 402 | 71 | 100 | 25 | 74 | .249 |
| American League Totals | | 1269 | 4791 | 980 | 1528 | 306 | 1202 | .319 |
| National League Totals | | 125 | 402 | 71 | 100 | 25 | 74 | .249 |
| Major League Totals | | 1394 | 5193 | 1051 | 1628 | 331 | 1276 | .313 |

### WORLD SERIES RECORD

| Year Club | League | G. | AB. | R. | H. | HR. | RBI. | B.A. |
|---|---|---|---|---|---|---|---|---|
| 1934—Detroit | Amer. | 7 | 28 | 4 | 9 | 1 | 7 | .321 |
| 1935—Detroit | Amer. | 2 | 6 | 1 | 1 | 1 | 2 | .167 |
| 1940—Detroit | Amer. | 7 | 28 | 5 | 10 | 1 | 6 | .357 |
| 1945—Detroit | Amer. | 7 | 23 | 7 | 7 | 2 | 7 | .304 |
| World Series Totals | | 23 | 85 | 17 | 27 | 5 | 22 | .318 |

## CLARK CALVIN (OLD FOX) GRIFFITH

| Year Club | League | G. | IP. | W. | L. | Pct. |
|---|---|---|---|---|---|---|
| 1888—Bloomington | Cent.-Int. St. | 14 | .... | 10 | 4 | .714 |
| 1888—Milwaukee | Western | 23 | .... | 12 | 10 | .545 |
| 1889—Milwaukee | Western | 31 | .... | 18 | 13 | .581 |
| 1890—Milwaukee | Western | 34 | .... | 27 | 7 | .794 |
| 1891—St. Louis-Boston | Amer. Assn. | 24 | 225 | 17 | 7 | .708 |
| 1892—Tacoma | P. N. W. | 24 | .... | 13 | 7 | .650 |
| 1893—Oakland | Pacific Coast | 48 | .... | 30 | 18 | .625 |
| 1893—Chicago | National | 3 | 22 | 1 | 1 | .500 |
| 1894—Chicago | National | 32 | 274 | 21 | 11 | .656 |
| 1895—Chicago | National | 39 | 352 | 25 | 13 | .658 |
| 1896—Chicago | National | 35 | 319 | 22 | 13 | .629 |
| 1897—Chicago | National | 46 | 344 | 21 | 19 | .525 |
| 1898—Chicago | National | 37 | 316 | 26 | 10 | .722 |
| 1899—Chicago | National | 39 | 319 | 22 | 13 | .629 |
| 1900—Chicago | National | 27 | 249 | 14 | 13 | .519 |
| 1901—Chicago | American | 32 | 257 | 24 | 7 | *.774 |
| 1902—Chicago | American | 25 | 216 | 15 | 9 | .625 |
| 1903—New York | American | 24 | 214 | 14 | 10 | .583 |
| 1904—New York | American | 12 | 92 | 7 | 5 | .583 |
| 1905—New York | American | 16 | 100 | 9 | 6 | .600 |
| 1906—New York | American | 17 | 61 | 2 | 2 | .500 |
| 1907—New York | American | 4 | 6 | 0 | 0 | .000 |
| 1909—Cincinnati | National | 1 | 1 | 0 | 1 | .000 |
| 1910—Cincinnati | National | | (One game as pinch-hitter) | | | |

| Year | Club | League | G. | IP. | W. | L. | Pct. |
|---|---|---|---|---|---|---|---|
| 1912—Washington | American | | 1 | 1 | 0 | 0 | .000 |
| 1913—Washington | American | | 1 | 1 | 0 | 0 | .000 |
| 1914—Washington | American | | 1 | 1 | 0 | 0 | .000 |
| American League Totals | | | 133 | 949 | 71 | 39 | .645 |
| National League Totals | | | 259 | 2196 | 152 | 94 | .618 |
| American Association Totals | | | 24 | 225 | 17 | 7 | .708 |
| Major League Totals | | | 416 | 3370 | 240 | 140 | .632 |

## BURLEIGH ARLAND (OLD STUBBLEBEARD) GRIMES

| Year | Club | League | G. | IP. | W. | L. | Pct. | ERA. |
|---|---|---|---|---|---|---|---|---|
| 1912—Eau Claire | Minn.-Wis. | (League disbanded July 1) | | | | | | |
| 1913—Ottumwa | Cent. Assn. | | 9 | 70 | 6 | 2 | .750 | .... |
| 1913—Chattanooga | Southern | | 17 | 112 | 6 | 7 | .462 | .... |
| 1914—Chat.-Birm. | Southern | | 4 | 10 | 0 | 2 | .000 | .... |
| 1914—Richmond | Virginia | | 39 | 296 | 23 | 13 | .639 | .... |
| 1915—Birmingham | Southern | | 41 | 296 | 17 | 13 | .567 | .... |
| 1916—Birmingham | Southern | | 40 | 276 | 20 | 11 | .645 | .... |
| 1916—Pittsburgh | National | | 6 | 46 | 2 | 3 | .400 | 2.35 |
| 1917—Pittsburgh | National | | 37 | 194 | 3 | 16 | .158 | 3.53 |
| 1918—Brooklyn | National | | *40 | 270 | 19 | 9 | .679 | 2.13 |
| 1919—Brooklyn | National | | 25 | 181 | 10 | 11 | .476 | 3.48 |
| 1920—Brooklyn | National | | 40 | 304 | 23 | 11 | *.676 | 2.22 |
| 1921—Brooklyn | National | | 37 | 302 | ●22 | 13 | .629 | 2.83 |
| 1922—Brooklyn | National | | 35 | 256 | 17 | 14 | .548 | 4.75 |
| 1923—Brooklyn | National | | 39 | *327 | 21 | 18 | .538 | 3.58 |
| 1924—Brooklyn | National | | 38 | *311 | 22 | 13 | .629 | 3.82 |
| 1925—Brooklyn | National | | 33 | 247 | 12 | *19 | .387 | 5.03 |
| 1926—Brooklyn | National | | 30 | 225 | 12 | 13 | .480 | 3.72 |
| 1927—New York | National | | 39 | 260 | 19 | 8 | .704 | 3.53 |
| 1928—Pittsburgh | National | | *48 | *331 | ●25 | 14 | .641 | 2.99 |
| 1929—Pittsburgh | National | | 33 | 233 | 17 | 7 | .708 | 3.13 |
| 1930—Bos.-St.L. | National | | 33 | 201 | 16 | 11 | .593 | 4.07 |
| 1931—St. Louis | National | | 29 | 212 | 17 | 9 | .654 | 3.65 |
| 1932—Chicago | National | | 30 | 141 | 6 | 11 | .353 | 4.79 |
| 1933—Chi.-St.L. | National | | 21 | 84 | 3 | 7 | .300 | 3.75 |
| 1934—St.L.-Pitt. | National | | 12 | 35 | 3 | 3 | .500 | 6.43 |
| 1934—New York | American | | 10 | 18 | 1 | 2 | .333 | 5.50 |
| 1935—Bloomington | I.I.I. | | 21 | 119 | 10 | 5 | .667 | ..... |
| American League Totals | | | 10 | 18 | 1 | 2 | .333 | 5.50 |
| National League Totals | | | 605 | 4160 | 269 | 210 | .562 | 3.52 |
| Major League Totals | | | 615 | 4178 | 270 | 212 | .560 | 3.52 |

### WORLD SERIES RECORD

| Year | Club | League | G. | IP. | W. | L. | Pct. | ERA. |
|---|---|---|---|---|---|---|---|---|
| 1920—Brooklyn | National | | 3 | 19⅓ | 1 | 2 | .333 | 4.19 |
| 1930—St. Louis | National | | 2 | 17 | 0 | 2 | .000 | 3.71 |
| 1931—St. Louis | National | | 2 | 17⅔ | 2 | 0 | 1.000 | 2.04 |
| 1932—Chicago | National | | 2 | 2⅔ | 0 | 0 | .000 | 23.63 |
| World Series Totals | | | 9 | 56⅔ | 3 | 4 | .429 | 4.05 |

## ROBERT MOSES (LEFTY) GROVE

| Year | Club | League | G. | IP. | W. | L. | Pct. | ERA. |
|---|---|---|---|---|---|---|---|---|
| 1920—Martinsburg | Blue Ridge | | 6 | 59 | 3 | 3 | .500 | .... |
| 1920—Baltimore | International | | 19 | 123 | 12 | 2 | .857 | 3.80 |
| 1921—Baltimore | International | | 47 | 313 | 25 | 10 | .714 | 2.56 |
| 1922—Baltimore | International | | 41 | 209 | 18 | 8 | .692 | 2.80 |
| 1923—Baltimore | International | | *52 | 303 | 27 | 10 | .730 | 3.12 |
| 1924—Baltimore | International | | 47 | 236 | *27 | 6 | *.813 | 3.01 |
| 1925—Philadelphia | American | | 45 | 197 | 10 | 12 | .455 | 4.75 |
| 1926—Philadelphia | American | | 45 | 258 | 13 | 13 | .500 | *2.51 |
| 1927—Philadelphia | American | | 51 | 262 | 20 | 13 | .606 | 3.19 |
| 1928—Philadelphia | American | | 39 | 262 | ●24 | 8 | .750 | 2.58 |
| 1929—Philadelphia | American | | 42 | 275 | 20 | 6 | *.769 | *2.81 |
| 1930—Philadelphia | American | | *50 | 291 | *28 | 5 | *.848 | *2.54 |
| 1931—Philadelphia | American | | 41 | 289 | *31 | 4 | *.886 | *2.06 |
| 1932—Philadelphia | American | | 44 | 292 | 25 | 10 | .714 | *2.84 |
| 1933—Philadelphia | American | | 45 | 275 | ●24 | 8 | *.750 | 3.21 |
| 1934—Boston | American | | 22 | 109 | 8 | 8 | .500 | 6.52 |
| 1935—Boston | American | | 35 | 273 | 20 | 12 | .625 | *2.70 |
| 1936—Boston | American | | 35 | 253 | 17 | 12 | .586 | *2.81 |
| 1937—Boston | American | | 32 | 262 | 17 | 9 | .654 | 3.02 |
| 1938—Boston | American | | 24 | 164 | 14 | 4 | .778 | *3.07 |
| 1939—Boston | American | | 23 | 191 | 15 | 4 | *.789 | *2.54 |
| 1940—Boston | American | | 22 | 153 | 7 | 6 | .538 | 4.00 |
| 1941—Boston | American | | 21 | 134 | 7 | 7 | .500 | 4.37 |
| Major League Totals | | | 616 | 3940 | 300 | 141 | .680 | 3.06 |

### WORLD SERIES RECORD

| Year | Club | League | G. | IP. | W. | L. | Pct. | ERA. |
|---|---|---|---|---|---|---|---|---|
| 1929—Philadelphia | American | | 2 | 6⅓ | 0 | 0 | .000 | 0.00 |
| 1930—Philadelphia | American | | 3 | 19 | 2 | 1 | .667 | 1.42 |
| 1931—Philadelphia | American | | 3 | 26 | 2 | 1 | .667 | 2.42 |
| World Series Totals | | | 8 | 51⅓ | 4 | 2 | .667 | 1.75 |

## CHARLES JAMES (CHICK) HAFEY

| Year | Club | League | G. | AB. | R. | H. | HR. | RBI. | B.A. |
|---|---|---|---|---|---|---|---|---|---|
| 1923—Fort Smith | W. Assn. | | 141 | 573 | 83 | 163 | 16 | ..... | .284 |
| 1924—Houston | Tex. | | 126 | 481 | 82 | 173 | 9 | 90 | .360 |

| Year | Club | League | G. | AB. | R. | H. | HR. | RBI. | B.A. |
|---|---|---|---|---|---|---|---|---|---|
| 1924—St. Louis | Nat. | | 24 | 91 | 10 | 23 | 2 | 22 | .253 |
| 1925—Syracuse | Int. | | 21 | 84 | 17 | 24 | 2 | 8 | .286 |
| 1925—St. Louis | Nat. | | 93 | 358 | 36 | 108 | 5 | 57 | .302 |
| 1926—St. Louis | Nat. | | 78 | 225 | 30 | 61 | 4 | 38 | .271 |
| 1927—St. Louis | Nat. | | 103 | 346 | 62 | 114 | 18 | 63 | .329 |
| 1928—St. Louis | Nat. | | 138 | 520 | 101 | 175 | 27 | 111 | .337 |
| 1929—St. Louis | Nat. | | 134 | 517 | 101 | 175 | 29 | 125 | .338 |
| 1930—St. Louis | Nat. | | 120 | 446 | 108 | 150 | 26 | 107 | .336 |
| 1931—St. Louis | Nat. | | 122 | 450 | 94 | 157 | 16 | 95 | *.349 |
| 1932—Cincinnati | Nat. | | 83 | 253 | 34 | 87 | 2 | 36 | .344 |
| 1933—Cincinnati | Nat. | | 144 | 568 | 77 | 172 | 7 | 62 | .303 |
| 1934—Cincinnati | Nat. | | 140 | 535 | 75 | 157 | 18 | 67 | .293 |
| 1935—Cincinnati | Nat. | | 15 | 59 | 10 | 20 | 1 | 9 | .339 |
| 1936—Cincinnati | Nat. | | (Voluntarily Retired) | | | | | | |
| 1937—Cincinnati | Nat. | | 89 | 257 | 39 | 67 | 9 | 41 | .261 |
| Major League Totals | | | 1283 | 4625 | 777 | 1466 | 164 | 833 | .317 |

### WORLD SERIES RECORD

| Year | Club | League | G. | AB. | R. | H. | HR. | RBI. | B.A. |
|---|---|---|---|---|---|---|---|---|---|
| 1926—St. Louis | Nat. | | 7 | 27 | 2 | 5 | 0 | 0 | .185 |
| 1928—St. Louis | Nat. | | 4 | 15 | 0 | 3 | 0 | 0 | .200 |
| 1930—St. Louis | Nat. | | 6 | 22 | 2 | 6 | 0 | 2 | .273 |
| 1931—St. Louis | Nat. | | 6 | 24 | 1 | 4 | 0 | 0 | .167 |
| World Series Totals | | | 23 | 88 | 5 | 18 | 0 | 2 | .205 |

## JESSE JOSEPH (POP) HAINES

| Year | Club | League | G. | IP. | W. | L. | Pct. | ERA. |
|---|---|---|---|---|---|---|---|---|
| 1913—Dayton | Central | (Pitched one game, last day of season vs. Evansville) | | | | | | |
| 1914—Saginaw | S. Mich. | | 33 | 258 | 17 | 14 | .548 | ...... |
| 1914—Fort Wayne | Central | (No records available) | | | | | | |
| 1915—Saginaw | S. Mich. | (League disbanded July 1—no records available) | | | | | | |
| 1916—Springfield | Central | | 41 | 310 | 23 | 12 | .657 | 1.68 |
| 1917—Springfield | Central | | 35 | 275 | 19 | 10 | .655 | ...... |
| 1918—Topeka-Hutch'on | Western | | 16 | 132 | 12 | 4 | .750 | ...... |
| 1918—Cincinnati | National | | 1 | 5 | 0 | 0 | .000 | 1.80 |
| 1919—Tulsa | Western | | 14 | 101 | 5 | 9 | .357 | ...... |
| 1919—Kansas City | Amer. Assn. | | 28 | 213 | 21 | 5 | .808 | 2.11 |
| 1920—St. Louis | National | | *47 | 302 | 13 | 20 | .394 | 2.98 |
| 1921—St. Louis | National | | 37 | 244 | 18 | 12 | .600 | 3.50 |
| 1922—St. Louis | National | | 29 | 183 | 11 | 9 | .550 | 3.84 |
| 1923—St. Louis | National | | 37 | 266 | 20 | 13 | .606 | 3.11 |
| 1924—St. Louis | National | | 35 | 223 | 8 | 19 | .296 | 4.40 |
| 1925—St. Louis | National | | 29 | 207 | 13 | 14 | .481 | 4.57 |
| 1926—St. Louis | National | | 33 | 183 | 13 | 4 | .765 | 3.25 |
| 1927—St. Louis | National | | 38 | 301 | 24 | 10 | .706 | 2.72 |
| 1928—St. Louis | National | | 33 | 240 | 20 | 8 | .714 | 3.19 |
| 1929—St. Louis | National | | 28 | 180 | 13 | 10 | .565 | 5.70 |
| 1930—St. Louis | National | | 29 | 182 | 13 | 8 | .619 | 4.30 |
| 1931—St. Louis | National | | 19 | 122 | 12 | 3 | .800 | 3.02 |
| 1932—St. Louis | National | | 20 | 85 | 3 | 5 | .375 | 4.76 |
| 1933—St. Louis | National | | 32 | 115 | 9 | 6 | .600 | 2.50 |
| 1934—St. Louis | National | | 37 | 90 | 4 | 4 | .500 | 3.50 |
| 1935—St. Louis | National | | 30 | 115 | 6 | 5 | .545 | 3.60 |
| 1936—St. Louis | National | | 25 | 99 | 7 | 5 | .583 | 3.91 |
| 1937—St. Louis | National | | 16 | 66 | 3 | 3 | .500 | 4.50 |
| Major League Totals | | | 555 | 3208 | 210 | 158 | .571 | 3.64 |

### WORLD SERIES RECORD

| Year | Club | League | G. | IP. | W. | L. | Pct. | ERA. |
|---|---|---|---|---|---|---|---|---|
| 1926—St. Louis | National | | 3 | 16⅔ | 2 | 0 | 1.000 | 1.08 |
| 1928—St. Louis | National | | 1 | 6 | 0 | 1 | .000 | 4.50 |
| 1930—St. Louis | National | | 1 | 9 | 1 | 0 | 1.000 | 1.00 |
| 1934—St. Louis | National | | 1 | ⅔ | 0 | 0 | .000 | 0.00 |
| World Series Totals | | | 6 | 32⅓ | 3 | 1 | .750 | 1.67 |

## WILLIAM ROBERT (SLIDING BILLY) HAMILTON

| Year | Club | League | G. | AB. | R. | H. | HR. | SB. | B.A. |
|---|---|---|---|---|---|---|---|---|---|
| 1888—Worcester | N. Eng. | | 61 | 247 | 76 | 87 | 0 | 70 | .352 |
| 1888—Kansas City | A. A. | | 35 | 128 | 17 | 32 | 0 | 23 | .250 |
| 1889—Kansas City | A. A. | | 137 | 532 | 145 | 160 | 3 | *117 | .301 |
| 1890—Philadelphia | Nat. | | 123 | 496 | 131 | 161 | 2 | 102 | .325 |
| 1891—Philadelphia | Nat. | | 133 | 529 | *142 | *179 | 2 | *115 | *.338 |
| 1892—Philadelphia | Nat. | | 136 | 539 | 131 | 178 | 3 | 56 | .330 |
| 1893—Philadelphia | Nat. | | 82 | 349 | 111 | 138 | 5 | 41 | .395 |
| 1894—Philadelphia | Nat. | | 131 | 559 | *196 | 223 | 4 | *99 | .399 |
| 1895—Philadelphia | Nat. | | 121 | 517 | *166 | 203 | 5 | *95 | .393 |
| 1896—Boston | Nat. | | 131 | 523 | 153 | 190 | 2 | 93 | .363 |
| 1897—Boston | Nat. | | 125 | 506 | *153 | 174 | 3 | 70 | .344 |
| 1898—Boston | Nat. | | 109 | 417 | 111 | 153 | 3 | 59 | .367 |
| 1899—Boston | Nat. | | 81 | 294 | 62 | 90 | 1 | 19 | .306 |
| 1900—Boston | Nat. | | 135 | 524 | 103 | 174 | 1 | 29 | .332 |
| 1901—Boston | Nat. | | 99 | 349 | 70 | 102 | 3 | 19 | .292 |
| 1902—Haverhill | N. Eng. | | 66 | 243 | 67 | 82 | 2 | 26 | .337 |
| 1903—Haverhill | N. Eng. | | 37 | 132 | 37 | 60 | 4 | 27 | .446 |
| 1904—Haverhill | N. Eng. | | 113 | 408 | *113 | *168 | 0 | *74 | *.412 |
| 1905—Harrisburg | Tri-St. | | (No Record Available) | | | | | | |
| 1906—Harrisburg | N.Eng. | | 14 | 51 | 1 | 10 | 0 | ... | .196 |
| 1906—Harrisburg | Tri.-St. | | 43 | 155 | 33 | 43 | 0 | 16 | .278 |
| 1907—Haverhill | N. Eng. | | 91 | 324 | 50 | 108 | 0 | 29 | *.333 |

| Year | Club | League | G. | AB. | R. | H. | HR. | RBI. | B.A. |
|---|---|---|---|---|---|---|---|---|---|
| 1908—Haverhill | N. Eng. | 85 | 300 | 63 | 87 | 1 | 39 | .290 |
| 1909—Lynn | N. Eng. | 109 | 376 | 61 | 125 | 0 | 23 | *.332 |
| 1910—Lynn | N. Eng. | 41 | 112 | 14 | 28 | 0 | 5 | .250 |
| American Association Totals | | 172 | 660 | 162 | 192 | 3 | 140 | .291 |
| National League Totals | | 1406 | 5602 | 1529 | 1965 | 34 | 797 | .351 |
| Major League Totals | | 1578 | 6262 | 1690 | 2157 | 37 | 937 | .344 |

## STANLEY RAYMOND (BUCKY) HARRIS

| Year | Club | League | G. | AB. | R. | H. | HR. | RBI. | B.A. |
|---|---|---|---|---|---|---|---|---|---|
| 1916—Muskegon | Central | 55 | 169 | 8 | 28 | .... | .... | .166 |
| 1917—Norfolk | Virginia | 15 | 50 | 4 | 6 | 0 | 2 | .120 |
| 1917—Reading | N.Y.S. | 75 | 280 | 44 | 70 | .... | .... | .250 |
| 1918—Buffalo | Int. | 85 | 320 | 51 | 77 | 0 | .... | .241 |
| 1919—Buffalo | Int. | 120 | 447 | 68 | 126 | 2 | .... | .282 |
| 1919—Washington | Amer. | 8 | 28 | 0 | 6 | 0 | 4 | .214 |
| 1920—Washington | Amer. | 137 | 506 | 76 | 152 | 1 | 68 | .300 |
| 1921—Washington | Amer. | 154 | 584 | 82 | 169 | 0 | 54 | .289 |
| 1922—Washington | Amer. | 154 | 602 | 95 | 162 | 2 | 40 | .269 |
| 1923—Washington | Amer. | 145 | 532 | 60 | 150 | 2 | 70 | .282 |
| 1924—Washington | Amer. | 143 | 544 | 88 | 146 | 1 | 58 | .268 |
| 1925—Washington | Amer. | 144 | 551 | 91 | 158 | 1 | 66 | .287 |
| 1926—Washington | Amer. | 141 | 537 | 94 | 152 | 1 | 63 | .283 |
| 1927—Washington | Amer. | 128 | 475 | 98 | 127 | 1 | 55 | .267 |
| 1928—Washington | Amer. | 99 | 358 | 34 | 73 | 0 | 28 | .204 |
| 1929—Detroit | Amer. | 7 | 11 | 3 | 1 | 0 | 0 | .091 |
| 1930—Detroit | Amer. | | | | (Did not play) | | | |
| 1931—Detroit | Amer. | 4 | 8 | 1 | 1 | 0 | 0 | .125 |
| Major League Totals | | 1264 | 4736 | 722 | 1297 | 9 | 506 | .274 |

### WORLD SERIES RECORD

| Year | Club | League | G. | AB. | R. | H. | HR. | RBI. | B.A. |
|---|---|---|---|---|---|---|---|---|---|
| 1924—Washington | Amer. | 7 | 33 | 5 | 11 | 2 | 7 | .333 |
| 1925—Washington | Amer. | 7 | 23 | 2 | 2 | 0 | 0 | .087 |
| World Series Totals | | 14 | 56 | 7 | 13 | 2 | 7 | .232 |

### RECORD AS MANAGER

| Year | Club | League | Position | W. | L. |
|---|---|---|---|---|---|
| 1924—Washington | American | First | 92 | 62 |
| 1925—Washington | American | First | 96 | 55 |
| 1926—Washington | American | Fourth | 81 | 69 |
| 1927—Washington | American | Third | 85 | 69 |
| 1928—Washington | American | Fourth | 75 | 79 |
| 1929—Detroit | American | Sixth | 70 | 84 |
| 1930—Detroit | American | Fifth | 75 | 79 |
| 1931—Detroit | American | Seventh | 61 | 93 |
| 1932—Detroit | American | Fifth | 76 | 75 |
| 1933—Detroit | American | Fifth | 75 | 79 |
| 1934—Boston | American | Fourth | 76 | 76 |
| 1935—Washington | American | Sixth | 67 | 86 |
| 1936—Washington | American | Fourth | 82 | 71 |
| 1937—Washington | American | Sixth | 73 | 80 |
| 1938—Washington | Americcn | Fifth | 75 | 76 |
| 1939—Washington | American | Sixth | 65 | 87 |
| 1940—Washington | American | Seventh | 64 | 90 |
| 1941—Washington | American | *Sixth | 70 | 84 |
| 1942—Washington | American | Seventh | 62 | 89 |
| 1943—Philadelphia† | National | Sixth | 39 | 52 |
| 1944—Buffalo | International | Fourth | 78 | 76 |
| 1945—Buffalo | International | *Sixth | 64 | 89 |
| 1947—New York | American | First | 97 | 57 |
| 1948—New York | American | Third | 94 | 60 |
| 1949—San Diego | Pacific Coast | *Fourth | 96 | 92 |
| 1950—Washington | American | Fifth | 67 | 87 |
| 1951—Washington | American | Seventh | 62 | 92 |
| 1952—Washington | American | Fifth | 78 | 76 |
| 1953—Washington | American | Fifth | 76 | 76 |
| 1954—Washington | American | Sixth | 66 | 88 |
| 1955—Detroit | American | Fifth | 79 | 75 |
| Major League Totals | | | 2078 | 2146 |

*Tied for position.
†Replaced as manager by Fred Fitzsimmons, July 28, 1943.

### WORLD SERIES RECORD

| Year | Club | League | W. | L. |
|---|---|---|---|---|
| 1924—Washington | American | 4 | 3 |
| 1925—Washington | American | 3 | 4 |
| 1947—New York | American | 4 | 3 |

## CHARLES LEO (GABBY) HARTNETT

| Year | Club | League | G. | AB. | R. | H. | HR. | RBI. | B.A. |
|---|---|---|---|---|---|---|---|---|---|
| 1921—Worcester | East. | 100 | 345 | 38 | 91 | 3 | .... | .264 |
| 1922—Chicago | Nat. | 31 | 72 | 4 | 14 | 0 | 4 | .194 |
| 1923—Chicago | Nat. | 85 | 231 | 28 | 62 | 8 | 39 | .268 |
| 1924—Chicago | Nat. | 111 | 354 | 56 | 106 | 16 | 67 | .299 |
| 1925—Chicago | Nat. | 117 | 398 | 61 | 115 | 24 | 67 | .289 |
| 1926—Chicago | Nat. | 93 | 284 | 35 | 78 | 8 | 41 | .275 |
| 1927—Chicago | Nat. | 127 | 449 | 56 | 132 | 10 | 80 | .294 |
| 1928—Chicago | Nat. | 120 | 388 | 61 | 117 | 14 | 57 | .302 |
| 1929—Chicago | Nat. | 25 | 22 | 2 | 6 | 1 | 9 | .273 |
| 1930—Chicago | Nat. | 141 | 508 | 84 | 172 | 37 | 122 | .339 |
| 1931—Chicago | Nat. | 116 | 380 | 53 | 107 | 8 | 70 | .282 |
| 1932—Chicago | Nat. | 121 | 406 | 52 | 110 | 12 | 52 | .271 |
| 1933—Chicago | Nat. | 140 | 490 | 55 | 135 | 16 | 88 | .276 |

| Year | Club | League | G. | AB. | R. | H. | HR. | RBI. | B.A. |
|---|---|---|---|---|---|---|---|---|---|
| 1934—Chicago | Nat. | 130 | 438 | 58 | 131 | 22 | 90 | .299 |
| 1935—Chicago | Nat. | 116 | 413 | 67 | 142 | 13 | 91 | .344 |
| 1936—Chicago | Nat. | 121 | 424 | 49 | 130 | 7 | 64 | .307 |
| 1937—Chicago | Nat. | 110 | 356 | 47 | 126 | 12 | 82 | .354 |
| 1938—Chicago | Nat. | 88 | 299 | 40 | 82 | 10 | 59 | .274 |
| 1939—Chicago | Nat. | 97 | 306 | 36 | 85 | 12 | 59 | .278 |
| 1940—Chicago | Nat. | 37 | 64 | 3 | 17 | 1 | 12 | .266 |
| 1941—New York | Nat. | 64 | 150 | 20 | 45 | 5 | 26 | .300 |
| 1942—Indianapolis | A. A. | 72 | 186 | 17 | 41 | 4 | 24 | .220 |
| 1943—Jersey City | Int. | 16 | 16 | 0 | 4 | 0 | 5 | .250 |
| 1944—Jersey City | Int. | 31 | 11 | 1 | 2 | 0 | 6 | .182 |
| Major League Totals | | 1990 | 6432 | 867 | 1912 | 236 | 1179 | .297 |

### WORLD SERIES RECORD

| Year | Club | League | G. | AB. | R. | H. | HR. | RBI. | B.A. |
|---|---|---|---|---|---|---|---|---|---|
| 1929—Chicago | Nat. | 3 | 3 | 0 | 0 | 0 | 0 | .000 |
| 1932—Chicago | Nat. | 4 | 16 | 2 | 5 | 1 | 1 | .313 |
| 1935—Chicago | Nat. | 6 | 24 | 1 | 7 | 1 | 2 | .292 |
| 1938—Chicago | Nat. | 3 | 11 | 0 | 1 | 0 | 0 | .091 |
| World Series Totals | | 16 | 54 | 3 | 13 | 2 | 3 | .241 |

## HARRY EDWIN HEILMANN

| Year | Club | League | G. | AB. | R. | H. | HR. | RBI. | B.A. |
|---|---|---|---|---|---|---|---|---|---|
| 1913—Portland | N. W. | 122 | 417 | 55 | 127 | 11 | .... | .305 |
| 1914—Detroit | Amer. | 66 | 182 | 25 | 41 | 2 | 22 | .225 |
| 1915—San Francisco | P. C. | 98 | 371 | 57 | 135 | 12 | .... | .364 |
| 1916—Detroit | Amer. | 136 | 451 | 57 | 127 | 2 | 76 | .282 |
| 1917—Detroit | Amer. | 150 | 556 | 57 | 156 | 5 | 84 | .281 |
| 1918—Detroit | Amer. | 79 | 286 | 34 | 79 | 5 | 44 | .276 |
| 1919—Detroit | Amer. | 140 | 537 | 74 | 172 | 8 | 95 | .320 |
| 1920—Detroit | Amer. | 145 | 543 | 66 | 168 | 9 | 90 | .309 |
| 1921—Detroit | Amer. | 149 | 602 | 114 | *237 | 19 | 139 | *.394 |
| 1922—Detroit | Amer. | 118 | 455 | 92 | 162 | 21 | 92 | .356 |
| 1923—Detroit | Amer. | 144 | 524 | 121 | 211 | 18 | 115 | *.403 |
| 1924—Detroit | Amer. | 153 | 570 | 107 | 197 | 10 | 114 | .346 |
| 1925—Detroit | Amer. | 150 | 573 | 97 | 225 | 13 | 134 | *.393 |
| 1926—Detroit | Amer. | 141 | 502 | 90 | 184 | 9 | 103 | .367 |
| 1927—Detroit | Amer. | 141 | 505 | 106 | 201 | 14 | 120 | *.398 |
| 1928—Detroit | Amer. | 151 | 558 | 83 | 183 | 14 | 107 | .328 |
| 1929—Detroit | Amer. | 125 | 453 | 86 | 156 | 15 | 120 | .344 |
| 1930—Cincinnati | Nat. | 142 | 459 | 79 | 153 | 19 | 91 | .333 |
| 1931—Cincinnati | Nat. | | | | (Out of game all season) | | | |
| 1932—Cincinnati | Nat. | 15 | 31 | 3 | 8 | 0 | 6 | .258 |
| American League Totals | | 1988 | 7297 | 1209 | 2499 | 164 | 1455 | .343 |
| National League Totals | | 157 | 490 | 82 | 161 | 19 | 97 | .329 |
| Major League Totals | | 2145 | 7787 | 1291 | 2660 | 183 | 1552 | .342 |

## WILLIAM JENNINGS HERMAN

| Year | Club | League | G. | AB. | R. | H. | HR. | RBI. | B.A. |
|---|---|---|---|---|---|---|---|---|---|
| 1928—Vicksburg | Cot.St. | 106 | 364 | 63 | 121 | 4 | .... | .332 |
| 1928—Louisville | A. A. | 4 | 15 | 3 | 5 | 0 | 4 | .333 |
| 1929—Dayton | Cent. | 138 | 529 | 96 | 174 | 13 | 79 | .329 |
| 1929—Louisville | A. A. | 24 | 93 | 17 | 30 | 1 | 13 | .323 |
| 1930—Louisville | A. A. | 143 | 617 | 108 | 188 | 8 | 86 | .305 |
| 1931—Louisville | A. A. | 118 | 486 | 100 | 170 | 7 | 59 | .350 |
| 1931—Chicago | Nat. | 25 | 98 | 14 | 32 | 0 | 16 | .327 |
| 1932—Chicago | Nat. | ●154 | 656 | 102 | 206 | 1 | 51 | .314 |
| 1933—Chicago | Nat. | 153 | 619 | 82 | 173 | 0 | 44 | .279 |
| 1934—Chicago | Nat. | 113 | 456 | 79 | 138 | 3 | 42 | .303 |
| 1935—Chicago | Nat. | 154 | 666 | 113 | *227 | 7 | 83 | .341 |
| 1936—Chicago | Nat. | 153 | 632 | 101 | 211 | 5 | 93 | .334 |
| 1937—Chicago | Nat. | 138 | 564 | 106 | 189 | 8 | 65 | .335 |
| 1938—Chicago | Nat. | ●152 | 624 | 86 | 173 | 1 | 56 | .277 |
| 1939—Chicago | Nat. | 156 | 623 | 111 | 191 | 7 | 70 | .307 |
| 1940—Chicago | Nat. | 135 | 558 | 77 | 163 | 5 | 57 | .292 |
| 1941—Chi.-Brook | Nat. | 144 | 572 | 81 | 163 | 3 | 41 | .285 |
| 1942—Brooklyn | Nat. | *155 | 571 | 76 | 146 | 2 | 65 | .256 |
| 1943—Brooklyn | Nat. | 153 | 585 | 76 | 193 | 2 | 100 | .330 |
| 1944-45—Brooklyn | Nat. | | | | (In Military Service) | | | |
| 1946—Brk.-Bos. | Nat. | 122 | 436 | 56 | 130 | 3 | 50 | .298 |
| 1947—Pittsburgh | Nat. | 15 | 47 | 3 | 10 | 0 | 6 | .213 |
| 1948—Minneapolis | A. A. | 10 | 31 | 9 | 14 | 2 | 9 | .452 |
| 1949— | | | | | (Out of Organized Ball) | | | |
| 1950—Oakland | P. C. | 71 | 202 | 32 | 62 | 4 | 29 | .307 |
| Major League Totals | | 1922 | 7707 | 1163 | 2345 | 47 | 839 | .304 |

### WORLD SERIES RECORD

| Year | Club | League | G. | AB. | R. | H. | HR. | RBI. | B.A. |
|---|---|---|---|---|---|---|---|---|---|
| 1932—Chicago | Nat. | 4 | 18 | 5 | 4 | 0 | 1 | .222 |
| 1935—Chicago | Nat. | 6 | 24 | 3 | 8 | 1 | 6 | .333 |
| 1938—Chicago | Nat. | 4 | 16 | 1 | 3 | 0 | 0 | .188 |
| 1941—Brooklyn | Nat. | 4 | 8 | 0 | 1 | 0 | 0 | .125 |
| World Series Totals | | 18 | 66 | 9 | 16 | 1 | 7 | .242 |

## HARRY BARTHOLOMEW HOOPER

| Year | Club | League | G. | AB. | R. | H. | HR. | RBI. | B.A. |
|---|---|---|---|---|---|---|---|---|---|
| 1907—Oak.-Sacra'to | Calif. St. | 36 | 139 | 26 | 43 | 1 | .... | .309 |
| 1908—Sacramento | Calif. St. | 77 | 294 | 47 | 101 | .... | .... | .344 |
| 1909—Boston | Amer. | 81 | 255 | 29 | 72 | 0 | 16 | .282 |
| 1910—Boston | Amer. | 155 | 584 | 81 | 156 | 2 | 33 | .267 |
| 1911—Boston | Amer. | 130 | 524 | 93 | 163 | 4 | 43 | .311 |

| Year Club | League | G. | AB. | R. | H. | HR. | RBI. | B.A. |
|---|---|---|---|---|---|---|---|---|
| 1912—Boston | Amer. | 147 | 590 | 98 | 143 | 2 | 46 | .242 |
| 1913—Boston | Amer. | 148 | 585 | 100 | 169 | 4 | 40 | .289 |
| 1914—Boston | Amer. | 141 | 530 | 85 | 137 | 1 | 44 | .258 |
| 1915—Boston | Amer. | 149 | 566 | 90 | 133 | 2 | 48 | .235 |
| 1916—Boston | Amer. | 151 | 575 | 75 | 156 | 1 | 33 | .271 |
| 1917—Boston | Amer. | 151 | 559 | 89 | 143 | 3 | 43 | .256 |
| 1918—Boston | Amer. | 126 | 474 | 81 | 137 | 1 | 46 | .289 |
| 1919—Boston | Amer. | 128 | 491 | 76 | 131 | 3 | 48 | .267 |
| 1920—Boston | Amer. | 139 | 536 | 91 | 167 | 7 | 53 | .312 |
| 1921—Chicago | Amer. | 108 | 419 | 74 | 137 | 8 | 58 | .327 |
| 1922—Chicago | Amer. | 152 | 602 | 111 | 183 | 11 | 80 | .304 |
| 1923—Chicago | Amer. | 145 | 576 | 87 | 166 | 10 | 65 | .288 |
| 1924—Chicago | Amer. | 130 | 476 | 107 | 156 | 10 | 62 | .328 |
| 1925—Chicago | Amer. | 127 | 442 | 62 | 117 | 6 | 55 | .265 |
| 1926— | | | | | (Out of Organized Ball) | | | |
| 1927—Missions | P. C. | 78 | 218 | 35 | 62 | 1 | 19 | .284 |
| Major League Totals | | 2308 | 8784 | 1429 | 2466 | 75 | 813 | .281 |

### WORLD SERIES RECORD

| Year Club | League | G. | AB. | R. | H. | HR. | RBI. | B.A. |
|---|---|---|---|---|---|---|---|---|
| 1912—Boston | Amer. | 8 | 31 | 3 | 9 | 0 | 2 | .290 |
| 1915—Boston | Amer. | 5 | 20 | 4 | 7 | 2 | 3 | 350 |
| 1916—Boston | Amer. | 5 | 21 | 6 | 7 | 0 | 1 | .333 |
| 1918—Boston | Amer. | 6 | 20 | 0 | 4 | 0 | 0 | .200 |
| World Series Totals | | 24 | 92 | 13 | 27 | 2 | 6 | .293 |

## ROGERS (RAJAH) HORNSBY

| Year Club | League | G. | AB. | R. | H. | HR. | RBI. | B.A. |
|---|---|---|---|---|---|---|---|---|
| 1914—Hugo-Denison | Tex.-Ok | 113 | 393 | 47 | 91 | 3 | .... | .232 |
| 1915—Denison | W. A. | 119 | 429 | 75 | 119 | 4 | .... | .277 |
| 1915—St. Louis | Nat. | 18 | 57 | 5 | 14 | 0 | 4 | .246 |
| 1916—St. Louis | Nat. | 139 | 495 | 63 | 155 | 6 | 60 | .313 |
| 1917—St. Louis | Nat. | 145 | 523 | 86 | 171 | 8 | 70 | .327 |
| 1918—St. Louis | Nat. | 115 | 416 | 51 | 117 | 5 | 59 | .281 |
| 1919—St. Louis | Nat. | 138 | 512 | 68 | 163 | 8 | 68 | .318 |
| 1920—St. Louis | Nat. | 149 | 589 | 96 | ★218 | 9 | ●94 | ★.370 |
| 1921—St. Louis | Nat. | ★154 | 592 | ★131 | ★235 | 21 | ★126 | ★.397 |
| 1922—St. Louis | Nat. | 154 | 623 | ★141 | ★250 | ★42 | ★152 | ★.401 |
| 1923—St. Louis | Nat. | 107 | 424 | 89 | 163 | 17 | 83 | .384 |
| 1924—St. Louis | Nat. | 143 | 536 | ●121 | ★227 | 25 | 94 | ★.424 |
| 1925—St. Louis | Nat. | 138 | 504 | 133 | 203 | ★39 | ★143 | ★.403 |
| 1926—St. Louis | Nat. | 134 | 527 | 96 | 167 | 11 | 93 | .317 |
| 1927—New York | Nat. | ●155 | 568 | ●133 | 205 | 26 | 125 | .361 |
| 1928—Boston | Nat. | 140 | 486 | 99 | 188 | 21 | 94 | ★.387 |
| 1929—Chicago | Nat. | ★156 | 602 | ★156 | 229 | 39 | 149 | .380 |
| 1930—Chicago | Nat. | 42 | 104 | 15 | 32 | 2 | 18 | .308 |
| 1931—Chicago | Nat. | 100 | 357 | 64 | 118 | 16 | 90 | .331 |
| 1932—Chicago | Nat. | 19 | 58 | 10 | 13 | 1 | 7 | .224 |
| 1933—St. Louis | Nat. | 46 | 83 | 9 | 27 | 2 | 21 | .325 |
| 1933—St. Louis | Amer. | 11 | 9 | 2 | 3 | 1 | 2 | .333 |
| 1934—St. Louis | Amer. | 24 | 23 | 2 | 7 | 1 | 11 | .304 |
| 1935—St. Louis | Amer | 10 | 24 | 1 | 5 | 0 | 3 | .208 |
| 1936—St. Louis | Amer. | 2 | 5 | 1 | 2 | 0 | 2 | .400 |
| 1937—St. Louis | Amer. | 20 | 56 | 7 | 18 | 1 | 11 | .321 |
| 1938—Baltimore | Int. | 16 | 27 | 2 | 2 | 0 | 0 | .074 |
| 1939—Chattanooga | South. | 3 | 3 | 1 | 2 | 1 | 2 | .667 |
| 1940—Oklahoma City | Tex. | 1 | 1 | 0 | 1 | 0 | 0 | 1.000 |
| 1942—Ft. Worth | Tex. | 1 | 4 | 0 | 1 | 0 | 2 | .250 |
| National League Totals | | 2192 | 8056 | 1566 | 2895 | 298 | 1550 | .359 |
| American League Totals | | 67 | 117 | 13 | 35 | 3 | 29 | .299 |
| Major League Totals | | 2259 | 8173 | 1579 | 2930 | 301 | 1579 | .358 |

### WORLD SERIES RECORD

| Year Club | League | G. | AB. | R. | H. | HR. | RBI. | B.A. |
|---|---|---|---|---|---|---|---|---|
| 1926—St. Louis | Nat | 7 | 28 | 2 | 7 | 0 | 4 | .250 |
| 1929—Chicago | Nat. | 5 | 21 | 4 | 5 | 0 | 1 | .238 |
| World Series Totals | | 12 | 49 | 6 | 12 | 0 | 5 | .245 |

## WAITE CHARLES (SCHOOLBOY) HOYT

| Year Club | League | G. | IP. | W. | L. | Pct. | ERA. |
|---|---|---|---|---|---|---|---|
| 1916—Mt. Carmel | Pa. State | 6 | .... | 5 | 1 | .833 | ...... |
| 1916—Hartford-Lynn | Eastern | 10 | 71 | 4 | 5 | .444 | ...... |
| 1917—Memphis | Southern | 17 | 103 | 3 | 9 | .250 | ...... |
| 1917—Montreal | International | 28 | 215 | 7 | 17 | .292 | 2.51 |
| 1918—Nashville | Southern | 19 | 137 | 5 | 10 | .333 | ...... |
| 1918—New York | National | 1 | 1 | 0 | 0 | .000 | 0.00 |
| 1918—Newark | International | 5 | 43 | 2 | 3 | .400 | 2.09 |
| 1919—Boston | American | 13 | 105 | 4 | 6 | .400 | 3.26 |
| 1920—Boston | American | 22 | 121 | 6 | 6 | .500 | 4.39 |
| 1921—New York | American | 44 | 282 | 19 | 13 | .594 | 3.10 |
| 1922—New York | American | 37 | 265 | 19 | 12 | .613 | 3.43 |
| 1923—New York | American | 37 | 239 | 17 | 9 | .654 | 3.01 |
| 1924—New York | American | 46 | 247 | 18 | 13 | .581 | 3.79 |
| 1925—New York | American | 46 | 243 | 11 | 14 | .440 | 4.00 |
| 1926—New York | American | 40 | 218 | 16 | 12 | .571 | 3.84 |
| 1927—New York | American | 36 | 256 | ●22 | 7 | ★.759 | 2.64 |
| 1928—New York | American | 42 | 273 | 23 | 7 | .767 | 3.36 |
| 1929—New York | American | 30 | 202 | 10 | 9 | .526 | 4.23 |
| 1930—N.Y.-Detroit | American | 34 | 183 | 11 | 10 | .524 | 4.72 |

| Year Club | League | G. | IP. | W. | L. | Pct. | ERA. |
|---|---|---|---|---|---|---|---|
| 1931—Detroit-Phila. | American | 32 | 203 | 13 | 13 | .500 | 4.97 |
| 1932—Brooklyn-N.Y. | National | 26 | 124 | 6 | 10 | .375 | 4.35 |
| 1933—Pittsburgh | National | 36 | 117 | 5 | 7 | .417 | 2.92 |
| 1934—Pittsburgh | National | 48 | 191 | 15 | 6 | .714 | 2.92 |
| 1935—Pittsburgh | National | 39 | 164 | 7 | 11 | .389 | 3.40 |
| 1936—Pittsburgh | National | 22 | 117 | 7 | 5 | .583 | 2.69 |
| 1937—Pittsburgh-Brooklyn | National | 38 | 195 | 8 | 9 | .471 | 3.42 |
| 1938—Brooklyn | National | 6 | 16 | 0 | 3 | .000 | 5.06 |
| American League Totals | | 459 | 2837 | 189 | 131 | .591 | 3.68 |
| National League Totals | | 216 | 925 | 48 | 51 | .485 | 3.31 |
| Major League Totals | | 675 | 3762 | 237 | 182 | .566 | 3.59 |

### WORLD SERIES RECORD

| Year Club | League | G. | IP. | W. | L. | Pct. | ERA. |
|---|---|---|---|---|---|---|---|
| 1921—New York | American | 3 | 27 | 2 | 1 | .667 | 0.00 |
| 1922—New York | American | 2 | 8 | 0 | 1 | .000 | 1.13 |
| 1923—New York | American | 1 | 2⅓ | 0 | 0 | .000 | 15.43 |
| 1926—New York | American | 2 | 15 | 1 | 1 | .500 | 1.20 |
| 1927—New York | American | 1 | 7⅓ | 1 | 0 | 1.000 | 4.91 |
| 1928—New York | American | 2 | 18 | 2 | 0 | 1.000 | 1.50 |
| 1931—Philadelphia | American | 1 | 6 | 0 | 1 | .000 | 4.50 |
| World Series Totals | | 12 | 83⅔ | 6 | 4 | .600 | 1.83 |

## CARL OWEN (KING CARL) HUBBELL

| Year Club | League | G. | IP. | W. | L. | Pct. | ERA. |
|---|---|---|---|---|---|---|---|
| 1923—Cushing | Oklahoma State | | (No records available) | | | | |
| 1924—Cushing | Oklahoma State | | (No records available) | | | | |
| 1924—Ardmore | West Assn. | 2 | 12 | 1 | 0 | 1.000 | ...... |
| 1924—Oklahoma City | Western | 2 | 15 | 1 | 1 | .500 | ...... |
| 1925—Oklahoma City | Western | 45 | 284 | 17 | 13 | .567 | ...... |
| 1926—Toronto | Int. | 31 | 93 | 7 | 7 | .500 | 3.77 |
| 1927—Decatur | I.I.I. | 23 | 185 | 14 | 7 | .667 | 2.53 |
| 1927—Fort Worth | Texas | 2 | 3 | 0 | 1 | .000 | ...... |
| 1928—Beaumont | Texas | 21 | 185 | 12 | 9 | .571 | 2.97 |
| 1928—New York | National | 20 | 124 | 10 | 6 | .625 | 2.83 |
| 1929—New York | National | 39 | 268 | 18 | 11 | .621 | 3.69 |
| 1930—New York | National | 37 | 242 | 17 | 12 | .586 | 3.87 |
| 1931—New York | National | 36 | 248 | 14 | 12 | .538 | 2.65 |
| 1932—New York | National | 40 | 284 | 18 | 11 | .621 | 2.50 |
| 1933—New York | National | 45 | ★309 | ★23 | 12 | .657 | ★1.66 |
| 1934—New York | National | 49 | 313 | 21 | 12 | .636 | ★2.30 |
| 1935—New York | National | 42 | 303 | 23 | 12 | .657 | 3.27 |
| 1936—New York | National | 42 | 304 | ★26 | 6 | ★.813 | ★2.31 |
| 1937—New York | National | 39 | 262 | ★22 | 8 | ★.733 | 3.19 |
| 1938—New York | National | 24 | 179 | 13 | 10 | .565 | 3.07 |
| 1939—New York | National | 29 | 154 | 11 | 9 | .550 | 2.75 |
| 1940—New York | National | 31 | 214 | 11 | 12 | .478 | 3.66 |
| 1941—New York | National | 26 | 164 | 11 | 9 | .550 | 3.57 |
| 1942—New York | National | 24 | 157 | 11 | 8 | .579 | 3.96 |
| 1943—New York | National | 12 | 66 | 4 | 4 | .500 | 4.91 |
| Major League Totals | | 535 | 3591 | 253 | 154 | .622 | 2.98 |

### WORLD SERIES RECORD

| Year Club | League | G. | IP. | W. | L. | Pct. | ERA. |
|---|---|---|---|---|---|---|---|
| 1933—New York | National | 2 | 20 | 2 | 0 | 1.000 | 0.00 |
| 1936—New York | National | 2 | 16 | 1 | 1 | .500 | 2.25 |
| 1937—New York | National | 2 | 14⅓ | 1 | 1 | .500 | 3.77 |
| World Series Totals | | 6 | 50⅓ | 4 | 2 | .667 | 1.79 |

## MILLER JAMES HUGGINS

| Year Club | League | G. | AB. | R. | H. | HR. | SB. | B.A. |
|---|---|---|---|---|---|---|---|---|
| 1899—Mansfield | Int. St. | | (No Records available) | | | | | |
| 1900— | | | (Played semi-pro baseball) | | | | | |
| 1901—St. Paul | West. | 129 | 474 | 79 | 153 | 2 | 17 | .322 |
| 1902—St. Paul | A. A. | 129 | 466 | 75 | 153 | 0 | 34 | .328 |
| 1903—St. Paul | A. A. | 124 | 444 | 91 | 137 | 0 | 48 | .308 |
| 1904—Cincinnati | Nat. | 140 | 491 | 96 | 129 | 2 | 13 | .263 |
| 1905—Cincinnati | Nat. | 149 | 564 | 117 | 154 | 1 | 27 | .273 |
| 1906—Cincinnati | Nat. | 146 | 545 | 81 | 159 | 0 | 41 | .292 |
| 1907—Cincinnati | Nat. | ★156 | 561 | 64 | 139 | 1 | 28 | .248 |
| 1908—Cincinnati | Nat. | 135 | 498 | 65 | 119 | 0 | 30 | .239 |
| 1909—Cincinnati | Nat. | 46 | 159 | 18 | 34 | 0 | 11 | .213 |
| 1910—St. Louis | Nat. | 151 | 547 | 101 | 145 | 1 | 34 | .265 |
| 1911—St. Louis | Nat. | 136 | 509 | 106 | 133 | 1 | 37 | .261 |
| 1912—St. Louis | Nat. | 120 | 431 | 82 | 131 | 0 | 35 | .304 |
| 1913—St. Louis | Nat. | 121 | 382 | 74 | 109 | 0 | 23 | .285 |
| 1914—St. Louis | Nat. | 148 | 509 | 85 | 134 | 1 | 32 | .263 |
| 1915—St. Louis | Nat. | 107 | 353 | 57 | 85 | 2 | 13 | .241 |
| 1916—St. Louis | Nat. | 18 | 9 | 2 | 3 | 0 | 0 | .333 |
| Major League Totals | | 1573 | 5558 | 948 | 1474 | 9 | 324 | .265 |

### RECORD AS MANAGER

| Year Club | League | Position | W. | L. |
|---|---|---|---|---|
| 1913—St. Louis | National | Eighth | 51 | 99 |
| 1914—St. Louis | National | Third | 81 | 72 |
| 1915—St. Louis | National | Sixth | 72 | 81 |
| 1916—St. Louis | National | Seventh† | 60 | 93 |
| 1917—St. Louis | National | Third | 82 | 70 |
| 1918—New York | American | Fourth | 60 | 63 |

| Year Club | League | Position | W. | L. |
|---|---|---|---|---|
| 1919—New York | American | Third | 80 | 59 |
| 1920—New York | American | Third | 95 | 59 |
| 1921—New York | American | First | 98 | 55 |
| 1922—New York | American | First | 94 | 60 |
| 1923—New York | American | First | 98 | 54 |
| 1924—New York | American | Second | 89 | 63 |
| 1925—New York | American | Seventh | 69 | 85 |
| 1926—New York | American | First | 91 | 63 |
| 1927—New York | American | First | 110 | 44 |
| 1928—New York | American | First | 101 | 53 |
| 1929—New York | American | Second | 88 | 66 |
| Major League Totals | | | 1419 | 1139 |

†Tied for position.

### WORLD SERIES RECORD

| Year Club | League | W. | L. |
|---|---|---|---|
| 1921—New York | American | 3 | 5 |
| 1922—New York | American | 0 | 4 |
| 1923—New York | American | 4 | 2 |
| 1926—New York | American | 3 | 4 |
| 1927—New York | American | 4 | 0 |
| 1928—New York | American | 4 | 0 |

## MONFORD MERRILL (MONTE) IRVIN
### ORGANIZED BALL PLAYING RECORD

| Year Club | League | G. | AB. | R. | H. | HR. | RBI. | B.A. |
|---|---|---|---|---|---|---|---|---|
| 1949—Jersey City | Int. | 63 | 204 | 55 | 76 | 9 | 52 | .373 |
| 1949—New York | Nat. | 36 | 76 | 7 | 17 | 0 | 7 | .224 |
| 1950—Jersey City | Int. | 18 | 51 | 28 | 26 | 10 | 33 | .510 |
| 1950—New York | Nat. | 110 | 374 | 61 | 112 | 15 | 66 | .299 |
| 1951—New York | Nat. | 151 | 558 | 94 | 174 | 24 | ★121 | .312 |
| 1952—New York | Nat. | 46 | 126 | 10 | 39 | 4 | 21 | .310 |
| 1953—New York | Nat. | 124 | 444 | 72 | 146 | 21 | 97 | .329 |
| 1954—New York | Nat. | 135 | 432 | 62 | 113 | 19 | 64 | .262 |
| 1955—New York | Nat. | 51 | 150 | 16 | 38 | 1 | 17 | .253 |
| 1955—Minneapolis | A. A. | 75 | 250 | 57 | 88 | 14 | 52 | .352 |
| 1956—Chicago | Nat. | 111 | 339 | 44 | 92 | 15 | 50 | .271 |
| Major League Totals | | 764 | 2499 | 366 | 731 | 99 | 443 | .293 |

### WORLD SERIES RECORD

| Year Club | League | G. | AB. | R. | H. | HR. | RBI. | B.A. |
|---|---|---|---|---|---|---|---|---|
| 1951—New York | Nat. | 6 | 24 | 3 | 11 | 0 | 2 | .458 |
| 1954—New York | Nat. | 4 | 9 | 1 | 2 | 0 | 2 | .222 |
| World Series Totals | | 10 | 33 | 4 | 13 | 0 | 4 | ·.394 |

## TRAVIS CALVIN (STONEWALL or JAX) JACKSON

| Year Club | League | G. | AB. | R. | H. | HR. | RBI. | B.A. |
|---|---|---|---|---|---|---|---|---|
| 1921—Little Rock | South. | 39 | 130 | 11 | 26 | 1 | 12 | .200 |
| 1922—Little Rock | South. | 147 | 521 | 59 | 146 | 7 | .... | .280 |
| 1922—New York | Nat. | 3 | 8 | 1 | 0 | 0 | 0 | .000 |
| 1923—New York | Nat. | 96 | 327 | 45 | 90 | 4 | 37 | .275 |
| 1924—New York | Nat. | 151 | 596 | 81 | 180 | 11 | 76 | .302 |
| 1925—New York | Nat. | 112 | 411 | 51 | 117 | 9 | 59 | .285 |
| 1926—New York | Nat. | 111 | 385 | 64 | 126 | 8 | 51 | .327 |
| 1927—New York | Nat. | 127 | 469 | 67 | 149 | 14 | 98 | .318 |
| 1928—New York | Nat. | 150 | 537 | 73 | 145 | 14 | 77 | .270 |
| 1929—New York | Nat. | 149 | 551 | 92 | 162 | 21 | 94 | .294 |
| 1930—New York | Nat. | 116 | 431 | 70 | 146 | 13 | 82 | .339 |
| 1931—New York | Nat. | 145 | 555 | 65 | 172 | 5 | 71 | .310 |
| 1932—New York | Nat. | 52 | 195 | 23 | 50 | 4 | 38 | .256 |
| 1933—New York | Nat. | 53 | 122 | 11 | 30 | 0 | 12 | .246 |
| 1934—New York | Nat. | 137 | 523 | 75 | 140 | 16 | 101 | .268 |
| 1935—New York | Nat. | 128 | 511 | 74 | 154 | 9 | 80 | .301 |
| 1936—New York | Nat. | 126 | 465 | 41 | 107 | 7 | 53 | .230 |
| 1937—Jersey City | Int. | 6 | 20 | 0 | 5 | 0 | 1 | .250 |
| 1938—Jersey City | Int. | 10 | 17 | 0 | 5 | 0 | 2 | .294 |
| Major League Totals | | 1656 | 6086 | 833 | 1768 | 135 | 929 | .291 |

### WORLD SERIES RECORD

| Year Club | League | G. | AB. | R. | H. | HR. | RBI. | B.A. |
|---|---|---|---|---|---|---|---|---|
| 1923—New York | Nat. | 1 | 1 | 0 | 0 | 0 | 0 | .000 |
| 1924—New York | Nat. | 7 | 27 | 3 | 2 | 0 | 1 | .074 |
| 1933—New York | Nat. | 5 | 18 | 3 | 4 | 0 | 2 | .222 |
| 1936—New York | Nat. | 6 | 21 | 1 | 4 | 0 | 1 | .190 |
| World Series Totals | | 19 | 67 | 7 | 10 | 0 | 4 | .149 |

## HUGH AMBROSE (EE-YAH) JENNINGS

| Year Club | League | G. | AB. | R. | H. | HR. | SB. | B.A. |
|---|---|---|---|---|---|---|---|---|
| 1890—Allentown | E. Int.-St. | 13 | 50 | 8 | 16 | ... | | .320 |
| 1891—Louisville | A. A. | 81 | 316 | 46 | 95 | 1 | 14 | .300 |
| 1892—Louisville | Nat. | 152 | 584 | 66 | 137 | 2 | 24 | .232 |
| 1893—Louis.-Balt. | Nat. | 38 | 135 | 12 | 25 | 2 | 1 | .192 |
| 1894—Baltimore | Nat. | 128 | 505 | 136 | 168 | 4 | 36 | .332 |
| 1895—Baltimore | Nat. | 131 | 528 | 159 | 204 | 4 | 60 | .385 |
| 1896—Baltimore | Nat. | 129 | 523 | 125 | 208 | 0 | 73 | .398 |
| 1897—Baltimore | Nat. | 115 | 436 | 131 | 154 | 2 | 60 | .353 |
| 1898—Baltimore | Nat. | 143 | 533 | 136 | 173 | 0 | 31 | .325 |
| 1899—Brkn.-Balt. | Nat. | 63 | 223 | 44 | 67 | 0 | 18 | .300 |
| 1900—Brooklyn | Nat. | 112 | 440 | 62 | 119 | 2 | 35 | .270 |

| Year Club | League | G. | AB. | R. | H. | HR. | RBI. | B.A. |
|---|---|---|---|---|---|---|---|---|
| 1901—Philadelphia | Nat. | 81 | 302 | 38 | 83 | 1 | 13 | .274 |
| 1902—Philadelphia | Nat. | 78 | 289 | 31 | 80 | 1 | 8 | .277 |
| 1903—Brooklyn | Nat. | 6 | 17 | 2 | 4 | 0 | 0 | .235 |
| 1903—Baltimore | East. | 32 | 122 | 26 | 40 | 0 | 9 | .328 |
| 1904—Baltimore | East. | 92 | 332 | 65 | 97 | 1 | 23 | .292 |
| 1905—Baltimore | East. | 56 | 179 | 24 | 45 | 0 | 3 | .251 |
| 1906—Baltimore | East. | 75 | 242 | 24 | 60 | 0 | 2 | .248 |
| 1907—Detroit | Amer. | 2 | 4 | 0 | 1 | 0 | 0 | .250 |
| 1908—Detroit | Amer. | 1 | 0 | 0 | 0 | 0 | 0 | .000 |
| 1909—Detroit | Amer. | 2 | 4 | 1 | 2 | 0 | 0 | .500 |
| 1912—Detroit | Amer. | 1 | 1 | 0 | 0 | 0 | 0 | .000 |
| 1918—Detroit | Amer. | 1 | 0 | 0 | 0 | 0 | 0 | .000 |
| American Association Totals | | 81 | 316 | 46 | 95 | 1 | 14 | .300 |
| American League Totals | | 7 | 9 | 1 | 3 | 0 | 0 | .333 |
| National League Totals | | 1176 | 4515 | 942 | 1422 | 18 | 359 | .315 |
| Major League Totals | | 1264 | 4840 | 989 | 1520 | 19 | 373 | .314 |

## WALTER PERRY (BARNEY) JOHNSON

| Year Club | League | G. | IP. | W. | L. | Pct. | ERA. |
|---|---|---|---|---|---|---|---|
| 1907—Washington | Amer. | 14 | 110 | 5 | 9 | .357 | .... |
| 1908—Washington | Amer. | 36 | 257 | 14 | 14 | .500 | .... |
| 1909—Washington | Amer. | 40 | 297 | 13 | 25 | .342 | .... |
| 1910—Washington | Amer. | ●45 | ★374 | 25 | 17 | .595 | .... |
| 1911—Washington | Amer. | 40 | 322 | 25 | 13 | .658 | .... |
| 1912—Washington | Amer. | 50 | 368 | 32 | 12 | .727 | .... |
| 1913—Washington | Amer. | 48 | ★346 | ★36 | 7 | .837 | ★1.14 |
| 1914—Washington | Amer. | ★51 | ★372 | ★28 | 18 | .609 | 1.72 |
| 1915—Washington | Amer. | 47 | ★337 | ★27 | 13 | .675 | 1.55 |
| 1916—Washington | Amer. | 48 | ★371 | ★25 | 20 | .556 | 1.89 |
| 1917—Washington | Amer. | 47 | 328 | 23 | 16 | .590 | 2.28 |
| 1918—Washington | Amer. | 39 | 325 | ★23 | 13 | .639 | ★1.27 |
| 1919—Washington | Amer. | 39 | 290 | 20 | 14 | .588 | ★1.49 |
| 1920—Washington | Amer. | 21 | 144 | 8 | 10 | .444 | 3.13 |
| 1921—Washington | Amer. | 35 | 264 | 17 | 14 | .548 | 3.51 |
| 1922—Washington | Amer. | 41 | 280 | 15 | 16 | .484 | 2.99 |
| 1923—Washington | Amer. | 42 | 261 | 17 | 12 | .586 | 3.48 |
| 1924—Washington | Amer. | 38 | 278 | ★23 | 7 | ★.767 | ★2.72 |
| 1925—Washington | Amer. | 30 | 229 | 20 | 7 | .741 | 3.07 |
| 1926—Washington | Amer. | 33 | 262 | 15 | 16 | .484 | 3.61 |
| 1927—Washington | Amer. | 18 | 108 | 5 | 6 | .455 | 5.08 |
| 1928—Newark | Int. | 1 | 0 | 0 | 0 | .000 | 0.00 |
| Major League Totals | | 802 | 5923 | 416 | 279 | .599 | .... |

### WORLD SERIES RECORD

| Year Club | League | G. | IP. | W. | L. | Pct. | ERA. |
|---|---|---|---|---|---|---|---|
| 1924—Washington | American | 3 | 24 | 1 | 2 | .333 | 2.25 |
| 1925—Washington | American | 3 | 26 | 2 | 1 | .667 | 2.08 |
| World Series Totals | | 6 | 50 | 3 | 3 | .500 | 2.16 |

## ADRIAN (ADDIE) JOSS

| Year Club | League | G. | IP. | W. | L. | Pct. |
|---|---|---|---|---|---|---|
| 1900—Toledo | Inter-State | 49 | .... | 19 | 16 | .543 |
| 1901—Toledo | Western Assn. | 41 | 353 | 25 | 15 | .625 |
| 1902—Cleveland | American | 32 | 269 | 17 | 13 | .567 |
| 1903—Cleveland | American | 32 | 284 | 18 | 13 | .581 |
| 1904—Cleveland | American | 25 | 192 | 14 | 10 | .583 |
| 1905—Cleveland | American | 33 | 289 | 20 | 12 | .625 |
| 1906—Cleveland | American | 34 | 282 | 21 | 9 | .700 |
| 1907—Cleveland | American | 42 | 339 | 27 | 10 | .730 |
| 1908—Cleveland | American | 42 | 324 | 24 | 12 | .667 |
| 1909—Cleveland | American | 33 | 243 | 14 | 13 | .519 |
| 1910—Cleveland | American | 13 | 107 | 5 | 5 | .500 |
| Major League Totals | | 286 | 2329 | 160 | 97 | .623 |

## ALBERT WILLIAM KALINE

| Year Club | League | G. | AB. | R. | H. | HR. | RBI. | B.A. |
|---|---|---|---|---|---|---|---|---|
| 1953—Detroit | Amer. | 30 | 28 | 9 | 7 | 1 | 2 | .250 |
| 1954—Detroit | Amer. | 138 | 504 | 42 | 139 | 4 | 43 | .276 |
| 1955—Detroit | Amer. | 152 | 588 | 121 | ★200 | 27 | 102 | ★.340 |
| 1956—Detroit | Amer. | 153 | 617 | 96 | 194 | 27 | 128 | .314 |
| 1957—Detroit | Amer. | 149 | 577 | 83 | 170 | 23 | 90 | .295 |
| 1958—Detroit | Amer. | 146 | 543 | 84 | 170 | 16 | 85 | .313 |
| 1959—Detroit | Amer. | 136 | 511 | 86 | 167 | 27 | 94 | 327 |
| 1960—Detroit | Amer. | 147 | 551 | 77 | 153 | 15 | 68 | .278 |
| 1961—Detroit | Amer. | 153 | 586 | 116 | 190 | 19 | 82 | .324 |
| 1962—Detroit | Amer. | 100 | 398 | 78 | 121 | 29 | 94 | .304 |
| 1963—Detroit | Amer. | 145 | 551 | 89 | 172 | 27 | 101 | .312 |
| 1964—Detroit | Amer. | 146 | 525 | 77 | 154 | 17 | 68 | .293 |
| 1965—Detroit | Amer. | 125 | 399 | 72 | 112 | 18 | 72 | .281 |
| 1966—Detroit | Amer. | 142 | 479 | 85 | 138 | 29 | 88 | .288 |
| 1967—Detroit | Amer. | 131 | 458 | 94 | 141 | 25 | 78 | .308 |
| 1968—Detroit | Amer. | 102 | 327 | 49 | 94 | 10 | 53 | .287 |
| 1969—Detroit | Amer. | 131 | 456 | 74 | 124 | 21 | 69 | .272 |
| 1970—Detroit | Amer. | 131 | 467 | 64 | 130 | 16 | 71 | .278 |
| 1971—Detroit | Amer. | 133 | 405 | 69 | 119 | 15 | 54 | .294 |
| 1972—Detroit | Amer. | 106 | 278 | 46 | 87 | 10 | 32 | .313 |
| 1973—Detroit | Amer. | 91 | 310 | 40 | 79 | 10 | 45 | .255 |
| 1974—Detroit | Amer. | 147 | 558 | 71 | 146 | 13 | 64 | .262 |
| Major League Totals | | 2834 | 10116 | 1622 | 3007 | 399 | 1583 | .297 |

## CHAMPIONSHIP SERIES RECORD

| Year Club | League | G. | AB. | R. | H. | HR. | RBI. | B.A. |
|---|---|---|---|---|---|---|---|---|
| 1972—Detroit | Amer. | 5 | 19 | 3 | 5 | 1 | 1 | .263 |

## WORLD SERIES RECORD

| Year Club | League | G. | AB. | R. | H. | HR. | RBI. | B.A. |
|---|---|---|---|---|---|---|---|---|
| 1968—Detroit | Amer. | 7 | 29 | 6 | 11 | 2 | 8 | .379 |

## TIMOTHY J. (TIM) KEEFE

| Year Club | League | G. | IP. | W. | L. | Pct. | ShO. |
|---|---|---|---|---|---|---|---|
| 1879—Utica-New Bedford | Nat. Assn. | 24 | .... | .... | .... | .... | .... |
| 1880—Albany | Nat. Assn. | 18 | .... | .... | .... | .... | .... |
| 1880—Troy | National | 12 | 105 | 6 | 6 | .500 | 0 |
| 1881—Troy | National | 45 | 404 | 18 | 27 | .400 | 4 |
| 1882—Troy | National | 43 | 376 | 17 | 26 | .395 | 1 |
| 1883—Metropolitan | Amer. Assn. | *68 | *619 | 41 | 27 | .603 | 5 |
| 1884—Metropolitan | Amer. Assn. | 56 | 483 | 37 | 17 | .685 | 4 |
| 1885—New York | National | 46 | 400 | 32 | 13 | .711 | 7 |
| 1886—New York | National | *64 | *535 | ●42 | 20 | .677 | 2 |
| 1887—New York | National | 56 | 476 | 35 | 19 | .648 | 2 |
| 1888—New York | National | 51 | 434 | *35 | 11 | *.761 | ●8 |
| 1889—New York | National | 47 | 363 | 28 | 13 | .683 | 3 |
| 1890—New York | Players | 30 | 227 | 17 | 11 | .607 | 1 |
| 1891—N.Y.-Philadelphia | National | 19 | 131 | 5 | 11 | .313 | 0 |
| 1892—Philadelphia | National | 39 | 312 | 19 | 16 | .543 | 3 |
| 1893—Philadelphia | National | 22 | 178 | 10 | 7 | .588 | 0 |
| American Association Totals | | 124 | 1102 | 78 | 44 | .639 | 9 |
| National League Totals | | 444 | 3714 | 247 | 169 | .594 | 30 |
| Players League Totals | | 30 | 227 | 17 | 11 | .607 | 1 |
| Major League Totals | | 598 | 5043 | 342 | 224 | .604 | 40 |

## WORLD SERIES RECORD

| Year Club | League | G. | IP. | W. | L. | Pct. | ShO. |
|---|---|---|---|---|---|---|---|
| 1884—Metropolitan | American Assn. | 2 | 15 | 0 | 2 | .000 | 0 |
| 1888—New York | National | 4 | 35 | 4 | 0 | 1.000 | 0 |
| 1889—New York | National | 2 | 11 | 0 | 1 | .000 | 0 |
| World Series Totals | | 8 | 61 | 4 | 3 | .571 | 0 |

## WILLIAM H. (WEE WILLIE) KEELER

| Year Club | League | G. | AB. | R. | H. | HR. | SB. | B.A. |
|---|---|---|---|---|---|---|---|---|
| 1892—Binghamton | East. | 93 | 410 | 109 | 153 | 2 | 12 | *.373 |
| 1892—New York | Nat. | 13 | 49 | 6 | 15 | 0 | 5 | .306 |
| 1893—N.Y.-Brooklyn | Nat. | 29 | 90 | 19 | 30 | 2 | 7 | .333 |
| 1893—Binghamton | East. | 15 | 68 | 9 | 20 | 1 | 3 | .294 |
| 1894—Baltimore | Nat. | 128 | 593 | 164 | 218 | 5 | 30 | .368 |
| 1895—Baltimore | Nat. | 131 | 560 | 161 | 221 | 4 | 57 | .395 |
| 1896—Baltimore | Nat. | 127 | 546 | 154 | 214 | 4 | 73 | .392 |
| 1897—Baltimore | Nat. | 128 | 562 | 147 | *243 | 0 | 63 | *.432 |
| 1898—Baltimore | Nat. | 128 | 564 | 126 | 214 | 0 | 26 | *.379 |
| 1899—Brooklyn | Nat. | 143 | 571 | *141 | 215 | 1 | 44 | .377 |
| 1900—Brooklyn | Nat. | 137 | 568 | 106 | *208 | 4 | 39 | .366 |
| 1901—Brooklyn | Nat. | 136 | 589 | 124 | 209 | 2 | 31 | .355 |
| 1902—Brooklyn | Nat. | 132 | 550 | 84 | 188 | 0 | 23 | .342 |
| 1903—New York | Amer. | 132 | 515 | 98 | 164 | 0 | 25 | .318 |
| 1904—New York | Amer. | 143 | 539 | 76 | 185 | 2 | 22 | .343 |
| 1905—New York | Amer. | 149 | 560 | 81 | 169 | 4 | 19 | .302 |
| 1906—New York | Amer. | 152 | 592 | 96 | 180 | 2 | 23 | .304 |
| 1907—New York | Amer. | 107 | 423 | 50 | 99 | 0 | 7 | .234 |
| 1908—New York | Amer. | 91 | 323 | 38 | 85 | 1 | 14 | .263 |
| 1909—New York | Amer. | 99 | 360 | 44 | 95 | 1 | 10 | .264 |
| 1910—New York | Nat. | 19 | 10 | 5 | 3 | 0 | 1 | .300 |
| 1911—Toronto | East. | 39 | 155 | 26 | 43 | 0 | 4 | .277 |
| American League Totals | | 873 | 3312 | 483 | 977 | 10 | 120 | .295 |
| National League Totals | | 1251 | 5252 | 1237 | 1978 | 22 | 399 | .377 |
| Major League Totals | | 2124 | 8564 | 1720 | 2955 | 32 | 519 | .345 |

## GEORGE CLYDE KELL

| Year Club | League | G. | AB. | R. | H. | HR. | RBI. | B.A. |
|---|---|---|---|---|---|---|---|---|
| 1940—Newport | NE. Ark. | 48 | 169 | 14 | 27 | 0 | 14 | .160 |
| 1941—Newport | NE. Ark. | 118 | 462 | 71 | *143 | 1 | 75 | .310 |
| 1942—Lancaster | Int.-St. | 127 | 465 | 56 | 139 | 0 | 30 | .299 |
| 1943—Lancaster | Int.-St. | 138 | 555 | *120 | *220 | 5 | 79 | *.396 |
| 1943—Philadelphia | Amer. | 1 | 5 | 1 | 1 | 0 | 1 | .200 |
| 1944—Philadelphia | Amer. | 139 | 514 | 51 | 138 | 0 | 44 | .268 |
| 1945—Philadelphia | Amer. | 147 | 567 | 50 | 154 | 4 | 56 | .272 |
| 1946—Phila.-Detroit | Amer. | 131 | 521 | 70 | 168 | 4 | 52 | .322 |
| 1947—Detroit | Amer. | 152 | 588 | 75 | 188 | 5 | 93 | .320 |
| 1948—Detroit | Amer. | 92 | 368 | 47 | 112 | 2 | 44 | .304 |
| 1949—Detroit | Amer. | 134 | 522 | 97 | 179 | 3 | 59 | *.343 |
| 1950—Detroit | Amer. | ●157 | *641 | 114 | *218 | 8 | 101 | .340 |
| 1951—Detroit | Amer. | 147 | 598 | 92 | *191 | 2 | 59 | .319 |
| 1952—Det.-Boston | Amer. | 114 | 428 | 52 | 133 | 7 | 57 | .311 |
| 1953—Boston | Amer. | 134 | 460 | 68 | 141 | 12 | 73 | .307 |
| 1954—Bos.-Chicago | Amer. | 97 | 326 | 40 | 90 | 5 | 58 | .276 |
| 1955—Chicago | Amer. | 128 | 429 | 44 | 134 | 8 | 81 | .312 |
| 1956—Chi.-Balt. | Amer. | 123 | 425 | 52 | 115 | 9 | 48 | .271 |
| 1957—Baltimore | Amer. | 99 | 310 | 28 | 92 | 9 | 44 | .297 |
| Major League Totals | | 1795 | 6702 | 881 | 2054 | 78 | 870 | .306 |

## JOSEPH JAMES KELLEY

| Year Club | League | G. | AB. | R. | H. | HR. | SB. | B.A. |
|---|---|---|---|---|---|---|---|---|
| 1891—Lowell | N. Eng. | 57 | 245 | 50 | 81 | ... | 21 | .331 |
| 1891—Bos.-Pittsburgh | Nat. | 14 | 52 | 8 | 12 | 0 | 0 | .231 |
| 1892—Omaha | West. | 49 | 203 | 32 | 67 | ... | 18 | .330 |
| 1892—Pitts.-Balt. | Nat. | 66 | 232 | 30 | 57 | 0 | 7 | .246 |
| 1893—Baltimore | Nat. | 124 | 490 | 120 | 153 | 9 | 38 | .312 |
| 1894—Baltimore | Nat. | 129 | 509 | 167 | 199 | 6 | 45 | .391 |
| 1895—Baltimore | Nat. | 131 | 510 | 148 | 189 | 10 | 59 | .371 |
| 1896—Baltimore | Nat. | 130 | 516 | 147 | 191 | 8 | 90 | .370 |
| 1897—Baltimore | Nat. | 129 | 503 | 113 | 196 | 5 | 50 | .390 |
| 1898—Baltimore | Nat. | 124 | 467 | 71 | 153 | 3 | 22 | .328 |
| 1899—Brooklyn | Nat. | 144 | 540 | 107 | 178 | 6 | 31 | .330 |
| 1900—Brooklyn | Nat. | 118 | 453 | 92 | 144 | 6 | 26 | .318 |
| 1901—Brooklyn | Nat. | 120 | 493 | 77 | 152 | 4 | 20 | .308 |
| 1902—Baltimore | Amer. | 60 | 222 | 50 | 69 | 1 | 12 | .311 |
| 1902—Cincinnati | Nat. | 37 | 156 | 24 | 51 | 1 | 3 | .327 |
| 1903—Cincinnati | Nat. | 104 | 383 | 85 | 121 | 3 | 18 | .316 |
| 1904—Cincinnati | Nat. | 123 | 449 | 75 | 126 | 0 | 15 | .281 |
| 1905—Cincinnati | Nat. | 87 | 321 | 43 | 89 | 1 | 8 | .277 |
| 1906—Cincinnati | Nat. | 127 | 465 | 43 | 106 | 1 | 9 | .228 |
| 1907—Toronto | East. | 91 | 314 | 32 | 101 | 1 | 15 | .322 |
| 1908—Boston | Nat. | 62 | 228 | 25 | 59 | 2 | 5 | .259 |
| 1909—Toronto | East. | 107 | 357 | 49 | 96 | 1 | 11 | .269 |
| 1910—Toronto | East. | 46 | 110 | 13 | 31 | 0 | 4 | .282 |
| American League Totals | | 60 | 222 | 50 | 69 | 1 | 12 | .311 |
| National League Totals | | 1769 | 6767 | 1375 | 2176 | 65 | 446 | .322 |
| Major League Totals | | 1829 | 6989 | 1425 | 2245 | 66 | 458 | .321 |

## PITCHING RECORD

| Year Club | League | G. | I.P. | W. | L. | Pct. |
|---|---|---|---|---|---|---|
| 1891—Lowell | New England | 14 | 121 | 10 | 3 | .769 |

## GEORGE LANGE (HIGH POCKETS) KELLY

| Year Club | League | G. | AB. | R. | H. | HR. | RBI. | B.A. |
|---|---|---|---|---|---|---|---|---|
| 1914—Victoria | N. W. | 141 | 436 | 45 | 109 | 7 | ..... | .250 |
| 1915—Victoria | N. W. | 94 | 361 | 57 | 107 | 5 | ..... | .297 |
| 1915—New York | Nat. | 17 | 38 | 2 | 6 | 1 | 5 | .158 |
| 1916—New York | Nat. | 49 | 76 | 4 | 12 | 0 | 2 | .158 |
| 1917—N.York-Pitts. | Nat. | 19 | 30 | 2 | 2 | 0 | 0 | .067 |
| 1917—Rochester | Int. | 32 | 120 | 16 | 36 | 4 | ..... | .300 |
| 1918—New York | Nat. | | | (In Military Service) | | | | |
| 1919—Rochester | Int. | 103 | 376 | 72 | 134 | 15 | ..... | .356 |
| 1919—New York | Nat. | 32 | 107 | 12 | 31 | 1 | 13 | .290 |
| 1920—New York | Nat. | 155 | 590 | 69 | 157 | 11 | ●94 | .266 |
| 1921—New York | Nat. | 149 | 587 | 95 | 181 | *23 | 122 | .308 |
| 1922—New York | Nat. | 151 | 592 | 96 | 194 | 17 | 107 | .328 |
| 1923—New York | Nat. | 145 | 560 | 82 | 172 | 16 | 103 | .307 |
| 1924—New York | Nat. | 144 | 571 | 91 | 185 | 21 | ●136 | .324 |
| 1925—New York | Nat. | 147 | 586 | 87 | 181 | 20 | 99 | .309 |
| 1926—New York | Nat. | 136 | 499 | 70 | 151 | 13 | 80 | .303 |
| 1927—Cincinnati | Nat. | 61 | 222 | 27 | 60 | 5 | 21 | .270 |
| 1928—Cincinnati | Nat. | 116 | 402 | 46 | 119 | 3 | 58 | .296 |
| 1929—Cincinnati | Nat. | 147 | 577 | 73 | 169 | 5 | 103 | .293 |
| 1930—Cin.-Chicago | Nat. | 90 | 354 | 40 | 109 | 8 | 54 | .308 |
| 1930—Minneapolis | A. A. | 34 | 147 | 25 | 53 | 6 | 38 | .361 |
| 1931—Minneapolis | A. A. | 155 | 606 | 84 | 194 | 20 | 112 | .320 |
| 1932—Brooklyn | Nat. | 64 | 202 | 23 | 49 | 4 | 22 | .243 |
| 1932—Jersey City | Int. | 47 | 153 | 18 | 45 | 6 | 31 | .294 |
| 1933—Oakland | P. C. | 21 | 56 | 5 | 13 | 1 | 6 | .232 |
| Major League Totals | | 1622 | 5993 | 819 | 1778 | 148 | 1019 | .297 |

## WORLD SERIES RECORD

| Year Club | League | G. | AB. | R. | H. | HR. | RBI. | B.A. |
|---|---|---|---|---|---|---|---|---|
| 1921—New York | Nat. | 8 | 30 | 3 | 7 | 0 | 3 | .233 |
| 1922—New York | Nat. | 5 | 18 | 0 | 5 | 0 | 2 | .278 |
| 1923—New York | Nat. | 6 | 22 | 1 | 4 | 0 | 1 | .182 |
| 1924—New York | Nat. | 7 | 31 | 7 | 9 | 1 | 4 | .290 |
| World Series Totals | | 26 | 101 | 11 | 25 | 1 | 10 | .248 |

## MICHAEL JOSEPH (KING) KELLY

| Year Club | League | G. | AB. | R. | H. | HR. | SB. | B.A. |
|---|---|---|---|---|---|---|---|---|
| 1878—Cincinnati | Nat. | 59 | 231 | 29 | 65 | 0 | ..... | .281 |
| 1879—Cincinnati | Nat. | 76 | 342 | 78 | 119 | 3 | ..... | .348 |
| 1880—Chicago | Nat. | 82 | 335 | 71 | 98 | 1 | ..... | .293 |
| 1881—Chicago | Nat. | 80 | 353 | 84 | 114 | 2 | ..... | .323 |
| 1882—Chicago | Nat. | 84 | 377 | 81 | 115 | 1 | ..... | .305 |
| 1883—Chicago | Nat. | 98 | 430 | 92 | 109 | 3 | ..... | .253 |
| 1884—Chicago | Nat. | 107 | 448 | *120 | 153 | 12 | ..... | .341 |
| 1885—Chicago | Nat. | 107 | 438 | *124 | 126 | 9 | ..... | .288 |
| 1886—Chicago | Nat. | 118 | 451 | *155 | 175 | 4 | 53 | *.388 |
| 1887—Boston | Nat. | 114 | 525 | 119 | 207 | 8 | 84 | .394 |
| 1888—Boston | Nat. | 105 | 440 | 85 | 140 | 9 | 56 | .318 |
| 1889—Boston | Nat. | 125 | 507 | 120 | 149 | 7 | 68 | .293 |
| 1890—Boston | Players | 90 | 352 | 89 | 114 | 3 | 40 | .324 |
| 1891—Cin.-Bos.(N.L.) | A. A. | 77 | 264 | 50 | 73 | 2 | 16 | .276 |
| 1891—Boston | Nat. | 24 | 96 | 14 | 23 | 0 | 24 | .240 |
| 1892—Boston | Nat. | 72 | 279 | 40 | 56 | 1 | 24 | .201 |
| 1893—New York | Nat. | 16 | 54 | 8 | 17 | 0 | 5 | .315 |

| Year Club | League | G. | AB. | R. | H. | HR. | RBI. | B.A. |
|---|---|---|---|---|---|---|---|---|
| 1894—Allentown | Pa. State | 75 | 325 | 82 | 99 | 3 | .... | .305 |
| 1894—Allen.-Yonkers | Eastern | 15 | 61 | 11 | 23 | 0 | .... | .377 |
| American Association Totals | | 77 | 264 | 50 | 73 | 2 | 16 | .276 |
| Players League Totals | | 90 | 352 | 89 | 114 | 3 | 40 | .324 |
| National League Totals | | 1267 | 5306 | 1220 | 1666 | 60 | .... | .314 |
| Major League Totals | | 1434 | 5922 | 1359 | 1853 | 65 | .... | .313 |

## RALPH McPHERRAN KINER

| Year Club | League | G. | AB. | R. | H. | HR. | RBI. | B.A. |
|---|---|---|---|---|---|---|---|---|
| 1941—Albany | East. | ●141 | 509 | 94 | 142 | 11 | 66 | .279 |
| 1942—Albany | East. | ★141 | 483 | 84 | 124 | ★14 | 75 | .257 |
| 1943—Toronto | Int. | 43 | 144 | 22 | 34 | 2 | 13 | .236 |
| 1943-44-45—Pittsburgh | Nat. | | | (In Military Service) | | | | |
| 1946—Pittsburgh | Nat. | 144 | 502 | 63 | 124 | ★23 | 81 | .247 |
| 1947—Pittsburgh | Nat. | 152 | 565 | 118 | 177 | ●51 | 127 | .313 |
| 1948—Pittsburgh | Nat. | ●156 | 555 | 104 | 147 | ●40 | 123 | .265 |
| 1949—Pittsburgh | Nat. | 152 | 549 | 116 | 170 | ★54 | ★127 | .310 |
| 1950—Pittsburgh | Nat. | 150 | 547 | 112 | 149 | ★47 | 118 | .272 |
| 1951—Pittsburgh | Nat. | 151 | 531 | ●124 | 164 | ★42 | 109 | .309 |
| 1952—Pittsburgh | Nat. | 149 | 516 | 90 | 126 | ●37 | 87 | .244 |
| 1953—Pitts.-Chi. | Nat. | ★158 | 562 | 100 | 157 | 35 | 116 | .279 |
| 1954—Chicago | Nat. | 147 | 557 | 88 | 159 | 22 | 73 | .285 |
| 1955—Cleveland | Amer. | 113 | 321 | 56 | 73 | 18 | 54 | .243 |
| National League Totals | | 1359 | 4884 | 915 | 1373 | 351 | 961 | .281 |
| American League Totals | | 113 | 321 | 56 | 78 | 18 | 54 | .243 |
| Major League Totals | | 1472 | 5205 | 971 | 1451 | 369 | 1015 | .279 |

## CHARLES HERBERT (CHUCK) KLEIN

| Year Club | League | G. | AB. | R. | H. | HR. | RBI. | B.A. |
|---|---|---|---|---|---|---|---|---|
| 1927—Evansville | I.I.I. | 14 | 49 | 10 | 16 | 2 | .... | .327 |
| 1928—Fort Wayne | Cent. | 88 | 359 | 85 | 119 | 26 | .... | .331 |
| 1928—Philadelphia | Nat. | 64 | 253 | 41 | 91 | 11 | 34 | .360 |
| 1929—Philadelphia | Nat. | 149 | 616 | 126 | 219 | ★43 | 145 | .356 |
| 1930—Philadelphia | Nat. | ●156 | 648 | ★158 | 250 | 40 | 170 | .386 |
| 1931—Philadelphia | Nat. | 148 | 594 | ●121 | 200 | ★31 | ★121 | .337 |
| 1932—Philadelphia | Nat. | ●154 | 650 | ★152 | ★226 | ★38 | 137 | .348 |
| 1933—Philadelphia | Nat. | 152 | 606 | 101 | ★223 | ★28 | ★120 | ★.368 |
| 1934—Chicago | Nat. | 115 | 435 | 78 | 131 | 20 | 80 | .301 |
| 1935—Chicago | Nat. | 119 | 434 | 71 | 127 | 21 | 73 | .293 |
| 1936—Chi.-Phil. | Nat. | 146 | 601 | 102 | 184 | 25 | 104 | .306 |
| 1937—Philadelphia | Nat. | 115 | 406 | 74 | 132 | 15 | 57 | .325 |
| 1938—Philadelphia | Nat. | 129 | 458 | 53 | 113 | 8 | 61 | .247 |
| 1939—Phi.-Pit. | Nat. | 110 | 317 | 45 | 90 | 12 | 56 | .284 |
| 1940—Philadelphia | Nat. | 116 | 354 | 39 | 77 | 7 | 37 | .218 |
| 1941—Philadelphia | Nat. | 50 | 73 | 6 | 9 | 1 | 3 | .123 |
| 1942—Philadelphia | Nat. | 14 | 14 | 0 | 1 | 0 | 0 | .071 |
| 1943—Philadelphia | Nat. | 12 | 20 | 0 | 2 | 0 | 3 | .100 |
| 1944—Philadelphia | Nat. | 4 | 7 | 1 | 1 | 0 | 0 | .143 |
| Major League Totals | | 1753 | 6486 | 1168 | 2076 | 300 | 1201 | .320 |

### WORLD SERIES RECORD

| Year Club | League | G. | AB. | R. | H. | HR. | RBI. | B.A. |
|---|---|---|---|---|---|---|---|---|
| 1935—Chicago | Nat. | 5 | 12 | 2 | 4 | 1 | 2 | .333 |

## SANFORD (SANDY) KOUFAX

| Year Club | League | G. | IP. | W. | L. | Pct. | ERA. |
|---|---|---|---|---|---|---|---|
| 1955—Brooklyn | National | 12 | 42 | 2 | 2 | .500 | 3.00 |
| 1956—Brooklyn | National | 16 | 59 | 2 | 4 | .333 | 4.88 |
| 1957—Brooklyn | National | 34 | 104 | 5 | 4 | .556 | 3.89 |
| 1958—Los Angeles | National | 40 | 159 | 11 | 11 | .500 | 4.47 |
| 1959—Los Angeles | National | 35 | 153 | 8 | 6 | .571 | 4.06 |
| 1960—Los Angeles | National | 37 | 175 | 8 | 13 | .381 | 3.91 |
| 1961—Los Angeles | National | 42 | 256 | 18 | 13 | .581 | 3.52 |
| 1962—Los Angeles | National | 28 | 184 | 14 | 7 | .667 | ★2.54 |
| 1963—Los Angeles | National | 40 | 311 | ●25 | 5 | .833 | ★1.88 |
| 1964—Los Angeles | National | 29 | 223 | 19 | 5 | ★.792 | ★1.74 |
| 1965—Los Angeles | National | 43 | ★336 | ★26 | 8 | ★.765 | ★2.04 |
| 1966—Los Angeles | National | 41 | ★323 | ★27 | 9 | .750 | ★1.73 |
| Major League Totals | | 397 | 2325 | 165 | 87 | .655 | 2.76 |

### WORLD SERIES RECORD

| Year Club | League | G. | IP. | W. | L. | Pct. | ERA. |
|---|---|---|---|---|---|---|---|
| 1959—Los Angeles | National | 2 | 9 | 0 | 1 | .000 | 1.00 |
| 1963—Los Angeles | National | 2 | 18 | 2 | 0 | 1.000 | 1.50 |
| 1965—Los Angeles | National | 3 | 24 | 2 | 1 | .667 | 0.38 |
| 1966—Los Angeles | National | 1 | 6 | 0 | 1 | .000 | 1.50 |
| World Series Totals | | 8 | 57 | 4 | 3 | .571 | 0.95 |

## NAPOLEON (LARRY) LAJOIE

| Year Club | League | G. | AB. | R. | H. | HR. | SB. | B.A. |
|---|---|---|---|---|---|---|---|---|
| 1896—Fall River | N. Eng. | 80 | 380 | 94 | 163 | 16 | .... | ★.429 |
| 1896—Philadelphia | Nat. | 39 | 174 | 37 | 57 | 4 | 4 | .328 |
| 1897—Philadelphia | Nat. | 126 | 545 | 107 | 198 | ★10 | 22 | .363 |
| 1898—Philadelphia | Nat. | 147 | 610 | 113 | 200 | 5 | 33 | .328 |
| 1899—Philadelphia | Nat. | 72 | 308 | 70 | 117 | 6 | 14 | .380 |
| 1900—Philadelphia | Nat. | 102 | 451 | 95 | 156 | 7 | 25 | .346 |
| 1901—Philadelphia | Amer. | 131 | 543 | ★145 | ★229 | ★14 | 27 | ★.422 |
| 1902—Phila.-Cleveland | Amer. | 87 | 352 | 81 | 129 | 7 | 19 | .366 |
| 1903—Cleveland | Amer. | 126 | 488 | 90 | 173 | 7 | 22 | ★.355 |
| 1904—Cleveland | Amer. | 140 | 554 | 92 | ★211 | 5 | 31 | ★.381 |
| 1905—Cleveland | Amer. | 65 | 249 | 29 | 82 | 2 | 11 | .329 |
| 1906—Cleveland | Amer. | 152 | 602 | 88 | ★214 | 0 | 20 | .355 |
| 1907—Cleveland | Amer. | 137 | 509 | 53 | 153 | 2 | 24 | .301 |
| 1908—Cleveland | Amer. | ★157 | 581 | 77 | 168 | 2 | 15 | .289 |
| 1909—Cleveland | Amer. | 128 | 469 | 56 | 152 | 1 | 13 | .324 |
| 1910—Cleveland | Amer. | ★159 | ★591 | 94 | ★227 | 4 | 27 | ★.384 |
| 1911—Cleveland | Amer. | 90 | 315 | 36 | 115 | 2 | 13 | .365 |
| 1912—Cleveland | Amer. | 117 | 448 | 66 | 165 | 0 | 18 | .368 |
| 1913—Cleveland | Amer. | 137 | 465 | 67 | 156 | 1 | 17 | .335 |
| 1914—Cleveland | Amer. | 121 | 419 | 37 | 108 | 0 | 14 | .258 |
| 1915—Philadelphia | Amer. | 129 | 490 | 40 | 137 | 1 | 10 | .280 |
| 1916—Philadelphia | Amer. | 113 | 426 | 33 | 105 | 2 | 15 | .246 |
| 1917—Toronto | Int. | 151 | 581 | 83 | ★221 | 5 | 4 | .380 |
| 1918—Indianapolis | A. A. | 78 | 291 | 39 | 82 | 2 | 10 | .282 |
| American League Totals | | 1989 | 7501 | 1084 | 2524 | 50 | 296 | .336 |
| National League Totals | | 486 | 2088 | 422 | 728 | 32 | 100 | .349 |
| Major League Totals | | 2475 | 9589 | 1506 | 3252 | 82 | 396 | .339 |

## ROBERT GRANVILLE LEMON
### PITCHING RECORD

| Year Club | League | G. | IP. | W. | L. | Pct. | ERA. |
|---|---|---|---|---|---|---|---|
| 1938—Oswego | Can.-Amer. | 1 | 1 | 0 | 0 | .000 | 0.00 |
| 1941—Wilkes-Barre | Eastern | 1 | 1 | 0 | 1 | .000 | 9.00 |
| 1946—Cleveland | American | 32 | 94 | 4 | 5 | .444 | 2.49 |
| 1947—Cleveland | American | 37 | 167 | 11 | 5 | .688 | 3.45 |
| 1948—Cleveland | American | 43 | ★294 | 20 | 14 | .588 | 2.82 |
| 1949—Cleveland | American | 37 | 280 | 22 | 10 | .688 | 2.99 |
| 1950—Cleveland | American | 44 | ★288 | ★23 | 11 | .676 | 3.84 |
| 1951—Cleveland | American | 42 | 263 | 17 | ★14 | .548 | 3.52 |
| 1952—Cleveland | American | 42 | ★310 | 22 | 11 | .667 | 2.50 |
| 1953—Cleveland | American | 41 | ★287 | 21 | 15 | .583 | 3.36 |
| 1954—Cleveland | American | 36 | 258 | ●23 | 7 | .767 | 2.72 |
| 1955—Cleveland | American | 35 | 211 | ●18 | 10 | .643 | 3.88 |
| 1956—Cleveland | American | 39 | 255 | 20 | 14 | .588 | 3.04 |
| 1957—Cleveland | American | 21 | 117 | 6 | 11 | .353 | 4.62 |
| 1958—Cleveland | American | 11 | 25 | 0 | 1 | .000 | 5.40 |
| 1958—San Diego | P. Coast | 12 | 56 | 2 | 5 | .286 | 4.34 |
| Major League Totals | | 460 | 2849 | 207 | 128 | .618 | 3.23 |

### WORLD SERIES RECORD

| Year Club | League | G. | IP. | W. | L. | Pct. | ERA. |
|---|---|---|---|---|---|---|---|
| 1948—Cleveland | American | 2 | 16⅓ | 2 | 0 | 1.000 | 1.65 |
| 1954—Cleveland | American | 2 | 13⅓ | 0 | 2 | .000 | 6.75 |
| World Series Totals | | 4 | 29⅔ | 2 | 2 | .500 | 3.94 |

### BATTING RECORD

| Year Club | League | G. | AB. | R. | H. | HR. | RBI. | B.A. |
|---|---|---|---|---|---|---|---|---|
| 1938—Springfield | M.-Atl. | 7 | 18 | 1 | 4 | 0 | 2 | .222 |
| 1938—Oswego | C.-A. | 75 | 282 | 44 | 88 | 7 | 34 | .312 |
| 1939—Springfield | M.-Atl. | 80 | 307 | 44 | 90 | 3 | 39 | .293 |
| 1939—New Orleans | South. | 52 | 207 | 30 | 64 | 0 | 22 | .309 |
| 1940—Wilkes-Barre | East. | 92 | 321 | 37 | 82 | 2 | 53 | .255 |
| 1941—Wilkes-Barre | East. | ★141 | ★562 | ★109 | ★169 | 4 | 43 | .301 |
| 1941—Cleveland | Amer. | 5 | 4 | 0 | 1 | 0 | 0 | .250 |
| 1942—Baltimore | Int. | 148 | 596 | 95 | 160 | 21 | 80 | .268 |
| 1942—Cleveland | Amer. | 5 | 5 | 0 | 0 | 0 | 0 | .000 |
| 1943-44-45—Cleveland | Amer. | | | (In Military Service) | | | | |
| 1946—Cleveland | Amer. | 55 | 89 | 9 | 16 | 1 | 4 | .180 |
| 1947—Cleveland | Amer. | 47 | 56 | 11 | 18 | 2 | 5 | .321 |
| 1948—Cleveland | Amer. | 52 | 119 | 20 | 34 | 5 | 21 | .286 |
| 1949—Cleveland | Amer. | 46 | 108 | 17 | 29 | 7 | 19 | .269 |
| 1950—Cleveland | Amer. | 72 | 136 | 21 | 37 | 6 | 26 | .272 |
| 1951—Cleveland | Amer. | 56 | 102 | 11 | 21 | 3 | 13 | .206 |
| 1952—Cleveland | Amer. | 54 | 124 | 14 | 28 | 2 | 9 | .226 |
| 1953—Cleveland | Amer. | 51 | 112 | 12 | 26 | 2 | 17 | .232 |
| 1954—Cleveland | Amer. | 40 | 98 | 11 | 21 | 2 | 10 | .214 |
| 1955—Cleveland | Amer. | 49 | 78 | 11 | 19 | 1 | 9 | .244 |
| 1956—Cleveland | Amer. | 43 | 93 | 8 | 18 | 5 | 12 | .194 |
| 1957—Cleveland | Amer. | 25 | 46 | 2 | 3 | 1 | 1 | .065 |
| 1958—Cleveland | Amer. | 15 | 13 | 1 | 3 | 0 | 1 | .231 |
| 1958—San Diego | P.C. | 32 | 69 | 2 | 18 | 0 | 7 | .261 |
| Major League Totals | | 615 | 1183 | 148 | 274 | 37 | 147 | .232 |

## FREDERICK CHARLES (LINDY) LINDSTROM

| Year Club | League | G. | AB. | R. | H. | HR. | RBI. | B.A. |
|---|---|---|---|---|---|---|---|---|
| 1922—Toledo | A. A. | 18 | 23 | 3 | 7 | 0 | 1 | .304 |
| 1923—Toledo | A. A. | 147 | 581 | 77 | 157 | 1 | 39 | .270 |
| 1924—New York | Nat. | 52 | 79 | 19 | 20 | 0 | 4 | .253 |
| 1925—New York | Nat. | 104 | 356 | 43 | 102 | 4 | 33 | .287 |
| 1926—New York | Nat. | 140 | 543 | 90 | 164 | 9 | 76 | .302 |
| 1927—New York | Nat. | 138 | 562 | 107 | 172 | 7 | 58 | .306 |
| 1928—New York | Nat. | 153 | 646 | 99 | ★231 | 14 | 107 | .358 |
| 1929—New York | Nat. | 130 | 549 | 99 | 175 | 15 | 91 | .319 |
| 1930—New York | Nat. | 148 | 609 | 127 | 231 | 22 | 106 | .379 |
| 1931—New York | Nat. | 78 | 303 | 38 | 91 | 5 | 36 | .300 |

| Year Club | League | G. | AB. | R. | H. | HR. | RBI. | B.A. |
|---|---|---|---|---|---|---|---|---|
| 1932—New York | Nat. | 144 | 595 | 83 | 161 | 15 | 92 | .271 |
| 1933—Pittsburgh | Nat. | 138 | 538 | 70 | 167 | 5 | 55 | .310 |
| 1934—Pittsburgh | Nat. | 97 | 383 | 59 | 111 | 4 | 49 | .290 |
| 1935—Chicago | Nat. | 90 | 342 | 49 | 94 | 3 | 62 | .275 |
| 1936—Brooklyn | Nat. | 26 | 106 | 12 | 28 | 0 | 10 | .264 |
| Major League Totals | | 1438 | 5611 | 895 | 1747 | 103 | 779 | .311 |

### WORLD SERIES RECORD

| Year Club | League | G. | AB. | R. | H. | HR. | RBI. | B.A. |
|---|---|---|---|---|---|---|---|---|
| 1924—New York | Nat. | 7 | 30 | 1 | 10 | 0 | 4 | .333 |
| 1935—Chicago | Nat. | 4 | 15 | 0 | 3 | 0 | 0 | .200 |
| World Series Totals | | 11 | 45 | 1 | 13 | 0 | 4 | .289 |

## ALFONSO RAMON (SENOR) LOPEZ

| Year Club | League | G. | AB. | R. | H. | HR. | RBI. | B.A. |
|---|---|---|---|---|---|---|---|---|
| 1925—Tampa | Fla. St. | 51 | 134 | 13 | 30 | 0 | 0 | .224 |
| 1926—Tampa | Fla. St. | 116 | 419 | 64 | 132 | 1 | .... | .315 |
| 1927—Jacksonville | So'East | 128 | 416 | 58 | 115 | 3 | .... | .276 |
| 1928—Macon | Sally | 114 | 389 | 67 | 127 | 14 | 64 | .326 |
| 1928—Brooklyn | Nat. | 3 | 12 | 0 | 0 | 0 | 0 | .000 |
| 1929—Atlanta | South. | 143 | 490 | 70 | 160 | 10 | 85 | .327 |
| 1930—Brooklyn | Nat. | 128 | 421 | 60 | 130 | 6 | 57 | .309 |
| 1931—Brooklyn | Nat. | 111 | 360 | 38 | 97 | 0 | 40 | .269 |
| 1932—Brooklyn | Nat. | 126 | 404 | 44 | 111 | 1 | 43 | .275 |
| 1933—Brooklyn | Nat. | 126 | 372 | 39 | 112 | 3 | 41 | .301 |
| 1934—Brooklyn | Nat. | 140 | 439 | 58 | 120 | 7 | 54 | .273 |
| 1935—Brooklyn | Nat. | 128 | 379 | 50 | 95 | 3 | 39 | .251 |
| 1936—Boston | Nat. | 128 | 426 | 46 | 103 | 8 | 50 | .242 |
| 1937—Boston | Nat. | 105 | 334 | 31 | 68 | 3 | 38 | .205 |
| 1938—Boston | Nat. | 71 | 236 | 19 | 63 | 1 | 14 | .267 |
| 1939—Boston | Nat. | 131 | 412 | 32 | 104 | 8 | 49 | .252 |
| 1940—Bos.-Pitts. | Nat. | 95 | 293 | 35 | 80 | 3 | 41 | .273 |
| 1941—Pittsburgh | Nat. | 114 | 317 | 33 | 84 | 5 | 43 | .265 |
| 1942—Pittsburgh | Nat. | 103 | 289 | 17 | 74 | 1 | 26 | .256 |
| 1943—Pittsburgh | Nat. | 118 | 372 | 40 | 98 | 1 | 39 | .263 |
| 1944—Pittsburgh | Nat. | 115 | 331 | 27 | 76 | 1 | 34 | .230 |
| 1945—Pittsburgh | Nat. | 91 | 243 | 22 | 53 | 0 | 18 | .218 |
| 1946—Pittsburgh | Nat. | 56 | 150 | 13 | 46 | 1 | 12 | .307 |
| 1947—Cleveland | Amer. | 61 | 126 | 9 | 33 | 0 | 14 | .262 |
| 1948—Indianapolis | A. A. | 43 | 127 | 13 | 34 | 2 | 21 | .268 |
| American League Totals | | 61 | 126 | 9 | 33 | 0 | 14 | .262 |
| National League Totals | | 1889 | 5790 | 604 | 1514 | 52 | 638 | .261 |
| Major League Totals | | 1950 | 5916 | 613 | 1547 | 52 | 652 | .261 |

### RECORD AS MANAGER

| Year Club | League | Position | W. | L. |
|---|---|---|---|---|
| 1948—Indianapolis | Amer. Assoc. | First | 100 | 54 |
| 1949—Indianapolis | Amer. Assoc. | Second | 93 | 61 |
| 1950—Indianapolis | Amer. Assoc. | Second | 85 | 67 |
| 1951—Cleveland | American | Second | 93 | 61 |
| 1952—Cleveland | American | Second | 93 | 61 |
| 1953—Cleveland | American | Second | 92 | 62 |
| 1954—Cleveland | American | First | 111 | 43 |
| 1955—Cleveland | American | Second | 93 | 61 |
| 1956—Cleveland | American | Second | 88 | 66 |
| 1957—Chicago | American | Second | 90 | 64 |
| 1958—Chicago | American | Second | 82 | 72 |
| 1959—Chicago | American | First | 94 | 60 |
| 1960—Chicago | American | Third | 87 | 67 |
| 1961—Chicago | American | Fourth | 86 | 76 |
| 1962—Chicago | American | Fifth | 85 | 77 |
| 1963—Chicago | American | Second | 94 | 68 |
| 1964—Chicago | American | Second | 98 | 64 |
| 1965—Chicago | American | Second | 95 | 67 |
| 1968—Chicago | American | Eighth† | 33 | 48 |
| 1969—Chicago | American | Fourth | 8 | 9 |
| Major League Totals | | | 1422 | 1026 |

†Tied for position.

### WORLD SERIES RECORD

| Year Club | League | W. | L. |
|---|---|---|---|
| 1954—Cleveland | American | 0 | 4 |
| 1959—Chicago | American | 2 | 4 |

## THEODORE AMAR (TED) LYONS

| Year Club | League | G. | IP. | W. | L. | Pct. | ERA. |
|---|---|---|---|---|---|---|---|
| 1923—Chicago | American | 9 | 23 | 2 | 1 | .667 | 6.26 |
| 1924—Chicago | American | 41 | 216 | 12 | 11 | .522 | 4.88 |
| 1925—Chicago | American | 43 | 263 | ●21 | 11 | .656 | 3.25 |
| 1926—Chicago | American | 39 | 284 | 18 | 16 | .529 | 3.01 |
| 1927—Chicago | American | 39 | ●308 | ●22 | 14 | .611 | 2.83 |
| 1928—Chicago | American | 39 | 240 | 15 | 14 | .517 | 3.98 |
| 1929—Chicago | American | 37 | 259 | 14 | 20 | .412 | 4.10 |
| 1930—Chicago | American | 42 | ★298 | 22 | 15 | .595 | 3.78 |
| 1931—Chicago | American | 22 | 101 | 4 | 6 | .400 | 4.01 |
| 1932—Chicago | American | 33 | 231 | 10 | 15 | .400 | 3.27 |
| 1933—Chicago | American | 36 | 228 | 10 | ★21 | .323 | 4.38 |
| 1934—Chicago | American | 30 | 205 | 11 | 13 | .458 | 4.87 |
| 1935—Chicago | American | 23 | 191 | 15 | 8 | .652 | 3.02 |

| Year Club | League | G. | IP. | W. | L. | Pct. | ERA. |
|---|---|---|---|---|---|---|---|
| 1936—Chicago | American | 26 | 182 | 10 | 13 | .435 | 5.14 |
| 1937—Chicago | American | 22 | 169 | 12 | 7 | .632 | 4.15 |
| 1938—Chicago | American | 23 | 195 | 9 | 11 | .450 | 3.69 |
| 1939—Chicago | American | 21 | 173 | 14 | 6 | .700 | 2.76 |
| 1940—Chicago | American | 22 | 186 | 12 | 8 | .600 | 3.24 |
| 1941—Chicago | American | 22 | 187 | 12 | 10 | .545 | 3.71 |
| 1942—Chicago | American | 20 | 180 | 14 | 6 | .700 | ★2.10 |
| 1943-44-45—Chicago | American | | (In Military Service) | | | | |
| 1946—Chicago | American | 5 | 43 | 1 | 4 | .200 | 2.30 |
| Major League Totals | | 594 | 4162 | 260 | 230 | .531 | 3.67 |

## MICKEY CHARLES MANTLE

| Year Club | League | G. | AB. | R. | H. | HR. | RBI. | B.A. |
|---|---|---|---|---|---|---|---|---|
| 1949—Independence | K-O-M | 89 | 323 | 54 | 101 | 7 | 63 | .313 |
| 1950—Joplin | W. A. | 137 | 519 | ★141 | ★199 | 26 | 136 | ★.383 |
| 1951—New York | Amer. | 96 | 341 | 61 | 91 | 13 | 65 | .267 |
| 1951—Kansas City | A. A. | 40 | 166 | 32 | 60 | 11 | 50 | .361 |
| 1952—New York | Amer. | 142 | 549 | 94 | 171 | 23 | 87 | .311 |
| 1953—New York | Amer. | 127 | 461 | 105 | 136 | 21 | 92 | .295 |
| 1954—New York | Amer. | 146 | 543 | ★129 | 163 | 27 | 102 | .300 |
| 1955—New York | Amer. | 147 | 517 | 121 | 158 | ★37 | 99 | .306 |
| 1956—New York | Amer. | 150 | 533 | ★132 | 188 | ★52 | ★130 | ★.353 |
| 1957—New York | Amer. | 144 | 474 | ★121 | 173 | 34 | 94 | .365 |
| 1958—New York | Amer. | 150 | 519 | ★127 | 158 | ★42 | 97 | .304 |
| 1959—New York | Amer. | 144 | 541 | 104 | 154 | 31 | 75 | .285 |
| 1960—New York | Amer. | 153 | 527 | ★119 | 145 | ★40 | 94 | .275 |
| 1961—New York | Amer. | 153 | 514 | ●132 | 163 | 54 | 128 | .317 |
| 1962—New York | Amer. | 123 | 377 | 96 | 121 | 30 | 89 | .321 |
| 1963—New York | Amer. | 65 | 172 | 40 | 54 | 15 | 35 | .314 |
| 1964—New York | Amer. | 143 | 465 | 92 | 141 | 35 | 111 | .303 |
| 1965—New York | Amer. | 122 | 361 | 44 | 92 | 19 | 46 | .255 |
| 1966—New York | Amer. | 108 | 333 | 40 | 96 | 23 | 56 | .288 |
| 1967—New York | Amer. | 144 | 440 | 63 | 108 | 22 | 55 | .245 |
| 1968—New York | Amer. | 144 | 435 | 57 | 103 | 18 | 54 | .237 |
| Major League Totals | | 2401 | 8102 | 1677 | 2415 | 536 | 1509 | .298 |

### WORLD SERIES RECORDS

| Year Club | League | G. | AB. | R. | H. | HR. | RBI. | B.A. |
|---|---|---|---|---|---|---|---|---|
| 1951—New York | Amer. | 2 | 5 | 1 | 1 | 0 | 0 | .200 |
| 1952—New York | Amer. | 7 | 29 | 5 | 10 | 2 | 3 | .345 |
| 1953—New York | Amer. | 6 | 24 | 3 | 5 | 2 | 7 | .208 |
| 1955—New York | Amer. | 3 | 10 | 1 | 2 | 1 | 1 | .200 |
| 1956—New York | Amer. | 7 | 24 | 6 | 6 | 3 | 4 | .250 |
| 1957—New York | Amer. | 6 | 19 | 3 | 5 | 1 | 2 | .263 |
| 1958—New York | Amer. | 7 | 24 | 4 | 6 | 2 | 3 | .250 |
| 1960—New York | Amer. | 7 | 25 | 8 | 10 | 3 | 11 | .400 |
| 1961—New York | Amer. | 2 | 6 | 0 | 1 | 0 | 0 | .167 |
| 1962—New York | Amer. | 7 | 25 | 2 | 3 | 0 | 0 | .120 |
| 1963—New York | Amer. | 4 | 15 | 1 | 2 | 1 | 1 | .133 |
| 1964—New York | Amer. | 7 | 24 | 8 | 8 | 3 | 8 | .333 |
| World Series Totals | | 65 | 230 | 42 | 59 | 18 | 40 | .257 |

## HENRY EMMETT (HEINIE) MANUSH

| Year Club | League | G. | AB. | R. | H. | HR. | RBI. | B.A. |
|---|---|---|---|---|---|---|---|---|
| 1921—Edmonton | W. Can. | 83 | 327 | 52 | 105 | ★9 | .... | .321 |
| 1922—Omaha | West. | 167 | 652 | 148 | 245 | 20 | .... | .376 |
| 1923—Detroit | Amer. | 109 | 308 | 59 | 103 | 4 | 54 | .334 |
| 1924—Detroit | Amer. | 120 | 422 | 83 | 122 | 9 | 68 | .289 |
| 1925—Detroit | Amer. | 99 | 278 | 46 | 84 | 5 | 47 | .303 |
| 1926—Detroit | Amer. | 136 | 498 | 95 | 188 | 14 | 86 | ★.378 |
| 1927—Detroit | Amer. | 151 | 593 | 102 | 177 | 6 | 90 | .298 |
| 1928—St. Louis | Amer. | 154 | 638 | 104 | ★241 | 13 | 108 | .378 |
| 1929—St. Louis | Amer. | 142 | 574 | 85 | 204 | 6 | 81 | .355 |
| 1930—St. L.-Wash. | Amer. | 137 | 554 | 100 | 194 | 9 | 94 | .350 |
| 1931—Washington | Amer. | 146 | 616 | 110 | 189 | 6 | 70 | .307 |
| 1932—Washington | Amer. | 149 | 625 | 121 | 214 | 14 | 116 | .342 |
| 1933—Washington | Amer. | 153 | 658 | 115 | ★221 | 5 | 95 | .336 |
| 1934—Washington | Amer. | 137 | 556 | 88 | 194 | 11 | 89 | .349 |
| 1935—Washington | Amer. | 119 | 479 | 68 | 131 | 4 | 56 | .273 |
| 1936—Boston | Amer. | 82 | 313 | 43 | 91 | 0 | 45 | .291 |
| 1937—Brooklyn | Nat. | 132 | 466 | 57 | 155 | 4 | 73 | .333 |
| 1938—Brook.-Pitts. | Nat. | 32 | 64 | 11 | 16 | 0 | 10 | .250 |
| 1938—Toronto | Int. | 81 | 277 | 38 | 86 | 3 | 39 | .310 |
| 1939—Pittsburgh | Nat. | 10 | 12 | 0 | 0 | 0 | 1 | .000 |
| 1939—Toronto | Int. | 66 | 228 | 32 | 55 | 0 | 19 | .241 |
| 1940—Rocky Mount | Pied. | 32 | 107 | 13 | 30 | 1 | 16 | .280 |
| 1941—Greensboro | Pied. | 12 | 32 | 7 | 10 | 0 | 7 | .313 |
| 1942—Greensboro | Pied. | | (Less than ten games) | | | | | |
| 1943—Roanoke | Pied. | 10 | 8 | 0 | 0 | 0 | 1 | .000 |
| 1944—Scranton | East. | | (Less than ten games) | | | | | |
| 1945—Martinsville | Car. | | (Less than ten games) | | | | | |
| American League Totals | | 1834 | 7112 | 1219 | 2353 | 106 | 1099 | .331 |
| National League Totals | | 174 | 542 | 68 | 171 | 4 | 84 | .315 |
| Major League Totals | | 2008 | 7654 | 1287 | 2524 | 110 | 1183 | .330 |

### WORLD SERIES RECORD

| Year Club | League | G. | AB. | R. | H. | HR. | RBI. | B.A. |
|---|---|---|---|---|---|---|---|---|
| 1933—Washington | Amer. | 5 | 18 | 2 | 2 | 0 | 0 | .111 |

## JAMES WALTER VINCENT (RABBIT) MARANVILLE

| Year | Club | League | G. | AB. | R. | H. | HR. | RBI. | B.A. |
|---|---|---|---|---|---|---|---|---|---|
| 1911—New Bedford | N. Eng. | | 117 | 422 | 41 | 96 | 2 | .... | .227 |
| 1912—New Bedford | N. Eng. | | 122 | 452 | 65 | 128 | 4 | .... | .283 |
| 1912—Boston | Nat. | | 26 | 86 | 8 | 18 | 0 | 7 | .209 |
| 1913—Boston | Nat. | | 143 | 571 | 68 | 141 | 2 | 44 | .247 |
| 1914—Boston | Nat. | | •156 | 586 | 74 | 144 | 4 | 72 | .246 |
| 1915—Boston | Nat. | | 149 | 509 | 51 | 124 | 2 | 47 | .244 |
| 1916—Boston | Nat. | | 155 | 604 | 79 | 142 | 4 | 36 | .235 |
| 1917—Boston | Nat. | | 142 | 561 | 69 | 146 | 3 | 41 | .260 |
| 1918—Boston | Nat. | | 11 | 38 | 3 | 12 | 0 | 3 | .316 |
| 1919—Boston | Nat. | | 131 | 480 | 44 | 128 | 5 | 43 | .267 |
| 1920—Boston | Nat. | | 134 | 493 | 48 | 131 | 1 | 43 | .266 |
| 1921—Pittsburgh | Nat. | | 153 | 612 | 90 | 180 | 1 | 70 | .294 |
| 1922—Pittsburgh | Nat. | | 155 | *672 | 115 | 198 | 0 | 63 | .295 |
| 1923—Pittsburgh | Nat. | | 141 | 581 | 78 | 161 | 1 | 41 | .277 |
| 1924—Pittsburgh | Nat. | | 152 | 594 | 62 | 158 | 2 | 71 | .266 |
| 1925—Chicago | Nat. | | 75 | 266 | 37 | 62 | 0 | 23 | .233 |
| 1926—Brooklyn | Nat. | | 78 | 234 | 32 | 55 | 0 | 24 | .235 |
| 1927—Rochester | Int. | | 135 | 507 | 81 | 151 | 1 | 63 | .298 |
| 1927—St. Louis | Nat. | | 9 | 29 | 0 | 7 | 0 | 1 | .241 |
| 1928—St. Louis | Nat. | | 112 | 366 | 40 | 88 | 1 | 34 | .240 |
| 1929—Boston | Nat. | | 146 | 560 | 87 | 159 | 0 | 55 | .284 |
| 1930—Boston | Nat. | | 142 | 558 | 85 | 157 | 2 | 43 | .281 |
| 1931—Boston | Nat. | | 145 | 562 | 69 | 146 | 0 | 33 | .260 |
| 1932—Boston | Nat. | | 149 | 571 | 67 | 134 | 0 | 37 | .235 |
| 1933—Boston | Nat. | | 143 | 478 | 46 | 104 | 0 | 38 | .218 |
| 1934—Boston | Nat. | (Broke leg in exhibition game and did not play) | | | | | | | |
| 1935—Boston | Nat. | | 23 | 67 | 3 | 10 | 0 | 5 | .149 |
| 1936—Elmira | NYP | | 123 | 427 | 65 | 138 | 0 | 54 | .323 |
| 1939—Albany | East. | | 6 | 17 | 3 | 2 | 0 | 2 | .118 |
| Major League Totals | | | 2670 | 10078 | 1255 | 2605 | 28 | 874 | .258 |

### WORLD SERIES RECORD

| Year | Club | League | G. | AB. | R. | H. | HR. | RBI. | B.A. |
|---|---|---|---|---|---|---|---|---|---|
| 1914—Boston | Nat. | | 4 | 13 | 1 | 4 | 0 | 3 | .308 |
| 1928—St. Louis | Nat. | | 4 | 13 | 2 | 4 | 0 | 0 | .308 |
| World Series Totals | | | 8 | 26 | 3 | 8 | 0 | 3 | .308 |

## JUAN ANTONIO MARICHAL (SANCHEZ)

| Year | Club | League | G. | IP. | W. | L. | Pct. | ERA. |
|---|---|---|---|---|---|---|---|---|
| 1958—Michigan City | Midwest | | 35 | *245 | *21 | 8 | .724 | *1.87 |
| 1959—Springfield | Eastern | | 37 | *271 | *18 | 13 | .581 | *2.39 |
| 1960—Tacoma | P. Coast | | 18 | 139 | 11 | 5 | .688 | 3.11 |
| 1960—San Francisco | National | | 11 | 81 | 6 | 2 | .750 | 2.67 |
| 1961—San Francisco | National | | 29 | 185 | 13 | 10 | .565 | 3.89 |
| 1962—San Francisco | National | | 37 | 263 | 18 | 11 | .621 | 3.35 |
| 1963—San Francisco | National | | 41 | *321 | •25 | 8 | .758 | 2.41 |
| 1964—San Francisco | National | | 33 | 269 | 21 | 8 | .724 | 2.48 |
| 1965—San Francisco | National | | 39 | 295 | 22 | 13 | .629 | 2.14 |
| 1966—San Francisco | National | | 37 | 307 | 25 | 6 | .806 | 2.23 |
| 1967—San Francisco | National | | 26 | 202 | 14 | 10 | .583 | 2.76 |
| 1968—San Francisco | National | | 38 | *326 | *26 | 9 | .743 | 2.43 |
| 1969—San Francisco | National | | 37 | 300 | 21 | 11 | .656 | *2.10 |
| 1970—San Francisco | National | | 34 | 243 | 12 | 10 | .545 | 4.11 |
| 1971—San Francisco | National | | 37 | 279 | 13 | 11 | .621 | 2.94 |
| 1972—San Francisco | National | | 25 | 165 | 6 | 16 | .273 | 3.71 |
| 1973—San Francisco | National | | 34 | 207 | 11 | 15 | .423 | 3.83 |
| 1974—Boston | American | | 11 | 57 | 5 | 1 | .833 | 4.89 |
| 1975—Los Angeles | National | | 2 | 6 | 0 | 1 | .000 | 13.50 |
| National League Totals | | | 460 | 3449 | 238 | 141 | .628 | 2.86 |
| American League Totals | | | 11 | 57 | 5 | 1 | .833 | 4.89 |
| Major League Totals | | | 471 | 3506 | 243 | 142 | .631 | 2.89 |

### CHAMPIONSHIP SERIES RECORD

| Year | Club | League | G. | IP. | W. | L. | Pct. | ERA. |
|---|---|---|---|---|---|---|---|---|
| 1971—San Francisco | National | | 1 | 8 | 0 | 1 | .000 | 2.25 |

### WORLD SERIES RECORD

| Year | Club | League | G. | IP. | W. | L. | Pct. | ERA. |
|---|---|---|---|---|---|---|---|---|
| 1962—San Francisco | National | | 1 | 4 | 0 | 0 | .000 | 0.00 |

## RICHARD W. (RUBE) MARQUARD

| Year | Club | League | G. | IP. | W. | L. | Pct. | ERA. |
|---|---|---|---|---|---|---|---|---|
| 1907—Canton | Central | | 40 | | *23 | 13 | .639 | ...... |
| 1908—Indianapolis | Amer. Assn. | | *47 | *367 | *28 | 19 | .596 | ...... |
| 1908—New York | National | | 1 | 5 | 0 | 1 | .000 | ...... |
| 1909—New York | National | | 29 | 173 | 5 | 13 | .278 | ...... |
| 1910—New York | National | | 13 | 69 | 4 | 4 | .500 | ...... |
| 1911—New York | National | | 45 | 278 | 24 | 7 | *.774 | ...... |
| 1912—New York | National | | 43 | 295 | •26 | 11 | .703 | 2.56 |
| 1913—New York | National | | 42 | 288 | 23 | 10 | .697 | 2.50 |
| 1914—New York | National | | 39 | 268 | 12 | 22 | .353 | 3.06 |
| 1915—N.Y.-Brooklyn | National | | 33 | 194 | 11 | 10 | .524 | 4.04 |
| 1916—Brooklyn | National | | 36 | 205 | 13 | 6 | .684 | 1.58 |
| 1917—Brooklyn | National | | 37 | 233 | 19 | 12 | .613 | 2.55 |
| 1918—Brooklyn | National | | 34 | 239 | 9 | •18 | .333 | 2.64 |
| 1919—Brooklyn | National | | 8 | 59 | 3 | 3 | .500 | 2.29 |
| 1920—Brooklyn | National | | 28 | 190 | 10 | 7 | .588 | 3.22 |
| 1921—Cincinnati | National | | 39 | 266 | 17 | 14 | .548 | 3.38 |
| 1922—Boston | National | | 39 | 198 | 11 | 15 | .423 | 5.09 |
| 1923—Boston | National | | 38 | 239 | 11 | 14 | .440 | 3.73 |
| 1924—Boston | National | | 6 | 36 | 1 | 2 | .333 | 3.00 |
| 1925—Boston | National | | 26 | 72 | 2 | 8 | .200 | 5.75 |
| 1926—Providence | Eastern | | 7 | 44 | 3 | 1 | .750 | 3.68 |
| 1927—Baltimore | Intenational | | 6 | 30 | 1 | 2 | .333 | ...... |
| 1927—Birmingham | Southern | | 3 | 11 | 0 | 1 | .000 | ...... |
| 1928— | | (Out of Organized Ball) | | | | | | |
| 1929—Jacksonville | Southeastern | | 3 | 3 | 0 | 0 | .000 | ...... |
| 1930—Jacksonville | Southeastern | | 15 | 114 | 5 | 4 | .556 | 2.13 |
| 1931— | | (Umpire, Eastern League) | | | | | | |
| 1932—Atlanta | Southern | | 6 | 42 | 1 | 3 | .250 | ...... |
| Major League Totals | | | 536 | 3307 | 201 | 177 | .532 | 3.13 |

### WORLD SERIES RECORD

| Year | Club | League | G. | IP. | W. | L. | Pct. | ERA. |
|---|---|---|---|---|---|---|---|---|
| 1911—New York | National | | 3 | 11⅔ | 0 | 1 | .000 | 1.54 |
| 1912—New York | National | | 2 | 18 | 2 | 0 | 1.000 | 0.50 |
| 1913—New York | National | | 2 | 9 | 0 | 1 | .000 | 7.00 |
| 1916—Brooklyn | National | | 2 | 11 | 0 | 2 | .000 | 6.55 |
| 1920—Brooklyn | National | | 2 | 9 | 0 | 1 | .000 | 1.00 |
| World Series Totals | | | 11 | 58⅔ | 2 | 5 | .286 | 2.91 |

## EDWIN LEE MATHEWS, JR.

| Year | Club | League | G. | AB. | R. | H. | HR. | RBI. | B.A. |
|---|---|---|---|---|---|---|---|---|---|
| 1949—H. Point-Th'ville | N.C. St. | | 63 | 240 | 62 | 87 | 17 | 56 | .363 |
| 1950—Atlanta | South. | | 146 | 552 | 103 | 158 | 32 | 106 | .286 |
| 1951—Atlanta | South. | | 37 | 128 | 23 | 37 | 6 | 29 | .289 |
| 1951—Milwaukee | A. A. | | 12 | 9 | 2 | 3 | 1 | 5 | .333 |
| 1952—Boston | Nat. | | 145 | 528 | 80 | 128 | 25 | 58 | .242 |
| 1953—Milwakee | Nat. | | 157 | 579 | 110 | 175 | *47 | 135 | .302 |
| 1954—Milwaukee | Nat. | | 138 | 476 | 96 | 138 | 40 | 103 | .290 |
| 1955—Milwaukee | Nat. | | 141 | 499 | 108 | 144 | 41 | 101 | .289 |
| 1956—Milwaukee | Nat. | | 151 | 552 | 103 | 150 | 37 | 95 | .272 |
| 1957—Milwaukee | Nat. | | 148 | 572 | 109 | 167 | 32 | 94 | .292 |
| 1958—Milwaukee | Nat. | | 149 | 546 | 97 | 137 | 31 | 77 | .251 |
| 1959—Milwaukee | Nat. | | 148 | 594 | 118 | 182 | *46 | 114 | .306 |
| 1960—Milwaukee | Nat. | | 153 | 548 | 108 | 152 | 39 | 124 | .277 |
| 1961—Milwaukee | Nat. | | 152 | 572 | 103 | 175 | 32 | 91 | .306 |
| 1962—Milwaukee | Nat. | | 152 | 536 | 106 | 142 | 29 | 90 | .265 |
| 1963—Milwaukee | Nat. | | 158 | 547 | 82 | 144 | 23 | 84 | .263 |
| 1964—Milwaukee | Nat. | | 141 | 502 | 83 | 117 | 23 | 74 | .233 |
| 1965—Milwaukee | Nat. | | 156 | 546 | 77 | 137 | 32 | 95 | .251 |
| 1966—Atlanta | Nat. | | 134 | 452 | 72 | 113 | 16 | 53 | .250 |
| 1967—Houston | Nat. | | 101 | 328 | 39 | 78 | 10 | 38 | .238 |
| 1967—Detroit | Amer. | | 36 | 108 | 14 | 25 | 6 | 19 | .231 |
| 1968—Detroit | Amer. | | 31 | 52 | 4 | 11 | 3 | 8 | .212 |
| National League Totals | | | 2324 | 8377 | 1491 | 2279 | 503 | 1426 | .272 |
| American League Totals | | | 67 | 160 | 18 | 36 | 9 | 27 | .225 |
| Major League Totals | | | 2391 | 8537 | 1509 | 2315 | 512 | 1453 | .271 |

### WORLD SERIES RECORD

| Year | Club | League | G. | AB. | R. | H. | HR. | RBI. | B.A. |
|---|---|---|---|---|---|---|---|---|---|
| 1957—Milwaukee | Nat. | | 7 | 22 | 4 | 5 | 1 | 4 | .227 |
| 1958—Milwaukee | Nat. | | 7 | 25 | 3 | 4 | 0 | 3 | .160 |
| 1968—Detroit | Amer. | | 2 | 3 | 0 | 1 | 0 | 0 | .333 |
| World Series Totals | | | 16 | 50 | 7 | 10 | 1 | 7 | .200 |

## CHRISTOPHER (BIG SIX) MATHEWSON

| Year | Club | League | G. | IP. | W. | L. | Pct. | ERA. |
|---|---|---|---|---|---|---|---|---|
| 1899—Taunton | New England | | 17 | | 5 | 2 | .714 | ...... |
| 1900—Norfolk | Virginia | | 22 | 187 | 20 | 2 | .909 | ...... |
| 1900—New York | National | | 6 | 34 | 0 | 3 | .000 | ...... |
| 1901—New York | National | | 40 | 336 | 20 | 17 | .541 | ...... |
| 1902—New York | National | | 34 | 276 | 14 | 17 | .452 | ...... |
| 1903—New York | National | | 45 | 367 | 30 | 13 | .698 | ...... |
| 1904—New York | National | | 48 | 368 | 33 | 12 | .733 | ...... |
| 1905—New York | National | | 43 | 339 | *31 | 9 | .775 | ...... |
| 1906—New York | National | | 38 | 267 | 22 | 12 | .647 | ...... |
| 1907—New York | National | | 41 | 315 | *24 | 12 | .667 | ...... |
| 1908—New York | National | | *56 | *391 | *37 | 11 | .771 | ...... |
| 1909—New York | National | | 37 | 274 | 25 | 6 | .806 | ...... |
| 1910—New York | National | | 38 | 319 | *27 | 9 | .750 | ...... |
| 1911—New York | National | | 45 | 307 | 26 | 13 | .667 | ...... |
| 1912—New York | National | | 43 | •310 | 23 | 12 | .657 | 2.12 |
| 1913—New York | National | | 40 | 306 | 25 | 11 | .694 | *2.06 |
| 1914—New York | National | | 41 | 312 | 24 | 13 | .648 | 3.00 |
| 1915—New York | National | | 27 | 186 | 8 | 14 | .364 | 3.58 |
| 1916—N.Y.-Cinn. | National | | 13 | 74 | 4 | 4 | .500 | 3.04 |
| Major League Totals | | | 635 | 4781 | 373 | 188 | .665 | |

### WORLD SERIES RECORD

| Year | Club | League | G. | IP. | W. | L. | Pct. | ERA. |
|---|---|---|---|---|---|---|---|---|
| 1905—New York | National | | 3 | 27 | 3 | 0 | .000 | 0.00 |
| 1911—New York | National | | 3 | 27 | 1 | 2 | .333 | 2.00 |
| 1912—New York | National | | 3 | 28 | 0 | 2 | .000 | 1.57 |
| 1913—New York | National | | 2 | 19 | 1 | 1 | .500 | 0.95 |
| World Series Totals | | | 11 | 101 | 5 | 5 | .500 | 1.15 |

## WILLIE HOWARD MAYS, JR.

| Year | Club | League | G. | AB. | R. | H. | HR. | RBI. | B.A. |
|------|------|--------|-----|------|------|------|------|------|------|
| 1950—Trenton | Int. St. | | 81 | 306 | 50 | 108 | 4 | 55 | .353 |
| 1951—Minneapolis | A. A. | | 35 | 149 | 38 | 71 | 8 | 30 | .477 |
| 1951—New York | Nat. | | 121 | 464 | 59 | 127 | 20 | 68 | .274 |
| 1952—New York | Nat. | | 34 | 127 | 17 | 30 | 4 | 23 | .236 |
| 1953—New York | Nat. | (In Military Service) | | | | | | | |
| 1954—New York | Nat. | | 151 | 565 | 119 | 195 | 41 | 110 | ★.345 |
| 1955—New York | Nat. | | 152 | 580 | 123 | 185 | ★51 | 127 | .319 |
| 1956—New York | Nat. | | 152 | 578 | 101 | 171 | 36 | 84 | .296 |
| 1957—New York | Nat. | | 152 | 585 | 112 | 195 | 35 | 97 | .333 |
| 1958—San Francisco | Nat. | | 152 | 600 | ★121 | 208 | 29 | 96 | .347 |
| 1959—San Francisco | Nat. | | 151 | 575 | 125 | 180 | 34 | 104 | .313 |
| 1960—San Francisco | Nat. | | 153 | 595 | 107 | ★190 | 29 | 103 | .319 |
| 1961—San Francisco | Nat. | | 154 | 572 | ★129 | 176 | 40 | 123 | .308 |
| 1962—San Francisco | Nat. | | 162 | 621 | 130 | 189 | ★49 | 141 | .304 |
| 1963—San Francisco | Nat. | | 157 | 596 | 115 | 187 | 38 | 103 | .314 |
| 1964—San Francisco | Nat. | | 157 | 578 | 121 | 171 | ★47 | 111 | .296 |
| 1965—San Francisco | Nat. | | 157 | 558 | 118 | 177 | ★52 | 112 | .317 |
| 1966—San Francisco | Nat. | | 152 | 552 | 99 | 159 | 37 | 103 | .288 |
| 1967—San Francisco | Nat. | | 141 | 486 | 83 | 128 | 22 | 70 | .263 |
| 1968—San Francisco | Nat. | | 148 | 498 | 84 | 144 | 23 | 79 | .289 |
| 1969—San Francisco | Nat. | | 117 | 403 | 64 | 114 | 13 | 58 | .283 |
| 1970—San Francisco | Nat. | | 139 | 478 | 94 | 139 | 28 | 83 | .291 |
| 1971—San Francisco | Nat. | | 136 | 417 | 82 | 113 | 18 | 61 | .271 |
| 1972—S. F.-N.Y. | Nat. | | 88 | 244 | 35 | 61 | 8 | 22 | .250 |
| 1973—New York | Nat. | | 66 | 209 | 24 | 44 | 6 | 25 | .211 |
| Major League Totals | | | 2992 | 10881 | 2062 | 3283 | 660 | 1903 | .302 |

### CHAMPIONSHIP SERIES RECORD

| Year | Club | League | G. | AB. | R. | H. | HR. | RBI. | B.A. |
|------|------|--------|-----|------|------|------|------|------|------|
| 1971—San Francisco | Nat. | | 4 | 15 | 2 | 4 | 1 | 3 | .267 |
| 1973—New York | Nat. | | 1 | 3 | 1 | 1 | 0 | 1 | .333 |
| Championship Series Totals | | | 5 | 18 | 3 | 5 | 1 | 4 | .278 |

### WORLD SERIES RECORD

| Year | Club | League | G. | AB. | R. | H. | HR. | RBI. | B.A. |
|------|------|--------|-----|------|------|------|------|------|------|
| 1951—New York | Nat. | | 6 | 22 | 1 | 4 | 0 | 1 | .182 |
| 1954—New York | Nat. | | 4 | 14 | 4 | 4 | 0 | 3 | .286 |
| 1962—San Francisco | Nat. | | 7 | 28 | 3 | 7 | 0 | 1 | .250 |
| 1973—New York | Nat. | | 3 | 7 | 1 | 2 | 0 | 1 | .286 |
| World Series Totals | | | 20 | 71 | 9 | 17 | 0 | 6 | .239 |

## JOSEPH VINCENT (MARSE JOE) McCARTHY

### RECORD AS MANAGER

| Year | Club | League | Position | W. | L. |
|------|------|--------|----------|-----|-----|
| 1913—Wilkes-Barre | New York State | Second | 84 | 56 |
| 1919—Louisville* | Amer. Assoc. | Third | 39 | 30 |
| 1920—Louisville | Amer. Assoc. | Second | 88 | 79 |
| 1921—Louisville | Amer. Assoc. | First | 98 | 70 |
| 1922—Louisville | Amer. Assoc. | Sixth | 77 | 91 |
| 1923—Louisville | Amer. Assoc. | Third | 91 | 77 |
| 1924—Louisville | Amer. Assoc. | Third | 90 | 75 |
| 1925—Louisville | Amer. Assoc. | First | 102 | 61 |
| 1926—Chicago | National | Fourth | 82 | 72 |
| 1927—Chicago | National | Fourth | 85 | 68 |
| 1928—Chicago | National | Third | 91 | 63 |
| 1929—Chicago | National | First | 98 | 54 |
| 1930—Chicago† | National | Second | 86 | 64 |
| 1931—New York | American | Second | 94 | 59 |
| 1932—New York | American | First | 107 | 47 |
| 1933—New York | American | Second | 91 | 59 |
| 1934—New York | American | Second | 94 | 60 |
| 1935—New York | American | Second | 89 | 60 |
| 1936—New York | American | First | 102 | 51 |
| 1937—New York | American | First | 102 | 52 |
| 1938—New York | American | First | 99 | 53 |
| 1939—New York | American | First | 106 | 45 |
| 1940—New York | American | Third | 88 | 66 |
| 1941—New York | American | First | 101 | 53 |
| 1942—New York | American | First | 103 | 51 |
| 1943—New York | American | First | 98 | 56 |
| 1944—New York | American | Third | 83 | 71 |
| 1945—New York | American | Fourth | 81 | 71 |
| 1946—New York‡ | American | Second | 22 | 13 |
| 1948—Boston x | American | Second | 96 | 59 |
| 1949—Boston | American | Second | 96 | 58 |
| 1950—Boston y | American | Fourth | 32 | 30 |
| Major League Totals | | | 2126 | 1335 |

### WORLD SERIES RECORD

| Year | Club | League | W. | L. |
|------|------|--------|-----|-----|
| 1929—Chicago | National | 1 | 4 |
| 1932—New York | American | 4 | 0 |
| 1936—New York | American | 4 | 2 |
| 1937—New York | American | 4 | 1 |
| 1938—New York | American | 4 | 0 |

| Year | Club | League | W. | L. |
|------|------|--------|-----|-----|
| 1939—New York | American | 4 | 0 |
| 1941—New York | American | 4 | 1 |
| 1942—New York | American | 1 | 4 |
| 1943—New York | American | 4 | 1 |

*Replaced Pat Flaherty as manager, July 22, with club in third place.
†Resigned as manager, September 24, 1930, replaced by Rogers Hornsby.
‡Resigned as manager, May 24, 1946, replaced by William Dickey.
xIncludes game lost in playoff for league championship.
yResigned as manager, June 23, 1950, replaced by Steve O'Neill.

## THOMAS FRANCIS MICHAEL McCARTHY

| Year | Club | League | G. | AB. | R. | H. | HR. | SB. | B.A. |
|------|------|--------|-----|------|------|------|------|------|------|
| 1884—Boston | U.A. | | 53 | 218 | 37 | 45 | 0 | .... | .206 |
| 1885—Boston | Nat. | | 40 | 148 | 16 | 27 | ... | .... | .182 |
| 1886—Philadelphia | Nat. | | 8 | 27 | 6 | 5 | ... | 0 | .185 |
| 1887—Philadelphia | Nat. | | 18 | 72 | 7 | 15 | ... | 15 | .208 |
| 1888—St. Louis | A.A. | | 131 | 510 | 106 | 141 | ... | 109 | .276 |
| 1889—St. Louis | A.A. | | 140 | 603 | 136 | 179 | 2 | 59 | .297 |
| 1890—St. Louis | A.A. | | 132 | 539 | ★134 | 189 | 6 | 91 | .351 |
| 1891—St. Louis | A.A. | | 125 | 527 | 115 | 163 | 8 | 37 | .309 |
| 1892—Boston | Nat. | | 152 | 602 | 116 | 147 | 4 | 59 | .244 |
| 1893—Boston | Nat. | | 116 | 441 | 108 | 159 | 5 | 49 | .361 |
| 1894—Boston | Nat. | | 126 | 536 | 118 | 187 | 13 | 40 | .349 |
| 1895—Boston | Nat. | | 116 | 454 | 89 | 132 | 2 | 24 | .291 |
| 1896—Brooklyn | Nat. | | 101 | 378 | 62 | 96 | 3 | 23 | .254 |
| Union Association Totals | | | 53 | 218 | 37 | 45 | 0 | .... | .206 |
| American Association Totals | | | 528 | 2179 | 491 | 672 | 16 | 296 | .308 |
| National League Totals | | | 677 | 2658 | 522 | 768 | 27 | 210 | .289 |
| Major League Totals | | | 1258 | 5055 | 1050 | 1485 | 43 | 506 | .294 |

### WORLD SERIES RECORD

| Year | Club | League | G. | AB. | R. | H. | HR. | SB. | B.A. |
|------|------|--------|-----|------|------|------|------|------|------|
| 1888—St. Louis | A.A. | | 10 | 41 | 9 | 10 | 1 | 6 | .244 |

## CORNELIUS (CONNIE MACK) McGULLICUDDY

### RECORD AS MANAGER

| Year | Club | League | Position | W. | L. |
|------|------|--------|----------|-----|-----|
| 1894—Pittsburgh† | National | Seventh | 11 | 11 |
| 1895—Pittsburgh | National | Seventh | 71 | 61 |
| 1896—Pittsburgh | National | Sixth | 66 | 63 |
| 1897—Milwaukee | Western | Fourth | 85 | 51 |
| 1898—Milwaukee | Western | Third | 82 | 57 |
| 1889—Milwaukee | Western | Sixth | 55 | 68 |
| 1900—Milwaukee | American | Second | 79 | 58 |
| 1901—Philadelphia | American | Fourth | 74 | 62 |
| 1902—Philadelphia | American | First | 83 | 53 |
| 1903—Philadelphia | American | Second | 75 | 60 |
| 1904—Philadelphia | American | Fifth | 81 | 70 |
| 1905—Philadelphia | American | First | 92 | 56 |
| 1906—Philadelphia | American | Fourth | 78 | 67 |
| 1907—Philadelphia | American | Second | 88 | 57 |
| 1908—Philadelphia | American | Sixth | 68 | 84 |
| 1909—Philadelphia | American | Second | 95 | 58 |
| 1910—Philadelphia | American | First | 102 | 48 |
| 1911—Philadelphia | American | First | 101 | 50 |
| 1912—Philadelphia | American | Third | 90 | 62 |
| 1913—Philadelphia | American | First | 96 | 57 |
| 1914—Philadelphia | American | First | 99 | 53 |
| 1915—Philadelphia | American | Eighth | 43 | 109 |
| 1916—Philadelphia | American | Eighth | 36 | 117 |
| 1917—Philadelphia | American | Eighth | 55 | 98 |
| 1918—Philadelphia | American | Eighth | 52 | 76 |
| 1919—Philadelphia | American | Eighth | 36 | 104 |
| 1920—Philadelphia | American | Eighth | 48 | 106 |
| 1921—Philadelphia | American | Eighth | 53 | 100 |
| 1922—Philadelphia | American | Seventh | 65 | 89 |
| 1923—Philadelphia | American | Sixth | 69 | 83 |
| 1924—Philadelphia | American | Fifth | 71 | 81 |
| 1925—Philadelphia | American | Second | 88 | 64 |
| 1926—Philadelphia | American | Third | 83 | 67 |
| 1927—Philadelphia | American | Second | 91 | 63 |
| 1928—Philadelphia | American | Second | 98 | 55 |
| 1929—Philadelphia | American | First | 104 | 46 |
| 1930—Philadelphia | American | First | 102 | 52 |
| 1931—Philadelphia | American | First | 107 | 45 |
| 1932—Philadelphia | American | Second | 94 | 60 |
| 1933—Philadelphia | American | Third | 79 | 72 |
| 1934—Philadelphia | American | Fifth | 68 | 82 |
| 1935—Philadelphia | American | Eighth | 58 | 91 |
| 1936—Philadelphia | American | Eighth | 53 | 100 |
| 1937—Philadelphia | American | Seventh | 54 | 97 |
| 1938—Philadelphia | American | Eighth | 53 | 99 |
| 1939—Philadelphia | American | Seventh | 55 | 97 |
| 1940—Philadelphia | American | Eighth | 54 | 100 |
| 1941—Philadelphia | American | Eighth | 64 | 90 |
| 1942—Philadelphia | American | Eighth | 55 | 99 |
| 1943—Philadelphia | American | Eighth | 49 | 105 |
| 1944—Philadelphia | American | *Fifth | 72 | 82 |
| 1945—Philadelphia | American | Eighth | 52 | 98 |

| Year Club | League | Position | W. | L. |
|---|---|---|---|---|
| 1946—Philadelphia | American | Eighth | 49 | 105 |
| 1947—Philadelphia | American | Fifth | 78 | 76 |
| 1948—Philadelphia | American | Fourth | 84 | 70 |
| 1949—Philadelphia | American | Fifth | 81 | 73 |
| 1950—Philadelphia | American | Eighth | 52 | 102 |
| Major League Totals | | | 3775 | 4025 |

### WORLD SERIES RECORD

| Year Club | League | W. | L. |
|---|---|---|---|
| 1905—Philadelphia | American | 1 | 4 |
| 1910—Philadelphia | American | 4 | 1 |
| 1911—Philadelphia | American | 4 | 2 |
| 1913—Philadelphia | American | 4 | 1 |
| 1914—Philadelphia | American | 0 | 4 |
| 1929—Philadelphia | American | 4 | 1 |
| 1930—Philadelphia | American | 4 | 2 |
| 1931—Philadelphia | American | 3 | 4 |

*Tied for position.
†Replaced Al Buckenberger as manager, September 3, with club in seventh place.

## JOSEPH JEROME (IRON MAN) McGINNITY

| Year Club | League | G. | IP. | W. | L. | Pct. | ShO. |
|---|---|---|---|---|---|---|---|
| 1893—Montgomery | Southern | 31 | 193 | 10 | 19 | .345 | .... |
| 1894—Kansas City | Western | 20 | 124 | 8 | 10 | .444 | .... |
| 1898—Peoria | West. Assn. | 16 | 104 | 10 | 3 | .769 | .... |
| 1899—Baltimore | National | 49 | 380 | ●28 | 17 | .622 | 4 |
| 1900—Brooklyn | National | *45 | 347 | *29 | 9 | *.763 | 1 |
| 1901—Baltimore | American | *48 | *378 | 26 | 21 | .553 | 1 |
| 1902—Baltimore | American | 25 | 199 | 13 | 10 | .565 | 0 |
| 1902—New York | National | 19 | 153 | 8 | 8 | .500 | 1 |
| 1903—New York | National | *55 | *434 | *31 | 20 | .608 | 3 |
| 1904—New York | National | *51 | *408 | *35 | 8 | *.814 | *9 |
| 1905—New York | National | ●46 | 320 | 21 | 15 | .588 | 2 |
| 1906—New York | National | *45 | 340 | *27 | 12 | .692 | 3 |
| 1907—New York | National | *47 | 310 | 18 | 18 | .500 | 3 |
| 1908—New York | National | 37 | 186 | 11 | 7 | .611 | 5 |
| 1909—Newark | Eastern | *55 | *422 | *29 | 16 | .644 | .... |
| 1910—Newark | Eastern | *61 | *408 | *30 | 19 | .612 | .... |
| 1911—Newark | Eastern | 43 | 278 | 12 | 19 | .387 | .... |
| 1912—Newark | International | 37 | 261 | 16 | 10 | .615 | .... |
| 1913—Tacoma | Northwestern | *68 | *436 | 22 | 19 | .537 | .... |
| 1914—Tacoma | Northwestern | 49 | 326 | 20 | *21 | .488 | .... |
| 1914—Venice | Pacific Coast | 8 | 37 | 1 | 4 | .200 | .... |
| 1915—Tacoma | Northwestern | 45 | *355 | 21 | 15 | .583 | .... |
| 1916—Butte | Northwestern | 43 | 291 | 20 | 13 | .606 | .... |
| 1917—Butte-Great Falls | Northwestern | 16 | 119 | 7 | 6 | .538 | .... |
| 1918—Vancouver | P. C.-Int. | 9 | .... | 2 | 6 | .250 | .... |
| 1922—Danville | I. I. I. | 16 | 79 | 1 | 6 | .143 | .... |
| 1922—Dubuque | Miss. Valley | 19 | 91 | 5 | 8 | .385 | .... |
| 1923—Dubuque | Miss. Valley | 42 | 206 | 15 | 12 | .556 | .... |
| 1925—Dubuque | Miss. Valley | 15 | 85 | 6 | 6 | .500 | .... |
| American League Totals | | 73 | 577 | 39 | 31 | .557 | 1 |
| National League Totals | | 394 | 2878 | 208 | 114 | .646 | 31 |
| Major League Totals | | 467 | 3455 | 247 | 145 | .630 | 32 |

### WORLD SERIES RECORD

| Year Club | League | G. | IP. | W. | L. | Pct. | ERA. |
|---|---|---|---|---|---|---|---|
| 1905—New York | National | 2 | 17 | 1 | 1 | .500 | 0.00 |

## JOHN JOSEPH (LITTLE NAPOLEON) McGRAW
### RECORD AS MANAGER

| Year Club | League | Position | W. | L. |
|---|---|---|---|---|
| 1899—Baltimore | National | Fourth | 86 | 62 |
| 1901—Baltimore | American | Fifth | 68 | 65 |
| 1902—Baltimore | American | Seventh | 28 | 34 |
| 1902—New York | National | Eighth | 25 | 38 |
| 1903—New York | National | Second | 84 | 55 |
| 1904—New York | National | First | 106 | 47 |
| 1905—New York | National | First | 105 | 48 |
| 1906—New York | National | Second | 96 | 56 |
| 1907—New York | National | Fourth | 82 | 71 |
| 1908—New York | National | Second | 98 | 56 |
| 1909—New York | National | Third | 92 | 61 |
| 1910—New York | National | Second | 91 | 63 |
| 1911—New York | National | First | 99 | 54 |
| 1912—New York | National | First | 103 | 48 |
| 1913—New York | National | First | 101 | 51 |
| 1914—New York | National | Second | 84 | 70 |
| 1915—New York | National | Eighth | 69 | 83 |
| 1916—New York | National | Fourth | 86 | 66 |
| 1917—New York | National | First | 98 | 56 |
| 1918—New York | National | Second | 71 | 53 |
| 1919—New York | National | Second | 87 | 53 |
| 1920—New York | National | Second | 86 | 68 |
| 1921—New York | National | First | 94 | 59 |
| 1922—New York | National | First | 93 | 61 |
| 1923—New York | National | First | 95 | 58 |

| Year Club | League | Position | W. | L. |
|---|---|---|---|---|
| 1924—New York | National | First | 93 | 60 |
| 1925—New York | National | Second | 86 | 66 |
| 1926—New York | National | Fifth | 74 | 77 |
| 1927—New York | National | Third | 92 | 62 |
| 1928—New York | National | Second | 93 | 61 |
| 1929—New York | National | Third | 84 | 67 |
| 1930—New York | National | Third | 87 | 67 |
| 1931—New York | National | Second | 87 | 65 |
| 1932—New York | National | Eighth | 17 | 23 |
| Major League Totals | | | 2840 | 1984 |

### WORLD SERIES RECORD

| Year Club | League | W. | L. |
|---|---|---|---|
| 1905—New York | National | 4 | 1 |
| 1911—New York | National | 2 | 4 |
| 1912—New York | National | 3 | 4 |
| 1913—New York | National | 1 | 4 |
| 1917—New York | National | 2 | 4 |
| 1921—New York | National | 5 | 3 |
| 1922—New York | National | 4 | 0 |
| 1923—New York | National | 2 | 4 |
| 1924—New York | National | 3 | 4 |

## WILLIAM BOYD (DEACON) McKECHNIE
### RECORD AS MANAGER

| Year Club | League | Position | W. | L. |
|---|---|---|---|---|
| 1915—Newark† | Federal | Fifth | 53 | 45 |
| 1922—Pittsburgh‡ | National | Fourth | 47 | 26 |
| 1923—Pittsburgh | National | Third | 87 | 67 |
| 1924—Pittsburgh | National | Third | 90 | 63 |
| 1925—Pittsburgh | National | First | 95 | 58 |
| 1926—Pittsburgh | National | Third | 84 | 69 |
| 1928—St. Louis | National | First | 95 | 59 |
| 1929—Rochester§ | International | First | 60 | 20 |
| 1929—St. Louis x | National | Fourth | 35 | 29 |
| 1930—Boston | National | Sixth | 70 | 84 |
| 1931—Boston | National | Seventh | 64 | 90 |
| 1932—Boston | National | Fifth | 77 | 77 |
| 1933—Boston | National | Fourth | 83 | 71 |
| 1934—Boston | National | Fourth | 78 | 73 |
| 1935—Boston | National | Eighth | 38 | 115 |
| 1936—Boston | National | Sixth | 71 | 83 |
| 1937—Boston | National | Fifth | 79 | 73 |
| 1938—Cincinnati | National | Fourth | 82 | 68 |
| 1939—Cincinnati | National | First | 97 | 57 |
| 1940—Cincinnati | National | First | 100 | 53 |
| 1941—Cincinnati | National | Third | 88 | 66 |
| 1942—Cincinnati | National | Fourth | 76 | 76 |
| 1943—Cincinnati | National | Second | 87 | 67 |
| 1944—Cincinnati | National | Third | 89 | 65 |
| 1945—Cincinnati | National | Seventh | 61 | 93 |
| 1946—Cincinnati | National | Sixth | 67 | 87 |
| Major League Totals | | | 1840 | 1669 |

### WORLD SERIES RECORD

| Year Club | League | W. | L. |
|---|---|---|---|
| 1925—Pittsburgh | National | 4 | 3 |
| 1928—St. Louis | National | 0 | 4 |
| 1939—Cincinnati | National | 0 | 4 |
| 1940—Cincinnati | National | 4 | 3 |

†Replaced Bill Phillips as manager with club tied for fifth place, June 19.
‡Replaced George Gibson as manager with club in sixth place, July 15.
§xSwapped jobs with Billy Southworth, taking over Cardinals in fourth place, July 23.

## JOSEPH MICHAEL (DUCKY) MEDWICK

| Year Club | League | G. | AB. | R. | H. | HR. | RBI. | B.A. |
|---|---|---|---|---|---|---|---|---|
| 1930—Scottdale | Mid. Atl. | 75 | 332 | 75 | 139 | 22 | 100 | .419 |
| 1931—Houston | Texas | *161 | 616 | 99 | 188 | *19 | *126 | .305 |
| 1932—Houston | Texas | 139 | 560 | 113 | 198 | 26 | 111 | .354 |
| 1932—St. Louis | Nat. | 26 | 106 | 13 | 37 | 2 | 12 | .349 |
| 1933—St. Louis | Nat. | 148 | 595 | 92 | 182 | 18 | 98 | .306 |
| 1934—St. Louis | Nat. | 149 | 620 | 110 | 198 | 18 | 106 | .319 |
| 1935—St. Louis | Nat. | 154 | 634 | 132 | 224 | 23 | 126 | .353 |
| 1936—St. Louis | Nat. | 155 | 636 | 115 | *223 | 18 | *138 | .351 |
| 1937—St. Louis | Nat. | *156 | *633 | *111 | *237 | ●31 | *154 | *.374 |
| 1938—St. Louis | Nat. | 146 | 590 | 100 | 190 | 21 | *122 | .322 |
| 1939—St. Louis | Nat. | 150 | 606 | 98 | 201 | 14 | 117 | .332 |
| 1940—St. L.-Brook. | Nat. | 143 | 581 | 83 | 175 | 17 | 86 | .301 |
| 1941—Brooklyn | Nat. | 133 | 538 | 100 | 171 | 18 | 88 | .318 |
| 1942—Brooklyn | Nat. | 142 | 553 | 69 | 166 | 4 | 96 | .300 |
| 1943—Brook.-N.Y. | Nat. | 126 | 497 | 54 | 138 | 5 | 70 | .278 |
| 1944—New York | Nat. | 128 | 490 | 64 | 165 | 7 | 85 | .337 |
| 1945—N.Y.-Bos. | Nat. | 92 | 310 | 31 | 90 | 3 | 37 | .290 |
| 1946—Brooklyn | Nat. | 41 | 77 | 7 | 24 | 2 | 18 | .312 |
| 1947—St. Louis | Nat. | 75 | 150 | 19 | 46 | 4 | 28 | .307 |
| 1948—St. Louis | Nat. | 20 | 19 | 0 | 4 | 0 | 2 | .211 |
| 1948—Houston | Texas | 35 | 87 | 8 | 24 | 2 | 20 | .276 |
| 1949—Miami Beach | Fla. Int. | 106 | 375 | 53 | 121 | 10 | 72 | .323 |

294

| Year | Club | League | G. | AB. | R. | H. | HR. | RBI. | B.A. |
|---|---|---|---|---|---|---|---|---|---|
| 1951—Raleigh | Carolina | | 60 | 158 | 22 | 45 | 4 | 33 | .285 |
| 1952—Tampa | Fla. Int. | | 11 | 9 | 0 | 3 | 0 | 6 | .333 |
| Major League Totals | | | 1984 | 7635 | 1198 | 2471 | 205 | 1383 | .324 |

### WORLD SERIES RECORD

| Year | Club | League | G. | AB. | R. | H. | HR. | RBI. | B.A. |
|---|---|---|---|---|---|---|---|---|---|
| 1934—St. Louis | Nat. | | 7 | 29 | 4 | 11 | 1 | 5 | .379 |
| 1941—Brooklyn | Nat. | | 5 | 17 | 1 | 4 | 0 | 0 | .235 |
| World Series Totals | | | 12 | 46 | 5 | 15 | 1 | 5 | .326 |

## JOHN ROBERT (BIG CAT) MIZE

| Year | Club | League | G. | AB. | R. | H. | HR. | RBI. | B.A. |
|---|---|---|---|---|---|---|---|---|---|
| 1930—Greensboro | Pied. | | 12 | 31 | 5 | 6 | 0 | 2 | .194 |
| 1931—Greensboro | Pied. | | 94 | 341 | 69 | 115 | 9 | 64 | .337 |
| 1932—Elmira | NYP | | 106 | 405 | 60 | 132 | 8 | 78 | .326 |
| 1933—Greensboro | Pied. | | 98 | 378 | 108 | 136 | 22 | 104 | .360 |
| 1933—Rochester | Int. | | 42 | 159 | 27 | 56 | 8 | 32 | .352 |
| 1934—Rochester | Int. | | 90 | 313 | 49 | 106 | 17 | 66 | .339 |
| 1935—Rochester | Int. | | 65 | 252 | 37 | 80 | 12 | 44 | .317 |
| 1936—St. Louis | Nat. | | 126 | 414 | 76 | 136 | 19 | 93 | .329 |
| 1937—St. Louis | Nat. | | 145 | 560 | 103 | 204 | 25 | 113 | .364 |
| 1938—St. Louis | Nat. | | 149 | 531 | 85 | 179 | 27 | 102 | .337 |
| 1939—St. Louis | Nat. | | 153 | 564 | 104 | 197 | *28 | 108 | *.349 |
| 1940—St. Louis | Nat. | | 155 | 579 | 111 | 182 | *43 | *137 | .314 |
| 1941—St. Louis | Nat. | | 126 | 473 | 67 | 150 | 16 | 100 | .317 |
| 1942—New York | Nat. | | 142 | 541 | 97 | 165 | 26 | *110 | .305 |
| 1943-44-45—New York | Nat. | | | | (In Military Service) | | | | |
| 1946—New York | Nat. | | 101 | 377 | 70 | 127 | 22 | 70 | .337 |
| 1947—New York | Nat. | | 154 | 586 | *137 | 177 | ●51 | *138 | .302 |
| 1948—New York | Nat. | | 152 | 560 | 110 | 162 | ●40 | 125 | .289 |
| 1949—New York | Nat. | | 106 | 388 | 59 | 102 | 18 | 62 | .263 |
| 1949—New York | Amer. | | 13 | 23 | 4 | 6 | 1 | 2 | .261 |
| 1950—Kansas City | A.A. | | 26 | 94 | 18 | 28 | 5 | 18 | .298 |
| 1950—New York | Amer. | | 90 | 274 | 43 | 76 | 25 | 72 | .277 |
| 1951—New York | Amer. | | 113 | 332 | 37 | 86 | 10 | 49 | .259 |
| 1952—New York | Amer. | | 78 | 137 | 9 | 36 | 4 | 29 | .263 |
| 1953—New York | Amer. | | 81 | 104 | 6 | 26 | 4 | 27 | .250 |
| American League Totals | | | 375 | 870 | 99 | 230 | 44 | 179 | .264 |
| National League Totals | | | 1509 | 5573 | 1019 | 1781 | 315 | 1158 | .320 |
| Major League Totals | | | 1884 | 6443 | 1118 | 2011 | 359 | 1337 | .312 |

### WORLD SERIES RECORD

| Year | Club | League | G. | AB. | R. | H. | HR. | RBI. | B.A. |
|---|---|---|---|---|---|---|---|---|---|
| 1949—New York | Amer. | | 2 | 2 | 0 | 2 | 0 | 2 | 1.000 |
| 1950—New York | Amer. | | 4 | 15 | 0 | 2 | 0 | 0 | .133 |
| 1951—New York | Amer. | | 4 | 7 | 2 | 2 | 0 | 1 | .286 |
| 1952—New York | Amer. | | 5 | 15 | 3 | 6 | 3 | 6 | .400 |
| 1953—New York | Amer. | | 3 | 3 | 0 | 0 | 0 | 0 | .000 |
| World Series Totals | | | 18 | 42 | 5 | 12 | 3 | 9 | .286 |

## STANLEY FRANK (THE MAN) MUSIAL

| Year | Club | League | G. | AB. | R. | H. | HR. | RBI. | B.A. |
|---|---|---|---|---|---|---|---|---|---|
| 1938—Williamson | Mt. St. | | 26 | 62 | 5 | 16 | 1 | 6 | .258 |
| 1939—Williamson | Mt. St. | | 23 | 71 | 10 | 25 | 1 | 9 | .352 |
| 1940—Daytona Beach | Fla. St. | | 113 | 405 | 55 | 126 | 1 | 70 | .311 |
| 1941—Springfield | W. Assoc. | | 87 | 348 | 100 | 132 | *26 | 94 | .379 |
| 1941—Rochester | Int. | | 54 | 221 | 43 | 72 | 3 | 21 | .326 |
| 1941—St. Louis | Nat. | | 12 | 47 | 8 | 20 | 1 | 7 | .426 |
| 1942—St. Louis | Nat. | | 140 | 467 | 87 | 147 | 10 | 72 | .315 |
| 1943—St. Louis | Nat. | | ●157 | 617 | 108 | *220 | 13 | 81 | *.357 |
| 1944—St. Louis | Nat. | | 146 | 568 | 112 | ●197 | 12 | 94 | .347 |
| 1945—St. Louis | Nat. | | | | (In Military Service) | | | | |
| 1946—St. Louis | Nat. | | ●156 | *624 | *124 | *228 | 16 | 103 | *.365 |
| 1947—St. Louis | Nat. | | 149 | 587 | 113 | 183 | 19 | 95 | .312 |
| 1948—St. Louis | Nat. | | 155 | 611 | *135 | *230 | 39 | *131 | *.376 |
| 1949—St. Louis | Nat. | | *157 | 612 | 128 | *207 | 36 | 123 | .338 |
| 1950—St. Louis | Nat. | | 146 | 555 | 105 | 192 | 28 | 109 | *.346 |
| 1951—St. Louis | Nat. | | 152 | 578 | *124 | 205 | 32 | 108 | *.355 |
| 1952—St. Louis | Nat. | | ●154 | 578 | ●105 | *194 | 21 | 91 | *.336 |
| 1953—St. Louis | Nat. | | 157 | 593 | 127 | 200 | 30 | 113 | .337 |
| 1954—St. Louis | Nat. | | 153 | 591 | ●120 | 195 | 35 | 126 | .330 |
| 1955—St. Louis | Nat. | | ●154 | 562 | 97 | 179 | 33 | 108 | .319 |
| 1956—St. Louis | Nat. | | 156 | 594 | 87 | 184 | 27 | *109 | .310 |
| 1957—St. Louis | Nat. | | 134 | 502 | 82 | 176 | 29 | 102 | *.351 |
| 1958—St. Louis | Nat. | | 135 | 472 | 64 | 159 | 17 | 62 | .337 |
| 1959—St. Louis | Nat. | | 115 | 341 | 37 | 87 | 14 | 44 | .255 |
| 1960—St. Louis | Nat. | | 116 | 331 | 49 | 91 | 17 | 63 | .275 |
| 1961—St. Louis | Nat. | | 123 | 372 | 46 | 107 | 15 | 70 | .288 |
| 1962—St. Louis | Nat. | | 135 | 433 | 57 | 143 | 19 | 82 | .330 |
| 1963—St. Louis | Nat. | | 124 | 337 | 34 | 86 | 12 | 58 | .255 |
| Major League Totals | | | 3026 | 10972 | 1949 | 3630 | 475 | 1951 | .331 |

### WORLD SERIES RECORD

| Year | Club | League | G. | AB. | R. | H. | HR. | RBI. | B.A. |
|---|---|---|---|---|---|---|---|---|---|
| 1942—St. Louis | Nat. | | 5 | 18 | 2 | 4 | 0 | 2 | .222 |
| 1943—St. Louis | Nat. | | 5 | 18 | 2 | 5 | 0 | 0 | .278 |
| 1944—St. Louis | Nat. | | 6 | 23 | 2 | 7 | 1 | 2 | .304 |
| 1946—St. Louis | Nat. | | 7 | 27 | 3 | 6 | 0 | 4 | .222 |
| World Series Totals | | | 23 | 86 | 9 | 22 | 1 | 8 | .256 |

### PITCHING RECORD

| Year | Club | League | G. | IP. | W. | L. | Pct. | ERA. |
|---|---|---|---|---|---|---|---|---|
| 1938—Williamson | Mt. State | | 20 | 110 | 6 | 6 | .500 | 4.66 |
| 1939—Williamson | Mt. State | | 13 | 92 | 9 | 2 | .818 | 4.30 |
| 1940—Daytona Beach | Fla. State | | 28 | 223 | 18 | 5 | *.783 | 2.62 |
| 1952—St. Louis | National | | 1 | 0 | 0 | 0 | .000 | 0.00 |
| Major League Totals | | | 1 | 0 | 0 | 0 | .000 | 0.00 |

## CHARLES AUGUSTUS (KID) NICHOLS

| Year | Club | League | G. | CG. | IP. | W. | L. | Pct. | ShO. |
|---|---|---|---|---|---|---|---|---|---|
| 1887—Kansas City | Western | | ... | ... | ... | ... | 12 | ... | ... |
| 1888—Memphis | Southern | | 15 | ... | ... | ... | 8 | ... | ... |
| 1888—Kansas City | West. Assn. | | 18 | ... | ... | ... | ... | ... | ... |
| 1889—Omaha | West. Assn. | | 48 | ... | ... | 36 | 12 | .750 | ... |
| 1890—Boston | National | | 48 | 47 | 424 | 27 | 19 | .587 | *7 |
| 1891—Boston | National | | 52 | 45 | 423 | 30 | 17 | .638 | 5 |
| 1892—Boston | National | | 53 | 49 | 454 | 35 | 16 | .686 | 5 |
| 1893—Boston | National | | 52 | 43 | 414 | 34 | 14 | .708 | 1 |
| 1894—Boston | National | | 50 | 40 | 417 | 32 | 13 | .711 | ●3 |
| 1895—Boston | National | | 47 | 42 | 394 | 26 | 16 | .619 | 1 |
| 1896—Boston | National | | 49 | 37 | 375 | 30 | 14 | .682 | 3 |
| 1897—Boston | National | | *46 | 37 | 358 | 31 | 11 | .738 | 2 |
| 1898—Boston | National | | 50 | 40 | 388 | 31 | 12 | .721 | 5 |
| 1899—Boston | National | | 42 | 37 | 349 | 21 | 19 | .525 | 4 |
| 1900—Boston | National | | 29 | 25 | 226 | 13 | 16 | .448 | ●4 |
| 1901—Boston | National | | 38 | 33 | 326 | 19 | 16 | .543 | 4 |
| 1902—Kansas City | Western | | 37 | ... | ... | 27 | 7 | .794 | ... |
| 1903—Kansas City | Western | | 35 | ... | ... | 21 | 12 | .636 | ... |
| 1904—St. Louis | National | | 36 | 35 | 317 | 21 | 13 | .618 | 3 |
| 1905—St. Louis-Phila | National | | 24 | 20 | 191 | 11 | 11 | .500 | 1 |
| 1906—Philadelphia | National | | 4 | 1 | 11 | 0 | 1 | .000 | 0 |
| Major League Totals | | | 620 | 531 | 5067 | 361 | 208 | .634 | 48 |

## JAMES HENRY (ORATOR JIM) O'ROURKE

| Year | Club | League | G. | AB. | R. | H. | HR. | SB. | B.A. |
|---|---|---|---|---|---|---|---|---|---|
| 1872—Mansfield | Nat. Assn. | | ... | ... | ... | ... | ... | ... | ... |
| 1873—Boston | Nat. Assn. | | 57 | 297 | 79 | 103 | ... | ... | .347 |
| 1874—Boston | Nat. Assn. | | 70 | 334 | 80 | 115 | ... | ... | .344 |
| 1875—Boston | Nat. Assn. | | 69 | ... | ... | ... | ... | ... | .306 |
| 1876—Boston | Nat. | | 70 | 327 | 61 | 102 | 2 | ... | .312 |
| 1877—Boston | Nat. | | 49 | 211 | 54 | 74 | 0 | ... | .351 |
| 1878—Boston | Nat. | | 60 | 255 | 44 | 70 | 1 | ... | .275 |
| 1879—Providence | Nat. | | 80 | 359 | 69 | 126 | 4 | ... | .351 |
| 1880—Boston | Nat. | | 84 | 355 | 70 | 100 | ●6 | ... | .282 |
| 1881—Buffalo | Nat. | | 83 | 348 | 71 | 105 | 0 | ... | .302 |
| 1882—Buffalo | Nat. | | 84 | 370 | 62 | 104 | 2 | ... | .281 |
| 1883—Buffalo | Nat. | | 93 | 430 | 99 | 141 | 1 | ... | .328 |
| 1884—Buffalo | Nat. | | 104 | 448 | 112 | 157 | 4 | ... | *.350 |
| 1885—New York | Nat. | | 112 | 477 | 119 | 143 | 4 | ... | .300 |
| 1886—New York | Nat. | | 104 | 440 | 106 | 136 | 1 | 14 | .309 |
| 1887—New York | Nat. | | 103 | 433 | 73 | 149 | 2 | 46 | .344 |
| 1888—New York | Nat. | | 107 | 409 | 50 | 112 | 4 | 25 | .274 |
| 1889—New York | Nat. | | 128 | 502 | 89 | 161 | 3 | 33 | .321 |
| 1890—New York | Play. | | 111 | 469 | 112 | 172 | 8 | 26 | .367 |
| 1891—New York | Nat. | | 136 | 554 | 94 | 167 | 5 | 25 | .301 |
| 1892—New York | Nat. | | 112 | 447 | 63 | 133 | 0 | 23 | .298 |
| 1893—Washington | Nat. | | 129 | 527 | 76 | 161 | 2 | 19 | .306 |
| 1904—New York | Nat. | | 1 | 4 | 1 | 1 | 0 | 0 | .250 |
| 1904—Bridgeport | Conn. | | 65 | 245 | 28 | 70 | 0 | 2 | .286 |
| 1905—Bridgeport | Conn. | | 68 | 238 | 15 | 60 | 1 | 3 | .252 |
| 1906—Bridgeport | Conn. | | 93 | 348 | 26 | 85 | 0 | 5 | .244 |
| 1907—Bridgeport | Conn. | | 24 | 83 | 3 | 16 | ... | ... | .193 |
| National League Totals | | | 1639 | 6896 | 1313 | 2142 | 41 | ... | .311 |
| Players League Totals | | | 111 | 469 | 112 | 172 | 8 | 26 | .367 |
| Major League Totals | | | 1750 | 7365 | 1425 | 2314 | 49 | ... | .314 |

## MELVIN THOMAS OTT

| Year | Club | League | G. | AB. | R. | H. | HR. | RBI. | B.A. |
|---|---|---|---|---|---|---|---|---|---|
| 1926—New York | Nat. | | 35 | 60 | 7 | 23 | 0 | 4 | .383 |
| 1927—New York | Nat. | | 82 | 163 | 23 | 46 | 1 | 19 | .282 |
| 1928—New York | Nat. | | 124 | 435 | 69 | 140 | 18 | 77 | .322 |
| 1929—New York | Nat. | | 150 | 545 | 138 | 179 | 42 | 151 | .328 |
| 1930—New York | Nat. | | 148 | 521 | 122 | 182 | 25 | 119 | .349 |
| 1931—New York | Nat. | | 138 | 497 | 104 | 145 | 29 | 115 | .292 |
| 1932—New York | Nat. | | ●154 | 566 | 119 | 180 | *38 | 123 | .318 |
| 1933—New York | Nat. | | 152 | 580 | 98 | 164 | 23 | 103 | .283 |
| 1934—New York | Nat. | | 153 | 582 | 119 | 190 | ●35 | *135 | .326 |
| 1935—New York | Nat. | | 152 | 593 | 113 | 191 | 31 | 114 | .322 |
| 1936—New York | Nat. | | 150 | 534 | 120 | 175 | *33 | 135 | .328 |
| 1937—New York | Nat | | 151 | 545 | 99 | 160 | *31 | 95 | .294 |
| 1938—New York | Nat. | | 150 | 527 | *116 | 164 | *36 | 116 | .311 |
| 1939—New York | Nat. | | 125 | 396 | 85 | 122 | 27 | 80 | .308 |
| 1940—New York | Nat. | | 151 | 536 | 89 | 155 | 19 | 79 | .289 |
| 1941—New York | Nat. | | 148 | 525 | 89 | 150 | 27 | 90 | .286 |
| 1942—New York | Nat. | | 152 | 549 | *118 | 162 | *30 | 93 | .295 |
| 1943—New York | Nat. | | 125 | 380 | 65 | 89 | 18 | 47 | .234 |
| 1944—New York | Nat. | | 120 | 399 | 91 | 115 | 26 | 82 | .288 |
| 1945—New York | Nat. | | 135 | 451 | 73 | 139 | 21 | 79 | .308 |
| 1946—New York | Nat. | | 31 | 68 | 2 | 5 | 1 | 4 | .074 |
| 1947—New York | Nat. | | 4 | 4 | 0 | 0 | 0 | 0 | .000 |
| Major League Totals | | | 2730 | 9456 | 1859 | 2876 | 511 | 1860 | .304 |

WORLD SERIES RECORD

| Year | Club | League | G. | AB. | R. | H. | HR. | RBI. | B.A. |
|---|---|---|---|---|---|---|---|---|---|
| 1933—New York | Nat. | 5 | 18 | 3 | 7 | 2 | 4 | .389 |
| 1936—New York | Nat. | 6 | 23 | 4 | 7 | 1 | 3 | .304 |
| 1937—New York | Nat. | 5 | 20 | 1 | 4 | 1 | 3 | .200 |
| World Series Totals | | 16 | 61 | 8 | 18 | 4 | 10 | .295 |

## LEROY ROBERT (SATCHEL) PAIGE

| Year | Club | League | G. | IP. | W. | L. | Pct. | ERA. |
|---|---|---|---|---|---|---|---|---|
| 1948—Cleveland | American | 21 | 73 | 6 | 1 | .857 | 2.47 |
| 1949—Cleveland | American | 31 | 83 | 4 | 7 | .364 | 3.04 |
| 1950— | (Out of Organized Ball) | | | | | | |
| 1951—St. Louis | American | 23 | 62 | 3 | 4 | .429 | 4.79 |
| 1952—St. Louis | American | 46 | 138 | 12 | 10 | .545 | 3.07 |
| 1953—St. Louis | American | 57 | 117 | 3 | 9 | .250 | 3.54 |
| 1954-55— | (Out of Organized Ball) | | | | | | |
| 1956—Miami | International | 37 | 111 | 11 | 4 | .733 | 1.86 |
| 1957—Miami | International | 40 | 119 | 10 | 8 | .556 | 2.42 |
| 1958—Miami | International | 28 | 110 | 10 | 10 | .500 | 2.95 |
| 1959-60— | (Out of Organized Ball) | | | | | | |
| 1961—Portland | Pacific Coast | 5 | 25 | 0 | 0 | .000 | 2.88 |
| 1962-63-64— | (Out of Organized Ball) | | | | | | |
| 1965—Kansas City | American | 1 | 3 | 0 | 0 | .000 | 0.00 |
| 1966—Peninsula | Carolinas | 1 | 2 | 0 | 0 | .000 | 9.00 |
| Major League Totals | | 179 | 476 | 28 | 31 | .475 | 3.29 |

WORLD SERIES RECORD

| Year | Club | League | G. | IP. | W. | L. | Pct. | ERA. |
|---|---|---|---|---|---|---|---|---|
| 1948—Cleveland | American | 1 | ⅔ | 0 | 0 | .000 | 0.00 |

## HERBERT JEFFERIS PENNOCK

| Year | Club | League | G. | IP. | W. | L. | Pct. | ERA. |
|---|---|---|---|---|---|---|---|---|
| 1912—Philadelphia | American | 17 | 50 | 1 | 2 | .333 | ...... |
| 1913—Philadelphia | American | 14 | 33 | 2 | 1 | .667 | 5.13 |
| 1914—Philadelphia | American | 28 | 152 | 11 | 4 | .733 | 2.78 |
| 1915—Providence | International | 13 | 90 | 6 | 4 | .600 | |
| 1915—Phila.-Boston | American | 16 | 58 | 3 | 6 | .333 | 6.36 |
| 1916—Boston | American | 9 | 27 | 0 | 2 | .000 | 3.00 |
| 1916—Buffalo | International | 15 | 113 | 7 | 6 | .538 | 1.67 |
| 1917—Boston | American | 24 | 101 | 5 | 5 | .500 | 3.30 |
| 1918—Boston | American | (In Military Service) | | | | | |
| 1919—Boston | American | 32 | 219 | 16 | 8 | .667 | 2.71 |
| 1920—Boston | American | 37 | 242 | 16 | 13 | .552 | 3.68 |
| 1921—Boston | American | 32 | 223 | 12 | 14 | .462 | 4.04 |
| 1922—Boston | American | 32 | 202 | 10 | 17 | .370 | 4.32 |
| 1923—New York | American | 35 | 238 | 19 | 6 | ★.760 | 3.14 |
| 1924—New York | American | 40 | 286 | 21 | 9 | .700 | 2.83 |
| 1925—New York | American | 47 | ★277 | 16 | 17 | .485 | 2.96 |
| 1926—New York | American | 40 | 266 | 23 | 11 | .676 | 3.62 |
| 1927—New York | American | 34 | 210 | 19 | 8 | .704 | 3.00 |
| 1928—New York | American | 28 | 211 | 17 | 6 | .739 | 2.56 |
| 1929—New York | American | 27 | 158 | 9 | 11 | .450 | 4.90 |
| 1930—New York | American | 25 | 156 | 11 | 7 | .611 | 4.33 |
| 1931—New York | American | 25 | 189 | 11 | 6 | .647 | 4.29 |
| 1932—New York | American | 22 | 147 | 9 | 5 | .643 | 4.59 |
| 1933—New York | American | 23 | 65 | 7 | 4 | .636 | 5.54 |
| 1934—Boston | American | 30 | 62 | 2 | 0 | 1.000 | 3.05 |
| Major League Totals | | 617 | 3572 | 240 | 162 | .597 | 3.54 |

WORLD SERIES RECORD

| Year | Club | League | G. | IP. | W. | L. | Pct. | ERA. |
|---|---|---|---|---|---|---|---|---|
| 1914—Philadelphia | American | 1 | 3 | 0 | 0 | .000 | 0.00 |
| 1923—New York | American | 3 | 17⅓ | 2 | 0 | 1.000 | 3.63 |
| 1926—New York | American | 3 | 22 | 2 | 0 | 1.000 | 1.23 |
| 1927—New York | American | 1 | 9 | 1 | 0 | 1.000 | 1.00 |
| 1932—New York | American | 2 | 4 | 0 | 0 | .000 | 2.25 |
| World Series Totals | | 10 | 55⅓ | 5 | 0 | 1.000 | 1.95 |

## EDWARD S. PLANK

| Year | Club | League | G. | IP. | W. | L. | Pct. | ERA. |
|---|---|---|---|---|---|---|---|---|
| 1901—Philadelphia | American | 33 | 262 | 17 | 11 | .607 | ..... |
| 1902—Philadelphia | American | 36 | 295 | 20 | 15 | .571 | ..... |
| 1903—Philadelphia | American | ★43 | 338 | 23 | 16 | .590 | ..... |
| 1904—Philadelphia | American | 44 | 365 | 26 | 17 | .605 | ..... |
| 1905—Philadelphia | American | 41 | ●346 | 25 | 12 | .676 | ..... |
| 1906—Philadelphia | American | 26 | 211 | 19 | 6 | ★.760 | ..... |
| 1907—Philadelphia | American | 43 | 344 | 24 | 16 | .600 | ..... |
| 1908—Philadelphia | American | 34 | 245 | 14 | 16 | .467 | ..... |
| 1909—Philadelphia | American | 34 | 265 | 19 | 10 | .655 | ..... |
| 1910—Philadelphia | American | 38 | 250 | 16 | 10 | .615 | ..... |
| 1911—Philadelphia | American | 40 | 257 | 22 | 8 | .733 | ..... |
| 1912—Philadelphia | American | 37 | 260 | 26 | 6 | .813 | ..... |
| 1913—Philadelphia | American | 41 | 244 | 18 | 10 | .643 | 2.59 |
| 1914—Philadelphia | American | 34 | 185 | 15 | 7 | .682 | 2.87 |
| 1915—St. Louis | Federal | 42 | 269 | 21 | 11 | .656 | ★2.01 |
| 1916—St. Louis | American | 37 | 236 | 16 | 15 | .516 | 2.33 |
| 1917—St. Louis | American | 20 | 131 | 5 | 6 | .455 | 1.79 |
| Major League Totals | | 581 | 4234 | 305 | 181 | .628 | ..... |

WORLD SERIES RECORD

| Year | Club | League | G. | IP. | W. | L. | Pct. | ERA. |
|---|---|---|---|---|---|---|---|---|
| 1905—Philadelphia | American | 2 | 17 | 0 | 2 | .000 | 1.06 |
| 1911—Philadelphia | American | 2 | 9⅔ | 1 | 1 | .500 | 1.86 |
| 1913—Philadelphia | American | 2 | 19 | 1 | 1 | .500 | 0.95 |
| 1914—Philadelphia | American | 1 | 9 | 0 | 1 | .000 | 1.00 |
| World Series Totals | | 7 | 54⅔ | 2 | 5 | .286 | 1.15 |

## CHARLES (OLD HOSS) RADBOURN

| Year | Club | League | G. | IP. | W. | L. | Pct. | ShO. |
|---|---|---|---|---|---|---|---|---|
| 1878—Peoria Reds | Independent | Batted .289 and fielded .810 in 28 games | | | | | |
| 1879—Dubuque | N.W.L. | Batted .387 and fielded .916 in 47 games | | | | | |
| 1880—Buffalo | National | Batted .143 and fielded .937 in 6 games | | | | | |
| 1881—Providence | National | 41 | 327 | 25 | 11 | ★.694 | 3 |
| 1882—Providence | National | 52 | 471 | 31 | 19 | .620 | ●6 |
| 1883—Providence | National | ★76 | 642 | ★49 | 25 | .662 | 4 |
| 1884—Providence | National | ★74 | ★679 | ★60 | 12 | ★.833 | 11 |
| 1885—Providence | National | 49 | 448 | 26 | 20 | .565 | 2 |
| 1886—Boston | National | 57 | 511 | 27 | 30 | .474 | 3 |
| 1887—Boston | National | 47 | 429 | 24 | 23 | .511 | 1 |
| 1888—Boston | National | 24 | 209 | 7 | 16 | .304 | 1 |
| 1889—Boston | National | 32 | 276 | 20 | 11 | .645 | 1 |
| 1890—Boston | Players | 40 | 347 | 27 | 12 | .692 | 1 |
| 1891—Cincinnati | National | 25 | 204 | 12 | 12 | .500 | 2 |
| National League Totals | | 477 | 4196 | 281 | 179 | .611 | 34 |
| Players League Totals | | 40 | 347 | 27 | 12 | .692 | 1 |
| Major League Totals | | 517 | 4543 | 308 | 191 | .617 | 35 |

WORLD SERIES RECORD

| Year | Club | League | G. | IP. | W. | L. | Pct. | ShO. |
|---|---|---|---|---|---|---|---|---|
| 1884—Providence | National | 3 | 22 | 3 | 0 | 1.000 | 0 |

## EDGAR CHARLES (SAM) RICE

| Year | Club | League | G. | AB. | R. | H. | HR. | RBI. | B.A. |
|---|---|---|---|---|---|---|---|---|---|
| 1914—Petersburg | Va. | 31 | 71 | 9 | 22 | 0 | ..... | .310 |
| 1915—Petersburg | Va. | 62 | 156 | 16 | 47 | 0 | ..... | .301 |
| 1915—Washington | Amer. | 4 | 8 | 0 | 3 | 0 | 0 | .375 |
| 1916—Washington | Amer. | 58 | 197 | 26 | 59 | 1 | 16 | .299 |
| 1917—Washington | Amer. | 155 | 586 | 77 | 177 | 0 | 68 | .302 |
| 1918—Washington | Amer. | 7 | 23 | 3 | 8 | 0 | 3 | .348 |
| 1919—Washington | Amer. | ●141 | 557 | 80 | 179 | 3 | 72 | .321 |
| 1920—Washington | Amer. | 153 | 624 | 83 | 211 | 3 | 80 | .336 |
| 1921—Washington | Amer. | 143 | 561 | 83 | 185 | 4 | 79 | .330 |
| 1922—Washington | Amer. | 154 | ★633 | 91 | 187 | 6 | 69 | .295 |
| 1923—Washington | Amer. | 148 | 595 | 117 | 188 | 3 | 75 | .316 |
| 1924—Washington | Amer. | 154 | ★646 | 106 | ★216 | 1 | 76 | .334 |
| 1925—Washington | Amer. | 152 | 649 | 111 | 227 | 1 | 87 | .350 |
| 1926—Washington | Amer. | 152 | ★641 | 98 | ●216 | 3 | 76 | .337 |
| 1927—Washington | Amer. | 142 | 603 | 98 | 179 | 2 | 65 | .297 |
| 1928—Washington | Amer. | 148 | 616 | 95 | 202 | 2 | 55 | .328 |
| 1929—Washington | Amer. | 150 | 616 | 119 | 199 | 1 | 62 | .323 |
| 1930—Washington | Amer. | 147 | 593 | 121 | 207 | 1 | 73 | .349 |
| 1931—Washington | Amer. | 120 | 413 | 81 | 128 | 0 | 42 | .310 |
| 1932—Washington | Amer. | 106 | 288 | 58 | 93 | 1 | 34 | .323 |
| 1933—Washington | Amer. | 73 | 85 | 19 | 25 | 1 | 12 | .294 |
| 1934—Cleveland | Amer. | 97 | 335 | 48 | 98 | 1 | 33 | .293 |
| Major League Totals | | 2404 | 9269 | 1514 | 2987 | 34 | 1077 | .322 |

WORLD SERIES RECORD

| Year | Club | League | G. | AB. | R. | H. | HR. | RBI. | B.A. |
|---|---|---|---|---|---|---|---|---|---|
| 1924—Washington | Amer. | 7 | 29 | 2 | 6 | 0 | 1 | .207 |
| 1925—Washington | Amer. | 7 | 33 | 5 | 12 | 0 | 3 | .364 |
| 1933—Washington | Amer. | 1 | 1 | 0 | 1 | 0 | 0 | 1.000 |
| World Series Totals | | 15 | 63 | 7 | 19 | 0 | 4 | .302 |

PITCHING RECORD

| Year | Club | League | G. | IP. | W. | L. | Pct. | ERA. |
|---|---|---|---|---|---|---|---|---|
| 1914—Petersburg | Virginia | 15 | 123 | 9 | 2 | .818 | .... |
| 1915—Petersburg | Virginia | 29 | 233 | 11 | 12 | .478 | .... |
| 1915—Washington | American | 4 | 18 | 1 | 0 | .000 | 2.00 |
| 1916—Washington | American | 5 | 21⅓ | 0 | 1 | .000 | 2.94 |
| Major League Totals | | 9 | 39⅓ | 1 | 1 | .500 | 2.52 |

## EPPA (JEPTHA) RIXEY

| Year | Club | League | G. | IP. | W. | L. | Pct. | ERA. |
|---|---|---|---|---|---|---|---|---|
| 1912—Philadelphia | National | 23 | 162 | 10 | 10 | .500 | 2.50 |
| 1913—Philadelphia | National | 35 | 156 | 9 | 5 | .643 | 3.12 |
| 1914—Philadelphia | National | 24 | 103 | 2 | 11 | .154 | 4.37 |
| 1915—Philadelphia | National | 29 | 177 | 11 | 12 | .478 | 2.39 |
| 1916—Philadelphia | National | 38 | 287 | 22 | 10 | .688 | 1.85 |
| 1917—Philadelphia | National | 39 | 281 | 16 | ●21 | .432 | 2.27 |
| 1918—Philadelphia | National | (In Military Service) | | | | | |
| 1919—Philadelphia | National | 23 | 154 | 6 | 12 | .333 | 3.97 |
| 1920—Philadelphia | National | 41 | 284 | 11 | ★22 | .333 | 3.49 |
| 1921—Cincinnati | National | 40 | 301 | 19 | 18 | .514 | 2.78 |
| 1922—Cincinnati | National | 40 | ★313 | ★25 | 13 | .658 | 3.54 |
| 1923—Cincinnati | National | 42 | 309 | 20 | 15 | .571 | 2.80 |
| 1924—Cincinnati | National | 35 | 238 | 15 | 14 | .517 | 2.76 |

| Year Club | League | G. | IP. | W. | L. | Pct. | ERA. |
|---|---|---|---|---|---|---|---|
| 1925—Cincinnati | National | 39 | 287 | 21 | 11 | .656 | 2.89 |
| 1926—Cincinnati | National | 37 | 233 | 14 | 8 | .636 | 3.40 |
| 1927—Cincinnati | National | 34 | 220 | 12 | 10 | .545 | 3.48 |
| 1928—Cincinnati | National | 43 | 291 | 19 | 18 | .514 | 3.43 |
| 1929—Cincinnati | National | 35 | 201 | 10 | 13 | .435 | 4.16 |
| 1930—Cincinnati | National | 32 | 164 | 9 | 13 | .409 | 5.10 |
| 1931—Cincinnati | National | 22 | 127 | 4 | 7 | .364 | 3.90 |
| 1932—Cincinnati | National | 25 | 112 | 5 | 5 | .500 | 2.65 |
| 1933—Cincinnati | National | 16 | 94 | 6 | 3 | .667 | 3.16 |
| Major League Totals | | 692 | 4494 | 266 | 251 | .515 | 3.15 |

### WORLD SERIES RECORD

| Year Club | League | G. | IP. | W. | L. | Pct. | ERA. |
|---|---|---|---|---|---|---|---|
| 1915—Philadelphia | National | 1 | 6⅔ | 0 | 1 | .000 | 2.70 |

## ROBIN EVAN ROBERTS

| Year Club | League | G. | IP. | W. | L. | Pct. | ERA. |
|---|---|---|---|---|---|---|---|
| 1948—Wilmington | Int. State | 11 | 96 | 9 | 1 | ★.900 | ★2.06 |
| 1948—Philadelphia | National | 20 | 147 | 7 | 9 | .438 | 3.18 |
| 1949—Philadelphia | National | 43 | 227 | 15 | 15 | .500 | 3.69 |
| 1950—Philadelphia | National | 40 | 304 | 20 | 11 | .645 | 3.02 |
| 1951—Philadelphia | National | 44 | ★315 | 21 | 15 | .583 | 3.03 |
| 1952—Philadelphia | National | 39 | ★330 | ★28 | 7 | .800 | 2.59 |
| 1953—Philadelphia | National | 44 | ★347 | ●23 | 16 | .590 | 2.75 |
| 1954—Philadelphia | National | 45 | ★337 | ★23 | 15 | .605 | 2.96 |
| 1955—Philadelphia | National | 41 | ★305 | ★23 | 14 | .622 | 3.28 |
| 1956—Philadelphia | National | 43 | 297 | 19 | ●18 | .514 | 4.45 |
| 1957—Philadelphia | National | 39 | 250 | 10 | ★22 | .313 | 4.07 |
| 1958—Philadelphia | National | 35 | 270 | 17 | 14 | .548 | 3.23 |
| 1959—Philadelphia | National | 35 | 257 | 15 | 17 | .469 | 4.27 |
| 1960—Philadelphia | National | 35 | 237 | 12 | 16 | .429 | 4.03 |
| 1961—Philadelphia | National | 26 | 117 | 1 | 10 | .091 | 5.85 |
| 1962—Baltimore | American | 27 | 191 | 10 | 9 | .526 | 2.78 |
| 1963—Baltimore | American | 35 | 251 | 14 | 13 | .519 | 3.33 |
| 1964—Baltimore | American | 31 | 204 | 13 | 7 | .650 | 2.91 |
| 1965—Baltimore | American | 20 | 115 | 5 | 7 | .417 | 3.37 |
| 1965—Houston | National | 10 | 76 | 5 | 2 | .714 | 1.89 |
| 1966—Houston-Chicago | National | 24 | 112 | 5 | 8 | .385 | 4.82 |
| 1967—Reading | Eastern | 11 | 80 | 5 | 3 | .625 | 2.48 |
| American League Totals | | 113 | 761 | 42 | 36 | .538 | 3.09 |
| National League Totals | | 563 | 3928 | 244 | 209 | .539 | 3.45 |
| Major League Totals | | 676 | 4689 | 286 | 245 | .539 | 3.40 |

### WORLD SERIES RECORD

| Year Club | League | G. | IP. | W. | L. | Pct. | ERA. |
|---|---|---|---|---|---|---|---|
| 1950—Philadelphia | National | 2 | 11 | 0 | 1 | .000 | 1.64 |

## BROOKS CALBERT ROBINSON, JR.

| Year Club | League | G. | AB. | R. | H. | HR. | RBI. | B.A. |
|---|---|---|---|---|---|---|---|---|
| 1955—York | Pied. | 95 | 354 | 72 | 117 | 11 | 67 | .331 |
| 1955—Baltimore | Amer. | 6 | 22 | 0 | 2 | 0 | 1 | .091 |
| 1956—San Antonio | Texas | 154 | 577 | 72 | 157 | 9 | 74 | .272 |
| 1956—Baltimore | Amer. | 15 | 44 | 5 | 10 | 1 | 1 | .227 |
| 1957—San Antonio | Texas | 33 | 124 | 10 | 33 | 1 | 9 | .266 |
| 1957—Baltimore | Amer. | 50 | 117 | 13 | 28 | 2 | 14 | .239 |
| 1958—Baltimore | Amer. | 145 | 463 | 31 | 110 | 3 | 32 | .238 |
| 1959—Vancouver | P. C. | 42 | 163 | 20 | 54 | 6 | 30 | .331 |
| 1959—Baltimore | Amer. | 88 | 313 | 29 | 89 | 4 | 24 | .284 |
| 1960—Baltimore | Amer. | 152 | 595 | 74 | 175 | 14 | 88 | .294 |
| 1961—Baltimore | Amer. | ●163 | ★668 | 89 | 192 | 7 | 61 | .287 |
| 1962—Baltimore | Amer. | ●162 | 634 | 77 | 192 | 23 | 86 | .303 |
| 1963—Baltimore | Amer. | ★161 | 589 | 67 | 148 | 11 | 67 | .251 |
| 1964—Baltimore | Amer. | ●163 | 612 | 82 | 194 | 28 | ★118 | .317 |
| 1965—Baltimore | Amer. | 144 | 559 | 81 | 166 | 18 | 80 | .297 |
| 1966—Baltimore | Amer. | 157 | 620 | 91 | 167 | 23 | 100 | .269 |
| 1967—Baltimore | Amer. | 158 | 610 | 88 | 164 | 22 | 77 | .269 |
| 1968—Baltimore | Amer. | ●162 | 608 | 65 | 154 | 17 | 75 | .253 |
| 1969—Baltimore | Amer. | 156 | 598 | 73 | 140 | 23 | 84 | .234 |
| 1970—Baltimore | Amer. | 158 | 608 | 84 | 168 | 18 | 94 | .276 |
| 1971—Baltimore | Amer. | 156 | 589 | 67 | 160 | 20 | 92 | .272 |
| 1972—Baltimore | Amer. | 153 | 556 | 48 | 139 | 8 | 64 | .250 |
| 1973—Baltimore | Amer. | 155 | 549 | 53 | 141 | 9 | 72 | .257 |
| 1974—Baltimore | Amer. | 153 | 553 | 46 | 159 | 7 | 59 | .288 |
| 1975—Baltimore | Amer. | 144 | 482 | 50 | 97 | 6 | 53 | .201 |
| 1976—Baltimore | Amer. | 71 | 218 | 16 | 46 | 3 | 11 | .211 |
| 1977—Baltimore | Amer. | 24 | 47 | 3 | 7 | 1 | 4 | .149 |
| Major League Totals | | 2896 | 10654 | 1232 | 2848 | 268 | 1357 | .267 |

### CHAMPIONSHIP SERIES RECORD

| Year Club | League | G. | AB. | R. | H. | HR. | RBI. | B.A. |
|---|---|---|---|---|---|---|---|---|
| 1969—Baltimore | Amer. | 3 | 14 | 1 | 7 | 0 | 0 | .500 |
| 1970—Baltimore | Amer. | 3 | 12 | 3 | 7 | 0 | 1 | .583 |
| 1971—Baltimore | Amer. | 3 | 11 | 2 | 4 | 1 | 3 | .364 |
| 1973—Baltimore | Amer. | 5 | 20 | 1 | 5 | 0 | 2 | .250 |
| 1974—Baltimore | Amer. | 4 | 12 | 1 | 1 | 1 | 1 | .083 |
| Championship Series Totals | | 18 | 69 | 8 | 24 | 2 | 7 | .348 |

### WORLD SERIES RECORD

| Year Club | League | G. | AB. | R. | H. | HR. | RBI. | B.A. |
|---|---|---|---|---|---|---|---|---|
| 1966—Baltimore | Amer. | 4 | 14 | 2 | 3 | 1 | 1 | .214 |
| 1969—Baltimore | Amer. | 5 | 19 | 0 | 1 | 0 | 2 | .053 |
| 1970—Baltimore | Amer. | 5 | 21 | 5 | 9 | 2 | 6 | .429 |
| 1971—Baltimore | Amer. | 7 | 22 | 2 | 7 | 0 | 5 | .318 |
| World Series Totals | | 21 | 76 | 9 | 20 | 3 | 14 | .263 |

## FRANK ROBINSON

| Year Club | League | G. | AB. | R. | H. | HR. | RBI. | B.A. |
|---|---|---|---|---|---|---|---|---|
| 1953—Ogden | Pion. | 72 | 270 | 70 | 94 | 17 | 83 | .348 |
| 1954—Tulsa | Tex. | 8 | 30 | 4 | 8 | 0 | 1 | .267 |
| 1954—Columbia | Sally | 132 | 491 | ★112 | 165 | 25 | 110 | .336 |
| 1955—Columbia | Sally | 80 | 243 | 50 | 64 | 12 | 52 | .263 |
| 1956—Cincinnati | Nat. | 152 | 572 | ★122 | 166 | 38 | 83 | .290 |
| 1957—Cincinnati | Nat. | 150 | 611 | 97 | 197 | 29 | 75 | .322 |
| 1958—Cincinnati | Nat. | 148 | 554 | 90 | 149 | 31 | 83 | .269 |
| 1959—Cincinnati | Nat. | 146 | 540 | 106 | 168 | 36 | 125 | .311 |
| 1960—Cincinnati | Nat. | 139 | 464 | 86 | 138 | 31 | 83 | .297 |
| 1961—Cincinnati | Nat. | 153 | 545 | 117 | 176 | 37 | 124 | .323 |
| 1962—Cincinnati | Nat. | 162 | 609 | ★134 | 208 | 39 | 136 | .342 |
| 1963—Cincinnati | Nat. | 140 | 482 | 79 | 125 | 21 | 91 | .259 |
| 1964—Cincinnati | Nat. | 156 | 568 | 103 | 174 | 29 | 96 | .306 |
| 1965—Cincinnati | Nat. | 156 | 582 | 109 | 172 | 33 | 113 | .296 |
| 1966—Baltimore | Am. | 155 | 576 | ★122 | 182 | ★49 | ★122 | ★.316 |
| 1967—Baltimore | Am. | 129 | 479 | 83 | 149 | 30 | 94 | .311 |
| 1968—Baltimore | Am. | 130 | 421 | 69 | 113 | 15 | 52 | .268 |
| 1969—Baltimore | Am. | 148 | 539 | 111 | 166 | 32 | 100 | .308 |
| 1970—Baltimore | Am. | 132 | 471 | 88 | 144 | 25 | 78 | .306 |
| 1971—Baltimore | Am. | 133 | 455 | 82 | 128 | 28 | 99 | .281 |
| 1972—Los Angeles | Nat. | 103 | 342 | 41 | 86 | 19 | 59 | .251 |
| 1973—California | Amer. | 147 | 534 | 85 | 142 | 30 | 97 | .266 |
| 1974—Calif.-Cleve. | Amer. | 144 | 477 | 81 | 117 | 22 | 68 | .245 |
| 1975—Cleveland | Amer. | 49 | 118 | 19 | 28 | 9 | 24 | .237 |
| 1976—Cleveland | Amer. | 36 | 67 | 5 | 15 | 3 | 10 | .224 |
| National League Totals | | 1605 | 5869 | 1084 | 1759 | 343 | 1068 | .300 |
| American League Totals | | 1203 | 4137 | 745 | 1184 | 243 | 744 | .286 |
| Major League Totals | | 2808 | 10006 | 1829 | 2943 | 586 | 1812 | .294 |

### CHAMPIONSHIP SERIES RECORD

| Year Club | League | G. | AB. | R. | H. | HR. | RBI. | B.A. |
|---|---|---|---|---|---|---|---|---|
| 1969—Baltimore | Amer. | 3 | 12 | 1 | 4 | 1 | 2 | .333 |
| 1970—Baltimore | Amer. | 3 | 10 | 3 | 2 | 1 | 2 | .200 |
| 1971—Baltimore | Amer. | 3 | 12 | 2 | 1 | 0 | 1 | .083 |
| Championship Series Totals | | 9 | 34 | 6 | 7 | 2 | 5 | .206 |

### WORLD SERIES RECORD

| Year Club | League | G. | AB. | R. | H. | HR. | RBI. | B.A. |
|---|---|---|---|---|---|---|---|---|
| 1961—Cincinnati | Nat. | 5 | 15 | 3 | 3 | 1 | 4 | .200 |
| 1966—Baltimore | Amer. | 4 | 14 | 4 | 4 | 2 | 3 | .286 |
| 1969—Baltimore | Amer. | 5 | 16 | 2 | 3 | 1 | 1 | .188 |
| 1970—Baltimore | Amer. | 5 | 22 | 5 | 6 | 2 | 4 | .273 |
| 1971—Baltimore | Amer. | 7 | 25 | 5 | 7 | 2 | 2 | .280 |
| World Series Totals | | 26 | 92 | 19 | 23 | 8 | 14 | .250 |

## JACK ROOSEVELT ROBINSON

| Year Club | League | G. | AB. | R. | H. | HR. | RBI. | B.A. |
|---|---|---|---|---|---|---|---|---|
| 1946—Montreal | Int. | 124 | 444 | ●113 | 155 | 3 | 66 | ★.349 |
| 1947—Brooklyn | Nat. | 151 | 590 | 125 | 175 | 12 | 48 | .297 |
| 1948—Brooklyn | Nat. | 147 | 574 | 108 | 170 | 12 | 85 | .296 |
| 1949—Brooklyn | Nat. | 156 | 593 | 122 | 203 | 16 | 124 | ★.342 |
| 1950—Brooklyn | Nat. | 144 | 518 | 99 | 170 | 14 | 81 | .328 |
| 1951—Brooklyn | Nat. | 153 | 548 | 106 | 185 | 19 | 88 | .338 |
| 1952—Brooklyn | Nat. | 149 | 510 | 104 | 157 | 19 | 75 | .308 |
| 1953—Brooklyn | Nat. | 136 | 484 | 109 | 159 | 12 | 95 | .329 |
| 1954—Brooklyn | Nat. | 124 | 386 | 62 | 120 | 15 | 59 | .311 |
| 1955—Brooklyn | Nat. | 105 | 317 | 51 | 81 | 8 | 36 | .256 |
| 1956—Brooklyn | Nat. | 117 | 357 | 61 | 98 | 10 | 43 | .275 |
| Major League Totals | | 1382 | 4877 | 947 | 1518 | 137 | 734 | .311 |

### WORLD SERIES RECORD

| Year Club | League | G. | AB. | R. | H. | HR. | RBI. | B.A. |
|---|---|---|---|---|---|---|---|---|
| 1947—Brooklyn | Nat. | 7 | 27 | 3 | 7 | 0 | 3 | .259 |
| 1949—Brooklyn | Nat. | 5 | 16 | 2 | 3 | 0 | 2 | .188 |
| 1952—Brooklyn | Nat. | 7 | 23 | 4 | 4 | 1 | 2 | .174 |
| 1953—Brooklyn | Nat. | 6 | 25 | 3 | 8 | 0 | 1 | .320 |
| 1955—Brooklyn | Nat. | 6 | 22 | 5 | 4 | 0 | 1 | .182 |
| 1956—Brooklyn | Nat. | 7 | 24 | 5 | 6 | 1 | 2 | .250 |
| World Series Totals | | 38 | 137 | 22 | 32 | 2 | 12 | .234 |

## WILBERT (ROBBY) ROBINSON

### RECORD AS MANAGER

| Year Club | League | Position | W. | L. |
|---|---|---|---|---|
| 1902—Baltimore | American | Eighth | 22 | 54 |
| 1914—Brooklyn | National | Fifth | 75 | 79 |
| 1915—Brooklyn | National | Third | 80 | 72 |
| 1916—Brooklyn | National | First | 94 | 60 |

| Year Club | League | Position | W. | L. |
|---|---|---|---|---|
| 1917—Brooklyn | National | Seventh | 70 | 81 |
| 1918—Brooklyn | National | Fifth | 57 | 69 |
| 1919—Brooklyn | National | Fifth | 69 | 71 |
| 1920—Brooklyn | National | First | 93 | 61 |
| 1921—Brooklyn | National | Fifth | 77 | 75 |
| 1922—Brooklyn | National | Sixth | 76 | 78 |
| 1923—Brooklyn | National | Sixth | 76 | 78 |
| 1924—Brooklyn | National | Second | 92 | 62 |
| 1925—Brooklyn | National | Sixth† | 68 | 85 |
| 1926—Brooklyn | National | Sixth | 71 | 82 |
| 1927—Brooklyn | National | Sixth | 65 | 88 |
| 1928—Brooklyn | National | Sixth | 77 | 76 |
| 1929—Brooklyn | National | Sixth | 70 | 83 |
| 1930—Brooklyn | National | Fourth | 86 | 68 |
| 1931—Brooklyn | National | Fourth | 79 | 73 |
| Major League Totals | | | 1397 | 1395 |

†Tied for position

### WORLD SERIES RECORD

| Year Club | League | W. | L. |
|---|---|---|---|
| 1916—Brooklyn | National | 1 | 4 |
| 1920—Brooklyn | National | 2 | 5 |

## EDD J. ROUSH

| Year Club | League | G. | AB. | R. | H. | HR. | RBI. | B.A. |
|---|---|---|---|---|---|---|---|---|
| 1912—Evansville | Kitty | 41 | 148 | 17 | 43 | 2 | ..... | .284 |
| 1913—Evansville | Central | 89 | 344 | 42 | 109 | 5 | ..... | .317 |
| 1913—Chicago | Amer. | 9 | 10 | 2 | 1 | 0 | 0 | .100 |
| 1913—Lincoln | West. | 10 | 35 | ..... | 6 | 0 | ..... | .171 |
| 1914—Indianapolis | Federal | 74 | 165 | 26 | 55 | 1 | ..... | .333 |
| 1915—Newark | Federal | 145 | 550 | 73 | 164 | 3 | ..... | .298 |
| 1916—N.Y.-Cin. | Nat. | 108 | 341 | 38 | 91 | 0 | 19 | .267 |
| 1917—Cincinnati | Nat. | 136 | 522 | 82 | 178 | 4 | 62 | *.341 |
| 1918—Cincinnati | Nat. | 113 | 435 | 61 | 145 | 5 | 61 | .333 |
| 1919—Cincinnati | Nat. | 133 | 504 | 73 | 162 | 3 | 69 | *.321 |
| 1920—Cincinnati | Nat. | 149 | 579 | 81 | 196 | 4 | 90 | .339 |
| 1921—Cincinnati | Nat. | 112 | 418 | 68 | 147 | 4 | 71 | .352 |
| 1922—Cincinnati | Nat. | 49 | 165 | 29 | 58 | 1 | 24 | .352 |
| 1923—Cincinnati | Nat. | 138 | 527 | 88 | 185 | 6 | 88 | .351 |
| 1924—Cincinnati | Nat. | 121 | 483 | 67 | 168 | 3 | 72 | .348 |
| 1925—Cincinnati | Nat. | 134 | 540 | 91 | 183 | 8 | 83 | .339 |
| 1926—Cincinnati | Nat. | 144 | 563 | 95 | 182 | 7 | 70 | .323 |
| 1927—New York | Nat. | 140 | 570 | 83 | 173 | 7 | 58 | .304 |
| 1928—New York | Nat. | 46 | 163 | 20 | 41 | 2 | 13 | .252 |
| 1929—New York | Nat. | 115 | 450 | 76 | 146 | 8 | 52 | .324 |
| 1930—Cincinnati | Nat. | | | (Out of Organized Ball) | | | | |
| 1931—Cincinnati | Nat. | 101 | 376 | 46 | 102 | 1 | 41 | .271 |
| American League Totals | | 9 | 10 | 2 | 1 | 0 | 0 | .100 |
| National League Totals | | 1739 | 6636 | 998 | 2157 | 63 | 882 | .325 |
| Major League Totals | | 1748 | 6646 | 1000 | 2158 | 63 | 882 | .325 |

### WORLD SERIES RECORD

| Year Club | League | G. | AB. | R. | H. | HR. | RBI. | B.A. |
|---|---|---|---|---|---|---|---|---|
| 1919—Cincinnati | Nat. | 8 | 28 | 6 | 6 | 0 | 7 | .214 |

## CHARLES HERBERT (RED) RUFFING

| Year Club | League | G. | IP. | W. | L. | Pct. | ERA. |
|---|---|---|---|---|---|---|---|
| 1923—Danville | I.I.I. | 39 | 239 | 12 | 16 | .429 | ..... |
| 1924—Boston | Amer. | 8 | 23 | 0 | 0 | .000 | 6.65 |
| 1924—Dover | East. Shore | 15 | 94 | 4 | 7 | .364 | |
| 1925—Boston | Amer. | 37 | 217 | 9 | 18 | .333 | 5.02 |
| 1926—Boston | Amer. | 37 | 166 | 6 | 15 | .286 | 4.39 |
| 1927—Boston | Amer. | 26 | 158 | 5 | 13 | .278 | 4.67 |
| 1928—Boston | Amer. | 42 | 289 | 10 | *25 | .286 | 3.89 |
| 1929—Boston | Amer. | 35 | 244 | 9 | *22 | .290 | 4.87 |
| 1930—Boston-New York | Amer. | 38 | 222 | 15 | 8 | .652 | 4.38 |
| 1931—New York | Amer. | 37 | 237 | 16 | 14 | .533 | 4.41 |
| 1932—New York | Amer. | 35 | 259 | 18 | 7 | .720 | 3.09 |
| 1933—New York | Amer. | 35 | 235 | 9 | 14 | .391 | 3.91 |
| 1934—New York | Amer. | 36 | 256 | 19 | 11 | .633 | 3.94 |
| 1935—New York | Amer. | 30 | 222 | 16 | 11 | .593 | 3.12 |
| 1936—New York | Amer. | 33 | 271 | 20 | 12 | .625 | 3.85 |
| 1937—New York | Amer. | 31 | 256 | 20 | 7 | .741 | 2.99 |
| 1938—New York | Amer. | 31 | 247 | *21 | 7 | *.750 | 3.32 |
| 1939—New York | Amer. | 28 | 233 | 21 | 7 | .750 | 2.94 |
| 1940—New York | Amer. | 30 | 226 | 15 | 12 | .556 | 3.38 |
| 1941—New York | Amer. | 23 | 186 | 15 | 6 | .714 | 3.53 |
| 1942—New York | Amer. | 24 | 194 | 14 | 7 | .667 | 3.20 |
| 1943-44—New York | Amer. | | | (In Military Service) | | | |
| 1945—New York | Amer. | 11 | 87 | 7 | 3 | .700 | 2.90 |
| 1946—New York | Amer. | 8 | 61 | 5 | 1 | .833 | 1.77 |
| 1947—Chicago | Amer. | 9 | 53 | 3 | 5 | .375 | 6.11 |
| Major League Totals | | 624 | 4342 | 273 | 225 | .548 | 3.80 |

### WORLD SERIES RECORD

| Year Club | League | G. | IP. | W. | L. | Pct. | ERA. |
|---|---|---|---|---|---|---|---|
| 1932—New York | Amer. | 1 | 9 | 1 | 0 | 1.000 | 4.00 |
| 1936—New York | Amer. | 2 | 14 | 0 | 1 | .000 | 4.50 |

| Year Club | League | G. | IP. | W. | L. | Pct. | ERA. |
|---|---|---|---|---|---|---|---|
| 1937—New York | Amer. | 1 | 9 | 1 | 0 | 1.000 | 1.00 |
| 1938—New York | Amer. | 2 | 18 | 2 | 0 | 1.000 | 1.50 |
| 1939—New York | Amer. | 1 | 9 | 1 | 0 | 1.000 | 1.00 |
| 1941—New York | Amer. | 1 | 9 | 1 | 0 | 1.000 | 1.00 |
| 1942—New York | Amer. | 2 | 17⅔ | 1 | 1 | .500 | 4.08 |
| World Series Totals | | 10 | 85⅔ | 7 | 2 | .778 | 2.63 |

## AMOS WILSON RUSIE

| Year Club | League | G. | W. | L. | Pct. | ShO. |
|---|---|---|---|---|---|---|
| 1889—Indianapolis | National | 23 | 13 | 10 | .565 | 1 |
| 1890—New York | National | 60 | 29 | 30 | .492 | 4 |
| 1891—New York | National | 54 | 32 | 19 | .627 | *6 |
| 1892—New York | National | 62 | 31 | 28 | .525 | 2 |
| 1893—New York | National | *48 | 29 | 18 | .617 | ●4 |
| 1894—New York | National | 49 | *36 | 13 | .735 | ●3 |
| 1895—New York | National | 43 | 22 | 21 | .512 | ●4 |
| 1896—New York | National | | | (Holdout all season) | | |
| 1897—New York | National | 37 | 29 | 8 | *.784 | ●3 |
| 1898—New York | National | 33 | 20 | 10 | .667 | 4 |
| 1899-1900—New York | National | | | (Under suspension) | | |
| 1901—Cincinnati | National | 3 | 0 | 1 | .000 | 0 |
| Major League Totals | | 412 | 241 | 158 | .604 | 31 |

### TEMPLE CUP RECORD

| Year Club | League | G. | I.P. | W. | L. | Pct. |
|---|---|---|---|---|---|---|
| 1894—New York | National | 2 | 18 | 2 | 0 | 1.000 |

## GEORGE HERMAN (BABE) RUTH

| Year Club | League | G. | AB. | R. | H. | HR. | RBI. | B.A. |
|---|---|---|---|---|---|---|---|---|
| 1914—Balt.-Prov | Int. | 46 | 121 | 22 | 28 | 1 | ..... | .231 |
| 1914—Boston | Amer. | 5 | 10 | 1 | 2 | 0 | 0 | .200 |
| 1915—Boston | Amer. | 42 | 92 | 16 | 29 | 4 | 20 | .315 |
| 1916—Boston | Amer. | 67 | 136 | 18 | 37 | 3 | 16 | .272 |
| 1917—Boston | Amer. | 52 | 123 | 14 | 40 | 2 | 10 | .325 |
| 1918—Boston | Amer. | 95 | 317 | 50 | 95 | ●11 | 64 | .300 |
| 1919—Boston | Amer. | 130 | 432 | *103 | 139 | *29 | *112 | .322 |
| 1920—New York | Amer. | 142 | 458 | *158 | 172 | *54 | *137 | .376 |
| 1921—New York | Amer. | 152 | 540 | *177 | 204 | *59 | *171 | .378 |
| 1922—New York | Amer. | 110 | 406 | 94 | 128 | 35 | 99 | .315 |
| 1923—New York | Amer. | 152 | 520 | *151 | 205 | *41 | *131 | .394 |
| 1924—New York | Amer. | 153 | 529 | *143 | 200 | *46 | 121 | *.378 |
| 1925—New York | Amer. | 98 | 359 | 61 | 104 | 25 | 66 | .290 |
| 1926—New York | Amer. | 152 | 495 | *139 | 184 | *47 | *145 | .372 |
| 1927—New York | Amer. | 151 | 540 | *158 | 192 | *60 | 164 | .356 |
| 1928—New York | Amer. | 154 | 536 | *163 | 173 | *54 | ●142 | .323 |
| 1929—New York | Amer. | 135 | 499 | 121 | 172 | *46 | 154 | .345 |
| 1930—New York | Amer. | 145 | 518 | 150 | 186 | *49 | 153 | .359 |
| 1931—New York | Amer. | 145 | 534 | 149 | 199 | ●46 | 163 | .373 |
| 1932—New York | Amer. | 133 | 457 | 120 | 156 | 41 | 137 | .341 |
| 1933—New York | Amer. | 137 | 459 | 97 | 138 | 34 | 103 | .301 |
| 1934—New York | Amer. | 125 | 365 | 78 | 105 | 22 | 84 | .288 |
| 1935—Boston | Nat. | 28 | 72 | 13 | 13 | 6 | 12 | .181 |
| American League Totals | | 2475 | 8325 | 2161 | 2860 | 708 | 2192 | .344 |
| National League Totals | | 28 | 72 | 13 | 13 | 6 | 12 | .181 |
| Major League Totals | | 2503 | 8397 | 2174 | 2873 | 714 | 2204 | .342 |

### WORLD SERIES RECORD

| Year Club | League | G. | AB. | R. | H. | HR. | RBI. | B.A. |
|---|---|---|---|---|---|---|---|---|
| 1915—Boston | Amer. | 1 | 1 | 0 | 0 | 0 | 0 | .000 |
| 1916—Boston | Amer. | 1 | 5 | 0 | 0 | 0 | 1 | .000 |
| 1918—Boston | Amer. | 3 | 5 | 0 | 1 | 0 | 2 | .200 |
| 1921—New York | Amer. | 6 | 16 | 3 | 5 | 1 | 4 | .313 |
| 1922—New York | Amer. | 5 | 17 | 1 | 2 | 0 | 1 | .118 |
| 1923—New York | Amer. | 6 | 19 | 8 | 7 | 3 | 3 | .368 |
| 1926—New York | Amer. | 7 | 20 | 6 | 6 | 4 | 5 | .300 |
| 1927—New York | Amer. | 4 | 15 | 4 | 6 | 2 | 7 | .400 |
| 1928—New York | Amer. | 4 | 16 | 9 | 10 | 3 | 4 | .625 |
| 1932—New York | Amer. | 4 | 15 | 6 | 5 | 2 | 6 | .333 |
| World Series Totals | | 41 | 129 | 37 | 42 | 15 | 33 | .326 |

### PITCHING RECORD

| Year Club | League | G. | IP. | W. | L. | Pct. | ERA. |
|---|---|---|---|---|---|---|---|
| 1914—Balti.-Providence | International | 35 | 245 | 22 | 9 | .710 | ..... |
| 1914—Boston | American | 4 | 23 | 2 | 1 | .667 | 3.91 |
| 1915—Boston | American | 32 | 218 | 18 | 8 | .692 | 2.44 |
| 1916—Boston | American | 44 | 324 | 23 | 12 | .657 | *1.75 |
| 1917—Boston | American | 41 | 326 | 24 | 13 | .649 | 2.02 |
| 1918—Boston | American | 20 | 166 | 13 | 7 | .650 | 2.22 |
| 1919—Boston | American | 17 | 133 | 9 | 5 | .643 | 2.97 |
| 1920—New York | American | 1 | 4 | 1 | 0 | 1.000 | 4.50 |
| 1921—New York | American | 2 | 9 | 2 | 0 | 1.000 | 9.00 |
| 1930—New York | American | 1 | 9 | 1 | 0 | 1.000 | 3.00 |
| 1933—New York | American | 1 | 9 | 1 | 0 | 1.000 | 5.00 |
| Major League Totals | | 163 | 1221 | 94 | 46 | .671 | 2.28 |

### WORLD SERIES PITCHING RECORD

| Year Club | League | G. | IP. | W. | L. | Pct. | ERA. |
|---|---|---|---|---|---|---|---|
| 1916—Boston | American | 1 | 14 | 1 | 0 | 1.000 | 0.64 |
| 1918—Boston | American | 2 | 17 | 2 | 0 | 1.000 | 1.06 |
| World Series Totals | | 3 | 31 | 3 | 0 | 1.000 | 0.87 |

## RAYMOND WILLIAM (CRACKER) SCHALK

| Year | Club | League | G. | AB. | R. | H. | HR. | RBI. | B.A. |
|------|------|--------|----|----|----|----|-----|------|------|
| 1911—Taylorville | Ill.-Mo. | 47 | 161 | 27 | 64 | .... | ..... | .398 |
| 1911—Milwaukee | A. A. | 31 | 76 | 9 | 18 | 0 | ..... | .237 |
| 1912—Milwaukee | A. A. | 80 | 266 | 19 | 72 | 3 | ..... | .271 |
| 1912—Chicago | Amer. | 23 | 63 | 7 | 18 | 0 | 6 | .286 |
| 1913—Chicago | Amer. | 128 | 401 | 38 | 98 | 1 | 42 | .244 |
| 1914—Chicago | Amer. | 135 | 392 | 30 | 106 | 0 | 37 | .270 |
| 1915—Chicago | Amer. | 135 | 413 | 46 | 110 | 1 | 48 | .266 |
| 1916—Chicago | Amer. | 129 | 410 | 36 | 95 | 0 | 36 | .232 |
| 1917—Chicago | Amer. | 140 | 424 | 48 | 96 | 3 | 53 | .226 |
| 1918—Chicago | Amer. | 108 | 333 | 35 | 73 | 0 | 24 | .219 |
| 1919—Chicago | Amer. | 131 | 394 | 57 | 111 | 0 | 40 | .282 |
| 1920—Chicago | Amer. | 151 | 485 | 64 | 131 | 1 | 61 | .270 |
| 1921—Chicago | Amer. | 128 | 416 | 32 | 105 | 0 | 47 | .252 |
| 1922—Chicago | Amer. | 142 | 442 | 57 | 124 | 4 | 60 | .281 |
| 1923—Chicago | Amer. | 123 | 382 | 42 | 87 | 1 | 44 | .228 |
| 1924—Chicago | Amer. | 57 | 153 | 15 | 30 | 1 | 11 | .196 |
| 1925—Chicago | Amer. | 125 | 343 | 44 | 94 | 0 | 52 | .274 |
| 1926—Chicago | Amer. | 82 | 226 | 26 | 60 | 0 | 32 | .265 |
| 1927—Chicago | Amer. | 16 | 26 | 2 | 6 | 0 | 2 | .231 |
| 1928—Chicago | Amer. | 2 | 1 | 0 | 1 | 0 | 1 | 1.000 |
| 1929—New York | Nat. | 5 | 2 | 0 | 0 | 0 | 0 | .000 |
| 1932—Buffalo | Int. | 1 | 3 | 1 | 2 | 0 | 0 | .667 |
| American League Totals | | 1755 | 5304 | 579 | 1345 | 12 | 596 | .254 |
| National League Totals | | 5 | 2 | 0 | 0 | 0 | 0 | .000 |
| Major League Totals | | 1760 | 5306 | 579 | 1345 | 12 | 596 | .253 |

### WORLD SERIES RECORD

| Year | Club | League | G. | AB. | R. | H. | HR. | RBI. | B.A. |
|------|------|--------|----|----|----|----|-----|------|------|
| 1917—Chicago | Amer. | 6 | 19 | 1 | 5 | 0 | 0 | .263 |
| 1919—Chicago | Amer. | 8 | 23 | 1 | 7 | 0 | 2 | .304 |
| World Series Totals | | 14 | 42 | 2 | 12 | 0 | 2 | .286 |

## JOSEPH WHEELER SEWELL

| Year | Club | League | G. | AB. | R. | H. | HR. | RBI. | B.A. |
|------|------|--------|----|----|----|----|-----|------|------|
| 1920—New Orleans | South. | 92 | 346 | 58 | 100 | 2 | ..... | .289 |
| 1920—Cleveland | Amer. | 22 | 70 | 14 | 23 | 0 | 12 | .329 |
| 1921—Cleveland | Amer. | 154 | 572 | 101 | 182 | 4 | 91 | .318 |
| 1922—Cleveland | Amer. | 153 | 558 | 80 | 167 | 2 | 83 | .299 |
| 1923—Cleveland | Amer. | 153 | 553 | 98 | 195 | 3 | 109 | .353 |
| 1924—Cleveland | Amer. | 153 | 594 | 99 | 188 | 4 | 106 | .316 |
| 1925—Cleveland | Amer. | 155 | 608 | 78 | 204 | 1 | 98 | .336 |
| 1926—Cleveland | Amer. | 154 | 578 | 91 | 187 | 4 | 85 | .324 |
| 1927—Cleveland | Amer. | 153 | 569 | 83 | 180 | 1 | 92 | .316 |
| 1928—Cleveland | Amer. | ●155 | 588 | 79 | 190 | 4 | 70 | .323 |
| 1929—Cleveland | Amer. | 152 | 578 | 90 | 182 | 7 | 73 | .315 |
| 1930—Cleveland | Amer. | 109 | 353 | 44 | 102 | 0 | 48 | .289 |
| 1931—New York | Amer. | 130 | 484 | 102 | 146 | 6 | 64 | .302 |
| 1932—New York | Amer. | 125 | 503 | 95 | 137 | 11 | 68 | .272 |
| 1933—New York | Amer. | 135 | 524 | 87 | 143 | 2 | 54 | .273 |
| Major League Totals | | 1903 | 7132 | 1141 | 2226 | 49 | 1053 | .312 |

### WORLD SERIES RECORD

| Year | Club | League | G. | AB. | R. | H. | HR. | RBI. | B.A. |
|------|------|--------|----|----|----|----|-----|------|------|
| 1920—Cleveland | Amer. | 7 | 23 | 0 | 4 | 0 | 0 | .174 |
| 1932—New York | Amer. | 4 | 15 | 4 | 5 | 0 | 3 | .333 |
| World Series Totals | | 11 | 38 | 4 | 9 | 0 | 3 | .237 |

## ALOYSIUS HARRY (BUCKETFOOT) SIMMONS

| Year | Club | League | G. | AB. | R. | H. | HR. | RBI. | B.A. |
|------|------|--------|----|----|----|----|-----|------|------|
| 1922—Milwaukee | A. A. | 19 | 50 | 9 | 11 | 1 | 7 | .220 |
| 1922—Aberdeen | Dakota | 99 | 395 | 91 | ★144 | 10 | ..... | .365 |
| 1923—Shreveport | Tex. | 144 | 525 | 96 | 189 | 12 | 99 | .360 |
| 1923—Milwaukee | A. A. | 24 | 98 | 20 | 39 | 0 | 16 | .398 |
| 1924—Philadelphia | Amer. | 152 | 594 | 69 | 183 | 8 | 102 | .308 |
| 1925—Philadelphia | Amer. | 153 | ★658 | 122 | ★253 | 24 | 129 | .384 |
| 1926—Philadelphia | Amer. | 147 | 581 | 90 | 199 | 19 | 109 | .343 |
| 1927—Philadelphia | Amer. | 106 | 406 | 86 | 159 | 15 | 108 | .392 |
| 1928—Philadelphia | Amer. | 119 | 464 | 78 | 163 | 15 | 107 | .351 |
| 1929—Philadelphia | Amer. | 143 | 581 | 114 | 212 | 34 | ★157 | .365 |
| 1930—Philadelphia | Amer. | 138 | 554 | ★152 | 211 | 36 | 165 | ★.381 |
| 1931—Philadelphia | Amer. | 128 | 513 | 105 | 200 | 22 | 128 | ★.390 |
| 1932—Philadelphia | Amer. | 154 | ★670 | 144 | ★216 | 35 | 151 | .322 |
| 1933—Chicago | Amer. | 146 | 605 | 85 | 200 | 14 | 119 | .331 |
| 1934—Chicago | Amer. | 138 | 558 | 102 | 192 | 18 | 104 | .344 |
| 1935—Chicago | Amer. | 128 | 525 | 68 | 140 | 16 | 79 | .267 |
| 1936—Detroit | Amer. | 143 | 568 | 96 | 186 | 13 | 112 | .327 |
| 1937—Washington | Amer. | 103 | 419 | 60 | 117 | 8 | 84 | .279 |
| 1938—Washington | Amer. | 125 | 470 | 79 | 142 | 21 | 95 | .302 |
| 1939—Bos.-Cin. | Nat. | 102 | 351 | 39 | 96 | 7 | 44 | .274 |
| 1940—Philadelphia | Amer. | 37 | 81 | 7 | 25 | 1 | 19 | .309 |
| 1941—Philadelphia | Amer. | 9 | 24 | 1 | 3 | 0 | 1 | .125 |
| 1942—Philadelphia | Amer. | (Served as coach.) | | | | | | |
| 1943—Boston | Amer. | 40 | 133 | 9 | 27 | 1 | 12 | .203 |
| 1944—Philadelphia | Amer. | 4 | 6 | 1 | 3 | 0 | 2 | .500 |
| American League Totals | | 2113 | 8410 | 1468 | 2831 | 300 | 1783 | .337 |
| National League Totals | | 102 | 351 | 39 | 96 | 7 | 44 | .274 |
| Major League Totals | | 2215 | 8761 | 1507 | 2927 | 307 | 1827 | .334 |

## WORLD SERIES RECORD

| Year | Club | League | G. | AB. | R. | H. | HR. | RBI. | B.A. |
|------|------|--------|----|----|----|----|-----|------|------|
| 1929—Philadelphia | Amer. | 5 | 20 | 6 | 6 | 2 | 5 | .300 |
| 1930—Philadelphia | Amer. | 6 | 22 | 4 | 8 | 2 | 4 | .364 |
| 1931—Philadelphia | Amer. | 7 | 27 | 4 | 9 | 2 | 8 | .333 |
| 1939—Cincinnati | Nat. | 1 | 4 | 1 | 1 | 0 | 0 | .250 |
| World Series Totals | | 19 | 73 | 15 | 24 | 6 | 17 | .329 |

## GEORGE HAROLD (GORGEOUS GEORGE) SISLER

| Year | Club | League | G. | AB. | R. | H. | HR. | RBI. | B.A. |
|------|------|--------|----|----|----|----|-----|------|------|
| 1915—St. Louis | Amer. | 81 | 274 | 28 | 78 | 3 | 29 | .285 |
| 1916—St. Louis | Amer. | 151 | 580 | 83 | 177 | 4 | 74 | .305 |
| 1917—St. Louis | Amer. | 135 | 539 | 60 | 190 | 2 | 55 | .353 |
| 1918—St. Louis | Amer. | 114 | 452 | 69 | 154 | 2 | 45 | .341 |
| 1919—St. Louis | Amer. | 132 | 511 | 96 | 180 | 10 | 83 | .352 |
| 1920—St. Louis | Amer. | ●154 | ★631 | 137 | ★257 | 19 | 122 | ★.407 |
| 1921—St. Louis | Amer. | 138 | 582 | 125 | 216 | 12 | 104 | .371 |
| 1922—St. Louis | Amer. | 142 | 586 | ★134 | ★246 | 8 | 105 | ★.420 |
| 1923—St. Louis | Amer. | (Out with eye trouble) | | | | | | |
| 1924—St. Louis | Amer. | 151 | 636 | 94 | 194 | 9 | 74 | .305 |
| 1925—St. Louis | Amer. | 150 | 649 | 100 | 224 | 12 | 105 | .345 |
| 1926—St. Louis | Amer. | 150 | 613 | 78 | 178 | 7 | 71 | .289 |
| 1927—St. Louis | Amer. | 149 | 614 | 87 | 201 | 5 | 97 | .327 |
| 1928—Washington | Amer. | 20 | 49 | 1 | 12 | 0 | 2 | .245 |
| 1928—Boston | Nat. | 118 | 491 | 71 | 167 | 4 | 68 | .340 |
| 1929—Boston | Nat. | 154 | 629 | 67 | 205 | 2 | 79 | .326 |
| 1930—Boston | Nat. | 116 | 431 | 54 | 133 | 3 | 67 | .309 |
| 1931—Rochester | Int. | 159 | 613 | 86 | 186 | 3 | 81 | .303 |
| 1932—Shrev.-Tyler | Texas | 70 | 258 | 28 | 74 | 1 | 23 | .287 |
| American League Totals | | 1667 | 6716 | 1092 | 2307 | 93 | 966 | .344 |
| National League Totals | | 388 | 1551 | 192 | 505 | 9 | 214 | .326 |
| Major League Totals | | 2055 | 8267 | 1284 | 2812 | 102 | 1180 | .340 |

### PITCHING RECORD

| Year | Club | League | G. | IP. | W. | L. | Pct. | ERA. |
|------|------|--------|----|----|----|----|------|------|
| 1915—St. Louis | American | 15 | 70 | 4 | 4 | .500 | 2.83 |
| 1916—St. Louis | American | 3 | 27 | 1 | 2 | .333 | 1.00 |
| 1920—St. Louis | American | 1 | 1 | 0 | 0 | .000 | 0.00 |
| 1925—St. Louis | American | 1 | 2 | 0 | 0 | .000 | 0.00 |
| 1926—St. Louis | American | 1 | 2 | 0 | 0 | .000 | 0.00 |
| 1928—Boston | National | 1 | 1 | 0 | 0 | .000 | 0.00 |
| Major League Totals | | 22 | 103 | 5 | 6 | .455 | 2.13 |

## EDWIN DONALD (DUKE) SNIDER

| Year | Club | League | G. | AB. | R. | H. | HR. | RBI. | B.A. |
|------|------|--------|----|----|----|----|-----|------|------|
| 1944—Montreal | Int. | 2 | 2 | 0 | 0 | 0 | 0 | .000 |
| 1944—Newport News | Pied. | 131 | 507 | 87 | 149 | ★9 | 50 | .294 |
| 1945—Newport News | Pied. | (In Military Service) | | | | | | |
| 1946—Fort Worth | Tex. | 68 | 232 | 36 | 58 | 5 | 30 | .250 |
| 1947—St. Paul | A.A. | 66 | 269 | 59 | 85 | 12 | 46 | .316 |
| 1947—Brooklyn | Nat. | 40 | 83 | 6 | 20 | 0 | 5 | .241 |
| 1948—Montreal | Int. | 77 | 275 | 67 | 90 | 17 | 77 | .327 |
| 1948—Brooklyn | Nat. | 53 | 160 | 22 | 39 | 5 | 21 | .244 |
| 1949—Brooklyn | Nat. | 146 | 552 | 100 | 161 | 23 | 92 | .292 |
| 1950—Brooklyn | Nat. | 152 | 620 | 109 | ★199 | 31 | 107 | .321 |
| 1951—Brooklyn | Nat. | 150 | 606 | 96 | 168 | 29 | 101 | .277 |
| 1952—Brooklyn | Nat. | 144 | 534 | 80 | 162 | 21 | 92 | .303 |
| 1953—Brooklyn | Nat. | 153 | 590 | ★132 | 198 | 42 | 126 | .336 |
| 1954—Brooklyn | Nat. | 149 | 584 | ●120 | 199 | 40 | 130 | .341 |
| 1955—Brooklyn | Nat. | 148 | 538 | ★126 | 166 | 42 | ★136 | .309 |
| 1956—Brooklyn | Nat. | 151 | 542 | 112 | 158 | ★43 | 101 | .292 |
| 1957—Brooklyn | Nat. | 139 | 508 | 91 | 139 | 40 | 92 | .274 |
| 1958—Los Angeles | Nat. | 106 | 327 | 45 | 102 | 15 | 58 | .312 |
| 1959—Los Angeles | Nat. | 126 | 370 | 59 | 114 | 23 | 88 | .308 |
| 1960—Los Angeles | Nat. | 101 | 235 | 38 | 57 | 14 | 36 | .243 |
| 1961—Los Angeles | Nat. | 85 | 233 | 35 | 69 | 16 | 56 | .296 |
| 1962—Los Angeles | Nat. | 80 | 158 | 28 | 44 | 5 | 30 | .278 |
| 1963—New York | Nat. | 129 | 354 | 44 | 86 | 14 | 45 | .243 |
| 1964—San Francisco | Nat. | 91 | 167 | 16 | 35 | 4 | 17 | .210 |
| Major League Totals | | 2143 | 7161 | 1259 | 2116 | 407 | 1333 | .295 |

### WORLD SERIES RECORD

| Year | Club | League | G. | AB. | R. | H. | HR. | RBI. | B.A. |
|------|------|--------|----|----|----|----|-----|------|------|
| 1949—Brooklyn | Nat. | 5 | 21 | 2 | 3 | 0 | 0 | .143 |
| 1952—Brooklyn | Nat. | 7 | 29 | 5 | 10 | 4 | 8 | .345 |
| 1953—Brooklyn | Nat. | 6 | 25 | 3 | 8 | 1 | 5 | .320 |
| 1955—Brooklyn | Nat. | 7 | 25 | 5 | 8 | 4 | 7 | .320 |
| 1956—Brooklyn | Nat. | 7 | 23 | 5 | 7 | 1 | 4 | .304 |
| 1959—Los Angeles | Nat. | 4 | 10 | 1 | 2 | 1 | 2 | .200 |
| World Series Totals | | 36 | 133 | 21 | 38 | 11 | 26 | .286 |

## WARREN EDWARD SPAHN

| Year | Club | League | G. | IP. | W. | L. | Pct. | ERA. |
|------|------|--------|----|----|----|----|------|------|
| 1940—Bradford | Pony | 12 | 66 | 5 | 4 | .556 | 2.73 |
| 1941—Evansville | I.I.I. | 28 | 212 | ★19 | 6 | ★.760 | ★1.83 |
| 1942—Hartford | Eastern | 33 | 248 | 17 | 12 | .586 | 1.96 |
| 1942—Boston | National | 4 | 16 | 0 | 0 | .000 | 5.63 |
| 1943-44-45—Boston | National | (In Military Service) | | | | | | |

| Year | Club | League | G. | IP. | W. | L. | Pct. | ERA. |
|---|---|---|---|---|---|---|---|---|
| 1946—Boston | National | | 24 | 126 | 8 | 5 | .615 | 2.93 |
| 1947—Boston | National | | 40 | ★290 | 21 | 10 | .677 | ★2.33 |
| 1948—Boston | National | | 36 | 257 | 15 | 12 | .556 | 3.71 |
| 1949—Boston | National | | 38 | ★302 | ★21 | 14 | .600 | 3.07 |
| 1950—Boston | National | | 41 | 293 | ★21 | 17 | .553 | 3.16 |
| 1951—Boston | National | | 39 | 311 | 22 | 14 | .611 | 2.98 |
| 1952—Boston | National | | 40 | 290 | 14 | 19 | .424 | 2.98 |
| 1953—Milwaukee | National | | 35 | 266 | ●23 | 7 | .767 | ★2.10 |
| 1954—Milwaukee | National | | 39 | 283 | 21 | 12 | .636 | 3.15 |
| 1955—Milwaukee | National | | 39 | 246 | 17 | 14 | .548 | 3.26 |
| 1956—Milwaukee | National | | 39 | 281 | 20 | 11 | .645 | 2.79 |
| 1957—Milwaukee | National | | 39 | 271 | ★21 | 11 | .656 | 2.69 |
| 1958—Milwaukee | National | | 38 | ★290 | ●22 | 11 | ●.667 | 3.07 |
| 1959—Milwaukee | National | | 40 | ★292 | ●21 | 15 | .583 | 2.96 |
| 1960—Milwaukee | National | | 40 | 268 | ●21 | 10 | .677 | 3.49 |
| 1961—Milwaukee | National | | 38 | 263 | ●21 | 13 | .618 | ★3.01 |
| 1962—Milwaukee | National | | 34 | 269 | 18 | 14 | .563 | 3.04 |
| 1963—Milwaukee | National | | 33 | 260 | 23 | 7 | .767 | 2.60 |
| 1964—Milwaukee | National | | 38 | 174 | 6 | 13 | .316 | 5.28 |
| 1965—N.Y.-San Fran. | National | | 36 | 198 | 7 | 16 | .304 | 4.00 |
| 1966—Mexico City Tigers | Mexican | | 3 | 10 | 1 | 1 | .500 | 4.50 |
| 1967—Tulsa | Pacific Coast | | 3 | 7 | 0 | 1 | .000 | 6.43 |
| Major League Totals | | | 750 | 5246 | 363 | 245 | .597 | 3.08 |

### WORLD SERIES RECORD

| Year | Club | League | G. | IP. | W. | L. | Pct. | ERA. |
|---|---|---|---|---|---|---|---|---|
| 1948—Boston | Nat. | | 3 | 12 | 1 | 1 | .500 | 3.00 |
| 1957—Milwaukee | Nat. | | 2 | 15⅓ | 1 | 1 | .500 | 4.70 |
| 1958—Milwaukee | Nat. | | 3 | 28⅔ | 2 | 1 | .667 | 1.88 |
| World Series Totals | | | 8 | 56 | 4 | 3 | .571 | 2.89 |

## TRISTRAM (SPOKE or GRAY EAGLE) SPEAKER

| Year | Club | League | G. | AB. | R. | H. | HR. | RBI. | B.A. |
|---|---|---|---|---|---|---|---|---|---|
| 1906—Cleburne | No. Tex. | | 84 | 287 | 35 | 77 | .... | ..... | .268 |
| 1907—Houston | Texas | | 118 | 468 | 70 | 147 | .... | ..... | ★.314 |
| 1907—Boston | Amer. | | 7 | 20 | 0 | 3 | 0 | 0 | .150 |
| 1908—Little Rock | South. | | 127 | 471 | ★81 | ★165 | 3 | .... | ★.350 |
| 1908—Boston | Amer. | | 31 | 116 | 12 | 26 | 0 | 10 | .224 |
| 1909—Boston | Amer. | | 143 | 544 | 73 | 168 | 7 | 79 | .309 |
| 1910—Boston | Amer. | | 141 | 538 | 92 | 183 | 7 | 62 | .340 |
| 1911—Boston | Amer. | | 141 | 500 | 88 | 167 | 8 | 80 | .334 |
| 1912—Boston | Amer. | | 153 | 580 | 136 | 222 | 10 | 98 | .383 |
| 1913—Boston | Amer. | | 141 | 520 | 94 | 190 | 3 | 81 | .365 |
| 1914—Boston | Amer. | | ●158 | 571 | 100 | ★193 | 4 | 86 | .338 |
| 1915—Boston | Amer. | | 150 | 547 | 108 | 176 | 0 | 63 | .322 |
| 1916—Cleveland | Amer. | | 151 | 546 | 102 | ★211 | 2 | 83 | ★.386 |
| 1917—Cleveland | Amer. | | 142 | 523 | 90 | 184 | 2 | 65 | .352 |
| 1918—Cleveland | Amer. | | 128 | 475 | 73 | 151 | 0 | 61 | .318 |
| 1919—Cleveland | Amer. | | 134 | 494 | 83 | 146 | 2 | 69 | .296 |
| 1920—Cleveland | Amer. | | 150 | 552 | 137 | 214 | 8 | 107 | .388 |
| 1921—Cleveland | Amer. | | 132 | 506 | 107 | 183 | 3 | 74 | .362 |
| 1922—Cleveland | Amer. | | 131 | 426 | 85 | 161 | 11 | 71 | .378 |
| 1923—Cleveland | Amer. | | 150 | 574 | 133 | 218 | 17 | 130 | .380 |
| 1924—Cleveland | Amer. | | 136 | 486 | 94 | 167 | 9 | 65 | .344 |
| 1925—Cleveland | Amer. | | 117 | 429 | 79 | 167 | 12 | 87 | .389 |
| 1926—Cleveland | Amer. | | 150 | 539 | 96 | 164 | 7 | 86 | .304 |
| 1927—Washington | Amer. | | 141 | 523 | 71 | 171 | 2 | 73 | .327 |
| 1928—Philadelphia | Amer. | | 64 | 191 | 28 | 51 | 3 | 32 | .267 |
| 1929—Newark | Int. | | 48 | 138 | 36 | 49 | 5 | 20 | .355 |
| 1930—Newark | Int. | | 11 | 31 | 3 | 13 | 0 | 3 | .419 |
| Major League Totals | | | 2791 | 10200 | 1881 | 3516 | 117 | 1562 | .345 |

### WORLD SERIES RECORD

| Year | Club | League | G. | AB. | R. | H. | HR. | RBI. | B.A. |
|---|---|---|---|---|---|---|---|---|---|
| 1912—Boston | Amer. | | 8 | 30 | 4 | 9 | 0 | 2 | .300 |
| 1915—Boston | Amer. | | 5 | 17 | 2 | 5 | 0 | 0 | .294 |
| 1920—Cleveland | Amer. | | 7 | 25 | 6 | 8 | 0 | 1 | .320 |
| World Series Totals | | | 20 | 72 | 12 | 22 | 0 | 3 | .306 |

## CHARLES DILLON (CASEY) STENGEL

| Year | Club | League | G. | AB. | R. | H. | HR. | RBI. | B.A. |
|---|---|---|---|---|---|---|---|---|---|
| 1910—Kankakee | No. Assn. | | (League disbanded in July) | | | | | | |
| 1910—Shelb.-Mays. | Bl.Grass | | 69 | 233 | 27 | 52 | 2 | .... | .223 |
| 1911—Aurora | Wis.-Ill. | | 121 | 420 | 76 | ★148 | 4 | .... | .352 |
| 1912—Montgomery | South. | | 136 | 479 | 85 | 139 | .... | .... | .290 |
| 1912—Brooklyn | Nat. | | 17 | 57 | 9 | 18 | 1 | 12 | .316 |
| 1913—Brooklyn | Nat. | | 124 | 438 | 60 | 119 | 7 | 44 | .272 |
| 1914—Brooklyn | Nat. | | 126 | 412 | 55 | 130 | 4 | 56 | .316 |
| 1915—Brooklyn | Nat. | | 132 | 459 | 52 | 109 | 3 | 43 | .237 |
| 1916—Brooklyn | Nat. | | 127 | 462 | 66 | 129 | 8 | 53 | .279 |
| 1917—Brooklyn | Nat. | | 150 | 549 | 69 | 141 | 6 | 69 | .257 |
| 1918—Pittsburgh | Nat. | | 39 | 122 | 18 | 30 | 1 | 13 | .246 |
| 1919—Pittsburgh | Nat. | | 89 | 321 | 38 | 94 | 4 | 40 | .293 |
| 1920—Philadelphia | Nat. | | 129 | 445 | 53 | 130 | 9 | 50 | .292 |
| 1921—Phila.-N.Y. | Nat. | | 42 | 81 | 11 | 23 | 0 | 6 | .284 |
| 1922—New York | Nat. | | 84 | 250 | 48 | 92 | 7 | 48 | .368 |
| 1923—New York | Nat. | | 75 | 218 | 39 | 74 | 5 | 43 | .339 |
| 1924—Boston | Nat. | | 131 | 461 | 57 | 129 | 5 | 39 | .280 |
| 1925—Boston | Nat. | | 12 | 13 | 0 | 1 | 0 | 2 | .077 |

| Year | Club | League | G. | AB. | R. | H. | HR. | RBI. | B.A. |
|---|---|---|---|---|---|---|---|---|---|
| 1925—Worcester | East. | | 100 | 334 | 73 | 107 | 10 | .... | .320 |
| 1926—Toledo | A.A. | | 88 | 201 | 40 | 66 | 0 | 27 | .328 |
| 1927—Toledo | A.A. | | 18 | 17 | 3 | 3 | 1 | 3 | .176 |
| 1928—Toledo | A.A. | | 26 | 32 | 5 | 14 | 0 | 12 | .438 |
| 1929—Toledo | A.A. | | 20 | 31 | 2 | 7 | 0 | 9 | .226 |
| 1931—Toledo | A.A. | | 2 | 8 | 1 | 3 | 0 | 0 | .375 |
| Major League Totals | | | 1277 | 4288 | 575 | 1219 | 60 | 518 | .284 |

### WORLD SERIES RECORD

| Year | Club | League | G. | AB. | R. | H. | HR. | RBI. | B.A. |
|---|---|---|---|---|---|---|---|---|---|
| 1916—Brooklyn | Nat. | | 4 | 11 | 2 | 4 | 0 | 0 | .364 |
| 1922—New York | Nat. | | 2 | 5 | 0 | 2 | 0 | 0 | .400 |
| 1923—New York | Nat. | | 6 | 12 | 3 | 5 | 2 | 4 | .417 |
| World Series Totals | | | 12 | 28 | 5 | 11 | 2 | 4 | .393 |

### RECORD AS MANAGER

| Year | Club | League | Position | W. | L. |
|---|---|---|---|---|---|
| 1925—Worcester† | Eastern | | Third | 70 | 55 |
| 1926—Toledo | Amer. Assoc. | | Fourth | 87 | 77 |
| 1927—Toledo | Amer. Assoc. | | First | 101 | 67 |
| 1928—Toledo | Amer. Assoc. | | Sixth | 79 | 88 |
| 1929—Toledo | Amer. Assoc. | | Eighth | 67 | 100 |
| 1930—Toledo | Amer. Assoc. | | Third | 88 | 66 |
| 1931—Toledo | Amer. Assoc. | | Eighth | 68 | 100 |
| 1934—Brooklyn | National | | Sixth | 71 | 81 |
| 1935—Brooklyn | National | | Fifth | 70 | 83 |
| 1936—Brooklyn‡ | National | | Seventh | 67 | 87 |
| 1938—Boston | National | | Fifth | 77 | 75 |
| 1939—Boston | National | | Seventh | 63 | 88 |
| 1940—Boston | National | | Seventh | 65 | 87 |
| 1941—Boston | National | | Seventh | 62 | 92 |
| 1942—Boston | National | | Seventh | 59 | 89 |
| 1943—Boston§ | National | | Sixth | 68 | 85 |
| 1944—Milwaukee x | Amer. Assoc. | | First | 91 | 49 |
| 1945—Kansas City | Amer. Assoc. | | Seventh | 65 | 86 |
| 1946—Oakland | Pacific Coast | | Second | 111 | 72 |
| 1947—Oakland | Pacific Coast | | Fourth | 96 | 90 |
| 1948—Oakland | Pacific Coast | | First | 114 | 74 |
| 1949—New York | American | | First | 97 | 57 |
| 1950—New York | American | | First | 98 | 56 |
| 1951—New York | American | | First | 98 | 56 |
| 1952—New York | American | | First | 95 | 59 |
| 1953—New York | American | | First | 99 | 52 |
| 1954—New York | American | | Second | 103 | 51 |
| 1955—New York | American | | First | 96 | 58 |
| 1956—New York | American | | First | 97 | 57 |
| 1957—New York | American | | First | 98 | 56 |
| 1958—New York | American | | First | 92 | 62 |
| 1959—New York | American | | Third | 79 | 75 |
| 1960—New York | American | | First | 97 | 57 |
| 1962—New York | National | | Tenth | 40 | 120 |
| 1963—New York | National | | Tenth | 51 | 111 |
| 1964—New York | National | | Tenth | 53 | 109 |
| 1965—New York y | National | | Tenth | 31 | 64 |
| Major League Totals | | | | 1926 | 1867 |

†Named president-manager when Boston Braves purchased club, while in eighth place, May 22, 1925.

‡Ousted as manager at close of 1936 season, but continued to draw salary in 1937 under terms of contract.

§Struck by an auto while crossing street in Boston on April 20, suffering a broken leg, returning to bench in July. Released as manager in December, 1943.

xReplaced Charlie Grimm, who moved up to Chicago Cubs, as manager with club in first place, May 5, 1944.

yRetired, July 24, 1965; replaced by Wes Westrum.

### WORLD SERIES RECORD

| Year | Club | League | W. | L. |
|---|---|---|---|---|
| 1949—New York | American | | 4 | 1 |
| 1950—New York | American | | 4 | 0 |
| 1951—New York | American | | 4 | 2 |
| 1952—New York | American | | 4 | 3 |
| 1953—New York | American | | 4 | 2 |
| 1955—New York | American | | 3 | 4 |
| 1956—New York | American | | 4 | 3 |
| 1957—New York | American | | 3 | 4 |
| 1958—New York | American | | 4 | 3 |
| 1960—New York | American | | 3 | 4 |

## WILLIAM HAROLD TERRY

| Year | Club | League | G. | AB. | R. | H. | HR. | RBI. | B.A. |
|---|---|---|---|---|---|---|---|---|---|
| 1915—Newnan | Ga.-Ala. | | 8 | .... | .... | .... | .... | .... | ..... |
| 1916—Shreveport | Tex. | | 19 | 29 | 3 | 7 | 0 | .... | .241 |
| 1917—Shreveport | Tex. | | 95 | 208 | 15 | 48 | 4 | .... | .231 |
| 1918-19-20-21— | | | (Played semi-pro ball) | | | | | | |
| 1922—Toledo | A. A. | | 88 | 235 | 41 | 79 | 14 | 61 | .336 |
| 1923—Toledo | A. A. | | 109 | 427 | 73 | 161 | 15 | 82 | .377 |
| 1923—New York | Nat. | | 3 | 7 | 1 | 1 | 0 | 0 | .143 |
| 1924—New York | Nat. | | 77 | 163 | 26 | 39 | 5 | 24 | .239 |

| Year | Club | League | G. | AB. | R. | H. | HR. | RBI. | B.A. |
|---|---|---|---|---|---|---|---|---|---|
| 1925—New York | Nat. | | 133 | 489 | 75 | 156 | 11 | 70 | .319 |
| 1926—New York | Nat. | | 98 | 225 | 26 | 65 | 5 | 43 | .289 |
| 1927—New York | Nat. | | 150 | 580 | 101 | 189 | 20 | 121 | .326 |
| 1928—New York | Nat. | | 149 | 568 | 100 | 185 | 17 | 101 | .326 |
| 1929—New York | Nat. | | 150 | 607 | 103 | 226 | 14 | 117 | .372 |
| 1930—New York | Nat. | | 154 | 633 | 139 | ★254 | 23 | 129 | ★.401 |
| 1931—New York | Nat. | | 153 | 611 | ●121 | 213 | 9 | 112 | .349 |
| 1932—New York | Nat. | | ●154 | 643 | 124 | 225 | 28 | 117 | .350 |
| 1933—New York | Nat. | | 123 | 475 | 68 | 153 | 6 | 58 | .322 |
| 1934—New York | Nat. | | 153 | 602 | 109 | 213 | 8 | 83 | .354 |
| 1935—New York | Nat. | | 145 | 596 | 91 | 203 | 6 | 64 | .341 |
| 1936—New York | Nat. | | 79 | 229 | 36 | 71 | 2 | 39 | .310 |
| Major League Totals | | | 1721 | 6428 | 1120 | 2193 | 154 | 1078 | .341 |

## PITCHING RECORD

| Year | Club | League | G. | IP. | W. | L. | Pct. | ERA. |
|---|---|---|---|---|---|---|---|---|
| 1915—Newnan | Ga.-Ala. | | 8 | .... | 7 | 1 | .875 | ..... |
| 1916—Shreveport | Texas | | 19 | 84 | 6 | 2 | .750 | 1.07 |
| 1917—Shreveport | Texas | | 40 | 246 | 14 | 11 | .560 | 3.00 |
| 1922—Toledo | Amer. Assn. | | 26 | 127 | 9 | 9 | .500 | 4.26 |

## WORLD SERIES RECORD

| Year | Club | League | G. | AB. | R. | H. | HR. | RBI. | B.A. |
|---|---|---|---|---|---|---|---|---|---|
| 1924—New York | Nat. | | 5 | 14 | 3 | 6 | 1 | 1 | .429 |
| 1933—New York | Nat. | | 5 | 22 | 3 | 6 | 1 | 1 | .273 |
| 1936—New York | Nat. | | 6 | 25 | 1 | 6 | 0 | 5 | .240 |
| World Series Totals | | | 16 | 61 | 7 | 18 | 2 | 7 | .295 |

## SAMUEL L. (BIG SAM) THOMPSON

| Year | Club | League | G. | AB. | R. | H. | HR. | SB. | B.A. |
|---|---|---|---|---|---|---|---|---|---|
| 1884—Evansville | N.W. | | 5 | 23 | 5 | 9 | 0 | 0 | .391 |
| 1885—Indianapolis | West. | | 30 | 136 | 38 | 43 | 1 | .... | .316 |
| 1885—Detroit | Nat. | | 63 | 254 | 58 | 77 | 7 | .... | .303 |
| 1886—Detroit | Nat. | | 122 | 503 | 100 | 156 | 8 | 13 | .310 |
| 1887—Detroit | Nat. | | 127 | 576 | 118 | 234 | 10 | 22 | .406 |
| 1888—Detroit | Nat. | | 55 | 238 | 51 | 67 | 6 | 5 | .282 |
| 1889—Philadelphia | Nat. | | 128 | 533 | 103 | 158 | ★20 | 24 | .296 |
| 1890—Philadelphia | Nat. | | 132 | 549 | 114 | ●172 | 4 | 25 | .313 |
| 1891—Philadelphia | Nat. | | 133 | 551 | 108 | 163 | 7 | 33 | .296 |
| 1892—Philadelphia | Nat. | | 151 | 602 | 109 | 183 | 9 | 30 | .304 |
| 1893—Philadelphia | Nat. | | 130 | 583 | 130 | ★220 | 11 | 18 | .377 |
| 1894—Philadelphia | Nat. | | 102 | 458 | 115 | 185 | 13 | 29 | .404 |
| 1895—Philadelphia | Nat. | | 118 | 533 | 131 | 210 | 16 | 24 | .394 |
| 1896—Philadelphia | Nat. | | 119 | 517 | 103 | 158 | ●13 | 11 | .306 |
| 1897—Philadelphia | Nat. | | 3 | 13 | 2 | 3 | 0 | 0 | .231 |
| 1898—Philadelphia | Nat. | | 14 | 63 | 13 | 23 | 2 | 1 | .365 |
| 1906—Detroit | Amer. | | 8 | 31 | 4 | 7 | 0 | 0 | .226 |
| American League Totals | | | 8 | 31 | 4 | 7 | 0 | 0 | .226 |
| National League Totals | | | 1397 | 5973 | 1255 | 2009 | 126 | 235 | .336 |
| Major League Totals | | | 1405 | 6004 | 1259 | 2016 | 126 | 235 | .336 |

## WORLD SERIES RECORD

| Year | Club | League | G. | AB. | R. | H. | BA. |
|---|---|---|---|---|---|---|---|
| 1887—Detroit | Nat. | | 15 | 61 | 9 | 23 | .377 |

## JOSEPH BERT TINKER

| Year | Club | League | G. | AB. | R. | H. | HR. | SB. | B.A. |
|---|---|---|---|---|---|---|---|---|---|
| 1900—Denver | West. | | 32 | 137 | 18 | 30 | ... | 8 | .219 |
| 1900—Gr't F'ls-Helena | Mont. St. | | 57 | 236 | 39 | 76 | ... | 12 | .322 |
| 1901—Portland | P. NW. | | 106 | 424 | 74 | 123 | ... | 37 | .290 |
| 1902—Chicago | Nat. | | 133 | 501 | 54 | 137 | 2 | 28 | .273 |
| 1903—Chicago | Nat. | | 124 | 460 | 67 | 134 | 2 | 27 | .291 |
| 1904—Chicago | Nat. | | 141 | 488 | 55 | 108 | 3 | 41 | .221 |
| 1905—Chicago | Nat. | | 149 | 547 | 70 | 135 | 2 | 31 | .247 |
| 1906—Chicago | Nat. | | 148 | 523 | 75 | 122 | 1 | 30 | .233 |
| 1907—Chicago | Nat. | | 113 | 402 | 36 | 89 | 1 | 20 | .221 |
| 1908—Chicago | Nat. | | ●157 | 548 | 67 | 146 | 6 | 30 | .266 |
| 1909—Chicago | Nat. | | 143 | 516 | 56 | 132 | 4 | 23 | .256 |
| 1910—Chicago | Nat. | | 132 | 473 | 48 | 136 | 3 | 20 | .288 |
| 1911—Chicago | Nat. | | 143 | 536 | 61 | 149 | 4 | 30 | .278 |
| 1912—Chicago | Nat. | | 142 | 550 | 80 | 155 | 0 | 25 | .282 |
| 1913—Cincinnati | Nat. | | 110 | 382 | 47 | 121 | 1 | 10 | .317 |
| 1914—Chicago | Fed. | | 127 | 440 | 53 | 114 | 2 | 24 | .259 |
| 1915—Chicago | Fed. | | 30 | 69 | 7 | 19 | 0 | 3 | .275 |
| 1916—Chicago | Nat. | | 7 | 10 | 0 | 1 | 0 | 0 | .100 |
| 1917—Columbus | A. A. | | 22 | 51 | 5 | 6 | 0 | 4 | .118 |
| 1921—Orlando | Fla. St. | | 2 | 3 | 1 | 1 | 0 | 0 | .333 |
| Major League Totals | | | 1642 | 5936 | 716 | 1565 | 29 | 315 | .264 |

## WORLD SERIES RECORD

| Year | Club | League | G. | AB. | R. | H. | HR. | SB. | B.A. |
|---|---|---|---|---|---|---|---|---|---|
| 1906—Chicago | Nat. | | 6 | 18 | 4 | 3 | 0 | 2 | .167 |
| 1907—Chicago | Nat. | | 5 | 13 | 4 | 2 | 0 | 3 | .154 |
| 1908—Chicago | Nat. | | 5 | 19 | 2 | 5 | 1 | 5 | .263 |
| 1910—Chicago | Nat. | | 5 | 18 | 2 | 6 | 0 | 0 | .333 |
| World Series Totals | | | 21 | 68 | 12 | 16 | 1 | 10 | .235 |

## HAROLD JOSEPH (PIE) TRAYNOR

| Year | Club | League | G. | AB. | R. | H. | HR. | RBI. | B.A. |
|---|---|---|---|---|---|---|---|---|---|
| 1920—Portsmouth | Va. | | 104 | 392 | 50 | 106 | 8 | 57 | .270 |
| 1920—Pittsburgh | Nat. | | 17 | 52 | 6 | 11 | 0 | 2 | .212 |
| 1921—Birmingham | South. | | 131 | 527 | 101 | 177 | 5 | 53 | .336 |
| 1921—Pittsburgh | Nat. | | 7 | 19 | 0 | 5 | 0 | 2 | .263 |
| 1922—Pittsburgh | Nat. | | 142 | 571 | 89 | 161 | 4 | 81 | .282 |
| 1923—Pittsburgh | Nat. | | 153 | 616 | 108 | 208 | 12 | 101 | .338 |
| 1924—Pittsburgh | Nat. | | 142 | 545 | 86 | 160 | 5 | 82 | .294 |
| 1925—Pittsburgh | Nat. | | 150 | 591 | 114 | 189 | 6 | 106 | .320 |
| 1926—Pittsburgh | Nat. | | 152 | 574 | 83 | 182 | 3 | 92 | .317 |
| 1927—Pittsburgh | Nat. | | 149 | 573 | 93 | 196 | 5 | 106 | .342 |
| 1928—Pittsburgh | Nat. | | 144 | 569 | 91 | 192 | 3 | 124 | .337 |
| 1929—Pittsburgh | Nat. | | 130 | 540 | 94 | 192 | 4 | 108 | .356 |
| 1930—Pittsburgh | Nat. | | 130 | 497 | 90 | 182 | 9 | 119 | .366 |
| 1931—Pittsburgh | Nat. | | 155 | 615 | 81 | 183 | 2 | 68 | .298 |
| 1932—Pittsburgh | Nat. | | 135 | 513 | 74 | 169 | 2 | 68 | .329 |
| 1933—Pittsburgh | Nat. | | ●154 | 624 | 85 | 190 | 1 | 82 | .304 |
| 1934—Pittsburgh | Nat. | | 119 | 444 | 62 | 137 | 1 | 61 | .309 |
| 1935—Pittsburgh | Nat. | | 57 | 204 | 24 | 57 | 1 | 36 | .279 |
| 1936—Pittsburgh | Nat. | | | | | (Did not play) | | | |
| 1937—Pittsburgh | Nat. | | 5 | 12 | 3 | 2 | 0 | 0 | .167 |
| Major League Totals | | | 1941 | 7559 | 1183 | 2416 | 58 | 1273 | .320 |

## WORLD SERIES RECORD

| Year | Club | League | G. | AB. | R. | H. | HR. | RBI. | B.A. |
|---|---|---|---|---|---|---|---|---|---|
| 1925—Pittsburgh | Nat. | | 7 | 26 | 2 | 9 | 1 | 4 | .346 |
| 1927—Pittsburgh | Nat. | | 4 | 15 | 1 | 3 | 0 | 0 | .200 |
| World Series Totals | | | 11 | 41 | 3 | 12 | 1 | 4 | .293 |

## ARTHUR CHARLES (DAZZY) VANCE

| Year | Club | League | G. | IP. | W. | L. | Pct. | ERA. |
|---|---|---|---|---|---|---|---|---|
| 1912—Red Cloud | Neb. State | | 36 | .... | 11 | 15 | .423 | ..... |
| 1913—Superior | Neb. State | | 25 | .... | 11 | 14 | .440 | ..... |
| 1914—Hastings | Neb. State | | 26 | .... | 17 | 4 | ★.810 | ..... |
| 1914—St. Joseph | Western | | 21 | 134 | 9 | 8 | .529 | 2.96 |
| 1915—Pittsburgh | National | | 1 | 3 | 0 | 1 | .000 | 6.00 |
| 1915—St. Joseph | Western | | 39 | 264 | 17 | 15 | .531 | 2.93 |
| 1915—New York | American | | 8 | 28 | 0 | 3 | .000 | 3.54 |
| 1916—Columbus | Amer. Assn. | | 14 | 50 | 2 | 2 | .500 | 4.50 |
| 1917—Toledo | Amer. Assn. | | 15 | 71 | 2 | 6 | .250 | 2.28 |
| 1917—Memphis | Southern | | 16 | 122 | 6 | 8 | .429 | ..... |
| 1918—Memphis | Southern | | 16 | 117 | 8 | 6 | .571 | ..... |
| 1918—Rochester | International | | 9 | 72 | 3 | 5 | .375 | 3.88 |
| 1918—New York | American | | 2 | 2 | 0 | 0 | .000 | 18.00 |
| 1919—Sacramento | Pacific Coast | | 48 | 294 | 10 | 18 | .357 | 2.82 |
| 1920—Mem.-New Orleans | Southern | | 45 | 284 | 16 | 17 | .485 | ..... |
| 1921—New Orleans | Southern | | 38 | 253 | 21 | 11 | .656 | 3.52 |
| 1922—Brooklyn | National | | 36 | 246 | 18 | 12 | .600 | 3.70 |
| 1923—Brooklyn | National | | 37 | 280 | 18 | 15 | .545 | 3.50 |
| 1924—Brooklyn | National | | 35 | 309 | ★28 | 6 | .824 | ★2.16 |
| 1925—Brooklyn | National | | 31 | 265 | ★22 | 9 | .710 | 3.53 |
| 1926—Brooklyn | National | | 24 | 169 | 9 | 10 | .474 | 3.89 |
| 1927—Brooklyn | National | | 34 | 273 | 16 | 15 | .516 | 2.70 |
| 1928—Brooklyn | National | | 38 | 280 | 22 | 10 | .688 | ★2.09 |
| 1929—Brooklyn | National | | 31 | 231 | 14 | 13 | .519 | 3.90 |
| 1930—Brooklyn | National | | 35 | 259 | 17 | 15 | .531 | ★2.61 |
| 1931—Brooklyn | National | | 30 | 219 | 11 | 13 | .458 | 3.37 |
| 1932—Brooklyn | National | | 27 | 176 | 12 | 11 | .522 | 4.19 |
| 1933—St. Louis | National | | 28 | 99 | 6 | 2 | .750 | 3.55 |
| 1934—Cincinnati-St.L. | National | | 25 | 77 | 1 | 3 | .250 | 4.56 |
| 1935—Brooklyn | National | | 20 | 51 | 3 | 2 | .600 | 4.41 |
| American League Totals | | | 10 | 30 | 0 | 3 | .000 | 4.50 |
| National League Totals | | | 432 | 2937 | 197 | 137 | .590 | 3.23 |
| Major League Totals | | | 442 | 2967 | 197 | 140 | .585 | 3.24 |

## WORLD SERIES RECORD

| Year | Club | League | G. | IP. | W. | L. | Pct. | ERA. |
|---|---|---|---|---|---|---|---|---|
| 1934—St. Louis | National | | 1 | 1⅓ | 0 | 0 | .000 | 0.00 |

## GEORGE EDWARD (RUBE) WADDELL

| Year | Club | League | G. | IP. | W. | L. | Pct. | ShO. |
|---|---|---|---|---|---|---|---|---|
| 1897—Louisville | National | | 2 | 13 | 0 | 1 | .000 | 0 |
| 1898—Detroit | Western | | 9 | .... | 4 | 4 | .500 | .... |
| 1899—Col.-Grand Rapids | American | | 42 | 330 | 27 | 13 | .675 | .... |
| 1899—Louisville | National | | 10 | 80 | 7 | 2 | .778 | 1 |
| 1900—Pittsburgh | National | | 29 | 212 | 9 | 11 | .450 | 2 |
| 1900—Milwaukee | American | | 15 | 129 | 10 | 3 | .769 | 2 |
| 1901—Pittsburgh-Chicago | National | | 31 | 250 | 13 | 16 | .448 | 0 |
| 1902—Los Angeles | Pacific Coast | | 20 | 178 | 12 | 8 | .600 | 2 |
| 1902—Philadelphia | American | | 33 | 275 | 23 | 7 | .767 | 3 |
| 1903—Philadelphia | American | | 39 | 323 | 21 | 16 | .568 | 4 |
| 1904—Philadelphia | American | | 46 | 384 | 25 | 19 | .568 | 8 |
| 1905—Philadelphia | American | | ★46 | 324 | ★26 | 11 | .703 | 7 |
| 1906—Philadelphia | American | | 43 | 272 | 15 | 17 | .469 | 8 |
| 1907—Philadelphia | American | | 44 | 285 | 19 | 13 | .594 | 7 |
| 1908—St. Louis | American | | 43 | 286 | 19 | 14 | .576 | 5 |
| 1909—St. Louis | American | | 31 | 220 | 11 | 14 | .440 | 5 |
| 1910—St. Louis | American | | 10 | 34 | 3 | 1 | .750 | 0 |

| Year—Club | League | G. | IP. | W. | L. | Pct. | ShO. |
|---|---|---|---|---|---|---|---|
| 1910—Newark | Eastern | 15 | 97 | 5 | 3 | .625 | .... |
| 1911—Minneapolis | Amer. Assn. | 54 | 300 | 20 | 17 | .541 | .... |
| 1912—Minneapolis | Amer. Assn. | 33 | 151 | 12 | 6 | .667 | .... |
| 1913—Virginia | Northern | 15 | 84 | 3 | 9 | .250 | .... |
| American League Totals | | 335 | 2403 | 162 | 112 | .591 | 47 |
| National League Totals | | 72 | 555 | 29 | 30 | .492 | 3 |
| Major League Totals | | 407 | 2958 | 191 | 142 | .574 | 50 |

## JOHN PETER (HONUS) WAGNER

| Year—Club | League | G. | AB. | R. | H. | HR. | RBI. | B.A. |
|---|---|---|---|---|---|---|---|---|
| 1895—Steubenville | Int. St. | 44 | .... | .... | .... | .... | .... | .402 |
| 1895—Mansfield | Ohio St. | | (No records available) | | | | | |
| 1895—Adrian | Mich. St. | 20 | .... | .... | .... | .... | .... | .365 |
| 1895—Warren | Iron-Oil | 65 | .... | .... | .... | .... | .... | .369 |
| 1896—Paterson | Atl. | 109 | 416 | 106 | 145 | .... | .... | .349 |
| 1897—Paterson | Atlantic | 74 | 301 | 61 | 114 | .... | .... | .379 |
| 1897—Louisville | Nat. | 61 | 241 | 38 | 83 | 2 | .... | .344 |
| 1898—Louisville | Nat. | 148 | 591 | 80 | 180 | 10 | .... | .305 |
| 1899—Louisville | Nat. | 144 | 549 | 102 | 197 | 7 | .... | .359 |
| 1900—Pittsburgh | Nat. | 134 | 528 | 107 | 201 | 4 | .... | ★.381 |
| 1901—Pittsburgh | Nat. | 141 | 556 | 100 | 196 | 6 | .... | .353 |
| 1902—Pittsburgh | Nat. | 137 | 538 | ★105 | 177 | 3 | .... | .329 |
| 1903—Pittsburgh | Nat. | 129 | 512 | 97 | 182 | 5 | .... | ★.355 |
| 1904—Pittsburgh | Nat. | 132 | 490 | 97 | 171 | 4 | .... | ★.349 |
| 1905—Pittsburgh | Nat. | 147 | 548 | 114 | 199 | 6 | .... | .363 |
| 1906—Pittsburgh | Nat. | 140 | 516 | ●103 | 175 | 2 | .... | ★.339 |
| 1907—Pittsburgh | Nat. | 142 | 515 | 98 | 180 | 6 | ★91 | ★.350 |
| 1908—Pittsburgh | Nat. | 151 | 568 | 100 | ★201 | 10 | ★106 | ★.354 |
| 1909—Pittsburgh | Nat. | 137 | 495 | 92 | 168 | 5 | ★102 | ★.339 |
| 1910—Pittsburgh | Nat. | 150 | 556 | 90 | ●178 | 4 | 84 | .320 |
| 1911—Pittsburgh | Nat. | 130 | 473 | 87 | 158 | 9 | 108 | ★.334 |
| 1912—Pittsburgh | Nat. | 145 | 558 | 91 | 181 | 7 | 94 | .324 |
| 1913—Pittsburgh | Nat. | 114 | 413 | 51 | 124 | 3 | 55 | .300 |
| 1914—Pittsburgh | Nat. | 150 | 552 | 60 | 139 | 1 | 46 | .252 |
| 1915—Pittsburgh | Nat. | 156 | 566 | 68 | 155 | 6 | 78 | .274 |
| 1916—Pittsburgh | Nat. | 123 | 432 | 45 | 124 | 1 | 38 | .287 |
| 1917—Pittsburgh | Nat. | 74 | 230 | 15 | 61 | 0 | 22 | .265 |
| Major League Totals | | 2785 | 10427 | 1740 | 3430 | 101 | .... | .329 |

### WORLD SERIES RECORD

| Year—Club | League | G. | AB. | R. | H. | HR. | RBI. | B.A. |
|---|---|---|---|---|---|---|---|---|
| 1903—Pittsburgh | Nat. | 8 | 27 | 2 | 6 | 0 | 3 | .222 |
| 1909—Pittsburgh | Nat. | 7 | 24 | 4 | 8 | 0 | 7 | .333 |
| World Series Totals | | 15 | 51 | 6 | 14 | 0 | 10 | .275 |

## RODERICK JOHN (BOBBY) WALLACE

| Year—Club | League | G. | AB. | R. | H. | HR. | SB. | B.A. |
|---|---|---|---|---|---|---|---|---|
| 1894—Cleveland | Nat. | 4 | 13 | 0 | 2 | 0 | 0 | .154 |
| 1895—Cleveland | Nat. | 27 | 97 | 16 | 21 | 0 | 3 | .216 |
| 1896—Cleveland | Nat. | 33 | 130 | 17 | 30 | 1 | 1 | .231 |
| 1897—Cleveland | Nat. | 131 | 522 | 99 | 177 | 4 | 17 | .339 |
| 1898—Cleveland | Nat. | 153 | 591 | 81 | 159 | 3 | 9 | .269 |
| 1899—St. Louis | Nat. | 151 | 576 | 90 | 174 | 12 | 11 | .302 |
| 1900—St. Louis | Nat. | 129 | 489 | 72 | 133 | 5 | 10 | .272 |
| 1901—St. Louis | Nat. | 135 | 556 | 69 | 179 | 2 | 17 | .322 |
| 1902—St. Louis | Amer. | 133 | 495 | 71 | 142 | 1 | 19 | .287 |
| 1903—St. Louis | Amer. | 136 | 519 | 63 | 127 | 1 | 11 | .245 |
| 1904—St. Louis | Amer. | 139 | 550 | 57 | 150 | 2 | 19 | .273 |
| 1905—St. Louis | Amer. | ★156 | 587 | 67 | 159 | 1 | 13 | .271 |
| 1906—St. Louis | Amer. | 139 | 476 | 64 | 123 | 2 | 24 | .258 |
| 1907—St. Louis | Amer. | 147 | 538 | 56 | 138 | 0 | 16 | .257 |
| 1908—St. Louis | Amer. | 137 | 487 | 59 | 123 | 1 | 5 | .253 |
| 1909—St. Louis | Amer. | 116 | 403 | 36 | 96 | 1 | 7 | .238 |
| 1910—St. Louis | Amer. | 138 | 508 | 47 | 131 | 0 | 12 | .258 |
| 1911—St. Louis | Amer. | 125 | 410 | 35 | 95 | 0 | 8 | .232 |
| 1912—St. Louis | Amer. | 99 | 323 | 39 | 78 | 0 | 3 | .241 |
| 1913—St. Louis | Amer. | 52 | 147 | 11 | 31 | 0 | 2 | .211 |
| 1914—St. Louis | Amer. | 26 | 73 | 3 | 16 | 0 | 1 | .219 |
| 1915—St. Louis | Amer. | 9 | 13 | 1 | 3 | 0 | 0 | .231 |
| 1916—St. Louis | Amer. | 14 | 18 | 0 | 5 | 0 | 0 | .278 |
| 1917—Wichita | West. | 33 | 123 | 9 | 34 | 0 | 4 | .276 |
| 1917—St. Louis | Nat. | 8 | 10 | 0 | 1 | 0 | 0 | .100 |
| 1918—St. Louis | Nat. | 32 | 98 | 3 | 15 | 0 | 1 | .153 |
| American League Totals | | 1566 | 5547 | 609 | 1417 | 9 | 140 | .255 |
| National League Totals | | 803 | 3082 | 447 | 891 | 27 | 69 | .289 |
| Major League Totals | | 2369 | 8629 | 1056 | 2308 | 36 | 209 | .267 |

### PITCHING RECORD

| Year—Club | League | G. | CG. | ShO. | IP. | W. | L. | Pct. |
|---|---|---|---|---|---|---|---|---|
| 1894—Cleveland | National | 4 | 2 | 0 | 26 | 2 | 1 | .667 |
| 1895—Cleveland | National | 27 | 21 | 1 | 222 | 12 | 13 | .480 |
| 1896—Cleveland | National | 22 | 12 | 2 | 144 | 10 | 7 | .588 |
| 1902—St. Louis | American | 1 | 0 | ... | .... | 0 | 0 | .... |
| Major League Totals | | 54 | 35 | 3 | 392 | 24 | 21 | .534 |

### TEMPLE CUP PITCHING RECORD

| Year—Club | League | G. | CG. | ShO. | IP. | W. | L. | Pct. |
|---|---|---|---|---|---|---|---|---|
| 1896—Cleveland | National | 1 | 1 | 0 | 8 | 0 | 1 | .000 |

### TEMPLE CUP BATTING RECORD

| Year—Club | League | G. | AB. | R. | H. | HR. | SB. | B.A. |
|---|---|---|---|---|---|---|---|---|
| 1896—Cleveland | Nat. | 3 | 5 | 1 | 1 | 0 | 0 | .200 |

## EDWARD AUGUSTIN WALSH

| Year—Club | League | G. | IP. | W. | L. | Pct. | ShO. |
|---|---|---|---|---|---|---|---|
| 1902—Wilkes-Barre | Pa. State | 4 | 36 | 1 | 2 | .333 | .... |
| 1902—Meriden | Connecticut | 21 | 182 | 15 | 5 | .750 | .... |
| 1903—Meriden | Connecticut | 23 | 182 | 11 | 10 | .524 | .... |
| 1903—Newark | Eastern | 19 | 117 | 9 | 5 | .643 | .... |
| 1904—Chicago | American | 18 | 113 | 6 | 3 | .667 | 1 |
| 1905—Chicago | American | 22 | 138 | 8 | 3 | .727 | 1 |
| 1906—Chicago | American | 42 | 281 | 17 | 13 | .567 | ★10 |
| 1907—Chicago | American | ★56 | ★419 | 24 | 18 | .600 | 5 |
| 1908—Chicago | American | ★66 | ★465 | ★40 | 15 | ★.727 | ★12 |
| 1909—Chicago | American | 31 | 230 | 15 | 11 | .577 | ★8 |
| 1910—Chicago | American | ●45 | 370 | 18 | ★20 | .474 | 7 |
| 1911—Chicago | American | ★56 | ★369 | 27 | 18 | .600 | 5 |
| 1912—Chicago | American | ★62 | ★393 | 27 | 17 | .614 | 6 |
| 1913—Chicago | American | 16 | 98 | 8 | 3 | .727 | 1 |
| 1914—Chicago | American | 9 | 45 | 2 | 3 | .400 | 1 |
| 1915—Chicago | American | 3 | 27 | 3 | 0 | 1.000 | 1 |
| 1916—Chicago | American | 2 | 3 | 0 | 1 | 1.000 | 0 |
| 1917—Boston | National | 4 | 18 | 0 | 1 | .000 | 0 |
| 1919—Milwaukee | Amer. Assn. | 4 | 21 | 2 | 2 | .500 | .... |
| 1920—Bridgeport | Eastern | 3 | 22 | 1 | 1 | .500 | .... |
| American League Totals | | 428 | 2951 | 195 | 125 | .609 | 58 |
| National League Totals | | 4 | 18 | 0 | 1 | .000 | 0 |
| Major League Totals | | 432 | 2969 | 195 | 126 | .607 | 58 |

### WORLD SERIES RECORD

| Year—Club | League | G. | IP. | W. | L. | Pct. | ShO. |
|---|---|---|---|---|---|---|---|
| 1906—Chicago | American | 2 | 15 | 2 | 0 | 1.000 | 1 |

## LLOYD JAMES (LITTLE POISON) WANER

| Year—Club | League | G. | AB. | R. | H. | HR. | RBI. | B.A. |
|---|---|---|---|---|---|---|---|---|
| 1925—San Francisco | P.C. | 31 | 44 | 7 | 11 | 0 | 1 | .250 |
| 1926—San Francisco | P.C. | 6 | 20 | 0 | 4 | 0 | .... | .200 |
| 1926—Columbia | So. Atl. | 121 | 498 | 95 | 172 | 6 | 33 | .345 |
| 1927—Pittsburgh | Nat. | 150 | 629 | ●133 | 223 | 2 | 27 | .355 |
| 1928—Pittsburgh | Nat. | 152 | ★659 | 121 | 221 | 5 | 61 | .335 |
| 1929—Pittsburgh | Nat. | 151 | ★662 | 134 | 234 | 5 | 74 | .353 |
| 1930—Pittsburgh | Nat. | 68 | 260 | 32 | 94 | 1 | 36 | .362 |
| 1931—Pittsburgh | Nat. | 154 | ★681 | 90 | ★214 | 4 | 57 | .314 |
| 1932—Pittsburgh | Nat. | 134 | 565 | 90 | 188 | 2 | 38 | .333 |
| 1933—Pittsburgh | Nat. | 121 | 500 | 59 | 138 | 0 | 26 | .276 |
| 1934—Pittsburgh | Nat. | 140 | 611 | 95 | 173 | 1 | 48 | .283 |
| 1935—Pittsburgh | Nat. | 122 | 537 | 83 | 166 | 0 | 46 | .309 |
| 1936—Pittsburgh | Nat. | 106 | 414 | 67 | 133 | 1 | 31 | .321 |
| 1937—Pittsburgh | Nat. | 129 | 537 | 80 | 177 | 1 | 45 | .330 |
| 1938—Pittsburgh | Nat. | 147 | 619 | 79 | 194 | 5 | 57 | .313 |
| 1939—Pittsburgh | Nat. | 112 | 379 | 49 | 108 | 0 | 24 | .285 |
| 1940—Pittsburgh | Nat. | 72 | 166 | 30 | 43 | 0 | 3 | .259 |
| 1941—Pitt.-Bos.-Cinn. | Nat. | 77 | 219 | 26 | 64 | 0 | 11 | .292 |
| 1942—Philadelphia | Nat. | 101 | 287 | 23 | 75 | 0 | 10 | .261 |
| 1943—Brooklyn | Nat. | | (Voluntarily retired) | | | | | |
| 1944—Brook.-Pitts. | Nat. | 34 | 28 | 5 | 9 | 0 | 3 | .321 |
| 1945—Pittsburgh | Nat. | 23 | 19 | 5 | 5 | 0 | 1 | .263 |
| Major League Totals | | 1993 | 7772 | 1201 | 2459 | 27 | 598 | .316 |

### WORLD SERIES RECORD

| Year—Club | League | G. | AB. | R. | H. | HR. | RBI. | B.A. |
|---|---|---|---|---|---|---|---|---|
| 1927—Pittsburgh | Nat. | 4 | 15 | 5 | 6 | 0 | 0 | .400 |

## PAUL GLEE (BIG POISON) WANER

| Year—Club | League | G. | AB. | R. | H. | HR. | RBI. | B.A. |
|---|---|---|---|---|---|---|---|---|
| 1923—San Francisco | P.C. | 112 | 325 | 54 | 120 | 3 | 39 | .369 |
| 1924—San Francisco | P.C. | 160 | 587 | 113 | 209 | 8 | 97 | .356 |
| 1925—San Francisco | P.C. | 174 | 699 | 167 | 280 | 11 | 130 | ★.401 |
| 1926—Pittsburgh | Nat. | 144 | 536 | 101 | 180 | 8 | 79 | .336 |
| 1927—Pittsburgh | Nat. | ●155 | 623 | 114 | ★237 | 9 | ★131 | ★.380 |
| 1928—Pittsburgh | Nat. | 152 | 602 | ★142 | 223 | 6 | 86 | .370 |
| 1929—Pittsburgh | Nat. | 151 | 596 | 131 | 200 | 15 | 100 | .336 |
| 1930—Pittsburgh | Nat. | 145 | 589 | 117 | 217 | 8 | 77 | .368 |
| 1931—Pittsburgh | Nat. | 150 | 559 | 88 | 180 | 6 | 70 | .322 |
| 1932—Pittsburgh | Nat. | ●154 | 630 | 107 | 215 | 8 | 82 | .341 |
| 1933—Pittsburgh | Nat. | ●154 | 618 | 101 | 191 | 7 | 70 | .309 |
| 1934—Pittsburgh | Nat. | 146 | 599 | ★122 | ★217 | 14 | 90 | ★.362 |
| 1935—Pittsburgh | Nat. | 139 | 549 | 98 | 176 | 11 | 78 | .321 |
| 1936—Pittsburgh | Nat. | 148 | 585 | 107 | 218 | 5 | 94 | ★.373 |
| 1937—Pittsburgh | Nat. | 154 | 619 | 94 | 219 | 2 | 74 | .354 |
| 1938—Pittsburgh | Nat. | 148 | 625 | 77 | 175 | 6 | 69 | .280 |
| 1939—Pittsburgh | Nat. | 125 | 461 | 62 | 151 | 3 | 45 | .328 |
| 1940—Pittsburgh | Nat. | 89 | 238 | 32 | 69 | 1 | 32 | .290 |
| 1941—Brook-Bost. | Nat. | 106 | 329 | 45 | 88 | 2 | 50 | .267 |
| 1942—Boston | Nat. | 114 | 333 | 43 | 86 | 1 | 39 | .258 |
| 1943—Brooklyn | Nat. | 82 | 225 | 29 | 70 | 1 | 26 | .311 |
| 1944—Brooklyn | Nat. | 83 | 136 | 16 | 39 | 0 | 16 | .287 |

| Year | Club | League | G. | AB. | R. | H. | HR. | RBI. | B.A. |
|---|---|---|---|---|---|---|---|---|---|
| 1944—New York | Amer. | 9 | 7 | 1 | 1 | 0 | 1 | .143 |
| 1945—New York | Amer. | 1 | 0 | 0 | 0 | 0 | 0 | .000 |
| 1946—Miami | Fla. Int. | 62 | 80 | 12 | 26 | 0 | 12 | .325 |
| American League Totals | | 10 | 7 | 1 | 1 | 0 | 1 | .143 |
| National League Totals | | 2539 | 9452 | 1626 | 3151 | 113 | 1308 | .333 |
| Major League Totals | | 2549 | 9459 | 1627 | 3152 | 113 | 1309 | .333 |

WORLD SERIES RECORD

| Year | Club | League | G. | AB. | R. | H. | HR. | RBI. | B.A. |
|---|---|---|---|---|---|---|---|---|---|
| 1927—Pittsburgh | Nat. | 4 | 15 | 0 | 5 | 0 | 3 | .333 |

## JOHN MONTGOMERY WARD

| Year | Club | League | G. | AB. | R. | H. | HR. | SB. | B.A. |
|---|---|---|---|---|---|---|---|---|---|
| 1877—Athletics | League Alliance club—no record available | | | | | | | | .203 |
| 1878—Providence | Nat. | 35 | 128 | 14 | 26 | 1 | .... | .203 |
| 1879—Providence | Nat. | 82 | 362 | 71 | 104 | 2 | .... | .287 |
| 1880—Providence | Nat. | 82 | 340 | 49 | 77 | 0 | .... | .226 |
| 1881—Providence | Nat. | 83 | 352 | 56 | 85 | 0 | .... | .241 |
| 1882—Providence | Nat. | 83 | 355 | 58 | 87 | 0 | .... | .245 |
| 1883—New York | Nat. | 88 | 379 | 76 | 98 | 7 | .... | .259 |
| 1884—New York | Nat. | 109 | 466 | 99 | 116 | 2 | .... | .249 |
| 1885—New York | Nat. | 111 | 446 | 72 | 101 | 0 | .... | .226 |
| 1886—New York | Nat. | 122 | 491 | 82 | 134 | 2 | 36 | .273 |
| 1887—New York | Nat. | 129 | 574 | 113 | 213 | 1 | *111 | .371 |
| 1888—New York | Nat. | 122 | 510 | 70 | 128 | 2 | 38 | .251 |
| 1889—New York | Nat. | 114 | 479 | 86 | 143 | 1 | 62 | .299 |
| 1890—Brooklyn | Play. | 128 | 558 | 135 | *207 | 4 | 71 | .371 |
| 1891—Brooklyn | Nat. | 104 | 438 | 85 | 126 | 0 | 80 | .288 |
| 1892—Brooklyn | Nat. | 148 | 610 | 109 | 167 | 2 | *94 | .274 |
| 1893—New York | Nat. | 134 | 557 | 129 | 194 | 2 | *72 | .348 |
| 1894—New York | Nat. | 136 | 552 | 99 | 145 | 0 | 41 | .262 |
| National League Total | | 1682 | 7039 | 1268 | 1944 | 22 | 534 | .276 |
| Players League Totals | | 128 | 558 | 135 | 207 | 4 | 71 | .371 |
| Major League Totals | | 1810 | 7597 | 1403 | 2151 | 26 | 605 | .283 |

PITCHING RECORD

| Year | Club | League | G. | CG. | W. | L. | Pct. | ShO. |
|---|---|---|---|---|---|---|---|---|
| 1878—Providence | National | 35 | 35 | 22 | 13 | .629 | 6 |
| 1879—Providence | National | 65 | 58 | *44 | 18 | *.710 | 2 |
| 1880—Providence | National | 63 | 58 | 40 | 23 | .635 | *9 |
| 1881—Providence | National | 36 | 33 | 18 | 18 | .500 | 3 |
| 1882—Providence | National | 32 | 30 | 19 | 13 | .594 | 4 |
| 1883—New York | National | 33 | 24 | 12 | 14 | .462 | 1 |
| 1884—New York | National | 9 | 5 | 3 | 3 | .500 | 0 |
| Major League Totals | | 273 | 243 | 158 | 102 | .608 | 25 |

WORLD SERIES RECORD

| Year | Club | League | G. | AB. | R. | H. | HR. | SB. | B.A. |
|---|---|---|---|---|---|---|---|---|---|
| 1888—New York | Nat. | 8 | 29 | 4 | 11 | 0 | 6 | .379 |
| 1889—New York | Nat. | 9 | 37 | 10 | 15 | 0 | 8 | .405 |
| World Series Totals | | 17 | 66 | 14 | 26 | 0 | 14 | .394 |

## MICHAEL FRANCIS (MICKEY) WELCH

| Year | Club | League | G. | IP. | W. | L. | Pct. | ShO. |
|---|---|---|---|---|---|---|---|---|
| 1878—Auburn | National Assn. | ... | ... | ... | ... | ..... | .. |
| 1879—Holyoke | National Assn. | ... | ... | ... | ... | ..... | .. |
| 1880—Troy | National | 65 | 574 | 34 | 30 | .531 | 4 |
| 1881—Troy | National | 40 | 362 | 21 | 18 | .538 | 4 |
| 1882—Troy | National | 34 | 292 | 14 | 16 | .467 | 5 |
| 1883—New York | National | 54 | 422 | 25 | 23 | .521 | 4 |
| 1884—New York | National | 65 | 555 | 39 | 21 | .650 | 4 |
| 1885—New York | National | 56 | 496 | 44 | 11 | .800 | 7 |
| 1886—New York | National | 59 | 499 | 33 | 22 | .600 | 1 |
| 1887—New York | National | 41 | 346 | 22 | 15 | .595 | 2 |
| 1888—New York | National | 47 | 425 | 26 | 19 | .578 | 5 |
| 1889—New York | National | 45 | 364 | 27 | 12 | .692 | 3 |
| 1890—New York | National | 37 | 294 | 17 | 13 | .567 | 2 |
| 1891—New York | National | 22 | 160 | 5 | 9 | .357 | 0 |
| 1892—New York | National | 1 | 5 | 0 | 0 | .000 | 0 |
| 1892—Troy | Eastern | 31 | | 17 | 14 | .548 | .. |
| Major League Totals | | 566 | 4794 | 307 | 209 | .595 | 41 |

## ZACHARIAH DAVIS (ZACK) WHEAT

| Year | Club | League | G. | AB. | R. | H. | HR. | RBI. | B.A. |
|---|---|---|---|---|---|---|---|---|---|
| 1908—Shreveport | Texas | 92 | 239 | 49 | 91 | 1 | .... | .268 |
| 1909—Mobile | South. | 129 | 460 | 58 | 112 | 2 | .... | .246 |
| 1909—Brooklyn | Nat. | 26 | 102 | 15 | 31 | 0 | 4 | .304 |
| 1910—Brooklyn | Nat. | ●156 | 606 | 78 | 172 | 2 | 54 | .284 |
| 1911—Brooklyn | Nat. | 136 | 534 | 55 | 153 | 5 | 76 | .287 |
| 1912—Brooklyn | Nat. | 123 | 453 | 70 | 138 | 8 | 62 | .305 |
| 1913—Brooklyn | Nat. | 138 | 535 | 64 | 161 | 7 | 71 | .301 |
| 1914—Brooklyn | Nat. | 145 | 533 | 66 | 170 | 9 | 88 | .319 |
| 1915—Brooklyn | Nat. | 146 | 528 | 64 | 136 | 5 | 70 | .258 |
| 1916—Brooklyn | Nat. | 149 | 568 | 76 | 177 | 9 | 76 | .312 |
| 1917—Brooklyn | Nat. | 109 | 362 | 38 | 113 | 1 | 40 | .312 |
| 1918—Brooklyn | Nat. | 105 | 409 | 39 | 137 | 0 | 48 | *.335 |
| 1919—Brooklyn | Nat. | 137 | 536 | 70 | 159 | 5 | 68 | .297 |

| Year | Club | League | G. | AB. | R. | H. | HR. | RBI. | B.A. |
|---|---|---|---|---|---|---|---|---|---|
| 1920—Brooklyn | Nat. | 148 | 583 | 89 | 191 | 9 | 73 | .328 |
| 1921—Brooklyn | Nat. | 148 | 568 | 91 | 182 | 14 | 85 | .320 |
| 1922—Brooklyn | Nat. | 152 | 600 | 92 | 201 | 16 | 112 | .335 |
| 1923—Brooklyn | Nat. | 98 | 349 | 63 | 131 | 8 | 65 | .375 |
| 1924—Brooklyn | Nat. | 141 | 566 | 92 | 212 | 14 | 97 | .375 |
| 1925—Brooklyn | Nat. | 150 | 616 | 125 | 221 | 14 | 103 | .359 |
| 1926—Brooklyn | Nat. | 111 | 411 | 68 | 119 | 5 | 35 | .290 |
| 1927—Philadelphia | Amer. | 88 | 247 | 34 | 80 | 1 | 38 | .324 |
| 1928—Minneapolis | A.A. | 82 | 194 | 17 | 60 | 5 | 30 | .309 |
| American League Totals | | 88 | 247 | 34 | 80 | 1 | 38 | .324 |
| National League Totals | | 2318 | 8859 | 1255 | 2804 | 131 | 1227 | .317 |
| Major League Totals | | 2406 | 9106 | 1289 | 2884 | 132 | 1265 | .317 |

WORLD SERIES RECORD

| Year | Club | League | G. | AB. | R. | H. | HR. | RBI. | B.A. |
|---|---|---|---|---|---|---|---|---|---|
| 1916—Brooklyn | Nat. | 5 | 19 | 2 | 4 | 0 | 1 | .211 |
| 1920—Brooklyn | Nat. | 7 | 27 | 2 | 9 | 0 | 2 | .333 |
| World Series Totals | | 12 | 46 | 4 | 13 | 0 | 3 | .283 |

## THEODORE SAMUEL (THE KID) WILLIAMS

| Year | Club | League | G. | AB. | R. | H. | HR. | RBI. | B.A. |
|---|---|---|---|---|---|---|---|---|---|
| 1936—San Diego | P. C. | 42 | 107 | 18 | 29 | 0 | 11 | .271 |
| 1937—San Diego | P. C. | 138 | 454 | 66 | 132 | 23 | 98 | .291 |
| 1938—Minneapolis | A. A. | 148 | 528 | *130 | 193 | *43 | *142 | *.366 |
| 1939—Boston | Amer. | 149 | 565 | 131 | 185 | 31 | *145 | .327 |
| 1940—Boston | Amer. | 144 | 561 | *134 | 193 | 23 | 113 | .344 |
| 1941—Boston | Amer. | 143 | 456 | *135 | 185 | *37 | 120 | *.406 |
| 1942—Boston | Amer. | 150 | 522 | *141 | 186 | *36 | *137 | *.356 |
| 1943-44-45—Boston | Amer. | (In Military Service) | | | | | | |
| 1946—Boston | Amer. | 150 | 514 | *142 | 176 | 38 | 123 | .342 |
| 1947—Boston | Amer. | 156 | 528 | *125 | 181 | *32 | *114 | *.343 |
| 1948—Boston | Amer. | 137 | 509 | 124 | 188 | 25 | 127 | *.369 |
| 1949—Boston | Amer. | ●155 | 566 | *150 | 194 | *43 | ●159 | .343 |
| 1950—Boston | Amer. | 89 | 334 | 82 | 106 | 28 | 97 | .317 |
| 1951—Boston | Amer. | 148 | 531 | 109 | 169 | 30 | 126 | .318 |
| 1952—Boston | Amer. | 6 | 10 | 2 | 4 | 1 | 3 | .400 |
| 1953—Boston | Amer. | 37 | 91 | 17 | 37 | 13 | 34 | .407 |
| 1954—Boston | Amer. | 117 | 386 | 93 | 133 | 29 | 89 | .345 |
| 1955—Boston | Amer. | 98 | 320 | 77 | 114 | 28 | 83 | .356 |
| 1956—Boston | Amer. | 136 | 400 | 71 | 138 | 24 | 82 | .345 |
| 1957—Boston | Amer. | 132 | 420 | 96 | 163 | 38 | 87 | *.388 |
| 1958—Boston | Amer. | 129 | 411 | 81 | 135 | 26 | 85 | *.328 |
| 1959—Boston | Amer. | 103 | 272 | 32 | 69 | 10 | 43 | .254 |
| 1960—Boston | Amer. | 113 | 310 | 56 | 98 | 29 | 72 | .316 |
| Major League Totals | | 2292 | 7706 | 1798 | 2654 | 521 | 1839 | .344 |

PITCHING RECORD

| Year | Club | League | G. | IP. | W. | L. | Pct. | ERA. |
|---|---|---|---|---|---|---|---|---|
| 1936—San Diego | Pacific Coast | 1 | 1⅓ | 0 | 0 | .000 | 13.50 |
| 1940—Boston | American | 1 | 2 | 0 | 0 | .000 | 4.50 |

WORLD SERIES RECORD

| Year | Club | League | G. | AB. | R. | H. | HR. | RBI. | B.A. |
|---|---|---|---|---|---|---|---|---|---|
| 1946—Boston | Amer. | 7 | 25 | 2 | 5 | 0 | 1 | .200 |

## LEWIS ROBERT (HACK) WILSON

| Year | Club | League | G. | AB. | R. | H. | HR. | RBI. | B.A. |
|---|---|---|---|---|---|---|---|---|---|
| 1921—Martinsburg | B. Ridge | 30 | 101 | 17 | 36 | 5 | .... | .356 |
| 1922—Martinsburg | B. Ridge | 84 | 322 | 66 | 118 | *30 | .... | .366 |
| 1923—Portsmouth | Va. | 115 | 448 | 96 | 174 | *19 | *101 | *.388 |
| 1923—New York | Nat. | 3 | 10 | 0 | 2 | 0 | 0 | .200 |
| 1924—New York | Nat. | 107 | 383 | 62 | 113 | 10 | 57 | .295 |
| 1925—New York | Nat. | 62 | 180 | 28 | 43 | 6 | 30 | .239 |
| 1925—Toledo | A.A. | 55 | 210 | 42 | 72 | 4 | 36 | .343 |
| 1926—Chicago | Nat. | 142 | 529 | 97 | 170 | *21 | 109 | .321 |
| 1927—Chicago | Nat. | 146 | 551 | 119 | 175 | ●30 | 129 | .318 |
| 1928—Chicago | Nat. | 145 | 520 | 89 | 163 | ●31 | 120 | .313 |
| 1929—Chicago | Nat. | 150 | 574 | 135 | 198 | 39 | *159 | .345 |
| 1930—Chicago | Nat. | 155 | 585 | 146 | 208 | *56 | *190 | .356 |
| 1931—Chicago | Nat. | 112 | 395 | 66 | 103 | 13 | 61 | .261 |
| 1932—Brooklyn | Nat. | 135 | 481 | 77 | 143 | 23 | 123 | .297 |
| 1933—Brooklyn | Nat. | 117 | 360 | 41 | 96 | 9 | 54 | .267 |
| 1934—Brook.-Phila | Nat. | 74 | 192 | 24 | 47 | 6 | 30 | .245 |
| 1935—Albany | Int. | 59 | 175 | 30 | 46 | 3 | 29 | .263 |
| Major League Totals | | 1348 | 4760 | 884 | 1461 | 244 | 1062 | .307 |

WORLD SERIES RECORD

| Year | Club | League | G. | AB. | R. | H. | HR. | RBI. | B.A. |
|---|---|---|---|---|---|---|---|---|---|
| 1924—New York | Nat. | 7 | 30 | 1 | 7 | 0 | 3 | .233 |
| 1929—Chicago | Nat. | 5 | 17 | 2 | 8 | 0 | 0 | .471 |
| World Series Totals | | 12 | 47 | 3 | 15 | 0 | 3 | .319 |

## EARLY (GUS) WYNN, JR.

| Year | Club | League | G. | IP. | W. | L. | Pct. | ERA. |
|---|---|---|---|---|---|---|---|---|
| 1937—Sanford | Florida State | 35 | 235 | 16 | 11 | .593 | 3.41 |
| 1938—Charlotte | Piedmont | 29 | 179 | 10 | 11 | .476 | 5.28 |
| 1939—Charlotte | Piedmont | 34 | 243 | 15 | 14 | .517 | 3.96 |
| 1939—Washington | American | 3 | 20 | 0 | 2 | .000 | 5.85 |

| Year Club | League | G. | IP. | W. | L. | Pct. | ERA. |
|---|---|---|---|---|---|---|---|
| 1940—Charlotte | Piedmont | 31 | 144 | 9 | 7 | .563 | 4.25 |
| 1941—Springfield | Eastern | 34 | 257 | 16 | 12 | .571 | 2.56 |
| 1941—Washington | American | 5 | 40 | 3 | 1 | .750 | 1.58 |
| 1942—Washington | American | 30 | 190 | 10 | 16 | .385 | 5.12 |
| 1943—Washington | American | 37 | 257 | 18 | 12 | .600 | 2.91 |
| 1944—Washington | American | 33 | 208 | 8 | *17 | .320 | 3.38 |
| 1945—Washington | American | | | (In Military Service) | | | |
| 1946—Washington | American | 17 | 107 | 8 | 5 | .615 | 3.11 |
| 1947—Washington | American | 33 | 247 | 17 | 15 | .531 | 3.64 |
| 1948—Washington | American | 33 | 198 | 8 | 19 | .296 | 5.82 |
| 1949—Cleveland | American | 26 | 165 | 11 | 7 | .611 | 4.15 |
| 1950—Cleveland | American | 32 | 214 | 18 | 8 | .692 | *3.20 |
| 1951—Cleveland | American | 37 | *274 | 20 | 13 | .606 | 3.02 |
| 1952—Cleveland | American | 42 | 286 | 23 | 12 | .657 | 2.90 |
| 1953—Cleveland | American | 36 | 252 | 17 | 12 | .586 | 3.93 |
| 1954—Cleveland | American | 40 | *271 | ●23 | 11 | .676 | 2.72 |
| 1955—Cleveland | American | 32 | 230 | 17 | 11 | .607 | 2.82 |
| 1956—Cleveland | American | 38 | 278 | 20 | 9 | .690 | 2.72 |
| 1957—Cleveland | American | 40 | 263 | 14 | 17 | .452 | 4.31 |
| 1958—Chicago | American | 40 | 240 | 14 | 16 | .467 | 4.13 |
| 1959—Chicago | American | 37 | *256 | *22 | 10 | .688 | 3.16 |
| 1960—Chicago | American | 36 | 237 | 13 | 12 | .520 | 3.49 |
| 1961—Chicago | American | 17 | 110 | 8 | 2 | .800 | 3.52 |
| 1962—Chicago | American | 27 | 168 | 7 | 15 | .318 | 4.45 |
| 1963—Cleveland | American | 20 | 55 | 1 | 2 | .333 | 2.29 |
| Major League Totals | | 691 | 4566 | 300 | 244 | .551 | 3.54 |

### WORLD SERIES RECORD

| Year Club | League | G. | IP. | W. | L. | Pct. | ERA. |
|---|---|---|---|---|---|---|---|
| 1954—Cleveland | American | 1 | 7 | 0 | 1 | .000 | 3.86 |
| 1959—Chicago | American | 3 | 13 | 1 | 1 | .500 | 5.54 |
| World Series Totals | | 4 | 20 | 1 | 2 | .333 | 4.95 |

### DENTON TRUE (CY) YOUNG

| Year Club | League | G. | IP. | W. | L. | Pct. | ShO. |
|---|---|---|---|---|---|---|---|
| 1890—Canton | Tri-State | 31 | 260 | 15 | 15 | .500 | 0 |
| 1890—Cleveland | National | 17 | 150 | 9 | 7 | .563 | 0 |
| 1891—Cleveland | National | 54 | 430 | 27 | 20 | .574 | 0 |
| 1892—Cleveland | National | 53 | 455 | 36 | 11 | *.766 | *9 |
| 1893—Cleveland | National | 53 | 426 | 32 | 16 | .667 | 1 |
| 1894—Cleveland | National | 52 | 409 | 25 | 22 | .532 | 2 |
| 1895—Cleveland | National | 47 | 373 | *35 | 10 | .778 | ●4 |
| 1896—Cleveland | National | 51 | 414 | 29 | 16 | .644 | ●5 |
| 1897—Cleveland | National | ●47 | 338 | 21 | 18 | .538 | 2 |
| 1898—Cleveland | National | 46 | 378 | 25 | 14 | .641 | 1 |
| 1899—St. Louis | National | 44 | 369 | 26 | 15 | .634 | 4 |
| 1900—St. Louis | National | 41 | 321 | 20 | 18 | .526 | ●4 |
| 1901—Boston | American | 43 | 371 | *33 | 10 | .767 | ●5 |
| 1902—Boston | American | *45 | *386 | *32 | 10 | .762 | 3 |
| 1903—Boston | American | 40 | *342 | *28 | 10 | .737 | *7 |
| 1904—Boston | American | 43 | 380 | 26 | 16 | .619 | *10 |
| 1905—Boston | American | 38 | 321 | 18 | 19 | .486 | 5 |
| 1906—Boston | American | 39 | 288 | 13 | ●21 | .382 | 0 |
| 1907—Boston | American | 43 | 343 | 22 | 15 | .595 | 6 |
| 1908—Boston | American | 36 | 299 | 21 | 11 | .656 | 3 |
| 1909—Cleveland | American | 35 | 295 | 19 | 15 | .559 | 3 |
| 1910—Cleveland | American | 21 | 163 | 7 | 10 | .412 | 1 |
| 1911—Cleveland | American | 7 | 46 | 3 | 4 | .429 | 0 |
| 1911—Boston | National | 11 | 80 | 4 | 5 | .444 | 2 |
| American League Totals | | 390 | 3234 | 222 | 141 | .612 | 43 |
| National League Totals | | 516 | 4143 | 289 | 172 | .627 | 34 |
| Major League Totals | | 906 | 7377 | 511 | 313 | .620 | 77 |

#### TEMPLE CUP RECORD

| Year Club | League | G. | IP. | W. | L. | Pct. | ShO. |
|---|---|---|---|---|---|---|---|
| 1895—Cleveland | National | 3 | 27 | 3 | 0 | 1.000 | 0 |
| 1896—Cleveland | National | 1 | 9 | 0 | 1 | .000 | 0 |
| Temple Cup Totals | | 4 | 36 | 3 | 1 | .750 | 0 |

#### WORLD SERIES RECORD

| Year Club | League | G. | IP. | W. | L. | Pct. | ShO. |
|---|---|---|---|---|---|---|---|
| 1903—Boston | American | 4 | 34 | 2 | 1 | .667 | 0 |

### ROSS MIDDLEBROOK (PEP) YOUNGS

| Year Club | League | G. | AB. | R. | H. | HR. | RBI. | B.A. |
|---|---|---|---|---|---|---|---|---|
| 1914—Austin | Tex. | 10 | 31 | ..... | 3 | 0 | ..... | .097 |
| 1915—Brenham | Mid. Tex. | | No averages. League disbanded June 19. | | | | | |
| 1915—Waxahachie | Cent. Tex. | | League disbanded in July. No averages. | | | | | |
| 1916—Sherman | W. A. | 137 | *539 | *103 | *195 | 4 | ..... | *.362 |
| 1917—Rochester | Int. | 140 | 506 | 85 | 180 | 1 | ..... | .356 |
| 1917—New York | Nat. | 7 | 26 | 5 | 9 | 0 | 1 | .346 |
| 1918—New York | Nat. | 121 | 474 | 70 | 143 | 1 | 29 | .302 |
| 1919—New York | Nat. | 130 | 489 | 73 | 152 | 2 | 43 | .311 |
| 1920—New York | Nat. | 153 | 581 | 92 | 204 | 6 | 78 | .351 |
| 1921—New York | Nat. | 141 | 504 | 90 | 165 | 3 | 102 | .327 |
| 1922—New York | Nat. | 149 | 559 | 105 | 185 | 7 | 86 | .331 |
| 1923—New York | Nat. | 152 | 596 | *121 | 200 | 3 | 87 | .336 |
| 1924—New York | Nat. | 133 | 526 | 112 | 187 | 10 | 74 | .356 |
| 1925—New York | Nat. | 130 | 500 | 82 | 132 | 6 | 53 | .264 |
| 1926—New York | Nat. | 95 | 372 | 62 | 114 | 4 | 43 | .306 |
| Major League Totals | | 1211 | 4627 | 812 | 1491 | 42 | 596 | .322 |

### WORLD SERIES RECORD

| Year Club | League | G. | AB. | R. | H. | HR. | RBI. | B.A. |
|---|---|---|---|---|---|---|---|---|
| 1921—New York | Nat. | 8 | 25 | 3 | 7 | 0 | 4 | .280 |
| 1922—New York | Nat. | 5 | 16 | 2 | 6 | 0 | 2 | .375 |
| 1923—New York | Nat. | 6 | 23 | 2 | 8 | 1 | 3 | .348 |
| 1924—New York | Nat. | 7 | 27 | 3 | 5 | 0 | 2 | .185 |
| World Series Totals | | 26 | 91 | 10 | 26 | 1 | 11 | .286 |

This book does not include the Negro league records of the 10 former black baseball greats who have been added to the Hall of Fame over the years, or the playing records of those Hall of Famers whose enshrinement was based on a successful managerial career. Those inducted for off-the-field contributions—the game's founders, pioneers and executives—are covered solely in profile form.

Major league records of all players in this book are based on performances in the following leagues:

National League—1876 through 1982.

American Association—1882 through 1891.

Union Association—1884.

Players League—1890.

American League—1901 through 1982.

Federal League records of 1914-15, although carried in the players' year-by-year performances, are not included in the players' major league career totals. This league was not recognized at that time by The Sporting News, the commissioner, Kenesaw Mountain Landis, or the American and National leagues as a major league.

# Additions

# To

# Baseball Hall of Fame
# (1984-85)

# Luis Aparicio

**By the mid-1960s, Luis Aparicio was one of baseball's top shortstops and performing his magic for the Orioles.**

In major league baseball's first 110 years, few players, regardless of position, were accorded accolades so generously as was Luis Ernesto Aparicio, whose 18-year major league career consisted of American League stops at Chicago, Baltimore and Boston.

Observers competed constantly for superlatives to describe the skills of the diminutive shortstop from Venezuela.

Marty Marion, "Mr. Shortstop" of the 1940s and Luis' first major league manager, readily conceded that Aparicio's talents exceeded his own. "He must be better," Marion asserted. "He covers twice as much ground as I did."

Casey Stengel, manager of the Yankees, added this tribute: "If that kid gets any better you might as well call in the second baseman and third baseman because he gobbles up everything within a mile of him."

Not long after Luis was named the American League's Rookie of the Year in 1956 for his .266 batting average and fielding brilliance with the White Sox, a 50-year observer of the major leagues added further praise.

"That kid is the greatest shortstop of all time," said Donie Bush, who had seen them all since the heyday of Honus Wagner. "What makes Aparicio so outstanding are his lightning reflexes. They're the greatest I've ever seen. He breaks fast and is so quick with his hands that his glove is right there no matter how erratic or sharp the ball may hop."

In Luis' prime it was not uncommon for fans to arrive at the park in time for fielding practice and to cheer wildly when Aparicio defied a coach's effort to drive a baseball past him.

The name of Aparicio was familiar to Venezuelans long before Luis was born. For 25 years his father reigned as the foremost shortstop in the country. He retired only when his son shoved him aside.

Reports of the teen-age wonder filtered northward in the early 1950s and touched off a heated contest for his services. The White Sox won the bidding over the Cleveland Indians when Chicago General Manager Frank Lane advised his agent in Venezuela, "Tell the owners of the team (the Venezuelan club for which Aparicio was playing winter ball) that we'll send no more players down there if we don't get Aparicio."

The strategy worked, although by 1957 Lane had cause for regret. By the time Luis had completed his two-year apprenticeship at Waterloo (Three-I League) and Memphis (Southern Association) and was making breathtaking plays for the White Sox, Lane, the newly appointed front-office chief of the Indians, was bemoaning his earlier success.

**Luis Aparicio's consistent bat and baserunning abilities sparked the Chicago White Sox for many years and he combined with second baseman Nellie Fox (left, above right) to form a potent double-play combination.**

White Sox executives realized early that they possessed an extraordinary prospect in the 5-foot-8, 155-pound Aparicio. Conversations with officials of other teams invariably contained the query: "What will you take for that kid shortstop at Memphis?"

That "kid shortstop" was an immediate sensation on the South Side of Chicago. When the Sox blossomed as the "Go-Go" team of the majors, it was Aparicio who led them on the basepaths.

When the White Sox broke the Yankees' four-year grip on the A.L. pennant in 1959, Aparicio stole 56 bases, one of nine consecutive seasons he led the league in steals. In the World Series, won by the Los Angeles Dodgers in six games, Luis batted .308 with seven singles and a double.

In 1966, when the Orioles swept the Dodgers in the Series, Aparicio fielded virtually flawlessly for Baltimore and batted .250.

As a youngster, Luis worked diligently to polish his skills as a fielder and it was not until he achieved major league stardom that he devoted hours to improving his hitting. Dividends followed almost instant-ly. From a previous high mark of .277, attained in 1960, Luis climbed to .280 in 1969 and contended for the A.L. batting title for much of the 1970 season before finishing at .313.

A year later, however, Aparicio's batting touch was gone. In one stretch with his new club, the Red Sox, Luis went hitless in 44 at-bats. When the slump ended with a single, Fenway Park fans gave Aparicio a standing ovation.

Several days later a letter, written on White House stationery, was dropped into Luis' mailbox. In it, President Richard Nixon complimented Aparicio on his gentlemanly conduct during the hitless period and expressed gratitude for the countless thrills he had provided the chief executive through the years.

The nation's fans took little note of Aparicio's batting deficiencies in '71 and voted him a starting berth in that summer's All-Star Game, one of 10 appearances Luis made in the midsummer classic.

Aparicio was 39 when he called it a career at the close of the 1973 campaign. Even at that advanced stage he was able to bat .271.

# Lou Brock

The St. Louis Cardinals were en route from Los Angeles to Houston in mid-June 1964 when General Manager Bing Devine turned to his companion in the next seat and revealed that the Cards, in search of an outfielder since the retirement of Stan Musial the previous fall, had an opportunity to acquire Lou Brock from the Chicago Cubs.

"What are we waiting for?" Manager Johnny Keane replied. On the strength of that conversation, St. Louis took a giant step toward three pennants in a five-year period and Brock took a huge stride toward the Hall of Fame.

To the untrained eye, the trade lacked headline quality. In giving up Ernie Broglio, a former 20-game winner who had notched 18 victories in 1963, and two others for Brock, a .251 hitter at that juncture of the '64 season, and a couple of others, there was little to excite hopes for the first St. Louis pennant since 1946.

How little the critics knew! Broglio won only seven more games in his major league career. Brock, at 25, proved to be an all-time bargain on baseball's flesh mart, a record basestealer, collector of 3,000 hits and a Hall of Fame selectee in his first year of eligibility.

Louis Clark Brock, a native of El Dorado, Ark., was an unheralded student at Southern University in Baton Rouge, La., in 1958 when he reported for the baseball team and almost immediately collapsed in the outfield under a hot sun.

A medical examination revealed he was suffering from a lack of salt. The youngster confessed he had not been eating regularly and was subsisting mainly by dropping into friends' homes at mealtime.

With his dietary habits corrected, Lou batted nearly .500 in his sophomore and junior seasons and then accepted a $30,000 bonus to sign with the Chicago Cubs organization in 1960.

In 1961, the 5-foot-11, 170-pound prospect played for St. Cloud (Northern League), where he won the batting championship of the Class-C league with a mark of .361 and was tops in games, hits, runs and doubles. Late in the year, he joined the Cubs and singled off Robin Roberts of the Phillies on his first trip to the plate in the big leagues. Lou made two errors in that game, though, and failed to get another hit during the late-season stint (finishing with one hit in 11 at-bats).

In two full seasons with the Cubs, Brock did little to generate public acclaim. His batting averages were below .265 and he struck out much too often. In 1963, he fanned 122 times while drawing only 31 walks.

In the field, he left much to be desired. Bleacherites

In 1965 (above), Lou Brock was a first-year Cardinal beginning the long journey to the 3,000-hit milestone, which ended with a tip of the cap in 1979.

assailed him with cries of "Brock, as in rock." A rival manager insisted that "Brock double-dribbles everything hit to him."

"I did not feel that I belonged in the major leagues," Lou remembered years later, "until one day early in 1964. A player lined a long drive to right-center field. I raced over from my position in right field and leaped against the brick wall. I didn't think I had a chance to make the catch, but when I came down the ball was in my glove. Then and there I decided I could play in the major leagues."

Installed as the regular left fielder for the Cardinals, Brock batted .348 for the balance of the 1964 season and raised his mark for the year to .315. He climaxed the season with a .300 average (9 for 30) in the World Series as the Cardinals upset the Yankees in seven games.

For the next 15 years Lou played a dominant role in the major leagues. When he stole 63 bases in 1965, it marked the first of a record 12 consecutive seasons in which he swiped 50 or more sacks.

The Cardinal star made his first All-Star Game appearance in 1967 and, although he went hitless in two at-bats in that game, he compiled a .375 batting average in five midsummer classics.

After batting .299 in 1967 and posting career highs of 21 home runs and 76 runs batted in, Brock led the Cardinals to a World Series triumph over the Red Sox

with a .414 batting average and a record seven stolen bases. One year later, in the 1968 World Series against Detroit, Lou batted .464 and again stole seven bases. His career Series batting average of .391 established a record for players with at least 20 games.

Brock was 35 years old when he attained one of his most cherished goals in 1974. His 118 stolen bases eclipsed the major league record of 104 set by Maury Wills of the Los Angeles Dodgers in 1962.

With the season stolen-base record secure—at least until it was surpassed by Oakland's Rickey Henderson eight years later—Lou set his sights on two more goals. He achieved the first in the seventh inning of a game at San Diego on August 29, 1977, when he stole his 893rd base to pass the lifetime major league mark established by Ty Cobb. (He finished his career with 938 steals.)

Brock appeared in only 92 games in 1978, however, and batted .221. Seeking to disprove a "washed-up" tag, he made a determined effort to close on a high note in 1979. At age 40, the outfielder played in 120 games, during which he became the 14th player to register 3,000 big-league hits (getting the milestone hit August 13 against Dennis Lamp of the Cubs), and he finished the season with a batting average of .304.

On that glittering performance, the onetime poor farm boy was voted The Sporting News' N.L. Comeback Player of the Year and he called it a career.

**Lou Brock raised plenty of dust and more than a few eyebrows with his baserunning success.**

# Don Drysdale

Off the field, he was the soul of congeniality, but when he toed the pitching mound, the 6-foot-6 right-hander could be as mean as the proverbial junkyard dog.

Few players could match Donald Scott Drysdale as a Jekyll-and-Hyde personality—or as a pitcher. In 14 seasons as a Dodger, he won 209 games, established a record for consecutive innings of scoreless pitching and ignited a brawl or two with an intimidating style born of competitive fire.

He was described as "having the face of a choirboy, the physique of Goliath and the competitive instincts of a tarantula."

To another, Big D had "the image of an ogre, a man who would knock his mother down on Mother's Day if there were anything at stake and a man who would kick a small dog just because it got in his way."

Walter Alston, Don's only major league manager, remarked, "I've never seen a pitcher so unafraid of batters."

Another commented, "He has a private war with anybody who stands up at the plate; he'll knock down anyone who tries to take advantage of him."

Two such batters were Johnny Logan of the Braves and Frank Robinson of the Reds. Their direct action against Big D triggered bench-clearing brawls.

To Roy Campanella, his catcher at the start of his big-league career, Drysdale was "sweet and mean—a sweet pitcher and a mean competitor."

Drysdale, who did not pitch until his senior year at Van Nuys, Calif., High School and then won nine of 10 decisions, acquired his master's degree in mound methodology from Sal (The Barber) Maglie, who believed that a close shave for a batter was a good thing . . . for a pitcher.

The son of a repairman for a West Coast telephone company, Drysdale signed with the Dodgers' Bakersfield (California League) farm club fresh out of high school. A second season at Montreal (International) completed his apprenticeship. At age 19, Drysdale became a Brooklyn Dodger.

Don was an apt pupil for Maglie, the veteran pitcher who joined the Dodgers a month into Drysdale's rookie season of 1956. Firing a 95-mile-an-hour fastball and a wide-sweeping curve, both with a sidearm motion, Big D set batters back on their heels muttering darkly to themselves.

Drysdale made his first major league start on April 23, 1956, against the Phillies and struck out the side in the first inning. Don won his debut, 6-1.

Drysdale won four more games in 1956 and appeared in one World Series game that fall against the

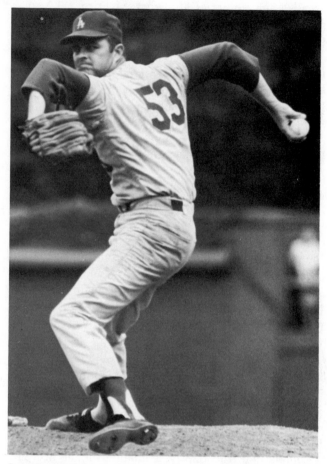

Don Drysdale's powerful right arm and ruthless determination spelled trouble for opposing batters.

Yankees. He blossomed as a regular starter the next year and contributed 17 victories to the Dodgers' third-place finish.

As Drysdale matured as a pitcher, his temper tantrums showed "development" as well. No segment of the baseball community escaped his rage, not even himself. Once, yanked from a game in which he blew a 5-0 first-inning lead, he took on a bat bag, loaded with bats, and lost the kicking match.

Once, when an umpire reported to league headquarters that Don intentionally hit a batter with a pitch, for which he drew a $50 fine, Drysdale bristled. "What am I supposed to do," he stormed, "throw everything down the pike and let 'em hit it out? I can't change my style if it costs me $5,000 in fines."

Headlines clearly reflected Don's behavioral patterns. "Angry Drysdale Blasts Coaches," reported one. "Hot Drysdale Roars 'Trade Me,'" said another. Others were: "Drysdale Vows to Sue N.L. If Fined" and "Drysdale Blows Up Over Fans' Dumb Questions."

But there were other headlines, too, attesting to his greatness as an athlete, such as when he won the Cy

Young Award in 1962 with a 25-9 record, or when he tied a National League season mark for home runs by a pitcher by hitting seven (Drysdale performed that feat twice), or when he established a major league record by hurling 58 consecutive scoreless innings.

That shutout-innings streak started on May 14, 1968, when Drysdale defeated the Cubs, 1-0. In quick succession, he then blanked the Astros, 1-0; the Cardinals, 2-0; the Astros, 5-0; the Giants, 3-0, and the Pirates, 5-0.

With 54 straight scoreless innings to his credit, Drysdale faced the Phillies on June 8, needing only two more shutout innings to break the record of 55⅔ straight scoreless innings set by Walter Johnson of Washington in 1913. Big D went out and blanked Philadelphia through four innings before singles by Tony

Taylor and Clay Dalrymple and a sacrifice fly by Howie Bedell snapped the string in the fifth.

Drysdale won only 14 games that season, however, and posted a 5-4 record in 1969 before calling it a career. A chronic shoulder ailment forced him into retirement at age 33.

Before the '69 season closed, the Dodgers and more than 30,000 fans tendered the big warrior a formal farewell. Gifts of all descriptions were showered on the author of 49 career shutouts and three World Series victories. Among the tributes was a wire from California Gov. Ronald Reagan that read:

" 'Big D' once meant Dallas. Now it's you alone. In a day when young people are looking for heroes and too often finding the wrong kind, you are the epitome of the value of athletics."

**Dodger righthander Don Drysdale was mobbed by teammates after completing his fifth consecutive shut-** out in 1968 en route to his major league-record streak of 58 straight scoreless innings.

# Rick Ferrell

Some of the most significant facts about a player's career are not always contained in statistical summaries, but rather in yellowing magazines and newspapers. Such was true in the 18-year American League career of Richard Benjamin Ferrell, a catcher of distinction with the St. Louis Browns, Boston Red Sox and Washington Senators.

Before attaining major league stardom, Rick Ferrell won 17 of 18 professional fights and claimed the championship of North Carolina in the lightweight division.

Before he entered the majors, he was declared a free agent and accepted a bonus of $25,000 to sign with the St. Louis Browns.

As a major league star, Rick formed a battery with his younger brother, Wesley, with Boston and Washington and, late in his career, was handed the unenviable task of catching the deliveries of four knuckleball pitchers on the same club, the Washington Senators.

The fact that he was charged with 21 passed balls in one season failed to dim Ferrell's reputation as a premier catcher.

One of seven brothers born to a North Carolina farmer, Rick Ferrell became a catcher by necessity. "When several brothers decide to become pitchers," he explained, "somebody has to catch 'em, and I took the job."

Rick was a student at Guilford College in North Carolina when he accepted $1,500 to play for the Detroit organization in 1926. Later, he was ordered to join the parent club in training at San Antonio, and a telegram was sent to Tigers Manager George Moriarty to give the recruit a thorough trial.

Moriarty took one glance at the youngster, without a bat in his hands, and announced, "One look at him and you know he'll never hit a lick."

Ferrell was assigned to Columbus of the American Association for whom, in 1928, he batted .333 and attracted major league scouts in profusion. Fancy offers were made for the 21-year-old prospect.

Enter Commissioner Kenesaw Mountain Landis. The Tigers, it developed, had loaned Ferrell to Columbus on a "gentleman's agreement," whereby he would revert to Detroit at season's end. When word reached Tiger officials that Columbus was about to ignore their verbal pact, the Tigers notified Landis, who declared Rick a free agent. Moments after the announcement, Ferrell signed with the St. Louis Browns for $25,000.

It was as a Brownie that Ferrell enjoyed his most memorable days. After batting .306 for St. Louis in 1931, Rick hit a career-high .315 for the Browns in

**Rick Ferrell's outstanding catching ability was his ticket to baseball's Hall of Fame.**

1932.

In 1933, when the first All-Star Game was staged in Chicago, Rick was named to the American League squad and looked forward to a leisurely afternoon with Bill Dickey doing the catching. To his surprise, Ferrell, traded from the Browns to the Red Sox two months earlier, was named the starting catcher. He played the entire nine innings, handling the deliveries of Lefty Gomez, Lefty Grove and Alvin Crowder as the A.L. won, 4-2.

In sharp contrast to his tempestuous brother Wes, Rick was of a placid nature. Little disturbed him, and when he batted against his brother, who was winning 20 games regularly for Cleveland, he bore down a little harder.

On April 29, 1931, Wes was working on a no-hitter for the Indians against St. Louis when Rick cracked a sharp grounder to the left side. The shortstop's throw pulled the first baseman off the bag and the official scorer ruled an error. Wes got his no-hitter, but years later he conceded, "I still think it was a hit."

When Rick completed his major league career with a lifetime batting average of .281, he had caught an American League-record 1,806 games.

# Harmon Killebrew

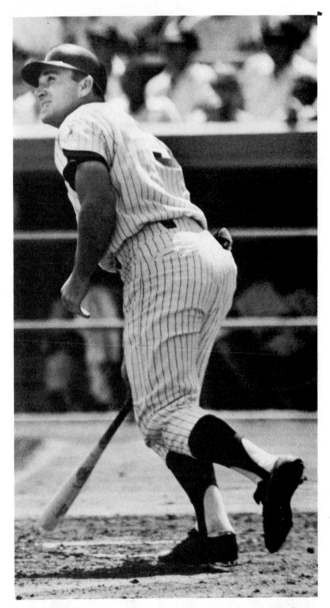

As youth gave way to experience, Harmon Killebrew developed into one of the top power hitters in history.

Ossie Bluege would have bet, willingly and eagerly, that he had seen all that there was to see when he received an order to scout a young slugger in Payette, Idaho, in the spring of 1954.

The farm director of the Washington Senators, a former major league player and manager, was directed by his boss, Clark Griffith, to check on the phenom in the same state where, in 1907, an earlier Washington scout had found a fireballing righthanded pitcher named Walter Johnson. Perhaps the Senators could uncover another gold mine.

Bluege was ill prepared for what he saw. In an Idaho-Oregon Border League semipro game, Harmon Clayton Killebrew clouted a 435-foot home run. Check-

ing out the 17-year-old slugger, Bluege learned that he was batting .847 and that he had collected 12 hits— four home runs, three triples and five singles—in as many at-bats.

Bluege was flabbergasted. He wired Griffith that "the sky's the limit," and the club owner, for the first time in his career, offered a bonus contract to a prospect.

Before Killebrew accepted, however, there was a matter of honor to be taken care of. Days earlier he had played golf with Earl Johnson and promised the Boston Red Sox scout that he would not sign with a major league club without giving Johnson a chance to match the proposal.

Washington's three-year offer was in the form of a $30,000 package, an annual salary of $6,000, the major league minimum, and a yearly bonus of $4,000. Johnson refused to match the offer and Griffith obtained one of baseball's greatest bargains.

Soft-spoken Harmon became an instant curiosity in the nation's capital. Baseball folks were unaccustomed to seeing muscular machines at Griffith Stadium but, reported the teen-ager, bulging biceps ran in the family. The former all-state high school quarterback explained that his father had been a collegiate fullback and his paternal grandfather, a Civil War veteran, was reputed to be the strongest man in the Union Army.

To improve on his inherited muscles, Harmon added, he had, in his younger years, wrestled 10-gallon milk pails—full of milk. "That," he said, "will put muscles on you even if you don't try."

Killebrew was not an instant success as a major leaguer. In his early years in the pro ranks, he tried to learn discipline as a batter and to throw like a third baseman rather than like a passing quarterback.

"It took me five years to catch up with major league pitching," he noted. Those years were split between Washington, Charlotte, N.C., Indianapolis and Chattanooga. But when he did catch up, pitchers paid an enormous price.

On opening day of the 1959 season, his first year as a Senators regular, Harmon walloped a homer against Baltimore and later, during a 17-game stretch, he enjoyed five two-homer games. On the final day of the season, he clouted his 42nd homer to tie Cleveland's Rocky Colavito for the league title.

After two seasons as a Washington idol, Killebrew accompanied the Senators franchise to the Minneapolis-St. Paul area, where it was renamed the Minnesota Twins.

Harmon made the transition smoothly and homers continued to fly to distant spots. The clouts were not of the line-drive variety, but high, majestic pokes that invited measurement by public-relations people.

Killebrew won four A.L. home run titles outright, shared two crowns and hit 40 or more homers in a season eight times (reaching 49 twice, in 1964 and 1969). He appeared in 11 All-Star Games, including the 1968 contest at Houston in which, stretching for a throw, he suffered a leg injury and was limited to 100 games that year.

Killebrew was named the American League's Most Valuable Player in 1969, when he also won the first of two consecutive designations by The Sporting News as the A.L. Player of the Year.

**The punch of Bob Allison (left) and Harmon Killebrew kept Minnesota fans happy through the 1960s.**

Along the way Harmon also tied a major league record by hitting two or more homers in each A.L. park in one season (1962), equaled a league mark for most homers in a doubleheader (four) and established a league record for most lifetime homers by a righthanded batter (573).

After hitting only 13 homers in 1974, the 38-year-old slugger was released by the Twins and signed to play with the Kansas City Royals for $125,000, exceeding his top Minnesota salary by $15,000.

Appearing in 106 games (mostly as a designated hitter), Harmon belted 14 homers in 1975 and then retired. "The artificial turf took it out of my legs," he explained, "and I wanted no more of it."

Killebrew intended to enter the cattle business in the Northwest, but plans did not work out. He attended classes to obtain a securities license, and when he achieved that goal, Killebrew and several partners organized an insurance-securities company in Boise, Idaho, approximately 50 miles from his home in Ontario, Ore. Harmon also entered the broadcasting field.

As he carved out new careers, Killebrew could not help but wonder what his home run total would have been had he accepted less money to play for the Red Sox in 1954. Playing half of his games in Fenway Park, with its inviting left-field wall for righthanded hitters, could have swelled his homer total immeasurably.

"When I made my first trip to Boston," he recalled, "and walked out on the field, the wall seemed so close that I could touch it."

# Pee Wee Reese

From 1947 through 1956, when the Brooklyn Dodgers won six National League pennants and were in the thick of every flag race, nobody contributed more handsomely or more consistently than the shortstop known as the Little Colonel.

He was christened Harold Henry Reese, but since the age of 12 he had been known as Pee Wee, a tribute to marble-shooting skills that carried him to the finals of the Louisville championship tournament.

Reese was captain of the Dodgers. During Pee Wee's 15 seasons with Brooklyn (he also played one season for the Los Angeles Dodgers), the Dodgers won seven pennants, finished second six times and wound up in third place twice. The Little Colonel was the solid performer, the one who made the dazzling plays to choke off rallies and delivered the clutch hits to ignite Brooklyn rallies. It was Reese to whom teammates looked for counsel and advice on and off the field, the one who cooled inflamed tempers in a turbulent clubhouse.

With it all, Pee Wee was a reluctant Dodger. He had graduated from the same church league team that sent Billy Herman into professional baseball. In two seasons with his hometown Louisville team of the American Association, Reese batted in the high .270s and in his second year stole 35 bases.

In the late 1930s the Colonels were owned by the Boston Red Sox and it was assumed that Reese would succeed an aging Joe Cronin as shortstop for the American League club. Reese himself counted on the move.

But Cronin, it developed, was not quite ready to abdicate and Reese was placed on the market. When that bit of intelligence reached Brooklyn, Larry MacPhail, major-domo of the Dodgers, dispatched scout Ted McGrew to check out Reese. McGrew's report sounded too lavish for MacPhail, who ordered Andy High on a similar mission.

When High was equally as extravagant in his praise, MacPhail decided to take a look himself and his evaluation surpassed the other two. The Dodgers acquired Reese for approximately $75,000 in players and cash.

Reese was in Kansas City, preparing to play in the 1939 American Association All-Star Game, when the announcement was made. He was crestfallen. For years he had heard about the Brooklyn Daffiness Boys under Wilbert Robinson—and he wanted no part of such an organization. When Pee Wee studied the situation, however—and received $3,750 as his share of the sale price—his attitude softened. In time, he admitted that the deal "was the break of my life."

When Jackie Robinson broke the modern major

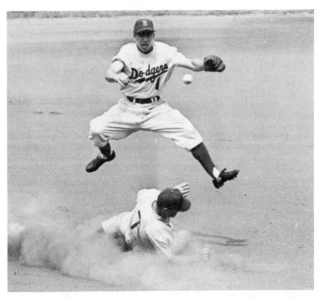

**Pee Wee Reese sparked the Dodgers to seven pennants and six second-place finishes in his Hall of Fame career.**

league color line in 1947, Kentuckian Reese rallied to the defense of his teammate. During an exhibition game in Fort Worth where raucous, racist spectators belabored Jackie, Reese strolled to Robinson's side, draped an arm encouragingly over his shoulders and spoke a few soothing words. The harassment subsided.

A similar situation developed in Boston during the early part of the '47 season. Reese repeated his earlier actions and once more the air was cleared.

Jackie never forgot Pee Wee's kindnesses.

"I could talk about that fellow for an hour, or a day or a year," Robinson said years later. "Everybody respects and follows that fellow. In my book, there's none finer."

Reese batted .300 only once, reaching .309 in 1954. His most productive RBI season was 1951 when he drove in 84 runs, and his best power season was 1949 when he smacked 16 home runs.

Always a threat on the bases, Reese led the National League with 30 stolen bases in 1952.

Reese appeared in seven World Series, during which he batted a composite .272 and helped Brooklyn to its only Series championship in 1955. He accompanied the Dodgers to Los Angeles when the storied franchise relocated there after the 1957 season.

After concluding his playing career in 1958 with a lifetime batting mark of .269, Pee Wee served as a Dodgers coach in 1959 and then retired from baseball, declining all offers of a managerial position. At the time of his election to the Hall of Fame in 1984, the Little Colonel was a representative of the Hillerich & Bradsby Co., manufacturer of Louisville Slugger bats.

# Enos Slaughter

In the summer of 1959, a national magazine published a feature article that bore the heading "Last of the Old Pros." A subhead read: "For half of his 42 years, the old Warhorse has been ripping the game apart with his hustling, hell-for-leather brand of ball. If he ever runs out of gas, there won't be any more like him."

Enos Slaughter started running early. He remembered clearly the exact time and place and repeated the story frequently as an example of the benefits to be derived from his full-scale approach to the game.

Slaughter was in his second season of professional ball in 1936 and playing for Columbus, Ga., of the South Atlantic League when he started his program of constant running. Discouraged by what he considered his own inferior play, Enos walked from his outfield position toward the dugout at the close of an inning. As he crossed the foul line, he was greeted by his manager, Eddie Dyer, who barked: "Are you tired, kid? If so, I'll get some help for you."

The 20-year-old North Carolinian was stung by the remark. "I suddenly realized," he remembered afterward, "people don't care how sorry I felt for myself. That's when I started running."

The next season, with Columbus, O., of the American Association, the newly energized outfielder won a batting championship with a mark of .382 and gained a new nickname, "Country," which was tacked on by his manager, Burt Shotton.

The hard-driving 22-year-old joined the St. Louis Cardinals in 1938 and batted a creditable .276. But he really blossomed in 1939 when, playing with the reckless abandon of the old Gas House Gang, he batted .320, drove in 86 runs and led National League outfielders in putouts and assists.

The fact that Slaughter was able to play at all in '39 was remarkable. Hunting with his father on New Year's Day, Enos handled infected rabbits and contracted tularemia, a fever that killed his father three days later.

When spring-training time arrived, Slaughter still was suffering from chills and lightheadedness. Against the pleadings of his mother and advice of his doctor, however, he reported to the Florida camp. His manager, Ray Blades, never learned of the handicap under which the young sophomore performed.

Playing hurt was a trademark for Enos. In 1941, in an effort to avoid a collision with center fielder Terry Moore, Slaughter dived into a concrete wall and suffered a fractured collarbone. He returned to action before the injury healed and when he swung at a pitch and missed, the skin tore and blood spurted forth.

**Enos Slaughter literally hustled his way into the hearts of fans throughout the baseball world.**

The following season, Slaughter led the league with 188 hits and 17 triples before contracting the flu preceding the World Series. Hours in the steam room enabled him to shake the disease, but Slaughter remained weak at the start of the Series against the New York Yankees. It made little difference. The stocky right fielder scintillated on defense and delivered key hits as the Birds upset the favored Yankees.

After a three-year stint in military service during World War II, Slaughter returned to the Cardinals in 1946. He rapped 18 homers and led the majors with 130 runs batted in (establishing personal big-league highs in those departments) and sparked the Birds into the World Series against Boston. In the fifth game, a St. Louis defeat, Slaughter was hit on the right elbow. The pain brought tears to the eyes of the old Warhorse who, apparently for the only time in his career, asked to be removed from a game.

Heat packs were applied during the ensuing 24-hour train ride from Boston to St. Louis, but the Cardinals' team physician expressed doubt that Slaughter would be ready for the sixth game. A blood clot had formed. If it burst, dire consequences were predicted.

But Enos played. Swinging the bat with one hand and playing in pain, he executed a difficult catch in the sixth game. In Game 7, after belting an eighth-inning single, Slaughter raced home from first base on Harry Walker's hit to left-center field. The daring baserunning caught the Red Sox by surprise and gave the Cards a Series-clinching 4-3 victory.

Slaughter was 38 when, in April 1954, he was traded to the Yankees in a deal that sent promising minor league outfielder Bill Virdon, among others, to St. Louis. Enos remained in the major leagues for six more seasons and appeared in the 1956, 1957 and 1958 World Series with the Yankees.

# Arky Vaughan

In the 1941 All-Star Game at Detroit, Arky Vaughan cracked two-run homers in the seventh and eighth innings, and when the National League carried a 5-3 lead into the last half of the ninth inning, few in the crowd of 54,000-plus would have doubted that the Pittsburgh shortstop would be the hero of the contest.

But a four-run American League rally, capped by Ted Williams' dramatic three-run homer, sent the senior circuit to a 7-5 defeat and left Vaughan's achievement all but forgotten.

The incident typified the career of Joseph Floyd Vaughan, a superlative performer who labored for many years away from the spotlight. His .318 lifetime batting average, speed and excellent arm were frequently overlooked in favor of less-talented athletes. Vaughan engaged in no colorful antics and uttered no spicy comments, letting his natural talents speak for themselves.

Arky, so named by a California playmate when he learned that Vaughan was born in Arkansas, might have become a Yankee great if it had been possible for a New York scout to be in two places at once. Arky was a young shortstop for a semipro team in Fullerton, Calif., and had started to attract notice when Bill Essick, a Yankee scout, drew up his schedule for a Sunday near the holiday season. Essick had a choice. He could check out either Vaughan in Fullerton or a young catcher in Long Beach. He chose the latter course. Eventually, he signed the backstop, Willard Hershberger, who went on to play for the Cincinnati Reds until his death by suicide in 1940.

When Essick checked on Vaughan at a later date, he learned that the shortstop had been signed by Art Griggs, president and manager of the Wichita club of the Western League.

One season of schooling was all Arky required for advancement to the majors. A .338 batting average, 21 homers and 81 runs batted in convinced the Pirates that he was ready, and they never had cause to reconsider their decision.

In 10 seasons with Pittsburgh, Vaughan never batted below .300 and attained his high-water mark of .385 in 1935 when he won the National League batting championship and was named the league's Most Valuable Player by The Sporting News. He drove in more than 90 runs four times, topped by 99 in 1935. He also tied an N.L. record by leading the league in bases on balls for three consecutive years, 1934 through 1936.

After a decade with the Pirates, Vaughan was traded to Brooklyn, where he spent two seasons before going into voluntary retirement. World War II was in

Arky Vaughan's potent bat and quick hands helped solidify Pittsburgh's infields in the 1930s.

progress and, with a younger brother in the military service, Arky's full-time attention was demanded on his 2,000-acre ranch in Potter Valley, Calif.

In 1947, after selling all but 400 acres of his spread, Vaughan felt baseball's siren song again. He was only 35 and had remained trim by maintaining the rugged outdoor life style he had favored since childhood. He was a part-time third baseman and outfielder in 1947 and '48 for the Dodgers, batting .325 and .244 before drawing his release. One season with San Francisco (Pacific Coast League) completed his career.

In retirement, Arky loved to spend hours fishing near Eagleville, Calif., on Lost Lake, a deep body of water in the crater of an extinct volcano. On August 30, 1952, after promising his wife he would return in time to accompany her and three of their children on a drive to a neighboring town, Arky set out on another fishing expedition, his last. When a companion made a vigorous cast, their boat capsized. Vaughan was an excellent swimmer, but both anglers disappeared about 65 feet from shore. The 40-year-old former player was believed to have suffered a heart attack while trying to rescue his friend. Both men drowned.

# Hoyt Wilhelm

Progress in professional baseball could be painfully slow in the years immediately following World War II. For instance, a young pitcher who had participated in the Battle of the Bulge not too many months earlier compiled a 21-8 record for Mooresville in 1946 and found himself in the same Class D North Carolina State League in 1947.

A 20-7 record in that second season caught the fancy of a rival manager, who recommended the pitcher to the New York Giants. For a modest $2,000, the National League team acquired future Hall of Famer James Hoyt Wilhelm.

Wilhelm, born July 26, 1923, at Huntersville, N.C., first learned of the freak pitch in 1939 when broadcasts of Washington Senators games into North Carolina reported Dutch Leonard's success with the butterfly pitch. When a local newspaper published an illustrated article on the mechanics of throwing a knuckler, teen-ager Hoyt studied diagrams closely and developed the pitch to a high degree of efficiency.

By 1950 Wilhelm had advanced to Minneapolis of the Triple-A American Association. Hoyt won 15 games for the Millers in '50 and posted 11 victories in '51, earning an invitation to the Giants' spring-training camp in 1952.

At Phoenix, New York Manager Leo Durocher was smitten by Wilhelm's dancing pitches, particularly after Coach Fred Fitzsimmons, an old knuckleballer himself, suggested that Hoyt abandon his sidearm style and throw with a three-quarter motion in order to improve his control.

Wilhelm was three months from his 29th birthday when he made his major league debut on April 18, 1952, hurling one-third of an inning against Brooklyn. But the game he savored most in his freshman campaign took place on April 23. Relieving in the third inning, Wilhelm hurled 5⅓ innings to gain credit for a 9-5 triumph over Boston. Moreover, on his first trip to the plate as a major leaguer, Hoyt joined an exclusive society by clouting a home run. It not only was his first homer in the majors, but also his last.

Wilhelm won 15 games and lost three as a rookie. His winning percentage (.833), earned-run average (2.43) and total appearances (71) led the N.L.

Although he frequently expressed a desire to become a starting pitcher, Hoyt remained a fireman exclusively in five seasons with the Giants (1952 through 1956) and one season with the Cardinals (1957, a year in which he was sold to Cleveland in the final 10 days of the season). But in 1958, after 363 relief appearances, he was given a starting nod by Indians Manager Bobby Bragan.

**Hoyt Wilhelm knuckled down and brought relief to numerous major league bullpens.**

Traded to Baltimore in late August of '58, Hoyt started four times for the Orioles and turned one of those assignments into a singular event in his 21-year career. On September 20, he authored his only no-hit game. Making only 99 pitches, 87 of them knuckleballs, Hoyt defeated the Yankees, 1-0.

Wilhelm enjoyed his most active season as a starter in 1959 when he opened 27 games. He reeled off nine straight wins at the start of the season and did not taste defeat until June 15. Although his ERA (2.19) was the lowest in the American League, Wilhelm won only six games after his streak was snapped and finished 15-11 for the sixth-place Orioles.

Hoyt made his final major league start as a member of the White Sox in 1963. The next season, he trudged out of the Chicago bullpen 73 times, his personal high, and compiled an ERA of 1.99. It was one of six times that Hoyt bettered the 2.00 mark as a fireman.

After stints with the Angels, Braves, Cubs and Dodgers, Wilhelm's long, winding trail came to a close on July 21, 1972, when he was released by Los Angeles. That was five days before his 49th birthday.

When the curtain fell, the talented Tar Heel owned lifetime big-league records for relief victories (124), games finished (651), games as a reliever (1,018), most innings in relief (1,870) and most games pitched overall (1,070).

Although saves were not part of the official statistics during most of Wilhelm's career, researchers have determined that he preserved leads 227 times.

His election in 1985 gave Wilhelm the distinction of being the first relief specialist, and the first knuckleballer, to be enshrined at Cooperstown.

# Career Records of Hall of Fame Additions

*Denotes led League. ●Denotes tied for league lead.

## LUIS ERNESTO APARICIO

| Year | Club | League | G. | AB. | R. | H. | HR. | RBI. | B.A. |
|---|---|---|---|---|---|---|---|---|---|
| 1954—Waterloo | I.I.I. | 94 | 390 | 85 | 110 | 4 | 47 | .282 |
| 1955—Memphis | South. | 150 | 564 | 92 | 154 | 6 | 51 | .273 |
| 1956—Chicago | Amer. | 152 | 533 | 69 | 142 | 3 | 56 | .266 |
| 1957—Chicago | Amer. | 143 | 575 | 82 | 148 | 3 | 41 | .257 |
| 1958—Chicago | Amer. | 145 | 557 | 76 | 148 | 2 | 40 | .266 |
| 1959—Chicago | Amer. | 152 | 612 | 98 | 157 | 6 | 51 | .257 |
| 1960—Chicago | Amer. | 153 | 600 | 86 | 166 | 2 | 61 | .277 |
| 1961—Chicago | Amer. | 156 | 625 | 90 | 170 | 6 | 45 | .272 |
| 1962—Chicago | Amer. | 153 | 581 | 72 | 140 | 7 | 40 | .241 |
| 1963—Baltimore | Amer. | 146 | 601 | 73 | 150 | 5 | 45 | .250 |
| 1964—Baltimore | Amer. | 146 | 578 | 93 | 154 | 10 | 37 | .266 |
| 1965—Baltimore | Amer. | 144 | 564 | 67 | 127 | 8 | 40 | .225 |
| 1966—Baltimore | Amer. | 151 | *659 | 97 | 182 | 6 | 41 | .276 |
| 1967—Baltimore | Amer. | 134 | 546 | 55 | 127 | 4 | 31 | .233 |
| 1968—Chicago | Amer. | 155 | 622 | 55 | 164 | 4 | 36 | .264 |
| 1969—Chicago | Amer. | 156 | 599 | 77 | 168 | 5 | 51 | .280 |
| 1970—Chicago | Amer. | 146 | 552 | 86 | 173 | 5 | 43 | .313 |
| 1971—Boston | Amer. | 125 | 491 | 56 | 114 | 4 | 45 | .232 |
| 1972—Boston | Amer. | 110 | 436 | 47 | 112 | 3 | 39 | .257 |
| 1973—Boston | Amer. | 132 | 499 | 56 | 135 | 0 | 49 | .271 |
| Major League Totals | | 2599 | 10230 | 1335 | 2677 | 83 | 791 | .262 |

### WORLD SERIES RECORD

| Year | Club | League | G. | AB. | R. | H. | HR. | RBI. | B.A. |
|---|---|---|---|---|---|---|---|---|---|
| 1959—Chicago | Amer. | 6 | 26 | 1 | 8 | 0 | 0 | .308 |
| 1966—Baltimore | Amer. | 4 | 16 | 0 | 4 | 0 | 2 | .250 |
| World Series Totals | | 10 | 42 | 1 | 12 | 0 | 2 | .286 |

## LOUIS CLARK BROCK

| Year | Club | League | G. | AB. | R. | H. | HR. | RBI. | B.A. |
|---|---|---|---|---|---|---|---|---|---|
| 1961—St. Cloud | Northern | ●128 | 501 | *117 | *181 | 14 | 82 | *.361 |
| 1961—Chicago | National | 4 | 11 | 1 | 1 | 0 | 0 | .091 |
| 1962—Chicago | National | 123 | 434 | 73 | 114 | 9 | 35 | .263 |
| 1963—Chicago | National | 148 | 547 | 79 | 141 | 9 | 37 | .258 |
| 1964—Chi.-St. Louis | National | 155 | 634 | 111 | 200 | 14 | 58 | .315 |
| 1965—St. Louis | National | 155 | 631 | 107 | 182 | 16 | 69 | .288 |
| 1966—St. Louis | National | 156 | 643 | 94 | 183 | 15 | 46 | .285 |
| 1967—St. Louis | National | 159 | *689 | ●113 | 206 | 21 | 76 | .299 |
| 1968—St. Louis | National | 159 | 660 | 92 | 184 | 6 | 51 | .279 |
| 1969—St. Louis | National | 157 | 655 | 97 | 195 | 12 | 47 | .298 |
| 1970—St. Louis | National | 155 | 664 | 114 | 202 | 13 | 57 | .304 |
| 1971—St. Louis | National | 157 | 640 | *126 | 200 | 7 | 61 | .313 |
| 1972—St. Louis | National | 153 | 621 | 81 | 193 | 3 | 42 | .311 |
| 1973—St. Louis | National | 160 | 650 | 110 | 193 | 7 | 63 | .297 |
| 1974—St. Louis | National | 153 | 635 | 105 | 194 | 3 | 48 | .306 |
| 1975—St. Louis | National | 136 | 528 | 78 | 163 | 3 | 47 | .309 |
| 1976—St. Louis | National | 133 | 498 | 73 | 150 | 4 | 67 | .301 |
| 1977—St. Louis | National | 141 | 489 | 69 | 133 | 2 | 46 | .272 |
| 1978—St. Louis | National | 92 | 298 | 31 | 66 | 0 | 12 | .221 |
| 1979—St. Louis | National | 120 | 405 | 56 | 123 | 5 | 38 | .304 |
| Major League Totals | | 2616 | 10332 | 1610 | 3023 | 149 | 900 | .293 |

### WORLD SERIES RECORD

| Year | Club | League | G. | AB. | R. | H. | HR. | RBI. | B.A. |
|---|---|---|---|---|---|---|---|---|---|
| 1964—St. Louis | National | 7 | 30 | 2 | 9 | 1 | 5 | .300 |
| 1967—St. Louis | National | 7 | 29 | 8 | 12 | 1 | 3 | .414 |
| 1968—St. Louis | National | 7 | 28 | 6 | 13 | 2 | 5 | .464 |
| World Series Totals | | 21 | 87 | 16 | 34 | 4 | 13 | .391 |

## DONALD SCOTT (BIG D) DRYSDALE

| Year | Club | League | G. | IP. | W. | L. | Pct. | ERA. |
|---|---|---|---|---|---|---|---|---|
| 1954—Bakersfield | Calif. | 15 | 112 | 8 | 5 | .615 | 3.45 |
| 1955—Montreal | Int. | 28 | 173 | 11 | 11 | .500 | 3.33 |
| 1956—Brooklyn | Nat. | 25 | 99 | 5 | 5 | .500 | 2.64 |
| 1957—Brooklyn | Nat. | 34 | 221 | 17 | 9 | .654 | 2.69 |
| 1958—Los Angeles | Nat. | 44 | 212 | 12 | 13 | .480 | 4.16 |
| 1959—Los Angeles | Nat. | 44 | 271 | 17 | 13 | .567 | 3.45 |
| 1960—Los Angeles | Nat. | 41 | 269 | 15 | 14 | .517 | 2.84 |
| 1961—Los Angeles | Nat. | 40 | 244 | 13 | 10 | .565 | 3.69 |
| 1962—Los Angeles | Nat. | 43 | *314 | *25 | 9 | .735 | 2.84 |
| 1963—Los Angeles | Nat. | 42 | 315 | 19 | 17 | .528 | 2.63 |
| 1964—Los Angeles | Nat. | 40 | *321 | 18 | 16 | .529 | 2.19 |
| 1965—Los Angeles | Nat. | 44 | 308 | 23 | 12 | .657 | 2.78 |
| 1966—Los Angeles | Nat. | 40 | 274 | 13 | 16 | .448 | 3.42 |
| 1967—Los Angeles | Nat. | 38 | 282 | 13 | 16 | .448 | 2.74 |
| 1968—Los Angeles | Nat. | 31 | 239 | 14 | 12 | .538 | 2.15 |
| 1969—Los Angeles | Nat. | 12 | 63 | 5 | 4 | .556 | 4.43 |
| Major League Totals | | 518 | 3432 | 209 | 166 | .557 | 2.95 |

### WORLD SERIES RECORD

| Year | Club | League | G. | IP. | W. | L. | Pct. | ERA. |
|---|---|---|---|---|---|---|---|---|
| 1956—Brooklyn | Nat. | 1 | 2 | 0 | 0 | .000 | 9.00 |
| 1959—Los Angeles | Nat. | 1 | 7 | 1 | 0 | 1.000 | 1.29 |
| 1963—Los Angeles | Nat. | 1 | 9 | 1 | 0 | 1.000 | 0.00 |
| 1965—Los Angeles | Nat. | 2 | 11⅔ | 1 | 1 | .500 | 3.86 |
| 1966—Los Angeles | Nat. | 2 | 10 | 0 | 2 | .000 | 4.50 |
| World Series Totals | | 7 | 39⅔ | 3 | 3 | .500 | 2.95 |

## RICK FERRELL

| Year | Club | League | G. | AB. | R. | H. | HR. | RBI. | B.A. |
|---|---|---|---|---|---|---|---|---|---|
| 1926—Kinston | Virginia | 64 | 192 | 24 | 51 | 2 | 20 | .266 |
| 1926—Columbus | A. A. | 5 | 14 | 2 | 4 | 0 | | .286 |
| 1927—Columbus† | A. A. | 104 | 345 | 42 | 86 | 2 | 44 | .249 |
| 1928—Columbus† | A. A. | 126 | 339 | 51 | 113 | 2 | 65 | .333 |
| 1929—St. Louis | Amer. | 64 | 144 | 21 | 33 | 0 | 20 | .229 |
| 1930—St. Louis | Amer. | 101 | 314 | 43 | 84 | 1 | 41 | .268 |
| 1931—St. Louis | Amer. | 117 | 386 | 47 | 118 | 3 | 57 | .306 |
| 1932—St. Louis | Amer. | 126 | 438 | 67 | 138 | 2 | 65 | .315 |
| 1933—St. L.‡-Boston | Amer. | 140 | 493 | 58 | 143 | 4 | 77 | .290 |
| 1934—Boston | Amer. | 132 | 437 | 50 | 130 | 1 | 48 | .297 |
| 1935—Boston | Amer. | 133 | 458 | 54 | 138 | 3 | 61 | .301 |
| 1936—Boston | Amer. | 121 | 410 | 59 | 128 | 8 | 55 | .312 |
| 1937—Boston§-Wash. | Amer. | 104 | 344 | 39 | 84 | 2 | 36 | .244 |
| 1938—Washington | Amer. | 135 | 411 | 55 | 120 | 1 | 58 | .292 |
| 1939—Washington | Amer. | 87 | 274 | 32 | 77 | 0 | 31 | .281 |
| 1940—Washington | Amer. | 103 | 326 | 35 | 89 | 0 | 28 | .273 |
| 1941—Wash'ton x-St.L. | Amer. | 121 | 387 | 38 | 99 | 2 | 36 | .256 |
| 1942—St. Louis | Amer. | 99 | 273 | 20 | 61 | 0 | 26 | .223 |
| 1943—St. Louis y | Amer. | 74 | 209 | 12 | 50 | 0 | 20 | .239 |
| 1944—Washington | Amer. | 99 | 339 | 14 | 94 | 0 | 25 | .277 |
| 1945—Washington | Amer. | 91 | 286 | 33 | 76 | 1 | 38 | .266 |
| 1947—Washington | Amer. | 37 | 99 | 10 | 30 | 0 | 12 | .303 |
| Major League Totals | | 1884 | 6028 | 687 | 1692 | 28 | 734 | .281 |

## HARMON CLAYTON (KILLER) KILLEBREW, JR.

| Year | Club | League | G. | AB. | R. | H. | HR. | RBI. | B.A. |
|---|---|---|---|---|---|---|---|---|---|
| 1954—Washington | Amer. | 9 | 13 | 1 | 4 | 0 | 3 | .308 |
| 1955—Washington | Amer. | 38 | 80 | 12 | 16 | 4 | 7 | .200 |
| 1956—Washington | Amer. | 44 | 99 | 10 | 22 | 5 | 13 | .222 |
| 1956—Charlotte | Sally | 70 | 249 | 61 | 81 | 15 | 63 | .325 |
| 1957—Chattanooga | South. | 142 | 519 | 90 | 145 | *29 | 101 | .279 |
| 1957—Washington | Amer. | 9 | 31 | 4 | 9 | 2 | 5 | .290 |
| 1958—Washington | Amer. | 13 | 31 | 2 | 6 | 0 | 2 | .194 |
| 1958—Indianapolis | A. A. | 38 | 121 | 14 | 26 | 2 | 10 | .215 |
| 1958—Chattanooga | South. | 86 | 299 | 58 | 92 | 17 | 54 | .308 |
| 1959—Washington | Amer. | 153 | 546 | 98 | 132 | ●42 | 105 | .242 |
| 1960—Washington | Amer. | 124 | 442 | 84 | 122 | 31 | 80 | .276 |
| 1961—Minnesota | Amer. | 150 | 541 | 94 | 156 | 46 | 122 | .288 |
| 1962—Minnesota | Amer. | 155 | 552 | 85 | 134 | *48 | *126 | .243 |
| 1963—Minnesota | Amer. | 142 | 515 | 88 | 133 | *45 | 96 | .258 |
| 1964—Minnesota | Amer. | 158 | 577 | 95 | 156 | *49 | 111 | .270 |
| 1965—Minnesota | Amer. | 113 | 401 | 78 | 108 | 25 | 75 | .269 |
| 1966—Minnesota | Amer. | 162 | 569 | 89 | 160 | 39 | 110 | .281 |
| 1967—Minnesota | Amer. | 163 | 547 | 105 | 147 | ●44 | 113 | .269 |
| 1968—Minnesota | Amer. | 100 | 295 | 40 | 62 | 17 | 40 | .210 |
| 1969—Minnesota | Amer. | ●162 | 555 | 106 | 153 | *49 | *140 | .276 |
| 1970—Minnesota | Amer. | 157 | 527 | 96 | 143 | 41 | 113 | .271 |
| 1971—Minnesota | Amer. | 147 | 500 | 61 | 127 | 28 | *119 | .254 |
| 1972—Minnesota | Amer. | 139 | 433 | 53 | 100 | 26 | 74 | .231 |
| 1973—Minnesota | Amer. | 69 | 248 | 29 | 60 | 5 | 32 | .242 |
| 1974—Minnesota | Amer. | 122 | 333 | 28 | 74 | 13 | 54 | .222 |
| 1975—Kansas City | Amer. | 106 | 312 | 25 | 62 | 14 | 44 | .199 |
| Major League Totals | | 2435 | 8147 | 1283 | 2086 | 573 | 1584 | .256 |

### WORLD SERIES RECORD

| Year | Club | League | G. | AB. | R. | H. | HR. | RBI. | B.A. |
|---|---|---|---|---|---|---|---|---|---|
| 1965—Minnesota | Amer. | 7 | 21 | 2 | 6 | 1 | 2 | .286 |

## PEE WEE REESE

| Year | Club | League | G. | AB. | R. | H. | HR. | RBI. | B.A. |
|---|---|---|---|---|---|---|---|---|---|
| 1938—Louisville | A. A. | 138 | 483 | 68 | 134 | 3 | 54 | .277 |
| 1939—Louisville | A. A. | 149 | 506 | 78 | 141 | 4 | 57 | .279 |
| 1940—Brooklyn | Nat. | 84 | 312 | 58 | 85 | 5 | 28 | .272 |
| 1941—Brooklyn | Nat. | 152 | 595 | 76 | 136 | 2 | 46 | .229 |
| 1942—Brooklyn | Nat. | 151 | 564 | 87 | 144 | 3 | 53 | .255 |
| 1943-44-45—Brooklyn | Nat. | (In Military Service) | | | | | | |
| 1946—Brooklyn | Nat. | 152 | 542 | 79 | 154 | 5 | 60 | .284 |
| 1947—Brooklyn | Nat. | 142 | 476 | 81 | 135 | 12 | 73 | .284 |
| 1948—Brooklyn | Nat. | 151 | 566 | 96 | 155 | 9 | 75 | .274 |

| Year Club | League | G. | AB. | R. | H. | HR. | RBI. | B.A. |
|---|---|---|---|---|---|---|---|---|
| 1949—Brooklyn | Nat. | 155 | 617 | ★132 | 172 | 16 | 73 | .279 |
| 1950—Brooklyn | Nat. | 141 | 531 | 97 | 138 | 11 | 52 | .260 |
| 1951—Brooklyn | Nat. | 154 | 616 | 94 | 176 | 10 | 84 | .286 |
| 1952—Brooklyn | Nat. | 149 | 559 | 94 | 152 | 6 | 58 | .272 |
| 1953—Brooklyn | Nat. | 140 | 524 | 108 | 142 | 13 | 61 | .271 |
| 1954—Brooklyn | Nat. | 141 | 554 | 98 | 171 | 10 | 69 | .309 |
| 1955—Brooklyn | Nat. | 145 | 553 | 99 | 156 | 10 | 61 | .282 |
| 1956—Brooklyn | Nat. | 147 | 572 | 85 | 147 | 9 | 46 | .257 |
| 1957—Brooklyn | Nat. | 103 | 330 | 33 | 74 | 1 | 29 | .224 |
| 1958—Los Angeles | Nat. | 59 | 147 | 21 | 33 | 4 | 17 | .224 |
| Major League Totals | | 2166 | 8058 | 1338 | 2170 | 126 | 885 | .269 |

### WORLD SERIES RECORD

| Year Club | League | G. | AB. | R. | H. | HR. | RBI. | B.A. |
|---|---|---|---|---|---|---|---|---|
| 1941—Brooklyn | Nat. | 5 | 20 | 1 | 4 | 0 | 2 | .200 |
| 1947—Brooklyn | Nat. | 7 | 23 | 5 | 7 | 0 | 4 | .304 |
| 1949—Brooklyn | Nat. | 5 | 19 | 2 | 6 | 1 | 2 | .316 |
| 1952—Brooklyn | Nat. | 7 | 29 | 4 | 10 | 1 | 4 | .345 |
| 1953—Brooklyn | Nat. | 6 | 24 | 0 | 5 | 0 | 0 | .278 |
| 1955—Brooklyn | Nat. | 7 | 27 | 5 | 8 | 0 | 2 | .296 |
| 1956—Brooklyn | Nat. | 7 | 27 | 3 | 6 | 0 | 2 | .222 |
| World Series Totals | | 44 | 169 | 20 | 46 | 2 | 16 | .272 |

## ENOS BRADSHER SLAUGHTER

| Year Club | League | G. | AB. | R. | H. | HR. | RBI. | B.A. |
|---|---|---|---|---|---|---|---|---|
| 1935—Martinsville | Bi-State | 109 | 422 | 68 | 115 | 18 | ..... | .273 |
| 1936—Columbus | Sally | 151 | 569 | 106 | 185 | 9 | 118 | .325 |
| 1937—Columbus | A. A. | 154 | 642 | ★147 | ★245 | 26 | 122 | ★.382 |
| 1938—St. Louis | Nat. | 112 | 395 | 59 | 109 | 8 | 58 | .276 |
| 1939—St. Louis | Nat. | 149 | 604 | 95 | 193 | 12 | 86 | .320 |
| 1940—St. Louis | Nat. | 140 | 516 | 96 | 158 | 17 | 73 | .306 |
| 1941—St. Louis | Nat. | 113 | 425 | 71 | 132 | 13 | 76 | .311 |
| 1942—St. Louis | Nat. | 152 | 591 | 100 | ★188 | 13 | 98 | .318 |
| 1943-44-45—St. Louis | Nat. | ..... | ..... | ..... | ..... | ..... | ..... | ..... |
| 1946—St. Louis | Nat. | ●156 | 609 | 100 | 183 | 18 | ★130 | .300 |
| 1947—St. Louis | Nat. | 147 | 551 | 100 | 162 | 10 | 86 | .294 |
| 1948—St. Louis | Nat. | 146 | 549 | 91 | 176 | 11 | 90 | .321 |
| 1949—St. Louis | Nat. | 151 | 568 | 92 | 191 | 13 | 96 | .336 |
| 1950—St. Louis | Nat. | 148 | 556 | 82 | 161 | 10 | 101 | .290 |
| 1951—St. Louis | Nat. | 123 | 409 | 48 | 115 | 4 | 64 | .281 |
| 1952—St. Louis | Nat. | 140 | 510 | 73 | 153 | 11 | 101 | .300 |
| 1953—St. Louis | Nat. | 143 | 492 | 64 | 143 | 6 | 89 | .291 |
| 1954—New York | Amer. | 69 | 125 | 19 | 31 | 1 | 19 | .248 |
| 1955—N.Y.-K.C. | Amer. | 118 | 276 | 50 | 87 | 5 | 35 | .315 |
| 1956—K.C.-N.Y. | Amer. | 115 | 306 | 52 | 86 | 2 | 27 | .281 |
| 1957—New York | Amer. | 96 | 209 | 24 | 53 | 5 | 34 | .254 |
| 1958—New York | Amer. | 77 | 138 | 21 | 42 | 4 | 19 | .304 |
| 1959—New York | Amer. | 74 | 99 | 10 | 17 | 6 | 21 | .172 |
| 1959—Milwaukee | Nat. | 11 | 18 | 0 | 3 | 0 | 1 | .167 |
| 1960—Houston | A.A. | 40 | 45 | 7 | 13 | 1 | 8 | .289 |
| 1961—Raleigh | Car. | 42 | 41 | 8 | 14 | 0 | 9 | .341 |
| American League Totals | | 549 | 1153 | 176 | 316 | 23 | 155 | .274 |
| National League Totals | | 1831 | 6793 | 1071 | 2067 | 146 | 1149 | .304 |
| Major League Totals | | 2380 | 7946 | 1247 | 2383 | 169 | 1304 | .300 |

### WORLD SERIES RECORD

| Year Club | League | G. | AB. | R. | H. | HR. | RBI. | B.A. |
|---|---|---|---|---|---|---|---|---|
| 1942—St. Louis | Nat. | 5 | 19 | 3 | 5 | 1 | 2 | .263 |
| 1946—St. Louis | Nat. | 7 | 25 | 5 | 8 | 1 | 2 | .320 |
| 1956—New York | Amer. | 6 | 20 | 6 | 7 | 1 | 4 | .350 |
| 1957—New York | Amer. | 5 | 12 | 2 | 3 | 0 | 0 | .250 |
| 1958—New York | Amer. | 4 | 3 | 1 | 0 | 0 | 0 | .000 |
| World Series Totals | | 27 | 79 | 17 | 23 | 3 | 8 | .291 |

## JOSEPH FLOYD (ARKY) VAUGHAN

| Year Club | League | G. | AB. | R. | H. | HR. | RBI. | B.A. |
|---|---|---|---|---|---|---|---|---|
| 1931—Wichita | West. | 132 | 494 | ★145 | 167 | 21 | 81 | .338 |
| 1932—Pittsburgh | Nat. | 129 | 497 | 71 | 158 | 4 | 61 | .318 |
| 1933—Pittsburgh | Nat. | 152 | 573 | 85 | 180 | 9 | 97 | .314 |
| 1934—Pittsburgh | Nat. | 149 | 558 | 115 | 186 | 12 | 94 | .333 |
| 1935—Pittsburgh | Nat. | 137 | 499 | 108 | 192 | 19 | 99 | ★.385 |
| 1936—Pittsburgh | Nat. | ●156 | 568 | ★122 | 190 | 9 | 78 | .335 |
| 1937—Pittsburgh | Nat. | 126 | 469 | 71 | 151 | 5 | 72 | .322 |
| 1938—Pittsburgh | Nat. | 148 | 541 | 88 | 174 | 7 | 68 | .322 |
| 1939—Pittsburgh | Nat. | 152 | 595 | 94 | 182 | 6 | 62 | .306 |
| 1940—Pittsburgh | Nat. | ★156 | 594 | ★113 | 178 | 7 | 95 | .300 |
| 1941—Pittsburgh | Nat. | 106 | 374 | 69 | 118 | 6 | 38 | .316 |
| 1942—Brooklyn | Nat. | 128 | 495 | 82 | 137 | 2 | 49 | .277 |
| 1943—Brooklyn | Nat. | 149 | 610 | ★112 | 186 | 5 | 66 | .305 |
| 1944-45-46—Brooklyn | Nat. | (Voluntarily retired) | | | | | | |
| 1947—Brooklyn | Nat. | 64 | 126 | 24 | 41 | 2 | 25 | .325 |
| 1948—Brooklyn | Nat. | 65 | 123 | 19 | 30 | 3 | 22 | .244 |
| 1949—San Francisco | P.C.L. | 97 | 281 | 50 | 81 | 2 | 26 | .288 |
| Major League Totals | | 1817 | 6622 | 1173 | 2103 | 96 | 926 | .318 |

### WORLD SERIES RECORD

| Year Club | League | G. | AB. | R. | H. | HR. | RBI. | B.A. |
|---|---|---|---|---|---|---|---|---|
| 1947—Brooklyn | Nat. | 3 | 2 | 0 | 1 | 0 | 0 | .500 |

## JAMES HOYT WILHELM

| Year Club | League | G. | IP. | W. | L. | Pct. | ERA. |
|---|---|---|---|---|---|---|---|
| 1942—Mooresville | N.C. St. | 23 | 108 | 10 | 3 | .769 | 4.25 |
| 1943-44-45—Mooresville | N.C. St. | (In Military Service) | | | | | |
| 1946—Mooresville | N.C. St. | ★34 | 233 | 21 | 8 | .724 | 2.47 |
| 1947—Mooresville | N.C. St. | 31 | ★250 | ★20 | 7 | .741 | 3.38 |
| 1948—Jacksonville | Sally | 6 | 11 | 0 | 0 | .000 | 8.18 |
| 1948—Knoxville | Tri-State | 24 | 189 | 13 | 9 | .591 | 3.62 |
| 1949—Jacksonville | Sally | 33 | 223 | 17 | 12 | .586 | 2.66 |
| 1950—Minneapolis | Am. Assoc. | 35 | 180 | 15 | 11 | .577 | 4.95 |
| 1951—Minneapolis | Am. Assoc. | 40 | ●210 | 11 | 14 | .440 | 3.94 |
| 1952—New York | National | ★71 | 159 | 15 | 3 | ★.833 | ★2.43 |
| 1953—New York | National | ★68 | 145 | 7 | 8 | .467 | 3.04 |
| 1954—New York | National | 57 | 111 | 12 | 4 | ●.750 | 2.11 |
| 1955—New York | National | 59 | 103 | 4 | 1 | .800 | 3.93 |
| 1956—New York | National | 64 | 89 | 4 | 9 | .308 | 3.84 |
| 1957—St. Louis | National | 40 | 55 | 1 | 4 | .200 | 4.25 |
| 1957—Cleveland | American | 2 | 4 | 1 | 0 | 1.000 | 2.25 |
| 1958—Cleveland-Baltimore | American | 39 | 131 | 3 | 10 | .231 | 2.34 |
| 1959—Baltimore | American | 32 | 226 | 15 | 11 | .577 | ★2.19 |
| 1960—Baltimore | American | 41 | 147 | 11 | 8 | .579 | 3.31 |
| 1961—Baltimore | American | 51 | 110 | 9 | 7 | .563 | 2.29 |
| 1962—Baltimore | American | 52 | 93 | 7 | 10 | .412 | 1.94 |
| 1963—Chicago | American | 55 | 136 | 5 | 8 | .385 | 2.65 |
| 1964—Chicago | American | 73 | 131 | 12 | 9 | .571 | 1.99 |
| 1965—Chicago | American | 66 | 144 | 7 | 7 | .500 | 1.81 |
| 1966—Chicago | American | 46 | 81 | 5 | 2 | .714 | 1.67 |
| 1967—Chicago | American | 49 | 89 | 8 | 3 | .727 | 1.31 |
| 1968—Chicago | American | 72 | 94 | 4 | 4 | .500 | 1.72 |
| 1969—California | American | 44 | 66 | 5 | 7 | .417 | 2.45 |
| 1969—Atlanta | National | 8 | 12 | 2 | 0 | 1.000 | 0.75 |
| 1970—Atlanta-Chicago | National | 53 | 82 | 6 | 5 | .545 | 3.40 |
| 1971—Spokane | Pac. Coast | 8 | 37 | 2 | 3 | .400 | 3.89 |
| 1971—Atlanta-Los Angeles | National | 12 | 20 | 0 | 1 | .000 | 2.70 |
| 1972—Los Angeles | National | 16 | 25 | 0 | 1 | .000 | 4.68 |
| American League Totals | | 622 | 1452 | 92 | 86 | .517 | 2.19 |
| National League Totals | | 448 | 801 | 51 | 36 | .586 | 3.12 |
| Major League Totals | | 1070 | 2253 | 143 | 122 | .540 | 2.52 |

### WORLD SERIES RECORD

| Year Club | League | G. | IP. | W. | L. | Pct. | ERA. |
|---|---|---|---|---|---|---|---|
| 1954—New York | National | 2 | 2⅓ | 0 | 0 | .000 | 0.00 |